THE ROUTLEDGE RESEARCH COMPANION TO THE HISTORY OF EVANGELICALISM

Evangelicalism, an inter-denominational religious movement that has grown to become one of the most pervasive expressions of world Christianity in the early twenty-first century, had its origins in the religious revivals led by George Whitefield, John Wesley and Jonathan Edwards in the middle decades of the eighteenth century. With its stress on the Bible, the cross of Christ, conversion and the urgency of mission, it quickly spread throughout the Atlantic world and then became a global phenomenon.

Over the past three decades evangelicalism has become the focus of considerable historical research. This research companion brings together a team of leading scholars writing broad-ranging chapters on key themes in the history of evangelicalism. It provides an authoritative and state-of-the-art review of current scholarship, and maps the territory for future research. Primary attention is paid to English-speaking evangelicalism, but the volume is transnational in its scope. Arranged thematically, chapters assess evangelicalism and the Bible, the atonement, spirituality, revivals and revivalism, worldwide mission in the Atlantic North and the Global South, eschatology, race, gender, culture and the arts, money and business, interactions with Roman Catholicism, Eastern Christianity, and Islam, and globalization. It demonstrates evangelicalism's multiple and contested identities in different ages and contexts.

The historical and thematic approach of this research companion makes it an invaluable resource for scholars and students alike worldwide.

Andrew Atherstone is Latimer Research Fellow at Wycliffe Hall, Oxford. He is author of *Archbishop Justin Welby: Risk-taker and Reconciler* (2014) and co-editor of *Evangelicalism and the Church of England in the Twentieth Century* (2014).

David Ceri Jones is Reader in Welsh and Atlantic History and Head of the Department of History and Welsh History at Aberystwyth University. He is co-editor of *George Whitefield: Life, Context, and Legacy* (2016), and *Evangelicalism and Fundamentalism in the United Kingdom in the Twentieth Century* (2013).

ROUTLEDGE STUDIES IN EVANGELICALISM

The study of evangelicalism is a well-developed discipline with a strong international readership. A major movement within global Christianity, it continues to attract considerable scholarly and 'popular' interest on both sides of the Atlantic and further afield. The Routledge Studies in Evangelicalism series publishes monographs and collaborative volumes of significant original research in any aspect of evangelical history or historical theology from the 18th century to the present, and is global in its scope. This series will appeal both to the flourishing community of scholars of religious history and to informed practitioners within the evangelical constituency.

Series editors:
Andrew Atherstone, Wycliffe Hall, Oxford, UK
David Ceri Jones, Aberystwyth University, UK

Philip Doddridge and the Shaping of Evangelical Dissent
Robert Strivens

The Routledge Research Companion to the History of Evangelicalism
Edited by Andrew Atherstone and David Ceri Jones

For more information about this series, please visit: https://www.routledge.com/religion/series/AEVANGE

THE ROUTLEDGE RESEARCH COMPANION TO THE HISTORY OF EVANGELICALISM

Edited by Andrew Atherstone and David Ceri Jones

LONDON AND NEW YORK

First published 2019
by Routledge
2 Park Square, Milton Park, Abingdon, Oxon OX14 4RN

and by Routledge
711 Third Avenue, New York, NY 10017

Routledge is an imprint of the Taylor & Francis Group, an informa business

© 2019 selection and editorial matter, Andrew Atherstone and David Ceri Jones; individual chapters, the contributors

The right of Andrew Atherstone and David Ceri Jones to be identified as the authors of the editorial material, and of the authors for their individual chapters, has been asserted in accordance with sections 77 and 78 of the Copyright, Designs and Patents Act 1988.

All rights reserved. No part of this book may be reprinted or reproduced or utilised in any form or by any electronic, mechanical, or other means, now known or hereafter invented, including photocopying and recording, or in any information storage or retrieval system, without permission in writing from the publishers.

Trademark notice: Product or corporate names may be trademarks or registered trademarks, and are used only for identification and explanation without intent to infringe.

British Library Cataloguing-in-Publication Data
A catalogue record for this book is available from the British Library

Library of Congress Cataloging-in-Publication Data
Names: Atherstone, Andrew, editor.
Title: The Routledge research companion to the history of Evangelicalism / edited by Andrew Atherstone and David Ceri Jones.
Description: New York : Routledge, 2018. | Series: Routledge studies in Evangelicalism | Includes bibliographical references and index.
Identifiers: LCCN 2018002286| ISBN 9781472438928 (hardback : alk. paper) | ISBN 9781315613604 (ebook)
Subjects: LCSH: Evangelicalism.
Classification: LCC BR1640 .R69 2018 | DDC 270.8/2--dc23
LC record available at https://lccn.loc.gov/2018002286

ISBN: 978-1-4724-3892-8 (hbk)
ISBN: 978-1-315-61360-4 (ebk)

Typeset in Bembo by
Servis Filmsetting Ltd, Stockport, Cheshire

 Printed in the United Kingdom
by Henry Ling Limited

CONTENTS

Preface   vii
Notes on contributors   ix

1 Evangelicals and evangelicalisms: contested identities   1
  Andrew Atherstone and David Ceri Jones

2 Evangelicals and the Bible   22
  Mark A. Noll

3 Evangelicals and the cross   39
  David Ceri Jones

4 Evangelical spirituality   57
  Peter J. Morden

5 Evangelicals, revival and revivalism   73
  Michael J. McClymond

6 Evangelicals and Rome   93
  John Maiden

7 Evangelicals and Eastern Christianity   110
  Tim Grass

8 Evangelicals and Islam   127
  Andrew Atherstone

9	Evangelicals and mission in the Atlantic North *Martin Spence*	146
10	Evangelicals and mission in the Global South *Michael Gladwin*	162
11	Evangelicals and the end of the world *Mark S. Sweetnam*	178
12	Evangelicals and race *John Coffey and Stephen Tuck*	198
13	Evangelicals and gender *Linda Wilson*	217
14	Evangelicals, culture and the arts *Peter Webster*	232
15	Evangelicals, money and business *Richard Turnbull*	248
16	Evangelicals and globalization *Philip Jenkins*	267

Select bibliography and further reading — 281
Index — 293

PREFACE

Encyclopaedic companion and handbook volumes in almost every academic discipline, and many of their sub-disciplines, have become highly fashionable in recent times. The study of evangelical religion has been no exception to this trend with *The Cambridge Companion to Evangelical Theology* (2007), edited by Timothy Larsen and Daniel J. Treier, and *The Oxford Handbook of Evangelical Theology* (2010), edited by Gerald McDermott, appearing in the last decade or so. As their titles indicate, both take a largely theological approach, charting evangelicals' key doctrinal and devotional preoccupations. McDermott's volume includes a section surveying evangelical teaching on a range of ethical questions, while Larsen and Treier prefer some closer contextual chapters looking at expressions of evangelical religion in various global contexts. Readers of the present Routledge volume might be justified in asking whether there is a need for another companion to evangelicalism.

Where this volume differs is in its thorough-going historical approach. This is a companion volume to the history of evangelicalism, and as such is concerned primarily to chart change and development within the evangelical movement over time. While it addresses theological ideas throughout, it is mostly concerned with how those ideas have been expressed in time and place. The choice of themes in the volume reflects this. Overtly theological chapters are limited to discussion of the two basic convictions of all evangelicals: Mark Noll explores the importance of the Bible, while the centrality of the atoning death of Christ is examined by David Ceri Jones. Other chapters look at the way in which these core evangelical convictions have been applied and lived out; an evangelical approach to spirituality is mapped by Peter Morden, and attitudes towards revivals and revivalism, so central to the mission strategy of evangelicals everywhere, are explored by Michael McClymond.

A trio of chapters pioneer some new perspectives by looking at evangelical relations with other Christian groups and other faiths. John Maiden and Tim Grass examine interactions with Roman Catholicism and Eastern Christianity respectively, in both cases highlighting a trajectory from suspicion and belligerence to cautious engagement, while Andrew Atherstone explores the various ways in which evangelicals have understood and reacted to Islam. In the next pair of chapters, Martin Spence and Michael Gladwin analyse evangelical approaches to mission, the former in the Atlantic North, the latter in the Global South. Both, in different ways, lay bare the sheer variety of evangelical attitudes to expansion and (in the case of the Atlantic North) retrenchment too. A clutch of chapters survey evangelical responses to issues in the wider culture. Mark S. Sweetnam looks at evangelical views of the future, revealing in the process their attitude to the present world. This sets the scene for John Coffey and Stephen Tuck's exploration of evangelical perspectives on race, a chapter that challenges future historians of evangelicalism fully to integrate black voices into their interpretation of the evangelical past. Linda Wilson, Peter Webster and Richard Turnbull probe evangelical views regarding gender, culture and the arts, and money, in each case demonstrating that evangelical opinions have evolved over time and defy simple categorization.

The companion takes full account of the contested nature of evangelical identities, brought into focus in the opening chapter by Atherstone and Jones, and evidenced in various ways in each contribution which follows. After fifteen chapters of historical analysis, stretching back to the eighteenth century, the volume concludes with a forward-looking chapter by Philip Jenkins that charts the global transformation that has taken place within evangelicalism in the later twentieth and twenty-first centuries, and prognosticates on what the future shape and character of the movement, if it is possible to talk of a coherent evangelical movement, might look like. This research companion provides a snapshot of the current state of historical scholarship in its areas of concern, and several chapters attempt to shift the focus away from the dominant Anglo-American perspective that has characterized evangelical historiography for generations. It also points to specific areas where new research is needed, some of which may open up entirely new vistas on the evangelical past.

Andrew Atherstone
David Ceri Jones

NOTES ON CONTRIBUTORS

Andrew Atherstone is Latimer Research Fellow at Wycliffe Hall, Oxford. He is author of *Archbishop Justin Welby: Risk-taker and Reconciler* (2014) and co-editor of *Evangelicalism and the Church of England in the Twentieth Century* (2014).

John Coffey is Professor of Early Modern History at the University of Leicester. His recent books include *Exodus and Liberation: Deliverance Politics from John Calvin to Martin Luther King Jr* (2014), and (as editor) *Heart Religion: Evangelical Piety in England and Ireland, 1690–1850* (2016).

Michael Gladwin is Senior Lecturer in History at St Mark's National Theological Centre in the School of Theology at Charles Sturt University, Canberra. He is author of *Captains of the Soul: A History of Australian Army Chaplains* (2013), and *Anglican Clergy in Australia, 1788–1850: Building a British World* (2015).

Tim Grass is a Senior Research Fellow at Spurgeon's College, London, and has been active in dialogue with the Orthodox churches for many years. His books include *Gathering to His Name: The Story of the Open Brethren in Britain and Ireland* (2006), and biographies of Edward Irving and F. F. Bruce.

Philip Jenkins is Distinguished Professor of History at Baylor University, Texas, and author of *The Next Christendom: The Rise of Global Christianity* (2011) and *The Great and Holy War: How World War I Became a Religious Crusade* (2014).

David Ceri Jones is Reader in Welsh and Atlantic History and Head of the Department of History and Welsh History at Aberystwyth University. He is co-editor of *George Whitefield: Life, Context, and Legacy* (2016), and *Evangelicalism and Fundamentalism in the United Kingdom in the Twentieth Century* (2013).

John Maiden is Senior Lecturer in Religious Studies at the Open University, co-editor of *Evangelicalism and the Church of England in the Twentieth Century* (2014), and author of *National Religion and the Prayer Book Controversy, 1927–28* (2009).

Notes on contributors

Michael J. McClymond is Professor of Modern Christianity at Saint Louis University, editor of *Encyclopedia of Religious Revivals in America* (2 vols, 2007) and co-author of *The Theology of Jonathan Edwards* (2012).

Peter J. Morden is Senior Pastor of South Parade Baptist Church, Leeds, and Distinguished Visiting Scholar at Spurgeon's College, London. He is author of *The Life and Thought of Andrew Fuller* (2015) and co-editor of *Pathways and Patterns in History* (2015).

Mark A. Noll is the Francis McAnaney Professor of History Emeritus at the University of Notre Dame and author most recently of *From Every Tribe and Nation* (2014) and *In the Beginning Was the Word: The Bible in American Public Life, 1492–1783* (2016).

Martin Spence is Associate Professor of History at Cornerstone University, Grand Rapids, Michigan, and author of *Heaven on Earth: Reimagining Time and Eternity in Nineteenth-Century British Evangelicalism* (2015).

Mark S. Sweetnam is Assistant Professor in the School of English at Trinity College, Dublin, and author of *John Donne and Religious Authority in the Reformed English Church* (2014).

Stephen Tuck is Professor of Modern History at Pembroke College, Oxford. He is author of *The Night Malcolm X Spoke at the Oxford Union: A Transatlantic Story of Antiracist Protest* (2014) and co-editor of *The Other Special Relationship: Race, Rights, and Riots in Britain and the United States* (2015).

Richard Turnbull is director of the Centre for Enterprise, Markets and Ethics, and former principal of Wycliffe Hall, Oxford. His books include *Anglican and Evangelical?* (2007), and *Shaftesbury: The Great Reformer* (2010).

Peter Webster is an independent scholar and consultant, and has published widely on contemporary British religious history. He is author of *Archbishop Ramsey: The Shape of the Church* (2015) and *Church and Patronage in 20th Century Britain: Walter Hussey and the Arts* (2017).

Linda Wilson is an Honorary Research Fellow at Bristol Baptist College and has published extensively on the history of women, men, spirituality and gender, including *Constrained by Zeal: Female Spirituality Amongst Nonconformists, 1825–75* (2000).

1

EVANGELICALS AND EVANGELICALISMS: CONTESTED IDENTITIES

Andrew Atherstone and David Ceri Jones

During the early days of the revivals led by George Whitefield and the Wesley brothers in the middle decades of the eighteenth century, use of the term 'evangelical' was relatively rare. Whitefield, the highest profile leader of the revivals in their first decade, although an Anglican clergyman, was reluctant to engage in too much defining of the new movement. 'My one design', he wrote in 1740, 'is to bring poor souls to Jesus Christ'.[1] To this end he preached a pared down message: I am determined, he wrote in his journal, to 'preach the new birth and the power of godliness, and not to insist so much on the form'.[2] While he was not averse to theological controversy when he felt it was necessary, Whitefield's determination 'to preach the simple gospel, to all who are willing to hear me, of whatever denomination',[3] was characteristic of his desire to focus on the practicalities of soul winning rather than the intricacies of theological disputing. When he came under pressure to support one ecclesiastical party or another, Whitefield blamed the Devil, who 'turns himself into an angel of light & stirs up God's Children to tempt me to come over to some particular party ... From those who would turn Religion into a Party, Good Lord deliver my soul.'[4] For Whitefield the evangelical movement was a broad tent, at the heart of which was a shared experience of the new birth.[5] Any diversion from that he regarded as a distraction.

A generation later, Charles Simeon, leader in Cambridge during the 'second spring' of the revivals, likewise seldom used 'evangelical' nomenclature. One of his university sermons, from November 1809, was published as *Evangelical and Pharisaic Righteousness Compared*,

---

[1] *A Letter from the Reverend Mr. Whitefield, to Some Church Members of the Presbyterian Perswasion, in Answer to Certain Scruples and Queries Relating to Some Passages in his Printed Sermons and Other Writings* (Boston, MA: S. Ireland and T. Green, 1740), p. 12.
[2] *A Continuation of the Reverend Mr. Whitefield's Journal, From a Few Days after his Return to Georgia to his Arrival at Falmouth on the 11th March 1741* (London: W. Strahan, 1741), p. 24.
[3] George Whitefield to Ebenezer Erskine (16 May 1741), *The Works of the Reverend George Whitefield*, edited by John Gillies (6 vols, Edinburgh: Edward and Charles Dilly, 1771), I: 262.
[4] George Whitefield to Howel Harris (13 August 1741), National Library of Wales, Calvinistic Methodist Archive, the Trevecka Letters, no. 366.
[5] See David Ceri Jones, 'George Whitefield and Heart Religion', in *Heart Religion: Evangelical Piety in England and Ireland, 1690–1850*, edited by John Coffey (Oxford: Oxford University Press, 2016), pp. 97–101.

not with any party connotation but as a synonym for righteousness as taught in the New Testament.[6] In his private correspondence, Simeon wrote to William Wilberforce about episcopal persecution of 'the Evangelical Clergy', and William Jay of Bath celebrated with Simeon at the revival and extension of 'evangelical religion', but these are rare examples.[7] In Oxford, John Hill (vice-principal of St Edmund Hall) stood at the nexus of the university's evangelical networks between the 1810s and 1840s, but adopted the 'evangelical' label only sparingly. Although he contrasted 'evangelical doctrine' with the threat of Tractarianism, his preferred description of like-minded believers was 'pious' or 'earnest'.[8] Nevertheless, 'evangelical' categories gathered pace during the early nineteenth century, and soon the idea of a coherent 'evangelicalism' was coined, initially as a term of abuse. One of the characters in *Dialogues on Prophecy* (1828), compiled by Henry Drummond and Edward Irving, blamed the demise of contemporary theology on 'modern evangelicalism' as originated by Whitefield and Wesley, men of 'warm affections, fervent imaginations, and small study'.[9] When *The Record* newspaper criticized Irving's prophetic circle, his journal, *The Morning Watch*, retorted that 'a greater semblance of truth is preserved by the Papacy, detestable apostasy though it be, than by the system called Evangelicalism'.[10] The journal predicted that if the personality of the Holy Spirit was displayed in the Church then 'the doctors of Evangelicalism' would foment 'a persecution as hot as ever was that set on foot by Nero'.[11] *The Edinburgh Review* soon picked up the new epithet, observing that 'the worst things about Evangelicalism' were its exclusiveness and misrepresentation of human nature.[12] Self-professed evangelicals themselves eventually embraced the concept of 'evangelicalism', although when J. C. Ryle attempted to define it for the Church Association in 1867, his approach was dismissed by a fellow Anglican Calvinist as mere 'Ryle-ism', a sectional affair like Puseyism.[13] During the Victorian period, many adopted an explicit 'evangelical' identity as a popular badge of honour, although when faced by doctrinal 'downgrade' among the Baptists in the late 1880s, C. H. Spurgeon famously protested: 'It is mere cant to cry, "We are evangelical, we are all evangelical", and yet decline to say what evangelical means'.[14] Meanwhile among the Congregationalists R. W. Dale highlighted apparent deficiencies within 'the old evangelicalism' and advocated a new brand for the modern Church.[15] In these shifting sands, the rightful ownership and definition of evangelical terminology was never fixed.

Addressing the students at Princeton Theological Seminary in Philadelphia, in September

---

6 Charles Simeon, *Evangelical and Pharisaic Righteousness Compared: A Sermon Preached Before the University of Cambridge, on Sunday, November 26th, 1809* (Cambridge: J. Smith, 1809).
7 Charles Simeon to William Wilberforce (18 November 1816), Bodleian Library, MS Wilberforce c.3, fos 154–5; William Jay to Charles Simeon (18 February 1811), Ridley Hall Archives, Cambridge.
8 See, for example, entries for 27 July 1830, 8 January 1832, 13 January 1835, 28 August 1846, 12 June 1847: Diary of John Hill, Bodleian Library, MS St Edmund Hall 67/1–20.
9 *Dialogues on Prophecy* (3 vols, London: James Nisbet, 1827–9), II: 345–6.
10 'On Religious Periodicals', *The Morning Watch; or Quarterly Journal on Prophecy* vol. 2 (December 1830), 919.
11 'On the Religious and Prophetic Aspect of the French Revolution of 1830', *The Morning Watch; or Quarterly Journal on Prophecy* vol. 2 (December 1830), 898.
12 'Pretended Miracles – Irving, Scott, and Erskine', *Edinburgh Review* vol. 53 (June 1831), 305.
13 J. C. Ryle, *Evangelical Religion: What It Is, and What It Is Not* (London: William Hunt, 1868); T. H. Gregg, *Evangelical-ISM! or, 'Evangelical Religion: What It Is' (As Interpreted by the Rev. J. C. Ryle, BA, Vicar of Stradbroke, Suffolk) 'Weighed in the Balances' (Of Holy Scripture, and the Thirty-Nine Articles) 'And Found Wanting'* (London: Marlborough and Co., 1868), p. 5.
14 'Notes', *The Sword and the Trowel* (October 1888), 563.
15 R. W. Dale, *The Old Evangelicalism and the New* (London: Hodder and Stoughton, 1889).

1915, Benjamin Warfield mourned the death of important theological words such as 'Redemption', 'Christianity', and 'Evangelical'. Taking his cue from the battlefields of the First World War, he declared:

> The religious terrain is full of the graves of good words which have died from lack of care – they stand as close in it as do the graves today in the flats of Flanders or among the hills of northern France. And these good words are still dying all around us. There is that good word 'Evangelical'. It is certainly moribund, if not already dead. Nobody any longer seems to know what it means. Even our Dictionaries no longer know.[16]

For example, the *Standard Dictionary* (1893) defined an evangelical as someone holding 'what the majority of Protestants regard as the fundamental doctrines of the gospel', or alternatively as 'spiritually minded and zealous for practical Christian living'.[17] Warfield asserted that 'there never was a more blundering, floundering attempt ever made to define a word'. Furthermore, to identify German Protestantism as the *Evangelische Kirche* had dragged the name 'into the bog' and robbed it of all its meaning, he lamented. Likewise, surveying America, he asked:

> Does anybody in the world know what 'Evangelical' means, in our current religious speech? The other day, a professedly evangelical pastor, serving a church which is certainly committed by its formularies to an evangelical confession, having occasion to report in one of our newspapers on a religious meeting composed practically entirely of Unitarians and Jews, remarked with enthusiasm upon the deeply evangelical character of its spirit and utterances.

'But the dying of the words is not the saddest thing which we see here', Warfield concluded. 'The saddest thing is the dying out of the hearts of men of the things for which the words stand.'[18] Perhaps he had in view contemporaries like the New York pastor Harry Emerson Fosdick, a prominent modernist, who insisted, 'I may be a liberal, but I'm evangelical, too!'[19]

In every generation, from the eighteenth century to the present, evangelical identity has been contested. This chapter examines the more recent evolution of these continuous debates, from the 1970s to the early twenty-first century. For scholars and participants of the movement in the Anglo-American world, controversy over definitions continues to dominate historical and theological discussions. In particular, this chapter analyses the development of competing taxonomies, attempts to delineate the essence or coherence of evangelicalism, and contrasting approaches to evangelical boundaries and membership.

---

16 Benjamin B. Warfield, '"Redeemer" and "Redemption"', *Princeton Theological Review* vol. 14 (April 1916), 198.
17 *A Standard Dictionary of the English Language*, edited by Isaac K. Funk and others (2 vols, New York: Funk and Wagnalls, 1893–5), I: 633.
18 Warfield, '"Redeemer" and "Redemption"', 198–200.
19 Robert Moats Miller, *Harry Emerson Fosdick: Preacher, Pastor, Prophet* (New York: Oxford University Press, 1985), p. 336.

Metaphors and taxonomies

Analysts of evangelicalism turn frequently to metaphor to express unity-in-diversity. Examples are legion – evangelical 'tribes',[20] an evangelical 'mosaic',[21] an evangelical 'kaleidoscope',[22] an evangelical 'rainbow' with a variety of hues,[23] an evangelical 'extended family' whose members are sometimes estranged.[24] Randall Balmer likened evangelicalism to the automobile manufacturer General Motors, an umbrella with multiple brands such as Chevrolet, Cadillac, Buick and GMC trucks.[25] Graham Kings preferred the image of an evangelical watercourse, interconnected but manifest in different guises as canal, river and rapids.[26] Taxonomies are likewise multitudinous, ranging from Oliver Barclay's simple polarities of 'conservative evangelicals' versus 'liberal evangelicals',[27] to Robert Webber's fourteen sub-categories (Fundamentalist, Dispensational, Conservative, Non-denominational, Reformed, Anabaptist, Wesleyan, Holiness, Pentecostal, Charismatic, Black, Progressive, Radical, Mainline).[28]

Timothy Weber counted four branches of the evangelical family tree (Classical, Pietistic, Fundamentalist, Progressive),[29] and Gabriel Fackre settled for six (Fundamentalist, Old, New, Justice and Peace, Charismatic, Ecumenical),[30] while Cullen Murphy's circus analogy identified no less than 'a lively 12-ring show in progress' within 'the vast tent of evangelical faith'.[31] Evangelicals affiliated to denominations could themselves be further subdivided. Anglican evangelicals, for example, were categorized in numerous ways during the twentieth century, such as the Traditional, Protestant, Evangelistic and Liberal strands described by E. C. Dewick in 1915, or the alliterative Pietist, Parochial, Puritan and Protestant strands identified by Michael Saward in 1987.[32] Continuing this taxonomic tradition, according to David Wells' trenchant

---

20 Pete Ward, 'The Tribes of Evangelicalism', in *The Post-Evangelical Debate* (London: Triangle, 1997), pp. 19–34.
21 Joel A. Carpenter, *Revive Us Again: The Reawakening of American Fundamentalism* (New York: Oxford University Press, 1997), p. 141; Grant Wacker, *Heaven Below: Early Pentecostals and American Culture* (Cambridge, MA: Harvard University Press, 2001), p. ix.
22 Timothy L. Smith, 'The Evangelical Kaleidoscope and the Call to Christian Unity', *Christian Scholar's Review* vol. 15 (1986), 125–40; Michael L. Cromartie, 'The Evangelical Kaleidoscope: A Survey of Recent Evangelical Political Engagement', in *Christians and Politics Beyond the Culture Wars: An Agenda for Engagement*, edited by David P. Gushee (Grand Rapids, MI: Baker, 2000), pp. 15–28.
23 Nigel Wright, *The Radical Evangelical: Seeking a Place to Stand* (London: SPCK, 1996), p. 12.
24 Robert K. Johnston, 'American Evangelicalism: An Extended Family', in *The Variety of American Evangelicalism*, edited by Donald W. Dayton and Robert K. Johnston (Knoxville, TN: University of Tennessee Press, 1991), pp. 252–72; Joseph M. Stowell, 'The Evangelical Family: Its Blessings and Boundaries', in *This We Believe: The Good News of Jesus Christ for the World*, edited by John N. Akers, John M. Armstrong and John D. Woodbridge (Grand Rapids, MI: Zondervan, 2000), pp. 205–19.
25 Randall Balmer, *Evangelicalism in America* (Waco, TX: Baylor University Press, 2016), p. xii.
26 Graham Kings, 'Canal, River, Rapids: Contemporary Evangelicalism in the Church of England', *Anvil* vol. 20 (2003), 167–84.
27 Oliver Barclay, *Evangelicalism in Britain 1935–1995: A Personal Sketch* (Leicester: Inter-Varsity Press, 1997), pp. 12–14.
28 Robert E. Webber, *Common Roots: The Original Call to an Ancient-Future Faith* (Grand Rapids, MI: Zondervan, 2009), pp. 56–7.
29 Timothy P. Weber, 'Premillennialism and the Branches of Evangelicalism', in *The Variety of American Evangelicalism*, edited by Dayton and Johnston, pp. 12–14.
30 Gabriel Fackre, *Ecumenical Faith in Evangelical Perspective* (Grand Rapids, MI: Eerdmans, 1993), pp. 22–3.
31 Cullen Murphy, 'Protestantism and the Evangelicals', *Wilson Quarterly* vol. 5 (Autumn 1981), 108.
32 Andrew Atherstone and John Maiden, 'Anglican Evangelicalism in the Twentieth Century: Identities and Contexts', in *Evangelicalism and the Church of England in the Twentieth Century: Reform, Resistance and Renewal*, edited by Andrew Atherstone and John Maiden (Woodbridge: Boydell Press, 2014), pp. 3–9.

cultural analysis the 'evangelical kingdom' had mutated by the twenty-first century into three distinct and competing constituencies – 'classic evangelicals' (in the school of Harold Ockenga, John Stott and Francis Schaeffer), 'marketers' (such as megachurch pastors Bill Hybels and Rick Warren), and 'emergents' (such as Brian McLaren and Rob Bell).[33] Faced by the remarkable diversity of theologies and subcultures encompassed by the 'evangelical' label, Donald Dayton reckoned it useless as an analytical category and appealed (unsuccessfully) for a moratorium on the term.[34]

Some participants disillusioned with evangelicalism, especially in its more conservative or fundamentalistic guises, have abandoned evangelical identity altogether.[35] Others, however, have attempted to reconfigure it. For example, in the United States where 'evangelical' is often confused with 'the Religious Right', some like Tony Campolo and the 'socially and politically progressive minority', prefer 'Red-Letter Christians' as a self-descriptor, focusing on the radical teaching of Jesus Christ.[36] In the United Kingdom, Dave Tomlinson pioneered an alternative nomenclature in *The Post-Evangelical*, launched at the Greenbelt Festival in 1995. Tomlinson was raised in the Brethren and became a leader in the early charismatic house churches, before founding Holy Joe's in a pub in Clapham, south London, which he envisaged as a refuge for disaffected churchgoers, 'people who do not fit into the mould and yet who love God and want to pursue their faith in an alternative way'. 'Post-evangelical' did not mean 'ex-evangelical', he insisted, but meant rather 'to take as given many of the assumptions of evangelical faith, while at the same time moving beyond its perceived limitations'. In Tomlinson's schema, evangelicalism was wedded to a bygone modernity, while post-evangelicalism chimed with the rise of late twentieth-century post-modernity. In particular, he criticized contemporary evangelicalism as an 'exclusive, middle-class club' which had made 'an idol out of the Bible', was paranoid about liberalism, allergic to ambiguity, and obsessed by religious taboos. 'Doctrinal correctness matters little to God and labels matter less', Tomlinson asserted; 'honesty, openness and a sincere searching for truth, on the other hand, matter a great deal'.[37] Maggi Dawn, a former member of Holy Joe's, celebrated that post-evangelicalism was breaking down traditional ecclesial boundaries, for example by integrating catholic sacramentalism with evangelical worship in a 'mix and match' approach. She concluded:

> Whether we end up being called New evangelicals, Post-evangelicals, Radical evangelicals, Catholic evangelicals or anything else doesn't matter that much. The label game is, in any case, usually governed by those on the outside of a movement. What matters is that we are authentically Christian.[38]

---

33 David Wells, *The Courage To Be Protestant: Truth-Lovers, Marketers and Emergents in the Postmodern World* (Nottingham: Inter-Varsity Press, 2008).
34 Donald W. Dayton, 'Some Doubts about the Usefulness of the Category "Evangelical"', in *The Variety of American Evangelicalism*, edited by Dayton and Johnston, p. 251.
35 Alan Jamieson, *A Churchless Faith: Faith Journeys Beyond the Churches* (London: SPCK, 2002); Gordon Lynch, *Losing My Religion? Moving on from Evangelical Faith* (London: Darton, Longman and Todd, 2003); *Leaving Fundamentalism: Personal Stories*, edited by G. Elijah Dann (Waterloo, Ontario: Wilfrid Laurier University Press, 2008); Kent Dobson, *Bitten by a Camel: Leaving Church, Finding God* (Minneapolis, MN: Fortress Press, 2017); Josie McSkimming, *Leaving Christian Fundamentalism and the Reconstruction of Identity* (Abingdon: Routledge, 2017).
36 Tony Campolo, *Letters to a Young Evangelical* (New York: Basic Books, 2006), p. 7.
37 Dave Tomlinson, *The Post-Evangelical* (London: Triangle, 1995), pp. 7, 40, 61, 68. See further, David Hilborn, *Picking Up the Pieces: Can Evangelicals Adapt to Contemporary Culture?* (London: Hodder and Stoughton, 1997), pp. 79–116.
38 Maggi Dawn, 'You Have to Change to Stay the Same', in *The Post-Evangelical Debate*, p. 56.

However, Graham Cray worried that post-evangelical was synonymous with 'post-biblical', and that like the 'liberal evangelicals' of the 1920s they were likely to fade away from evangelicalism altogether.[39] *Evangelicals Now* warned that it 'tears the heart out' of biblical religion.[40] In a scathing review, Alister McGrath dismissed *The Post-Evangelical* as one of 'the most superficial and inadequate treatments' he had ever read, 'depressingly muddled', ignorant of recent scholarship, and motivated primarily by Tomlinson's own 'deep personal alienation' from the movement.[41] Nigel Wright, a Baptist minister, also rejected post-evangelicalism as 'another form of supermarket Christianity', propagated by a sophisticated middle-class elite who lacked serious commitment to the whole people of God. Although he echoed Tomlinson's desire to 're-imagine' evangelicalism, he dismissed the post-evangelical category as a 'dead end' which undermined confidence in the gospel and was merely 'a form of parasite on the body evangelical, unable of itself to win converts'. The theological task, Wright argued, was not to grow beyond evangelicalism but to 'enrich it from within'. He preferred categories such as 'open', 'progressive', 'constructive', 'ecumenical', 'catholic' or 'unitive' evangelicalism, and issued his own rival manifesto in 1996 as *The Radical Evangelical*.[42] Tomlinson was ordained as an Anglican clergyman in 1997, and later dropped the language of 'post-evangelicalism' in favour of 'progressive orthodoxy',[43] but continued the same line of protest with books such as *How to be a Bad Christian . . . and a Better Human Being* (2012) and *Black Sheep and Prodigals: An Antidote to Black and White Religion* (2017).

In parallel with 'post-evangelicalism' was the construction of 'post-conservative evangelicalism' as a taxonomic category, coined by Roger Olson, author of volumes such as *Reformed and Always Reforming* (2007) and *How To Be Evangelical Without Being Conservative* (2008). He was determined not to relinquish his evangelical identity, but objected to the movement being 'hijacked by social and political conservatives and religious traditionalists'.[44] A 'post-conservative evangelical', he explained, views the task of theology as an open-ended pilgrimage, wants to be liberated from Enlightenment presuppositions, emphasizes spiritual experience rather than doctrinal belief, and holds lightly to tradition.[45] In most ecclesial disputes of this nature, protagonists from opposing parties seek to establish their position as the centre-ground, thus relegating alternative views to the periphery or wings of the movement.[46] Such was the deep disparity among late twentieth-century American evangelicals over numerous doctrinal and political issues, George Marsden noted, that 'no one, not even Billy Graham, could claim to stand at the center of so

---

39 Graham Cray, 'The Post-Evangelical Debate', in *The Post-Evangelical Debate*, pp. 7–8.
40 Mark Johnston, 'Post-Modern Holy Joes', *Evangelicals Now* (May 1996), 17.
41 Alister McGrath, 'Prophets of Doubt', *Alpha* (August 1996), 28–30. For reply to McGrath's 'dismissive generalisations, sweeping misrepresentations, and scathing put-downs', see Dave Tomlinson, 'Heralds of Hope?' *Alpha* (September 1996), 32–4.
42 Nigel Wright, 'Re-imagining Evangelicalism', in *The Post-Evangelical Debate*, pp. 99, 105, 108–9.
43 Dave Tomlinson, *The Post-Evangelical* (new edition, London: SPCK, 2014), p. xiii.
44 Roger E. Olson, *How To Be Evangelical Without Being Conservative* (Grand Rapids, MI: Zondervan, 2008), p. 202.
45 Roger E. Olson, *Reformed and Always Reforming: The Postconservative Approach to Evangelical Theology* (Grand Rapids, MI: Baker, 2007), pp. 51–65. In response, see Millard J. Erickson, *The Evangelical Left: Encountering Postconservative Evangelical Theology* (Grand Rapids, MI: Baker, 1997); *Reforming or Conforming? Post-Conservative Evangelicals and the Emerging Church*, edited by Gary L. W. Johnson and Ronald N. Gleason (Wheaton, IL: Crossway, 2008).
46 Andrew Atherstone, 'Identities and Parties', in *The Oxford Handbook of Anglican Studies*, edited by Mark D. Chapman, Sathianathan Clark and Martyn Percy (Oxford: Oxford University Press, 2015), p. 88.

divided a coalition'.[47] Yet this stark reality did not stop 'post-conservatives' and 'conservatives' from issuing rival manifestos to stake just such a claim to the evangelical heartlands, expressed in contrasting volumes like *Renewing the Center* (2000) and *Reclaiming the Center* (2004).[48]

The multiplicity of evangelical identities generates existential angst. It is difficult, as Kenneth Collins observed, to discern any overarching 'evangelical metanarrative'.[49] Witnessing the fragmentation of the American 'neo-evangelical' coalition which he had laboured so hard to build, Carl Henry penned *Evangelicals in Search of Identity* (1976) and reflected in *The Christian Century* magazine:

> Numerous crosscurrents now vex almost every effort at comprehensive evangelical liaison. At present no single leader or agency has the respect, magnetism or platform to summon all divergent elements to conference. Evangelical differences increasingly pose an identity crisis.[50]

At the same period, on the other side of the Atlantic, J. I. Packer spoke of an 'identity problem' among evangelicals in the Church of England. He warned of the 'radical erosion' of the evangelical cause, 'so that soon it will be a mere featureless blob, like the ruined, unrecognisable face of a weatherbeaten gargoyle'.[51] A fellow Anglican, David Samuel, mourned that 'evangelical' was now a meaningless word 'evacuated of any significance': 'Evangelicalism is now just what Tom, Dick or Harry make it to mean at any given moment. It is a nose of wax which may be moulded to suit the fancy of the wearer. How are the mighty fallen!'[52] In a rear-guard action, Wells led calls for a return to the confessional evangelicalism dominant between the 1940s and the 1970s, with unity expressed in common doctrines. He lamented the ambiguity of the title 'evangelical', whose 'essence, like the morning mist, is disappearing in the bright light of modern pluralism'.[53] In *No Place for Truth* (1993), Wells offered a more pungent assessment; as evangelicalism grows it 'spills out in all directions, producing a family of hybrids whose theological connections are quite baffling' – catholic evangelicals, feminist evangelicals, radical evangelicals, charismatic evangelicals and so on. 'What is now primary is not what is evangelical but what is adjectivally distinctive . . . It is, I believe, the dark prelude to death, when parasites have finally succeeded in bringing down their host. Amid the clamor of all these new models of evangelical faith there is the sound of a death rattle.'[54]

---

47 George Marsden, 'Unity and Diversity in the Evangelical Resurgence', *Altered Landscapes. Christianity in America, 1935–1985*, edited by David W. Lotz (Grand Rapids, MI: Eerdmans, 1989), p. 71.

48 Stanley J. Grenz, *Renewing the Center: Evangelical Theology in a Post-Theological Era* (Grand Rapids, MI: Baker, 2000); *Reclaiming the Center: Confronting Evangelical Accommodation in Postmodern Times*, edited by Millard J. Erickson, Paul Kjoss Helseth and Justin Taylor (Wheaton, IL: Crossway, 2004); David P. Gushee, *The Future of Faith in American Politics: The Public Witness of the Evangelical Center* (Waco, TX: Baylor University Press, 2008).

49 Kenneth J. Collins, *The Evangelical Moment: The Promise of an American Religion* (Grand Rapids, MI: Baker, 2005), p. 22.

50 Quoted in Jon R. Stone, *On the Boundaries of American Evangelicalism: The Postwar Evangelical Coalition* (Basingstoke: Macmillan, 1997), p. 172.

51 J. I. Packer, *The Evangelical Anglican Identity Problem: An Analysis* (Oxford: Latimer House, 1978), p. 13.

52 David Samuel, 'Evangelical Catholicity', *Evangelical Magazine* no. 72 (November 1972), 15.

53 David Wells, 'On Being Evangelical: Some Theological Differences and Similarities', in *Evangelicalism: Comparative Studies of Popular Protestantism in North America, the British Isles, and Beyond, 1700–1990*, edited by Mark A. Noll, David W. Bebbington and George A. Rawlyk (New York: Oxford University Press, 1994), p. 390.

54 David Wells, *No Place for Truth: or, Whatever Happened to Evangelical Theology?* (Grand Rapids, MI: Eerdmans, 1993), p. 134.

At the 1989 *Evangelical Affirmations* consultation in Chicago, co-sponsored by the National Association of Evangelicals and Trinity Evangelical Divinity School, Henry attempted to answer the pressing question 'Who are the evangelicals?' by reiterating his lifelong appeal for them to cohere around theological affirmations concerning the saving work of Christ and the authority of Scripture.[55] Yet in response to Henry, Nathan Hatch proclaimed that 'In truth, there is no such thing as evangelicalism.' The generic name masked the reality of accelerating 'centrifugal forces' generating a 'rampant pluralism', dominated by 'scores of self-appointed and independent-minded religious leaders'.[56] Jon Stone concurred, that despite energetic attempts to construct an evangelical coalition in postwar America, evangelicalism – as an *ism* – was 'a fiction'.[57] Lewis Smedes called evangelicalism 'a fantasy'.[58] While many mourned over evangelicalism's fatal weaknesses and prescribed necessary antidotes, like Mark Noll's *The Scandal of the Evangelical Mind* (1994) and Iain Murray's *Evangelicalism Divided* (2000), Darryl Hart proposed a more radical solution: 'Instead of trying to fix evangelicalism, born-again Protestants would be better off if they abandoned the category altogether. . . . Evangelicalism needs to be relinquished as a religious identity because it does not exist.' Like Samuel, he likened it to 'the wax nose of twentieth-century American Protestantism. Behind this proboscis, which has been nipped and tucked by savvy religious leaders, academics, and pollsters, is a face void of any discernible features.' Evangelicalism, Hart argued, was 'largely a constructed ideal without any real substance', a façade built by the self-styled 'neo-evangelicals' of the postwar generation. It had become such a 'popular category' in religious scholarship that it was no longer useful. In particular, he warned that the resurgence of evangelical history as an academic discipline had 'yielded the impression that something old has been discovered when it could actually be that scholars have taken something recent and read it selectively into the past'.[59] Nevertheless, despite these protests, the burgeoning literature on evangelicalism, and the search for evangelical identities, continues unabated.

In search of definitions

'Evangelicalism is probably the most over-defined religious movement in the world', observes Mark Smith. Indeed he argues that this obsession with self-definition is so pervasive that it may, ironically, be one of evangelicalism's defining characteristics.[60] This instinct was displayed by Martyn Lloyd-Jones (minister of Westminster Chapel, London) in his addresses to the International Fellowship of Evangelical Students in Austria in 1971 on the question, 'What is an Evangelical?' He emphasized the need to distinguish accurately 'between evangelicals and pseudo-evangelicals':

---

55 See further, Gregory Alan Thornbury, *Recovering Classic Evangelicalism: Applying the Wisdom and Vision of Carl F. H. Henry* (Wheaton, IL: Crossway, 2013); *Essential Evangelicalism: The Enduring Influence of Carl F. H. Henry*, edited by Matthew J. Hall and Owen Strachan (Wheaton, IL: Crossway, 2015).
56 Nathan O. Hatch, 'The Evangelicals: Response to Carl F. H. Henry', in *Evangelical Affirmations*, edited by Kenneth S. Kantzer and Carl F. H. Henry (Grand Rapids, MI: Academie Books, 1990), pp. 97–8.
57 Stone, *On the Boundaries of American Evangelicalism*, p. 2.
58 Lewis Smedes, 'Evangelicalism: A Fantasy', *Reformed Journal* vol. 30 (February 1980), 2–3.
59 D. G. Hart, *Deconstructing Evangelicalism: Conservative Protestantism in the Age of Billy Graham* (Grand Rapids, MI: Baker, 2004), pp. 16–18, 38.
60 Mark Smith, 'British Evangelical Identities: Locating the Discussion', in *British Evangelical Identities Past and Present: Aspects of the History and Sociology of Evangelicalism in Britain and Ireland*, edited by Mark Smith (Milton Keynes: Paternoster, 2008), pp. 1–2.

we must not take this term 'evangelical' for granted. We must rediscover its meaning. We must define it again. And we must be ready to fight for it and to defend it . . . the whole question of the meaning of 'evangelical' has been thrown again into the melting pot. We must be sure and certain that we know exactly what we mean when we employ this term.

Lloyd-Jones was concerned that some who had recently departed from traditional evangelicalism 'still try to claim that they are truly evangelical. Therefore the problem is this: to define exactly what an evangelical is, and who exactly is an evangelical.' Because it ultimately concerned the content of the gospel, precise definition was essential and he called upon his audience to be prepared to defend the meaning of the term 'even to our very "latest breath" '.[61]

And yet every definition is itself a contested battleground. To seek a workable definition of evangelicalism is, in the words of Leonard Sweet, 'to kick the hornet's nest'.[62] The constant evolution of evangelicalism across the generations presents a particular conundrum. 'I know what constituted an Evangelical in former times', wrote Lord Shaftesbury to his friend the evangelical barrister Alexander Haldane, 'I have no clear notion what constitutes one now.'[63] A century later, Colin Buchanan celebrated the growing strength of evangelicals in the Church of England but admitted that they were 'nothing like' their predecessors. 'They cannot be expected to mouth the same shibboleths. They will not fight for the same causes.' Indeed, he confessed that by the standards of an earlier generation 'it is doubtful if there are any evangelical ordinands in training today'.[64] The burgeoning of charismatic Anglicanism led *Christianity Today* in 1990 to conclude that although the proportion of young evangelicals in the Church of England was increasing, 'their evangelicalism is less and less like that promoted in the postwar resurgence'.[65] For Kevin Bauder, a self-styled evangelical fundamentalist, the threat to evangelical cohesion came from a different quarter. He complained that 'left-leaning evangelicals' had ceased to identify liberalism with apostasy, with serious consequences for the whole movement: 'Today the Left draws the entire evangelical movement like a huge theological magnet. Views that would have been seen as heterodox in 1947 or as anti-evangelical in 1975 are regarded as mainstream in 2011.'[66] Yet these evangelical evolutions had the ability both to include the previously heterodox and to exclude the previously orthodox. For example, Gerald Bray declared in 2005 that N. T. Wright could not be considered a 'conservative evangelical' because of his support for the consecration of women bishops. Yet Wright retorted that in their youth conservative evangelicalism had always been defined by one's views on the Bible and the atonement, and since he had not changed his position on either of those subjects he should not now be forcibly excluded from the 'conservative evangelical' constituency.[67]

61 'What is an Evangelical?' (1971), in D. M. Lloyd-Jones, *Knowing the Times: Addresses Delivered on Various Occasions, 1942–1977* (Edinburgh: Banner of Truth Trust, 1989), pp. 300, 305–6, 342.
62 Leonard I. Sweet, 'The Evangelical Tradition in America', in *The Evangelical Tradition in America*, edited by Leonard I. Sweet (Macon, GA: Mercer University Press, 1984), p. 86.
63 Edwin Hodder, *The Life and Work of the Seventh Earl of Shaftesbury* (3 vols, London: Cassell, 1887), III: 451.
64 Colin Buchanan, 'Released from the Ghetto', *Church of England Newspaper*, 11 March 1977.
65 David Neff and George K. Brushaber, 'The Remaking of English Evangelicalism: Signs, Wonders, and Worries in the Land of Canterbury', *Christianity Today* (5 February 1990), 26.
66 Kevin T. Bauder, 'Generic Evangelicalism: A Fundamentalist Response', in *The Spectrum of Evangelicalism*, edited by Andrew David Naselli and Collin Hansen (Grand Rapids, MI: Zondervan, 2011), pp. 148–9.
67 Gerald Bray, 'No Taxation Without Representation', *Churchman* vol. 119 (Autumn 2005), 195–8; N. T. Wright, 'Bishops, Women and the Bible: A Response', *Churchman* vol. 120 (Spring 2006), 7–9.

In this shifting terrain, definitions for evangelicalism which accurately reflect lived evangelical experience in multiple cultural and historical contexts across the globe, remain elusive. During the early burgeoning of scholarly interest in evangelicalism among historians, sociologists and political commentators, from the 1970s onwards, identifying the proper research field was a primary concern. Echoing Christopher Hill's playful image on the dilemmas of defining puritanism, Mark Noll likened the problem of evangelical definitions to a 'fearsome dragon' standing in the historian's path.[68] The inaugural conference in 1983 of the Institute for the Study of American Evangelicals at the Billy Graham Center, Wheaton College, Illinois, attempted to delineate 'evangelicalism' as a conceptual unity. George Marsden argued that despite the movement's evident diversity, it could be studied as 'a single phenomenon', and he posited that evangelicals were Christians who 'typically emphasize' five points:

(1) the Reformation doctrine of the final authority of Scripture (2) the real, historical character of God's saving work recorded in Scripture (3) eternal salvation only through personal trust in Christ (4) the importance of evangelism and missions (5) the importance of a spiritually transformed life.

Although evangelicals might disagree sharply over the details, these marks, according to Marsden, identified them as 'a distinct religious grouping', even a 'denomination'.[69] Among a host of similar formulae put forward experimentally during the 1980s, the version published by David Bebbington at the end of the decade came to dominate all subsequent historical conversations on evangelical identity. Addressing specifically the British context, he famously posited:

There are the four qualities that have been the special marks of Evangelical religion: *conversionism*, the belief that lives need to be changed; *activism*, the expression of the gospel in effort; *biblicism*, a particular regard for the Bible; and what may be called *crucicentrism*, a stress on the sacrifice of Christ on the cross. Together they form a quadrilateral of priorities that is the basis of Evangelicalism.[70]

These themes were unpacked more fully in Bebbington's analysis, but this succinct definition quickly became, in the words of W. R. Ward, the 'most quoted sentence in the whole historiography of evangelicalism'.[71] The Bebbington quadrilateral, due primarily to its simplicity and flexibility, proved serviceable for historians researching evangelicalism in other global contexts, and Derek Tidball reckoned it to be 'as near to a consensus as we might ever expect to reach'.[72]

Nevertheless, Bebbington's descriptive approach remained controversial and generated a literature of its own. Albert Mohler acknowledged that it was helpful to a limited extent, but 'as

---

68 Mark A. Noll, *Between Faith and Criticism: Evangelicals, Scholarship, and the Bible in America* (San Francisco, CA: Harper and Row, 1986), p. 1.
69 George Marsden 'The Evangelical Denomination', in *Evangelicalism and Modern America*, edited by George Marsden (Grand Rapids, MI: Eerdmans, 1984), pp. ix–x.
70 David W. Bebbington, *Evangelicalism in Modern Britain: A History from the 1730s to the 1980s* (London: Unwin Hyman, 1989), pp. 2–3.
71 W. R. Ward, 'The Making of the Evangelical Mind' (2004), in *Evangelicalism, Piety and Politics: The Selected Writings of W. R. Ward*, edited by Andrew Chandler (Farnham: Ashgate, 2014), p. 17.
72 Derek J. Tidball, *Who are the Evangelicals? Tracing the Roots of the Modern Movements* (London: Marshall Pickering, 1994), p. 14. See further Timothy Larsen, 'The Reception Given *Evangelicalism in Modern Britain* since its Publication in 1989', in *The Emergence of Evangelicalism: Exploring Historical Continuities*, edited by Michael A. G. Haykin and Kenneth J. Stewart (Nottingham: Apollos, 2008), pp. 21–36.

is so often the case with phenomenological definitions, these criteria are so vague as to be fairly useless in determining the limits of evangelical definition', because Roman Catholics or liberal Protestants might also fit the bill. Put more sharply, 'It utterly fails to identify in any helpful sense who is *not* an evangelical.'[73] Subsequent historians have sought to meet this challenge by adding to Bebbington's four marks. John Stackhouse, for instance, proposed orthodoxy/orthopraxy and transdenominationalism as additional features.[74] Likewise Timothy Larsen attempted a five-point definition of an evangelical:

1. an orthodox Protestant
2. who stands in the tradition of the global Christian networks arising from the eighteenth-century revival movements associated with John Wesley and George Whitefield;
3. who has a preeminent place for the Bible in her or his Christian life as the divinely inspired, final authority in matters of faith and practice;
4. who stresses reconciliation with God through the atoning work of Jesus Christ on the cross;
5. and who stresses the work of the Holy Spirit in the life of an individual to bring about conversion and an ongoing life of fellowship with God and service to God and others, including the duty of all believers to participate in the task of proclaiming the gospel to all people.

Points 3 to 5 encompassed Bebbington's quartet (combining 'conversionism' and 'activism' as aspects of pneumatology), while Point 1 excluded both Roman Catholics and liberal Protestants, and Point 2 located evangelicalism as a post eighteenth-century movement explicitly including Arminians and Calvinists.[75] Rob Warner argued that Bebbington's model was too 'static' and should be 'reconceptualised as twin and rival axes within pan-evangelicalism that energise the dynamic of evangelical rivalries, experiments and evolution'. He interpreted the contested nature of the late twentieth-century British movement by placing 'entrepreneurial' evangelicals on a conversionist-activist axis and 'theologically oriented' evangelicals on a biblicist-crucicentrist axis, each competing for dominance.[76]

These various working definitions, as Dayton observes, are often closely tied to the historian's source material – for example, whether they read primarily Presbyterian and Baptist literature or Methodist and Pentecostal literature, or whether their research focuses upon the nineteenth-century revivalist and holiness movements or the twentieth-century fundamentalist controversies. Marsden often categorized evangelicalism as 'conservative' or 'orthodox' in opposition to liberalism, whereas Dayton preferred to conceive of evangelicalism as 'radical' because of its ability to disrupt traditional churches.[77] Olson lamented these perennial attempts to define evangelicalism as 'an interesting but ultimately futile project. And yet it is one we

---

73 R. Albert Mohler, 'Confessional Evangelicalism', in *The Spectrum of Evangelicalism*, edited by Naselli and Hansen, pp. 73–4.
74 John G. Stackhouse, 'Generic Evangelicalism', in *The Spectrum of Evangelicalism*, edited by Naselli and Hansen, p. 124.
75 Timothy Larsen, 'Defining and Locating Evangelicalism', in *The Cambridge Companion to Evangelical Theology*, edited by Timothy Larsen and Daniel J. Treier (Cambridge: Cambridge University Press, 2007), pp. 1–14.
76 Rob Warner, *Reinventing English Evangelicalism, 1966–2001: A Theological and Sociological Study* (Milton Keynes: Paternoster, 2007), p. 20.
77 Donald W. Dayton, 'Re-Thinking Evangelicalism: "The Search for the Historical Evangelicalism: George Marsden's History of Fuller Seminary as a Case Study"' (1993), in *From the Margins: A Celebration of the Theological Work of Donald W. Dayton*, edited by Christian T. Collins Winn (Eugene, OR: Wipf and Stock, 2007), pp. 253–80.

scholars of evangelicalism cannot seem to give up on.'[78] Other historians were more sanguine. Acknowledging that classifications could be both highly complex and politically sensitive, Noll nonetheless reasoned that 'if common sense prevails, the difficulties are manageable'.[79]

While historians and sociologists tend to favour a phenomenological approach to evangelical identity, theologians and church leaders (especially of the conservative variety) have often argued for a propositional approach.[80] Of course this methodology could cut both ways. By interpreting 'evangelicalism' not as a demographic but as a doctrinal category towards which all Christians should strive, it could be decoupled from a conservative subculture. In *Not Evangelical Enough!* (2003), Iain Taylor asked not 'what *does* it mean' but 'What *should* it mean to be an evangelical? . . . That one is an "Evangelical" is of itself no guarantee that one is in fact properly evangelical, that is, in line with the gospel.'[81] Likewise Kevin Vanhoozer understood 'evangelical' to mean 'a guiding hope and eschatological reality, not an already-accomplished historical achievement'.[82]

For pollsters, an accurate conceptualization of evangelicalism is equally difficult.[83] As Conrad Hackett and Michael Lindsay show, most religious surveys of the population employ one of three methods, or a combination of them. Some count evangelical denominations, thus excluding non-Protestant respondents and those within doctrinally-mixed denominations such as Anglicanism. Others rely upon evangelical self-identification or enquire (as did the 1976 Gallup poll) whether respondents have had a 'born-again experience', which widens the scope to some within Roman Catholicism, Eastern Orthodoxy and Mormonism. Other pollsters ask a series of 'yes/no' questions in order to identify evangelical allegiance. These contrasting methodologies lead to wildly different results, with the estimated number of evangelicals in America fluctuating between one in two and one in twenty.[84]

One of the complexities, as Mark Smith notes, is that the essentials of evangelicalism are not easily 'dissected or distilled' because it is 'never met with in its pure form' but is

> always encountered as a hybrid with other sources of identity. . . . Presbyterian evangelicals and Baptist evangelicals, male evangelicals and female evangelicals, English evangelicals and Northern Irish evangelicals, black evangelicals and white evangelicals, reformed evangelicals and charismatic evangelicals, but never mere evangelicals. . . .

---

78 Roger E. Olson, 'Postconservative Evangelicalism', in *The Spectrum of Evangelicalism*, edited by Naselli and Hansen, p. 162.
79 Mark Noll, 'What is "Evangelical"?', in *The Oxford Handbook of Evangelical Theology*, edited by Gerald R. McDermott (Oxford: Oxford University Press, 2010), p. 22.
80 Samuel Crossley, 'Recent Developments in the Definition of Evangelicalism', *Foundations: An International Journal of Evangelical Theology* no. 70 (Spring 2016), 112–33.
81 Iain Taylor, 'Introduction', in *Not Evangelical Enough! The Gospel at the Centre*, edited by Iain Taylor (Carlisle: Paternoster, 2003), p. xv.
82 Kevin J. Vanhoozer and Daniel J. Treier, *Theology and the Mirror of Scripture: A Mere Evangelical Account* (London: Apollos, 2016), p. 10.
83 For analysis of American surveys, see Christian Smith, *American Evangelicalism: Embattled and Thriving* (Chicago, IL: University of Chicago Press, 1998); Christian Smith, *Christian America? What Evangelicals Really Want* (Berkeley: University of California Press, 2000); Corwin W. Smidt, *American Evangelicals Today* (Lanham, MA: Rowman and Littlefield, 2013). For analysis of a British survey, see *21st Century Evangelicals: Reflections on Research by the Evangelical Alliance*, edited by Greg Smith (Watford: Instant Apostle, 2015).
84 Conrad Hackett and D. Michael Lindsay, 'Measuring Evangelicalism: Consequences of Different Operationalization Strategies', *Journal for the Scientific Study of Religion* vol. 47 (September 2008), 499–514. See also 'Measuring Evangelicalism One Question at a Time', in Hart, *Deconstructing Evangelicalism*, pp. 85–106.

Evangelicalism may be indigenised within, corrupted by, in tension with, or transforming the contexts in which it is encountered (and perhaps all four simultaneously) but those contexts and the multiple refractions of evangelicalism they produce are an inescapable part of the phenomenon.[85]

Therefore historians, for whom context and practice loom large, often emphasize the inherent plurality of evangelical identities. The relative place of evangelicalism, when hybridized with denominational identities, is especially contested. Some equate evangelicalism with the gospel itself and thus of supreme and primary importance. John Stott, for instance, asserted that 'properly understood, the Christian faith, the catholic faith, the biblical faith and the evangelical faith are one and the same thing'.[86] In contrast, Hugh Gough (Archbishop of Sydney) explained that when it came to Anglican evangelicalism or evangelical Anglicanism, 'I am an Anglican first.'[87] Lloyd-Jones retorted that these inverted loyalties made Gough 'suspect as an evangelical'. The true evangelical, he insisted, must be 'evangelical first. He may be a Baptist, he may be a Presbyterian, he may be Episcopalian, but he is primarily, first and foremost, evangelical.'[88]

Such 'evangelical first' affirmations were especially difficult for denominational leaders responsible for mixed theological constituencies. As a seventeen-year-old, in May 1953, George Carey was converted through the ministry of an evangelical parish church in Dagenham, east London. However, three and a half decades later, shortly after his appointment as an Anglican bishop, he publicly criticized British evangelicalism as 'too constricting intellectually, too narrow academically and too stifling spiritually'. Acknowledging that 'I owe to evangelicalism my very soul', he nonetheless described himself as someone 'whose heart beats in time with the evangelical love of Jesus and a deep devotion to the biblical tradition, but whose head cannot go along with received evangelical teaching.'[89] On his elevation in 1991 as Archbishop of Canterbury, Carey resisted being put into 'a theological box',[90] and stated: 'no one will ever hear me calling *myself* an evangelical ... For me the most important thing is being a Christian, then being an Anglican, and those are the two most important words in my vocabulary.'[91] In a parallel trajectory, Justin Welby was converted as an undergraduate through the Cambridge Inter-Collegiate Christian Union in 1975, and on his appointment as Archbishop of Canterbury in 2013 he told the *Church Times*: 'I'd still describe myself as a conservative Evangelical if I had to put a label on it, but the trouble with the label is it brings so much baggage.' Pushed further at the Evangelical Alliance, he assented to being an evangelical in theology, but nevertheless made clear, 'Am I an evangelical in party terms? Absolutely not, because the Bible tells me we're not to have parties and groups and factions within the Church. So I don't buy into a party, but I do have a high view of Scripture and I'm deeply committed to proclaiming the gospel.' The *English Churchman*, a Protestant newspaper, dismissed the archbishop as 'a New Evangelical of

---

85 Smith, 'British Evangelical Identities', pp. 6–7.
86 John R. W. Stott, *Christ the Controversialist: A Study in Some Essentials of Evangelical Religion* (London: Tyndale Press, 1970), p. 33. See further John Stott, *Evangelical Truth: A Personal Plea for Unity* (Leicester: Inter-Varsity Press, 1999).
87 Marcia Cameron, *Phenomenal Sydney: Anglicans in a Time of Change, 1945–2013* (Eugene, OR: Wipf and Stock, 2016), p. 97.
88 Lloyd-Jones, 'What is an Evangelical?', p. 323.
89 George Carey, 'Parties in the Church of England', *Theology* vol. 91 (July 1988), 269–70.
90 George Carey, *I Believe* (London: SPCK, 1991), p. 7.
91 Mary Loudon, *Revelations: The Clergy Questioned* (London: Hamilton, 1994), p. 253. See further, Andrew Atherstone, 'Archbishop Carey's Ecumenical Vision', *Theology* vol. 106 (September 2003), 342–52.

a rather liberal, charismatic, modern and ecumenical persuasion'.[92] Welby's ambivalence about evangelical nomenclature and its place in his own religious identity was typical of his friends and mentors at Holy Trinity Brompton, in central London, where successive vicars Sandy Millar and Nicky Gumbel spoke of their dislike of 'unhelpful and divisive labels' and stereotypes such as 'evangelical' and 'charismatic', in favour simply of the title 'Christian'.[93]

These dilemmas were felt not only by archbishops, but also by members of Reformed denominations who likewise rejected an 'evangelical first' approach to Christian identity because it was undogmatic and unecclesial.[94] The Calvinist seceders from the Presbyterian Church in the United States of America (PCUSA) in the 1930s, led by J. Gresham Machen, reconstituted themselves as the Orthodox Presbyterian Church (OPC), committed to the Westminster standards. Significantly, they voted against calling themselves the Evangelical Presbyterian Church, partly because 'evangelical' bore the taint of Arminianism and revivalism.[95] The relationship between the Southern Baptist Convention and evangelicalism was likewise contested, fomented by deep ideological and cultural rivalries, with one Southern Baptist spokesman in 1976 emphatically rejecting evangelical identity because 'That's a Yankee word.'[96] Mohler was more conciliatory, calling for 'the rediscovery and reclamation of an authentic and distinctive Southern Baptist evangelicalism – *genuinely Baptist*, and *genuinely evangelical*'.[97] Yet he continued to describe himself as Baptist before evangelical, because 'the only way evangelicalism can be retained as a definable theological movement is by means of a glad and eager confessionalism'.[98] Rather than conceiving of evangelicalism as a 'big tent' in which ecclesiological distinctives are dissolved, Michael Horton preferred the analogy of evangelicalism as 'an old village green', surrounded by churches. Christians might gather on the green for parachurch ministries, but it was not ultimately where they belonged or would be most spiritually nourished.[99] Hart went further, refusing the label 'evangelical' altogether, in preference for a Presbyterian and Reformed self-identity. Yet he railed against the aggressive imperialism of the evangelical movement (which he associated with a 'low-church, revivalistic form of piety') for counting as adherents even those, like himself, who did not want to belong:

---

92 Andrew Atherstone, *Archbishop Justin Welby: Risk-taker and Reconciler* (London: Darton, Longman and Todd, 2014), pp. 195, 197.
93 Sandy Millar, *All I Want Is You: A Collection of Christian Reflections* (London: Alpha International, 2005), pp. 107–8; Nicky Gumbel, 'Alpha Plus', in *Why I Am Still An Anglican: Essays and Conversations*, edited by Caroline Chartres (London: Continuum, 2006), p. 96.
94 *Why We Belong: Evangelical Unity and Denominational Diversity*, edited by Anthony L. Chute, Christopher W. Morgan and Robert A. Peterson (Wheaton, IL: Crossway, 2013).
95 D. G. Hart and John Muether, *Fighting the Good Fight: A Brief History of the Orthodox Presbyterian Church* (Willow Grove, PA: Orthodox Presbyterian Church, 1995), pp. 50–3.
96 Joel A. Carpenter, 'Is "Evangelical" a Yankee Word? Relations Between Northern Evangelicals and the Southern Baptist Convention in the Twentieth Century', in *Southern Baptists and American Evangelicals: The Conversation Continues*, edited by David S. Dockery (Nashville, TN: Broadman and Holman, 1993), p. 78. See also, James Leo Garrett, E. Glenn Hinson and James E. Tull, *Are Southern Baptists 'Evangelicals'?* (Macon, GA: Mercer University Press, 1983); *Southern Baptists, Evangelicals, and the Future of Denominationalism*, edited by David S. Dockery (Nashville, TN: B&H Academic, 2011).
97 R. Albert Mohler, 'A Call for Baptist Evangelicals and Evangelical Baptists: Communities of Faith and a Common Quest for Identity', in *Southern Baptists and American Evangelicals*, edited by Dockery, p. 238.
98 Mohler, 'Generic Evangelicalism: A Confessional Evangelical Response', in *The Spectrum of Evangelicalism*, edited by Naselli and Hansen, p. 155.
99 Michael S. Horton, 'The Church After Evangelicalism', in *Renewing the Evangelical Mission*, edited by Richard Lints (Grand Rapids, MI: Eerdmans, 2013), p. 159.

> If my denomination is not a member of the National Association of Evangelicals, if I do not give to the Billy Graham Evangelistic Association, if I do not read *Christianity Today* for edification, and if I refuse to put an *ichthys* medallion on my car, why am I considered an evangelical? Do these scholars, parachurch officials, and pundits know something that I don't? Can they actually see into my heart?[100]

The elastic boundaries of evangelicalism made it a movement easy to join but difficult to leave, with many conscripted against their wills.

Guarding the boundaries

The purpose of the *Evangelical Affirmations* consultation, explained Kenneth Kantzer, was 'to determine what we mean by "evangelical". What are its boundaries? Who are in and who are out?'[101] Joel Beeke agreed that 'while much of what bears the name evangelical is shallow and even contrary to Scripture, the label itself is worth defending', though 'a slippery fish to catch'. In his view this required 'both a firm centre and clearly delineated boundaries. If evangelicalism has no boundaries, then it has no meaning.'[102] This clamour for definitional clarity is especially evident in North America, and Stackhouse discerns a correlation with the increased financial and political clout of the movement since the 1940s. Eligibility for an 'evangelical membership card' opens doors to the corridors of power within the institution's numerous seminaries, management boards and publishing houses. 'Boundaries will continue to be policed', therefore, 'because the property being guarded is so valuable.'[103] For example, D. A. Carson criticized the 'younger evangelical intellectuals' who had drifted from biblical authority and other core doctrines: 'But most of them still want to call themselves evangelicals: that is their power base, that is their prime readership, and it is that group that funds many of the colleges and seminaries where they teach.' Yet their output, in Carson's judgment, had become 'less and less "evangelical" in any useful historic or theological sense'.[104]

In each generation, on both sides of the Atlantic, the boundaries have been contested. Attitudes to Catholicism were a particular source of tension. Addressing the Fellowship of Evangelical Churchmen in 1961, Packer declared:

> You cannot add to evangelical theology without subtracting from it. By augmenting it, you cannot enrich it; you can only impoverish it. . . . What is more than evangelical is less than evangelical. Evangelical theology, by its very nature, cannot be supplemented; it can only be denied.[105]

However, Packer was himself accused of undermining that basic principle by contributing to *Growing into Union* (1970), an ecumenical proposal co-authored with Buchanan and two traditionalist Anglo-Catholics, Graham Leonard and Eric Mascall.[106] In the minds of some

---

100 Hart, *Deconstructing Evangelicalism*, p. 10. For a defence of confessionalism versus evangelicalism, see further D. G. Hart, *The Lost Soul of American Protestantism* (Lanham, MD: Rowman and Littlefield, 2002).
101 Kenneth S. Kantzer, 'Afterword: Where Do We Go From Here?', in *Evangelical Affirmations*, edited by Kantzer and Henry, p. 513.
102 Joel R. Beeke, *What is Evangelicalism?* (Darlington: Evangelical Press, 2012), pp. 14–15.
103 Stackhouse, 'Generic Evangelicalism', pp. 140, 142.
104 D. A. Carson, *The Gagging of God: Christianity Confronts Pluralism* (Leicester: Apollos, 1996), p. 453.
105 Quoted in Stott, *Christ the Controversialist*, pp. 32–3.
106 Andrew Atherstone, 'A Mad Hatter's Tea Party in the Old Mitre Tavern? Ecumenical Reactions to *Growing into Union*', *Ecclesiology* vol. 6 (January 2010), 39–67.

reviewers, Packer and Buchanan's participation in such a unity scheme threw their evangelical credentials into doubt. The *Evangelical Magazine of Wales* declared that the book had 'done well-nigh irretrievable damage within that which used to be called Evangelicalism, but which cannot without serious re-definition of terms be so called any longer.' They had 'dragged their anchors' and departed from 'historic, biblical Evangelicalism'.[107] Likewise *Peace and Truth*, journal of the Sovereign Grace Union, believed Packer and Buchanan had 'cut loose from their moorings' and proved themselves to be 'no longer Evangelicals'.[108] Michael Buss, a Baptist pastor in Islington, north London, was also left asking 'What is an evangelical?', and wrote on behalf of the British Evangelical Council:

> Already we have to fence the word with such qualifications as *conservative* or *Reformed*. If the word *evangelical* relates principally to our conviction that Scripture is the inspired, infallible and inerrant Word of God in its entirety and as such is our only authority for matters of faith and practice then we wonder how these authors may consistently call themselves *evangelical* for their book betrays our definition. Alternatively, if these men are truly evangelical we are tempted to say the word has lost all its meaning and we shall now even have to accept Rome's claim of being *evangelical*. Until we know clearly what an evangelical is the word will continue to be bandied about and cause more confusion than it is worth.[109]

Under this hostile scrutiny, Packer defended his right still to call himself an 'evangelical'. He argued that evangelicals should define themselves not negatively by what they opposed (such as Roman Catholicism) but positively by what they believed. He listed evangelicalism's six 'essential ingredients', to which he still subscribed: the authority of the Word of God, the finality of the gospel of Christ, the priesthood of all believers, the primacy of evangelism, the necessity of conversion and the lordship of the Holy Spirit. 'What a man is or is not against may show him to be a muddled or negligent or inconsistent Evangelical', Packer observed, 'but you may not deny his right to call himself an Evangelical while he maintains these principles as the basis of his Christian position.' He insisted that his authorship of *Growing into Union* implied no 'defection from evangelical essentials'.[110] Yet Lloyd-Jones dismissed Packer's claims as 'quite wrong' and as opening the door to a repetition of the Galatian heresy.[111] One of the casualties of the controversy was the Puritan Studies Conference in which the two men had collaborated since 1950. It was cancelled with explanation from Lloyd-Jones that it would be a 'farce' to continue because such were Packer's concessions to Catholicism that he was 'no more either Evangelical or Puritan'.[112] Similar questions were raised in the 1990s about Packer's participation in the ecumenical initiative 'Evangelicals and Catholics Together'.[113]

During the 1970s 'Battle for the Bible', the role of the inerrancy of Scripture as an evangelical boundary marker was vociferously debated. Ockenga observed:

---

107 'Unity – At a Price', *Evangelical Magazine of Wales* vol. 9 (August / September 1970), 3.
108 'The National Church', *Peace and Truth* vol. 49 (October 1970), 77–8.
109 B.E.C. *Newsletter* no. 5 (July 1970).
110 J. I. Packer, '"Growing into Union": A Reply to Some Criticisms', *Evangelical Magazine* no. 66 (April 1971), 3, 7.
111 Lloyd-Jones, 'What is an Evangelical?', p. 319.
112 Martyn Lloyd-Jones to Philip E. Hughes, 22 December 1970, in *D. Martyn Lloyd-Jones: Letters 1919–1981*, edited by Iain H. Murray (Edinburgh: Banner of Truth Trust, 1994), p. 182.
113 Mark Noll and Carolyn Nystrom, *Is the Reformation Over? An Evangelical Assessment of Contemporary Roman Catholicism* (Grand Rapids, MI: Baker, 2005), pp. 151–94.

The evidence that those who surrender the doctrine of inerrancy inevitably move away from orthodoxy is indisputable. It is apparent that those who give up an authoritative, dependable, authentic, trustworthy, and infallible Scripture must ultimately yield the right to use of the name 'evangelical'.[114]

Harold Lindsell (editor of *Christianity Today*) agreed that anyone who denied the doctrine of biblical infallibility 'cannot truly be an evangelical'.[115] However, faced by a backlash from those who felt disenfranchised, Lindsell acknowledged that he had no power to copyright the term. He concluded that the word 'evangelical' had been 'so debased that it has lost its usefulness', 'a confusing label and probably a lost cause'. Therefore he recommended inerrantists return to a 'fundamentalist' self-identity, despite its pejorative connotations, or call themselves 'Orthodox Protestants'.[116] Nevertheless the Evangelical Theological Society (ETS, founded 1949) discovered that a simple affirmation of biblical inerrancy was insufficient to protect its boundaries, revoking the membership of Robert Gundry in 1983 for denying the historicity of Matthew's Gospel and coming close to the expulsion of Clark Pinnock in 2003 for advocating open theism.[117] Pinnock defended his teaching on divine foreknowledge by asking rhetorically: 'Why can an evangelical not propose a different view of this matter? What church council has declared it to be impossible? Since when has this become the criterion of being orthodox or unorthodox, evangelical or not evangelical?'[118] Yet Bruce Ware, among others, argued that open theism was so destructive of core tenets of the Christian faith as to be 'unacceptable as a viable, legitimate model within evangelicalism'.[119] To this Pinnock retorted that his proposals were merely 'the logical next step in Arminian thinking, which has always been part of evangelicalism', and urged the ETS to resist 'the current move to make scholastic Calvinism (in effect) the only true evangelical theology'.[120]

In Britain, the Evangelical Alliance (EA, founded 1846) aimed to embrace all branches of evangelicalism, but its cohesion was regularly tested. Periodically it came to the brink of expelling unorthodox members, ranging from T. R. Birks in the 1870s for his teaching on hell, to Morris Cerullo in the 1990s for the prosperity gospel which pervaded his Mission to London crusades.[121] EA's doctrinal boundaries were especially scrutinized after one of its leading lights, Steve Chalke (Baptist minister and social justice campaigner), published *The Lost of Message of*

---

114 Harold J. Ockenga, 'Foreword', in Harold Lindsell, *The Battle for the Bible* (Grand Rapids, MI: Zondervan, 1976).
115 Lindsell, *The Battle for the Bible*, p. 210.
116 Harold Lindsell, *The Bible in the Balance* (Grand Rapids, MI: Zondervan, 1979), pp. 319–21.
117 Noll, *Between Faith and Criticism*, pp. 167–71; Norman L. Geisler and William C. Roach, *Defending Inerrancy: Affirming the Accuracy of Scripture for a New Generation* (Grand Rapids, MI: Baker, 2011), pp. 45–60.
118 Clark H. Pinnock, *Most Moved Mover: A Theology of God's Openness* (Carlisle: Paternoster, 2001), p. 110.
119 Bruce A. Ware, 'Defining Evangelicalism's Boundaries Theologically: Is Open Theism Evangelical?', *Journal of the Evangelical Theological Society* vol. 45 (June 2002), 212. See also, Wayne Grudem, 'Why, When, and for What Should We Draw New Boundaries?', in *Beyond the Bounds: Open Theism and the Undermining of Biblical Christianity*, edited by John Piper, Justin Taylor and Paul Kjoss Helseth (Wheaton, IL: Crossway, 2003), pp. 339–70.
120 Clark H. Pinnock, 'There Is Room For Us: A Reply to Bruce Ware', *Journal of the Evangelical Theological Society* vol. 45 (June 2002), 214, 219.
121 Ian Randall and David Hilborn, *One Body in Christ: The History and Significance of the Evangelical Alliance* (Carlisle: Paternoster, 2001), pp. 119–32; Nancy A. Schaefer, '"Some Will See Miracles": The Reception of Morris Cerullo World Evangelism in Britain', *Journal of Contemporary Religion* vol. 14 (1999), 111–26.

Jesus (2003).[122] Chalke affirmed the inherent goodness of humanity, downplayed God's wrath at sin, and parodied the doctrine of penal substitutionary atonement (in the most frequently quoted sentence of his book) as 'a form of cosmic child abuse – a vengeful Father, punishing his Son for an offence he has not even committed . . . in total contradiction to the statement "God is love".'[123] One stringent review lambasted it as an 'alarming, painful, dangerous book' which 'attacks the heart of biblical Christianity', and questioned why Chalke was given a platform at the Word Alive conference (part of Spring Harvest).[124] In particular, his right to call himself an 'evangelical' was widely questioned. The EA doctrinal basis affirmed 'The universal sinfulness and guilt of fallen man, making him subject to God's wrath and condemnation', and 'The substitutionary sacrifice of the incarnate Son of God as the sole and all-sufficient ground of redemption from the guilt and power of sin, and from its eternal consequences.'[125] When challenged that his teaching was inconsistent with his subscription, Chalke replied that 'substitutionary sacrifice' was not necessarily penal.[126] The EA executive reaffirmed penal substitution as clearly implied by its basis, but resisted calls for Chalke's expulsion. EA's theological advisor, David Hilborn, defended him as merely a popularizer, not a pioneer, since many evangelical scholars had previously dissented from the traditional doctrine.[127] As divisions deepened, Joel Edwards (EA's general director and a self-styled 'classical Pentecostal') acknowledged the serious implications for evangelical identity, but appealed for peace on all sides. '"What is an evangelical?" is a very important question', he wrote in a pastoral letter, 'But our challenge is far greater than what we do about a charismatic individual . . . we must avoid the word "evangelical" getting in the way of the words, "good news".'[128]

Nevertheless, some accused the EA leadership of placing evangelical unity above biblical truth. It was not merely an 'intramural' debate which could be conducted 'within the evangelical family', asserted Garry Williams: 'separation' was required.[129] *Evangelicals Now* believed that British evangelicalism had reached 'a crossroads', and Jonathan Stephen (pastor of Carey Baptist Church, Reading) warned:

> Just as in the 19th century 'Christianity' came to be defined in terms of whatever 'Christians' believed, so in the 21st century 'evangelicalism' has come to be defined by whatever 'evangelicals' believe. Either way, the inevitable result is liberalism. . . . This is yet another significant indication that popular evangelicalism is in theological freefall.[130]

---

122 Maxwell Wood, 'Penal Substitution in the Construction of British Evangelical Identity: Controversies in the Doctrine of the Atonement in the mid-2000s' (unpublished PhD thesis, Durham University, 2011).
123 Steve Chalke and Alan Mann, *The Lost Message of Jesus* (Grand Rapids, MI: Zondervan, 2003), p. 182.
124 Andrew Sach and Mike Ovey, 'Have We Lost the Message of Jesus?', *Evangelicals Now* (June 2004), 27.
125 Randall and Hilborn, *One Body in Christ*, p. 360. For the background to these affirmations, and their revision by EA in 2002–5, see David Hilborn, 'Atonement, Evangelicalism and the Evangelical Alliance: The Present Debate in Context', in *The Atonement Debate: Papers from the London Symposium on the Theology of Atonement*, edited by Derek Tidball, David Hilborn and Justin Thacker (Grand Rapids, MI: Zondervan, 2008), pp. 22–8.
126 Andy Peck, 'Evangelicals Debate the Cross', *Christianity* (December 2004), 10.
127 'EA Affirms Penal Substitution', *Christianity* (January 2005), 8.
128 Joel Edwards, 'A Letter from my Heart', *Christianity* (January 2005), 22.
129 Garry Williams, 'Penal Substitution: A Response to Recent Criticisms', in *The Atonement Debate*, edited by Tidball, Hilborn and Thacker, p. 188.
130 'A Public Debate on *The Lost Message*', *Evangelicals Now* (November 2004), 23.

Addressing the Fellowship of Independent Evangelical Churches (FIEC), Stephen lamented that the term 'evangelicalism' had 'become virtually meaningless. Virtually every conceivable religious deviation can now shelter under the umbrella of evangelicalism, if it so wishes'. He linked Chalke's denial of penal substitution with open theism and the 'new perspective' on Paul, as three examples of how 'a no-holds-barred, postmodern critique, implacably suspicious and arrogantly dismissive of the centuries-old convictions of Bible-centred Christianity, is wreaking havoc within professing evangelicalism'. The antidote, Stephen advocated, was a return to 'the confessional, conservative, classical evangelicalism that has been handed down to us'.[131]

These tensions over evangelical boundaries reached breaking point in 2013 when Chalke publicly affirmed his support for the British government's plans to extend marriage to same-sex couples.[132] Here, after much soul-searching, the Evangelical Alliance drew the line, and revoked the EA membership of Chalke's charity Oasis Trust (founded 1985), although he was permitted to retain his personal membership.[133] *Christianity* magazine spoke of 'the battle for the soul of evangelicalism', with homosexuality having become 'the defining litmus test for evangelical orthodoxy' in the twenty-first century, although Chalke continued to defend his entitlement to the name, interpreting 'evangelical' to mean a 'good news bringer'.[134] As further prominent individuals within the evangelical community, on both sides of the Atlantic, led calls for the 'full inclusion' of LGBT Christians, evangelical identities continued to fracture. After publishing *Changing Our Mind* (2014), the American ethicist David Gushee discovered he had crossed a 'line in the sand' and experienced 'the ashy chill of evangelical nuclear winter', having his name deleted from 'the invitation list of pretty much the entire evangelical world'.[135] Within the Church of England, David Runcorn proposed the labels 'Conserving Evangelicals' and 'Including Evangelicals' ('CEs' and 'IEs') for the two sides of the debate, thereby granting *bona fide* evangelical status to both.[136] Likewise Bishop Colin Fletcher desired that 'Evangelicals would accept each other as Evangelicals', regardless of their views on this question, without marginalizing or excluding one another from the movement.[137] Roy Clements (former pastor of Eden Baptist Church, Cambridge) identified as a 'gay evangelical', refusing to relinquish his membership of the evangelical movement. 'If I am now disowned by the evangelical establishment', he argued, 'it is because the goalposts have been moved – the term "evangelical Christian" has been hijacked and redefined.' He lamented that homosexuality had become an 'evangelical shibboleth', preferring to define evangelicals as those with a 'high view of Scripture'

---

131 Jonathan Stephen, 'The Current Crisis in Evangelicalism', *Evangelicals Now* (June 2005), 26–7.
132 Steve Chalke, 'The Bible and Homosexuality', *Christianity* (February 2013), 26–9. See further, Mark Vasey-Saunders, *The Scandal of Evangelicals and Homosexuality: English Evangelical Texts, 1960–2010* (Farnham: Ashgate, 2015).
133 Steve Clifford, *One: Unity in Diversity, A Personal Journey* (Oxford: Monarch, 2017), pp. 205–24.
134 Justin Brierley, 'The Battle for the Soul of Evangelicalism' and 'The Litmus Test for Orthodoxy', *Christianity* (June 2014), 5, 35–7.
135 David P. Gushee, *Still Christian: Following Jesus out of American Evangelicalism* (Louisville, KY: Westminster John Knox Press, 2017), pp. 129, 142. See also David P. Gushee, *Changing Our Mind: A Call from America's Leading Evangelical Ethics Scholar for Full Acceptance of LGBT Christians in the Church* (Canton, MI: Read the Spirit Books, 2014); Mark Achtemeier, *The Bible's Yes to Same-Sex Marriage: An Evangelical's Change of Heart* (Louisville, KY: Westminster John Knox Press, 2014).
136 David Runcorn, 'Evangelicals, Scripture and Same Sex Relationships: An "Including Evangelical" Perspective', in *Report of the House of Bishops Working Group on Human Sexuality* ('The Pilling Report') (London: Church House Publishing, 2013), p. 176.
137 Colin Fletcher, 'Challenging Times for Evangelicals', in *Journeys in Grace and Truth: Revisiting Scripture and Sexuality*, edited by Jayne Ozanne (London: Via Media, 2016), p. xxxi.

and respect for the rights of personal conscience.[138] The Accepting Evangelicals network (founded 2004) believed that 'the time has come to move towards the acceptance of faithful, loving same-sex partnerships at every level of church life', but rather than attempt to define evangelicalism it operated on the basis of self-definition, welcoming 'everyone who would call themselves Evangelical'.[139] It was only the latest conflict in the decades-long warfare over authentic evangelical identities.

Conclusion: global trajectories

Evangelicalism lacks a single pope, or a curia. As Mohler observes, there is no 'evangelical high court', and thus ultimately no mechanism for settling the ongoing disputes about identity which have wracked the movement since its inception.[140] To complicate matters further, the opening decades of the twenty-first century present fresh challenges for scholarly analysis, especially the rapid globalization of evangelicalism. Here the historical literature is still in its infancy, although gathering pace.[141] The title of the fifth and final volume of 'A History of Evangelicalism' from the Inter-Varsity Press – Brian Stanley's *The Global Diffusion of Evangelicalism* (2013) – is a deliberate *double entendre*. In one sense the movement has spread across geographical and cultural boundaries, to the furthest flung corners of the world. Although evangelical relationships have always been international, they are now 'multidirectional', from East to West and South to North.[142] The Scripture Union movement has exploded across the continent of Africa, autonomous and self-governing, no longer answerable to London. Indigenous evangelists have risen to prominence throughout the old empire, from Ghana to India, independent of missionary societies from Europe and North America. Evangelicals are no longer typically well-educated white Anglo-Americans but live in poverty and under political oppression in the southern hemisphere. Yet as a result of this global spread, the movement is increasingly 'diffuse' in another sense. Indeed, Stanley argues, it has become 'so diffuse as to be theologically unstable and incapable of definition'. The rapid growth of Pentecostalism, in particular, has accelerated the loss of evangelical cohesion. Nevertheless, predictions of evangelical disintegration are 'premature', Stanley maintains, because in the midst of theological realignments and angst-ridden arguments over evangelical boundaries, the movement always somehow finds the 'capacity to survive'.[143] The contest over evangelical identities since the 1970s has principally been located in the Anglo-American world, as this chapter has shown, but with evangelicalism's centre

---

138 Roy Clements, 'Why I am Still a Christian' and 'Why I am Still an Evangelical Christian' (two lectures to the Evangelical Fellowship for Lesbian and Gay Christians, 2014), www.eflgc.org.uk (accessed 13 October 2017). Compare Steve Chalke, 'What Might Jesus Say to Roy Clements about the Church and the Homosexual Debate', *Christianity+Renewal* (June 2001), 36–9.
139 Runcorn, 'Evangelicals, Scripture and Same Sex Relationships', p. 177.
140 Mohler, 'Generic Evangelicalism', p. 154.
141 See, for example, *Christianity Reborn: Evangelicalism's Global Expansion in the Twentieth Century*, edited by Donald M. Lewis (Grand Rapids, MI: Eerdmans, 2004); Mark Hutchinson and John Wolffe, *A Short History of Global Evangelicalism* (Cambridge: Cambridge University Press, 2012); *Global Evangelicalism: Theology, History and Culture in Regional Perspective*, edited by Donald M. Lewis (Downers Grove, IL: InterVarsity Press, 2014); Stephen Offutt, *New Centers of Global Evangelicalism in Latin America and Africa* (Cambridge: Cambridge University Press, 2015). For a popular survey, see *Evangelicals Around the World: A Global Handbook for the 21st Century*, edited by Brian C. Stiller, Todd M. Johnson, Karen Stiller and Mark Hutchinson (Nashville, TN: Thomas Nelson, 2015).
142 Brian Stanley, *The Global Diffusion of Evangelicalism: The Age of Billy Graham and John Stott* (Nottingham: Inter-Varsity Press, 2013), p. 61.
143 Stanley, *Global Diffusion*, pp. 237–9.

of gravity now increasingly in the Global South, new vistas and dilemmas are opened up. If diffusion does lead to disintegration, Stanley concludes, it cannot be blamed on a few radical preachers or professors in the West: 'The battle for the integrity of the gospel in the opening years of the twenty-first century is being fought not primarily in the lecture rooms of North American seminaries but in the shanty towns, urban slums and villages of Africa, Asia and Latin America.'[144] Historians of the evangelical movement in a global perspective have to face up to these new challenges for accurate scholarly analysis of evangelical identities, theologies and cultures. Many fresh fields of research lie ahead.

---

144 Stanley, *Global Diffusion*, p. 247.

2
EVANGELICALS AND THE BIBLE

Mark A. Noll

From one angle, evangelical appropriations of Scripture have represented only a refinement of dogmas and practices extending back to the dawn of Christianity itself. From another angle, evangelicals since the eighteenth century have generated from the Bible an extraordinary range of wildly creative, confusingly diverse, and often internally contradictory attitudes, uses, convictions, images, and material objects.

To illustrate the former, most contemporary evangelicals would accept the following statements, taken selectively, from the 1994 *Catechism of the Catholic Church* as also describing their convictions about the Bible: '"The divinely revealed realities, which are contained and presented in the text of Sacred Scripture, have been written down under the inspiration of the Holy Spirit." . . . God inspired the human authors of the sacred books. . . . The inspired books teach the truth. "Since therefore all that the inspired authors or sacred writers affirm should be regarded as affirmed by the Holy Spirit, we must acknowledge that the books of Scripture firmly, faithfully, and without error teach that truth which God, for the sake of our salvation, wished to see confided to the Sacred Scriptures."'[1] In other words, the main evangelical attitudes toward Scripture continue to replicate in many particulars the foundational historical reliance on the Bible shared by all Christian movements in all times and places.

But of course there is more. The great internal diversity in evangelical approaches to Scripture can be illustrated by evangelicals in the United States who in recent years have published at least thirty separate books canvassing 'three views' or 'four views' that evangelicals, in disagreement with one another, maintain on important doctrines or practices – and all advanced with a direct appeal to Scripture. In other words, although almost all evangelical groups are united in claiming to be guided first and foremost by the Bible, that guidance has fostered what one scholar calls 'pervasive interpretive pluralism'.[2]

---

1 *Catechism of the Catholic Church* (Ligouri, MO: Ligouri Press, 1994), p. 31 (paras. 105, 106, 107, with quotations from the dogmatic constitution, *Dei Verbum*, Second Vatican Council).
2 Christian Smith, *The Bible Made Impossible: Why Biblicism Is Not a Truly Evangelical Reading of Scripture* (Grand Rapids, MI: Brazos, 2011), p. 3.

Foundations

The evangelical movements of the eighteenth century gratefully repeated the professions about Scripture articulated by the first Protestants whom they considered their predecessors in faith. Those reformers, in turn, had consistently appealed to earlier figures whom they celebrated for having guided their teachings and their lives by the Bible. When John Calvin defined the authority of Scripture in his *Institutes of the Christian Religion*, he enlisted Augustine for his conclusion that the Bible authorized the church, instead of the other way around as the Catholics of his era insisted. Calvin also recruited Augustine for one of his own summary statements about the supremacy of Scripture: 'We must come, I say, to the Word, where God is truly and vividly described to us from his works . . . If we turn aside from the Word . . . we shall never reach the goal. . . . [then this quotation from Augustine] it is better to limp along this path than to dash with all speed outside it.'[3]

Evangelicals especially celebrated the intimate connection that early Protestants drew between the general truthfulness of Scripture and the particular work of redemption that God conveyed through the Bible's message. Most would have agreed with Calvin who firmly tied together Scripture as revealed truth from God and Scripture as saving truth made alive by the Holy Spirit: 'The same Spirit . . . who has spoken through the mouths of the prophets must penetrate into our hearts to persuade us that they faithfully proclaimed what had been divinely commanded.'[4]

Martin Luther's famous declaration before the Emperor, Charles V, at the Diet of Worms in 1521 established an evangelical baseline even more directly: 'I am bound by the Scriptures I have quoted and my conscience is captive to the Word of God. I cannot and I will not retract anything, since it is neither safe nor right to go against conscience.'[5] When Luther tied his own conscience to the authority of the Bible, he anticipated a great deal of later evangelical history. Scripture would be regarded as definitive and determinative truth from God, but the distinctive evangelical emphasis would stress the redeeming truth of the Bible speaking *to me*.

Scripture as such did not emerge as a particular focus for the earliest evangelical leaders. When in 1746, John Wesley offered to the public the first edition of his published sermons, he underscored with burning ardour his devotion to the Bible, but it was a devotion dedicated to one particular end: 'I want to know one thing, the way to heaven. . . . God himself has condescended to teach the way: for this very end he came from heaven. He hath written it down in a book. O give me that book! At any price give me the Book of God! I have it here. Here is knowledge enough for me. Let me be *homo unius libri* [a man of one book].' From this basis, Wesley dedicated his energies to proclaiming what he called 'the true, the scriptural, experimental religion'.[6] 'Experimental' – meaning experiential, lively, or simply true – was the key.

Samuel Hopkins wrote of his mentor Jonathan Edwards that he 'studied the Bible more than all other Books, and more than most other Divines do. . . . He took his religious Principles from the Bible, and not from any Human System or Body of Divinity.'[7] Similarly, George Whitefield

---

3 John Calvin, *Institutes of the Christian Religion*, translated by F. L. Battles, edited by J. T. McNeill (2 vols, Philadelphia, PA: Westminster, 1960), I: 73 (I.vi.3).
4 Calvin, *Institutes of the Christian Religion*, I: 79 (I.vii.4).
5 'Luther at the Diet of Worms, 1521', in *Luther's Works, vol. 32: Career of the Reformer II*, edited by G. W. Forell (Philadelphia, PA: Fortress, 1958), p. 112.
6 John Wesley, 'Preface' to *Sermons on Several Occasions* (1746), but reprinted in all subsequent editions of his sermons; quoted here from *The Works of John Wesley, vol. I: Sermons I*, edited by Albert Outler (Nashville, TN: Abingdon, 1984), pp. 105–6.
7 Samuel Hopkins, *The Life and Character of the Reverend Mr. Jonathan Edwards* (Boston, MA: Kneeland, 1765), pp. 40–1.

paused several times in his peripatetic itinerations to affirm the authority of Scripture, as in a sermon published in 1740: 'If we once get above our Bibles and cease making the written word of God our sole rule both as to faith and practice, we shall soon lie open to all manner of delusion and be in great danger of making shipwreck of faith and a good conscience.'[8] These opinions about the Bible were, however, commonplace in the Protestant world of their day.

Evangelicals like Wesley, Edwards and Whitefield set themselves apart instead by what they did with Scripture. Whitefield became the phenomenon of his age, not because he preached from the Bible, but because of how memorably he transformed each of his preaching texts into a dramatic invitation to experience the new birth. As examples, when he preached from Genesis 22:12 on 'Abraham Offering Up His Son Isaac', his conclusion urged his listeners 'to look to him [Christ] whom you have pierced, and mourn'.[9] When he preached on Isaiah 44:5, 'Christ the Believer's Husband', he concluded with an explicit gospel appeal: 'But you are blind, and miserable, and naked; to whom then should you fly for succour, but to Jesus, who came to open the eyes of the blind, to seek and save the miserable and lost, and clothe the naked with his perfect and spotless righteousness.'[10]

Similarly, Edwards' most famous sermon, 'Sinners in the Hands of an Angry God', began conventionally with a text, this one from Deuteronomy 32:35: 'Their foot shall slide in due time'. But then the existential drama with which he infused his application of the text was anything but conventional: 'The bow of God's wrath is bent, and the arrow made ready on the string, and Justice bends the arrow at your heart, and strains the bow, and it is nothing but the mere pleasure of God, and that of an angry God, without any promise or obligation at all, that keeps the arrow one moment from being made drunk with your blood.'[11] Later evangelicals followed the path set out by these early leaders. Evangelical innovations did not include new views of biblical inspiration. They did include scriptural revelation in service to an active, participatory and conversionist vision of the Christian life.

That focused application created significant landmarks of evangelical history.[12] The Bible come alive for personal spiritual renewal was always foundational. But almost as prevalent were differences of opinion over how Scripture should be used to shape Christian thinking and guide the Christian life. Intense, sometimes vitriolic contentions over whether the Bible better supported Calvinism, Arminianism or some alternative way of depicting redemption began in earnest by the late 1740s and have never stopped. Debates over whether Scripture mandated adult or infant baptism and whether it favoured Presbyterian, Episcopal, or Congregational church organization have likewise engaged evangelicals in endless appeals to individual passages and broad biblical themes. In the eighteenth century, evangelicals with Bibles in hand also stood on opposite sides of social questions – whether warfare could ever be approved by Bible-

---

8 George Whitefield, 'Walking with God' (1740), in *The Works of the Reverend George Whitefield*, edited by John Gillies (7 vols, London: E. & C. Dilly, 1771–2), V: 27.
9 George Whitefield, 'Abraham's Offering Up His Son Isaac' (1742), in *The Works of George Whitefield*, V: 49.
10 George Whitefield, 'On Christ the Believer's Husband' (1747), in *The Works of George Whitefield*, V: 196.
11 Jonathan Edwards, 'Sinners in the Hands of an Angry God' (1741), in *The Works of Jonathan Edwards, vol. 22: Sermons and Discourses, 1739–1742*, edited by Harry S. Stout, Nathan O. Hatch and Kyle P. Farley (New Haven, CT: Yale University Press, 2003), p. 411.
12 Many of those landmarks are treated in D. W. Bebbington, *Evangelicalism in Modern Britain: A History from the 1730s to the 1980s* (London: Unwin Hyman, 1989); John G. Stackhouse, *Canadian Evangelicalism in the Twentieth Century* (Toronto: University of Toronto Press, 1993); Douglas A. Sweeney, *The American Evangelical Story* (Grand Rapids, MI: Baker, 2005); and Stuart Piggin, *Spirit, Word, and World: Evangelical Christianity in Australia* (Brunswick East, Victoria: Acorn, 2012).

believing servants of Christ, whether slavery was sanctioned by the example of Old Testament patriarchs and the apparent approval by the Apostle Paul,[13] and in a fierce contest that has now faded from memory whether the American war for independence against Parliament could meet scriptural standards for a just war.[14] For evangelical history since the eighteenth century, it is important to note that these intra-evangelical contentions over disputed interpretations of Scripture regularly co-existed with general agreement concerning what the sweep of biblical revelation entailed for reconciliation between a holy God and sinful creatures.

Evangelical hymnody also reflected the strongly biblical emphases of the surge of evangelical faith. The transformation of ecclesiastical music propelled by Isaac Watts, Charles Wesley, and then a host of other evangelicals grew from the artful presentation of scriptural teaching in accessible and highly memorable hymns.[15] Unlike the earlier hymnody of English Protestantism, which remained tethered to metrical renditions of the Psalms, the Christ-centred praise that evangelical authors drew from Scripture overcame a deeply-ingrained fear of man-centred worship and became an evangelical gift to the entire Christian world.

When in 1719 Isaac Watts attempted a Christian exposition of Psalm 72 ('let the whole earth be filled with his glory'), the result was 'Jesus shall reign where-er the sun'. That hymn transformed a general biblical truth into a moving declaration that would later motivate missionaries from Britain and North America, but it would also inspire believers in far-flung corners of the world who responded to the missionaries' message.[16] Charles Wesley's 'Wrestling Jacob', first published in 1742, represented a meditation on Genesis 34 where the patriarch Jacob wrestled with 'a man . . . until the break of day'. In Wesley's verse, the story grew effortlessly into an account of coming to 'know Thee, Saviour, who Thou art, / Jesus the Feeble Sinner's Friend'.[17] When George Whitefield in 1753 published the first edition of his own hymn collection, its contents (much from Wesley and even more from Watts) offered a lively, infectious, but thoroughly biblical form of proclamation. The hymns' constantly repeated phrases – 'Messiah', 'man of grief', 'sacrifice', 'second Adam', 'redeeming Lamb', 'heavenly Lamb', 'Lamb-like Son of God' – drove home the evangelist's fixation on a scriptural message of redemption in Christ.[18] In such hymnody, the ancient text of Scripture came powerfully alive as an encouragement for lively Christian worship, but also for biblically-centred Christian life.

The bold appropriation of Scripture by laymen and laywomen may have been the most significant innovation of the eighteenth-century evangelical revivals. Again, it was not new for biblical teaching to inspire all levels within a Christian community. It was new to hear lay voices speaking boldly in public, to view ecclesiastical deference giving way to Spirit inspired self-assurance, and to witness women and ethnic minorities empowered by their personal understanding of Scripture. W. R. Ward's magisterial interpretations of early-modern evangelicalism placed special stress on how revivals breathed life into what he called 'that Cinderella

---

13 Mark A. Noll, 'The Bible and Slavery', in *Religion and the American Civil War*, edited by R. M. Miller, H. S. Stout and C. R. Wilson (New York: Oxford University Press, 1998), pp. 43–73.
14 Mark A. Noll, *In the Beginning Was the Word: The Bible in American Public Life, 1492–1783* (New York: Oxford University Press, 2015), pp. 296–315.
15 See especially J. R. Watson, *The English Hymn: A Critical and Historical Study* (Oxford: Clarendon Press, 1997), pp. 133–70, 230–64.
16 Isaac Watts, *The Psalms of David Imitated in the Language of the New Testament, And Apply'd to the Christian State and Worship* (London, 1719), pp. 186–7; Christopher Idle, *Stories of Our Favorite Hymns* (Grand Rapids, MI: Eerdmans, 1980), p. 24.
17 For text and editions, see *Representative Verse of Charles Wesley* (New York: Abingdon, 1962) edited by Frank Baker, pp. 37–9.
18 George Whitefield, *A Collection of Hymns for Social Worship* (London: William Strahan, 1753).

of Protestant doctrines, the priesthood of all believers' – that is, a doctrine that had been much proclaimed but little practised until the appearance of pietistic and evangelical renewal movements. 'Whatever Luther may have said about the priesthood of all believers', in Ward's account, 'it took more than a century and a half for the idea to receive full-scale treatment' in German pietism and Anglo-American evangelicalism.[19] Even if, as Ward also documented, the spiritual priesthood would be constrained when revivalism solidified into church structures and doctrinal orthodoxies, the evangelical injunction that *all* people needed to appropriate the scriptural message of salvation *for themselves* has marked evangelical movements wherever and whenever they have appeared.

The forthright boldness of a laity inspired by personal appropriation of the Bible marked the records left by one of the great events of the evangelical revival. After a series of memorable public meetings at Cambuslang, Scotland, in 1742, several ministers took testimonies from individuals whose lives had been transformed during this revival. In the published version of these testimonies, the ministers edited out the visions, voices and dreams that featured prominently in the accounts. But the ministers could only welcome the many instances where Scripture played the crucial part in turning men and women to Christ and bringing them assurance of salvation.[20]

Across the Atlantic the same personal appropriation of Scripture lay behind the remarkable life of Sarah Osborn, a humble and self-effacing resident of Newport, Rhode Island. Her energetic life of service, evangelism, and personal encouragement rested completely on her mastery of the Scriptures. Her conversion took place in 1738 through a private reading of Isaiah 54: 4–5 ('For thou shalt forget the shame of thy youth, and shalt not remember the reproach of thy widowhood any more. For thy Maker is thine husband, the LORD of Hosts is his name, and thy Redeemer the Holy One of Israel').[21] It was the same text that George Whitefield had movingly opened at Cambuslang and that had prompted some of the testimonies recorded by the Scottish ministers. For Osborn, although her long life passed through as many dark days as celebrations, constant recourse to Scripture made her the most influential citizen in Newport's religious life and an exemplar of holiness remembered long after her death.

A Baptist laywoman, Anne Steele, who came first in a long evangelical line of noteworthy female hymn writers, wrote of her own experience when she celebrated the written Word of God that had drawn her to Christ:

> Father of mercies, in thy word / What endless glory shines?
> Forever be thy name ador'd / For these celestial lines. . . .
> Here the Redeemer's welcome voice, / Spreads heavenly peace around;
> And life, and everlasting joys / Attend the blissful song.[22]

The empowering presence of Scripture reached even to the enslaved population in the British Atlantic world. David George had escaped from slavery, lived with Native Americans and had

---

19 W. R. Ward, *The Protestant Evangelical Awakening* (Cambridge: Cambridge University Press, 1992), p. 353; 'Pastoral Office and the General Priesthood in the Great Awakening', in W. R. Ward, *Faith and Faction* (London: Epworth, 1993), p. 177.
20 *The McCulloch Examinations of the Cambuslang Revival (1742): A Critical Edition*, edited by Keith Edward Beebe (Rochester, NY: Scottish History Society / Boydell, 2013).
21 Catherine A. Brekus, *Sarah Osborn's World: The Rise of Evangelical Christianity in Early America* (New Haven, CT: Yale University Press, 2013), p. 116.
22 Anne Steele, 'The Excellency of the Holy Scriptures', in *The Emergence of Evangelical Spirituality: The Age of Edwards, Newton, and Whitefield*, edited by Tom Schwanda (New York: Paulist Press, 2015), pp. 134–5.

been retaken into bondage when in the early 1770s he heard a black preacher, George Liele, expound Matthew 11:28 ('Come unto me all ye that labour, and are heavy laden, and I will give you rest'), which confirmed an evangelical conversion he had recently undergone.[23] George's later career – liberated by the British, active as preacher and church organizer in Georgia, Nova Scotia and Sierra Leone – continued to rest on a thoroughly personal appropriation of the Bible.

Evangelical laity took to heart the message that the Bible could guide the repentant soul to salvation in Christ. Yet once scriptural empowerment proved effective for personal redemption, that same empowerment could become disruptive. In Connecticut, Nathan Cole has been remembered for a breathless account of his opportunity to hear an outdoor sermon by George Whitefield in 1742 when the evangelist was at the height of his powers. Far less attention has been paid to Cole's later life when, after a profoundly evangelical conversion mediated by personally appropriated words of Scripture, he protested against activities by his town's officials because they were 'not in according to God's law'. He also separated from his local congregation for the same reason; he did not think it conformed to the biblical teaching he had discovered for himself.[24]

Similar occasions multiplied wherever evangelical religion spread. In their steady concentration on vital personal faith, evangelical movements brought the Bible to life with extraordinary force. But a force of that energetic magnitude could not be contained. It renewed churches but also divided them. It fuelled energetic social action, but sometimes with evangelicals lining up behind contradictory goals. It made Scripture into a spiritual dynamo but a dynamo whose energy spun off in many directions.

Continuity

After this beginning, evangelical attachment to Scripture continued to promote individual faith, inspire active faith and support faith of great diversity. Much subsequent history only extrapolated what had appeared with the first eighteenth-century evangelicals. At the same time, innovations also appeared as evangelicals followed the logic of their own convictions, dealt with causes of internal decay, generated new centres of both unity and disunity, interacted with major changes in British and America culture, and – most importantly – moved out into the world beyond Britain and North America.

Most obvious to evangelicals themselves has been dedicated, heartfelt and implicit trust in Scripture as the open doorway to peace with God. This confidence has always marked the larger-than-life place that widely recognized leaders – usually preachers or authors of popular literature – have enjoyed in evangelical history.[25]

---

23 Grant Gordon, *From Slavery to Freedom: The Life of David George, Pioneer Baptist Minister* (Hantsport, Nova Scotia: Lancelot, 1992), pp. 171–3.
24 Michael J. Crawford, 'The Spiritual Travels of Nathan Cole', *William and Mary Quarterly* vol. 33 (January 1976), 117.
25 Many of the figures mentioned in the next three paragraphs are profiled in Michael Gauvreau, *The Evangelical Century: College and Creed in English Canada from the Great Revival to the Great Depression* (Montreal: McGill-Queen's University Press, 1991); Allan Dwight Callahan, *The Talking Book: African Americans and the Bible* (New Haven, CT: Yale University Press, 2006); *Dictionary of Major Bible Interpreters*, edited by Donald McKim (Downers Grove, IL: InterVarsity Press, 2007); *Recovering Nineteenth-Century Women Interpreters of the Bible*, edited by Christiana de Groot and Marion Ann Taylor (Atlanta, GA: Society of Biblical Literature, 2007); Timothy Larsen, *A People of One Book: The Bible and the Victorians* (New York: Oxford University Press, 2011); *Handbook of Women Biblical Interpreters*, edited by Marion Ann Taylor and Agnes Choi (Grand Rapids, MI: Baker, 2012); *Dissent and the Bible in Britain, c. 1650–1950*, edited by Scott Mandelbrote and Michael Ledger-Lomas (Oxford: Oxford

In the nineteenth century, that confidence, in one form or another, undergirded the far-sighted organizational efforts of figures like Richard Allen, founder of the African Methodist Episcopal Church; Elias Boudinot, a prominent political leader who became first president of the American Bible Society; Alexander Campbell, an early leader of American Restorationist movements; William and Catherine Booth as founders of the Salvation Army; and Presbyterian George Monro Grant who became one of Canada's leading public figures in the last decades of the century. Conspicuous attention to Scripture likewise marked the careers of famous itinerant evangelists like the Americans Charles G. Finney and D. L. Moody, as well as the ministry of notable preachers like Charles Haddon Spurgeon of London's Metropolitan Tabernacle, Robert Murray M'Cheyne of Scotland, and Daniel Alexander Payne of the African Methodist Episcopal Church. Scripture infused the writings of popular authors like the active Anglican educational reformer Hannah More, the American Holiness advocate Phoebe Palmer, and William Blackstone whose million-selling *Jesus Is Coming* (1878) popularized a premillennial interpretation of Scripture. Theologians and Bible commentators went even further as they based their entire output on Scripture, with many gaining stature in their particular denominations and a few winning even wider attention like a number who prepared popular commentaries, including the Irish-born Methodist Adam Clarke, the Anglican Thomas Scott and the American Presbyterian Albert Barnes. Similar immersion in Scripture marked the work of Moses Stuart of Andover Seminary in Massachusetts, the United States' leading professional Bible scholar of the antebellum period, the widely respected American Presbyterian Charles Hodge, the Irish-born proponent of dispensational theology John Nelson Darby and the Canadian Methodist Nathanael Burwash.

Evangelical social reformers also took their marching orders from what they considered scriptural mandates, including William Wilberforce and his successor Thomas Fowell Buxton who badgered Parliament to outlaw slavery and then to protect aboriginal peoples throughout the British empire; or the prison stewards who in 1831–1832 so impressed Alexis de Tocqueville on his visit to the United States by providing Bibles to the incarcerated in US prisons; or the English Quaker Elizabeth Fry who became renowned for publicly declaiming the Scriptures to prisoners. Evangelicals also provided a great proportion of the reading audience that made Harriet Beecher Stowe's *Uncle Tom's Cabin* (1852), with many scenes featuring the consoling effects of Scripture, the best-selling American novel of the century, until displaced by Lew Wallace's *Ben Hur: A Tale of the Christ* (1880), which depended for its phenomenal success on a readership thoroughly familiar with gospel accounts of Jesus.[26] In Britain, books and paintings featuring incidents from the life of Jesus, which included a volume by Charles Dickens and several much-viewed works of art from members of the Pre-Raphaelite Brotherhood, looked to some evangelicals like sacrilege, but to many more as appropriate meditations on biblical material.

Over the last century and more, a similar orientation to Scripture has defined the popular preaching of Aimee Semple McPherson, Martyn Lloyd-Jones, Oral Roberts, Billy Graham and many more. It provided the resources for the worldwide reputation of the Anglican John Stott and the American Presbyterian Francis Schaeffer; for the German-born Pentecostal revivalist

---

University Press, 2013); *Evangelicals Around the World: A Global Handbook for the 21st Century*, edited by Britan Stiller (Nashville, TN: Thomas Nelson/World Evangelical Alliance, 2015).

26 For particularly insightful studies, see Charles H. Foster, *The Rungless Ladder: Harriet Beecher Stowe and New England Puritanism* (Durham, NC: Duke University Press, 1954), and *Bigger than Ben-Hur: The Book, its Adaptations, and their Audiences*, edited by Barbara Ryan and Milette Shamir (Syracuse, NY: Syracuse University Press, 2016).

Reinhard Bonnke; for theologians Mildred Wynkoop, Carl F. H. Henry, H. Orton Wiley and J. I. Packer; for Bible scholars F. F. Bruce, Derek Kidner and George Ladd; for popular writers like Hal Lindsey, whose *Late Great Planet Earth* (1970) sold tens of millions of copies, and authors of the phenomenally popular 'Left Behind' series of apocalyptic novels.

During the last century, as Anglo-American evangelical leadership has broadened into the entire world, a host of newer voices promoting a myriad of public tasks have worked from the same grounding in Scripture as a controlling orientation. These have included, as only the merest sample, Peter Ambuofa, a Solomon Islander evangelist who became leader of the South Sea Evangelical Mission; V. S. Azariah, a missionary organizer, faithful reformer, catechist, and the first native Indian Anglican bishop; Kwame Bediako, who indigenized theology for an African context and founded the Akrofi-Christaller Institute of Theology, Mission, and Culture in Accra, Ghana; Orlando Costas, a Puerto Rican theologian who enjoyed a distinguished teaching career in Costa Rica and the United States; Watchman Nee, organizer of the Little Flock (or Local Church) movement of indigenous Chinese congregations; Petrus Octavianus, founder of the Indonesian Missionary Fellowship and long-time head of the Indonesia Evangelical Mission Church; Pedro Arana Quírez, president of the Peruvian Bible Society; the Sadhu Sundar Singh, an Indian evangelist and mystic; and John Sung, an evangelist with an American doctorate in chemistry who became China's leading evangelist in the 1930s. The prominence of the Bible with so many figures who moved in so many directions testifies to the inescapably formidable presence of Scripture in all evangelical movements.

Yet the array of such figures can also leave an impression of simple confusion since the themes or parts of the Bible that these leaders stressed have varied so widely. While not overlooking that variety, it is significant that reliance on the Bible has also made it possible for pan-evangelical movements to craft formal declarations that have spoken cohesively for the diverse evangelical traditions. Through such statements, a protean landscape can appear much more coherent.

One such occasion took place in 1846 when 800 delegates from the European Continent, Britain and North America met for the inaugural meeting of the Evangelical Alliance. Sharp differences over whether the Bible should be read to condemn slavery threatened to torpedo the meeting. But once having set that issue aside, the delegates agreed on a brief nine-point Basis of Agreement. Of those points, six defined a common stance on God as Trinity and the way of salvation through Christ's atonement and the work of the Holy Spirit. But the foundation for the Basis was its first affirmation: 'The Divine inspiration, authority, and sufficiency of the Holy Scriptures'.[27]

One hundred and twenty-eight years later, a larger and much more international assembly gathered in Lausanne, Switzerland, to attempt a similar expression of common evangelical purpose. Although the spread of evangelical movements into the entire world would seem to have made any unified doctrinal statement all but impossible, the 2,700 globally representative delegates succeeded in issuing a doctrinal platform with the Bible as a foundation. Since its origin in 1974, this Lausanne Covenant has been either adopted or commended by a wide diversity of evangelical movements, organizations and institutions. Its statement on Scripture underscored historical evangelical emphases by organically linking the truth-telling character of the Bible to its purpose of redemption in Christ through the Holy Spirit:

> We affirm the divine inspiration, truthfulness and authority of both Old and New Testament Scriptures in their entirety as the only written Word of God, without error

---

[27] 'The Doctrinal Basis of the Evangelical Alliance', in *The Creeds of Christendom*, edited by Philip Schaff (3 vols, New York: Harper, 1919 [orig. 1877]), III: 827.

in all that it affirms, and the only infallible rule of faith and practice. We also affirm the power of God's Word to accomplish his purpose of salvation. The message of the Bible is addressed to all mankind. For God's revelation in Christ and in Scripture is unchangeable. Through it the Holy Spirit still speaks today. He illumines the minds of God's people in every culture to perceive its truth freshly through their own eyes and thus discloses to the whole church ever more of the many-coloured wisdom of God.[28]

A follow-up meeting of the Lausanne Continuing Movement, held in Manila in 1989, expressed even more succinctly the standard evangelical link between honouring the Bible as divine revelation and embracing its message as the way of salvation: 'We affirm that in the Scriptures of the Old and New Testaments God has given us an authoritative disclosure of his character and will, his redemptive acts and their meaning and his mandate for mission.'[29]

The importance of these nodes of unity should not be discounted. Yet they have always also co-existed with extensive debates among evangelicals over how scriptural teaching should define specific beliefs, church practices and stances in the world. Many of those debates have engendered incompatible or contradictory interpretations of Scripture. Thus, most of the original contentions over biblical interpretation remain contested: over, for example, the proportion of divine initiative and human response in redemption that continues to be debated among Calvinists, Arminians and many compromises; over the mode, subjects, and meaning of baptism; and over the biblically mandated (or suggested) forms of church organization.

Over the course of the last two centuries, an additional catalogue of contentious questions has divided evangelical biblical interpreters, with some such issues tolerated as secondary *adiaphora* (that is, questions to the side) or neglected altogether, while at other times rising up as causes for schismatic breaches of fellowship. The list of such issues is lengthy: whether conversion should ideally occur at a particular point in time or over a long period; whether growth in grace (also known as holiness and sanctification) occurs gradually, can take place instantly, and will or will not be completed in this lifetime; whether the Christian Sabbath should be observed on Saturday or Sunday, and what activities should or should not take place on that special day of the week. From the middle of the nineteenth century, evangelicals have differed substantially on whether to read the prophetic portions of Scripture as still to be fulfilled, fulfilled in the finished work of Christ, or in some other way. At the end of that century disagreements began over whether the gifts of the Holy Spirit described in the Book of Acts – like divine healing, speaking in tongues, and reception of special words of prophecy – could continue as a 'latter rain' (Joel 2: 23) bestowed upon believers today. The twentieth century witnessed vigorous debates over whether women could serve as church officers, ministers and pastors, and – as evangelical movements spread around the world – whether polygamy could be tolerated or had to be repudiated before someone could become a regular church member.

Similar contentions have attended attitudes toward whether evangelicals should engage in efforts to reform society, with some demanding activity, others denying the importance of such efforts, and still others vacillating between these polar positions. Further disagreements have divided evangelicals over which reforming efforts deserve Christian support, and then on which side Christian advocacy should act. Such issues as slavery, racial difference, the age of the

---

28 John Stott, *The Lausanne Covenant: An Exposition and Commentary* (Minneapolis, MN: World Wide Publications, 1975), p. 10.
29 Quoted in *One Faith: The Evangelical Consensus*, edited by J. I. Packer and Thomas C. Oden (Downers Grove, IL: InterVarsity Press, 2004), p. 39.

earth, the consumption of alcohol, nationalism, anti-communism, and more have often elicited contradictory biblical mandates.

Debates arising from how best to understand or use the Bible itself have made up a large category of evangelical disagreement. Especially in the early United States, where republican political ideology spoke so strongly against any external authority, some evangelicals chastised other evangelicals by claiming to follow 'no creed but the Bible' or 'the Bible alone'.[30] A different kind of controversy beset evangelical supporters of the British and Foreign Bible Society in its early years, with some defending the inclusion of the 'Apocrypha' in Bibles intended for Roman Catholic lands and others militantly opposed.[31]

In a word, evangelicals have testified to their high evaluation of Scripture by how much disagreement that common evaluation has generated, as well as by how much guidance, consolation, inspiration, and Christ-centred encouragement the Scriptures have provided.

Yet even when evangelicals have hotly debated contradictory biblical interpretations among themselves, many have been able to set those disagreements aside when they opened their hymnbooks. Throughout evangelical history, hymnbook editors (and more recently those who provide digital resources for projecting onto overhead screens) have enlivened principles of biblical adherence with hymns and spiritual songs keyed to specific biblical words, passages, or themes. The popularity of such compositions has been a constant. In 1858, as an example, two New England Congregationalists and Lowell Mason, a hymn-arranger and composer, published *The Sabbath Hymn Book*, a collection designed first for use in church, but also – in keeping with the individual focus of evangelical piety – 'to aid in the more private social devotions, in the conference room, the family, and the closet'.[32] The book's 1372 hymn texts included a minority of hymns paraphrased directly from Scripture, but to show the editors' commitment to a scriptural standard, they entitled all of their selections with verses from Scripture. The book included many eighteenth-century standards from Isaac Watts, Charles Wesley and others, but even more from recent compositions that, with this earlier hymnody, featured biblical stories, images, questions, circumstances or themes. Examples of such hymns included '"Tis midnight and on Olive's brow . . . 'Tis midnight in the garden now / The suffering Savior prays alone', by the American Congregationalist William Tappan (1822); 'My hope is built on nothing less . . . On Christ the solid rock I stand / All other ground is sinking sand', by the English Baptist Edward Mote (1834); 'Shall we gather at the river', by the American Baptist Robert Lowry (1864); '"Almost persuaded" now to believe'; and '"Almost persuaded" Christ to receive', by the American Methodist and Congregationalist Philip P. Bliss (1871).

During the nineteenth century, a few hymns became popular that, like the earlier composition by Anne Steele, focused on the Bible itself. One came in 1803 from an English Baptist layman, John Burton:

Holy Bible, book divine,
Precious treasure, thou art mine;
Mine to tell me whence I came;
Mine to teach me what I am.

---

30 Nathan O. Hatch, '*Sola Scriptura* and *Novus Ordo Seclorum*', in *The Bible in America: Essays in Cultural History*, edited by Nathan O. Hatch and Mark A. Noll (New York: Oxford University Press, 1982), pp. 59–78.
31 Leslie Howsam, *Cheap Bibles: Nineteenth-Century Publishing and the British and Foreign Bible Society* (Cambridge: Cambridge University Press, 1991), pp. 13–15.
32 Edwards Amasa Park, Austin Phelps and Lowell Mason, *The Sabbath Hymn Book for the Service of Song in the House of the Lord* (New York, 1858), p. ix.

By the second half of the century, it was appearing in more than a quarter of English-language hymnals.[33] Later, children in America and perhaps elsewhere joined the chorus as they enthusiastically sang, 'The B-I-B-L-E, yes, that's the book for me'.

To the present day, popular hymns have done almost as much to circulate biblical phrases, themes and narratives among evangelicals as the physical presence of Bibles. As one observer of worldwide evangelicalism recently noted:

> The gospel song – singable, sentimental, personal and in tune with musical tastes of the time – became the signature music of revival campaigns from the time of Moody. Its descendants – particularly in the charismatic and Pentecostal music produced by the Vineyard [originating in the U.S.], Hillsong [originating in Australia], and Scripture in Song [originating in New Zealand] movements – continue to shape the global culture of evangelical churches to this day.[34]

Among otherwise so disparate evangelical traditions, biblically-originated hymns and songs have provided a measure of both literal and metaphorical harmony.

The personal appropriation of Scripture by ordinary men and women that was so distinctive in the eighteenth century has also remained characteristic of evangelical movements. Lay efforts have always been crucial for organizations like the British and Foreign Bible Society (1804), the American Bible Society (1816) and the Gideons movement, founded in the early twentieth century and guided entirely by laymen in distributing billions of Bibles around the world.[35]

Important as such organizations have been for Bible distribution, evangelical Christianity has remained a force in the world mostly because the salvation-bestowing character of Scripture has existentially shaped the lives of individuals, families and groups. Examples beyond number could be cited, including many for African Americans among whom Scripture has always been an indispensable mainstay. Julia A. Foote, for example, a black evangelist in the latter half of the nineteenth century, was converted while reading the Bible. She continued to take strength from its pages throughout her life, including on the sad day on which her husband left for a long sea-voyage: 'While under this apparent cloud, I took the Bible to my closet, asking Divine aid. As I opened the book, my eyes fell on these words: "For thy Maker is thine husband". I then read the fifty-fourth chapter of Isaiah over and over again. It seemed to me that I had never seen it before. I went forth glorifying God.'[36]

Catherine Booth began her ministry in the London slums with great trepidation, but also with a determination to be sustained by Scripture. Her first encounter in the ministry that would become the Salvation Army involved a woman sunk into poverty because of her husband's drinking. Booth immediately read the Bible with him, whereupon he sobered up and became a founding member of a small group that met weekly under Booth's direction 'for reading the Scriptures' and for ensuring the continuing sobriety of such reformed alcoholics.[37]

---

33 See http://www.hymnary.org/text/holy_bible_book_divine (accessed 23 February 2018).
34 Wilbert R. Shenk, 'The Theological Impulse of Evangelical Expansion', in *Global Evangelicalism: Theology, History and Culture in Regional Perspective*, edited by Donald M. Lewis and Richard V. Pierard (Downers Grove, IL: InterVarsity Press, 2014), p. 50.
35 Mark A. Noll, 'The Gideons', in *The Oxford Companion to the Bible*, edited by Bruce M. Metzger and Michael D. Coggan (New York: Oxford University Press, 1993).
36 *A Brand Plucked from the Fire: An Autobiographical Sketch by Mrs. Julia A. J. Foote* (1886), in *Spiritual Narratives*, edited by Sue E. Houchins (New York: Oxford University Press, 1988), p. 61.
37 Timothy Larsen, 'The Bible and Varieties of Nineteenth-Century Dissent: Elizabeth Fry, Mary

A contemporary account comes from Zhao Xiao, a rising Chinese economist who, after visiting churches in trips to America, began to read the Bible in order to verify his convictions that God did not exist. 'Three months later', he has written, 'I admitted defeat. . . . [Scripture] talks about the history of the relationship between God and human beings, and this kind of book does not exist in China.' Yet in a distinctly Chinese denouement to this story, Zhao's encounter with Scripture has led him to author widely recognized publications on the importance of personal morality as a prerequisite for productive economic life.[38] Biographical accounts for individuals like Julia Foote, Catherine Booth and Zhao Xiao hint at the dynamism that remains central to evangelical biblical engagement.

New developments

Along with much in the last two centuries that represents straightforward extension from eighteenth-century origins, the history of evangelicals and the Bible has also witnessed a number of new developments. The wide range of those developments underscores the depth of evangelical commitment to Scripture but also the complexity of that commitment.

Evangelicals may have exerted their greatest international impact through the promotion of new Bible translations.[39] European pietists, rather than British evangelicals, showed what this promotion could mean, with Bartholomäus Ziegenbalg and Heinrich Plütschau pointing the way early in the eighteenth century when they translated the Bible into Tamil, an event that is still regarded as a literary landmark in the history of Tranquebar in South India. At the very end of the century, the English Baptist William Carey extended the impulse with translations of the Bible into Bengali and other Indian languages, translations that were the major legacy of Carey's pioneering missionary career. Soon thereafter, Robert Morrison's translation of the Bible into Chinese represented the major accomplishment of his work under the often reluctant sponsorship of Britain's East India Company. Among the first American foreign missionaries were Ann and Adoniram Judson whose Bible translations into Burmese began the history of Protestant Christianity in that part of southeast Asia. In New Zealand, William Williams of the Church Missionary Society began publishing sections of the New Testament in Maori in 1827. This translation served as Scripture for New Zealand's indigenous Christian community until it was revised after the Second World War by a committee that included Maori scholars.

The evangelical sponsorship of translation moved almost naturally toward native agency when local converts took the task in hand for themselves. Samuel Ajayi Crowther, the first African Anglican bishop, was also the first native speaker to prepare a Bible translation in his own language, in this case Yoruba. Crowther's extraordinary linguistic abilities also supported translations into Igbo and Nube. In the early twentieth century, Pandita Ramabai added work as a Bible translator (in Marathi) to the numerous social and educational activities she led at her Mukti Mission in the west of India.[40]

Carpenter, and Catherine Booth', in *Dissent and the Bible in Britain*, edited by Mandelbrote and Ledger-Lomas, p. 170.
38 Luis Bush with Brent Fulton, 'China's Next Generation: New Church, New China, New World', *Global Missiology* vol. 2 (24 January 2014).
39 See especially Lamin O. Sanneh, *Translating the Message: The Missionary Impact on Culture* (Maryknoll, NY: Orbis, 1989), and Andrew F. Walls, *The Missionary Movement in Christian History: Studies in the Transmission of Faith* (Maryknoll, NY: Orbis, 1996), pp. 26–42.
40 Matthew Oluremi Owadayo, 'Bishop Samuel Ajayi Crowther (1810-1891), in *Makers of the Church in Nigeria*, edited by Joseph Akinyele Omoyajowo (Lagos: CSS Bookshops, 1995), pp. 29-53; Padmini Sengupta, *Pandita Ramabai Saraswati: Her Life and Work* (London: Asia Publishing House, 1970).

Although evangelical initiatives in Bible translation have been promoted by many organizations in many parts of the world, the Wycliffe Bible Translators and this organization's academic arm, the Summer Institute of Linguistics, have become leaders in such efforts. Wycliffe came into existence under Cameron Townsend, a missionary to Guatemala who became disturbed that native speakers of Cakchiquel could not read the Bible in their native tongue.[41] After its establishment in 1942, Wycliffe initially recruited linguists and support staff from Western countries, but in recent decades it has drawn its well-educated workers from throughout the Christian world and employed an ever-increasing number of native informants in the target languages of new translations. A different example of evangelical dedication to the Scriptures, and also of American entrepreneurial initiative, has been *The Jesus Film*, a dramatization of the Gospel of Luke from 1979 that Campus Crusade for Christ has dubbed into over one thousand languages and shown as an evangelistic tool to billions of people throughout the world.

What might be considered a domestic counterpart to biblical translations into non-European languages has been the proliferation of new versions that now share the long-standing loyalty of English-speaking evangelicals to the King James Version (KJV) of 1611. For many evangelicals, this translation remains the Bible of choice. That loyalty is particularly strong among African American communities where powerful preaching – both quoting and modelled stylistically on the KJV – has provided a constant support through a very difficult history. Suspicion about modern versions among a few evangelicals has even led to a 'King James Only' movement where loyalty to this translation is defined on grounds of manuscript evidence and theological scruples that few others outside of this movement accept.

A broad range of evangelicals assisted efforts that led to the English Revised Version (1885) and the American Standard Version (1901), although neither ever came near to replacing the KJV.[42] When the Revised Standard Version appeared in 1952, quite a few American evangelicals objected to the translation of Isaiah 7:14 as 'a young woman shall conceive' (instead of 'a virgin') and continued to be nervous about the New Revised Standard Version (1989), even though these revisions were carried out by scholarly committees that included evangelicals like Bruce Metzger of Princeton Theological Seminary. Evangelicals in general took kindly to the New Testament paraphrase of the Anglican J. B. Phillips (1958) and the paraphrase of New Testament epistles, *Living Letters*, by an American editor/publisher, Kenneth Taylor (1956), a project that was completed as *The Living Bible* (1971) with eventual worldwide sales in the hundreds of millions. The American Bible Society's *Good News Bible/Today's English Version* (1966) gained considerable support among evangelicals, though versions sponsored by self-defined evangelical groups have done even better. These include the New King James Version (1982), the New International Version (1978) and the English Standard Version (2001). Whether or not all of these English-language versions could justify the immense efforts and considerable funding that produced them, they do testify to the determination that evangelicals share with other Christians to make the Scriptures understandable for as many readers as possible.

Herculean efforts in Bible translation outside of the English-speaking world have been transformative for the religious history of the whole human race. In the words of the Gambian-born scholar of world Christianity, Lamin Sanneh, 'Bible translation enabled Christianity to break the cultural filibuster of its Western domestication to create movements of resurgence and renewal

---

41 William Svelmoe, *A New Vision for Missions: William Cameron Townsend, the Wycliffe Bible Translators, and the Culture of Early Evangelical Missions, 1896–1945* (Tuscaloosa, AL: University of Alabama Press, 2008).

42 A superb study is Peter J. Thuesen, *In Discordance with the Scriptures: American Protestant Battles over Translating the Bible* (New York: Oxford University Press, 1999).

that transformed the religion into a world faith.'[43] If evangelicals are due much of the credit for this worldwide transformation, the result has been the emergence of evangelical and evangelical-like movements that have innovated freely in putting Scripture to use. Philip Jenkins, for example, has pointed out how Psalm 23, which for evangelicals in the West functions mostly as a source of devotional reassurance, has taken on additional political meanings when appropriated by believers in Kenya, Uganda, Korea, Namibia and Ghana. In the situations documented by Jenkins, this Psalm has been read as a challenge to corrupt political regimes – 'The Lord is my Shepherd; you aren't' – as well as a comfort in personal times of trial.[44] C. Rosalee Velloso Ewell, a Brazilian Baptist theologian and executive director of the Theological Commission for the World Evangelical Alliance, provides an illustration for how the globalization of evangelical faith has reverberated back to the West. With reference to the greater emphasis on social justice, alongside evangelization, at the Lausanne Congress of 1974, Ewell notes that: 'It was precisely the shift of the centers of Christianity from the North to the global South – which is made up of Central and Latin America, Africa, and most Asia – that helped Evangelicals recover this very important aspect of biblical theology . . . practices of justice and peace'.[45] The evangelical missionary drive, with its constant effort to disseminate the Scriptures, has been the major factor in making the Majority Christian world a shaper, as well as a receiver, of the gospel message.

Attention to influences arising from outside the English-speaking world illustrates the great difference that geography has meant for evangelicals, as with all religious movements. In other words, the locations where evangelicals put the Bible to use have influenced the character of that usage. An example is found in the very first attempts to craft a uniform evangelical doctrinal statement. At the first meeting of the Evangelical Alliance in 1846, one of the affirmations of its Basis was: 'The right and duty of Private Judgment in the interpretation of Holy Scripture'.[46] In the initial London publication of the Basis, this particular point came seventh. But when the Basis was published in the United States, it came second, immediately after the affirmation of the Bible's inspiration, authority and sufficiency.[47] American sensitivity about contentions over slavery meant that Americans wanted the historical Protestant insistence on 'Private Judgment' highlighted in a way that British and continental European sentiments did not require.

In the second half of the twentieth century, similar trans-Atlantic differences among evangelicals were obvious. Most of the new versions of the Bible, for instance, came out of the United States, where evangelical communities had long nourished a stronger entrepreneurial, individualistic and go-it-alone spirit than in Britain. Compared to their British contemporaries, American evangelicals also invested much more energy in controversies over whether the Bible should be considered 'inerrant'.[48] That difference could be partially explained by the long-standing populist and fragmenting character of American religious life in general, where

---

43 Lamin Sanneh, *Whose Religion Is Christianity? The Gospel Beyond the West* (Grand Rapids, MI: Eerdmans, 2003), p. 130.
44 Philip Jenkins, *The New Faces of Christianity: Believing the Bible in the Global South* (New York: Oxford University Press, 2006), pp. 147–8.
45 C. Rosalee Velloso Ewell, 'What Evangelicals Believe', in *Evangelicals Around the World*, p. 49.
46 *Evangelical Alliance: Report of the Proceedings of the Conference held . . . 1846* (London: Partridge and Oakley, 1847), p. 77.
47 'The Doctrinal Basis of the Evangelical Alliance', in *The Creeds of Christendom*, edited by Schaff, III: 827.
48 For the United States, see the books by Rogers and McKim, Carson and Woodbridge, and Hays and Ansberry, with full references in note 53 below. For the United Kingdom, see Bebbington, *Evangelicalism*, pp. 268–8, 271, 275; Derek J. Tidball, *Who Are the Evangelicals? Tracing the Roots of Today's Movement* (London: Marshall Pickering, 1994), pp. 79–97, and the books by Warner and Jones and Bebbington, with full references in note 53 below.

claims to follow 'the Bible alone' have magnified questions of scriptural authority, compared to the situation for British evangelicals who have functioned in some contexts (like the Church of England, the Church of Scotland and the major British universities) where such claims have never gained the same traction.

The deep and continuous evangelical dedication to Scripture has also been a factor in the history of the Bible as a physical object – and consequently its function as a merchandisable commodity. In a detailed study of the British and Foreign Bible Society, Leslie Howsam pointed out a gender dimension in early promotion of the Society that spoke of interwoven spirituality and commerce: 'When it came to organizing Associations, in places like Liverpool, the conflict was articulated in terms of gender. Women collected funds, to save souls, and men spent them – to publish books.'[49] When Bible printing and distribution became big business, conventional business thinking came to influence how evangelicals, along with others, looked to the Scriptures. The mixture of biblical devotion and biblical commerce was illustrated in Susan Warner's best-selling American novel from 1850, *Wide, Wide World*. It featured a protagonist, Ellen Montgomery, who in one memorable scene went shopping with her mother for Ellen's first Bible. Explicitly Christian use of Scripture came into play since Ellen had been reading passages describing heaven and the afterlife to her mother, who was very ill. But so also was nineteenth-century business in view as Warner showed her heroine enthusing over the great variety of Bibles available for purchase in every size, colour, binding and price. The scene, as summarized by Colleen McDannell, showed that by the mid-nineteenth century 'the Bible brought together faith, family, and fashion'.[50] Paul Gutjahr, author of the most comprehensive study of Scripture as a physical object in American history, has noted that when publishers responded to public demand by bringing out numerous Bibles in different sizes, with a range of bindings, and accompanied by many (or no) illustrations, 'these bindings and illustrations helped create Bibles that were purchased for reasons aside from the words they contained. Bindings increasingly became tools to mark levels of gentility and social status, not simply provide an appropriate protection reinforcing the Bible's precious words'.[51] This phenomenon has only become more prominent with the diversity of versions produced in recent times. Publishers of these versions offer not only alternative textual readings, but a huge array of special editions, sizes, prices, colours, targeted groups, and demographic niches. Without a steady market among evangelicals, the perennially flourishing trade in Bibles would be unimaginable.

While evangelical attachment to Scripture has often acted like a magnet to focus the devotion of diverse populations on a biblical presentation of redemption in Christ, that same devotion has also operated with magnetic force to repel others. In biographies of those who after being raised as evangelicals – and often expressing life-long attachment to the person of Jesus – but who then turned away, disillusionment with some aspect of evangelical scripturalism looms large. David Hempton has catalogued the issues that a number of well-known figures recorded for why they moved away from the evangelical faith in which they were nurtured – including the novelist George Eliot, Francis Newman, the brother of John Henry Newman, the American female reformers Sarah Grimké and Elizabeth Cady Stanton and the African American writer James Baldwin. Prominent among those difficulties have been 'the hard sayings of biblical narrative' or the 'moral repudiation of biblical ethics', factors that have often proven more important than

---

49 Howsam, *Cheap Bibles*, p. 204.
50 Colleen McDannell, *Material Christianity: Religion and Popular Culture in America* (New Haven, CT: Yale University Press, 1995), p. 99.
51 Paul C. Gutjahr, *An American Bible: A History of the Good Book in the United States, 1777–1880* (Stanford, CA: Stanford University Press, 1999), p. 177.

'difficulties presented by biblical criticism and Darwinian evolution'.[52] If evangelicals can be identified, above all, by their commitment to Scripture, so can that same commitment explain what has propelled some out and beyond evangelicalism.

On a scale of significance – and only after Bible translation and the spread of evangelical Bible-believing throughout the world – the most important development for evangelicals and the Bible since the eighteenth century has been the confrontation with modern learning. The first two generations of evangelicals were distinguished by their uses of Scripture, but not for the most part by their convictions about the Bible itself. That situation changed in the nineteenth century with the coming of biblical higher criticism to the English-speaking world, the rise of scientific thinking as the most authoritative form of public reason, and the specific challenge of new scientific discoveries. The response of evangelicals to these developments has generated a tsunami of writing, ranging from the most sophisticated to the most pedestrian.[53]

Evangelicals have never been convinced about many of the prominent features of modern biblical criticism – including its historicism (the view that all accounts in Scripture were a product of cultural assumptions of the periods when they were written), its evolutionism (the opinion that the religion of Scripture developed over time from the primitive to the refined), and its demythologizing (the assumption that supernatural events are best accounted for through natural explanations). Some evangelicals, however, have been able to appropriate aspects of modern criticism that they regard as resting on empirical investigation instead of presupposed historicism, evolutionism and demythologizing. Yet the many possibilities of such appropriation, along with considerable numbers of evangelicals who in principle reject all modern criticism, means that evangelicals express a vast range of opinions on whether, why, and how much modern criticism should be put to use.

It is the same with scientific aspirations as the norm for public discourse in general. Some evangelicals have approached Scripture with what B. M. Pietsch has called 'taxonomic thinking', or the modern assumption that genuine knowledge means 'quantification, precise measurement,

---

52 David Hempton, *Evangelical Disenchantment: Nine Portraits of Faith and Doubt* (New Haven, CT: Yale University Press, 2008), p. 191.
53 A few of the most informative titles, from an innumerable throng, that address the specific question of evangelicals and the Bible, or that show how important Scripture is within evangelical conceptions of theology, include James I. Packer, *'Fundamentalism' and the Word of God* (Grand Rapids, MI: Eerdmans, 1958); James Barr, *Fundamentalism* (Philadelphia, PA: Westminster, 1978); Jack B. Rogers and Donald McKim, *The Authority and Inspiration of the Bible* (San Francisco, CA: Harper & Row, 1979); *Hermeneutics, Authority, and Canon*, edited by D. A. Carson and John D. Woodbridge (Grand Rapids, MI: Zondervan, 1986); *The Variety of American Evangelicalism*, edited by Donald W. Dayton and Robert K. Johnson (Knoxville, TN: University of Tennessee Press, 1991); Mark A. Noll, *Between Faith and Criticism: Evangelicals, Scholarship, and the Bible in America* (Vancouver: Regent College Publishing, 2004); *The Bible and the University*, edited by David Lyle Jeffrey and C. Stephen Evans (Grand Rapids, MI: Zondervan, 2007); *The Cambridge Companion to Evangelical Theology*, edited by Timothy Larsen and Daniel J. Treier (Cambridge: Cambridge University Press, 2007); Rob Warner, *Reinventing English Evangelicalism, 1966–2001: A Theological and Sociological Study* (Milton Keynes: Paternoster, 2007); *The Oxford Handbook of Evangelical Theology*, edited by Gerald R. McDermott (Oxford: Oxford University Press, 2010); *Evangelicalism and Fundamentalism in the United Kingdom during the Twentieth Century*, edited by David W. Bebbington and David Ceri Jones (Oxford: Oxford University Press, 2013); *Evangelical Faith and the Challenge of Historical Criticism*, edited by Christopher M. Hays and Christopher B. Ansberry (London: SPCK, 2013); Kevin J. Vanhoozer and Daniel J. Treier, *Theology and the Mirror of Scripture: A Mere Evangelical Account* (Downers Grove, IL: InterVarsity Press, 2015); and for the world at large, Mark Hutchinson and John Wolffe, *A Short History of Global Evangelicalism* (Cambridge: Cambridge University Press, 2012).

classification, standardization, and "scientific" explanations'.[54] Other evangelicals have more self-consciously opted for what David Steinmetz memorably described as 'pre-critical exegesis', or an approach to Scripture that deliberately recovers typological, mystical, multivalent, and spiritual ways of approaching the Bible that were common before the Age of Enlightenment.[55] Most typically, evangelicals unselfconsciously mix together the modern, the pre-modern, the quasi-modern and the anti-modern as they read the Bible, with the result that a host of explicit and implicit influences have always shaped evangelical understandings of Scripture.

For discussions of the Bible and science, one of the main determinants has been geography. David Livingstone has explained, for example, why evangelicals in Princeton, Toronto and Edinburgh could accept some aspects of Darwin's theory of evolution, while those in Belfast and Columbia, South Carolina, did not. What might seem on the surface a struggle to align biblical revelation and scientific proposals 'turned out to be something else – the preservation of cultural identity, the control of educational institutions, sectarian rivalry, race relations'. In a world where evangelicals now exist in many more places than only a short time ago, Livingstone's emphasis on 'the salience of *place* and *politics* in religious engagements with scientific claims' should alert observers to the ways that geographical context shapes other understandings and uses of Scripture.[56]

The evangelical engagement with modern thought has operated within clear outer boundaries. Evangelicals have repudiated Unitarianism and efforts to strip their scriptural understanding of the Trinity, even if early generations of Unitarianism claimed to be only reading the biblical text closely.[57] Evangelicals have also repudiated thorough-going modernism that depicts God as immanent in the creation and the supernatural as only mythic but never actual. The terrain between these two extremes is the playing field where evangelicals read, study, apply, and argue about the Bible.

Conclusion

Evangelical attachment to Scripture in part reflects convictions shared with most other believers in the general history of Christianity. But it also reflects the particular character of a movement that in the words of a noteworthy recent book on evangelicalism worldwide, 'swings between its missional, experiential and doctrinal . . . touchpoints as it encounters new situations, negotiating between effectiveness and self-definition'.[58] Throughout evangelical history the Bible has been read incessantly, quickened personally, exalted theologically, interpreted democratically, sung passionately and debated endlessly. The plasticity of evangelical faith – sometimes focused on tasks (missional), sometimes emphasizing the believers' personal faith (experiential), and sometimes trying to define explicit standards for belief and practice (doctrinal) – goes far to explain the plasticity characterizing the history of evangelicals and the Bible.

---

54 B. M. Pietsch, *Dispensational Modernism* (New York: Oxford University Press, 2015), p. 18.
55 David Steinmetz, 'The Superiority of Pre-Critical Exegesis', *Theology Today* vol. 37 (April 1980), 27–38.
56 David N. Livingstone, *Dealing with Darwin: Place, Politics, and Rhetoric in Religious Engagements with Evolution* (Baltimore, MD: Johns Hopkins University Press, 2014), p. 198.
57 On the claim of a leading American Unitarian, William Ellery Channing, to be guided by 'whatever doctrines seem to us to be clearly taught in the Scriptures', see Mark A. Noll, *America's God: From Jonathan Edwards to Abraham Lincoln* (New York: Oxford University Press, 2002), p. 285.
58 Hutchinson and Wolffe, *A Short History of Global Evangelicalism*, p. 278.

3
EVANGELICALS AND THE CROSS

David Ceri Jones

From their very beginning, evangelicals wherever they have been found, have been preoccupied with the cross of Jesus Christ, that is, his atoning death and sacrifice on Good Friday, and his resurrection from the dead on Easter Sunday. Evangelicals have taken their cue from the Apostle Paul, who in his letter to the Corinthian church, spoke of his determination 'to know nothing but Jesus Christ and him crucified' (I Cor. 2: 2). For George Whitefield, whose preaching in London and Bristol in the mid and late 1730s effectively launched the evangelical revival in England, 'the doctrine of our regeneration, or new birth in Christ Jesus' was 'the most fundamental doctrine of our holy religion'.[1] For his friend John Wesley, there was barely a hair's breadth difference. The atonement, wrote Wesley, 'was properly the distinguishing point between Deism and Christianity', and towards the end of his life he exhorted his band of itinerant preachers that their 'main and constant business [was] to "preach Jesus Christ and him crucified"'.[2]

Through the nineteenth and twentieth centuries, despite much change elsewhere, evangelicals resolutely maintained their focus on the cross. In a sermon preached in 1878, the Baptist Charles Haddon Spurgeon said that the cross 'lightens our conscience, gladdens our hearts, inspires our devotion, and elevates our aspirations; we are wedded to it, and daily glory in it'.[3] Battling against modernism and theological liberalism at the beginning of the twentieth century, the authors of *The Fundamentals* (1910–1915) confidently asserted that: 'The atonement is Christianity in epitome. It is the heart of Christianity as a system; it is the distinguishing mark of the Christian religion'.[4] From a slightly different perspective, the Scottish Congregational theologian P. T. Forsyth commented: 'Christ is to us just what his cross is. All that Christ was in heaven or on earth was put into what he did there. . . . You do not understand Christ till

---

1 George Whitefield, *The Nature and Necessity of our New Birth in Christ Jesus, in Order to Salvation* (London: C. Rivington, 1737), p. 1.
2 Quoted in, Kenneth J. Collins, *The Theology of John Wesley: Holy Love and the Shape of Grace* (Nashville, TN: Abingdon Press, 2007), p. 99.
3 Quoted in, Mark Hopkins, *Nonconformity's Romantic Generation: Evangelical and Liberal Theologies in Victorian England* (Milton Keynes: Paternoster, 2004), pp. 146–7.
4 Dyson Hague, 'At-one-ment by Propitiation', in *The Fundamentals: A Testimony to the Truth*, edited by A. C. Dixon and R. A. Torrey (12 vols, Chicago, IL: Testimony Publishing Company, 1910), XI: 23.

you understand his cross'.[5] At the beginning of the twenty-first century, after over seventy years preaching to millions in stadiums around the globe, Billy Graham, in one of his final books, continued to proclaim that Christ 'paid for our freedom with his priceless life', and that salvation is still freely available 'to all who will take hold'.[6]

The hymns evangelicals have sung have dwelt on the cross more than any other single theme. In the popular *Olney Hymns* (1779), William Cowper graphically portrayed the cross as a blood-filled fountain:

> There is a fountain filled with blood
> Drawn from Immanuel's vein;
> And sinners plunged beneath that flood,
> Lose all their guilty stains
>
> The dying thief rejoiced to see
> That fountain in his day;
> And there have I, though vile as he,
> Washed all my sins away.[7]

The personal appropriation of the atoning work of Christ has been an indispensable part of the evangelical understanding of the cross. The so-called 'love song' of the 1904–1905 Welsh revival, 'Dyma gariad fel y moroedd' ('Here is love, vast as the ocean'), took up the theme of the love of God displayed at Calvary. Its second verse focused exclusively on the cross:

> On the Mount of Crucifixion
> Fountains opened deep and wide;
> Through the floodgates of God's mercy
> Flowed a vast and gracious tide.
> Grace and love, like mighty rivers,
> Poured incessant from above,
> And heaven's peace and perfect justice
> Kissed a guilty world in love.[8]

Sustained meditation on the atonement could sustain revival fires. The cross was also meant to overshadow and give shape to the whole of the Christian's life. Fanny Crosby's chorus expressed this more clearly than most:

> Jesus, keep me near the Cross:
> There a precious fountain,
> Free to all – a healing stream –
> Flows from Calvary's mountain.
>
> *In the Cross, in the Cross, be my glory ever;*
> *Till my raptured soul shall find rest beyond the river.*

---

5 P. T. Forsyth, *The Cruciality of the Cross* (London: Hodder and Stoughton, 1909), pp. 44–5.
6 Billy Graham, *The Reason for my Hope: Salvation* (Nashville, TN: Thomas Nelson, 2013), p. xii.
7 *Olney Hymns* (London: W. Oliver, 1797), no. 79; book 1, p. 98.
8 Translation from *Christian Hymns* (Bridgend: Evangelical Movement of Wales, 1977), no. 210.

> Near the Cross! O Lamb of God,
> Bring its scenes before me;
> Help me walk from day to day,
> With its shadow o'er me.[9]

For evangelicals, the sacrificial death of Christ has been at the heart of their expression of Christian faith; meditation upon it has been the meat and drink of their spirituality.[10]

Christians down the ages have understood the atoning work of Christ in many different ways, and have developed a number of theories or models to aid understanding.[11] Some have seen one or other of these models as best capturing the nature of Christ's redeeming work, while others have preferred to argue that each captures just one facet of Christ's death, and that only when taken together do we get a full picture. These models have included the ransom theory, championed by some of the early church fathers, in which Christ by his sufferings and death is held to have paid either God or the devil a ransom to free humanity from the debt that sin had incurred. So-called governmental theories, owing much to the seventeenth-century Dutch jurist, Hugo Grotius, have focused on the need to maintain God's justice, and have seen Christ's death as clearing all obstacles out of the way so that God can forgive sinners without punishing them.

The satisfaction view, developed by Anselm in the eleventh century, interprets Christ's death as a substitution, but avoids the language of punishment, by stressing that in his death Christ brought God the honour that he had been deprived because of human rebellion. More recently, the 'Christus Victor' approach, perhaps best associated with Gustav Aulén's work, regards the cross as a site of cosmic conflict between good and evil, in which Christ overcame the power of sin, death and the devil.[12] Other views include those which see Christ as being a scapegoat for human sin, and the recapitulation view, which argues that the atonement witnessed Christ succeeding where Adam had previously failed. More radically, others following the lead of twelfth-century theologian Peter Abelard have argued that Christ's death carried no redemptive value beyond the example it represented of human suffering. Following the teaching and example of Christ, in his life and his death, it is held, brings moral transformation.

Most evangelicals have certainly favoured a substitutionary view of Christ's sacrifice. That is, they have regarded Christ's passion as in some way in the place and stead of sinful humanity, and often they have added the language of punishment to that of substitution. Taking their lead from the sixteenth-century Protestant Reformer John Calvin, some have stressed that in his sufferings and death Christ bore the penalty and curse due for the sins of his people, and that in the process God's wrath against sin was propitiated, or appeased, and his justice fully satisfied.[13] However,

---

9 Ira D. Sankey, *Sacred Songs and Solos: Twelve Hundred Hymns* (London: Marshall, Morgan and Scott, 1921), no. 134.
10 David W. Bebbington, *Evangelicalism in Modern Britain: A History from the 1730s to the 1980s* (London: Unwin Hyman, 1989), pp.14–17.
11 For some recent introductory surveys to these models, see John Stott, *The Cross of Christ* (Leicester: Inter-Varsity Press, 1986); Mark D. Baker and Joel B. Green, *Recovering the Scandal of the Cross: Atonement in New Testament and Contemporary Contexts* (Carlisle: Paternoster, 2003); Gregory A. Boyd, Joel B. Green, Bruce R. Reichenbach and Thomas R. Schreiner, *The Nature of the Atonement: Four Views* (Downers Grove, IL: InterVarsity Press, 2006); Stephen R. Holmes, *The Wondrous Cross: Atonement and Penal Substitution in the Bible and History* (Milton Keynes: Paternoster, 2007); *T&T Clark Companion to Atonement*, edited by Adam J. Johnson (London: Continuum, 2016).
12 Gustav Aulén, *Christus Victor: An Historical Study of the Three Main Types of the Idea of the Atonement*, translated by A. G. Herbert (London: SPCK, 1931).
13 For Calvin's views, see John Calvin, *Institutes of the Christian Religion*, translated by F. L. Battles, edited

evidence of all of the other views on the atonement can be found in the preaching and writings of prominent figures from across the spectrum of evangelical opinion: while each approach has had its passionate advocates, none of them on their own have been regarded as fully expressing the richness of evangelical understandings of the cross. The atonement has consequently been a source of constant debate amongst evangelicals. This chapter explores some of these debates, and argues that while the cross has been integral to evangelical identity, it has also been highly contested, leading to conflicts over the nature of true evangelicalism.

Widening the atonement in the eighteenth century

Finding confident statements from first generation evangelicals concerning the centrality of a substitutionary view of the atonement is not difficult. During these decades most would have heartily agreed with the New England theologian Jonathan Edwards that the 'great Christian doctrine of Christ's satisfaction . . . is, as it were, the centre and hinge of all doctrines of pure revelation'.[14] In a sermon in January 1739, on a favourite evangelical text, Romans 3: 23–4, Charles Wesley went a step further and spoke of the atonement not only in substitutionary terms, but added penal language as well:

> God sent his only son our Saviour Christ into this world to fulfill the law for us, and by the shedding of his most precious blood, to make sacrifice and satisfaction or amends to his Father for our sins, and assuage his wrath and indignation conceived against us for the same.[15]

In his epic poem *Bywyd a Marwolaeth Theomemphus* (1764), the leading theologian of the Welsh Methodist revival, William Williams, put in the mouth of Theomemphus, the main protagonist, a similarly confident expression of penal substitution:

> He came to heal the wounded, was wounded in their stead;
> The heir of heaven was pierced for those through sin were dead;
> He sucked the awful poison the serpent gave to me,
> And from that deadly venom, he died on Calvary.[16]

Beyond early Methodism, the combination of substitutionary and penal language was no less clear. For the dissenting divine, Philip Doddridge, Christ 'was made a Curse for us, and endured the penalty which our sins had deserved',[17] while for John Witherspoon, the Scottish-American Presbyterian and President of the College of New Jersey (later Princeton), Christ's death was only fully understood as 'being a propitiation'. He wrote:

---

    by John T. McNeill (2 vols, Louisville, KY: Westminster John Knox Press, 2006), II: 503-11 (II. xvi.1-6).

14 Quoted in Michael J. McClymond and Gerald R. McDermott, *The Theology of Jonathan Edwards* (New York: Oxford University Press, 2012), p. 250.

15 John R. Tyson, '"I Preached at the Cross, As Usual": Charles Wesley and Redemption', in *Charles Wesley: Life, Literature and Legacy*, edited by Kenneth C. G. Newport and Ted A. Campbell (Peterborough: Epworth Press, 2007), p. 205.

16 Eifion Evans, *Pursued by God: A Selective Translation of the Welsh Religious Classic Theomemphus by William Williams of Pantycelyn* (Bridgend: Evangelical Press of Wales, 1996), p. 91.

17 Robert Strivens, *Philip Doddridge and the Shaping of Evangelical Dissent* (Farnham: Ashgate, 2015), p. 41.

> Without all question, every part of his humiliation was satisfactory to the divine justice, and contributed to appease the wrath of God ... The waves of divine wrath went over him; and he waded still deeper and deeper in this troubled ocean, till he was well nigh overwhelmed.[18]

The language of substitution, often with penal language as well, came most naturally to evangelicals when they wanted to explain the sacrificial death of Christ.

Yet there could also be significant variation in the way Christ's death was understood; sometimes alongside such clear expressions of penal substitution, other perspectives could harmoniously co-exist. The evangelical nonconformist Isaac Watts was a passionate defender of penal substitution, arguing that without it the 'blessed Gospel is shamefully curtailed, and depriv'd of some of its most important Designs and Honours'.[19] But he was also ready to speak of the atonement as a 'Recompence for the dishonour done to [God's] Government', and as 'a solemn spectacle and Wonder of other Worlds behind this, even the World of Angels, Principalities and Powers'.[20] Penal substitutionary, governmental and 'Christus Victor' theories meshed together. However, it was in his magnanimous approach to those who differed from his understanding of the atonement that Watts was perhaps most innovative. 'Far be it from me', he wrote, 'to imagine that every one must believe these things just after the same Order and in the same manner in which I have learnt to conceive of them'. There were others who had understood things differently. What mattered, he argued, was that all agreed that in his death Christ had made a 'proper Satisfaction for sin'.[21] It was a generous position.

Among those caught up in the evangelical revivals of the 1730s there was similar synthesis. There is some limited evidence that Jonathan Edwards grappled with some of the complexities of strictly penal views of the atonement, and there are hints here and there in Edwards' writings that he was attracted to a more governmental approach to Christ's death, although in the final analysis he never moved beyond the bounds of penal substitution.[22] In his analysis of the theology of John Wesley, Randy Maddox has demonstrated that Wesley could speak of the atonement in different ways at different times. Maddox characterized Wesley's position as a blended one, combining a 'Penalty Satisfaction *explanation* of the Atonement which has a Moral Influence *purpose*, and a Ransom *effect*'.[23]

As the spirit of the revivals spilled over its Methodist birthplace in the later eighteenth century, many of its characteristic emphases were taken up by leading figures in other denominations. In *The Complete Duty of Man* (1763), the Anglican evangelical Henry Venn, followed Wesley's synthesizing of various views of the atonement: Jesus, he wrote, 'was made sin, that is, a sin-offering, and a curse for us. He interposed his sacred body between the load of wrath from above, and us the heirs of wrath below', and in so doing, 'the debt of penal suffering, the debt of perfect obedience is paid to the law; the powers of hell are vanquished, and God is well

---

18 Kevin DeYoung, 'John Witherspoon and Late Reformed Orthodoxy', *Christianity and History Bulletin* vol. 8 (Spring 2016), 33.
19 Isaac Watts, *Sermons on Various Subjects: Divine and Moral* (2 vols, Boston, MA: Rogers and Fowle, 1746), II: 527.
20 Watts, *Sermons on Various Subjects*, II: 529–30.
21 Watts, *Sermons on Various Subjects*, II: 537–8.
22 See S. Mark Hamilton, 'Jonathan Edwards on the Atonement', *International Journal of Systematic Theology* vol. 15 (October 2013), 394–415.
23 Randy Maddox, *Responsible Grace: John Wesley's Practical Theology* (Nashville, TN: Kingswood Books, 1994), p. 109.

pleased'.[24] A similar approach was taken by Dan Taylor, the founder of the New Connexion of General Baptists in 1770, who fused a governmental, possibly Grotian understanding of the atonement, with the language of punishment and satisfaction.[25] His advocacy of a form of what became known as the governmental theory, presaged the more substantial attempts that would be made by later generations to replace penal substitution with this view altogether.

Despite these fairly tentative explorations of the precise meaning of the atonement, the chief point of controversy concerning the sacrificial death of Christ throughout much of the eighteenth century concerned not so much its substitutionary or penal nature, but who exactly it was intended to benefit. Questions regarding the extent of the atonement, whether Christ died for the world or just for a more limited group of his own people, the elect, absorbed considerable energy. It was the issue above all others that drove apart George Whitefield and John Wesley during the early stages of the evangelical revival, a fissure between Calvinists and Arminians that has remained ever-present within the evangelical movement. Wesley, a late-comer to the leadership of the English revival, found the Calvinism of the Methodists that Whitefield had gathered in Bristol in the mid-1730s deeply offensive. In a provocative sermon against predestination, he argued that election was the 'Horrible Decree',[26] because amongst other things it limited the freeness of the grace of God on offer in the gospel, and inevitably hindered evangelism. 'Christ died', Wesley wrote, 'not only for those that are saved, but also for them that perish'.[27] The grace and love of God are 'Free in all, and Free for all'.[28]

In his answer to Wesley's sermon, Whitefield reiterated his belief in election, but challenged Wesley's assertion that predestination made preaching the gospel all but redundant. Whitefield reiterated his belief in a limited or particular atonement – that Christ died for the elect alone:

> But blessed be God, our Lord knew for whom he died. There was an eternal Compact between the Father and the Son. A certain number was then given him, as the Purchase and Reward of his Obedience and Death. For these he prayed, John xvi. and not for the world. For these, and these only, he is now interceding, and with their Salvation he will be fully satisfied.[29]

However, for Whitefield this did not blunt evangelistic endeavour one bit. 'And since we know not who are Elect and who Reprobate', he wrote, 'we are to preach promiscuously to all'.[30] In Whitefield's hands Calvinism, at least in the moderate expression he favoured, far from being a hindrance to evangelism, proved to be an enormous motivation.

There were plenty still wedded to stricter forms of Calvinism, with its narrower application of the atonement. The Particular Baptist, John Gill's stress on eternal justification, the idea that the elect were justified before the foundation of the world, so elevated the secret decrees

---

24 Henry Venn, *The Complete Duty of Man: Or, a System of Doctrinal and Practical Christianity* (London: J. Newbery, 1763), pp. 195–6.
25 See Richard Pollard, '"To Revive Experimental Religion or Primitive Christianity in Faith and Practice": The Pioneering Evangelicalism of Dan Taylor (1738–1816)' (unpublished PhD thesis: University of Wales, 2014), p. 88.
26 John Wesley, *Free Grace: A Sermon Preach'd at Bristol* (Bristol: S. and F. Farley, 1739), p. 25.
27 Wesley, *Free Grace*, p. 5.
28 Wesley, *Free Grace*, p. 20.
29 George Whitefield, *A Letter to the Reverend Mr. John Wesley: In Answer to his Sermon, Entitled, Free-Grace* (London: W. Strahan, 1741), p. 26.
30 Whitefield, *A Letter to the Reverend Mr. John Wesley*, p. 11.

of God that evangelistic zeal inevitably suffered.[31] Sometimes, High Calvinist views could gain a considerable following, as in the case of the network of churches established in Surrey and Sussex by the eccentric pastor of Providence Chapel in London, William Huntington.[32] During the early decades of the nineteenth century some within the Welsh nonconformist community flirted seriously with hyper-Calvinsitic views, in part a reaction to the arrival of Wesleyan missionaries in north-east Wales. The Calvinistic Methodist leader John Elias dedicated himself to 'purge our pulpits for ever from the accusations that we do not have an atonement sufficient for the world'.[33] But by this point High Calvinist views were becoming increasingly rare among those eighteenth-century evangelicals who understood the death of Christ in Reformed terms.

George Whitefield had modelled a moderate evangelical Calvinism, holding election and a commitment to offering the gospel freely to all in something close to harmonic balance.[34] It was, of course, a rebalancing of Calvinism finely tuned to the more optimistic spirit of the age,[35] and there were many inspired by his example. The Bristol Baptist Academy became something of a proving ground for moderate Calvinists in that denomination.[36] Among a growing band of evangelicals in the Church of England, John Newton's views were not untypical. Holding to a belief in election, Newton preferred to argue that Christ's sacrifice was for 'sinners', a category large enough to be all-inclusive. It was an approach that owed much to the 'Book of Common Prayer', where the Lord's Supper liturgy says that Christ 'made there by his one oblation of himself once offered, a full perfect, and sufficient sacrifice, oblation and satisfaction for the sins of the whole world'.[37] This allowed him to say that the atonement was sufficient for all, and that none other was needed, without implying that all would necessarily be saved. It was an argument, according to Bruce Hindmarsh, 'that subordinated the whole question of the extent of the atonement to evangelical priorities'.[38] Despite often differing understandings of the extent of the atonement, whether it was intended for the world, or for a smaller subsection of it, in practice there was very little difference between the way in which moderate evangelical Calvinists and Arminians actually preached the cross.

Eighteenth-century evangelical engagement with the cross was not always preoccupied with the finer points of atonement theory. The cross was also the mainstay of evangelical devotional life. Sometimes meditation on the cross played a decisive role in conversion. Perhaps the classic example of this is the conversion narrative that Whitefield penned for his published journal.

---

31 Clive Jarvis, 'The Myth of High Calvinism?', in *Recycling the Past or Researching History? Studies in Baptist Historiography and Myths*, edited by Philip E. Thompson and Anthony R. Cross (Milton Keynes: Paternoster, 2005), pp. 234–40.
32 George M. Ella, *William Huntington: Pastor of Providence* (Darlington: Evangelical Press, 1994).
33 Owen Thomas, *The Atonement Controversy in Welsh Theological Literature and Debate, 1707–1841*, translated by John Aaron (Edinburgh: Banner of Truth Trust, 2002), p. 312. See also David Ceri Jones, '"Some of the Grandest and Most Illustrious Beauties of the Reformation": John Elias and the Battle over Calvinism in Early Nineteenth-Century Welsh Methodism', *Bulletin of the John Rylands Library: Reinventing the Reformation in the Nineteenth Century: A Cultural History*, vol. 90 (Spring 2014), 113–43.
34 David Ceri Jones, *George Whitefield and the Revival of Calvinism in Eighteenth-Century Britain* (London: The Congregational Memorial Hall Trust, 2014).
35 Bebbington, *Evangelicalism*, pp. 63–5.
36 Roger Hayden, *Continuity and Change: Evangelical Calvinism among Eighteenth-century Baptist Ministers Trained at the Bristol Academy, 1690–1791* (Milton-under-Wychwood: Nigel Lynn Publishing, 2006).
37 *The Book of Common Prayer: The Texts of 1549, 1559, and 1662*, edited by Brian Cummings (Oxford: Oxford University Press, 2011), p. 402.
38 D. Bruce Hindmarsh, *John Newton and the English Evangelical Tradition* (Grand Rapids, MI: Eerdmans, 1996), p. 165.

During a protracted period of conviction of sin, Whitefield found relief by emulating Christ in the final agonies of his crucifixion:

> it was suggested to me, that when *Jesus Christ* cried out, "I thirst," his sufferings were near at an End. Upon which, I cast myself down on the Bed, crying out, I thirst! I thirst! – Soon after this, I found and felt in myself that I was delivered from the Burden that had so heavily oppressed me![39]

However, there were few who matched the Moravians for their mystical devotion to the bodily sufferings of the dying Christ. In his study of early evangelical conversion narratives, Hindmarsh quotes the startling example of the barely literate Susannah Duree, who longed to:

> give my self Kuite up to my Deare Saver So that I may get In to Is Deare Sidhol and to a Bide theare for hever To hall he tarnety I can not find Rest any weare hels wich makes me wich to Sink kuite in to that Deare Sidhole thow I am so un faithful.[40]

Such overt focus on the physicality of the cross, including a preoccupation with the physical wounds of Christ, was exceptional.[41]

When their preaching focused on the gospel itself, some evangelicals said surprisingly little about the cross. Whitefield is the obvious example of this trend. For him the key issue was the new birth – regeneration – and it was his preaching on this theme that catapulted him to national fame in 1737. While he held that Christ died 'to be a Propitiation for our sins, to give his life a ransom for many',[42] it was not on this that he chose to dwell. In his oft-repeated sermon on the new birth he reasoned that because of the 'moral Impurity in our nature . . . it is necessary . . . that we should have a grant of God's Holy Spirit to change our natures, and to prepare us for the Enjoyment of that Happiness our Saviour has purchased by his precious blood'.[43] Whitefield tended to be more preoccupied with the inward awakening produced by the Holy Spirit in the soul, rather than by the objective accomplishments of Christ in his sacrificial death. Reference to the actual atonement is surprisingly rare in his published sermons. In marked contrast, the eccentric vicar of Everton in Bedfordshire, John Berridge, attributed the success of his ministry to his explicit focus on the penal substitutionary death of Christ:

> I told them very plainly, that they were children of wrath, and under the curse of God . . . and that none but Jesus Christ could deliver them from that curse . . . If we break God's law we immediately fall under the curse of it: and none can deliver us from this curse but Jesus Christ.[44]

---

39 *A Short Account of God's Dealings with the Reverend Mr. George Whitefield* (London: W. Strahan, 1740), pp. 48–9.
40 D. Bruce Hindmarsh, *The Evangelical Conversion Narrative: Spiritual Autobiography in Early Modern England* (Oxford: Oxford University Press, 2005), p. 179.
41 Explicit references to the cross are, for example, surprisingly absent in the conversion narratives of Whitefield's Calvinistic Methodists. See David Ceri Jones, 'Narratives of Conversion in English Calvinistic Methodism', in *Revival and Resurgence in Christian History*, edited by Kate Cooper and Jeremy Gregory (Woodbridge: Boydell and Brewer, 2008), pp. 128–41.
42 Whitefield, *The Nature and Necessity of our New Birth in Christ Jesus*, p. 17.
43 Whitefield, *The Nature and Necessity of our New Birth in Christ Jesus*, pp. 17–18.
44 John Berridge, *Justification by Faith: Being the Substance of a Letter from the Rev. Mr. Berridge in Cambridge to a Clergyman in Nottinghamshire, Giving an Account of a Great Work of God Wrought in His Own Heart* (London: E. Englesfield and J. Wakelin, 1762), pp. 20–1.

There was considerable flexibility in the evangelical use of cross in preaching to the unconverted.

The evangelical focus on the cross was not only limited to the beginnings of Christian life. Many evangelicals, both Calvinistic and Arminian, were alarmed at the spectre of Antinomianism, and so stressed the necessity of a life of good works as a sign of the reality of inward change and re-birth.[45] Some made explicit reference to the atoning work of Christ in this regard. In a letter to the evangelical philanthropist and anti-slavery campaigner, John Thornton, Berridge argued that 'all divine life, and all the precious fruits of it, pardon, peace and holiness, spring from the cross'. Progress in holiness, he argued, was dependent on 'clear views of the cross . . . We must feed on Christ's atonement every day, and derive all our life, the life of peace and holiness, from his death.'[46] Similarly, William Jay, the evangelical Congregational minister at the Argyle Chapel in Bath for over sixty years, urged that only 'the love of God shed abroad' in the heart of the Christian 'by his cross, will make them long to resemble him'.[47] For many the whole of the Christian life, not just its start, was a cross-shaped existence.

Redefining the atonement in the late eighteenth and nineteenth centuries

Among the early evangelicals there had been a broad commitment to substitutionary approaches to Christ's death; some added penal terminology, but others did not. While some had begun to tentatively explore other approaches, towards the end of the eighteenth-century voices arguing that the substitutionary view did not fully or adequately capture the perplexity of Christ's death became increasingly prominent. Advocates of what became known as the 'New Divinity' made the initial running. Joseph Bellamy, a close associate of Jonathan Edwards, argued that the atonement was, in the words of Oliver Crisp, a 'penal nonsubstitution'. Drawing on the views of Hugo Grotius, Bellamy favoured a version of the governmental theory of the atonement. The law of God, he stated, could not be abrogated without a major threat to God's justice; in his death Christ vindicated God's law by showing what is required of those who were condemned by it – that is punishment. The undeserving Christ was punished, and the merit he accrued as a consequence could be drawn upon to forgive sinners. For Bellamy that merit was sufficient for the whole world, but only actually applicable to the elect.[48] In his wake, there were others that took things much further. Edwards' son, Jonathan Edwards Jnr, propounded a full-blown governmental theory; he argued that Christ 'did not, in the literal sense, pay the debt we owed to God', but by means of his death vindicated God's law and justice. With the moral order intact, and God's justice satisfied, the way was clear for God to save by means of sovereign grace alone.[49]

This alternative language went through many iterations, as subsequent generations of New England theologians, such as those associated with the New Haven school and later Andover

---

45 David Ceri Jones, 'George Whitefield and Heart Religion', *Heart Religion: Evangelical Piety in England and Ireland, 1690–1850*, edited by John Coffey (Oxford: Oxford University Press, 2016), pp. 93–112.
46 John Berridge to John Thornton (18 August 1773), in *The Letters of John Berridge of Everton: A Singular Spirituality*, edited by Nigel P. Pibworth (Kitchiner, Ontario: Joshua Press, 2015), p. 198.
47 Quoted in Stephen Blair Waddell, 'William Jay of Bath (1769–1853)' (unpublished PhD thesis, University of Stirling, 2012), p. 140.
48 This section follows Oliver D. Crisp, 'The Moral Government of God: Jonathan Edwards and Joseph Bellamy on the Atonement', in *After Jonathan Edwards: The Courses of New England Theology*, edited by Oliver D. Crisp and Douglas A. Sweeney (New York: Oxford University Press, 2012), pp. 85–8.
49 See Douglas A. Sweeney, *Nathaniel Taylor, New Haven Theology and the Legacy of Jonathan Edwards* (New York: Oxford University Press, 2003), p. 105.

seminary, refined and adapted it further.[50] As some of their often tortuous theological manoeuvres trickled down to the popular level, they could be reduced to blunt statements that often lacked the nuance that characterized the work of their more careful expositors. In the hands of the revivalist Charles Finney, for example, this new view was stated in perhaps its starkest terms. Christ had died, he wrote, 'simply to remove an insurmountable obstacle out of the way of God's forgiving sinners'. In his death, Christ

> . . . had only satisfied public justice, by honouring the law both in his obedience and death; and therefore rendering it safe for God to pardon sin, and to pardon the sins of any man, and of all men, who would repent and believe in Christ.[51]

Among evangelicals in Britain, it was the Baptist Andrew Fuller who mediated such views to a wider constituency.

Advocating a governmental theory of the atonement, an innovation which led some to question his Calvinism altogether, it was Fuller's emphasis on 'duty faith' that both aroused most controversy and that was most widely followed. In the same way as the atonement was sufficient for the whole world, but only efficient to the elect, so when it came to the role of human responsibility in accepting the gospel, Fuller trod a similar tightrope. Following Edwards, he argued that all men and women had the natural ability to believe the gospel, but it was their moral inability that prevented them from accepting Christ, something that could only be overcome by the enlightening power of the Holy Spirit. For Fuller, a more capacious atonement led him to argue that all were commanded to believe the gospel – without exception. That in turn opened the way to more ambitious evangelistic labour.[52] These innovations were very much within the bounds of legitimate Reformed theological opinion, and they were taken on board enthusiastically in some quarters. Edward Williams, for example, the Welsh Congregationalist tutor at the Rotherham academy, had published *An Essay on the Equity of Divine Government and the Sovereignty of Divine Grace* in 1809, and was one of the founder members of the London Missionary Society.[53] He, like many others, thought that these ideas represented a more consistent Calvinism altogether.

In the middle and later nineteenth century, under the twin influences of first Romanticism and then Modernism, particularly in the form of German biblical criticism, much more radical reformulations of the doctrine of atonement took place. For the Romantics the idea of God as judge seemed outmoded, and the legal language that had been relied upon to define the purpose of the death of Christ jarred with the new more optimistic cultural mood. God, many argued, should be thought of as immanent rather than transcendent, more as a benevolent Father than a cosmic and distant ruler dispensing arbitrary justice. Gradually the incarnation of Christ, rather than his death, took centre stage.[54] The running was made by the Scot, John McLeod Campbell, who in his 1856 book *The Nature of the Atonement*, argued that it was Christ's identification with

---

50 For some of these developments, see *After Jonathan Edwards*, edited by Crisp and Sweeney, parts II & III.
51 Quoted in Charles E. Hambrick-Stowe, *Charles G. Finney and the Spirit of American Evangelicalism* (Grand Rapids, MI: Eerdmans, 1996), p. 34.
52 See Peter J. Morden, *Offering Christ to the World: Andrew Fuller (1754–1814) and the Revival of Particular Baptist Life* (Milton Keynes: Paternoster, 2003).
53 For Williams, see W. T. Owen, *Edward Williams D.D.: His Life, Thought and Influence* (Cardiff: University of Wales Press, 1963).
54 For this change and some if its wider implications, see Boyd Hilton, *The Age of Atonement: The Influence of Evangelicalism on Social and Economic Thought, 1785–1865* (Oxford: Clarendon Press, 1986).

humanity that was the key to understanding both his life and death. Christ lived vicariously in humanity's place, he wrote; in his death he made confession of sin on behalf of fallen human beings thereby recognizing the rightness of God the Father's estimation of sin and safeguarding his justice. While Christ's death was therefore still substitutionary, it was no longer penal.[55]

In a similar vein, the Birmingham Congregationalist R. W. Dale argued that Christ's death was a voluntary sacrifice which vindicated God's righteousness; as was becoming typical he laid equal stress on Christ's incarnation as his death, and maintained that by identifying so closely with human beings in his life, Christ was able to restore the broken relationship between God and humanity in his death.[56] In his *The Old Evangelicalism and the New* (1889), he contrasted the theology of the eighteenth-century evangelicals, with its exclusive stress on the atonement and regeneration, with the position of contemporary evangelicals who had, rightly in his opinion, restored the doctrine of the incarnation to centre stage.[57] Some of these reformulations of the doctrine of the atonement were still taking place within the broad parameters of the evangelical movement; initially they indicated the emergence of a liberal evangelical wing to that movement, but the theological trajectory of some of their advocates was to take them beyond evangelical belief.

By the end of the nineteenth century, other theological currents of a much more radical nature had overhauled the concept of atonement altogether, relegating it to an earlier more primitive stage in the development of the Christian faith. In its place, inspired by the German theologians Friedrich Schleiermacher and Albrecht Ritschl, were enthroned the universal fatherhood of God, and a theology that saw Christ's death as little more than an example of supreme self-sacrifice, certainly to be emulated, but carrying little intrinsic salvific or redemptive power. For some of the more radical voices, especially within nonconformity, the whole concept of atonement itself was regarded as outdated, ill-suited to the modern age.

The degree to which the atonement had become a thorny issue among evangelicals by the second half of the nineteenth century can be seen in the way in which the Evangelical Alliance tackled the doctrine in its basis of faith. Published in 1845, the clause on the atonement was concise and non-specific, speaking only of Christ's 'work of atonement for sinners of mankind'.[58] For many evangelicals, such imprecision was deeply troubling, and systemic of much greater theological drift. A little later J. C. Ryle, who would go on to serve as bishop of Liverpool, solemnly warned:

> As long as you live, beware of a religion in which there is not much of the cross. You live in times when the warning is sadly needful. . . . There are hundreds of places of worship, in this day, in which there is everything almost except the cross . . . Jesus Christ is not proclaimed in the pulpit. The Lamb of God is not lifted up, and salvation

---

55 T. F. Torrance, *Scottish Theology: From John Knox to John McLeod Campbell* (London: T. & T. Clark, 1996), pp. 297–317; Peter K. Stevenson, *God in Our Nature: The Incarnational Theology of John McLeod Campbell* (Milton Keynes: Paternoster, 2004).
56 R. W. Dale, *The Atonement* (London: Hodder and Stoughton, 1875). See also, Hopkins, *Nonconformity's Romantic Generation*, pp. 68–74; Alan P. F. Sell, *Christ and Controversy: The Person of Christ in Nonconformist Thought and Ecclesial Experience, 1600–2000* (Eugene, OR: Pickwick Publications, 2011), pp. 125–6.
57 See, for example, R. W. Dale, *The Old Evangelicalism and the New* (London: Hodder and Stoughton, 1889), p. 47.
58 Ian Randall and David Hilborn, *One Body in Christ: The History and Significance of the Evangelical Alliance* (Carlisle: Paternoster, 2001), p. 357.

by faith in Him is not freely proclaimed. And hence all is wrong. Beware of such places of worship.[59]

In comments on Psalm 85:10 in *The Treasury of David* (1870), C. H. Spurgeon, with his characteristic pungent wit, castigated 'modern thinkers who make sport of our Lord's substitutionary atonement'. He went on:

> The doctrine of atonement has been well described . . . as the admission that 'the Lord Jesus Christ did something or other, which somehow or other, was in some way or other connected with man's salvation'. This is their substitute for substitution.[60]

In the century that followed, the substitutionary view of the atonement that had been largely assumed by most evangelicals for over a century and a half, and that had hitherto been only lightly reshaped by others, came to greater prominence. When the principal of Princeton Theological Seminary, A. A. Hodge, published his exhaustive study of the atonement in 1867, identifying it along with biblical inspiration as one of the 'two doctrines just at present most generally brought into question',[61] the language of penal substitution stood in sharp relief. He wrote:

> It is not a pecuniary solution of debt, which ipso facto liberates upon the mere payment of the money. It is a vicarious penal satisfaction, which can be admitted in any case only at the arbitrary discretion of the sovereign; and which may have a redemptive bearing upon the case of none, of few, of many, or of all; and upon the elect case at whatsoever time and upon whatever conditions are predetermined by the mutual understanding of the Sovereign and of the voluntary substitute.[62]

As many within the churches at large were questioning the validity of an atonement altogether, many evangelicals began to argue that the penal substitutionary view, far from being just one approach among many to explain Christ's sacrificial death, should actually be seen as one of the defining characteristics of the evangelical movement as a whole.

Contesting the atonement in the twentieth century

As the twentieth century dawned, the 1904–1905 religious revival in Wales seemed to presage a bright future for evangelical Christianity, especially when the ripples from that revival stirred up revival movements elsewhere bringing into being a raft of new evangelical denominations, albeit with a Pentecostal flavour. Yet the excitement stirred by the revival was far from unique. In much the same way as they had done with the revivalist Evan Roberts a little earlier, in 1907 the national press latched on to the radical minister of London's City Temple, R. J. Campbell, turning him into a national celebrity almost overnight. Campbell, a highly charismatic figure, championed what quickly became known as the 'New Theology'. In reality, there was little that

---

59 J. C. Ryle, *Old Paths: Being Plain Statements on Some of the Weightier Matters of Christianity* (London: National Protestant Church Union, 1897), p. 249.
60 C. H. Spurgeon, *The Treasury of David: Containing an Original Exposition of the Book of Psalms* (7 vols, London: Marshall Brothers, 1869-85), III: 453.
61 Archibald Alexander Hodge, *The Atonement* (Philadelphia, PA: Presbyterian Board of Publication, 1867), p. 16.
62 Hodge, *The Atonement*, p. 341.

was actually new in what Campbell wrote, his skill rather lay in articulating the often abstruse theological ideas of others, albeit in more popular form.

Campbell's discussion of the atonement took up three chapters of his book, *The New Theology* (1907) – it was the subject dealt with at more length than any other. The traditional view of the atonement, he wrote, 'does not possess a living interest for the mind of to-day',[63] and 'has wrought a good deal of mischief in the past and bewilderment in the present'.[64] The atonement for Campbell had nothing whatsoever to do with punishment, rather it was an expression of the 'fundamental oneness of God and man'.[65] Jesus, he said, had lived a life of perfect self-sacrifice thereby revealing the divine life within him. Any human being could do likewise. 'If you want to see the atonement at work', he wrote, 'go wherever love is ministering to human necessity and you see the very same spirit which was in Jesus . . . Shew me a Christlike life and I will show you a part of the atonement of Christ'.[66] The task of the Church was not to preach a supernatural redemption, but to enflesh the life of Christ, to realize his kingdom on earth, by improving the social conditions of the poor and dispossessed.[67] Allied to the emerging Independent Labour Party in Britain, the Social Gospel became, for a time, a powerful force,[68] but its concept of salvation was far removed from the traditional preoccupations of evangelicals. For some advocates of the social gospel, such as John Morgan Jones in Wales, talk of theories of the atonement were just stumbling blocks put between people and the gospel of Jesus Christ.[69]

For many evangelicals at the beginning of the twentieth century, it seemed as though every aspect of the faith was up for grabs. When the process of theological redefinition turned to the death of Christ, it looked like the very gospel was at stake. The backlash from conservative evangelicals was loud and sustained; in denominations in Britain and America, the newly dubbed Fundamentalists sought to fight back against the inexorable tide of liberal and modernist ideas. In their manifesto, *The Fundamentals* (1910–1915), a series of twelve booklets covering the essentials of the Christian faith, bankrolled by Lyman Stewart, a Californian oilman, and sent to every English-speaking Protestant minister around the world, the indispensability of the penal substitutionary view of the atonement was asserted in no uncertain terms. Franklin Johnson's essay affirmed that the 'Christian world as a whole believes in a substitutionary atonement'.[70] The moral influence theory, so much in vogue, he dismissed as the preferred choice of those who denied the inspiration and inerrancy of Scripture. Both went hand in hand.

While British fundamentalists were never quite as belligerent as their American counterparts, there were a number of flashpoints in which the doctrine of the atonement played a significant part. Within the Church of England, controversy between conservative and more liberal evangelical voices focused around liberalizing tendencies within the Church Missionary Society;[71] in a book of essays summarizing the conservative evangelical position, C. H. Titterton accused

---

63 R. J. Campbell, *The New Theology* (New York: Macmillan, 1907), p. 111.
64 Campbell, *The New Theology*, pp. 113–4.
65 Campbell, *The New Theology*, p. 132.
66 Campbell, *The New Theology*, p. 162.
67 For Campbell and his 'New Theology', see Keith Robbins, 'The Spiritual Pilgrimage of Rev. R. J. Campbell', *Journal of Ecclesiastical History* vol. 30 (April 1979), 261–76.
68 For some American context on the social gospel, see Christopher H. Evans, *The Kingdom is Always but Coming: A Life of Walter Rauschenbusch* (Grand Rapids, MI: Eerdmans, 2004).
69 Robert Pope, *Seeking God's Kingdom: The Nonconformist Social Gospel in Wales, 1906–1939* (Cardiff: University of Wales Press, 1999), p. 71.
70 Franklin Johnson, 'The Atonement', in *The Fundamentals*, edited by Dixon and Torrey, VI: 50.
71 See Andrew Atherstone, 'Evangelicalism and Fundamentalism in the Inter-war Church of England', in *Evangelicalism and Fundamentalism in the United Kingdom in the Twentieth Century*, edited by David W. Bebbington and David Ceri Jones (Oxford: Oxford University Press, 2013), pp. 63–4.

those who had abandoned forensic language when explaining the atonement of 'toning down . . . Divine revelation, a toning down which emasculates the Atonement of its vital saving truths and makes the . . . New Covenant sealed by the Saviour's precious blood of none effect'.[72] Among conservative evangelical Baptists, there was consternation when the liberal T. R. Glover, a classical scholar at Cambridge, was nominated to the presidency of the Baptist Union in 1923. His dismissal of substitutionary atonement, which he argued in a 1931 publication is 'hardly to be found in the New Testament',[73] laid bare for all to see the gulf of views on the death of Christ which could be found in most of the British mainline denominations by this point. They represented a major challenge to evangelical identity.

However, by the 1930s the tide was beginning to change. The horrors of the Great War and the growing spectre of Nazism, brought home the reality of evil, something that some of the more liberalizing voices had underplayed. The renewed supernaturalism of many of the Neo-Orthodox theologians saw a focus once more on the objective realities of Christ's sacrificial death. Karl Barth came close to affirming substitutionary atonement, although he was more reluctant to stress some of its penal dimensions.[74] Equally influential was the work of the Swedish theologian Gustav Aulén; his *Christus Victor* (1930) identified three approaches to the atonement, one which, indebted to Anselm, stressed the substitutionary aspect of the atonement, another which focused on its role to effect moral change, and a third, favoured by Aulén himself, which charted a middle way, arguing that the atonement was a 'cosmic drama', in which Christ won 'a victory over the hostile powers' and 'brings to pass a new relation, a relation of reconciliation, between God and the world'.[75] Under attack for so long, there were suddenly persuasive and scholarly voices calling for a return to more traditional understandings of the sacrificial death of Christ.

They coincided with the renaissance of conservative evangelicalism in Britain and America, though the latter preferred the designation neo-evangelicalism. The first inklings of this upturn in Britain could be detected in the universities; at Cambridge the split between evangelicals and liberals within the Student Christian Movement in 1910 was specifically over the SCM's equivocation over penal substitutionary atonement.[76] The Inter-Varsity Fellowship which came into being in 1928 as an alternative to the SCM for more conservative evangelicals enshrined within its doctrinal basis a commitment to a penal substitutionary view of Christ's sacrificial death:

> Sinful human beings are redeemed from the guilt, penalty and power of sin only through the sacrificial death once and for all time of their representative and substitute, Jesus Christ, the only mediator between them and God.[77]

---

72 C. H. Titterton, 'The Atonement', in *Evangelicalism: By Members of the Fellowship of Evangelical Churchmen*, edited by J. Russell Howden (London: Thynne and Jarvis, 1925), p. 59.
73 T. R. Glover, *Fundamentals* (London: Baptist Union Publication Department, 1931), p. 12, quoted in David W. Bebbington, 'British Baptist Crucicentrism since the Late Eighteenth Century: Part 2', *Baptist Quarterly* vol. 44 (2012), 283.
74 Karl Barth, *Church Dogmatics, IV. 1: The Doctrine of Reconciliation*, edited by G. W. Bromiley and T. F. Torrance (London: T. & T. Clark, 2009), §59, pp. 204–77.
75 Aulén, *Christus Victor*, p. 21.
76 See, for example, the recollections of one of the evangelical dissentients: Norman P. Grubb, *Once Caught, No Escape: My Life Story* (Cambridge: Lutterworth Press, 1969), p. 56. See also, David Goodhew, 'The Rise of the Cambridge Inter-Collegiate Christian Union, 1910–1971', *Journal of Ecclesiastical History* vol. 54 (January 2003), 63–4.
77 http://www.uccf.org.uk/about/doctrinal-basis.htm (accessed 24 February 2018).

T. C. Hammond, an Irish Anglican, who wrote what can best be described as the doctrinal handbook for the IVF, *In Understanding be Men* (1936), urged evangelical students to 'fiercely contend' for views of the atonement which had the propitiatory work of Christ at their heart.[78] It was a clarion call. Attacks against the concept of propitiation continued. In his commentaries on Romans and on the letters of the apostle John, as well as through his role in the production of the New English Bible, the theologian C. H. Dodd argued that the concept of propitiation was totally foreign to the New Testament.[79]

By mid-century there were still more persuasive voices on the British evangelical scene exemplifying a new found confidence in the penal substitutionary view. The ministry of Martyn Lloyd-Jones was key in the resurgence of Calvinism within postwar evangelicalism. Lloyd-Jones had been helped in his understanding of the atonement by the slightly mixed-bag of R. W. Dale, P. T. Forsyth and James Denney,[80] three figures who were hardly of one mind in the interpretations they adopted. He played an important role in formulating the doctrinal basis of the International Fellowship of Evangelical Students in 1946, adopting the IVF statement on the atonement verbatim,[81] and his own ministry consistently maintained the central importance of penal substitution, although even he could sometimes hint that penal language did not do complete justice to the richness of the biblical testimony concerning Christ's sacrificial death.[82]

There were also other voices who took the opportunity to restate the centrality of penal substitution. A new and abridged edition of James Denney's *The Death of Christ* (1902) was issued under the auspices of Tyndale House,[83] a new research centre at Cambridge designed to encourage serious evangelical scholarly engagement with the New Testament. Denney's work was important because he had singled out penal substitution as the point 'which ultimately divides interpreters of Christianity into evangelical and non-evangelical'.[84] Leon Morris, an Australian Anglican theologian, published a series of comprehensive studies over a forty-year period, once again reiterating the centrality of the language of penal substitution.[85] In the postwar years, penal substitution had been brought to the foreground of evangelical identity. When the newly formed Evangelical Movement of Wales drew up its basis of faith in the late 1940s, Christ's 'substitutionary, atoning death on the cross' was given pride of place.[86]

The advent of charismatic renewal in the 1960s brought renewed challenge to evangelical understandings of the cross. While penal substitution was not ignored by charismatics, their

---

78 T. C. Hammond, *In Understanding be Men: A Handbook of Christian Doctrine* (London: Inter-Varsity Fellowship, 1936), p. 122.
79 See C. H. Dodd, *The Epistle of Paul to the Romans* (London: Hodder and Stoughton, 1932), pp. 54–5; *The Johannine Epistles* (London: Hodder and Stoughton, 1946), pp. 25–6.
80 David Ceri Jones, 'Lloyd-Jones and Wales', in *Engaging with Martyn Lloyd-Jones: The Life and Legacy of 'the Doctor'*, edited by Andrew Atherstone and David Ceri Jones (Nottingham: Apollos, 2011), pp. 65–6.
81 John Brencher, *Martyn Lloyd-Jones (1899–1981) and Twentieth-Century Evangelicalism* (Carlisle: Paternoster, 2002), p. 219.
82 In a series of sermons on 'Great Doctrines' between 1952 and 1955, Lloyd-Jones preached three times on the subject of the atonement. In two of the sermons he defended penal substitution, but in the third argued just as strongly for the 'Christus Victor' view, specifically naming Gustav Aulén's book of the same name. Martyn Lloyd-Jones, *Great Doctrines Series, vol. 1: God the Father, God the Son* (London: Hodder and Stoughton, 1996), Ch. 31.
83 James Denney, *The Death of Christ*, edited by R. V. Tasker (London: Tyndale Press, 1951).
84 James Denney, *The Atonement and the Modern Mind* (London: Hodder and Stoughton, 1903), p. 82.
85 The most important of his works are Leon Morris, *The Apostolic Preaching of the Cross* (London: Tyndale Press, 1955); *The Cross in the New Testament* (Exeter: Paternoster, 1965).
86 Noel Gibbard, *The First Forty Years: The History of the Evangelical Movement of Wales, 1948–98* (Bridgend: Bryntirion Press, 2002), p. 167.

emphasis was often on the achievements of Christ's death beyond individual salvation. Their early twentieth-century predecessors, the Pentecostals, had maintained that Christ's atoning work made provision not just for spiritual but also physical healing. The fourfold gospel, they said, consisted not just of personal salvation, but also Holy Spirit baptism, divine healing, and the imminent second coming of Christ. In the pages of *Confidence*, the first Pentecostal magazine in Britain, the Sunderland Anglican Alexander Boddy published an article by his wife, who exercised her own healing ministry, asserting;

> On Calvary we can rejoice to-day that the Redeemer fulfilled the Scriptures and bore away not only our sin, but our sickness.[87]

Pioneering Pentecostal leaders such as George Jeffreys, who with his brother Stephen, established the Elim denomination in 1916, were typical in including opportunities for healing at their evangelistic services, including at Jeffreys' mammoth Easter campaigns at the Royal Albert Hall in the mid-1930s.[88] Physical healing was often as important as spiritual; indeed the former was often seen as confirmation of the later.

Leading charismatics have continued to believe that Christ's atonement included healing from disease and sickness. The former Anglican clergyman and founder of Kingdom Faith Ministries, Colin Urquhart, was only unusual in the vividness of the imagery he deployed:

> When Jesus stood bearing the lashes from the Roman soldiers, all our physical pain and sicknesses were being heaped upon him . . . It is as if one lash for cancer, another for bone disease, another for heart disease, and so on. *Everything that causes physical pain was laid on Jesus as the nails were driven into His hands and feet.*[89]

The American John Wimber, leader of the so-called Third Wave of renewal in the 1980s, used the phrase 'power evangelism' to describe his view that Christians should expect to see supernatural signs and wonders to authenticate the message of the cross. 'Healing', Wimber said, is a 'gospel advancer'.[90] Often this stress on healing was combined with a more general stress on wholeness and prosperity, financial, spiritual and physical. The prevalence of larger than life personalities such as Benny Hinn and Reinhard Bonnke teaching a gospel of health and wealth characterizes much of the evangelical world, especially in the Global South.[91]

The sense that the evangelical focus on penal substitution had become blurred lay behind the English Anglican J. I. Packer's decision to pick penal substitution as his subject for his Tyndale Biblical Theology Lecture for 1973. This approach to the cross, he wrote, 'is a distinguishing mark of the worldwide evangelical fraternity'.[92] While he recognized that there were other legitimate perspectives on the atonement, he mounted a detailed case for the centrality of penal substitution, engaging closely with some of its main critics both historically and of more recent vintage. 'Can we', he urged in his conclusion, 'justify ourselves in holding a view of the

---

87 'Health and Healing in Jesus', *Confidence: A Pentecostal Paper for Great Britain* no. 2 (May 1908), 16.
88 Malcolm R. Hathaway, 'The Elim Pentecostal Church: Origins, Development and Distinctives', in *Pentecostal Perspectives*, edited by Keith Warrington (Carlisle: Paternoster, 1998), pp. 17–18.
89 Colin Urquhart, *Receive your Healing* (London: Hodder and Stoughton, 1986), p. 38
90 John Wimber and Kevin Springer *Power Healing* (London: Hodder and Stoughton, 1986), p. 60.
91 See Kate Bowler, *Blessed: A History of the American Prosperity Gospel* (New York: Oxford University Press, 2013).
92 James I. Packer, 'What did the Cross Achieve? The Logic of Penal Substitution', *Tyndale Bulletin* vol. 25 (1974), 3.

atonement into which penal substitution does not enter? Ought we not to reconsider whether penal substitution is not, after all, the heart of the matter?'[93] However, his voice was increasingly falling on deaf ears, particularly within his own Church of England. The final published statement issued by the second National Evangelical Anglican Congress in 1977 affirmed evangelical agreement about the importance of the death of Christ, but reflected the preference of many to 'lay greater stress on the relative significance of . . . other biblical pictures'.[94] Despite the efforts of others to shore up confidence in penal substitution – John Stott's *The Cross of Christ* (1986) was a particularly exhaustive treatment by one of the evangelical movement's most respected leaders – unanimity on the nature of Christ's sacrificial death was increasingly hard to find.

If anything the chorus of voices questioning penal substitution has grown louder in more recent times.[95] Furthermore, that criticism is no longer confined to just the speculations of theologians, but has some high profile advocates. One of these, the Baptist minister and minor television personality, Steve Chalke, outraged many in 2003 when he referred to the notion of penal substitution as 'a form of cosmic child abuse'.[96] Others, using slightly less pejorative language, have also levelled criticisms of the traditional evangelical approach to the atonement.[97] The Evangelical Alliance held a public debate in the immediate aftermath of the furore over Chalke's remarks; in a public statement they distanced themselves from his views, reaffirming the EA's commitment to penal substitution. They accepted that while the Bible does use other metaphors and pictures to speak of the cross, it never does so at the expense of penal substitutionary atonement.[98] The most vigorous response to Chalke came from the Reformed wing of the British evangelical movement; three authors from the conservative evangelical Anglican college, Oak Hill in London, expressed their deep concern that 'Christ will be robbed of his glory, that believers will be robbed of their assurance and that preachers will be robbed of their confidence in "the old, old story" of the life-transforming power of the cross of Christ' if belief in penal substitution were abandoned altogether.[99] A newly penned hymn by Stuart Townend, 'In Christ Alone', prominently and explicitly affirmed penal substitution: in the second half of its first verse

> Till on that cross as Jesus died,
> The wrath of God was satisfied –
> For every sin on Him was laid;
> Here in the death of Christ I live.[100]

---

93 Packer, 'What did the Cross Achieve?', 45.
94 *The Nottingham Statement* (London: Falcon Press, 1977), p. 13.
95 See, for example, Colin E. Gunton, *The Actuality of Atonement: A Study of Metaphor, Rationality and the Christian Tradition* (Edinburgh: T. & T. Clark, 1988), and some of the contributors to *Atonement Today*, edited by John Goldingay (London: SPCK, 1995).
96 Steve Chalke and Alan Mann, *The Lost Message of Jesus* (Grand Rapids, MI: Zondervan, 2003), p. 182.
97 See, for example, Brian D. McLaren, *The Story we Find Ourselves In: Further Adventures of a New Kind of Christian* (San Francisco: Jossey-Bass, 2003), pp. 100–8; Tom Wright, *The Day the Revolution Began: Rethinking the Meaning of Jesus' Crucifixion* (London: SPCK, 2016).
98 Evangelical Alliance Board Statement on the Atonement, http://www.eauk.org/church/resources/theological-articles/upload/Board-Statement-on-penal-substitutionary-atonement.pdf (accessed 23 February 2018). Papers from this symposium were published as *The Atonement Debate: Papers from the London Symposium on the Theology of Atonement*, edited by Derek Tidball, David Hilborn and Justin Thacker (Grand Rapids, MI: Zondervan, 2008).
99 Steve Jeffrey, Michael Ovey and Andrew Sach, *Pierced for Our Transgressions: Rediscovering the Glory of Penal Substitution* (Wheaton, IL: Crossway Books, 2007), p. 21.
100 *Christian Hymns* (Bridgend: Evangelical Movement of Wales, 2004), no. 647.

It has taken on an almost anthemic quality among some on the more conservative wings of the contemporary evangelical movement, although it is also appreciated in other not exclusively evangelical contexts, such as at the enthronement of the Archbishop of Canterbury in 2013. However, it has been common practice to change these lines (without Townend's permission) to: 'Till on the cross as Jesus died, the love of God was magnified'.[101] For many in the present day, the heart of the evangelical understanding of the gospel is at stake once more.

That the cross of Jesus Christ has been at the heart of evangelical self-understanding since the eighteenth century is plain. In one of his final books in 1999, John Stott, by this time the elder statesman of British, if not worldwide evangelicalism, issued an 'appeal to the rising generation' urging a renewed focus on those things which evangelicals around the world held in common, what he called 'essential evangelical truth'.[102] He roused evangelicals to 'protect' the doctrine of penal substitutionary atonement 'from misunderstanding and hedge it about with every possible safeguard'.[103] As this chapter has shown, evangelical understandings of the sacrificial death of Christ have been liable to change and development over time. While a commitment to penal substitution was largely taken for granted in the eighteenth century, it was rarely held on its own. Through the later eighteenth and nineteenth centuries there were efforts to adapt penal substitution, particularly with the development of governmental approaches to the atonement, but these gave way in the later nineteenth century to much more radical attempts at redefinition. During the twentieth century, the atonement has remained a contested doctrine, and more recent attempts to discredit it from within the evangelical movement itself have led some evangelicals to argue that penal substitution is effectively the only approach that does full justice to the significance of Christ's death and passion. If the cross of Christ has been at the heart of evangelical identity, evangelical understanding of it has often been less than unanimous.

---

101 'Keith Getty on What Makes "In Christ Alone" Accepted and Contested' (2013), at https://www.thegospelcoalition.org/article/keith-getty-on-what-makes-in-christ-alone-beloved-and-contested (accessed 24 February 2018).
102 John Stott, *Evangelical Truth: A Personal Plea for Unity* (Leicester: Inter-Varsity Press, 1999), p. 10.
103 Stott, *Evangelical Truth*, p. 91.

4

EVANGELICAL SPIRITUALITY

Peter J. Morden

The Anglican clergyman William Haslam was famously converted by his own sermon. He had been ordained nearly ten years when, one Sunday in 1851, he stood up to deliver a homily in his Cornish church, taking as his text Matthew 22: 42 and the question Jesus asked the Pharisees: 'What think ye of Christ?' A man of High Church principles, Haslam's approach to Christianity had been challenged by the revivalist fervour of Cornish Methodists and a personal meeting with a local evangelical clergyman who told him bluntly, 'you are not converted'.[1] Haslam was greatly shaken, and in the midst of his sermon he realized that he was 'no better' than the Pharisees: they did not believe in Jesus as God's Son and Saviour and neither did he. In his best-selling autobiography, *From Death into Life*, he recalled:

> I felt a wonderful light and joy coming into my soul . . . Whether it was something in my words, or my manner, or my look, I know not; but all of a sudden a local preacher, who happened to be in the congregation, stood up, and putting up his arms, shouted out in the Cornish manner, 'The parson is converted! The parson is converted! Hallelujah!' and in another moment his voice was lost in the shouts and praises of three or four hundred of the congregation. Instead of rebuking this extraordinary 'brawling', as I should have done in a former time, I joined in the outburst of praise.[2]

From that time on, Haslam 'began to preach the gospel' with fervour, stressing his own personal experience of the Bible's message of salvation through faith in Jesus Christ. Indeed, he was 'not ashamed to declare everywhere' what God had done for his soul. Formerly he had struggled to prepare and deliver sermons, but now he happily preached three times a Sunday and led many weekday revival services as well. Writing in 1880, he reckoned he had preached on average over six hundred times a year in the twenty-nine years following his dramatic conversion experience, which transformed his life and ministry.[3]

This famous narrative of the 'parson converted by his own sermon' illustrates some of the

---

1 William Haslam, *From Death into Life: or, Twenty Years of My Ministry* (London: Morgan and Scott, 1880), p. 55.
2 Haslam, *Death into Life*, pp. 60–1.
3 Haslam, *Death into Life*, p. 64.

primary features of evangelical spirituality – understood in this chapter to mean both the interior life of the soul and the ways that life is expressed in public and private spheres.[4] The most obvious characteristic in Haslam's account is his emphasis on the necessity of personal conversion to Christ. His story also highlights the importance of biblical preaching, missional activity, and personal experience, which have likewise been typical of the evangelical movement. His autobiography captures some of the vibrancy that is a hallmark of evangelical spirituality at its best.

This chapter seeks to delineate evangelical spirituality as it has been expressed historically, with an emphasis on the eighteenth and nineteenth centuries which were the 'formative eras' of the movement.[5] Because of constraints of space, there is a special focus on English evangelicalism, although wider global developments are also given attention. Seven leading themes of evangelical spirituality are analysed. Of course, there has been much diversity of thought and practice within the movement, but through careful consideration of the different interlinked themes the lineaments of a distinctively evangelical spirituality come into focus. It is argued that there is a richness in evangelical spirituality which has often not been recognized, even by adherents of the movement. At the close of the chapter attention is also given to some more recent trends, as well as to future challenges.

A convertive piety

As already noted, the experience of conversion is foundational for evangelical spirituality. To be converted is, to use Haslam's stark phrase, to pass from 'death unto life'. In describing what happens at conversion, evangelicals have given attention both to God's work in 'saving the sinner' and also to the human response that is required to appropriate that saving work. The New England Congregationalist Jonathan Edwards insisted that conversion was first and foremost a 'great and glorious work' of God's power, 'at once changing the heart, and infusing life into the dead soul'.[6] This emphasis on regeneration – the new birth – is typical of evangelicalism. But Edwards also stressed the Reformation doctrine of 'justification by faith alone' and this was characteristic of the movement also.[7] As John Wesley wrote in his journal in 1738, after his heart had been 'strangely warmed' at a Moravian meeting at Aldersgate Street, London: 'I felt I did trust in Christ, Christ alone for salvation, and an assurance was given me that he had taken away *my* sins, even *mine*, and saved *me* from the law of sin and death'.[8] Divine action and human response are both in evidence. God is at work granting salvation, but 'trust' is necessary for God's gift to be received.

Evangelicals often described their conversion experiences in ways which were extremely vivid and colourful, with the moment of conversion coming suddenly, albeit often after a long

---

4 For a similar approach to the study of spirituality, see Linda Wilson, *Constrained by Zeal: Female Spirituality Among Nonconformists, 1825–1875* (Carlisle: Paternoster, 2000), p. 4.
5 Ian M. Randall, *What a Friend We Have in Jesus: The Evangelical Tradition* (London: Darton, Longman and Todd, 2005), p. 24.
6 Jonathan Edwards, 'A Faithful Narrative of the Surprising Work of God', in *The Works of Jonathan Edwards, vol. IV: The Great Awakening*, edited by Clarence C. Goen (New Haven, CT: Yale University Press, 1972), p. 177.
7 Edwards, 'A Faithful Narrative', p. 148.
8 *The Works of John Wesley, vol. 18: Journals and Diaries (1735–38)*, edited by W. Reginald Ward and Richard P. Heitzenrater (Nashville, TN: Abingdon Press, 1988), p. 250. Whether Wesley's experience equates to his conversion has been hotly debated; see Henry D. Rack, *Reasonable Enthusiast: John Wesley and the Rise of Methodism* (London: Epworth, 1989), pp. 145–57.

period of intense struggle.[9] Yet from the early days of the movement there was an acknowledgement that, as Edwards stated, some would not be able to fix on the 'precise time' they experienced salvation. Whether the 'converting light' dawned suddenly or gradually was a secondary consideration; the crucial fact was that the light truly shone, dispelling the darkness.[10] It was the reality of conversion, rather than the manner in which it came, that evangelicals generally insisted upon. As Charles Haddon Spurgeon wrote, 'It is not everyone who can remember the very day and hour of his deliverance'.[11]

True conversion led to a changed life. The eighteenth-century Baptist evangelical Samuel Pearce described the effects of his own conversion: 'The change produced in my views, feelings, and conduct, was so evident to myself, that I could no more doubt of its being from God, than of my existence. I had the witness in myself, and was filled with peace and joy unspeakable'.[12] Pearce's testimony is redolent of Wesley's in his emphasis on the inner 'witness' of felt experience. But especially noteworthy is Pearce's observations on the effect his conversion had on his 'views, feelings, and conduct'. His life was transformed. Conversion, according to Spurgeon, was the 'great change'.[13] Those who had truly exercised saving faith would show this by living transformed lives. Conversion was nothing less than the gateway to true spirituality for evangelicals: without it only a dry moralism was possible. Consequently, the line between the 'unconverted' and the 'converted' was sharply drawn. Unless the line was crossed there could be no authentic spirituality.

Assurance of salvation

Evangelicals were able to live transformed lives partly because a robust doctrine of assurance left them free to develop their relationship with Christ with confidence. Haslam, Wesley and Pearce all, according to their own testimonies, experienced assurance of salvation immediately following their conversions. This confidence was typical of evangelicalism and became a feature of evangelical hymnody, as seen, for example, in the lines of the American hymn-writer Fanny J. Crosby:

> Blessed Assurance, Jesus is mine!
> Oh, what a foretaste of glory divine!
> Heir of Salvation, purchase of God;
> Born of his Spirit, washed in his blood.
> *This is my story, this is my song,*
> *Praising my Saviour all the day long.*[14]

Crosby's lyrics remain popular among evangelicals the world over. They express the joyful assurance that is characteristic of much evangelical spirituality.

Spurgeon articulated the doctrine of assurance vigorously:

---

9 D. Bruce Hindmarsh, *The Evangelical Conversion Narrative: Spiritual Autobiography in Early Modern England* (Oxford: Oxford University Press, 2005).
10 Edwards, 'A Faithful Narrative', p. 177.
11 C. H. Spurgeon, *Autobiography: Compiled from his Diary, Letters, and Records by his Wife and his Private Secretary* (4 vols, London: Passmore and Alabaster, 1897–99), I: 108.
12 Andrew Fuller, *Memoirs of the Late Rev. Samuel Pearce* (Clipstone: J. W. Morris, 1800), p. 75.
13 Spurgeon, *Autobiography*, I: 97.
14 *Sacred Songs and Solos: Revised and Enlarged*, compiled by Ira D. Sankey (London: Morgan and Scott, n.d.), no. 873.

Has Jesus saved me? I dare not speak with any hesitation here; I know He has. His word is true, therefore I am saved. My evidence that I am saved does not lie in the fact that I preach, or that I do this or that. All my hope lies in this, that Jesus Christ came to save sinners. I am a sinner, I trust Him, then He came to save me, and I am saved; I live habitually in the enjoyment of this blessed fact, and it is long since I have doubted the truth of it, for I have His own word to sustain my faith.[15]

Spurgeon's confidence – indeed certainty – was grounded in the gospel and in the promises of God found in 'his word', the Bible. Some evangelicals were not so certain of their salvation. One exception was John Newton who continued to struggle with questions of assurance after his conversion.[16] Nevertheless, the confident faith of Spurgeon was more typical.[17] In this he was influenced by the Enlightenment, admittedly a complex and diverse cultural phenomenon (indeed, many scholars argue it is better to speak of multiple 'enlightenments').[18] Nevertheless, central to enlightened thinking, as David Bebbington states, was a belief in 'the ability of human reason to discover truth'. That which had been 'found by investigation' following a careful weighing of the evidence could 'be known with confidence'.[19] Spurgeon's focus on 'evidence' and his assured epistemology betray his debt to the Enlightenment, which also shaped the evangelical approach to assurance more generally.[20] Here is an example of how evangelical piety has been moulded by intellectual and cultural currents, although adherents of the movement usually insisted their practice was derived solely from Scripture.[21] Indeed, the ability to adapt to different cultural contexts is one of the notable features of evangelicalism and has marked its spirituality.

Biblicism

Biblicism is a third foundational tenet of evangelical spirituality. Here again contemporary cultural trends influenced evangelical attitudes, alongside a range of other factors including temperament, background and ecclesiology. At their best, evangelicals have recognized this. George Whitefield frequently spoke about the importance of the Bible. In a sermon on walking with God, he wrote: 'If we once get above our Bibles and cease making the written word of God our sole rule both as to faith and practice, we shall soon lie open to all manner of delusion and be in great danger of making shipwreck of faith and a good conscience'.[22] In another of his early

---

15 Spurgeon, *Autobiography*, I: 112.
16 D. Bruce Hindmarsh, *John Newton and the English Evangelical Tradition* (Oxford: Clarendon, 1996), pp. 63–6.
17 See David W. Bebbington, *Evangelicalism in Modern Britain: A History from the 1730s to the 1980s* (London: Unwin Hyman, 1989), pp. 6–7, 42–50; David W. Bebbington, 'Response', in *The Emergence of Evangelicalism: Exploring Historical Continuities*, edited by Michael A. G. Haykin and Kenneth J. Stewart (Leicester: Inter-Varsity Press, 2008), pp. 420–2.
18 Bruce K. Ward, *Redeeming the Enlightenment: Christianity and the Liberal Virtues* (Grand Rapids, MI: Eerdmans, 2010), pp. 2–3; John G. A. Pocock, 'Historiography and Enlightenment: A View of their History', *Modern Intellectual History* vol. 5 (April 2008), 83.
19 David W. Bebbington, *Holiness in Nineteenth-Century England* (Carlisle: Paternoster, 2000), pp. 33, 35.
20 Bebbington, *Evangelicalism*, pp. 42–55.
21 Spurgeon was also shaped by Romanticism. On this, see Peter J. Morden, *Communion with Christ and his People: The Spirituality of C. H. Spurgeon (1834–92)* (Oxford: Regent's Park College, 2010), pp. 113–4, 117–8, 160–1.
22 George Whitefield, 'Walking with God', in *Six Sermons on the Following Subjects* (London: W. Strahan, 1750), p. 88.

published sermons on the importance of 'family religion', Whitefield stressed that 'Reading the Word of GOD . . . is a Duty incumbent on every private Person', and that the head of every family 'ought to look upon himself as a Prophet, and therefore . . . as bound to instruct those under his Charge in the Knowledge of the Word of GOD'.[23] For evangelicals the Bible was to be the only rule of faith and practice.

However, the pioneering Baptist missionary statesman, Andrew Fuller, was acutely aware of how difficult a thoroughgoing biblicism was in practice. In a private covenant he made with God in 1780, near the beginning of his ministry, he reflected on how many evangelicals in his own day professed 'to be searching after truth [and] to have Xt [Christ] & the inspired writers on their side', and yet they still came to significantly different conclusions on important matters. Fuller was conscious of his own fallibility too, that he was 'as liable to err' as others had done. To put it another way, 'exegesis' could easily become 'eisegesis': reading into a Bible passage one's own presuppositions and preferences and having those preconceived ideas confirmed. Nevertheless, Fuller was determined to be as biblical as possible. At the heart of his covenant lies the following passage:

> O Let not the sleight of wicked men, who lie in wait to deceive, nor ev'n the pious character of good men (who yet may be under great mistakes), draw me aside . . . Nor do thou suffer my own *fancy* to misguide me. Lord, thou hast given me a determination, to take up no principle at second hand; but to search for everything at the pure fountainhead, *thy Word*.[24]

Fuller was aware of some of the major pitfalls of engagement with the text of Scripture; for example, professing to search after the 'truth' whilst in reality using the Bible to support opinions already arrived at by another route. Yet his avowed commitment to go back to the 'fountainhead' of the Bible was well-meaning and genuine.

Evangelical spirituality aspires to biblicism: the Bible is understood to be God's word and therefore authoritative for the believer. The aim is that it shapes those who engage with it. John C. Ryle, the Victorian tract-writer, urged:

> [R]ead the Bible in a spirit of obedience and self-application. Sit down to the study of it with a daily determination that *you* will live by its rules, rest on its statements, and act on its commands. Consider, as you travel through every chapter, 'How does this affect *my* position and course of conduct? What does this teach *me*?' It is poor work to read the Bible from mere curiosity, and for speculative purposes, in order to fill your head and store your mind with opinions, while you do not allow the book to influence your heart and life. The Bible is read best which is practised most.[25]

---

23 George Whitefield, *The Great Duty of Family Religion: A Sermon Preached at the Parish Church of Saint Vedast, Foster-lane* (London: W. Bowyer, 1738), pp. 8–9.
24 Covenant (10 January 1780), inserted in Andrew Fuller's Shorthand Sermons, with some Meditations in Longhand, Books I–V, Bristol Baptist College (G 95 A), Book III, pp. 22–3. For a more complete discussion of Fuller's biblicism, see Peter J. Morden, *The Life and Thought of Andrew Fuller (1754–1815)* (Milton Keynes: Paternoster, 2015), pp. 50–3, 66–7.
25 'Bible-Reading', in John C. Ryle, *Practical Religion: Being Plain Papers on the Daily Duties, Experience, Dangers, and Privileges of Professing Christians* (London: National Protestant Church Union, 1897), p. 132.

Bible reading was to make a practical difference to people's lives. It was not enough simply to read Scripture or to memorize it. 'Heart and life' were to be fashioned and refashioned through reading, reflection and appropriate action.

Evangelical engagement with Scripture included the daily, personal study recommended by Ryle, often twice a day, morning and evening, alongside corporate devotions within the household.[26] When Spurgeon told the students at his Pastors' College (founded in 1856) that 'morning and evening sacrifice' should 'sanctify' their homes he had family prayer in mind.[27] Bible study in small groups was also a staple of evangelical spirituality, ever since pioneered by the Wesleyans in the eighteenth century.[28] In addition, biblical preaching was a form of corporate engagement, with the message of the text expounded and applied to the lives of the congregation. Evangelical interpretation of Scripture is not as individualistic as has sometimes been supposed. The daily 'Quiet Time' has been regarded as almost the sum and substance of evangelical spirituality, but on the contrary the Bible has moulded evangelical devotional practice in a variety of ways, both personal and corporate.

Prayer

Bible study has often gone hand-in-hand with prayer. Sometimes the personal devotional practices of evangelicals could be veiled in a cloud of secrecy. George Whitefield revealed little about his personal spiritual habits in his published journal, whereas John Wesley meticulously recorded every moment of each day in his, reportedly thinking little of the Christian who did not spend at least four hours each day in private prayer – 'the grand means of drawing near to God'.[29] Although he was known personally to rise at four o'clock each morning for private devotions, in his 'Large Minutes' in the late 1740s he recommended a daily mix of private, family and public prayers, with private prayers taking place each morning and evening.[30]

Andrew Fuller, like many evangelical diarists, frequently commented on his devotional life, revealing a great emphasis on both private and family prayer.[31] Linda Wilson has shown in detail that the prayer lives of many nineteenth-century evangelical women were fervent and rich.[32] In addition, corporate prayer meetings have been significant. Jonathan Edwards' *An Humble Attempt to Promote Explicit Agreement and Visible Union of God's People in Extraordinary Prayer* (1748), urged the establishment of regular prayer meetings at which 'fervent and constant' prayer would be offered for the pouring out of the Holy Spirit and the rapid extension of God's kingdom around the world.[33] This treatise was still in circulation a generation later, on the other side of the Atlantic, where it left a deep impression upon Fuller and his fellow

---

26 Hence the titles of Spurgeon's best-selling devotional books, *Morning By Morning: Or, Daily Readings for the Family or the Closet* (London: Passmore and Alabaster, 1865) and *Evening By Evening: Or, Readings at Eventide for the Family or the Closet* (London: Passmore and Alabaster, 1868).
27 C. H. Spurgeon, *Lectures To My Students: A Selection from Addresses Delivered to the Students of the Pastors' College, Metropolitan Tabernacle* (3 vols, London: Passmore and Alabaster, 1875–94), I: 40–1.
28 See Randall, *What a Friend*, pp. 48–9.
29 Quoted in Randy Maddox, *Responsible Grace: John Wesley's Practical Theology* (Nashville, TN: Kingswood Books, 2004), p. 214.
30 Ted A. Campbell, 'Means of Grace and Forms of Piety', in *The Oxford Handbook of Methodist Studies*, edited by William J. Abraham and James E. Kirby (Oxford: Oxford University Press, 2009), pp. 282–3.
31 Diary and Spiritual Thoughts [1784–1801], Bristol Baptist College (G 95 b), e.g., 23 August 1784 (family prayer); 5 August 1784, 11 January 1785, 22 February 1785 (personal, private prayer).
32 Wilson, *Constrained by Zeal*, pp. 112–6.
33 *The Works of Jonathan Edwards*, edited by Edward Hickman (2 vols, Edinburgh: Banner of Truth Trust, 1974), II: 312.

evangelical pastors in the Northamptonshire Association of Calvinistic Baptist Churches. In 1784 they established monthly prayer meetings in their different congregations, along the lines set out by Edwards, with a special focus on prayer for the global spread of the gospel. In the late nineteenth century, the main prayer gathering at Spurgeon's Metropolitan Tabernacle took place on a Monday night, usually with over a thousand people present, a level of attendance which the pastor regarded as a sure sign of the health of the church. Concerning these occasions, he wrote:

> I think that many of these . . . meetings for prayer will never be forgotten by us who have been privileged to be present at them . . . I know that, very often, as I have gone home, I have felt that the spirit of prayer has been so manifestly poured out in our midst that we have been carried right up to the gates of Heaven.[34]

The Monday prayer meeting was for Spurgeon a 'means of grace' and, specifically, a means of communion with God.[35] Such times were essential to his own personal spirituality.

Both Fuller and Spurgeon advocated extempore prayer, with Spurgeon going so far as to reject all set prayers and liturgy. He believed that the practice of reading prayers encouraged empty, formal devotion, which militated against prayer from the 'heart'.[36] In contrast, evangelical Anglicans continued to use the Book of Common Prayer and several produced devotional aids for family worship which included written prayers.[37] Nevertheless, caution regarding repetitive forms regularly surfaced within the movement. Whitefield lamented that when 'the spirit of prayer began to be lost, then forms of prayer were invented'.[38] Wesley was also decidedly cool regarding the use of written prayers.[39] Likewise Ryle warned his readers:

> We may insensibly get into the habit of using the fittest possible words, and offering the most Scriptural petitions; and yet we may do it all by rote, without feeling it, and walk daily round an old beaten path, like a horse in a mill. . . . If the skeleton and outline of our prayers be by habit almost a form, let us strive that the clothing and filling up of our prayers be as far as possible of the Spirit. As to praying out of a book, it is a habit I cannot praise. If we can tell our doctors the state of our bodies without a book, we ought to be able to tell the state of our souls to God.[40]

Ryle's reasoning here was remarkably similar to Spurgeon's. Their common concern was a fear of dry 'religion', the antithesis of deep personal engagement. Once again, experience can be seen as vital to evangelical spirituality. Spurgeon expressed the ideal epigrammatically: 'Prayer with the heart is the heart of prayer'.[41]

---

34 C. H. Spurgeon, *Only a Prayer Meeting* (London: Passmore and Alabaster, 1901), p. 27; *The Sword and The Trowel: A Record of Combat With Sin and Labour For The Lord* (November 1883), p. 609.
35 Spurgeon, *Only a Prayer Meeting*, pp. 27, 31.
36 Spurgeon, *Morning by Morning*, p. vii; 'A Loving Entreaty', *Metropolitan Tabernacle Pulpit* (London: Passmore and Alabaster, 1861–1917), XXIX: 551 (sermon number 1743, delivered 7 October 1883).
37 John Wolffe, *The Expansion of Evangelicalism: The Age of Wilberforce, More, Chalmers and Finney* (Leicester: Inter-Varsity Press, 2006), pp. 148–9.
38 *George Whitefield's Journals* (London: Banner of Truth Trust, 1959), p. 483.
39 Randall, *What a Friend*, pp. 77, 79–80.
40 'Prayer', in Ryle, *Practical Religion*, pp. 87–8.
41 C. H. Spurgeon, 'Thought-Reading Extraordinary', *Metropolitan Tabernacle Pulpit*, XXX: 536 (sermon number 1802, delivered 5 October 1884).

The cross

The keynote of personal experience can also be heard in evangelical engagement with the cross of Christ. The eighteenth-century English Baptist poet, Anne Steele, declared in one of her hymns, 'Deep are the wounds which sin hath made', before posing the question, 'Where shall the sinner find a cure?' In answer she directed people to the cross:

> See, in the Saviour's dying blood,
> Life, health, and bliss, abundant flow;
> 'Tis only this dear, sacred flood
> Can ease thy pain and heal thy woe.[42]

It was 'only' the 'dying blood' of Christ which could 'heal' the sinner. Christ was the great physician and he did his work through the cross. Steele expressed these sentiments with real commitment and deep feeling. She wrote of Christ's death as if her life depended on it, as indeed she believed it did. The doctrine of penal substitution ran through her poetry. In one stanza she proclaimed: 'The spotless, bleeding, dying Lamb / Beneath avenging justice fell',[43] and in another:

> Was it for sin, for mortal guilt,
> The Saviour gave his vital blood?
> For sin the amazing anguish felt,
> The wrath of an offended God?[44]

Christ was righteous – the 'spotless' lamb of God – who experienced the full force of God's wrath against sin on the cross. 'Avenging justice' fell on him, and through this substitutionary sacrifice 'guilty souls' were rescued from hell. Such sentiments, popular among many hymn-writers, were sung in public worship throughout the English-speaking evangelical world. They shaped evangelical spirituality as firmly crucicentric, with emphasis on one particular understanding of the atonement.

The death of Christ on the cross was not only the means of salvation; it was also a spur to entire devotion to God. As the Congregational minister Isaac Watts wrote in one of the most enduring of all eighteenth-century hymns:

> When I survey the wondrous cross,
> On which the prince of glory died.
> My richest gain I count but loss,
> And pour contempt on all my pride.
>
> Were the whole realm of nature mine,
> That were an offering far too small.
> Love so amazing, so divine,
> Demands my soul, my life, my all.[45]

---

42 Anne Steele, 'Christ the Physician of Souls', in J. R. Broome, *A Bruised Reed: The Life and Times of Anne Steele* (Trowbridge: Gospel Standard Trust, 2007), Part 2, 'Hymns of Anne Steele', no. 28, p. 271.
43 'Redemption by Christ Alone', 'Hymns of Anne Steele', no. 71, p. 284.
44 'Sin the Cause of Christ's Death', 'Hymns of Anne Steele', no. 104, p. 294.
45 *Sacred Songs and Solos*, no. 115.

The cross was the place where one 'died to self', counting all things 'loss' for the sake of Christ. Famously for the Moravians, especially in the 1740s, meditation on the physical sufferings of the crucified Christ, were at the heart of their devotional experience.[46] Count Zinzendorf gave expression to this in his hymns:

> I thirst, Thou wounded Lamb of God,
> To wash me in Thy cleansing blood,
> To dwell within Thy wounds; then pain
> Is sweet, and life or death is gain.[47]

Not all evangelicals warmed to such intense – some would say gory – language, but the atonement called forth the most ardent expressions of evangelical devotion nonetheless. Charles Simeon's conversion in 1779 was stimulated by reading a treatise by Bishop Thomas Wilson on the Lord's Supper in which he learnt about Christ's sacrifice for sin, as he recalled in his autobiography: 'The thought rushed into my mind, What! May I transfer all my guilt to another?'[48] Years later, Simeon continued to assert:

> I have never for a moment lost my hope and confidence in my adorable Saviour; for though, alas! I have had deep and abundant cause for humiliation, I have never ceased to wash in that fountain that was opened for sin and uncleanness, or to cast myself upon the tender mercy of my reconciled God.[49]

On his death bed, Simeon expressed a desire to lie before God 'as a poor, wretched, hell-deserving sinner . . . but I would also look to Him as my all-forgiving God – and as my all-sufficient God – and as my all-atoning God'. He was determined to remain 'at the foot of the cross, looking unto Jesus'.[50] Frances Ridley Havergal likewise spoke of the 'Precious, precious blood of Jesus', and exclaimed: 'O *precious* blood! Lord, let it rest on me!'[51] Another of her poems begins:

> I know the crimson stain of sin,
> Defiling all without, within;
> But now rejoicingly I know
> That He has washed me white as snow.
> I praise Him for the cleansing tide,
> Because I know that Jesus died.[52]

This crucicentrism did not mean that evangelicals regarded the incarnation and resurrection as unimportant. Yet the cross, as Spurgeon expressed it, was 'the centre of our system'.[53] Similarly,

---

46 Craig D. Attwood, 'Understanding Zinzendorf's Blood and Wounds Theology', *Journal of Moravian History* vol. 1 (Fall 2006), 31–47.
47 *Christian Hymns* (Bridgend: Evangelical Movement of Wales, 1977), no. 597.
48 William Carus, *Memoirs of the Life of the Rev. Charles Simeon* (London: Hatchard, 1847), p. 9.
49 'Circumstances of my Inward Experience' (1819), in Carus, *Memoirs of Simeon*, p. 518.
50 Matthew Morris Preston, *Memoranda of the Rev. Charles Simeon* (London: Richard Watts, 1840), pp. 82–3, 93–4.
51 'The Precious Blood of Jesus' and 'The Opened Fountain', in Frances Ridley Havergal, *Loyal Responses; or, Daily Melodies for the King's Minstrels* (London: James Nisbet, 1878), pp. 32, 34–6.
52 'Knowing', in Havergal, *Loyal Responses*, p. 40.
53 Quoted in Derek Tidball, *The Message of the Cross* (Leicester: Inter-Varsity Press, 2001), p. 22.

Samuel Pearce believed the atonement was the 'leading truth of the New Testament'; indeed, the theme of his ministry 'from first to last' was Christ crucified.[54] Crucicentrism has been one of the distinguishing marks of classic evangelical spirituality.

Holiness

Evangelicals insisted that salvation is not by 'works' but by 'grace', yet they also pursued personal holiness, emphasizing that the gospel must make a difference to the way life is lived. There were some in Samuel Pearce's congregation in Birmingham who were, as Fuller expressed it, 'infected' with an 'antinomian spirit', believing that Christians were exempt from the moral law. By contrast, Pearce exhorted his hearers to press on in 'practical godliness'.[55] He himself was described as 'seraphic' because of this passion. Ryle declared in the preface to his widely-read *Holiness* (1877) that sanctification was as important as justification, and that: 'Sound Protestant and Evangelical doctrine is useless if it is not accompanied by a holy life'.[56] This broad commitment to holiness was shared by others across the evangelical spectrum.

There were further commonalities. For example, the vision of holiness advocated by evangelicals tended to be holiness 'in the world'. Spurgeon insisted that holy living did not mean 'avoiding men with monkish fanaticism'.[57] He rejected the 'otherworldliness' he believed characterized Roman Catholicism and Anglo-Catholicism. Writing on the Oxford Movement, Norman Vance contends its adherents tended to downplay 'everyday human society as the proper sphere of Christian activity'.[58] Such a tendency was anathema to Spurgeon, who attacked High Church spirituality on just this point as not Christlike. 'Nobody', he maintained, 'mixed more with sinners than did our Lord'.[59] Certainly, Christians were to live 'separate' lives, in the sense of being distinctive. Spurgeon told students at his Pastors' College that if any were found attending the theatre it would be their 'first and last time'.[60] Nevertheless, evangelical holiness was to be a holiness lived out in the press of everyday life.

Alongside these common features, there have been significant varieties in evangelical attitudes to holiness. David Bebbington identified three broad streams which each enjoyed considerable support among British evangelicals by the end of the nineteenth century. First, there was the Wesleyan tradition, which was mainly confined to Methodism and often identified with 'sinless perfectionism'. There were important distinctions between Wesley's own views and later Wesleyan holiness teaching – for example, Methodist teachers tended to downplay Wesley's emphasis upon gradual progress towards 'perfect love' and instead 'preach up' the possibility of receiving sanctification instantly. Nevertheless, as the tradition evolved, Wesley's name continued to be invoked.[61]

The second approach was propounded by evangelical Calvinists such as Spurgeon and Ryle, who rejected the possibility of sinless perfection in this life. A believer would, ideally, make

---

54 Fuller, *Pearce*, pp. 247, 269.
55 Fuller, *Pearce*, pp. 86–7.
56 John C. Ryle, *Holiness, and Other Kindred Subjects* (London: William Hunt, 1877), p. vi.
57 C. H. Spurgeon, 'Holiness, The Law of God's House', *Metropolitan Tabernacle Pulpit*, XXVII: 513 (sermon number 1618, delivered 11 September 1881).
58 Norman Vance, *The Sinews of the Spirit: The Ideal of Christian Manliness in Victorian Literature and Religious Thought* (Cambridge: Cambridge University Press, 1985), pp. 6, 31.
59 Spurgeon, 'Holiness, The Law of God's House', p. 513.
60 *Kentish Mercury*, 24 September 1886, in 'Loose-Leaf Scrap Folder, March – October 1886', p. 65, Spurgeon's College, Heritage Room (2G).
61 Bebbington, *Holiness*, pp. 65–72.

steady progress towards holiness, but the further they journeyed, the more God would reveal to them about their sinfulness. Growth in godliness was to be achieved not by 'receiving sanctification' passively, but through the believer's action. Ryle contended that 'true holiness' did not consist merely of 'believing and feeling' but of 'doing'. 'Active personal exertion' was required; indeed, he spoke of a 'holy violence, a conflict, a warfare, a fight, a soldier's life, a wrestling'.[62] Of course, this could only be achieved in the power of the Holy Spirit. Nevertheless, the Christian was called to pursue holiness through active effort and struggle.

A third approach was associated with the Keswick Convention in the Lake District from the 1870s. Although it shared certain characteristics with Wesleyan holiness teaching, according to Ian Randall it 'denied traditional Wesleyan convictions that Christians could experience entire sanctification'. Rather the Keswick tradition taught that 'sin was not eradicated but "perpetually counteracted"' through 'entry into "the rest of faith"'. A Christian could move on, not to sinless perfection, but to a 'higher' or 'deeper' Christian life through a crisis experience. Contrary to the Calvinist view, resting faith rather than active works was the path to holiness.[63] Keswick came to occupy a prominent place in the late-nineteenth-century English evangelical landscape, but it divided evangelical opinion.[64] Some, like Haslam and Havergal, were attracted to its brand of evangelical piety; but others like Spurgeon and Ryle were repulsed. Indeed, Ryle's *Holiness* was published as an antidote to Keswick.[65] In summary, although there were commonalities in evangelical attitudes to holiness, there was also significant diversity on how it was to be achieved, a disagreement which has continued to the present day.

Mission

Evangelical spirituality has often been expressed through energetic activism. For Ryle, the ideal was to spend 'and be spent' in God's service.[66] In one of Havergal's earliest and most emotive poems, Christ asks the reader: 'I gave My life for thee; What hast thou given Me? . . . I spent long years for thee; Hast thou spent *one* for Me?'[67] Her popular 'Consecration Hymn' dedicated the whole of life to God's service as a 'lively sacrifice', including her time, hands, feet, voice, lips, money, intellect, will, heart and love.[68]

Most often this activism has worked itself out in mission. Vigorous pursuit of conversions has been commonplace. As a young convert, Spurgeon engaged in a torrent of evangelistic work. According to his diary, in the week following his baptism as a believer, which took place on 3 May 1850, he taught in his church's afternoon Sunday school (which had an evangelistic focus), went visiting and distributing tracts with another church member, attended a teachers' prayer meeting, a teachers' business meeting and a missionary prayer meeting.[69] The following week one entry reads, 'Went to Sunday-school at 9, stayed till service at 10.30, out at 12.15;

---

62 Ryle, *Holiness*, pp. x, xvi.
63 Ian M. Randall, *Evangelical Experiences: A Study in the Spirituality of English Evangelicalism 1918–1939* (Carlisle: Paternoster, 1999), p. 14, citing *The Keswick Jubilee Souvenir* (London, 1921).
64 Charles Price and Ian M. Randall, *Transforming Keswick* (Carlisle: Paternoster, 2000), p. 60.
65 For Haslam, see *Dictionary of Evangelical Biography, 1730–1860*, edited by Donald M. Lewis (2 vols, Oxford: Blackwell, 1995), I: 529; for Spurgeon, see Morden, *Communion with Christ*, pp. 244, 250–3.
66 John C. Ryle, '"First Words": An Opening Address Delivered at the First Liverpool Diocesan Conference, 1881', edited by Martin Wellings, in *Evangelicalism in the Church of England, c.1790–c.1900*, edited by Mark Smith and Stephen Taylor (Woodbridge: Boydell, 2004), p. 326.
67 'I Did This For Thee! What Hast Thou Done for Me?', in Frances Ridley Havergal, *The Ministry of Song* (second edition, London: Christian Book Society, 1871), p. 93.
68 'Consecration Hymn', in Havergal, *Loyal Responses*, pp. 9–10.
69 Diary entries, 4 May, 5 May, 6 May and 8 May 1850, in Spurgeon, *Autobiography*, I: 135–36.

Sunday-school at 1.45, service 3 till 4, visiting till 5'. The diarist was not exaggerating when he remarked that his day had been 'closely occupied'.[70] Spurgeon found such activity exhilarating and it fed his spirituality. Following some time spent distributing tracts later that month, he was ecstatic; at the beginning of the work he had been 'all but dumb concerning spiritual things', but as he gave out his booklets and sought to commend Christ through personal conversation, he quickly felt 'the working of the Lord'.[71] Evangelistic activity could be a route to joy and increased communion with God. In the 1790s, Fuller helped to found the Baptist Missionary Society, and wrote:

> Within the last year or two, we have formed a Missionary Society . . . My heart has been greatly interested in this work. Surely I never felt more genuine love to God and to his cause in my life. I bless God that this work has been a means of reviving my soul. If nothing else comes of it, I and many others have obtained a spiritual advantage.[72]

Fuller's own spiritual life was stimulated by his investment in mission.

Evangelicals practised holistic mission which encompassed social engagement. For example, the Anglican Hannah More established Sunday schools across England, including at Cheddar and Nailsea in Somerset, where she received considerable help from Methodists. These schools taught poor children basic skills in reading, as well as the gospel, part of an array of social provision including adult evening classes and women's benefit clubs. In 1796, More reported to her friend William Wilberforce, who helped to finance her work, that much 'good' was being done by her various institutions.[73] Wilberforce himself provides perhaps the most prominent example of evangelical socio-political involvement, but he was one of many.[74] Often evangelicals blended social action with evangelism. When Hamburg was devastated by fire in 1842, Johann Gerhardt Oncken and his Baptist congregation offered their premises to the city's authorities for housing the homeless, and approximately eighty people were given shelter and food there for eight months. Many of those who had been helped started attending the services and responded to the call to conversion.[75] Engaging vigorously in mission was a hallmark of evangelical spirituality.

Recent developments

Although evangelical spirituality in the twentieth century maintained the seven emphases analysed above, arguably the most significant new development was the advent of Pentecostalism. Its beginnings have traditionally been traced to North America, especially the ministry of the black holiness preacher, William Seymour, at Azusa Street, Los Angeles.[76] Nevertheless, recent

---

70 Diary entry, 12 May 1850, in Spurgeon, *Autobiography*, I: 137.
71 Diary entry, 18 May 1850, in Spurgeon, *Autobiography*, I: 138.
72 John Ryland Jr, *The Life and Death of the Rev. Andrew Fuller* (second edition, London: Button and Son, 1818), p. 155.
73 Anne Stott, 'Hannah More and the Blagdon Controversy, 1799–1802', in *Evangelicalism in the Church of England,* edited by Smith and Taylor, p. 11.
74 For an overview of this theme, see Wolffe, *Expansion of Evangelicalism*, pp. 151–215.
75 Ian M. Randall, *Communities of Conviction: Baptist Beginnings in Europe* (Schwarzenfeld: Neufeld Verlag, 2009), pp. 55–6.
76 Estrelda Y. Alexander, *Black Fire: One Hundred Years of African American Pentecostalism* (Downers Grove, IL: InterVarsity Press, 2011); Gastón Espinosa, *William J. Seymour and the Origins of Global Pentecostalism: A Biography and Documentary History* (Durham, NC: Duke University Press, 2014); Marne L. Campbell,

accounts have convincingly argued for 'several largely independent originating centres', with India and Chile among the more important.[77] Features of Pentecostal spirituality included an emphasis on a post-conversion experience of the Holy Spirit (often described as 'baptism in the Spirit'), with an expectation of glossolalia and physical healing. From the 1960s charismatic renewal, encouraged by ecumenical Pentecostal pioneers like the South African David du Plessis, began to make its mark upon historic denominations in the West in ways Pentecostalism had not.[78] Early evangelical leaders of the renewal in a British context included Michael Harper and David Watson (Anglican), Tom Smail (Church of Scotland) and Douglas McBain (Baptist).[79] New church groupings were also established that were both charismatic and self-consciously evangelical.[80] Many Pentecostal emphases were carried over into the renewal movement, which Bebbington has argued was shaped by the 'expressive revolution' of 1960s counter-culture.[81] Once again, popular evangelical spirituality was being moulded by its cultural milieu.

In a British context, the increased incidence of 'reverse mission' from Global South to Global North is redrawing the map of Christianity, particularly in large urban centres such as Birmingham and London.[82] This presents both a challenge and an opportunity. Jonathan Oloyede, convenor of the Global Day of Prayer in London, called for a partnership between what he termed the 'indigenous' church in Britain and the 'international' church, a partnership for prayer and holistic mission, often bringing charismatics, Pentecostals and other evangelicals together. Such partnering, worked out in various ways on a local level, will probably be significant for the future of evangelical spirituality in Britain and might provide a model for other Western nations also. In many ways the Global Day of Prayer, an international movement originating in South Africa in 2001, represents a call to focus on some of the classic emphases that have been characteristic of the evangelical movement at its strongest.[83] Likewise 'Thy Kingdom Come', a global prayer initiative launched by the Archbishops of Canterbury and York in 2016, is expressive of an ecumenically-minded evangelical spirituality, bringing older and newer churches together across the denominations.[84]

Another significant development in the late twentieth century was a resurgence of interest in 'spirituality' among evangelicals,[85] stimulated by writers and poets such as James Houston,

---

Making Black Los Angeles: Class, Gender, and Community, 1850–1917 (Chapel Hill, NC: University of North Carolina Press, 2016), pp. 132–66.

77 Tim Grass, *Modern Church History* (London: SCM, 2008), p. 215. For recent scholarship, see Allan Anderson, *To the Ends of the Earth: Pentecostalism and the Transformation of World Christianity* (Oxford: Oxford University Press, 2013); Allan Anderson, *An Introduction to Pentecostalism: Global Charismatic Christianity* (second edition, Cambridge: Cambridge University Press, 2014).

78 Joshua Ziefle, *David du Plessis and the Assemblies of God: The Struggle for the Soul of a Movement* (Leiden: Brill, 2012).

79 For a helpful account by a participant observer, see Douglas McBain, *Fire Over the Waters: Renewal Among Baptists and Others From the 1960s to the 1990s* (London: Darton, Longman and Todd, 1997).

80 William K. Kay, *Apostolic Networks in Britain: New Ways of Being Church* (Milton Keynes: Paternoster, 2007).

81 Bebbington, *Evangelicalism*, pp. 238–9.

82 Rebecca Catto, 'Reverse Mission: From the Global South to Mainline Churches', Hugh Osgood, 'The Rise of Black Churches', and Colin Marsh, 'The Diversification of English Christianity: The Example of Birmingham', in *Church Growth in Britain: 1980 to the Present*, edited by David Goodhew (Farnham: Ashgate, 2012), pp. 91–125, 193–205; and *Turning the Tables on Mission: Stories of Christians From the Global South in the UK*, edited by Israel Olofinjana (Watford: Instant Apostle, 2013).

83 See www.gdoplondon.com (accessed 29 May 2017).

84 See www.thykingdomcome.global (accessed 29 May 2017).

85 Randall, *What a Friend*, pp. 20–1.

Eugene Peterson, Luci Shaw and Dallas Willard.[86] In 1988, Richard Foster, an American Quaker, founded Renovaré, an organization which helped to rekindle interest in spiritual formation among evangelicals on both sides of the Atlantic. Willard, a Southern Baptist, was one evangelical who was extremely influential within Renovaré. They became increasingly open to the spiritual resources of other Christian traditions, from Celtic to Catholic, and Foster's *Streams of Living Waters* (1999) encouraged this trend.[87] Monasticism, Ignatian prayer, pilgrimage, and eucharistic devotion, previously anathema to evangelicals, saw a surge in popularity.[88] Some evangelicals expressed dissatisfaction with their own tradition, believing it had little to offer beyond the daily 'Quiet Time' and relentless and unreflective activism. Derek Tidball sounded a note of caution, while at the same time attempting to chart a positive way forward:

> It is easy in today's world to come up with a hybrid spirituality which is no longer evangelical or to transform the evangelical tradition so much that what results ceases to be evangelical. The challenge then is so to breathe life into tradition that it does, as it can, answer the deepest inner searches of contemporary seekers and provide a clear but humble pathway through the supermarket variety of spiritualities on offer.[89]

A number of writers have taken up the challenge of encouraging evangelicals to appreciate their own spiritual tradition better. From the 1950s, Calvinistic evangelicals like Martyn Lloyd-Jones, James I. Packer, and the Banner of Truth Trust publishing house, turned to the sixteenth and seventeenth-century puritans to resource contemporary evangelicalism.[90] In the twenty-first century the market for classics of Reformed spirituality remains buoyant, encouraged by the influence of contemporary Reformed writers such as John Piper.[91] Surveying a broader range of evangelicalism, Ian Randall provided a careful and incisive exposition of different dimensions of spirituality in *What a Friend We Have in Jesus* (2005), and an increasing number of historical studies of evangelical piety are now available.[92] Alister McGrath, in books such as *Beyond the*

---

86 See, for example, James M. Houston, *The Heart's Desire: Satisfying the Hunger of the Soul* (Vancouver: Regent College, 2001); Eugene H. Peterson, *Subversive Spirituality* (Vancouver: Regent College, 1997); Luci Shaw, *Water Lines: New and Selected Poems* (Grand Rapids, MI: Eerdmans, 2003); Dallas Willard, *Renovation of the Heart: Putting on the Character of Christ* (Leicester: Inter-Varsity Press, 2002).
87 Richard J. Foster, *Streams of Living Water: Celebrating the Great Traditions of Christian Faith* (London: Harper Collins, 1999).
88 See, for example, Dennis Okholm, *Monk Habits for Everyday People: Benedictine Spirituality for Protestants* (Grand Rapids, MI: Brazos Press, 2007); Hillary Kaell, *Walking Where Jesus Walked: American Christians and Holy Land Pilgrimage* (New York: New York University Press, 2014); Wes Markofski, *New Monasticism and the Transformation of American Evangelicalism* (New York: Oxford University Press, 2015); Tony Collins, *Taking my God for a Walk: A Publisher on Pilgrimage* (Oxford: Monarch, 2016).
89 Derek Tidball, *Who Are the Evangelicals? Tracing the Roots of the Modern Movements* (London: Marshall Pickering, 1994), p. 215.
90 James I. Packer, *Among God's Giants: Aspects of Puritan Christianity* (Eastbourne: Kingsway, 1991); Joel R. Beeke, *Puritan Reformed Spirituality* (Darlington: Evangelical Press, 2006); John J. Murray, *Catch the Vision: Roots of the Reformed Recovery* (Darlington: Evangelical Press, 2007); John Coffey, 'Lloyd-Jones and the Protestant Past', in *Engaging with Martyn Lloyd-Jones: The Life and Legacy of 'The Doctor'*, edited by Andrew Atherstone and David Ceri Jones (Nottingham: Apollos, 2011), pp. 293–325.
91 For Piper see, for example, John Piper, *Desiring God: Meditations of a Christian Hedonist* (third edition, Leicester: Inter-Varsity Press, 2004); Collin Hansen, *Young, Restless, Reformed: A Journalist's Journey with the New Calvinists* (Wheaton, IL: Crossway, 2008), Ch. 2.
92 See, for example, Ian M. Randall, *Spirituality and Social Change: The Contribution of F. B. Meyer (1847–1929)* (Carlisle: Paternoster, 2003); Daniel C. Goodwin, *Into Deep Waters: Evangelical Spirituality and Maritime Calvinistic Baptist Ministers, 1790–1855* (Montreal: McGill-Queen's University Press,

Quiet Time (1995) and *The Journey* (1999), drew extensively upon this legacy but also sought to 'breathe life' into the historical material by prompting readers to engage imaginatively with it and apply appropriate lessons to their own lives.[93] His aim was not just the recovery of the evangelical heritage; he wanted to encourage contemporary evangelicals and other Christians in the practice of their faith. Writing in 1994, McGrath described evangelicalism as 'the slumbering giant in the world of spirituality'.[94] Thus as the historic writings of evangelicalism are laid bare, resources are unearthed which inform Christian piety today.

The mining of historic evangelical spirituality has the added potential to renew the evangelical tradition, correcting imbalances that may have crept in. For example, an overstress within some branches of contemporary evangelicalism on joyful intimacy with God can prove pastorally unhelpful to those who are struggling in their faith through suffering or doubts. Even midlife crisis can lead to spiritual turmoil, as expressed by Nick Page, a member of the Renovaré network, in *The Dark Night of the Shed* (2015), a humorous echo of St John of the Cross's 'Dark Night of the Soul'.[95] Unsurprisingly, when told their experience of God is defective, some become disillusioned and look elsewhere for resources for their continuing spiritual journey, perhaps abandoning evangelicalism altogether. Yet there is a critique already at hand within the evangelical tradition itself which highlights the dangers of overemphasizing experience. It is found, for example, in the words of Samuel Walker of Truro, an eighteenth-century Anglican evangelical clergyman, who declared that many Methodists he had personally encountered wrongly 'thought believing to be feeling'. He continued: 'faith by them hath been placed in the affections instead of the heart; the consequence of which hath been doubting, when the stir of the affections hath been less'.[96] Walker encouraged Christians to focus on the objective reality of the gospel and the promises of God, because feelings are significant but secondary. In this and multiple other ways, historic evangelical spirituality has the potential to inject new 'life' into the tradition, thus contributing to the task identified by Tidball. There is much that remains to be rediscovered. The piety of evangelical women is just one under-researched area;[97] the impact of African spirituality on Western evangelicalism is another.[98] There are many unexplored pathways down which scholars can travel, drawing the varied contours of evangelical piety onto the larger map of Christian spirituality.

2010); Michael A. G. Haykin, *Joy Unspeakable and Full of Glory: The Piety of Samuel and Sarah Pearce* (Kitchener, Ontario: Joshua Press, 2012).

93 Alister E. McGrath, *Beyond the Quiet Time: Towards a Practical Evangelical Spirituality* (London: Triangle, 1995); Alister E. McGrath, *The Journey: A Pilgrim in the Lands of the Spirit* (London: Hodder and Stoughton, 1999).

94 Alister E. McGrath, *Evangelicalism and the Future of Christianity* (London: Hodder and Stoughton, 1994), p. 142.

95 Nick Page, *The Dark Night of the Shed: Men, the Midlife Crisis, Spirituality, and Sheds* (London: Hodder and Stoughton, 2015).

96 Edwin Sidney, *The Life and Ministry of the Rev. Samuel Walker* (second edition, London: Seeley and Burnside, 1838), p. 154.

97 Recent helpful studies include Cynthia Y. Aalders, *To Express the Ineffable: The Hymns and Spirituality of Anne Steele* (Milton Keynes: Paternoster, 2008); Linda Wilson, 'Sarah Terrett, Katherine Robinson and Edith Pearce: Three Nonconformist Women and Public Life in Bristol, 1870–1910', in *Grounded in Grace: Essays to Honour Ian M. Randall*, edited by Pieter J. Lalleman, Peter J. Morden, and Anthony R. Cross (London: Baptist Historical Society / Spurgeon's College, 2013), pp. 118–32; Wilson, *Constrained by Zeal*.

98 Ian M. Randall, 'The East African Revival and British Evangelical Spirituality, from the 1930s to the 1950s', in *Pathways and Patterns in History: Essays on Baptists, Evangelicals and the Modern World in Honour of David Bebbington*, edited by Anthony R. Cross, Peter J. Morden, and Ian M. Randall (London: Baptist Historical Society / Spurgeon's College, 2015), pp. 255–77.

Conclusion

Andrew Fuller once attended some Christian meetings which, he wrote in his diary in 1786, he found personally 'encouraging'. Nevertheless, as he reflected on the preaching he had heard (one of the messages having been given by himself), he confided that he 'wanted more spirituality'.[99] Fuller did not explain this comment, but it is suggestive of the archetypal evangelical quest for a deeper personal experience of God, worked out through spiritual disciplines such as engagement with God through the Bible and prayer, as well as other practices detailed in this chapter. If such a quest has been typical, then so too is the emphasis on mission that Fuller exemplified as an indefatigable enthusiast for the Baptist Missionary Society. Through such cross-cultural engagement, evangelical piety became a global piety. If the impact of evangelical spirituality has been considerable in the first three centuries of the movement, its continuing impact as the twenty-first century unfolds may prove to be greater still.

---

99 Diary entry, 6 June 1786, in Ryland, *Fuller*, p. 118.

5

EVANGELICALS, REVIVAL AND REVIVALISM

Michael J. McClymond

Writers use the terms 'revival' and/or 'revivalism' to denote a period of renewed religious experience, fervour or devotion. Michael Watts referred to the British evangelical revival of the eighteenth and early nineteenth centuries as 'an attempt to return, after the spiritual lethargy of the late seventeenth century, to the religious fervour of an earlier age'.[1] *Webster's Third New International Dictionary* defines the term 'revival' as 'a period of religious awakening: renewed interest in religion with 'meetings often characterized by emotional excitement'.[2] The concept and experience of Christian revival are not unique to English-speaking Protestantism. Foreign equivalents for the English term 'revival' include: *Erweckung* (German), *réveil* (French), *avivamiento* (Spanish), *fen xing* (Chinese), and *bu hung* (Korean). To call a religious gathering a 'revival' is to suggest that an intensification of experience has occurred. A gathered multitude does not as such constitute a 'revival'. What distinguishes a 'revival' is a deepening of religious feeling and expression. 'Revivals' are corporate, experiential events. In 'revival' there is often a spiritual contagion – an infectious influence transmitted by proximity – causing one person's spiritual experiences to spill over to others. The term 'renewal' is not as well defined as revival, and yet it suggests a return of zeal or vitality to a group of Christian believers who have declined in their devotion.

Since the early eighteenth century, reports of Christian revivals from differing geographic regions and cultural groups have shown common themes. Participants in revivals speak of their vivid sense of spiritual things, great joy and faith, deep sorrow over sin, passionate desire to evangelize others, and heightened feelings of love for God and fellow humanity. In times of revival, people often crowd into available buildings for religious services, filling them beyond capacity. Services may last from morning until midnight. News of a revival usually travels rapidly, and sometimes the reports of revival – in person, print or broadcast media – touch off new revivals in distant localities. During a revival, clergy and other Christian workers may receive many requests for their services. Sometimes people openly confess their sins in public settings. Another mark of revivals is generosity – individuals willing to give their time, money or resources to support the work of the revival. Revivals are typically controversial, drawing fierce

---

1 Michael R. Watts, *The Dissenters: From the Reformation to the French Revolution* (Oxford: Clarendon Press, 1978), p. 374.
2 *Webster's Third New International Dictionary* (Springfield, MA: Meriam-Webster, 1961).

opposition as well as loyal support. Often there are unusual bodily manifestations in revivals, such as falling down, rolling on the ground, involuntary muscle movements, laughing, shouting and spiritual dancing. Another common feature in revivals is the occurrence of so-called signs and wonders, such as the healing of the sick, prophecies, visions or dreams revealing secret knowledge, deliverance or exorcism from the power of Satan and the demonic, and speaking in tongues.

It would be a mistake to presume that Christian revivals are all about experience and so have nothing to do with religious doctrines or theological concepts. Philosophers of religion have generally rejected the notion of a 'pure religious experience' that is initially uninterpreted and then subsequently conceptualized. They argue that the notion of an uninterpreted experience is incoherent, and that experiences necessarily imply and involve concepts and conceptualization as well as sensations or perceptions.[3] The historical record bears this out: revivals have often provoked theological debates. Themes discussed in the wake of Christian revivals include the nature of sin, the meaning of faith and repentance, the place of prayer in triggering revival, the signs or marks of true conversion, the significance of bodily manifestations in revivals, spiritual discernment and the distinction between genuine and counterfeit spirituality, the activity and effects of Satan and the demonic, the dangers of religious fanaticism, the role of laypersons and especially the issue of lay preaching or exhorting, the role of women in the church, the limits of ministerial authority, the resolution of conflicts between ministers and laypeople, the possible grounds for ministers or laypersons to separate from congregations or denominations that oppose revivals, the need for new associations and collaborations among proponents of revival, and the call for social reform and social justice.

The present chapter is divided into six sections. The first portion touches briefly on the 'religious school' of theologically-based interpreters of Christian revivals, and then moves on to consider a range of social-scientific interpreters who approached this topic with methodologies drawn from the fields of psychology, political science, economics, anthropology and sociology. The second part considers a number of historians of Christian revival since the 1950s, including William McLoughlin, Jon Butler, W. Reginald Ward, Mark Shaw, Kenneth Jeffrey, and David Bebbington. The third, fourth and fifth sections of the chapter consider briefly a number of key themes in the study of revivals – the question of causation, bodily phenomena in revivals and the global diversity of revivals. The sixth and concluding portion of the chapter offers a sketch of a new paradigm for research that builds on David Bebbington's insights regarding local Christian revivals in Victorian-era, English-speaking Protestantism, yet extends this approach from the nineteenth into the twentieth century, to more fully account for Pentecostal-Charismatic revivals.[4] In the conclusion, I argue that Bebbington's three traditions of Christian revival from the early 1700s through the late 1800s need to be supplemented and complemented

---

3 Wayne Proudfoot, *Religious Experience* (Berkeley, CA: University of California Press, 1987), and *Mysticism and Religious Traditions*, edited by Steven T. Katz (New York: Oxford University Press, 1983).

4 Because of space limitations, this chapter will not treat a number of basic themes pertaining to revivals that the author has covered elsewhere. See Michael J. McClymond, 'Theology of Revivals', in *The Encyclopedia of Christianity, Si–Z, Volume 5*, edited by Erwin Fahlbusch et al. (Grand Rapids, MI: Eerdmans, 2008), pp. 341–9; Michael J. McClymond, 'Charismatic Gifts: Healing, Tongue-Speaking, Prophecy, and Exorcism', in *Wiley-Blackwell Companion to World Christianity*, edited by Lamin Sanneh and Michael J. McClymond (Oxford: Wiley-Blackwell, 2016). On the measurable social effects of revivals on individuals and on society, limited to the United States, see Michael J. McClymond, *Embodying the Spirit: New Perspectives on North American Revivalism* (Baltimore, MD: Johns Hopkins University Press, 2004), pp. 22–31.

by two additional models distinctive to Pentecostalism. Drawing from Mark Shaw's study of twentieth-century Christian revivals in Africa, Asia, and Latin America, this new paradigm for research seeks to balance local and global dimensions of revival, and to incorporate insights from Anthony Wallace's anthropological revitalization theory as a way of interpreting the cultural dynamics causing revival movements to assume a variety of local forms.

Social-scientific approaches

Prior to 1900, questions concerning theological doctrine and matters of religious practice shaped almost all of the literature that was published on Christian revival. Typically the underlying question was 'whether movement X was "of God" or "not of God"?' A given revival might be ascribed to God ('the power of the Holy Ghost'), to the flesh ('enthusiasm', 'fanaticism'), or to the devil ('a diabolical counterfeit of Christ'). Evangelical Christians wrote most of the pre-1900 literature, both supporting and criticizing particular revival movements. Literature written in this period by non-evangelical interpreters was far from being objective or fair-minded, since it was almost always polemical in orientation and directed to debunking revivals. During the eighteenth and nineteenth centuries, evangelical historians of revival generally adopted a providentialist model of history, according to which God's relationship with his people underwent periodic ups and downs. Like the children of Israel in the Old Testament, the church often stumbled for a season into sin and apostasy from God, while God in his mercy acted to restore the church to its faith and faithfulness through historical events that brought chastisement and through outpourings of the Holy Spirit engendering renewed life, vigour and conviction. John Gillies' *Historical Collections Relating to Remarkable Periods of the Success of the Gospel* (1754), an extensive compilation of revival narratives in the aftermath of the trans-Atlantic evangelical awakenings of the 1730s and 1740s, was based on just such a providentialist account of history.[5]

Similar assumptions underlay the multi-volume compilation of data on global Christian revivals published by J. Edwin Orr from the 1940s through the 1970s.[6] Kenneth Jeffrey speaks of a 'religious school' of authors on revival, including John Gillies, J. Edwin Orr and Iain Murray. The contemporary Calvinist Iain Murray affirmed that 'any explanation of the [1859] Revival other than that of an outpouring of the Spirit is considered inadequate'.[7] By relying exclusively on supernaturalist modes of explanation for revivals, this 'religious school' ruled

---

5 John Gillies, *Historical Collections Relating to Remarkable Periods of the Success of the Gospel* (Glasgow: Robert and Andrew Foulis, 1754).
6 J. Edwin Orr, *The Second Evangelical Awakening in Britain* (London: Marshall, Morgan and Scott, 1949); *The Second Evangelical Awakening in America* (London: Marshall, Morgan and Scott, 1952); *The Light of the Nations: Evangelical Renewal and Advance in the Nineteenth Century* (Grand Rapids, MI: Eerdmans, 1961); *The Flaming Tongue: The Impact of Twentieth Century Revivals* (Chicago, IL: Moody Press, 1973); *The Fervent Prayer: The Worldwide Impact of the Great Awakening of 1858* (Chicago: Moody Press, 1974); *The Eager Feet: Evangelical Awakenings, 1790–1830* (Chicago: Moody Press, 1975); *Evangelical Awakenings in Southern Asia* (Minneapolis, MN: Bethany Fellowship, 1975); *Evangelical Awakenings in Africa* (Minneapolis, MN: Bethany Fellowship, 1975); *Evangelical Awakenings in Eastern Asia* (Minneapolis, MN: Bethany Fellowship, 1975); *Evangelical Awakenings in Latin America* (Minneapolis, MN: Bethany Fellowship, 1978); *The Event of the Century: The 1857–1858 Awakening* (Wheaton, IL: International Awakening Press, 1989).
7 Kenneth S. Jeffrey, *When the Lord Walked the Land: The 1858–62 Revival in the North East of Scotland* (Carlisle: Paternoster, 2002), pp. 27–8. Iain Murray's work revives the nineteenth-century debates over the revivalist practices (especially as associated with Charles G. Finney) that many Calvinists saw as linked to Arminian theology and an exaggerated notion of human autonomy and self determination. Iain H. Murray, *Revival and Revivalism: The Making and Marring of American Evangelicalism, 1750–1858* (Edinburgh: Banner of Truth Trust, 1994).

out any need to investigate the historical, social and cultural factors at work in revivals. What resulted was a mistaken and misleading homogenization, whereby every revival was presumed in advance to be akin to every other revival. Whether happening in India or Indiana, in Scotland or in Swaziland, a revival was a revival. In contrast to this, David Bebbington's recent work on *Victorian Religious Revivals* (2013) has highlighted the irreducibly local and particular character of nineteenth-century revivals in English-speaking Protestant nations (Britain, the United States, Australia).[8] Since even English-speaking Protestant revivals in Bebbington's analysis were locally diverse, one might expect to find even greater diversity in far-flung global contexts, a conclusion that will be borne out in our discussion of revivals in the Pacific Islands, Africa, China, Korea, and Indonesia.

One of the first works clearly to break away from theological approaches to narrating or appraising Christian revivals was Frederick Davenport's *Primitive Traits in Religious Revivals: A Study in Mental and Social Evolution* (1905).[9] Davenport claimed to be offering the first truly 'scientific' account of revivals – where 'scientific' meant 'naturalistic'. Presuming a theory of social and cultural evolution, Davenport argued that revivals manifested the 'primitive' mindset of savages, women, the mentally unstable, and people of African descent. The argument rested on racist, misogynist and classist assumptions, and a presumption of the superior rationality of the Euro-American white male. Yet Davenport raised questions that later scholars felt compelled to address: why do revivals happen? What cause-and-effect relationships apply? Why do revivals so often spread – by a kind of contagion – from one person or community to another? What role do revival preachers play? How might one explain the bodily manifestations (e.g. falling, spasms, jerking, laughing, weeping, outcries, animal-like sounds) that are often reported in connection with revivals – and that participants describe as happening involuntarily in their bodies? What internal psychological or cultural-contextual factors favour or inhibit the emergence of religious revivals?

During the twentieth century, scholars used various academic disciplines to examine the phenomenon of religious revival. In the field of the psychology of religion, William James's *The Varieties of Religious Experience* (1902) is still considered a classic work.[10] To explain sudden religious conversion, James proposed a theory of 'unconscious incubation'. For James, what might seem like an instantaneous occurrence arrived at the end of a lengthy process. By analogy, one might think of a river frozen over in winter: the springtime thaw stretches over weeks, and then at last the ice cracks and water begins to flow. James's 'unconscious incubation' was implicitly naturalistic. No irruption or influx of divine influence was needed to explain religious conversion. The event of conversion was not so much a union of self with God, but a reintegration of the divided self.[11] By and large, psychologists of religion have followed James in remaining sceptical of supposedly sudden, interruptive, or disjunctive conversion experiences. They cite data to indicate that most people do not change over time in their core character traits. Lewis

---

8 David W. Bebbington, *Victorian Religious Revivals: Culture and Piety in Local and Global Contexts* (New York: Oxford University Press, 2013).
9 Frederick Morgan Davenport, *Primitive Traits in Religious Revivals: A Study in Mental and Social Evolution* (New York: Macmillan, 1905).
10 William James, *The Varieties of Religious Experience: A Study in Human Nature* (London: Longmans, Green, 1902).
11 To be sure, James referred to his own view as 'piecemeal supernaturalism', and insisted that his idea that religious experiences emerge through the human subconscious did not rule out the possibility of supernatural agency in the subconscious. Yet most academic psychologists who followed James embraced a more straightforward naturalism. Like James, Carl Gustav Jung interpreted 'salvation' as implying 'integration' of the self's disparate aspects.

Rambo, in *Understanding Religious Conversion* (1993), applied a negative-to-positive scale (e.g. −15, −10, −5, 0, +5, +10, +15) to signify the pre-conversion process leading up to conversion (negative numbers), the conversion experience (zero point), and the growth in religious belief and practice subsequent to conversion (positive numbers).[12] Rambo did not debunk the idea of conversion, but embedded it in a longer-term process.

Another psychological approach to Christian revivals appeared in Ann Taves' book, *Fits, Trances, and Visions* (1999).[13] Primarily focused on Anglo-American Protestantism, and on the involuntary experiences often associated with revivals (e.g. trances, speaking in tongues, visions), Taves structured her work as a dialogue between Christian supernaturalism, Enlightenment naturalism and a third or mediating tradition that interpreted religious experiences naturalistically and yet as valid. The subconscious, according to Taves, is a 'mediating term' between secular psychologists and religious believers, identifying 'the proximate, if not ultimate, explanation of the origins of religion'.[14] Taves notes that Christian advocates for revivals often explain them in exclusionary ways, by using supernaturalist interpretations for what happens in their own group ('a Holy Spirit outpouring'), and secularizing or diabolizing interpretations for similar phenomena in other groups ('the preacher manipulated the crowd', 'the false religionists with their demonic tongues'). Along these lines, Hank Hanegraaff attacked the 1990s Toronto Blessing as the 'counterfeit revival' of preachers who practiced hypnotism on their audiences.[15]

British scholars developed a political interpretation of Christian revivals. During the 1960s, E. P. Thompson's *The Making of the English Working Class* (1963) and E. J. Hobsbawn's *Labouring Men* (1964) claimed that radical religion and radical politics flourished together in the same places and at roughly the same times, and so sought to explain this seeming correlation.[16] Thompson built on the work of the French scholar, Élie Halévy, who, in writings published between 1905 and 1913, examined Britain in 1815 and asked why it had not undergone the sort of political revolution that occurred in France. On his view, Britain was favourable soil for revolution, and neither the British constitution nor the established church could explain the nation's political stability. Halévy found his answer in religious revivalism, stating that 'the despair of the working class was the raw material to which Methodist doctrine and discipline gave shape'. Methodism was an antidote to Jacobinism.[17] Based on Halévy, Thompson proposed an inverse relationship between religious and political radicalism. When lower-class movements of political protest become stalled, the energy of protest will be rechanneled into religious revival.

A review of E. P. Thompson's work by R. Currie and R. M. Hartwell pointed to his 'minimum of analysis' and his prejudicial commitment to Marxist theorizing. Currie and Hartwell could find 'no sign of a significant association between repression or failure of political activity and the expansion of Methodism'. David Hempton noted that Thompson's conclusions were based on selective data rather than the full range of evidence. In her study of the Primitive Methodists, Julia Werner saw 'no . . . clear picture' on the relation between political activity and

---

12 Lewis R. Rambo, *Understanding Religious Conversion* (New Haven, CT: Yale University Press, 1993).
13 Ann Taves, *Fits, Trances, and Visions: Experiencing Religion and Explaining Experience from Wesley to James* (Princeton, NJ: Princeton University Press, 1999).
14 Taves, *Fits, Trances, and Visions*, p. 280.
15 Hank Hanegraaff, *Counterfeit Revival* (Dallas, TX: Word, 1997).
16 E. P. Thompson, *The Making of the English Working Class* (Harmondsworth: Penguin, 1963); E. J. Hobsbawm, *Labouring Men: Studies in the History of Labour* (London, Weidenfeld and Nicolson, 1964), pp. 23–33.
17 Quoted in Elissa S. Itzkin, 'The Halévy Thesis – A Working Hypothesis? English Revivalism: Antidote for Revolution and Radicalism, 1789–1815', *Church History* vol. 44 (1974), 48.

religious revivals.[18] An obvious problem for Thompson's theory was that it seemed inapplicable to the early phases of evangelicalism. While the revivals that occurred between 1790 and 1810 might conceivably be explained in terms of a revolutionary situation, those of the 1730s and 1740s would be much harder to explain this way. Ned Landsman demonstrated that the 1742 Cambuslang Revival in Scotland occurred during a time of prosperity, as Glaswegian merchants found their industries beginning to flourish.[19] Thompson himself later conceded that 'revivalism is not a phenomenon which admits of a single hold-all explanation' and that 'different contexts may require different explanatory methods'.[20] Though critical of Thompson's theories, Kenneth Jeffrey argued that insecurity on financial, personal, social and theological levels plays a role in triggering Christian revivals. Economic threats, sudden and unexpected deaths and fears of warfare or disease have all correlated with the emergence of revivals.[21]

A different approach to revivals rests on the analogy of market or economic relations. In the so-called deprivation theory of religion, those who lack social status by the usual measures (i.e. birth, wealth, education, employment) compensate by ascribing to themselves an exalted religious identity. Based on the work of social scientist Charles Glock, Robert Mapes Anderson invoked the deprivation theory in *Vision of the Disinherited: The Making of American Pentecostalism* (1979).[22] Grant Wacker responded to Anderson in *Heaven Below* (2001) by demonstrating that early American Pentecostals, though not well-to-do, were mostly drawn not from the urban underclass but from the middle to lower-middle classes.[23] Michael Watts arrived at similar conclusions concerning early British Methodists, who generally had solid employment histories and middle-class backgrounds.[24] According to the deprivation theory, one would expect lower-class rather than the middle-class people to be most responsive to revivalism.

Since the 1990s, the 'supply side' theories of Rodney Stark and Roger Finke have largely supplanted earlier deprivation theories. In *Acts of Faith* (2000), Stark and Finke laid out their counterintuitive proposal that many people want their religion to be difficult rather than easy. Such persons will be drawn to religious movements with a black-and-white salvation message, vivid supernaturalism, unambiguous moral standards and sharp boundaries between members and non-members.[25] Nearly all revival movements in their earlier phases, eighteenth-century Methodism, nineteenth-century Holiness teaching, and twentieth-century Pentecostalism, exemplified these traits. Yet as they evolved over time, won social respectability and became more lax, they lost members. Stark and Finke argued that they did not lose members because of

18 R. Currie and R. M. Hartwell, 'The Making of the English Working Class?', *Economic History Review* vol. 18 (1965), 640; David Hempton, *The Religion of the People: Methodism and Popular Religion, c.1750–1900* (London: Routledge, 1996), p. 2; J. S. Werner, *The Primitive Methodist Connexion: Its Background and Early History* (Madison, WI: University of Wisconsin Press, 1984), p. 173.
19 Ned Landsman, 'Evangelicals and Their Hearers: Popular Interpretations of Revivalist Preaching in Eighteenth-Century Scotland', *Journal of British Studies* vol. 28 (1989), 124.
20 Thompson, *The Making of the English Working Class*, p. 919.
21 Jeffrey, *When the Lord Walked the Land*, pp. 33–6.
22 Robert Mapes Anderson, *Vision of the Disinherited: The Making of American Pentecostalism* (New York: Oxford University Press, 1979); Charles Glock, 'The Role of Deprivation in the Origin and Evolution of Religious Groups', in *Religion and Social Conflict*, edited by R. Lee and Martin Marty (Oxford: Oxford University Press, 1964), pp. 24–36.
23 Grant Wacker, *Heaven Below: Early Pentecostals and American Culture* (Cambridge, MA: Harvard University Press, 2001).
24 Michael Watts argued that early Methodist preachers, as a group, were not victims of social dislocation or disorganization: 'A high proportion seem to have enjoyed secure family life, steady work, and modest prosperity'. Watts, *The Dissenters*, p. 409.
25 Rodney Stark and Roger Finke, *Acts of Faith: Explaining the Human Side of Religion* (Berkeley, CA: University of California Press, 2000).

their strictness or otherworldliness, but because they were not strict or otherworldly enough. As Methodist numbers declined, newer Holiness and Pentecostal movements supplied the market for strict or austere religion.[26] Religious disestablishment, as first seen in the United States of America, created a religious marketplace in which individuals seeking intense religion could readily meet their needs. This, argued Stark, is why religious revivals had especially powerful and pervasive effects in the United States.

George Thomas found a close correlation between entrepreneurship and revivalist religion in the nineteenth-century United States, and suggested that revivalism can be seen as an adaptation of Christianity to fit the economic, social and cultural milieu of entrepreneurial capitalism. Self-determining individuals from the marketplace entered the house of worship on Sunday as self-determining individuals. 'The revivalist myth', said Thomas, 'was cognitively compelling because it corresponded to their everyday experience as shaped by the dominant cultural myth of individualism'.[27]

The anthropologist of religion I. M. Lewis, in *Ecstatic Religion* (1971), offered a cross-cultural perspective on spirit-possession and shamanism.[28] Lewis found that shamanistic religion not only allowed for spirit-beings to enter into the human body, but for particular human beings (i.e. the shaman) to venture into the spirit-world to obtain knowledge or power that could be applied to mundane issues. From Lewis's analysis, one might draw parallels between non-Christian shamanistic practices and those of twentieth-century Pentecostals, who, like the shamans, seek insight and information from the spiritual realm (by means of 'prophecy' or 'words of knowledge'). In *Fire From Heaven* (1995), Harvey Cox intimated that Korean Protestantism draws on pre-Christian Korean shamanism, a thesis disputed among Korean Christians.[29] Lewis found that in male dominated societies, spirit-possession often occurred among women. Spirit-possession cults among women thus 'play a significant part in the sex-war in traditional cultures and societies where women lack more obvious and direct means for forwarding their aims'.[30] Lewis's perspective might help to explain the prominence of female leadership in revivals and in the charismatic phenomena connected with them.

Sociological accounts of revivals have built on Max Weber's theory of the 'charismatic prophet', presented in *The Sociology of Religion* (1956 [1922]).[31] For Weber, religious 'prophets' claiming divine inspiration or 'charismatic authority' inaugurate religious change, yet come into inevitable conflict with 'priests' who seek to protect and maintain the existing institutional

---

26 Stark's theories find support in religious demographic data from the United States from 1800 to 1950. Michael McClymond, 'Diversity, Revival, Rivalry, and Reform: Protestant Christianity in the United States, 1800–1950', in *Cambridge History of Religions in America, volume 2: 1790–1945*, edited by Stephen J. Stein (Cambridge: Cambridge University Press, 2012), pp. 225–50.
27 George M. Thomas, *Revivalism and Cultural Change: Christianity, Nation Building, and the Market in the Nineteenth-Century United States* (Chicago, IL: University of Chicago Press, 1989), pp. 7, 83.
28 I. M. Lewis, *Ecstatic Religion: An Anthropological Study of Spirit Possession and Shamanism* (Harmondsworth: Penguin, 1971).
29 Harvey Cox, *Fire from Heaven: The Rise of Pentecostal Spirituality and the Reshaping of Religion in the Twenty-First Century* (Reading, MA: Addison-Wesley, 1995). On the possible link between Korean shamanism and Korean Protestantism and/or Pentecostalism, see Sung-Gun Kim, 'The Resurgence of Neo-Pentecostalism and Shamanism in Contemporary Korea', in *Global Pentecostalism: Encounters with Other Religious Traditions*, edited by David Westerlund (London: I. B. Tauris, 2009), pp. 137–56, and Sung-Deuk Oak, *The Making of Korean Christianity: Protestant Encounters with Korean Religions, 1876–1915* (Waco, TX: Baylor University Press, 2013).
30 Lewis, *Ecstatic Religion*, p. 31.
31 Max Weber, *The Sociology of Religion*, translated by Ephraim Fischoff (Boston, MA: Beacon Press, 1956).

forms of religion. In his *Revitalizations and Mazeways* (2003), Anthony Wallace further developed Weber's theory.[32] Wallace used the term 'revitalization movement' to cover indigenous religious movements referred to as 'nativistic movements', 'reform movements', 'cargo cults', or 'messianic movements'. Cultures function like organisms, argued Wallace, maintaining a state of homeostasis. Yet when a given culture moves out of alignment with perceived reality, people no longer see it as a protective force, and some individuals may seek deliberately to modify elements in the cultural system. The 'revitalization movement' occurs in stages: a steady state, a period of individual stress, a time of cultural distortion, a revitalization phase, and finally a new steady state. Wallace's theory is promising for research, since it allows one to interpret revivals in terms of historical, social and cultural factors in the context.

While Weber's sociology focused on the dynamics of religious change, Durkheim's sociology highlighted personal identity, social solidarity and experiences of 'collective effervescence'. John Corrigan and Sandra Sizer followed a less Weberian and more Durkheimian interpretation of revivals. The Revival of 1857–1858, Corrigan argued, provided American males an opportunity to show emotion – even through public weeping – and thus established the display of emotion as a badge of collective identity.[33] In her study of gospel hymnody, Sizer noted that people spoke of the relation with God or Jesus in terms of emotions 'articulated in a communal context'. Thus 'prayer, testimony, and exhortation were employed to create a community of intense feeling, in which individuals underwent similar experiences . . . and would thenceforth unite with others in matters of moral decision and social behavior'.[34]

Historical approaches

Among historians of the last century, William G. McLoughlin was an acknowledged leader in studying American revivals. His pioneering works included *Modern Revivalism: Charles Grandison Finney to Billy Graham* (1959), and *Revivals, Awakenings, and Reform: An Essay on Religion and Social Change in America, 1607–1977* (1978). McLoughlin defined revivalism as 'any series of spontaneous or organized meetings which produce religious conversions whether they occur in one church, a dozen churches, or in hundreds of churches under the leadership of a spectacular itinerant evangelist'.[35] In his later book he wrote: 'Revivalism is the Protestant ritual (at first spontaneous, but, since 1830, routinized) in which charismatic evangelists convey "the Word" of God to large masses of people, who, under this influence, experience what Protestants call conversion, salvation, regeneration, or spiritual rebirth'.[36] Common to both the earlier and later descriptions of revivals by McLoughlin was a stress on the dominating personality of the revivalist preacher, and on conversion as the revivalist's goal. Both assumptions might be questioned, when one considers that some revivals (for example, the revival of 1857–1858 in the United States) did not have a single, clearly denoted leader, and that many revivals from

---

32 Anthony F. C. Wallace, *Revitalization and Mazeways: Essays on Culture Change, volume 1*, edited by Robert S. Grumet (Lincoln, NE: University of Nebraska, 2003), pp. 9–29.
33 John Corrigan, *Business of the Heart: Religion and Emotion in the Nineteenth Century* (Berkeley, CA: University of California Press, 2002), p. 251.
34 Sandra S. Sizer, *Gospel Hymns and Social Religion: The Rhetoric of Nineteenth-Century Revivalism* (Philadelphia, PA: Temple University Press, 1978), p. 52.
35 William G. McLoughlin, *Modern Revivalism: Charles Grandison Finney to Billy Graham* (New York: Ronald Press, 1959), p. 7.
36 William G. McLoughlin, *Revivals, Awakenings, and Reform: An Essay on Religion and Social Change in America, 1607-1977* (Chicago, IL: University of Chicago Press, 1978), p. xiii.

the late nineteenth century onward focused on experiences other than conversion, for example, sanctification, Spirit-baptism, healing, or spiritual empowerment.[37]

An historical debate, initiated by historian Jon Butler, concerned the eighteenth-century American colonial revivals. Butler argued that revivals during the 1740s were isolated and sporadic, and that the idea of a single, trans-colonial event known as a 'Great Awakening' was an 'interpretive fiction' originating in the mid-1800s rather than the mid-1700s.[38] In certain respects, Butler's argument from the early 1980s anticipated the contemporary emphasis in David Bebbington and Kenneth Jeffrey to regard each local revival as possessing a local character, and so to resist large-scale generalizations that would homogenize or regularize revivals.

W. R. Ward's *The Protestant Evangelical Awakening* (1992) was a genuinely ground breaking historical study of Christian revivals.[39] Through a thorough, multi-lingual review of eighteenth-century literature, Ward traced Protestant awakenings in Britain back to persecuted German-speaking Protestants, in Silesia just after 1700, and in Salzburg (then within the Habsburg Empire) during the 1730s. In both cases Protestants were persecuted by Catholic authorities and driven from their homes and places of worship. In Ward's account, a 'Children's Revival' in Silesia took shape as younger people gathered out of doors for impromptu prayer, persuading their elders to join them, and not to let the loss of church buildings put an end to their corporate worship. While most scholars trace the origins of British evangelicalism to the Wesley brothers and to George Whitefield, Ward argued that three independent revivalistic movements – American, Moravian and Welsh – came into fruitful contact with one another and with Anglicanism through the Wesleys' labours at Oxford University. The 'Holy Club' was a point of convergence for spiritual currents originating elsewhere. Ward showed that it is simply not possible to narrate the story of the eighteenth-century evangelical awakening without referring to Continental Europe, the American colonies, and the British Isles.

Mark Shaw's, *Global Awakening: How Twentieth-Century Revivals Triggered a Christian Revolution* (2010) interpreted twentieth-century Christian revivals in a global, and comparative perspective.[40] Shaw saw revivals as 'charismatic people movements' that stir up eschatological vision and what Shaw called 'optimistic fatalism' – a confidence that no problem is too big for God to resolve. Revivals establish new forms of community as well as practical, activist expressions of faith. Revivals refashion social and ecclesial structures by transferring power from centre to periphery. People not previously given a voice, or a chance to lead, are suddenly thrust into the limelight. Women, people of colour, the young, and the less educated have all played central roles in Christian revivals of the past century. Shaw explained the internal process of revivals with reference to Anthony Wallace's theory of 'revitalization movements', which he simplified to a three-stage process of a problem stage, a paradigm stage and a power stage.

Kenneth Jeffrey's *When the Lord Walked the Land* (2002) and David Bebbington's *Victorian Religious Revivals* (2013) share a common interpretive paradigm. Jeffrey argued that the first and oldest tradition of evangelical revival was the seventeenth-century Scottish 'holy fair', or sacramental season, which had associated outbursts of spiritual awakening as early as the 1620s. The second revival tradition emerged in the eighteenth century, in British Methodism,

---

37 A critique of McLoughlin's view appears in McClymond, *Embodying the Spirit*, pp. 6–9.
38 Jon Butler, 'Enthusiasm Described and Decried: The Great Awakening as Interpretive Fiction', *Journal of American History* vol. 69 (1982), 305–25. Cited and critiqued in William McLoughlin, 'Timepieces and Butterflies', *Sociological Analysis* vol. 44 (1983), 107–8.
39 W. R. Ward, *The Protestant Evangelical Awakening* (Cambridge: Cambridge University Press, 1992).
40 Mark Shaw, *Global Awakening: How Twentieth-Century Revivals Triggered a Christian Revolution* (Downers Grove, IL: InterVarsity Press, 2010).

in which preachers gathered people in buildings or in the open air to hear gospel messages. In contrast to seventeenth-century teaching, Methodists presented conversion as occurring suddenly, and they generally welcomed exuberant and even noisy services of worship. In the growing cities of the nineteenth century, a third revival tradition developed that was orderly and business-like. A visiting evangelist, financially supported by wealthy businessmen, networked with local pastors, advertised throughout the city, and then led in a 'crusade' lasting several days, in which the evangelist called those deciding to follow Christ to come forward for an 'altar call' at the conclusion of the service. The American evangelist Charles G. Finney pioneered this approach, followed later by D. L. Moody, Billy Sunday, Aimee Semple McPherson, and Billy Graham.[41]

Bebbington referred to his work *Victorian Religious Revivals* (2013) as a 'celebration of the particular'.[42] Here he closely examined a number of local revivals, with reference to the twin themes of 'culture' and 'piety', yet without proposing any grand theory to explain how or why revivals occur. Bebbington spoke of nineteenth-century revivals as 'lay-led, excitable, Arminian, looking for instant conversions and experimenting with fresh methods'. Such revivals depended on 'planning' and were for a time 'an effective formula for church growth'.[43] Separate denominational patterns in revivals 'did not remain intact' and 'a process of synthesis' occurred as the nineteenth century wore on. By the early twentieth century, 'the style [of revivals] became cruder . . . as showmanship took over'.[44] 'Unplanned awakenings' still occurred, but by the late twentieth century they were 'more of a phenomenon of the lands traditionally regarded as mission fields'. In the recent decades, the 'older denominational traditions' of revival 'fell into decay', though 'Pentecostalism and charismatic renewal ensured that the ritual of revival did not die but rather was rejuvenated'.[45] While Bebbington offered a convincing account of Victorian revivals, he did not explain how revivals continued to evolve through the twentieth century and under the impact of Pentecostalism. From his account, one might mistakenly conclude that Christian revivals altered and adapted from the seventeenth until the nineteenth centuries yet not in the twentieth century.

Causal theories regarding revivals

Believers and scholars have interpreted revivals in divergent ways. Participants in revivals have often asserted that revivals are God's work and that no natural causes can explain them. Genuine revivals are due to a supernatural 'outpouring of the Holy Spirit', which, if due to any human factor at all, are a result of concerted prayer. On the other hand, some devout authors – including even Jonathan Edwards – have invoked natural causes alongside supernatural or divine factors as causes or reasons for revivals. In the aftermath of the revival of 1857–1858, Christian writers noted that the financial panic of 1857 helped to set the stage for the revival among New York City businessmen, and so they invoked natural alongside supernatural forms of explanation. Among scholars, there is no consensus as to why revivals occur. William McLoughlin provided a list of the supposed causal factors: natural or social catastrophes (floods, earthquakes, epidemics, wars, economic depressions), group psychology or the influence of charismatic personalities on multitudes of people; the decadence of ecclesiastical institutions and the consequent need to

---

41 Jeffrey, *When the Lord Walked the Land*, pp. xvii–xviii.
42 Bebbington, *Victorian Religious Revivals*, p. 52.
43 Bebbington, *Victorian Religious Revivals*, pp. 10–1.
44 Bebbington, *Victorian Religious Revivals*, p. 15.
45 Bebbington, *Victorian Religious Revivals*, pp. 16–8.

update or replace them; and a conflict between older modes of behaviour and belief and newer, emerging modes.

Today most scholars agree that the causes of revivals are complex and cannot be reduced to a single causal factor, and that poverty or economic distress alone are usually not the sole cause. If poverty were a major causal factor, then the 1930s would have been a golden age for religious revival – which it was not. Eras of religious revival do not seem to correlate with periods of social strain or turmoil. McLoughlin concluded that 'there can be no single cause for such wide-ranging transformations in thought and behaviour'.[46]

McLoughlin's approach to revivals, as noted, highlighted the personality and influence of the revivalist in causing revivals. A differing view is based on communications and networking. According to this view, revivals 'happen' when information and enthusiasm flow between otherwise isolated groups and they develop a sense of participation within a larger movement. The star preacher of the Great Awakening, George Whitefield, had a uncanny sense of how to connect evangelical believers who were scattered in different denominations, how to use the newspapers to gain publicity, and how even to employ the opposition against him in advancing his cause. Richard Lovelace stressed Whitefield's unifying influence among evangelicals, while Harry S. Stout identified Whitefield's theatricality and media skill as essential to his appeal.[47]

The theory of material or social deprivation, as noted above, holds that revivalist groups offer their members a superior religious status to compensate for their inferior social or economic status. While this theory might help to explain the spread of revivalist movements like Pentecostalism among America's – and later the world's – impoverished masses, it fails to explain why certain revivals (for example the charismatic renewal) have been influential among people of wealth and influence. The deprivation or compensation theory, argues Grant Wacker, does not account for the initiative, drive, and self-reliance of the leaders and laypersons participating in revivals. The theory portrays them as passive spectators to revival movements, and not as agents in their own individual and social transformation. Wacker, together with Alan Gilbert, Bernard Semmel, and John Corrigan, offered an interpretation of revivals that might be classified as functionalist. This perspective, indebted to the sociological perspective of Émile Durkheim, interprets revivalist religion in terms of its function in establishing personal identity and a sense of communal belonging. Wacker comments that early Pentecostalism was 'less an effort to escape adversity than a creative resource for dealing with it'.[48] Gilbert and Semmel viewed eighteenth-century British evangelicalism as a response to the 'anomie and social insecurity' that was caused by urban migration and separation from the life of traditional village communities. Early Methodism, they argued, offered a 'revolutionary message of liberty and equality' to masses of people alienated by the new industrial society.[49]

---

46 McLoughlin, *Revivals, Awakenings, and Reform*, p. 9.
47 Richard F. Lovelace, *Dynamics of Spiritual Life: An Evangelical Theology of Renewal* (Downers Grove, IL: InterVarsity Press, 1989), p. 39; Harry S. Stout, *The Divine Dramatist: George Whitefield and the Rise of Modern Evangelicalism* (Grand Rapids, MI: Eerdmans, 1991), pp. 60–1.
48 Wacker, *Heaven Below*, pp. 10, 200–1.
49 Michael J. Crawford, *Seasons of Grace: Colonial New England's Revival Tradition in its British Context* (New York: Oxford University Press, 1991), p. 8; citing Alan D. Gilbert, *Religion and Society in Industrial England: Church, Chapel, and Social Change, 1740–1914* (London: Longman, 1976), pp. 87–93, and Bernard Semmel, *The Methodist Revolution* (New York: Basic Books, 1973), pp. 5, 7–9, 198.

Bodily phenomena in revivals

Bodily actions such as falling, dancing and spasms, as well as vocalizations such as shouting, laughing and inarticulate groans and utterances played a part in many Christian revivals. The evangelical belief that salvation is gained through a crisis of conversion, and the quest for additional spiritual experiences such as Spirit-baptism, created an emotionally-charged environment where seekers might gain ecstatic release through bodily expressions.[50] Physical manifestations in revivals highlighted the role of lay interaction, emotional expression and the longing for the felt presence of God. For most eighteenth-century Christians, such phenomena were a likely sign of 'enthusiasm' – understood to be a product of delusion, madness or demonic inspiration. The New England minister, Charles Chauncy, articulated this view in his sermon 'Enthusiasm Described and Cautioned Against' (1742).[51] Interpreting enthusiasm as a spiritual disease, he commented on how it afflicted its victims' 'bodies, throwing them into convulsions and distortions, into quaking and tremblings'. Representing the rationalist strand in eighteenth-century Protestantism, Chauncy maintained that bodily manifestations in revival were a sign that passion had eclipsed reason. By contrast, Jonathan Edwards did not prioritize 'reason' over 'affections'. Because of the unity of soul and body, Edwards argued, those touched by spiritual truth might have bodily reactions as well.[52]

Yet Edwards's approach to bodily phenomena was too cautious for the Separate Baptists, Radical Congregationalists and Methodists who spread the revival fires into the American South. These groups engaged in exuberant worship with accompanying bodily phenomena. Christianity first made significant inroads among the enslaved black population in the United States during this phase of the Great Awakening. Most blacks were attracted to the ecstatic experiences offered in revivalism. Albert Raboteau showed that these elements of revivalism harkened back to traditional African religious practices of spirit-possession and ritual dance. As blacks converted to Christianity and participated in camp meetings, they entered a culturally sanctioned space where they continued in traditional patterns of religious ritual, although with new theological meanings attached.[53] The fusion of African performance traditions with revivalist Christianity created a more interactive approach to worship and placed a greater premium on bodily modes of knowledge and expression than had previously been seen in either British or American Methodism.

Bodily expressions were not unique to Methodists, especially during the Second Great Awakening in the United States (c.1795–c.1830). The famed Cane Ridge Kentucky revival of 1801 originated in a Scottish-style sacramental festival among American Presbyterians, though other Protestants participated as well. Cane Ridge featured perhaps the most widespread occurrence of diverse bodily phenomena in the history of American Revivalism. If eighteenth-

---

50 The discussion on bodily manifestations here draws extensively from Benjamin Wagner, 'Bodily Manifestations in Revivals', in *Encyclopedia of Religious Revivals in America*, edited by Michael J. McClymond (2 vols, Westport, CT: Greenwood Press, 2007), I: 55–8.
51 Charles Chauncy, 'Enthusiasm Described and Cautioned Against (1742)', in *The Great Awakening: Documents Illustrating the Crisis and Its Consequences*, edited by Alan Heimert and Perry Miller (Indianapolis, IN: Bobbs-Merrill Company, 1967).
52 Jonathan Edwards, '*The Distinguishing Marks of a Work of the Spirit of God* (1741)', in *The Works of Jonathan Edwards, volume 4*, edited by C. C. Goen (New Haven, CT: Yale University Press, 1972), pp. 215–88. Edwards's ideas regarding revival are discussed in Michael McClymond and Gerald McDermott, *The Theology of Jonathan Edwards* (New York: Oxford University Press, 2012), pp. 424–50.
53 Albert J. Raboteau, *Slave Religion: The 'Invisible Institution' in the Antebellum South* (New York: Oxford University Press, 1978).

century Puritans like Edwards expressed ambivalence about bodily expressions, such was not the case among promoters of the Cane Ridge revival. In his autobiography, Barton W. Stone offered a catalogue of the bodily exercises that occurred at Cane Ridge, which he took as unambiguous signs of God's work. The 'falling exercise' was the most common in the early stage of the revival. This trance-like condition would be punctuated by groaning, confession of sin, often ending in joy, sometimes accompanied by laughter, as the penitent experienced salvation. The 'jerks' were uncontrollable bodily tics that some have compared with epileptic seizures or Tourette's Syndrome. For Stone, involuntary jerking was a witness to God's power and a means whereby God brought people to humility prior to receiving salvation. Involuntary bodily phenomena of various sorts appeared also in connection with the great revival of 1859 in Northern Ireland.[54] In the mid-1990s, many of the same phenomena were reported in connection with the Toronto Blessing.[55]

The status given to the body in Pentecostalism can be understood in relation to two central practices, speaking in tongues and healing. Based on the New Testament book of Acts, Pentecostals believe that speaking in tongues is evidence of a post-conversion experience that they refer to as the baptism in (with/of) the Holy Spirit. Early accounts of tongues-speaking show that it was often a deeply embodied experience. Seekers of the experience typically had someone lay hands on them as they prayed. If the prayers were effective, the seeker would begin uttering unintelligible syllables, often accompanied by a sense of being physically overwhelmed. Many used the metaphor of electricity flowing through the body to describe the experience, while others used images of heat, fire or liquid waves.[56] The experience of Spirit-baptism convinced Pentecostals that they were physically filled with and affected by the Spirit.

Pentecostals had been prepared to view their body as a locus of the Spirit's activity through the late nineteenth-century divine healing movement. This movement taught that Christ's work on the cross secures physical healing for those who had faith. Physical healing taught the early Pentecostals that God wished to restore the whole person, and that message has become integral to the ministry of most Pentecostal revivalists. While focusing on speaking in tongues and healing, Pentecostals embraced the full range of involuntary exercises rejected by most mainline churches. With the emergence of the 1960s and 1970s Charismatic movement, Pentecostal practices such as speaking in tongues, divine healing and falling in the Spirit spread to mainline Protestant and Roman Catholic churches. During the 1990s, Pentecostals and

---

54 On physical phenomena in this and other revivals in Ulster, see James McCosh, *The Ulster Revival and Its Physiological Accidents* (Belfast: C. Aitchison, 1859); Henry G. Guinness, *The Revival in Ireland: Letters from Ministers and Medical Men in Ulster on the Revival of Religion in the North of Ireland* (Philadelphia, PA: S. & Alfred Martien, 1860); Arthur McNaughton, 'A Study of the Phenomena of Prostration Arising from Conviction of Sin' (unpublished PhD thesis, University of Edinburgh, 1937); Myrtle Hill, 'Ulster Awakened: the '59 Revival Reconsidered', *Journal of Ecclesiastical History* vol. 41 (1990), 443–62; Donald E. Meek, '"Falling Down as if Dead": Attitudes to Unusual Phenomena in the Skye Revival of 1841–1842', *Scottish Bulletin of Evangelical Theology* vol. 13 (1995), 116–28.

55 Literature on the Toronto Blessing is extensive, and is briefly surveyed in Michael J. McClymond, 'Discerning the Spirit: Conflicting Appeals to Jonathan Edwards in the 1990s Trans-Atlantic "Toronto Blessing" Revival', in *From Northampton to Azusa: Pentecostals and the Theology of Jonathan Edwards*, edited by Amos Young and Steven Studebaker (Bloomington, IN: Indiana University Press, forthcoming). Bodily phenomena in connection with the Toronto Blessing are discussed at length in Ronald A. N. Kydd, 'A Retrospectus / Prospectus on Physical Phenomena Centred on the "Toronto Blessing"', *Journal of Pentecostal Theology* vol. 12 (1998), 73–81; B. J. Oropeza, *A Time to Laugh: The Holy Laughter Phenomenon Examined* (Peabody, MA: Hendrickson Publishers, 1995); Nader Mikhaiel, *The Toronto Blessing and Slaying in the Spirit: The Telling Wonder* (Earlwood, NSW: N. Mikhaiel, 1996).

56 Wacker, *Heaven Below*.

charismatics flocked to Toronto Airport Christian Fellowship and to other revival centres to experience phenomena not unlike those of Cane Ridge and the early Pentecostal revivals.

Some theorists link these bodily behaviours to social marginality. In this interpretative framework, extraordinary bodily phenomena are an emotional catharsis arising from frustrations caused by social or material deprivation. Such somatic responses are thus reactionary and regressive. Yet some evidence opposes this interpretation. Paul Conkin showed that persons from all social levels were vulnerable to the bodily 'exercises' that occurred at Cane Ridge.[57] One might make the same point regarding the well-educated professionals who experienced bodily effects in the Toronto Blessing, or in its offshoot at London's Holy Trinity Brompton. Anthropologist Mary Douglas suggested that the bodily functions are a symbol of the social order. Conditions are favourable for bodily disinhibition wherever social control and order have become weak. Douglas's theory resonates with a common view that the 'excesses' of revivalism, including the bodily exercises, were products of the unsettled, backwoods nature of the American frontier. Given the impact of religious awakenings on urbanites and on the socially prominent, it is not clear that Douglas's theory is much better than the earlier deprivation theories.[58] To view somatic responses in revivals simply as reactionary or as regressive ignores their creative and expressive dimensions. Victor Turner argued that society exists in a dialectic between social order or structure and a period of disorder and liminality. Liminality occurs at the edge or boundary of normal social conditions and makes space for anti-structure and the emergence of new social arrangements. As a medium of social expression, the body plays a central role in the dialectic of structure and anti-structure.[59]

Early Pentecostal acceptance of women's spiritual authority – a socially radical position in a conservative Protestant context – was often based on women's demonstration of spiritual power (for example, healing) manifested in the liminal setting of a revival service. In charismatic or Spirit-oriented Christianity, the prominence of women leaders is noticeable. This would include the Kongolese prophetess, Beatriz Kimpa Vita (1684–1706), and the Kenyan leader, Gaudencia Aoko (1943–1988), a co-founder with Simeo Ondeto of the *Legio Maria* ('Legion of Mary') that broke from Roman Catholicism to become a separate church. The late nineteenth and earlier twentieth centuries brought a series of female Holiness, Pentecostal and Charismatic visionaries, healers and social reformers: Maria Woodworth-Etter (1844–1924), Pandita Ramabai of India (1858–1922), Carrie Judd Montgomery (1858–1946), Aimee Semple McPherson (1890–1944), Kathryn Kuhlman (1907–1976) and Heidi Baker of the United States and Mozambique (1959–).[60]

---

57 Paul K. Conkin, *Cane Ridge: America's Pentecost* (Madison, WI: University of Wisconsin Press, 1990).
58 Mary Douglas, *Natural Symbols: Explorations in Cosmology* (London: Routledge, 1996).
59 Victor Witter Turner, *The Ritual Process: Structure and Anti-Structure* (Chicago, IL: Aldine Publishing Company, 1969).
60 The lives of such female Charismatic preacher-healers were in some respects reminiscent of the great female mystics of the European Middle Ages, whose claim to attention rested largely on their reported visionary experiences – Hildegard of Bingen (1098–1179), Mechthild of Madgeburg (c.1207–c.1282), Julian of Norwich (c.1342– c.1416), and others. Bernard McGinn, '"To the Scandal of Men, Women are Prophesying": Female Seers of the High Middle Age', in *Fearful Hope: Approaching the New Millennium*, edited by Christopher Kleinhenz and Fannie LeMoine (Madison, WI: University of Wisconsin Press, 1999), pp. 59–85.

Global diversity

Throughout the 1970s and 1980s, the bulk of published literature on Christian revivals was devoted to the so-called Western world, Britain (England, Wales, Scotland, and Northern Ireland), the United States, Canada, Australia and, to a lesser extent, Germany, Switzerland and the countries of Scandinavia. In recent decades, a growing body of writing on African, Latin American, Caribbean, Asian, Oceanian, Middle Eastern and Southern or Eastern European revivals has emerged. Even a cursory examination of this recent literature shows the locally contextual ways that revivals originate and develop, and engage or challenge indigenous cultures in global contexts.[61]

In the nineteenth and early twentieth centuries, Christian revivals swept across the Pacific Islands, with the result that more than 90 per cent of the indigenous population became at least nominally Christian. The means by which many came to profess the faith has been called 'group conversion' or 'people movement'. Modern Western thinkers tend to see the individual person, or nuclear family, as the fundamental social unit. It is often forgotten that the Christianization of ancient Germanic and Slavic peoples often hinged on a ruler's conversion – like that of the Russian (or Kievan) Prince Vladimir, baptized in 988 CE. When a leader converted, so did his tribe or extended family. Moreover, a people's entry into the new faith involved competition between the old gods and the new God, the traditional priests and the new Christian emissaries. In Fiji, Tonga and Samoa the public destruction of fetish objects was a turning point. King Pomare II (d. 1821) of Tahiti broke a taboo when he devoured the sacred turtle. He also degraded the temple post by setting it as a pillar in his kitchen. Most people movements in the Pacific Islands were neither top-down decisions by a ruler nor choices made by isolated individuals. Rulers typically did not act alone but consulted the ruling elders and sometimes others as well.[62] The destruction of fetish objects was accomplished in a public ceremony in which the people played a role. The Pacific revivals thus challenge the notion that faith decisions must be solitary or that revivals take place through an aggregation of individual choices.

The Christian population of sub-Saharan Africa expanded tremendously during the last century, from less than 4 million in 1900 to more than 400 million by 2000. This expansion included thousands of African Indigenous Churches (AICs) that sprang up alongside Western-led missionary congregations or split off from them. African cultures generally presume that 'salvation' does not pertain merely to a spiritual dimension of human life but rather includes bodily health, family relations, social harmony, financial prosperity, and general human wellness. The failure of Western missionaries to appreciate and respond to this aspect of African cultures was a major reason for the emergence of the AICs. Another common feature of African cultures involves belief in the presence of malign, unholy forces associated with witchcraft or sorcery. A major function of African traditional religions, from time immemorial, has been to protect against evil spirits. If one begins with these two assumptions – that salvation means personal and

---

61 A multi-lingual bibliography of international Christian revivals appears as Michael J. McClymond and Michael Farley, 'A Select Bibliography on International Christian Revivals', in *Encyclopedia of Religious Revivals in America*, edited by McClymond, II: 527–602. A concise work comparing Christian revivals in various global contexts is Shaw, *Global Awakening*. For an overview of World Christianity, often touching on the theme of revival, see *Wiley-Blackwell Companion to World Christianity*, edited by Sanneh and McClymond.
62 Alan Richard Tippett, *People Movements in Southern Polynesia: Studies in the Dynamics of Church-Planting and Growth in Tahiti, New Zealand, Tonga, and Samoa* (Chicago, IL: Moody Press, 1971).

family wellness, and that evil forces stand against the experience of this wellness – then revival, healing and social restoration may be expected as the outcome when evil forces are removed.[63]

Revivals, in African contexts, are often concerned with the removal of evil spirits, curses and sorcery. Nigeria has prayer villages, where individuals or entire families undergo spiritual diagnosis to discern demons that are then neutralized through prayer. In the AICs of South Africa the healing process may involve spiritual preparation by the healer and the use of physical media. The healer must be pure before healing others, and the process often begins with prayer and fasting. The colours of clothing may be related to certain activities. White is for visions, while blue or red is for healing. Water or bathing is very important and is a part of the process of purification. Traditional medicines are compounded of ash, sugar, salt, seawater, and other ingredients; some are given to induce vomiting as a way to expel evil. Information on patients comes through dreams or visions, and candles are lit to clarify the visions. Praying occurs during dancing, and singing may be a way of invoking the Holy Spirit. Cords, flags and staves all function as symbols of protection.[64]

One major movement in Africa, known as the East African Revival, may be regarded as an extension of the British Holiness Movement associated with the Keswick Convention.[65] By the 1920s, some East Africans were only nominally Christian and had professed the faith for the sake of social advancement. Yet a 1929 meeting in Kampala, Uganda between a Cambridge-educated missionary doctor, Joe Church, stationed in Rwanda, and a young African, Simeoni Nsibambi, resulted in spiritual revitalization for both men. The resulting revival called Africans and missionaries alike to spiritual rededication. After the revival spread quietly in the early 1930s, ecstatic manifestations such as trances, weeping and shaking commenced in Rwanda in 1936, and within a year the movement spread to Burundi, Uganda and Kenya. By 1939, the revival reached Tanzania, southern Sudan and eastern Zaire (today the Democratic Republic of the Congo). Through the 1940s and 1950s, revival teams and conventions spread the message. Public confessions of sins, and public declarations of spiritual victory in Christ, were common features. Tension resulted when Africans, now calling themselves *balokole* ('saved ones'), suggested that the missionaries themselves needed to be revived. Within the Anglican Church, the danger of schism loomed large during 1941–1944 and yet no major division ensued. As a result, the various denominations of East African Christianity felt the influence of warm, evangelical Keswick piety from the 1940s through the 1970s and beyond. Brian Stanley called this an 'African initiative within a European tradition' – a culturally African movement that drew from British Holiness teaching.[66]

China experienced a revival in Manchuria during 1908 through the mediation of missionary Jonathan Goforth (1859–1936), who had been involved in the Korean Revival of 1907 and who wished to see it spread to China. Beginning in 1927, Shantung Province witnessed a revival that involved sudden conversions, powerful emotions and bodily manifestations. As in Korea, the Chinese revivals involved public confession of sins. Yet in early twentieth-century China, there was polarization between a conservative-revivalist and a liberal-ecumenical school of thought.[67] The conservatives promoted revival with a consistent biblical message of deliverance from sin

---

63 G. C. Oosthuizen, *The Healer-Prophet in Afro-Christian Churches* (Leiden: Brill, 1992).
64 Oosthuizen, *The Healer-Prophet*.
65 *The East African Revival: History and Legacies*, edited by Kevin Ward and Emma Wild-Wood (Farnham: Ashgate, 2011).
66 Brian Stanley, 'The East African Revival: European Initiative within a European Tradition', *Churchman* vol. 92 (1978), 6–22.
67 Chun Kwan Lee, 'The Theology of Revival in the Chinese Christian Church, 1900–1949: Its Emergence and Impact' (unpublished PhD thesis, Westminster Theological Seminary, 1988).

through Christ. They viewed revival as a work of the Holy Spirit. Despite the anti-Christian movements of the 1920s, revival regained momentum in China during the 1930s. Conservatives such as John Sung (1901–1944), Wang Ming-dao (1900–1991) and Watchman Nee (1903–1972) interpreted revival in terms of what C.K. Lee calls 'a theology of spiritual pursuit'. This involved a commitment not to social change but rather to a solitary pursuit of faith and holiness. By contrast, the liberal-ecumenical school promoted social involvement by participating in movements of social change and social reconstruction, both before and after 1949.

Since the Communist revolution, the unregistered house churches (with more than 100 million members as of 2013) have carried the fervour of revival into every region of China. During the anti Christian persecutions of 1966–1976, there were reports of signs and wonders among believers, including the healing of sickness and extraordinary escapes from prison and persecution in response to prayer. Beginning in the 1980s, Dennis Balcombe, a Bible smuggler and charismatic preacher, introduced tongues-speaking into the Chinese churches, and today it is estimated that about half of all the unregistered congregations could be classified as charismatic. Yet the 'Statement of Faith of Chinese House Churches' (1998) takes a middling position that tongues-speaking is neither required nor forbidden. Some revivalistic practices in the house churches are controversial, such as the noisy worship of the 'Shouters' and the tears of repentance during the gatherings of those known as 'Weepers'.[68]

Following the powerful 1907 revival in Korea, centred in the city of Pyongyang, Korean Christianity grew rapidly. In fact, the number of Korean Christians roughly doubled in every decade during the twentieth century, so that now about 35–40 per cent of the South Korean population is Christian. Pentecostalism entered Korea in 1928, and its remarkable growth in the later twentieth century is associated especially with the pastor Yonggi Cho (b. 1936) and his mother-in-law and prayer supporter, Ja-Sil Choe (1915–89).[69] In 2013 Cho's Yoido Full Gospel Central Church in Seoul had around 1 million active members and is at present the world's largest Christian congregation. Cho's personal theology has been influenced by the prosperity theology of such American teachers as Kenneth Hagin Sr., Kenneth Copeland and Oral Roberts. Cho's book *Triple Salvation* (1977) was based on the idea that God intends to give believers prosperity in their soul, healing in their body, and blessing in their varied life activities.[70]

In Indonesia, a Christian revival occurred following the failed Communist coup of 1965.[71] The revival in its origins was associated with the Indonesia Evangelists' Institute at Batu Malang, East Java, and it was especially strong in Timor from 1965 to 1969, with as many as 200,000 conversions reported. This revival had a strong lay orientation, and rather than centring on a professional evangelist, it involved groups of Christians coming together to witness, and

---

68 David Aikman, *Jesus in Beijing: How Christianity is Transforming China and Changing the Global Balance of Power* (Washington, DC: Regnery Publishing, 2003); Xi Lian, *Redeemed by Fire: The Rise of Popular Christianity in Modern China* (New Haven, CT: Yale University Press, 2010).
69 Ig-Jin Kim, *History and Theology of Korean Pentecostalism: Sunbogeum (Pure Gospel) Pentecostalism* (Zoetermeer: Boekencentrum, 2003).
70 Prosperity has been a major theme in global Pentecostalism since the 1960s. For an overview, see *Pentecostalism and Prosperity: The Socio-Economics of the Global Charismatic Movement*, edited by Katherine Attansai and Amos Young (New York: Palgrave Macmillan, 2012). Yet Pentecostals are not simply self-absorbed. Extensive field research in some twenty global locations by Donald Miller showed that Pentecostals today are increasingly involved in faith-based, social outreach. Donald Miller and Tetsunao Yamamori, *Global Pentecostalism: The New Face of Christian Social Engagement* (Berkeley, CA: University of California Press, 2007).
71 F. L. Cooley, 'The Revival in Timor', in *The Gospel and Frontier Peoples: A Report of a Consultation, December 1972*, edited by R. P. Beaver (South Pasadena, CA: William Carey Library, 1973), pp. 205–30.

experience, what was described as God's power. Teams of believers went out to the villages under the leadership of a person who claimed to have been led by the Holy Spirit. The Spirit revealed the names or faces of those who were to be included in the team as the leader's assistants. Teams ranged in size from three or four, up to twenty or so. They included young people and schoolteachers and were often led by simple, uneducated folk, in many cases women, though they also included church elders, deacons and pastors as members. Where they went and what they did was wholly dependent on what was taken to be the direct guidance of the Spirit, usually revealed through prayer. The teams spent hours each day in prayer for guidance and for power. Many healings of the sick and sudden conversions were reported. The 1960s revival in Indonesia thus centred on the equality of all believers under God and the need for moment-by-moment guidance from the Holy Spirit.

Conclusion: toward a new paradigm for interpreting revivals

As noted above, David Bebbington has proposed three historical paradigms for Christian revivals: seventeenth-century Scottish Presbyterian sacramental revivals (or 'holy fairs'), eighteenth-century early Methodist and evangelical revivals, and nineteenth-century modern mass evangelism.[72] While the first tradition seems to have become all-but-extinct in Christian practice today, the mass evangelistic methods of the last century remain a living force in the twenty-first century. Bebbington's work rightly recognizes the continuance of the third paradigm, and perhaps the second paradigm. At the same time, Bebbington's theory of revivals is in need of supplementation in light of newer paradigms for revival that emerged among Pentecostal-Charismatic Christians since 1900. In this conclusion, I identify two such paradigms that may be numbered in the sequence as twentieth-century 'healing evangelism' and twenty-first-century 'manifestational prayer'.

The first of the Pentecostal paradigms is 'healing evangelism', exemplified by William Branham, Oral Roberts, Kathryn Kuhlman, Francis and Judith MacNutt, Carlos Annacondia, Mahesh Chavda and countless other preacher-healers of the past and present, all around the world.[73] Already in the late nineteenth century, the divine healing movement announced its slogan of 'salvation for the soul, healing for the body'.[74] We can track the shifting paradigm for revivalism during the late nineteenth century by paying attention to the shifting meanings attached to the central revivalist ritual of the 'altar call' (known in Finney's day as the 'anxious bench').[75] When people came forward at a Maria Woodworth-Etter revival service during the 1890s, the 'altar call' was offered not only for forgiveness but also for healing. To be sure, Holiness preachers in Britain and America had already expanded the meaning of the revivalist's call to decision by setting forth a call to sanctification and/or consecration as well as a call

---

72 See Bebbington, *Victorian Religious Revivals*, Ch. 1.
73 A worldwide survey of Christian healing practices and healing evangelism appears in *Global Pentecostal and Charismatic Healing*, edited by Candy Gunther Brown (New York: Oxford University Press, 2011). The healing-evangelism paradigm proliferated during the 1940s and 1950s in the south-central portion of the United States (especially Oklahoma and Texas), as recounted in David Edwin Harrell Jr., *All Things are Possible: The Healing and Charismatic Revivals in Modern America* (Bloomington, IN: Indiana University Press, 1975).
74 Heather D. Curtis, *Faith in the Great Physician: Suffering and Divine Healing in American Culture, 1860–1900* (Baltimore, MD: Johns Hopkins University Press, 2007).
75 On the origins, development and significance of this ritual of coming forward, see Michael J. McClymond, 'Altar Call', in *Encyclopedia of Religious Revivals in America*, edited by McClymond, I: 15–7.

to conversion. With the rise of American Pentecostalism after 1901, and its teachings on Spirit-baptism, the 'altar call' became still more complex. People came forward for conversion, sanctification, freedom from addictions, healing of the body, Spirit-baptism, and so on. From the 1970s until the 1990s, Charismatic Christians added 'inner healing' and empowerment or the 'impartation' of spiritual gifts to the repertoire of what might be expected to happen when people were publicly prayed for in the front of the church.

In the 'ministry time' that occurs in churches today at the end of the service in a Vineyard Church, or after the liturgy is completed in a Spirit-oriented Protestant or Catholic parish, participants come forward and linger in the front of the sanctuary, praying and seeking from God whatever they might need. Outwardly observed, this is still an 'altar call' of the sort that one might long ago have observed in a Finney, Moody or Billy Graham revival service. Yet the 'healing evangelism' paradigm has decisively shifted the meaning of the ritual act of coming forward. Such 'ministry time' now occurs in evangelical churches that do not classify or name themselves as charismatic. One continuity with the earlier techniques of mass evangelism – Bebbington's nineteenth-century or third paradigm – is the presence of lay Christians to counsel fellow lay Christians at the front of the church.[76] Yet the laying on of hands in prayer, and the invocation for spiritual blessings to flow into the physical body of the seeker, are legacies of twentieth-century Pentecostalism rather than nineteenth-century evangelicalism.

In addition to healing evangelism, there is a yet newer paradigm that has been emerging in global Charismatic Christianity over the last twenty years. Because this view has not been characterized or discussed in academic literature, I will term it 'manifestational prayer' and characterize it as a fifth paradigm. It is associated with the 24/7 prayer movement and the 'houses of prayer' that have sprung up in the last two decades.[77] At the centre of this 'manifestational model' is an intense focus on God's presence, which is said to be 'drawn' or to be 'manifested' whenever God's people engage in faith-filled, heartfelt and prolonged prayer. The 'manifestational model' insists that God's presence as released through prayer is able to guide, direct, heal, save and reconcile – indeed, to meet every individual need of each individual seeker.

In this paradigm the preacher and preaching are de-emphasized. Moreover, a formalized 'altar call' is not needed, because the divine presence itself accomplishes everything – showing people where they need to repent, whether there is unforgiveness in their hearts, how they need to be healed and what direction to take in life decisions. On the surface, the 'manifestational model' seems to be wholly affective and non-cognitive. On examination, one finds though that participants are thinking through the implications and applications of their faith. They presuppose that it is the sovereign work of the Holy Spirit, rather than the initiative of the

---

76 The Association of Vineyard Churches in the USA, and its leader – John Wimber – through his British travels and ministry in the 1980s, played a decisive role in a 'democratization' of healing and worship practices, which were no longer focused on a visiting preacher-healer but on the believing community as whole, which Wimber viewed as the repository of healing power. See Michael J. McClymond, 'After Toronto: Randy Clark's Global Awakening, Heidi and Rolland Baker's Iris Ministries, and the Post-1990s Global Charismatic Networks', *Pneuma* vol. 38 (2016), 1–27. On the history of the Vineyard, see Bill Jackson, *The Quest for the Radical Middle: A History of the Vineyard* (Cape Town: Vineyard International Publishing, 1999).

77 A brief discussion of the house(s) of prayer movement appears in Michael J. McClymond, 'Charismatic Renewal and Neo-Pentecostalism: From American Origins to Global Permutations', in *The Cambridge Companion to Pentecostalism*, edited by Cecil Robeck and Amos Young (Cambridge: Cambridge University Press, 2014). The International House of Prayer (Kansas City, Missouri) commenced uninterrupted 24/7 prayer in 1999, and in Britain an independent 24/7 initiative began, also in 1999, led by Pete Greig of the Emmaus Road Community in Guildford. Pete Greig and Dave Roberts, *Red Moon Rising: How 24–7 Prayer is Awakening a Generation* (Winter Park, FL: Relevant Books, 2003).

preacher, that brings divine truth to the mind and so gives guidance to individual believers. In this paradigm there are certainly dangers of radical individualism and subjectivism in the way that God's guidance is sought and received. On the other hand, the stress on constant prayer and utter dependence on God stands in stark contrast to the sometimes mechanistic or formulaic applications of the mass evangelism model for revival.

The International House of Prayer (IHOP) in Kansas City, Missouri and other affiliated houses of prayer, seek to initiate local revivals not by sending out preachers, but rather teams of pray-ers, who go into a given city or neighbourhood and saturate the region with prayer, seeking to alter the 'spiritual atmosphere' to prepare for later evangelism. There is a strong emphasis on prayer with fasting, and conflict with evil spirits, seen as occupying a particular territory, and resisting the advancement of God's kingdom in that place. Also characteristic of the new paradigm is a focus on works of mercy, justice and reconciliation, viewed as manifestations of God's kingdom, and so as integral to the church's mission. Murder and other crimes, practices of idolatry and false religion, and attitudes of racial and ethnic hatred, are all regarded as barriers blocking the flow of the Holy Spirit, to be overcome through prayer and sometimes by interpersonal acts of reconciliation. An intriguing aspect to this new paradigm is the focus on land, territory and materiality, and the 'cleansing', 'healing' and 'blessing' not only of human beings but of the physical landscape and its plant and animal species.

Each of the five historic and contemporary paradigms for Christian revival is in need of further research and investigation, and this is particularly the case with the newest paradigm as just described. The five paradigms might be interpreted as a series of concentric circles: a newer paradigm did not displace those that preceded it, but incorporated them. Methodist revivals of the eighteenth century built on the earlier Presbyterian sacramental paradigm, while nineteenth-century mass evangelism modified the Methodist paradigm, and twentieth-century healing evangelism transformed the paradigm of mass evangelism. Of the five paradigms, it is only the first or Presbyterian 'sacramental' model that seems to have disappeared over time. Yet perhaps this original model will be repristinated in the twenty-first century: today's younger Protestants and Pentecostals are often more 'catholic' in their thinking than most of their forebears. Perhaps the Eucharist as well as preaching might become central to Christian revival?

To analyse the inner dynamics of Christian revivals, the model of 'revitalization movements' proposed by Anthony Wallace and championed by Mark Shaw offers advantages. The revitalization model is flexible enough to be applied to various global movements, as Shaw demonstrated with respect to movements in Africa, Asia and Latin America. Wallace's theory is not reductively naturalistic, but allows believers to see the hand of God at work in conferring divine insight or charisma to the human agents of revival. The revitalization model also allows one to build bridges between theological interpretation and cultural contexts, and to view each local revival as reflecting a particular, non-repeatable set of circumstances.

Research into Christian revivals ought to become at once more globalized and more localized. By stressing locality, scholars will be able to identify what is distinctive to each individual revival. By stressing globality, scholars will be forced to engage in side-by-side comparisons, which will bring to light the features that distinguish revivals in particular global regions. If Western scholars had not considered the 'people movements' of the Pacific Islands, they might never have realized just how individualistic their presuppositions on revival and conversion were. If they had not encountered the prayers of African Christians for physical healing, fertility and God's blessing on the land, Westerners might likewise not have understood their own spiritualized and rather deracinated views of human life and human nature. Studies of global Christian revivals in comparative perspective are likely to yield further insights.

6

EVANGELICALS AND ROME[1]

John Maiden

On 21 March 2013 Justin Welby was enthroned as Archbishop of Canterbury. There was much written in the secular and religious press about his evangelical charismatic background and the growing influence on Anglicanism of Holy Trinity Brompton, the birthplace of the Alpha evangelistic course. However, while charismatic Christianity had an important impact on Archbishop Welby, for the historian of evangelicalism another significant influence was Roman Catholic spirituality and teaching. Welby had a Roman Catholic spiritual director, the founder of the Eucharistein community in Switzerland. He had close connections with Chemin Neuf, the French ecumenical religious order founded by charismatic Jesuits in the 1970s; indeed he later invited some of its members to reside in Lambeth Palace. He furthermore was profoundly influenced by Catholic social thought – the ideas of 'the common good' and 'human flourishing'.[2] When in June 2013 he visited Pope Francis at the Vatican, he prayed at the tomb of John Paul II.

All this is arguably indicative of a broader historical development: the growing sense of mutuality between many evangelicals and Roman Catholics. In contrast, the longer history of evangelical attitudes towards Roman Catholicism has often been marked by competition and conflict. Evangelical anti-Catholicism is only one variety of a historic phenomenon with intellectual and popular dimensions and diverse exponents – conservative, liberal, religious and, more recently, secular. The substantial and multi-national historiography of anti-Catholicism demonstrates its 'societal force' and its significance for identity formation.[3] John Wolffe has suggested four main expressions: constitutional-national, theological, popular and socio-cultural.[4]

---

1 I am grateful to Professor John Wolffe for comments on an earlier draft of this chapter.
2 Andrew Atherstone, *Archbishop Justin Welby: Risk-taker and Reconciler* (London: Darton, Longman and Todd, 2014), pp. 98–102, 150–1, 167, 207–8, 230.
3 Yvonne Maria Werner and Jonas Harvard, 'European Anti-Catholicism in Comparative and Transnational Perspective – The Role of a Unifying Other: An Introduction', in *European Anti-Catholicism in a Comparative and Transnational Perspective*, edited by Yvonne Maria Werner and Jonas Harvard, *European Studies* vol. 31 (2013), 14. The historiography is vast; a helpful survey is M. A. Drury, 'Anti-Catholicism in Germany, Britain and the United States: A Review and Critique of Recent Scholarship', *Church History* vol. 70 (2001), 98–131.
4 John Wolffe, 'Protestant-Catholic Divisions in Europe and the United States: An Historical and Comparative Perspective', *Politics, Religion and Ideology* vol. 12 (2011), 241–56.

As a Christian movement which displays a strong kinship with the Reformation, in particular the authority of Scripture and salvation by faith through grace alone – alongside an emphasis on individualism and private judgment – evangelicalism has frequently regarded itself markedly at odds with Roman Catholicism.[5] To add to the sense of conflict and competition, the rise of evangelicalism occurred parallel to the resurgence of Catholicism in various Protestant contexts. The strength of evangelical antagonism with Romanism has often been remarked upon. In 1926, the political historian, Élie Halévy, writing of the early nineteenth century, asserted that 'from the very nature of their creed, the evangelicals were anti-Catholics'.[6] For some, it has been a distasteful characteristic of the movement. George Eliot, the English novelist, saw it as a key aspect of the Christianity of Dr John Cumming, minister of the National Scottish Church in Covent Garden, London. Her 1855 attack on Cumming in the *Westminster Review* asserted: 'The great majority of his published sermons are occupied with argument or philippic against Romanists and unbelievers'.[7] Cumming's apparent lack of love was repugnant to Eliot, who had turned her back on evangelicalism fourteen years earlier.[8]

However, as this chapter will also suggest, despite the historic strength of evangelical anti-Catholicism, there has been significant diversity in evangelical attitudes. There have been differences of emphasis and strategy where rivalries with 'Rome' were concerned. Furthermore, in various times and places there has been evidence of important commonalities between evangelicals and Catholics. While, as the opening paragraph might suggest, this has been increasingly the case in recent decades, there are also indications during earlier periods. A single chapter survey of evangelical–Catholic relations over the period covered by this volume necessarily has marked limitations. What follows only engages with the English-speaking world, and very largely with the North Atlantic context; the history of relations in areas of the Global South, notably in Latin America during the twentieth century, is often rather different. Furthermore, it mostly restricts its analysis to evangelical experiences and attitudes, saying far less about Catholic perspectives, including anti-Protestantism.[9] It looks through three chronological 'windows', each of fifty years, which together indicate long-term developments in evangelical–Catholic relations, as well as some ongoing themes. The windows are: early evangelicalism (c.1730–1780); nineteenth-century 'Protestant Crusades' (c.1830–1880); new evangelicalisms, Vatican II and the culture wars (c.1950–2000).

Early evangelicalism and anti-Catholicism (c.1730–1780)

Evangelicalism emerged during a period of widespread anxiety concerning Rome and its ambitions. Though not without its weaknesses, Linda Colley's central argument in *Britons*:

---

5 John Wolffe, 'Anti-Catholicism and Evangelical Identity in Britain and the United States, 1830–1860', in *Evangelicalism: Comparative Studies of Popular Protestantism in North America, the British Isles and Beyond, 1700–1990*, edited by David W. Bebbington, Mark A. Noll and George Rawlyk (New York: Oxford University Press, 1994), p. 183.
6 Élie Halévy, *History of the English People in the Nineteenth Century* (4 vols, London: Ernest Benn, 1924–47), II: 216.
7 George Eliot, 'Evangelical Teaching: Dr. Cumming', *Westminster Review* vol. 64 (October 1855), 439.
8 See discussion in David Hempton, *Evangelical Disenchantment: Nine Portraits of Faith and Doubt* (New Haven, CT: Yale University Press, 2008), pp. 24–5.
9 The literature on anti-Protestantism is far less expansive. But see, for example, Olaf Blaschke, 'Anti-Protestantism and anti-Catholicism in the Nineteenth Century: A Comparison', in *European Anti-Catholicism*, edited by Werner and Harvard, 115–34; Jay Dolan, 'Catholic Attitudes Toward Protestants', in *Uncivil Religion: Interreligious Hostility in America*, edited by Robert N. Bellah and Frederick E. Greenspahn (New York: Crossroad, 1987), pp. 72–85.

Forging the Nation, 1707–1837 (1992) remains broadly persuasive. In a context of rivalry and wars with France, and a Jacobite enemy within, Protestantism was 'the foundation that made the invention of Great Britain possible'.[10] Anti-Catholic ideology, materiality and performance was prevalent – for example, in frequent reprints of John Foxe's *Book of Martyrs*, the crude drawings by William Hogarth and the collective rituals of Bonfire night.[11] In a period of 'enlightenment', anti-Romanism remained influential within intellectual life. John Locke's *Letter Concerning Toleration* (1689) cast a shadow, with its exclusion of Roman Catholics, like atheists, from tolerance. The views of evangelicals often reflected such wider Protestant assumptions. George Whitefield, the leading personality of transatlantic evangelicalism in its first decades, described the dangers facing Britain in 1756 as the designs of 'France, of Rome and of hell'.[12] Often evangelicals reflected broader enlightenment assumptions. In the Church of Scotland, John Erskine, following Locke, regarded Rome as a threat both to freedom of thought and political liberties, and so counter-enlightenment. Erskine opposed the repeal of penal laws in Scotland on such grounds, but rejected the violence and intimidation by popular Protestantism.[13]

One irony of early evangelicalism is that its practitioners were sometimes accused of being crypto-Romanists. In the early stages of the Great Awakening, claims of supernatural interventions, including healings, could result in opponents of revivalism labelling it as Catholic superstition.[14] The Methodists frequently found themselves having to dodge accusations. Writings such as Bishop George Lavington's *Enthusiasm of Methodists and Papists Compared* (1749–1751) disseminated socially and politically damaging accusations, while the mob, unforgiving of religious difference, expressed anger.[15] The Jacobite threat of the 1740s prompted many breathless Methodist assertions of their loyal Protestantism in the press.[16] John Wesley wrote to King George II in 1744 assuring him that Methodists 'detest and abhor the fundamental doctrines of the Church of Rome, and are steadily attached to your Majesty's royal person and illustrious house'.[17] David Hempton's classic study asserts that the identification of Methodism with Popery had 'both theological and social foundations'.[18] Arminian theology clearly drew suspicions, including from Calvinist evangelicals, such as Welsh revivalist Howel Harris, who suspected

---

10 Linda Colley, *Britons: Forging the Nation, 1707–1837* (New Haven, CT: Yale University Press, 1992), pp. 53–4.
11 The literature is enormous, but see for example: G. F. A. Best, 'Popular Protestantism in Victorian Britain', in *Ideas and Institutions in Victorian Britain: Essays in Honour of George Kitson Clark*, edited by Robert Robson (London: G. Bell, 1967), pp. 115–42; Colin Haydon, *Anti-Catholicism in Eighteenth-Century England, c.1714–80* (Manchester: Manchester University Press, 1993); Danielle Thom, '"Sawney's Defence": Anti-Catholicism, Consumption and Performance in Eighteenth-Century Britain', *Victoria and Albert Online Journal* no. 7 (2015).
12 See correspondence with Bishop Zachary Pearce, including 16 February 1756: in *The Works of the Rev. George Whitefield M.A.*, edited by John Gillies (6 vols, London: Edward and Charles Dilly, 1771–2), III: 164.
13 Jonathan Yeager, *Enlightened Evangelicalism: The Life and Thought of John Esrkine* (New York: Oxford University Press, 2011), pp. 130–6.
14 Thomas S. Kidd, 'The Healing of Mercy Wheeler: Illness and Miracles among Early American Evangelicals', *William and Mary Quarterly* vol. 63 (2006), 149–70.
15 John Walsh, 'Methodism and the Mob in the Eighteenth Century', in *Popular Belief and Practice*, edited by G. J. Cuming and Derek Baker (Cambridge: Cambridge University Press, 1972), pp. 213–27.
16 David Ceri Jones, *'A Glorious Work in the World': Welsh Methodism and the International Evangelical Revival, 1735–1750* (Cardiff: University of Wales Press, 2004), pp. 324–5.
17 *The Works of the Rev. John Wesley* (10 vols, New York: Harper, 1827), II: 14.
18 David Hempton, *Methodism and Politics in British Society, 1750–1850* (London: Hutchinson, 1984), p. 31.

papist tendencies among their Arminian brethren.[19] Wesley's appreciation of Catholic mysticism strengthened suspicions, while 'enthusiasm' was deemed to mirror the supposed excesses of medieval Catholicism. Similarities between the Methodist and Roman Catholic communities, for example their reliance on itinerant clergy, likely also contributed to criticisms.[20]

It is not surprising, therefore, that early Methodism could display a 'powerful dislike of Popery'.[21] Some of the hymnody of Charles Wesley disseminated explicit anti-Rome messages. A hymn published at the time of the second Jacobite rebellion, for instance, suggested God superintended national security:

> Thou in danger's darkest hour
> Didst on our side appear,
> Snatch us from the wasting power
> Of Rome and Satan near:
> Whom the winds and seas obey,
> Thou, Lord, thy mighty arm didst shew,
> Chace [sic] the alien hosts away,
> And stop th' invading foe.[22]

From the mid-1740s, George Whitefield shifted from an exclusive conversionist message to reveal an imperial and anti-Catholic emphasis, with sermons such as 'Britain's Mercies, and Britain's Duty' (1746), delivered in Philadelphia, coming to typify an 'evangelical blending of politics, war and religion'.[23] Although there were inconsistencies in John Wesley's attitude, his overall sense of anti-Catholicism was clear.[24] He sometimes appeared more accommodating in his attitude towards Catholics which was likely situational, such as his irenic *Letter to a Roman Catholic* (1749) following dangerous rioting against Methodists in Cork, Ireland. In general, however, he displayed the widespread Protestant assumptions about Catholic Ireland and the Lockean view of Catholic religionists as a threat to freedom, the latter notably in the period of the Catholic Relief Act (1778).

Recent scholarship, nevertheless, has been drawn to the ambiguities in some early evangelical views of Roman Catholics. Revisionist literature, often the fruit of Catholic scholars, has attempted to draw out the 'Catholic' or even proto-ecumenist Wesleys.[25] Jean Orcibal identified the influences of continental spirituality on John Wesley, including on the development of the doctrine of perfection.[26] Significantly, Wesley acknowledged that some Catholics, living and dead, were true Christians. In a letter of 1744 he asserted that Thomas à Kempis and Francis

---

19 Jones, 'A Glorious Work in the World', p. 184.
20 Hempton, *Methodism and Politics in British Society*, pp. 31–3.
21 Haydon, *Anti-Catholicism*, p. 63.
22 *Hymns for Times of Trouble for the Year 1745* (Bristol: Felix Farley, 1745), pp. 49–50.
23 Thomas S. Kidd, *George Whitefield: America's Spiritual Founding Father* (New Haven, CT: Yale University Press, 2014), pp. 262–3.
24 Hempton, *Methodism and Politics in British Society*, pp. 34–9; David Butler, *Methodists and Papists: John Wesley and the Catholic Church in the Eighteenth Century* (London: Darton, Longman and Todd, 1995), p. 203.
25 For a critical survey, see Mark S. Massa, 'The Catholic Wesley: A Revisionist Prolegomenon', *Methodist History* vol. 12 (1983), 38–53.
26 Jean Orcibal, 'The Theological Originality of John Wesley and Continental Spirituality', in *A History of the Methodist Church in Great Britain*, edited by Rupert David and Gordon Rupp (4 vols, London: Epworth Press, 1965–88), I: 83–111.

de Sales were 'now in Abraham's bosom'.[27] In his sermon 'Of the Church', Wesley appeared to include some Roman Catholic congregations within the church catholic. Charles Wesley displayed some of the anti-Roman emphases of Protestant premillennialism from the 1750s, but in contrast to his brother he played a 'conciliatory' role in the controversy around the Catholic Relief Act.[28] There was a sense in which Charles Wesley, like Mary Fletcher, wife of John Fletcher (vicar of Madeley), believed 'holiness could not be confined within denominational boundaries'.[29] This issue came close to home following the conversion of Charles Wesley's son, Samuel, to Rome. In a letter to his nephew in August 1784, John Wesley wrote: 'Whether of this Church or that I care not; you may be saved in either, or damned in either'.[30] Such ambiguities in attitudes towards Catholicism – including the tension between the individual and the institution – have been a long-running theme in evangelicalism.

It is not surprising that early evangelicalism reflected many of the anti-Catholic prejudices of wider Protestant culture. Anxiety over Rome's spiritual and political tyranny were not necessarily distinct in the minds of revivalists such as Whitefield, who believed their freedom to spread the gospel relied on freedom from Papal influence.[31] The natural preoccupation of evangelicals was with things spiritual – 'heart religion' – but the political context could result in anti-Catholic polemic, or a merging of spiritual and earthly matters. Whitefield, for example, commented:

> I hope I shall always think it my bounden duty, next to inviting sinners to the blessed Jesus, to exhort my hearers to exert themselves against the first approaches of popish tyranny and arbitrary power. O that we may be enabled to watch and pray against all the opposition of Antichrist in our hearts; for after all, there lies the most dangerous man of sin.[32]

Following the American Revolution, and with the coming of the French Revolution in Europe, there was a lull in transatlantic anti-Catholicism. Evangelicals displayed an energetic range of reforming priorities, with Rome not generally a focus of attention. Indeed, there was sometimes peaceful co-existence, even co-operation, between evangelicals and Catholics. In the remote Western Scottish Highlands, for example, in the early decades of the nineteenth century there was sometimes co-operation between the evangelical missionaries of the Edinburgh Society and local priests and parents based on a mutual interest in children's education.[33] It was not until after the opening decades of the nineteenth century that anti-Catholicism became a key aspect of broader evangelical identity in the North Atlantic world.

---

27 John Wesley, *An Answer to the Rev. Mr. Church's Remarks*, in *The Works of John Wesley*, edited by John Emory (7 vols, New York: Carton and Porter, 1871), V: 267.
28 Peter Nockles, '"Emissaries of Babylon" or "Brothers in Christ"?', *Wesleyan and Methodist Studies* vol. 2 (2010), 16–17.
29 Nockles, '"Emissaries of Babylon" or "Brothers in Christ"?', 22–3.
30 Cited in Nockles, '"Emissaries of Babylon" or "Brothers in Christ"?', 19.
31 Kidd, *George Whitefield*, p. 263.
32 *A Select Collection of Letters of the Late Reverend George Whitefield* (3 vols, London: Edward and Charles Dilly, 1772), III: 146. See discussion in Kidd, *George Whitefield*, pp. 226–7.
33 Elizabeth Ritchie, 'The People, the Priests and the Protestants: Catholic Responses to Evangelical Missionaries in the Early Nineteenth-Century Scottish Highlands', *Church History* vol. 85 (2016), 275–301.

Evangelical anti-Catholicism and 'Protestant Crusades' (c.1830–1880)

There was an eruption of heated evangelical anti-Catholicism in Britain and the United States from the 1820s and Australia and Canada from the 1840s. Serious theological disagreement sometimes combined powerfully with anxieties over Rome's political and social threat. Analysing the period from 1830 until 1860, John Wolffe describes anti-Catholicism as 'very deeply rooted in evangelical identity and ideology',[34] and a key ingredient in the broader expression of anti-Catholicism.[35] Various general factors contributed to the upsurge. There was a shift from a positive post-millennial mindset towards pre-millennial eschatology; Irish immigration heightened rivalries in various English-speaking contexts; Protestants grew conscious of their declining cultural and political hegemony; and increasing Catholic institutional assertiveness, including Ultramontane religion, contributed to tensions. Added to this was the emergence of sacramental tendencies within Protestant denominations, notably ritualism within Anglicanism and Episcopalianism. Later, in *The Secret History of the Oxford Movement* (1898), Walter Walsh expressed the belief of many English evangelicals that the Church of England was 'literally honeycombed' with secret societies which acted as 'wire-pullers' to bring about corporate reunion with Rome.[36] Increasingly, evangelicals felt called to resist the advance of 'apostate' Rome.

Competition increased between evangelicals and Roman Catholics. Various Protestant societies were formed to evangelize or proselytize – for example, the Colonial Society (1819) to work in continental Europe; the Reformation Society (1827) to advance Protestantism in Ireland and then England, Scotland and Wales; the Irish Church Mission (1849); and the American and Foreign Christian Union (1849) which sought to convert Catholics in the United States, South America and Europe. A range of studies identify evangelical–Catholic rivalries. In towns and cities with growing Irish populations, evangelicals increased efforts to convert Catholics and improve moral and social conditions.[37] In Ireland itself, a period of relaxed religious relations was disturbed in the 1820s by militant Protestant evangelism, prompting a determined Catholic response.[38] In Francophone Lower Canada before the 1830s, cordial religious relations had existed, but increasing numbers of evangelicals and the arrival of Swiss and American mission agencies resulted in proselytization which had previously been frowned upon, so Ultramontane Catholics responded with their own revival meetings.[39] Mission rivalries were

---

34 Wolffe, 'Anti-Catholicism and Evangelical Identity', p. 184.
35 J. R. Wolffe, *The Protestant Crusade in Great Britain, 1829–1860* (Oxford: Clarendon Press, 1991). On the broader context of anti-Catholicism in the United States there is a vast literature, but see for example, R. A. Billington, *The Protestant Crusade* (New York: Macmillan, 1938); John Higham, *Strangers in the Land: Patterns of American Nativism, 1860–1925* (New Brunswick, NJ: Rutgers University Press, 2002).
36 Walter Walsh, *The Secret History of the Oxford Movement* (London: Swan Sonnenschein and Co., 1898), p. vi.
37 For example, on London, see Sheridan Gilley, 'Evangelical and Roman Catholic Missions to the Irish in London, 1830–1870' (unpublished PhD thesis, University of Cambridge, 1970); Sheridan Gilley, 'Papists, Protestants and the Irish in London, 1835–1970', in *Popular Belief and Practice*, edited by Cuming and Baker, pp. 259–66; Donald M. Lewis, *Lighten Their Darkness: The Evangelical Mission to Working-Class London, 1828–1860* (Westport, CT: Greenwood Press, 1986).
38 Desmond Bowen, *The Protestant Crusade in Ireland, 1800–1870: A Study of Protestant-Catholic Relations between the Act of Union and Disestablishment* (Dublin: Gill and Macmillan, 1978).
39 Robert Merrill Black, 'Different Visions: the Multiplication of Protestant Missions to French-Canadian Roman Catholics, 1834–1855', in *Canadian Protestant and Catholic Missions, 1820s–1960s: Historical Essays in Honour of John Webster Grant*, edited by John S. Moir and C. T. McIntire (New York: Peter Lang, 1988), pp. 47–73.

evident in remoter parts of the British Empire. Church Missionary Society (CMS) polemic in New Zealand resulted in Maori converts referring to one Catholic Bishop as the 'anti-Christ'.[40] Robert Choquette's illuminating account of mid-century competition in the Canadian North and West reveals intense anti-Catholicism and anti-Protestantism between Wesleyan Methodist or CMS workers and Catholic Oblate missionaries following the expansion of fur trades and mining opportunities. Robert Rundle, the only missionary in Alberta in 1841, wrote: 'The Roman Catholics are . . . casting a jealous eye over the plains of the Saskatchewan; I not only want to rescue . . . [the Indians] from the strongholds of heathenism but also to save them from the fascination and abominations of the Church of Rome'.[41] Choquette's study uses military metaphors of deployment, battles and beachheads to describe the Oblate missionary work and competition with Protestants.

Alongside theological concerns and competition for souls, the conviction that Rome was the antithesis of religious and political freedom and Protestant nationalism contributed to anti-Catholicism. In the United States, the final years of the religious and reforming impulses of the Second Great Awakening occurred in a context of rising Whig party opposition to the Irish Catholic 'menace', the emergence of nativism, and after the Civil War attempts by the Republican party to build a Protestant moral consensus culminating in the 1884 'Rum, Romanism and Rebellion' election. The narrative of the resurgence of anti-Catholicism is well rehearsed in the secondary literature. Following the burning of the Ursuline convent and school at Charlestown, Massachusetts, in 1834, various publications told lurid stories of priests and nuns. This was followed by growing conflict over education, with campaigns for and against the compulsory reading of the King James Bible in public schools in the 1840s, often framed by Protestants in terms of a struggle between 'Americans' and 'foreigners'.[42] The leading evangelical preacher and reformer Lyman Beecher's *A Plea for the West* (1835) became an influential text, warning of a threat to national destiny, American liberties and Protestant hegemony from an incoming tide of Catholic migrants to the trans-Appalachian west.[43] These newcomers, he argued, would be controlled by despotic central European powers by the hand of the priest. He wrote:

> But if, upon examination, it should appear that three-fourths of the foreign emigrants whose accumulating tide is rolling in upon us, are, through the medium of their religion and priesthood, as entirely accessible to the control of the potentates of Europe as if they were an army of soldiers, enlisted and officered, and spreading over the land; then, indeed, should we have just occasion to apprehend danger to our liberties.[44]

The danger, he argued, was 'a church and state union – another nation within the nation – the Greek in the midst of Troy'.[45]

Evangelicalism and nativism were not synonymous. The two ideologies were often seen

---

40 Tony Ballantyne, *Webs of Empire: Locating New Zealand's Colonial Past* (Vancouver: University of British Columbia Press, 2014), p. 158.
41 Cited in Robert Choquette, *The Oblate Assault on Canada's Northwest* (Ottawa: University of Ottawa Press, 1995), p. 138.
42 Tracy Fessenden, 'The Nineteenth-Century Bible Wars and the Separation of Church and State', *Church History* vol. 74 (2005), 784–811.
43 On Beecher, see also William M. Shea, *The Lion and the Lamb: Evangelicals and Catholics in America* (New York: Oxford University Press, 2004), pp. 62–6.
44 Lyman Beecher, *A Plea for the West* (Cincinnati, OH: Truman and Smith, 1835), pp. 56–7.
45 Beecher, *A Plea for the West*, p. 59

as incompatible – it seems, for example, few members of the American Protestant Society or American and Foreign Christian Union were involved in nativist politics.[46] However, notions of Protestant liberty and Catholic authoritarianism were widely accepted. Northern evangelicals attacked both Catholicism and pro-Slavery in the South as leftovers of the old European order, sometimes contrasting racial slavery with the mental slavery of Rome.[47] Furthermore evangelical anti-Catholicism became bound up with a sense of national mission. In *God's Hand on America* (1841), George Barrell Cheever, pastor of the Church of the Puritans, New York, contrasted his nation with despotic Catholic countries, arguing that divine Providence had raised up the American republic for a special purpose of world evangelization.[48] Just as British evangelicals caricatured Catholic Ireland, American Protestants thought of Mexico's Latin culture as priest-ridden, idolatrous and backward. Some evangelicals, particularly in the South and West, justified the Mexican-American war by emphasizing the evils of Romanism and possibilities for missionary activity.[49] Evangelicalism contributed significantly to the hostile mid-nineteenth-century atmosphere towards Roman Catholicism.

Following a hiatus from the 1780s, the resurgence of British anti-Catholicism came with debates over Catholic Emancipation, resulting in the Roman Catholic Relief Act (1829), controversies over the Irish Church and education, the Maynooth Act (1845), and Pope Pius IX's *Universalis Ecclesiae* (1850) restoring the Catholic hierarchy. Within the Church of England, the Clapham Sect had not been aggressively anti-Catholic. From the 1820s, however, a 'Recordite' (a term referring to the evangelical *Record* newspaper) leadership emerged which exhibited a 'more aggressive Evangelicalism, the doctrinal interpretations of which ultimately emanated from the postwar Evangelical revivals in Scotland and Geneva'.[50] The new evangelicalism tended to be pre-millennial in eschatology, strongly Erastian in its conception of church and state, and explicitly anti-Catholic.[51] While the Reformation Society focused primarily on conversionism, the Protestant Association (1835) allied its priorities with the Tory Party and used political means to fight Romanism and defend the 'Protestant constitution'.[52] As in America, a nationalistic Protestantism, emphasizing Britain as elect, was evident. One of the first uses of the word 'nationalism' in Britain was in an 1839 address by Hugh McNeile to the Protestant Association.[53] From the 1860s, Protestant Societies were increasingly focused on opposing Anglo-Catholic ritualism. This followed a broader cultural trend – Alec Corio argues that a 'cultural emancipation' of Roman Catholicism saw ritualism become Protestantism's new target.[54] The Church Association (1865) prosecuted ritualist priests and evangelical campaigning

---

46 Wolffe, 'Anti-Catholicism and Evangelical Identity', p. 187.
47 W. Jason Wallace, *Catholics, Slaveholders and the Dilemma of American Evangelicalism, 1835–1860* (Notre Dame, IN: University of Notre Dame Press, 2010). Some British evangelicals also made connections between physical and mental slavery, see Wolffe, *Protestant Crusade*, pp. 26, 132.
48 George B. Cheever, *God's Hand in America* (New York: M. W. Dodd, 1841).
49 John C. Pinherio, *Missionaries of Republicanism: A Religious History of the Mexican-American War* (Oxford: Oxford University Press, 2014), Ch. 7.
50 D. G. Paz, *Popular Anti-Catholicism in Mid-Victorian England* (Stanford, CA: Stanford University Press, 1992), p. 104.
51 On this new evangelicalism, see Wolffe, *Protestant Crusade*, pp. 29–34, 107–44; Paz, *Popular Anti-Catholicism*, pp. 104–9.
52 Wolffe, *Protestant Crusade*, pp. 29–106.
53 Wolffe, *Protestant Crusade*, p. 308. On wider Anglican evangelical views of Church and nation, see also Ralph Brown, 'The Evangelical Succession: Evangelical History and Denominational Identity', *Evangelical Quarterly* vol. 68 (1996), 3–13.
54 Alec Corio, 'Historical Perceptions of Roman Catholicism and National Identity, 1869–1919' (unpublished PhD thesis, Open University, 2013).

contributed to Parliament passing the Public Worship Regulation Act (1874).[55] Wesleyan Toryism was also committed to the Protestant constitution, resisting, for example, the government's Irish national education proposals of 1839 and Peel's Maynooth Bill.[56] Furthermore, Mats Selén has argued that Wesleyan opposition to Tractarianism in the established Church was important to the shaping of the denomination's own identity during the period.[57] More generally, however, if the sheer diversity of American evangelicalism weakened the overall coherence of anti-Catholicism, in the British Isles Church-State links limited pan-evangelical co-operation, even though British Nonconformity was robustly anti-Catholic.[58] Amongst dissenters, political liberalism, with its vigorous campaigns against the threat of Rome to national and international liberties, contributed to the diversity of evangelical anti-Catholicism.[59]

National studies provide valuable insights, but the complexities of evangelical anti-Catholicism are also contrastingly evident in both transnational and regional/local perspectives. Transnational networks disseminating pre-millennial eschatology were a stimulus for anti-popery. Canadian anti-evangelicalism, for example, was largely nourished by individuals, organizations and controversies originating in the United States and Britain. The re-establishment of the Catholic hierarchy in England in 1850 caused uproar. The arrival of the Irish evangelicals brought 'Second Reformation' zeal to Quebec, and opposition to Tractarianism became heated as in England.[60] Wolffe has described the 'interconnectedness of nineteenth-century anti-Catholicism' in the transatlantic context.[61] However, he also suggests that the internationalism of the Evangelical Alliance (1846) was limited by the 'national pride' of American and British evangelicals, and specifically tensions over slavery.[62] Regional and local level studies reveal the distinctive contexts shaping evangelical attitudes. A close study of the North-East of England has shown how both conservative and liberal anti-Catholicisms could prosper; the latter combining a Liberal and radical tradition with evangelical culture, for example in support of Italian independence.[63] The intricacies of local sectarian politics could also play a decisive role – the upsurge of evangelical anti-Catholicism in the 1880s in Boston, Massachusetts, was partly in response to perceptions of the growing power of Irish Catholics in city politics and policing.[64]

---

55 On the Church Association and evangelical anti-ritualism, see James Whisenant, *A Fragile Unity: Anti-Ritualism and the Division of Anglican Evangelicalism in the Nineteenth Century* (Milton Keynes: Paternoster, 2003). See also James Bentley, *Ritualism and Politics in Victorian Britain* (Oxford: Oxford University Press, 1978).

56 Hempton, *Methodism and Politics in British Society*, pp. 151–64, 191–4.

57 Mats Selén, *The Oxford Movement and Wesleyan Methodism in England, 1833–1882: A Study in Religious Conflict* (Lund: Lund University Press, 1992).

58 Wolffe, *Protestant Crusade*, pp. 134–43.

59 Jonathan Bush, *'Papists' and Prejudice: Popular Anti-Catholicism and Anglo-Irish Conflict in the North East of England, 1845–70* (Newcastle: Cambridge Scholars Publishing, 2013), Ch. 4.

60 J. R. Miller, 'Anti-Catholicism in Canada: From the British Conquest to the Great War', in *Creed and Culture: The Place of English-Speaking Catholics in Canadian Society, 1750-1930*, edited by Terence Murphy and Gerald Stortz (Montreal: McGill-Queen's University Press, 1993), pp. 37–8; Richard W. Vaudry, *Anglicans and the Atlantic World: High Churchmen, Evangelicals and the Quebec Connection* (Montreal: McGill-Queens University Press, 2003), pp. 142–5.

61 Wolffe, 'North Atlantic Anti-Catholicism in the Nineteenth Century: A Comparative Overview', in *European Anti-Catholicism*, edited by Werner and Harvard, 27.

62 Wolffe, 'Anti-Catholicism and Evangelical Identity', p. 191. See also, John Wolffe, 'Transatlantic Visitors and Evangelical Networks, 1829–61' in *International Religious Networks*, edited by Jeremy Gregory and Hugh McLeod (Woodbridge: Boydell, 2012), pp. 183–93.

63 Bush, *'Papists' and Prejudice*, p. 110.

64 M. L. Bendroth, *Fundamentalists in the City: Conflict and Division in Boston's Churches, 1885–1950* (New York: Oxford University Press, 2005).

There was, however, diversity in evangelical opinion. Anglican evangelicals disagreed about the appropriateness of involvement in political anti-Catholicism. The Reformation Society and the Protestant Association offered alternative 'spiritual' and 'political' approaches to the Catholic threat,[65] while the evangelical clergy of the Simeon Trust generally distanced themselves from both.[66] Moreover, moderate and militant Anglican evangelicals were divided over the use of courts to curtail Anglo-Catholic ritualism. Moderates opposed ritualism, but preferred alternative tactics. At the Islington Clerical Conference of 1883, Philip F. Eliot remarked: 'How, then, shall we carry on the battle, and how shall we contend with our brethren who differ from us? I answer – Out-teach them, out-preach them, out-pray them, out-shine them in holiness of life and charity of spirit!'[67] In the United States, while Lyman Beecher was vitriolic, Charles Finney, another leading New School Presbyterian, refused to single out Roman Catholicism, rarely mentioning it in his preaching, and regarded universalism, Old School Presbyterianism and Freemasonry as equal or greater threats.[68] There was also some ambiguity in the status of Roman Catholicism. Charles Hodge, although deeply hostile to Catholic doctrine, asserted that Catholic baptisms were valid, and in Paul Gutjahr's words, accepted that Roman Catholicism was 'within the fold of the universal Church because of its long and vitally important history'.[69] Hodge was in a minority – in 1845 only eight members of a Presbyterian General Assembly rejected a motion (six abstained) that Catholic baptism was invalid – however, his position stands out as notably nuanced.[70]

Despite the widespread competition, polemic and mutual antagonism in the mid-nineteenth century, the barriers between evangelicalism and Catholic or sacramental religion were neither always rigid nor impermeable. Just as Joseph Milner's *History of the Church of Christ* (1794–1809) had found evidence of 'real' Christianity amongst various popes and within the medieval Church,[71] so some evangelical literature continued to recognize the contribution and character of historic Catholic figures. English evangelical statesman Henry Venn's *The Missionary Life and Labours of Francis Xavier* (1862), while highly critical of Catholic doctrine and methods, was commendatory of Xavier's devotion and zeal.[72] Some evangelicals, too, moved towards 'higher' expressions of churchmanship. In Britain, although robustly opposed to Rome, the Catholic Apostolic Church moved ahead of 'all but the most advanced ritualists of the Church of England' in the 1850s and 1860s.[73] This was an extreme example, but in *Evangelical Churchmanship and Evangelical Eclecticism* (1883) the future bishop of Exeter, E. H. Bickersteth, suggested it was part of a broader development: 'Are Evangelical Churchmen in non-essential

---

65 Wolffe, *Protestant Crusade*, pp. 290–1.
66 Paz, *Popular Anti-Catholicism*, p. 104.
67 Cited in Whisenant, *A Fragile Unity*, p. 353.
68 Charles E. Hambrick-Stowe, 'Charles G. Finney and Evangelical Anti-Catholicism', *U. S. Catholic Historian* vol. 14 (1996), 42–8.
69 Paul C. Gutjahr, *Charles Hodge: Guardian of American Orthodoxy* (New York: Oxford University Press, 2011), p. 239. See also, Shea, *The Lion and the Lamb*, pp. 165–9.
70 Gutjahr, *Charles Hodge*, p. 235.
71 J. D. Walsh, 'Joseph Milner's Evangelical Church History', *Journal of Ecclesiastical History* vol. 10 (1959), 181.
72 Mark A. Smith, 'The Missionary Statesman and the Missionary Saint: Henry Venn's Life of Francis Xavier', in *British Evangelical Identities: Past and Present*, edited by Mark A. Smith (Milton Keynes: Paternoster, 2008), p. 250.
73 David Bebbington, *Evangelicalism in Modern Britain: A History from the 1730s to the 1980s* (London: Hyman Unwin, 1989), pp. 94–5.

matters of ritual – ritual which symbolizes no false doctrine – willing to use for the furtherance of the Gospel the prevalent aesthetic tastes of the age? Facts answer, Yes'.[74]

Relations between evangelicals and Catholics were not always defined by hostility or a hard proselytizing agenda. Despite the religious competition in the Canadian North and West, there was sometimes a 'love-hate' relationship between evangelicals and Catholics, with some anti-Catholic clergymen, such as Baptist C. C. McLaurin, admiring the sacrifice and zeal of Catholic priests in Western Canada.[75] Charles Finney felt warmth towards Clarence Augustus Walworth, of the Paulist Fathers, asserting that he appeared 'to be an earnest minister of Christ, given with heart and soul to the salvation of Roman Catholics', and suggested the encounter was as pleasant 'as we should have had if we had both been Protestants'.[76] The sense of commonality may have reflected the parallel revivalist impulses amongst Protestants and Catholics from the mid-nineteenth century in the United States.[77] Arguably another indication of some underlying affinity between evangelicalism and Catholicism were conversions. Walworth had himself first been converted during Charles Finney's second Rochester campaign in 1842. John Henry Newman is a well-known case of (albeit indirect) conversion. In his adolescence he had been converted into Calvinistic evangelicalism before later becoming a leading Tractarian and then converting to Rome. In *Apologia Pro Vita Sua* (1864) he suggested that at his conversion, 'I fell under the influences of a definite Creed, and received into my intellect impressions of dogma, which, through God's mercy, have never been effaced or obscured'.[78] A continuing sense of the importance of personal faith, dogma and growth in holiness remained with Newman.[79] A less famous, and more complex, case of conversion was that of Richard Sibthorp. Following an early attraction to Roman Catholicism he eventually become a leading London evangelical and founder member of the Islington Clerical Society; in 1841 he converted to Roman Catholicism and was ordained a priest before returning to Anglicanism, and then back to Catholicism. According to his biographer, as a Catholic priest 'his feelings, his language, his general teaching, were, in some very important respects, still evangelical'.[80] Even at the high point of nineteenth-century evangelical–Catholic rivalries there were significant ambiguities.

New evangelicalisms, Vatican II and 'culture wars' (c.1950–2000)

In the early twentieth century, there were greater signs of flux in the evangelical view of Catholicism. In the United States, in changing religious and political times marked by the 'apostasy' of liberalism and the threat of Communist atheism, some began to see potential commonalities and possibilities for engagement. Presbyterian J. Gresham Machen in his influential work *Christianity and Liberalism* (1924) recognized common loyalty to Scripture and creedal truths. Rome may have been a 'perversion' of Christian religion, he suggested, 'but naturalistic liberalism is not Christianity at all'.[81] In the 1930s, the politicized fundamentalist and staunchly

---

74 Cited in Whisenant, *A Fragile Unity*, p. 352.
75 Choquette, *The Oblate Assault*, pp. 181–3.
76 *The Memoirs of Charles G. Finney*, edited by Garth M. Rosell and Richard A. G. Dupuis (Grand Rapids, MI: Academie Books, 1989), pp. 443–4.
77 Hambrick-Stowe, 'Charles G. Finney and Evangelical Anti-Catholicism', 52.
78 John Henry Newman, *Apologia Pro Vita Sua: Being a Reply to a Pamphlet Entitled, 'What, Then, Does Dr Newman Mean?'* (London: Longman, Green and Co., 1864), p. 58.
79 John R. Connolly, *John Henry Newman: A View of Catholic Faith for the New Millennium* (Lanham, MD: Rowman and Littlefield, 2005), pp. 13–6.
80 John Fowler, *Richard Waldo Sibthorp: A Biography* (London: Skeffington, 1880), p. 177.
81 J. Gresham Machen, *Christianity and Liberalism* (New York: Macmillan, 1924), p. 52.

anti-Catholic, Carl McIntire saw individual Catholics as potential allies against the Communist threat.[82] However, opposition to Catholicism was still a common feature of evangelicalism and fundamentalism. While more pronounced in McIntire's *Christian Beacon,* it was also a feature of the neo-evangelicalism of the National Association of Evangelicals (NAE). Harold Ockenga's keynote address to the first convention of the NAE had raised an image of three clear and present dangers facing evangelicalism: Roman Catholicism, liberalism and secularism.[83]

Across American evangelicalism there remained a basic underlying fear of Roman Catholic power in relation to issues of church and state and the possibility of a Catholic president, as well as continuing concern over stories of Protestants facing persecution abroad. There was a significant mobilization of evangelical forces, with the involvement of the NAE and *Christianity Today,* to oppose Democrat candidate John F. Kennedy because of his Catholic faith.[84] Yet despite the sense of continuity in evangelical opposition to Rome, apocalyptic language was now rarely deployed by the neo-evangelicals. Furthermore, by the late 1950s there were some important signs of greater openness in the neo-evangelical *Christianity Today*, for example in the various book reviews and articles of G. C. Berkouwer, which indicated a greater willingness to engage.[85]

There were similar developments in British evangelicalism. Compared with earlier outcries, evangelical responses to the Roman Catholic Eucharistic Congress procession in London in 1908 and the Roman Catholic Relief Bill of 1926 were more limited.[86] The contemporary evangelical historian G. R. Balleine condemned the earlier political and litigious activities of the Church Association against Anglican ritualists, and in 1913 spoke out against 'a mere negative Protestantism'.[87] The notion of 'positive' Protestantism had a wider currency: the Wesleyan Methodist T. Dinsdale Young, for example, argued that the most effective antidote to Romanism was to preach a positive gospel.[88] However, distrust of both Roman Catholicism and sacramental trends within the Protestant denominations remained. When the Protestantism of the National Church seemed at stake, both conservative and liberal evangelicals responded to the perceived threat of Anglo-Catholicism; an alliance of Anglicans and Free Churchmen persuaded Parliament in 1927 and 1928 to reject controversial proposals for Prayer Book revision.[89] In the early 1960s, supposedly 'catholic' proposals for Anglican canon law revision were also opposed, this time unsuccessfully.[90] There was a continued emphasis on a national Reformation heritage. At a 1924 gathering of the World Evangelical Alliance, Sir Thomas Inskip, solicitor-general

---

82 Mark Ruotsila, *Fighting Fundamentalist: Carl McIntire and the Politicization of Fundamentalism* (New York: Oxford University Press, 2016), p. 37.
83 Harold Ockenga, 'Unvoiced Multitudes', in *Evangelical Action! A Report of the Organization of the National Association of Evangelicals for United Action* (Boston, MA: United Action Press, 1942).
84 Mark B. Chapman, 'American Evangelical Attitudes Toward Catholicism: World War II to Vatican II', *U.S. Catholic Historian* vol. 33 (Winter 2015–6), 37, 46–8. See also Shaun A. Casey, *The Making of a Catholic President: Kennedy vs. Nixon 1960* (New York: Oxford University Press, 2009), Ch. 5.
85 Chapman, 'American Evangelical Attitudes Toward Catholicism', 25–54.
86 John Maiden, *National Religion and the Prayer Book Controversy, 1927–28* (Woodbridge: Boydell, 2011), p. 181. See also John Maiden, 'Fundamentalism and Anti-Catholicism in Inter-War English Evangelicalism', in *Evangelicalism and Fundamentalism in the United Kingdom during the Twentieth Century,* edited by David W. Bebbington and David Ceri Jones (Oxford: Oxford University Press, 2013), pp. 151–70.
87 Cited in Andrew Atherstone, 'George Reginald Balleine: Historian of Anglican Evangelicalism', *Journal of Anglican Studies* vol. 12 (2014), 94.
88 T. Dinsdale Young, *Stars in Retrospect* (London: Hodder and Stoughton, 1920), pp. 159–60.
89 Maiden, *National Religion and the Prayer Book Controversy*.
90 John Maiden and Peter Webster, 'Parliament, the Church of England and the Last Gasp of Political Protestantism, 1963–4', *Parliamentary History* vol. 32 (2013), 361–77.

in the British Conservative government, spoke of the 'great right of private judgement which is inseparable from the open Bible, upon which the character of the British nation has been built'.[91] As in the United States, there were serious concerns for Protestants abroad, with the evangelical press continuing to report difficulties faced in countries such as Mexico and Spain, and organizations lobbying the British government. On both sides of the Atlantic, conversion and reconversion narratives, and critiques of Rome, by ex-Catholics continued to be published. Just as French-Canadian 'ex-priest' Father Chiniquy had condemned Rome from the 1860s, so former Catholics such as J. W. Poynter, in Britain, and Bryant Gray Harman, in the United States, continued in this tradition.[92]

While there were earlier signs of change, it was in the 1960s that concurrent developments opened up new possibilities for more constructive evangelical–Catholic relations. Pope John XXIII's decision to convene the Second Vatican Council (1962–1965) had major ramifications for Protestant–Catholic relations. Further research is still needed on evangelical responses. Certainly there seems to have been a perception that the Catholic hierarchy's changing attitudes towards the Bible might result in the renewal of individual Catholics; however, in the United States, evangelical comment on the Council often reinforced existing anti-Catholic assumptions. Many concluded that traditional 'heresies' remained in place and that Rome intended to gain control of Christendom through a world Church.[93] In Britain, Reformed evangelicals emphasized Rome's changelessness and cautioned that it might have a dangerous influence on the World Council of Churches. The eminent preacher Martyn Lloyd-Jones warned against the dangers of a global Church, publishing a sermon in 1966 which described Roman Catholicism as 'the devil's greatest masterpiece'. 'I would not hesitate with the Reformers of the sixteenth century to describe it as "apostasy"', he argued.[94]

However, while Vatican II hardly instantly transformed evangelical–Catholic relations, many leaders did look again at Rome. In *Revolution in Rome* (1973), American David F. Wells suggested Vatican II 'placed on Protestants an obligation to revise their thinking about Rome'. It was necessary to understand the heterogeneity of global Catholicism, and to engage seriously – and Christianly – with contemporary theological developments.[95] In 1989, one scholarly evangelical assessment likened the significance of Vatican II to *Perestroika* under Gorbachev – genuine change was underway, but there should not be naïve over-optimism.[96] Various formal ecumenical initiatives occurred. The earliest, from 1972, was the Pentecostal–Roman Catholic International Dialogue, where the agenda was to identify areas of convergence and commonality.[97] Then, between 1977 and 1984, the Evangelical–Roman Catholic Dialogue on Mission (ERCDOM), an initiative involving Lausanne evangelicals, including John Stott,

---

91 *The Reformation: It's Message for Today* (London: World Evangelical Alliance, 1924), p. 10.
92 Bryant Gray Harman, *To Rome and Back* (London: Protestant Truth Society, n.d.); J. W. Poynter, *Roman Catholic Propaganda* (London: Protestant Truth Society, n.d.).
93 Neil J. Young, '"A Saga of Sacrilege": Evangelicals Respond to the Second Vatican Council', in *American Evangelicals and the 1960s*, edited by Axel R. Shäfer (Madison, WI: University of Wisconsin Press, 2013), pp. 255–80.
94 D. M. Lloyd-Jones, *Roman Catholicism* (London: Evangelical Press, 1966), p. 2. See further, John Maiden, 'Martyn Lloyd-Jones and Roman Catholicism', in *Engaging with Martyn Lloyd-Jones: The Life and Legacy of 'the Doctor'*, edited by Andrew Atherstone and David Ceri Jones (Nottingham: Apollos, 2011), pp. 232–60.
95 David F. Wells, *Revolution in Rome* (London: Tyndale, 1973), p. 101.
96 Tony Lane, 'Evangelicals and Roman Catholicism', *Evangelical Quarterly* vol. 61 (1989), 351.
97 Cecil M. Robeck Jr., 'The Achievements of the Pentecostal–Catholic International Dialogue', in *Celebrating a Century of Ecumenism: Exploring the Achievements of International Dialogue*, edited by John A. Radno (Grand Rapids, MI: Eerdmans, 2012), pp. 163–94.

and participants selected by the Vatican Secretariat for Promoting Christian Unity, began to explore possibilities of greater engagement. The report of the conversations concluded that there existed a spectrum amongst evangelicals and Catholics: 'At one end . . . are those who can contemplate no co-operation of any kind. At the other are those who desire a very full co-operation. In between are many who still find some forms of common witness conscientiously impossible, while they find others to be the natural, positive expression of common concern and conviction'.[98] Some rhetoric during this period was ground-breaking. In England, the statement of the second National Evangelical Anglican Congress (1977) included the words, 'Seeing ourselves and Roman Catholics as fellow-Christians, we repent of attitudes that have seemed to deny it'.[99] Divisions became apparent between evangelicals over whether Rome was a true (if still doctrinally misguided) Church and the extent to which Roman Catholics should be evangelized.[100] The assumption remained that in many national contexts large numbers of nominal Roman Catholics needed conversion, and there was disagreement over the validity of the baptism of converts from Roman Catholicism.[101] However, increasingly on both sides, there was an attempt to distinguish between evangelism and proselytization and greater sensitivity to the damage caused by what ERCDOM described as 'unworthy witness': the 'unjust or uncharitable reference to the beliefs or practices of other religious communities in the hope of winning adherents'.[102]

A vital context of post-Vatican II evangelical attitudes was charismatic renewal.[103] Protestant 'neo-Pentecostalism' emerged from the 1950s and the Catholic renewal movement expanded rapidly from 1967. Ecumenical unity was a key feature of the diffuse charismatic movement, and evident both in interdenominational grassroots prayer meetings and larger charismatic conferences. In the words of Kevin Ranaghan, a prominent lay Catholic charismatic renewal leader in the United States, in 1971: 'Walls of separation long dividing people equally loved by Christ and truly dedicated to Him are beginning now, by the action of the Spirit, to crumble; fear, suspicion, ignorance, and hatred, are being dissipated in this vigorous and refreshing breeze'.[104] In Britain, alongside Anglicans it was Roman Catholics who provided most speakers at the Fountain Trust charismatic conferences.[105] One attender at the 1971 Fountain Trust event in Guildford Cathedral described occupying a pew on which sat 'a Roman Catholic layman with a rosary in hand, a Christian Brethren brother with a large Bible and an American lady who clasped the hand of the Anglican at her side as an expression of oneness in the Spirit'.[106] The charismatic 'new ecumenism' was seen as a 'reflection of the totality of the Spirit's impact across

---

98 Basil Meeking and John Stott, 'The Evangelical–Roman Catholic Dialogue on Mission, 1977–1984: A Report', *International Bulletin of Missionary Research* vol. 10 (1986), 20.
99 *The Nottingham Statement: The Official Statement of the Second National Evangelical Anglican Congress held in April 1977* (London: CPAS, 1977), p. 44.
100 Lane, 'Evangelicals and Roman Catholicism', 361–3.
101 *Christian Witness to Nominal Christians Among Roman Catholics*, The Thailand Report on Roman Catholics (Wheaton, IL: Lausanne Committee for World Evangelization, 1980), p. 7.
102 Meeking and Stott, 'The Evangelical–Roman Catholic Dialogue', 20.
103 Joshua R. Ziefle, *David du Plessis and the Assemblies of God: the Struggle for the Soul of the Movement* (Leiden: Brill: 2012), pp. 119–23; Connie Ho Yan Au, *Grassroots Unity in the Charismatic Renewal* (Eugene, OR: Wipf and Stock, 2011), pp. 44–5.
104 Kevin Ranaghan, 'Catholics and Pentecostals Meet in the Spirit', *Logos Journal* (November–December 1971), 20.
105 Au, *Grassroots Unity in the Charismatic Renewal*, p. 114.
106 Harry Sutton, 'The Charismatic Movement and the Universal Church', in *Agreement in the Faith: Talks between Anglicans and Roman Catholics: The Oxford Conference* (1975), p. 93.

the church's spectrum'.[107] Even as sectarian conflict flared again in Northern Ireland, some charismatics had hopes for the possibilities of reconciliation by the Spirit, with the charismatic press often reporting attempts to bridge the religious divide.[108] Anglican Cecil Kerr, of the Christian Renewal Centre in Northern Ireland, was one prominent activist for reconciliation, and described in 1975 'the Holy Spirit doing something which I would never have believed possible'.[109] The impact and significance of charismatic initiatives for reconciliation during the 'Troubles' requires further research and must be seen in a wider context where evangelicalism had potential to contribute to both conflict and reconciliation.[110]

Other sections of evangelicalism were resilient in opposing Rome. The widely-read cartoon tracts of Jack Chick continued to disseminate older Protestant criticisms.[111] In Reformed circles, in particular, intellectual critiques of Catholicism abounded. For example, Loraine Boettner's influential *Roman Catholicism* (1962) contended that 'interpretation of the Scriptures is so erroneous and its principles are so persistently unchristian that over the long period of time its influence for good is outweighed by its influence for evil. *It must, therefore, as a system, be judged to be a false church*'.[112] The instinct of many Pentecostals was to resist closer bonds. 'I rather suspect', warned one letter in the British charismatic *Renewal* magazine in 1974, 'that the charismatic renewal will eventually be used as a means to bring back the lost sheep to the fold of the infallible Church of Rome'.[113]

However, within wider evangelicalism there were various signs of partnership based on shared creedal and ethical orthodoxies. In Britain in the 1970s, the Nationwide Festival of Light brought together evangelical and Catholic morality campaigners against the permissive society, although it drew on the traditional Protestant imagery of the Spanish Armada to symbolize the invasion of Danish pornography![114] After *Roe v. Wade* American evangelicals increasingly allied with Catholics over abortion, while many British evangelicals admired the political efforts of the Catholic parliamentarian David Alton.[115] In Liverpool, David Sheppard and Derek Worlock, respectively the Anglican and Catholic bishops of the historically sectarian city, worked to promote the 'common good', for example following the upheaval of the Toxteth riots of 1981.[116] In the United States and Britain, and then from the 1990s in Eastern Europe and Latin America, Charles Colson's Prison Christian Fellowship was active in promoting ecumenical co-operation.[117] Furthermore, by the end of the twentieth century, the line between

---

107 Sutton, 'The Charismatic Movement and the Universal Church', p. 94.
108 See, for example, Barbara O'Reilly, 'Logos Report 2: Ireland', *Logos Journal* (January-February 1976), 55–8.
109 Cecil Kerr, 'The Charismatic Movement and the Universal Church', in *Agreement in the Faith*, pp. 101–3.
110 See, for example, Gladys Ganiel, *Evangelicalism and Conflict in Northern Ireland* (Basingstoke: Palgrave, 2008).
111 M. I. Borer and Adam Murphree, 'Jack Chick's Anti-Catholic Cartoons and the Flexible Boundaries of the Culture Wars', *Religion and American Culture: A Journal of Interpretation* vol. 18 (2008), 95–112.
112 Loraine Boettner, *Roman Catholicism* (Philadelphia, PA: Presbyterian and Reformed, 1962), p. 459.
113 Letter from Peter Krusi, *Renewal* no. 49 (February/March 1974), 9.
114 Matthew Grimley, 'Anglican Evangelicals and Anti-Permissiveness: The Nationwide Festival of Light, 1971–1983' in *Evangelicals and the Church of England in the Twentieth Century: Reform, Resistance and Renewal*, edited by Andrew Atherstone and John Maiden (Woodbridge: Boydell, 2014), pp. 183–205.
115 Lane, 'Evangelicals and Roman Catholicism', 364.
116 Maria Power, 'Reconciling State and Society? The Practice of the Common Good in the Partnership of Bishop David Sheppard and Archbishop Derek Worlock', *Journal of Religious History* vol. 40 (December 2016), 545–64.
117 Kendrick Oliver, 'The Origin and Development of Prison Fellowship International: Pluralism,

evangelicals and Catholics was increasingly blurred. American political scientists began to speak of 'evangelical orientated Catholics', while scholars of religion noticed the existence of 'catho-evangelicals'.[118] Conversion across denominational lines continued and the apparent increase in evangelicals joining the Catholic Church, including some well-known evangelical scholars, became a subject of interest, even if conversions now appeared less controversial.[119]

Conclusion

Christian Smith writes: 'Viewed in historical context, one can go to virtually any point in American evangelical history – but particularly beginning with the latter third of the nineteenth century – and readily detect in its elite discourse a sense of crisis, conflict, or threat'.[120] A similar argument might be made for evangelicalism in other national contexts. The most consistent evangelical concern was Roman Catholicism. This chapter has laid out a broad pattern, as follows. During the eighteenth century, evangelical attitudes towards Rome were largely a reflection of the wider and predominant attitudes of Protestant culture. In the mid-nineteenth century, however, evangelical attitudes hardened, and sharpened the theological edge of broader attitudes towards Rome. The anti-Catholic attitudes of evangelicals were increasingly more marked than in broader Anglophone culture. During the early twentieth century, while the perceived threats of theological liberalism and atheistic Communism watered-down the potency of evangelical anti-Catholicism, it nevertheless remained a key feature of the evangelical mindset, often appearing anachronistic as traditional antagonisms continued to wane. However, while Vatican II received an ambivalent response from evangelicals, the Council, the influence of charismatic renewal, and a growing sense of commonality in the face of 'cultural' threats resulted in a shift towards mutual recognition and co-operation. Perhaps the most telling evidence of this was the emergence of Evangelicals and Catholics Together (ECT), a significant *ad hoc* ecumenical project, described in a *Christianity Today* editorial as an 'Ecumenism of the trenches' in response to cultural changes which appeared unfriendly to traditional Christianity.[121] *Evangelicals and Catholics Together: The Christian Mission in the Third Millennium* (1994) unambiguously asserted that evangelicals and Catholics were 'brothers and sisters in Christ' united around the Apostles' Creed, argued that dialogue over areas of doctrinal disagreement was desirable, and recognized a pattern of co-operation on moral and economic matters.[122] ECT was an important sign of a trajectory of improving evangelical–Catholic relations during the second half of the twentieth century.

Although the geographical focus of this chapter has been the English-speaking and largely North Atlantic world, the shift in the centre of gravity of Christianity towards the Global South

---

Ecumenism and American Leadership in the Evangelical World, 1974–2006', *Journal of American Studies* vol. 51 (2017), 1221-42.

118 Andrew S. Grenville, 'The Awakened and Spirit-Moved: The Religious Experience of Canadian Evangelicals in the 1990s', in *Aspects of Canadian Evangelical Experience*, edited by G. A. Rawlyk (Toronto: McGill-Queen's University Press, 1997), pp. 417–31.

119 See, for example, *Path to Rome: Modern Journeys to the Catholic Church*, edited by Dwight Longenecker (Leominster: Gracewing, 2010); *Evangelical Exodus: Evangelical Seminarians and Their Paths to Rome*, edited by Douglas M. Beaumont (San Francisco: Ignatius Press, 2016).

120 Christian Smith, *American Evangelicalism: Embattled and Thriving* (Chicago, IL: University of Chicago Press, 1998), p. 122.

121 Timothy George, 'Catholics and Evangelicals in the Trenches', *Christianity Today*, 16 May 1994, 16.

122 'Evangelicals and Catholics Together: The Christian Mission in the Third Millennium', *First Things* (May 1994), 15–22. See also *Evangelicals and Catholics Together: Toward a Common Mission*, edited by Charles Colson and Richard John Neuhaus (London: Hodder and Stoughton, 1996).

has magnified the significance of evangelical–Catholic relations beyond Britain and North America. In different Global South contexts relations between the two groups have varied considerably, but the broader trajectory described above has not always been apparent. In some situations the absence of historic Protestant–Catholic conflict may have meant less division. The report on ERCDOM recognized that in parts of the 'Third World', the 'divisions which originated in Europe are felt with less intensity, and mutual trust has grown through united prayer and study of the Word of God'.[123] However, in Latin America, although there was some ecumenical co-operation in Chile for example, twentieth-century evangelical–Catholic relations were often marked by hostility.[124] Future research should contribute towards understanding of historical relations between evangelicalism and Catholicism in the Global South.

In the Anglophone world, while the broader pattern described above is useful, it should not obscure the existence of significant tensions and complexities within evangelicalism. The movement has been divided as well as united by its anti-Romanism. There have been tensions over the desirability of political Protestantism, and whether oppositional or 'positive' Protestantism was the most effective strategy. Throughout the history of evangelicalism there have been internal questions concerning the status of individual Catholics, Catholic congregations and the Roman Catholic Church itself. William Shea's important longitudinal study draws out two historic intellectual traditions among American evangelicals: one which regards the Catholic Church as heretical, the other as apostate.[125] These traditions have not held equal weight – the latter has been dominant – but, latently at least, the potentialities for constructive interchange pre-existed the 1960s. Furthermore, there have been some long-term ambiguities in evangelical attitudes. Various cases in this chapter suggest that while polemic and hostility has tended to run near the surface of evangelical–Catholic relations, there also exists a deeper level of affinity. Evangelicals have sometimes admired the piety or missionary zeal of Catholicism, or the aesthetics and materialities of sacramental worship; or recognized common ground in supernaturalism, or on moral and ethical matters. Despite the historic animosity in evangelical–Catholic relations, the two traditions have not been as diametrically opposed as at first meets the eye.

---

123 Meeking and Stott, 'The Evangelical–Roman Catholic Dialogue', 20.
124 Todd Hartch, *The Rebirth of Latin American Christianity* (New York: Oxford University Press, 2014), pp. 216–22.
125 Shea asserts: 'The issue – that is, is the Roman Catholic Church an apostate church and so not a Christian church, or it is, like the mainline Protestant churches, an heretical church – is old and is not nearly settled for evangelicals'. Shea, *The Lion and the Lamb*, p. 158.

7
EVANGELICALS AND EASTERN CHRISTIANITY

Tim Grass

It is often thought that the Western Protestants who have had most engagement with Eastern Christianity have been those holding high-church views; certainly that perspective has been dominant in ecumenical dialogue. However, this chapter offers evidence of substantial interaction between Eastern Christianity and another Western tradition, evangelicalism. It will outline and illustrate four main patterns which that engagement has taken, characterized as curiosity, assistance, confrontation, and dialogue and co-operation. They will be treated in order of their appearance in history, but all are apparent today in an engagement which is bewilderingly varied in its manifestations.

The ancient Eastern Christian churches comprise several distinct families. There are the Eastern Orthodox, who accepted the Chalcedonian definition of 451; the Oriental Orthodox, who did not accept Chalcedon but did accept the decrees of the first three ecumenical councils; and the Assyrians or Church of the East (formerly labelled Nestorians), who accepted only the decrees of the first two ecumenical councils. Most evangelical encounter with these churches has occurred in two regions, Orthodox Europe and the Middle East, and north and east Africa. More recently, the two traditions have encountered one another in the West, where (by contrast with the other regions) evangelicalism is usually the more established tradition and Orthodoxy is perceived as a newcomer.

Given that during the period of evangelicalism's existence most of the Eastern churches have lived under Muslim or Communist rule and so have been inhibited in their external witness, it is unsurprising that the initiative in constructive contacts between the two traditions has almost always been taken by Western evangelicals. Only now, and only in parts of the West, is that changing to any significant degree. This means that the Eastern churches have often seen themselves as being on the defensive against attempts to bring them under foreign domination or to draw away their members, or else as the recipients of external help in areas such as education, Bible translation and publication, social work and diplomatic advocacy. Yet their self-understanding as the church(es) of the Early Fathers and the ecumenical councils has, when given full play in their thinking about inter-Christian relations, made it impossible for them to regard Protestant churches as equal partners.

A complicating factor has been Roman Catholic missionary activity. Since the late medieval period, a key missionary objective had been to bring Eastern churches under Roman jurisdiction, usually allowing them to keep their Eastern liturgy. In several cases, these churches split, part remaining outside Roman authority, and part – the so-called 'Uniate' Churches – entering into communion with Rome. These should not be confused with Western-rite Catholics, and they often see themselves as Orthodox, in spite of their allegiance to Rome, but space precludes their discussion here. This history has sometimes made leaders of Eastern churches wary lest Protestant missionaries should likewise be seeking to bring them under a foreign jurisdiction; it has allowed Protestants and Orthodox to regard each other either as potential allies against Rome (as in the earliest contact) or as potential collaborators with it (where Protestants and Roman Catholics have shared minority status in Orthodox areas, the game may be somewhat different). In addition, during the 1830s and 1840s, evangelical mission stimulated increased Catholic activity in parts of the Middle East.[1] It should not be forgotten, either, that Western evangelicals have often interpreted Orthodoxy in terms of what they know of Catholicism, sometimes even asserting that there was 'no essential difference' between the two.[2] A more nuanced approach evident in the first half of the nineteenth century sometimes contrasted Orthodoxy favourably with Roman Catholicism on account of its approval of Bible circulation, an attitude which, missionaries hoped, could be drawn on for internal reform. In both cases, Roman Catholicism (as perceived by evangelicals) set the agenda, making it more difficult for evangelicals to understand Eastern Christianity on its own terms.

Curiosity

Before any kind of approach to Eastern Christianity could be formulated by Westerners, there had to be a measure of intellectual curiosity. During the immediate post-Reformation era, the Eastern presence in the West and the Western presence in the East tended to be restricted to diplomats and traders, who as expatriates enjoyed special provision for their worship needs. This rarely extended to wider interest in the religious scene of their host country.

There is more evidence of interest in Eastern Christianity on the part of German-speaking pietism. A. H. Francke (1663–1727) founded an Oriental Institute at Halle for the study of Eastern languages and the translation of pietist writings. John Wesley (1703–1791), whose life was changed by his contacts with pietism, is cited as an example of evangelical interest in Eastern theology; but Wesley appears to have read relatively little of the Greek Fathers, taking the texts he published from a volume of selections edited by a high Anglican, William Wake. Wesley edited these texts, removing most of their distinctive Eastern ideas, to make them fit the theology he wished his preachers to hold. Arguably, any reflection of patristic thought in his writings or his brother Charles' hymns was drawing on ideas generally current in the contemporary Church of England.[3]

We must look to the early nineteenth century, and the flourishing of Western Protestant mission, for evidence of evangelical interest in Eastern Christianity. This was an age of exploration, when learned societies and others sponsored expeditions to far-flung parts of the world. Discoveries made and contacts established were mediated to the public through published travelogues, a distinctive sub-group of these being what were sometimes entitled 'Christian

---

1 Heleen Murre-van den Berg, 'The Middle East: Western Missions and the Eastern Churches, Islam and Judaism', in *Cambridge History of Christianity, vol.8: World Christianities, c.1815–c.1914*, edited by Sheridan Gilley and Brian Stanley (Cambridge: Cambridge University Press, 2006), p. 461.
2 *Proceedings of the Church Missionary Society* vol. 50 (1849), lxxvi.
3 See Richard P. Heitzenrater, 'John Wesley's Reading of and References to the Early Church Fathers', in *Orthodox and Wesleyan Spirituality*, edited by S. T. Kimbrough Jr. (Crestwood, NY: St Vladimir's Seminary Press, 2002), pp. 25–32.

researches'.[4] These fed burgeoning Western interest in aspects of Eastern culture and language, an interest reflected in the growth of the academic outlook then known as Orientalism.[5] However, overlapping the academic interest, which was often motivated at least partially by missionary concern, was an approach which portrayed the East as degenerate, lax and corrupt, and as contrasting with the brisk commercial and political efficiency and evangelical uprightness of the West. The West, all too often, looked down on the East, or at least saw it as an object of pity, and this extended to Western attitudes towards Eastern Christianity. (There was some justification for this in the state of Eastern churches under Ottoman rule: for example, ecclesiastical offices were often sold to the highest bidders, who recouped the purchase price from those beneath them.) Such attitudes were reinforced where evangelicals belonged to Western nations seeking to make their presence felt politically in the region; resentment, often hidden, was one reaction of local Christians.

Following from these two factors, and slightly later in time, curiosity helped stimulate the growth of evangelical pilgrimage to the Holy Land: this was facilitated by the development of transport links and popular because of its perceived apologetic value, not only in bringing the Bible to life but also in confirming faith at a time when the evidences for Christianity were being questioned. However, this served only to confirm evangelicals in a negative estimate of Eastern Christianity. Protestant sensibilities rejected the ritualized worship, most notably the Holy Fire ceremony at Easter in Jerusalem, and were horrified at the infighting between different jurisdictions. Protestant and Orthodox pilgrims to the Holy Land were looking for two different things: one tradition sought to step inside the world of the Bible that its message might become more real to them, while the other honoured the holy sites as locations where God had manifested himself among human beings.[6] Evangelicals tended to look at nineteenth-century Palestine through Western eyes; they saw it as backward, poor and underdeveloped, due to its rejection of God's grace. Only when the inhabitants turned to a pure form of Christianity would divine judgment be reversed, and economic and political reform become possible.[7]

We can trace this curiosity about Eastern Christianity down to the present, but with a significant intermission. The twentieth century was a century of two parts. In the first, we have the post-revolutionary flight of many Russian intellectuals to the West; given the theological renaissance in those circles, especially in Paris, it would have been a propitious time for Western evangelicals to develop an interest in Orthodox theology, but the theological weakness and introversion evident in the Fundamentalist controversy of the 1920s meant that they rarely did so. As late as 1980, the Lausanne Movement could state of Protestant missionaries then working in Eastern Europe: 'there is hardly anyone well enough versed in Orthodox theology to make a meaningful approach possible'.[8]

But during recent decades, evangelical fascination with Eastern Christianity has grown significantly. Evangelical interest in patristic theology has deepened as part of a process of

---

4 Gareth Atkins, 'William Jowett's *Christian Researches*: British Protestants and Religious Plurality in the Mediterranean, Syria and the Holy Land, 1815–30', in *Christianity and Religious Plurality*, edited by Charlotte Methuen, Andrew Spicer and John Wolffe (Woodbridge: Boydell and Brewer, 2015), pp. 216–31.
5 See Nile Green, 'Parnassus of the Evangelical Empire: Orientalism and the English Universities, 1800–50', *Journal of Imperial and Commonwealth History* vol. 40 (2012), 337–55.
6 Ruth and Thomas Hummel, *Patterns of the Sacred: English Protestant and Russian Orthodox Pilgrims in the Nineteenth Century* (London: Scorpion Cavendish, 1995).
7 Hummel, *Patterns of the Sacred*, pp. 35, 37.
8 'Christian Witness to Nominal Christians among the Orthodox', Lausanne Occasional Paper 19 (1980), §3a.

paradigm shift in evangelical self-understanding. Eastern evangelicals, too, have developed significant interest in Orthodox theology: in particular, Romanian scholarship has secured (possibly grudging) respect and facilitated a limited measure of dialogue. More recently, this interest has broadened to include Orthodox missiology, as evangelicals have engaged in sustained missiological reflection. We may also note the ongoing evangelical / Pentecostal / charismatic quest for the authentic New Testament church: the evangelical Anglican convert to Orthodoxy, Fr Michael Harper (1930–2009), for example, regarded Orthodoxy as the logical conclusion of such a quest.[9]

Furthermore, from the 1960s, there was widespread interest in the plight of Christians under Communism. The sufferings of Eastern Christians, evangelicals and Orthodox alike, were reported by agencies such as Keston College, and some Western evangelicals rejoiced that the Spirit of Christ was at work in believers whose ways of worship (and distinctive doctrines) they would have written off. On the other hand, many found evidence to convince them that institutional Orthodoxy in Communist countries was fatally compromised by its negotiations with the state, confirming some in the belief that Orthodox were not truly Christian (there was similar suspicion of evangelicals deemed to have compromised with the authorities, such as the registered Baptists in Russia).

Finally, from the late 1980s evangelicals became aware of a trickle of departures from their ranks to Orthodoxy.[10] The primary significance of these lies in the awareness of Orthodoxy as a religious option which they have generated. Their critique of the weaknesses of para-church evangelicalism has not led to any change in the movement's ethos, but the ingestion of numbers of converts, many highly educated and evangelistically passionate, seems to have shaped the adaptation of Orthodoxy in the United States to a religiously plural environment.

We should not, however, overstate the level or extent of evangelical interest in Eastern Christianity. British church members have little awareness of Eastern Christianity (apart from perhaps supporting a local evangelical charitable work in an Orthodox country) or the presence of Eastern Christians in the West, although things may be somewhat different in America. There had been little evangelical response to Orthodox immigration, partly because Orthodox were not perceived as a threat, unlike Catholics, since they occupied a different place in nineteenth-century evangelical eschatological systems. Post-1945 immigration has been more significant numerically in Britain, especially with the accession of East European nations to the European Union, but as yet there is little substantive engagement with Orthodox communities; what evangelical ministry there is focuses more on winning people from Orthodoxy rather than constructively engaging with it.

Assistance

Pietist missionary zeal helped to give Western Protestants a concern for the fortunes of the whole Christian world. Pietists looked for positive interaction with Eastern Christianity, enabled by their focus on shared experience of Christ and downplaying of doctrinal issues. Francke and others hoped to come alongside Eastern Christians and contribute to the renewal of Eastern Christianity. Apart from the Halle Institution, Francke founded a Greek seminary in the city to provide training for Orthodox priests. And pietist outreach was not without fruit: in Russia, St

---

9 Michael Harper, *The True Light* (London: Hodder and Stoughton, 1997).
10 D. Oliver Herbel, *Turning to Tradition: Converts and the Making of an American Orthodox Church* (New York: Oxford University Press, 2014).

Tikhon of Zadonsk (1724–1783) was influenced by the works of the proto-pietist Johann Arndt (1555–1626), especially his *True Christianity*.[11]

But the real impetus to this approach was provided by post-millennialist eschatology. This gave many evangelicals the hope of an end-time ingathering, and the nascent missionary movement appeared to be taking the first steps towards it. At the end of the eighteenth century, the millennium seemed just around the corner. With the French Revolution and the rise to power of Napoleon, one Antichrist – the papacy – was tottering; the other – Islam – was seen as likely to fall soon afterwards, given the weakness of the contemporary Ottoman Empire. Missionaries could then expect a mighty harvest of souls, notably among Jews, whose ingathering was seen as precipitating a global turn to Christ, and Muslims. In this context the first evangelical missionary societies came into being. The two main Anglophone societies which began work in Orthodox areas were the Anglican Church Missionary Society (CMS; from 1815), whose workers were drawn mainly from England and Germany, and the Presbyterian and Congregationalist American Board of Commissioners for Foreign Missions (ABCFM; from 1819).

An initial objective of the ABCFM mission to the Levant was that of reaching Jewish people.[12] They and their land were seen as holding a key place in God's eschatological purposes. The establishment of the joint British-Prussian Jerusalem bishopric in 1841 demonstrates the strategic spiritual value which that city was deemed to possess, not just in terms of reaching Jews or Eastern Christians but also of reaching Muslims.

The call to take the gospel to Muslims proved to be highly significant in terms of the way it shaped mission strategy. To reach captive souls in Muslim lands, it was thought that the ancient churches of those lands would be the best agents. But (it was argued) they were corrupt, sunk in despair and lassitude as the result of centuries of Muslim domination. Their condition was seen as the result of divine judgment through Islam on account of their fall into error and corruption, an argument with a pedigree almost as old as Islam itself. Before they could reach anybody, therefore, they would need to be renewed. Such renewal, it was believed, must take place along evangelical lines. Unlike Roman Catholicism, the Eastern churches were thought to 'possess within themselves the principle and the means of reformation'.[13] William Jowett was therefore sent in 1815 to gather information, to explore possibilities for translating and distributing the Scriptures, and to influence the Eastern churches by whatever means possible.[14] At this stage, there were hopes not only that these churches would turn out to be remnants of an early and purer form of Christianity, but also that they might have preserved early biblical manuscripts.

The importance accorded to Bible translation and circulation meant that the British and Foreign Bible Society (founded in 1804) and its local counterparts became central to evangelical engagement with Eastern Christianity. It gave rise to a host of similar societies in various parts of Europe and the Near East. Fundamental to the strategy of these groups was the belief that circulation of vernacular Scriptures would itself lead to spiritual renewal; this was an expression of the Reformation-era conviction that faith comes by hearing, and hearing by the Word of God (Romans 10: 17). (Orthodox missionary strategy, too, had historically stressed vernacular

---

11 Ted A. Campbell, *The Religion of the Heart: A Study of European Religious Life in the Seventeenth and Eighteenth Centuries* (Columbia, SC: University of South Carolina Press, 1991), pp. 133–4.
12 Clifton J. Phillips, *Protestant America and the Pagan World: The First Half Century of the American Board of Commissioners for Foreign Missions, 1810–1860* (Cambridge, MA: Harvard University East Asian Research Center, 1969), p. 135.
13 Eugene Stock, *The History of the Church Missionary Society: Its Environment, its Men and its Work* (3 vols, London: Church Missionary Society, 1899), I: 226–7, citing *Missionary Register* vol. 17 (1829), 407.
14 Stock, *History of the Church Missionary Society*, I: 222–4.

translation of the Scriptures.)[15] The CMS established a bridgehead in Malta in 1815 which developed as a primary purpose the printing and distribution of Bibles and Scripture portions in various East European and Near Eastern languages. Some co-operation did take place with Churches and with local Bible societies, the best known being that founded in Russia in 1812 but closed down in 1826.[16] Similarly, translation of liturgical texts (also a key component of historic Orthodox mission strategy) was given priority, although it was an outgrowth of a sense of the superiority of evangelicalism to other forms of Christianity, rather than the superiority of Christianity to other forms of religion. Thus, the Book of Common Prayer was translated into various languages.[17]

Several further examples of this type of engagement are worth giving, because of the dominance for some time of this approach. The first is provided by Claudius Buchanan (1766–1815) and the CMS in India. In 1806 Buchanan visited the Syrian Orthodox in the Travancore region, and reported positively on their relative freedom from error. He even advocated a full union between the Syrian Orthodox Church and the Church of England, which would strengthen both parties to resist Roman activity, although he later admitted its impracticability.[18] In 1811 the CMS pictured the Syrian Orthodox as a communion for which sympathy should be felt due to its oppression by Rome:

> they have maintained a regular Episcopal Succession from the earliest ages, and in all important points accord with the faith of the Primitive Church; and have not departed into those errors, which have infected the Syrian Roman Catholics. . . . A few learned, prudent, and zealous clergymen would be received, as there is ground to hope, with open arms by this venerable Church. Their labours would tend, under the divine blessing, to revive and confirm the influence of the faith in that oppressed community; and might lead, ultimately, to a union between our Churches.[19]

Here were 'the Protestants of the East', a communion present in several countries which could be a source of missionaries to Muslims and pagans.[20] The Syrians were apprehensive that Protestants would try to subjugate their church, as the Catholics had done in 1599, but they were won over and the CMS set about educating children, training clergy, and translating the Bible into Malayalam. In 1818, a synod of the church instructed priests to conform their rites and doctrines to the teaching of the missionaries. However, the moral state of the clergy was low. Their educational level was no better, and from 1825 the church's leadership grew increasingly hostile. When Bishop Daniel Wilson insisted on its submission, memories were stirred of earlier Roman actions, and his demand was rejected. In 1836, relations were formally severed, and a CMS-supported church was set up, as well as the larger Mar Thoma Church, which wished to undertake reform independently of the missionaries but which was also forced to separate from the parent body.[21]

---

15 James J. Stamoolis, *Eastern Orthodox Mission Theology Today* (Maryknoll, NY: Orbis, 1986).
16 Stephen K. Batalden, *Russian Bible Wars: Modern Scriptural Translation and Cultural Authority* (Cambridge: Cambridge University Press, 2013), pp. 1–2.
17 *Missionary Register* vol. 8 (1820), 486; vol. 29 (1841), 333.
18 Hugh Pearson, *Memoirs of the Life and Writings of the Rev. Claudius Buchanan, D.D., late Vice-Provost of the College of Fort William in Bengal* (2 vols, Oxford: University Press, 1817), II: 328, 336, 453, 455.
19 *Proceedings of the Church Missionary Society* vol. 12 (1811–12), 413.
20 Pearson, *Claudius Buchanan*, II: 457.
21 Stock, *History of the Church Missionary Society*, I: 231–5; W. H. Taylor, *Antioch and Canterbury: The Syrian Orthodox Church and the Church of England, 1874–1928* (Piscataway, NJ: Gorgias Press, 2005),

Another example is the early work among Armenians and Nestorians of Turkey and North-West Persia. These churches were also presented in ways which resonated with Protestants – as being free of the perceived iconographic excesses of other Orthodox churches, and as needing to be strengthened and protected against the machinations of Roman missionaries. Moreover, whilst evangelicals disapproved of the non-Chalcedonian Christologies of these churches, their early separation from Rome and Byzantium had providentially preserved them from many other errors which later grew up in those communions. Armenians in particular were regarded as possessed of virtues which appealed to nineteenth-century industrialists and entrepreneurs: they were noble, hard-working, enterprising and present throughout the Middle Eastern world. This, and their church's relative freedom from impurity in doctrine and rite, marked them out as highly suitable disseminators of the gospel.[22] Furthermore, there was already a reform movement under way in the Armenian Apostolic Church, which welcomed the missionaries when they arrived in Constantinople.[23]

The Nestorians, rediscovered around 1830, were the ecclesiastical equivalent of the coelacanth, 'a living fossil, which it was necessary to study, to preserve and finally to convert'.[24] The ABCFM deemed it worth sending missionaries to them because of 'their extreme liberality towards other sects, their ideas of open communion, and their entire rejection of auricular confession'.[25] Justin Perkins of the ABCFM even suggested that Nestorius himself had been treated so harshly because he was 'far more evangelical than his opponents'. Their problem was 'spiritual death, rather than theological error'.[26] They were, however, in a situation of political weakness, and their openness to Western mission, whether Protestant or Catholic, was motivated in considerable measure by their need for political support. All the same, when Perkins arrived among them in 1834, his marching orders made it clear that his main objective was to enable their Church to play a part in reaching Asia, as it had done centuries before. Initially it appeared that efforts to stir the ancient Church to new life were being blessed.[27] But the failure of the missionaries to come to the aid of the Nestorians when they were attacked in the early 1840s, coupled with increasing opposition to aspects of Nestorian religious practice, along with what were perceived as high Anglican machinations, soured relations. Nevertheless, Perkins continued to oppose the creation of separate congregations, and by contrast with other ABCFM fields it was only after his final departure in 1869 that a separate Assyrian Protestant Church assumed formal existence.[28] Missionaries had been able to justify their strategy on the

---

pp. 5, 7–8; Robert Eric Frykenberg, *Christianity in India: From Beginnings to the Present* (Oxford: Oxford University Press, 2008), pp. 246–8.

22 Eli Smith and H. G. O. Dwight, *Missionary Researches in Armenia: Including a Journey through Asia Minor, and into Georgia and Persia, with a visit to the Nestorian and Chaldean Christians of Oormiah and Salmas* (London: George Wightman, 1834), advertisement; Samir Khalaf, *Protestant Missionaries in the Levant: Ungodly Puritans, 1820–60* (Abingdon: Routledge, 2012), p. 144.

23 Avedis Boynerian, 'The Importance of the Armenian Evangelical Churches for Christian Witness in the Middle East', *International Review of Mission* vol. 89 (2000), 76–7.

24 Christoph Baumer, *The Church of the East: An Illustrated History of Assyrian Christianity* (London: I. B. Tauris, 2008), p. 254.

25 Rufus Anderson, *History of the Missions of the American Board of Commissioners for Foreign Missions to the Oriental Churches* (2 vols, Boston, MA: Congregational Publishing Society, 1872), I: 86.

26 Justin Perkins, *A Residence of Eight Years in Persia, among the Nestorian Christians; with Notices of the Muhammedans* (Andover, MA: Allen, Morrill & Wardwell, 1843), pp. 3, 417.

27 Perkins, *A Residence of Eight Years in Persia*, p. 499.

28 Anderson, *History*, I: 216; Heleen Murre-van den Berg, 'Why Protestant Churches? The American Board and the Eastern Churches: Mission among "Nominal" Christians (1820–70)', in *Missions and Missionaries*, edited by Pieter Holtrop and Hugh McLeod (Woodbridge: Boydell and Brewer, 2000), pp. 108–9; Baumer, *Church of the East*, pp. 254–6.

basis that conversions were occurring and they were being allowed to preach in Nestorian churches.[29]

In Ethiopia (then known as Abyssinia), the CMS was active from 1829, seeing it as a bridgehead for reaching the heathen of Central Africa. The Ethiopian Orthodox Church was commended, in spite of its blemishes, for resisting the attacks of Romanism as well as Islam.[30] Here too the missionaries stressed the production and distribution of vernacular Scriptures as the main stimulus to church reform; one result was the formation in Eritrea from the 1860s of a renewal movement which was eventually forced to separate from Orthodoxy and developed into the Evangelical Church Mekane Yesus with assistance from Swedish Lutheran missionaries. The missionaries continued to uphold the principle of not proselytizing, as did later Anglican workers. By the 1920s, however, new missions were arriving on the scene which did not share this approach, and evangelical churches would see remarkable growth once missionaries were forced to withdraw in 1936.[31]

A significant aspect of this approach is education. The nineteenth century's growing confidence in all things Western, and the resulting cultural imperialism, was evident in the advocacy of Western-style education. This was a key plank of mission strategy in most of the fields under review. Some ABCFM institutions proved highly successful, such as the Syrian Protestant College, which developed into the American University of Beirut, and Robert College in Constantinople, both founded in 1863. Yet we may question whether the efforts devoted to education ever reaped much harvest in terms of converts to Christianity or reawakened Eastern Christians.

We see in this approach that Eastern Churches tended at first to welcome Western evangelicals coming alongside them, not least because the assistance proffered included education and medical care, and often came from powers deemed to have sufficient political and military clout to secure an improvement in the lot of Christians under Ottoman rule. All too often, however, it ran into problems and missionaries were forced to create separate churches for converts. Three main reasons may be given for their action: mission policy formulated from the home base, the need to provide for excommunicated converts, and the focus on providing a spiritual refuge for Muslims who were converted to Christ.

By the 1860s, this approach had begun to wane considerably in popularity. One problem was the conception of the relationship between spiritual renewal and institutional reform: the approach of seeking individual converts who would then be able to reform the ancient churches from within rested on a separation of soteriology from ecclesiology which was foreign to Eastern Christianity.[32] Even where the Scriptures circulated freely, that alone did not seem to be leading to any widespread rethinking of doctrine and practice, many missionaries concluded that it was impossible for the message of the gospel to be heard within those systems. Missionaries found themselves searching fruitlessly for individuals within the ancient churches of whose spiritual state they could be reasonably certain.

Another problem area was eschatology. There was a subtle shift in underlying outlook from eschatologically-inspired idealism to a more pragmatic focus on the need to create spiritual

---

29 Murre-van den Berg, 'Why Protestant Churches?', p. 112.
30 [Samuel Lee], 'A Brief History of the Church of Abyssinia', *Proceedings of the Church Missionary Society* vol. 18 (1817–18), 208.
31 Elizabeth Isichei, *A History of Christianity in Africa* (Grand Rapids, MI / Lawrenceville, NJ: Eerdmans / Africa World Press, 1995), p. 213; Tibebe Eshete, *The Evangelical Movement in Ethiopia: Resistance and Resilience* (Waco, TX: Baylor University Press, 2009), pp. 49–50.
32 Habib Badr, 'American Protestant Missionary Beginnings in Beirut and Istanbul: Policy, Politics, Practice and Response', *New Faith in Ancient Lands* vol. 32 (2006), 225.

homes for evangelical converts (and perhaps also to have something tangible to show to supporters at home). Expectation of Islam's eschatological decline was weakening, although the Western perception of it as terminally weak continued in a more secularized form. The eschatology of the new faith missions which proliferated from the 1860s was often pessimistic and pre-millennial, focusing on rescuing as many individuals as possible at the expense of longer-term objectives such as church reform and education. As propagated by the Brethren, who were active in many of the countries under review, this outlook saw 'Christendom' in whatever form as apostate and doomed, and urged the faithful to call awakened souls to leave religious 'Babylon' (Revelation 18: 4).

A third problem was that the Ottoman *millet* system made it very difficult for a Muslim to convert to Christianity, because it treated religion as intertwined with all aspects of society and daily life. Converts therefore tended to be from the Christian community, which provoked antagonism. In Turkey, for instance, after 1846 those converting to evangelical views and consequently excommunicated by the Armenian Church needed a separate church to be formed for them, but excommunication also entailed exclusion from the Armenian *millet* and hence brought civil as well as religious disadvantages. British officials therefore lobbied successfully for recognition of Protestantism as a *millet* in its own right.[33] In time, however, antagonism against evangelicals wore off and a measure of contact with the Armenian Church was resumed. Missionaries discouraged converts from seceding, and the original vision was partially fulfilled.[34]

Some still advocate coming alongside the ancient churches with a view to their being equipped to reach Muslims. A 1996 guide to Eastern Christianity produced for evangelical missionaries asked: 'If we are concerned that the non-Christians of these lands should hear the Good News of Christ, can we ignore the Ancient Churches? Do we expect God to bypass them all, and use only the witness of the small local evangelical minorities, and of foreigners?'[35] Other evangelicals advocate coming alongside spiritually alive Orthodox individuals as the best way of working towards the renewal of the Eastern churches. The Lausanne paper quoted earlier expressed the hope that individuals from both traditions would co-operate in outreach: 'we live with the expectation of seeing both Evangelicals and born-again Orthodox reaching nominal Christians in those nations with the Gospel'. It regarded what it saw as the born-again minority within Orthodoxy as a key group in reaching others: they needed help to grow and encouragement to witness so that 'the way may be prepared for a mighty Reformation and spiritual renewal within the Orthodox Church'.[36]

The accession of two thousand North American evangelicals to the Antiochian Orthodox Church in 1987 was arguably an instance of this pattern of engagement. For several decades, a number of Campus Crusade staff workers, led by Peter Gillquist, had been frustrated with the evangelical para-church mentality and had set out on a quest for the New Testament church. As they studied the Bible and the Fathers, they began to set up a new ecclesial structure, which in fact looked much like Orthodoxy. In time, they formed what became the Evangelical Orthodox Church, and the great majority of its membership was later received into canonical Orthodoxy.[37] They brought with them their entrepreneurial approach to evangelism and

33 Anderson, *History*, I: 424; Murre-van den Berg, 'Why Protestant Churches?', p. 105.
34 Kenneth Scott Latourette, *A History of the Expansion of Christianity, vol. 6: The Great Century in Northern Africa and Asia A.D.1800 – A.D.1914* (Exeter: Paternoster, 1971), p. 50.
35 Joyce Napper, *Christianity in the Middle East* (revised edition, Larnaca: Middle East Christian Outreach, 1996), pp. 5–6.
36 'Christian Witness to Nominal Christians among the Orthodox', §§4c(v), 4e(iii).
37 Herbel, *Turning to Tradition*, Chs 4–5.

church-planting – so they were coming alongside by joining an Eastern church, but with markedly Western, even American, notions concerning the lines along which renewal must take place. This gave rise to tensions, partly because whilst Orthodox missiology seeks to develop indigenous churches which are rooted in and sanctify the culture of the people, many Orthodox argued that the culture in question was a secularized Anglo-Saxon Protestant one.[38]

Divergent opinions have been expressed regarding the effectiveness of this approach. It has been argued that '[r]ather than strengthening the Christian presence in the Middle East, as had been their aim, missionaries contributed to the fragmentation, dispersion and even decimation through massacre of the Christian communities'.[39] But in the long run, there has been considerable renewal in parts of the Orthodox world, and observers have frequently argued that this has been due in part to Western input. More recent examples of renewal due to Western stimuli include the Lord's Army, a large renewal movement within Romanian Orthodoxy formed in the 1920s which has been influenced by evangelical thought and practice in several areas (such as the prominence of preaching), and the Coptic Orthodox Sunday School movement, which has played a key role since the 1940s in producing educated laity equipped to serve their church and wider Egyptian society.

Confrontation

Before too long, those who accepted the evangelical message began to experience persecution. Greece was to prove so barren a field that the ABCFM and CMS, along with the London Missionary Society, withdrew during the 1840s, asserting that the resurgence of xenophobic nationalism after independence had been achieved in 1821 made it impossible for foreigners, especially non-Orthodox, to secure a hearing. Russian Stundists (who had been influenced by German Mennonite migrants and whose initial development was within Orthodoxy) experienced opposition from the 1870s which was seen as instigated by the Orthodox. A related renewal movement among the St Petersburg aristocracy was suppressed by the state in 1884, as well as being forced to develop outside the Russian Orthodox Church.[40] Particularly under the procurator K. P. Pobedonostsev (in power 1871–1905), Orthodoxy worked with the state to repress evangelicalism in all forms. Elsewhere in Eastern Europe, E. H. Broadbent (1861–1945), an itinerant Brethren Bible teacher and mission strategist, recorded during 1935:

> The departure of the Greek Orthodox Church from the pure Word of God into tradition and superstition, by which it has for centuries held the masses of the people in ignorance – a Church which has always persecuted the people of God, those who have returned to the Scriptures and acted upon them, and which still continues to do this where it has the power, is one of the chief causes of the present infidelity. It is the swing of the pendulum.[41]

His colleague G. H. Lang (1874–1958) commented regarding 1940s Bulgaria: 'this is the Greek Orthodox Church in all places and all times when it has power'.[42] For Lang, as for many others,

---

38 Paisios Bukowsky Whitesides, 'Ethnics and Evangelicals: Theological Tensions within American Orthodox Christianity', *St Vladimir's Theological Quarterly* vol. 41 (1997), 28, 32.
39 Murre-van den Berg, 'Middle East', p. 470.
40 Edmund Heier, *Religious Schism in the Russian Aristocracy 1860–1900: Radstockism and Pashkovism* (The Hague: Martinus Nijhoff, 1970).
41 Manchester, John Rylands Library, Christian Brethren Archive, CBA 3067, E. H. Broadbent's diary, 1898–1937, fols 256–7.
42 G. H. Lang, *Edmund Hamer Broadbent: Saint and Pioneer* (London: Paternoster, 1949), p. 35.

the headship of Christ precluded fellowship with priestly religious systems, and rendered it necessary to urge believers to separate from them.[43] In every age, believers were a remnant, persecuted by the representatives of a 'Church' in which Christianity and Roman paganism were mingled.[44]

During the 1860s and 1870s, the Evangelical Alliance led the way in lobbying for religious liberty in Spain, Turkey, Russia and elsewhere, often on behalf of fellow evangelicals experiencing religious persecution, but by no means always: in 1861, it made representations on behalf of the 'Nestorians' in Persia.[45] Such activity was liable to bring evangelicalism into confrontation with Orthodoxy, especially in its Russian form, when Russian strategic military interests were in question. It was small wonder that some evangelicals initially welcomed the advent of Communist rule in Russia. All denominations were placed on an equal footing, and a brief window after 1917 allowed Baptists and others an unaccustomed measure of freedom to evangelize. This did not last, and evangelicals and Orthodox alike endured sometimes ferocious persecution and faced impossible decisions regarding co-operation with the authorities. With the collapse of Communist regimes, the religious liberty issue has returned in its pre-Communist form, for example in Belarus, and opposition owes something to Orthodox perception of evangelicals as American-inspired (and funded) sectarians.

Confrontation could also be provoked by Western religious disagreements. For instance, around 1850 the CMS found itself having to counter the charge of proselytism made by high Anglicans who were concerned to establish good diplomatic relations with the Eastern churches and hence to neutralize Roman overtures to them. Its defence was that its mission was to make available the Scriptures and win Easterners for Christ, even at the risk of their leaving the ancient communions.[46] Implicitly distancing the CMS from high-church thinking, one writer asserted that it was impossible to recognize the Eastern communions as like-minded churches on the basis of the possession of episcopal order, for that would imply that the differences between the two were non-essential; rather, 'they must be led to see that what they consider Christianity is not Christianity, and that what they regard as truth is not truth'. The missionary's aim was not to detach people from their church, but to preach the gospel; if that led to people separating, he was not to be held responsible.[47] Increasingly, the clear expectation was that it would.

The spread of this outlook gave rise to controversy at the World Missionary Conference in Edinburgh because Catholic and Orthodox countries were initially to be treated as 'unreached'; after intense debate, 'Edinburgh 1910 implicitly declared Protestant proselytism of Roman Catholics, and rather less clearly of Orthodox and Oriental Christians, to be no valid part of Christian mission.'[48] Yet this outlook has persisted, and was ironically repeated a century later at the Lausanne Movement's congress in Cape Town in 2010, where the expressed assumption that Orthodox counted as unreached peoples precipitated frank personal conversations between the few invited Orthodox observers and evangelical leaders, which resulted in the formation of the Lausanne-Orthodox Initiative (LOI).

Some of the confrontation has been rooted in an Orthodox perception of evangelicalism as something foreign, an 'invasive species' which if unchecked would threaten the life of the

---

43 Lang, *Edmund Hamer Broadbent*, p. 71.
44 Lang, *Edmund Hamer Broadbent*, pp. 88–9.
45 Ian Randall and David Hilborn, *One Body in Christ: The History and Significance of the Evangelical Alliance* (Carlisle: Paternoster, 2001), p. 98.
46 Stock, *The History of the Church Missionary Society*, II: 144–5.
47 'The Oriental Churches', *CMS Intelligencer* vol. 2 (1851), 171–7, 193–216, 219–39, at 194–5.
48 Brian Stanley, *The World Missionary Conference, Edinburgh 1910* (Grand Rapids, MI: Eerdmans, 2009), p. 72.

Orthodox churches.[49] Add to that the close identification of Orthodox allegiance and national identity, felt in Orthodox Europe and Ethiopia especially, and it is easy to see why evangelicalism could on occasion be seen as a threat to society and to national stability, and not merely to the Orthodox churches.

On the other hand, evangelical insensitivity when church-planting has contributed to confrontation. If coming alongside the ancient Churches was not going to work, and the missionary heart longed to see conversions to evangelical faith in Christ, then it was going to be necessary to provide converts with a spiritual home. It was a relatively small step from this to the conviction that separate congregations were not only necessary in practice, but also desirable in principle, because the ancient Churches were no place for anyone who came to a living Christian faith and wished to worship in a manner deemed scriptural.

A key thinker in the shift to a church-planting strategy by the ABCFM was its secretary, Rufus Anderson (1796–1880). The board had adopted a resolution in 1837 setting down the establishment of native churches as the primary object of its mission,[50] and by the mid-1840s he was arguing that work among Eastern Christians should be approached in the same way as work among the heathen, the objective in each case being the formation of indigenous churches with indigenous ministry.[51] At the end of his career, in 1872, he produced a history of the ABCFM's work among them, arguing that they were a legitimate object of mission. Those 'destitute of the knowledge of Christianity' (he was expounding the second article of the board's constitution) included Muslims and Jews, but also 'the Oriental Churches, as they were fifty years ago'. A key criterion for his assessment was the doctrine of justification: 'Of the doctrine of a justifying faith of the heart – the distinguishing doctrine of the Gospel – the people of the Oriental Churches are believed to have been wholly ignorant, before the arrival of Protestant missionaries among them.'[52] He now considered that even the Nestorian field, where missionaries had been late in forming separate churches, showed that 'the dead Church could not be galvanized into spiritual life. There was no way for the truly enlightened but to leave it, and form reunions on the Apostolic basis.'[53]

This church-planting approach was widely adopted. American Presbyterians aimed at the creation of a separate church from the beginning of their work in Egypt in 1854. This contrasted with the CMS, which aimed primarily at fostering the renewal of the Coptic Orthodox Church. Whilst a separate Anglican church came into being in 1921, the missionary Temple Gairdner (1873–1928) refused to seek converts from other Christian traditions (although they made up most of the membership); the Anglican church was seen as a bridge between Orthodox and evangelicals, and as well placed to engage in dialogue with Muslims.[54] Not surprisingly, the Presbyterian work produced a much larger church than the Anglican one.

Church-planting has given rise to vociferous complaints in Eastern Europe about evangelical intrusion on Orthodox 'canonical territory'.[55] But a church-planting strategy did not necessarily

---

49 Eshete, *The Evangelical Movement in Ethiopia*, p. 4.
50 Thomas Otakar Kutvirt, 'The Development of the Mission to the Armenians at Constantinople through 1846', *Armenian Review* vol. 37 (Winter 1984), 43.
51 Murre-van den Berg, 'Why Protestant Churches?', p. 102.
52 Anderson, *History*, I: viii, 3.
53 Anderson, *History*, II: 312.
54 Norman Horner, *A Guide to Christian Churches in the Middle East* (Elkhart, IN: Mission Focus, 1989), p. 68.
55 Canonical territory is the area seen by a particular Orthodox jurisdiction as lying within its responsibility; since only one Orthodox Church can have jurisdiction in any given area, the presence of other denominations or jurisdictions is seen as unacceptable.

preclude the earlier practice of seeking to come alongside the ancient Churches. Even after the formation of a separate Assyrian Protestant Church, for example, W. A. Shedd of the ABCFM continued to hope for the renewal of the communion from which it had separated:

> It is possible also that members of any one of the oriental churches, having a new vision of the gospel of Christ and of the mission of the church, may do the greatest good when separated from the parent body. I do not believe that such separation should be sought, but experience shows that it is inevitable. The reformation of the old churches themselves may be hastened by the presence alongside of bodies of Christians practising a simpler and more active faith.[56]

And, on occasion, different approaches could emerge from the same set of circumstances. In the 1920s, the Romanian Orthodox Church saw two renewal movements emerge from the same soil, both biblicist, moralist, lay-orientated and stressing personal faith in Christ. The Lord's Army remained within the church, not without some problems along the way, while the 'Christians according to the Scriptures' (registered in 1926), a Brethren-type movement led by the former Orthodox priest Teodor Popescu, was forced to develop outside it.[57]

The church-planting strategy received a massive but not always well focused boost after the collapse of East European Communism. Many Western missionaries entered the former Communist world with the conviction that they were 'bringing Jesus to' it. Where they sought to inform themselves regarding the religious background of the area where they would be working, their knowledge of Eastern European Christianity would have been shaped in part by what they had heard about the compromises it had made with Communism – and the compromisers were sometimes seen as including Eastern evangelicals, as well as Orthodox and Catholics. For such workers, it was axiomatic that they should aim to plant new congregations.

Dialogue and co-operation

Although this approach is discussed relatively late in the chapter, sixteenth-century Protestants quickly sought dialogue with Orthodox in order to join forces against Rome and/or the Ottoman Empire. Correspondence between Lutheran theologians from Tübingen and Patriarch Jeremias II of Constantinople elicited the closest thing to an official Orthodox statement on justification by faith in the patriarch's letter of 1576 expressing disagreement with Lutheran teaching.[58] The controversial views of his successor Cyril Lucaris (1572–1638), the so-called 'Calvinist patriarch' who had been educated in the West, precipitated a decisive Orthodox

---

56 W. A. Shedd, *Islam and the Oriental Churches* (Philadelphia, PA: Presbyterian Board of Publication and Sabbath-School Work, 1904), pp. 216–7, quoted by J. F. Coakley, *The Church of the East and the Church of England: A History of the Archbishop of Canterbury's Assyrian Mission* (Oxford: Oxford University Press, 1992), p. 64.
57 See Tom Keppeler, 'Oastea Domnului: The Army of the Lord in Romania', *Religion, State and Society* vol. 21 (1993), 221–7; Horia Azimioara, *From Darkness to Light: The Story of the Former Orthodox Priest Teodor Popescu* (Feschenberg: GBV, 2003).
58 George Mastrantonis, *Augsburg and Constantinople: The Correspondence between the Tübingen Theologians and Patriarch Jeremiah II of Constantinople on the Augsburg Confession* (Brookline, MA: Holy Cross Orthodox Press, 1982).

rejection of Reformation theology,[59] and it is unlikely that later encounter built on such contacts, although occasional references were made to them.[60]

Serious and open evangelical dialogue with ancient Eastern Christianity, in any formal manner, is a phenomenon largely restricted to the last three decades.[61] Apart from evangelical involvement in bilateral theological dialogues between world communions, as between Anglicans and Orthodox or Baptists and Orthodox, several dialogues have taken place between evangelicals and Orthodox. After the World Council of Churches assembly in 1991, Orthodox and evangelical delegates found they shared similar concerns, and this was a significant factor in the WCC convening a series of consultations and seminars bringing the two traditions together.[62] In Britain, the Evangelical Alliance sponsored a study group drawn from both traditions.[63] For a number of years from 1990, the Society for the Study of Eastern Orthodoxy and Evangelicalism met in the United States, while in recent years the Fellowship of St Alban and St Sergius sponsored a dialogue in Oxford. One-off consultations have also been held, as at the International Baptist Theological Seminary in Prague in 2001.[64] However, evangelicals have found it difficult to engage some Orthodox jurisdictions in such dialogues. Moreover, most dialogue has taken place in the West rather than the Orthodox world.

Dialogue objectives have shifted: as attempts to seek theological convergence proved elusive and frustrating, and yet the experience of fellowship remained compelling, a more pragmatic and some would say realistic approach has sought closer collaboration in mission, broadly defined; an example would be the Lausanne-Orthodox Initative, which held its first consultation in 2013.[65] To a considerable extent, this development reflects trends in the wider ecumenical world.

A persistent problem, however, has been the difficulty of moving from conversation to co-operation. Following Edinburgh 1910, there was a measure of co-operation between evangelicals and Eastern Christians, expressed primarily though common participation in para-church movements such as the Student Christian Movement. But relationships withered as evangelicals distanced themselves from organized ecumenism during the mid-twentieth century. Such

---

59 George Hadjiantoniou, *Protestant Patriarch: The Life of Cyril Lucaris (1572–1638), Patriarch of Constantinople* (Richmond, VA: John Knox Press, 1961); Gerald Bray, 'Justification and the Eastern Orthodox Churches', in *Here We Stand*, edited by J. I. Packer (London: Hodder and Stoughton, 1986), pp. 109, 112.

60 See, for example, William Jowett, *Christian Researches in the Mediterranean, from MDCCCXV to MDCCCXX in furtherance of the Objects of the Church Missionary Society, with an Appendix, containing the Journal of the Rev. James Connor, chiefly in Syria and Palestine* (London: Seeley, 1822), pp. 335–7.

61 Bradley Nassif, 'Eastern Orthodoxy and Evangelicalism: The Status of an Emerging Global Dialogue', in *Eastern Orthodox Theology: A Contemporary Reader*, edited by Daniel Clendenin (Grand Rapids, MI: Baker, 2003), pp. 211–48; 'Orthodox Dialogues with Evangelical Communities', in *Orthodoxy and Ecumenism: A Handbook of Theological Education* (Geneva: World Council of Churches, 2014), pp. 536–41; Tim Grass, 'Evangelical – Orthodox Dialogue: Past, Present and Future', *Transformation* vol. 27 (2010), 186–98.

62 *Proclaiming Christ Today: Orthodox-Evangelical Consultation, Alexandria, 10–15 July 1995*, edited by Huibert van Beek and Georges Lemopoulos (Geneva / Białystok: World Council of Churches, 1995); *Turn To God, Rejoice in Hope: Orthodox-Evangelical Consultation, Hamburg, 30 March – 4 April 1998* (Geneva, 1998); *Building Bridges between the Orthodox and Evangelical Traditions*, edited by Tim Grass, Jenny and Paul Rolph, and Ioan Sauca (Geneva: World Council of Churches, 2012).

63 *Evangelicalism and the Orthodox Church: A Report by the Evangelical Alliance (UK) Commission on Unity and Truth among Evangelicals (ACUTE)* (Carlisle: Paternoster, 2001).

64 *Baptists and the Orthodox Church: On the Way to Understanding*, edited by Ian M. Randall (Prague: International Baptist Theological Seminary, 2003).

65 For further details of this initiative, see its website at http://www.loimission.net (accessed 23 February 2018), and *The Mission of God: Studies in Orthodox and Evangelical Mission*, edited by Mark Oxbrow and Tim Grass (Oxford: Regnum, 2015).

co-operation as there was owed much to evangelical pragmatism. When Billy Graham visited Ethiopia (1960) and Russia (1984), working with the Orthodox was a natural application of his general principle of working with as broad a range of churches as possible. Graham's approach was untypical and earned him considerable criticism, but such campaigns have given evangelicals a higher degree of public visibility and acceptability in Orthodox areas.[66]

However, the ecumenical movement was the scene for mutual rediscovery from 1991, as noted above. Such dialogue has helped to create a climate in which co-operation has again become thinkable in such fields as translation and publishing (although Bible translation has been a contested area since the nineteenth century, each tradition condemning translations seen as permeated by the beliefs of the other), and welfare projects. Yet it is not cynicism to suggest that the more tenuous the link between a project and the worshipping life of local churches, the easier it is for evangelicals and Eastern Christians to co-operate in it. Whilst some co-operation has undoubtedly taken place under the auspices of global agencies such as Campus Crusade, CMS, Navigators and World Vision, local agencies are also being founded in which members of both traditions work together. Significantly, recent CMS policy has focused on the idea of entering into partnership with Orthodox jurisdictions and parishes through resourcing them in specific areas of their work.[67]

Conclusion

What factors have determined which of these approaches have been adopted? Doctrinally speaking, we have noticed how different eschatologies have shaped evangelical engagement with Eastern Christianity. Ecclesiology, however, has also played a defining role. Evangelical ecclesiology of various stripes has sometimes adopted an approach to Church history which sees the true Church as cast out and persecuted by the state-sponsored institutions of Christendom. A classic example was Broadbent's *The Pilgrim Church* (1931), which drew extensively on his own travels. Inevitably such an approach predisposes many against the Eastern Churches – until those, too, are persecuted and so come to share the marks of the true Church, as with the Nestorians in 1870s Turkey or Orthodox in 1960s Russia.

In terms of specific evangelical ecclesiologies, it is clear that Anglicans tended to feel that they had a head start in building relationships with the Eastern churches because of their episcopal order, which it was hoped would provide a model for reformed Orthodox jurisdictions. Indeed, even the ABCFM acknowledged this advantage, episcopacy being seen as paralleling the forms of civil government obtaining in the East; missionaries were reminded that their object was not to introduce a congregationalist or presbyterian polity.[68] Nowadays it is clear that belief in the local congregation (as opposed to a diocese or jurisdiction) as the primary ecclesiological unit makes the formation of new ones more likely, because of the ease with which it can be done and because it makes it harder for evangelicals with such an ecclesiology to see the marks of a true Christian congregation in Orthodox parishes around them. Baptistic missions, such as those of the Baptists, the Brethren, and the majority of Pentecostals, have often drawn on the congregationalist outlook and have proved more likely to adopt a negative attitude to Eastern Christianity than paedobaptistic ones. Baptistic denominations have often found it difficult to

---

66 Eshete, *The Evangelical Movement in Ethiopia*, p. 152; Billy Graham, *Just As I Am: The Autobiography of Billy Graham* (London: HarperCollins, 1997), pp. 517–27.
67 See *Together in Mission: Orthodox Churches Consult with the Church Mission Society, 25–30 April 2001, Moscow* (London: Church Mission Society, 2001).
68 *Missionary Register* vol. 26 (1838), 80; vol. 28 (1840), 80.

engage positively with Eastern Christianity, not least because they have been unable to accept infant baptism as valid and have therefore (re)baptized converts in an inversion of the practice of some Orthodox jurisdictions.

Differing understandings of soteriology have provided a major obstacle to closer or more constructive relations. Evangelical insistence on salvation received through faith alone has historically often been contrasted with an understanding of Orthodoxy which saw it as teaching something akin to 'salvation by works' (often understood in the light of contemporary Roman Catholicism). Considerable scholarly attention has been given to soteriological issues,[69] but dialogue statements have not yet offered a convincing account of how the respective views of two traditions can be regarded as compatible. However, changing understandings of such evangelical doctrines as justification by faith alone (as seen, for example, in the work of N. T. Wright[70] or that of Finnish Lutheran-Orthodox dialogue[71]) may offer new avenues of exploration.

As for external factors affecting the development of relationships, the political climate has alternately facilitated and hindered them, as we have seen. In the early nineteenth century, the Russian Bible Society was founded during the time of the 'Holy Alliance', when Tsar Alexander I was notably sympathetic to things Western, including Western mystical spirituality. The Ottoman Empire's fatal decay facilitated not only Western political intervention in the region but also Western religious intervention. By contrast, recent dialogue between Baptists and the Ecumenical Patriarchate was dealt a mortal blow by NATO bombing of Serbia in 1998; and the complications arising from Western involvement in Iraq and Syria cannot yet be adequately evaluated.

Political power could be used in various ways: to facilitate evangelical mission, as in early nineteenth-century India and late nineteenth-century Egypt, or to secure a greater measure of freedom for Eastern Christian communities, as in Turkey during the middle of the century; on the Orthodox side, it has not infrequently been used to repress evangelical activity. It can be argued that evangelicals, whose outlook was marked by a readiness to innovate, failed to grasp that centuries of political powerlessness under Muslim domination had made any form of development very difficult for churches in those lands; their priority had to be that of faithful maintenance of the tradition (as would later be the case in some Communist countries). For evangelicals, political powerlessness, when Orthodoxy was the religion of the rulers, strongly reinforced their negative attitude towards it.

Four areas call for further investigation. Some regions and missions are better researched than others. Although Eastern Europe contains a much larger number of Orthodox believers, from an Anglophone missions history perspective there is far more relevant research on the Middle East and Africa than on European Orthodoxy, Russia excepted. The lack of English-language discussion of evangelical engagement with Orthodoxy in Eastern Europe is the more significant given evangelicalism's strength in the region and the growing number of Eastern evangelical scholars engaging with aspects of Orthodox theology. Linked with this, is the relationship between evangelicalism and reform movements within twentieth-century Orthodoxy, notably in Armenia, Romania and Greece. Second, an aspect little mentioned here has been the encounter of Pentecostals and charismatics with Eastern Christianity; to the extent to which

---

69 For example, from the evangelical side, Edmund J. Rybarczyk, *Beyond Salvation: Eastern Orthodoxy and Classical Pentecostalism on becoming like Christ* (Carlisle: Paternoster, 2004); *Three Views on Eastern Orthodoxy and Evangelicalism*, edited by James J. Stamoolis (Grand Rapids, MI: Zondervan, 2004).
70 See N. T. Wright, *Justification: God's Plan and Paul's Vision* (London: SPCK, 2009).
71 *Union with Christ: The New Finnish Interpretation of Luther*, edited by Carl E. Braaten and Robert W. Jenson (Grand Rapids, MI: Eerdmans, 1998).

such Christians see themselves as different from evangelicals, this engagement has been marked by distinctive features, such as its focus on pneumatology. Third, more thought needs to be given to the relationship between changing evangelical understandings of missiology and attitudes towards Eastern Christianity. Finally, we cannot comprehend fully how evangelicals and Eastern Christians have related to one another outside Europe in Africa and the Middle East without giving full weight to the presence of a third tradition, which on one ancient reading was itself regarded as a Christian heresy – Islam. We therefore need to compare the various ways in which each tradition has engaged with Islam. In turn, this engagement could be compared fruitfully with that between evangelicalism, Orthodoxy and Communism. There is, then, plenty of scope for further research.

8

EVANGELICALS AND ISLAM

Andrew Atherstone

According to George Whitefield's famous quip in 1740, which he borrowed from John Wesley, the Archbishop of Canterbury, John Tillotson, 'knew no more about true Christianity than Mahomet', ignorant especially of justification by faith alone.[1] The evangelist's critics mirrored this abuse, mocking Whitefield as 'Mahomet-like' because of his ability to stir up ignorant enthusiasts and attract a 'giddy sensual Herd'. His disciples in the Great Awakening were compared to 'all true Mussulmans' who 'firmly believe the greatest Ideots [sic] or Madmen are the greatest Saints'.[2] For much of the eighteenth century, it was an effective polemical strategy to associate theological opponents with Islam and thus discredit or belittle them – whether Roman Catholics, Episcopalians, Quakers, Unitarians or evangelicals, as later for Mormons and fundamentalists. No first-hand knowledge of Islam was required. Mohammad, in the words of Thomas Kidd, 'could be portrayed as an example of a graceless legalist or a wild enthusiast, depending on the rhetorical needs of the moment'.[3] Jonathan Edwards' attacks upon Islam, for instance, were really a swipe at contemporary Deism.[4]

At later periods, Islam continued to be conscripted for intra-Christian controversy, often presented as the ultimate *reductio ad absurdum* to cap an argument. When John Henry Newman attempted to show in *Tract Ninety* (1841) that Roman Catholic theology was compatible with the Thirty-Nine Articles of Religion, Protestants replied that the same logic 'would allow a Mahometan to subscribe the Articles' or Professor Pusey, the Tractarian leader, 'to declare his belief in the Koran'.[5] Conversely, evangelicalism was likened to Islam by some Catholic

---

1 George Whitefield to Anon, 18 January 1740, in *Letters of George Whitefield for the Period 1734–1742* (Edinburgh: Banner of Truth Trust, 1976), p. 505.
2 Simon Lewis, 'A "Papal Emissary"? George Whitefield and Anti-Methodist Allegations of Popery, c.1738–c.1750', in *George Whitefield Tercentenary Essays*, edited by William Gibson and Thomas Smith, special issue of *Journal of Religious History, Literature and Culture* vol. 1 (November 2015), 21.
3 Thomas Kidd, *American Christians and Islam: Evangelical Culture and Muslims from the Colonial Period to the Age of Terrorism* (Princeton, NJ: Princeton University Press, 2009), p. 14.
4 Gerald McDermott, 'The Deist Connection: Jonathan Edwards and Islam', *Jonathan Edwards's Writings: Text, Context, Interpretation*, edited by Stephen Stein (Bloomington, IN: Indiana University Press, 1996), pp. 39–51.
5 Andrew Atherstone, *Oxford's Protestant Spy: The Controversial Career of Charles Golightly* (Milton Keynes: Paternoster, 2007), p. 160.

commentators for its rationalistic lack of beauty or sensuality. In Newman's novel *Loss and Gain* (1848) one of the characters, Mr White, an Anglican ritualist and aesthete, observes: 'Mahometanism is as cold and as dry as any Calvinistic meeting. The Mahometans have no altars or priests, nothing but a pulpit and a preacher.'[6] This methodology remained popular even at the turn of the twenty-first century, as evangelical polemicists capitalized on public perceptions of Islam to criticize their own opponents within the Church. Baptist preacher David Pawson, author of *Leadership is Male* (1988), used Islam's success at recruiting young men into its ranks to launch a protest at the perceived feminization of Western Christianity.[7] Wilfred Wong argued that the number of white Britons converting to Islam was proof that many wanted 'a faith which is sure of itself and has strict, unchanging tenets', unlike liberal Christianity which only succeeded in 'driving even more people away from the church.'[8] Meanwhile, John Stott, doyen among Anglican evangelicals, repudiated Christian fundamentalism by likening its teaching on biblical inspiration to an Islamic view of the mechanical dictation of the Qur'an to Muhammad via the Angel Gabriel.[9] On the other hand, Richard Dawkins and other critics of evangelicals labelled them the 'Christian Taliban', for their 'narrow bigotry', literalistic interpretation of Scripture, and hostility to modern thought.[10]

Although these casual rhetorical tropes continued to gain purchase, some Anglophone evangelicals engaged with Islam more seriously throughout the nineteenth and twentieth centuries as a result of missionary endeavours in North Africa, the Middle East and Asia,[11] and the rapid growth of Muslim populations in the West. This chapter examines five aspects of that engagement: the role of evangelical missionary exemplars; contrasting approaches to apologetics and disputation; evangelical concerns to unveil 'the true face of Islam'; prophetic predictions of Islam's imminent collapse or global domination; and the counting of Christian converts. Kidd's *American Christians and Islam* (2009) provides a penetrating analysis of the American literature, so this chapter focuses predominantly on British sources.

Missionary exemplars

William Carey and William Ward of the Baptist Missionary Society evangelized both Muslims and Hindus in Bengal from the 1790s,[12] while Pliny Fisk and Levi Parsons were sent out from Boston in 1819 by the American Board of Commissioners for Foreign Missions to pioneer gospel preaching to Muslims in the Levant.[13] Yet it was the British East India Company chaplain, Henry Martyn, who was lauded by Victorian evangelicals as the 'first modern missionary to

---

6 John Henry Newman, *Loss and Gain: The Story of a Convert*, edited by Sheridan Gilley (Leominster: Gracewing, 2014), p. 43.
7 David Pawson, *The Challenge of Islam to Christians* (London: Hodder and Stoughton, 2003), pp. 52–4.
8 Wilfred Wong, 'The Harvest is Plentiful', *Prophecy Today* vol. 20 (May / June 2004), 20.
9 John Stott, *Evangelical Truth: A Personal Plea for Unity* (Leicester: Inter-Varsity Press, 1999), p. 22. See also, Bill Musk, *The Certainty Trap: Can Christians and Muslims Afford the Luxury of Fundamentalism?* (Pasadena, CA: William Carey Library, 2008).
10 Richard Dawkins, *The God Delusion* (London: Bantam Press, 2006), p. 288.
11 For a helpful survey, see Lyle Vander Werff, *Christian Mission to Muslims, the Record: Anglican and Reformed Approaches in India and the Near East, 1800–1938* (Pasadena, CA: William Carey Library, 1977).
12 James Ryan West, 'Evangelizing Bengali Muslims, 1793–1813: William Carey, William Ward, and Islam' (unpublished PhD thesis, Southern Baptist Theological Seminary, 2014).
13 Christine Leigh Heyrman, *American Apostles: When Evangelicals Entered the World of Islam* (New York: Hill and Wang, 2015).

the Mohammedans'.[14] His months debating with Sufis at Shiraz, and his translations of the New Testament into Urdu, Persian and Arabic, before his untimely death, secured his reputation as the heroic exemplar for future generations, totemic of evangelical dreams for the conversion of Islam. Brian Stanley describes it as posthumous canonization, nothing less than the 'cult' of an evangelical saint.[15] At the centenary of Martyn's death in 1912, the American missionary Samuel Zwemer (founding editor of *The Moslem World*) called for a special day of prayer for Christian missions to Islam, exhorting his readers that after a hundred years 'the task is still unfinished, and Martyn's prophetic dreams are only beginning to see fulfilment'.[16] Zwemer was also a catalyst for the founding of the Henry Martyn School of Islamic Studies at Lahore in 1930, to train Christian workers in evangelism amongst Muslims.[17] Meanwhile in Egypt, Constance Padwick promoted Martyn's legacy and declared that she and her missionary colleagues were Martyn's 'spiritual kindred'.[18]

The globe-trotting exploits of the evangelical celebrity General Charles Gordon, and his assassination in the Sudan in 1885 by followers of the Mahdi, was another major stimulus to late-Victorian evangelical missions to the Islamic world.[19] The Cambridge Arabist, Ion Keith-Falconer, for example, went in 1886 as a Free Church of Scotland missionary to Aden, the doorway to Muslim Arabia, inspired in part by deep admiration for Gordon who he 'enshrined in his heart as one of his heroes'.[20] The general's example also motivated Douglas Thornton and Temple Gairdner who sailed for Cairo with the Church Missionary Society in 1898–1899. As an Oxford student Gairdner devoured Seton Churchill's hagiography, *General Gordon: The Christian Hero* (1890), and responded in his diary, 'Quo ducis Domine? In Africam, Domine?'[21] After studying a map of the Nile Valley, Thornton declared: 'It is the burden of my heart that all these tribes be reached. It was Gordon's wish . . .'.[22] Romantic tales of Gordon's devotion likewise inspired Llewellyn Gwynne to serve as a pioneer missionary in the Sudan from 1899. Shortly after arriving on the mission field he wrote to his former parishioners in Nottingham of 'the Christian influence of our great Gordon' who 'fell martyred' at the hands of the Dervishes: 'The standard of Christ once raised in all this great region has been thrown down. It must be planted here again. . . . Never must the Christian Church rest until she has retaken her own possessions.'[23] Gwynne became the first Anglican bishop of Khartoum and his cathedral was built in Gordon's honour with subscriptions from across the British Empire. It was consecrated

---

14 George Smith, *Henry Martyn, Saint and Scholar: First Modern Missionary to the Mohammedans* (London: Religious Tract Society, 1892).
15 Brian Stanley, 'An "Ardour" of Devotion: The Spiritual Legacy of Henry Martyn', in *India and the Indianness of Christianity*, edited by Richard Fox Young (Grand Rapids, MI: Eerdmans, 2009), pp. 108–26.
16 Samuel Zwemer, 'Henry Martyn', *Moslem World* vol. 2 (July 1912), 229.
17 Ian Douglas, 'Henry Martyn Institute of Islamic Studies', *Muslim World* vol. 51 (July 1961), 217–21; Diane D'Souza, 'Evangelism, Dialogue, Reconciliation: A Case Study of the Growth and Transformation of the Henry Martyn Institute', *Muslim World* vol. 91 (Spring 2001), 155–84.
18 Constance Padwick, *Henry Martyn: Confessor of the Faith* (London: Student Christian Movement, 1922), p. 12.
19 Andrew Porter, *Religion versus Empire: British Protestant Missionaries and Overseas Expansion, 1700–1914* (Manchester: Manchester University Press, 2004), pp. 222–3.
20 Robert Sinker, *Memorials of the Hon. Ion Keith-Falconer* (Cambridge: Deighton, Bell and Co., 1888), pp. 113–16.
21 Constance Padwick, *Temple Gairdner of Cairo* (London: SPCK, 1929), p. 66.
22 W. H. T. Gairdner, *D. M. Thornton: A Study in Missionary Ideals and Methods* (London: Hodder and Stoughton, 1909), p. 115.
23 Gwynne to parishioners of Emmanuel Church, Nottingham, 27 April 1900, in H. C. Jackson, *Pastor on the Nile: Being Some Account of the Life and Letters of Llewellyn H. Gwynne* (London: SPCK, 1960), p. 33.

in 1912, on 26 January, the anniversary of Gordon's death and its memorial chapel contained precious relics including Gordon's prayer carpet and an altar frontal fringed with gold braid from Gordon's uniform.[24] Such was Gwynne's adulation for his evangelical hero that when Gordon's reputation was destroyed by Lytton Strachey's *Eminent Victorians* (1918), the bishop's indignation could not 'adequately be expressed in words – at any rate by a parson'.[25] As late as 1945, on the sixtieth anniversary of Gordon's death, his career remained a stimulus to evangelical missions to the Sudan.[26]

Just as Gairdner and his associates were inspired by Martyn and Gordon, so they in turn inspired the next generation of evangelical missionaries to the Muslim world in the mid-twentieth century. Padwick's 1929 biography of Gairdner sold 13,000 copies in its first year and was quickly established as an evangelical classic.[27] It had a profound impact upon Kenneth Cragg, an undergraduate at Oxford in the early 1930s, who began missionary work in Lebanon in 1939 with the British Syria Mission and later served as a bishop and scholar in Jerusalem and Cairo. Cragg, one of the twentieth century's preeminent missiologists, explicitly claimed Gairdner's legacy, though he was more willing than Gairdner to identify theological commonalities between Islam and Christianity.[28]

Despite their deeply-ingrained anti-Catholicism, evangelicals in Muslim contexts modelled themselves not only upon their Protestant forebears but also upon the thirteenth-century Majorcan theologian and Franciscan tertiary, Ramon Lull, who initiated Christian missions to North Africa. One of Zwemer's earliest books was a biography of Lull, written as a challenge to the modern church to stop merely 'playing at missions' and earnestly seek to 'win the whole Mohammedan world for Christ'. The chief lesson he took from Lull's life was that 'our weapons against Islam should never be carnal. Love, and love alone, will conquer'.[29] As late as the 1950s, Cragg observed that 'For all our revision of their methods, the great Lulls and Martyns of the past still serve as our exemplars'.[30] By the early twenty-first century, however, Lull had been eclipsed in evangelical consciousness by another medieval Catholic, Francis of Assisi, whose audience with Sultan Malik al-Kamil at Damietta in 1219 at the height of the Crusades resonated with contemporary interfaith relations.[31] In *Waging Peace on Islam* (2000), Christine Mallouhi advocated the way of Francis as a model of Christian-Muslim engagement, 'not the emblazoned battle of power but the lowly path of love and service . . . not a declaration of war on God's enemies, but a message of indiscriminate love and salvation for all.'[32] Steve Bell called Francis 'a true icon of Christian grace towards Muslims'.[33]

---

24 Jackson, *Pastor on the Nile*, pp. 131–5.
25 Jackson, *Pastor on the Nile*, p. 139.
26 'Sixty Years After Gordon', *The Record*, 26 January 1945, p. 44.
27 Kenneth Cragg, 'Constance E. Padwick, 1886–1968', *Muslim World* vol. 59 (January 1969), 31.
28 Kenneth Cragg, 'Temple Gairdner's Legacy', *International Bulletin of Missionary Research* vol. 5 (October 1981), 164–7; James Tebbe, 'Kenneth Cragg in Perspective: A Comparison with Temple Gairdner and William Cantwell Smith', *International Bulletin of Missionary Research* vol. 26 (January 2002), 16–21.
29 Samuel Zwemer, *Raymund Lull: First Missionary to the Moslems* (New York: Funk and Wagnalls, 1902), pp. 150, 155–6.
30 Kenneth Cragg, 'The Christian Church and Islam Today', *Muslim World* vol. 42 (October 1952), 281.
31 For the reception history of this episode, see John Tolan, *Saint Francis and the Sultan: The Curious History of a Christian-Muslim Encounter* (Oxford: Oxford University Press, 2009).
32 Christine Mallouhi, *Waging Peace on Islam* (London: Monarch, 2000), pp. 33–4.
33 Steve Bell, *Grace for Muslims? The Journey from Fear to Faith* (Milton Keynes: Authentic, 2006), p. 58.

Apologetics and disputation

Set-piece public disputation, or *munazara*, was a popular form of theological engagement between Christians and Muslims in pre-Mutiny India. The German evangelical, Karl Gottlieb Pfander, pioneered this method of controversy with Islamic scholars, which reached a climax in the 'great debate' at Agra in 1854 against his articulate adversary Rahmatullah Kairanawi.[34] Pfander's aim was to make the gospel intellectually appealing, and his co-belligerent Thomas Valpy French (later bishop of Lahore) adopted similar methods, preaching regularly in the *bazaars* of the Punjab in the belief that it was better for missionaries to provoke enmity than to speak in a 'weak and subdued voice' as if 'afraid to be heard'.[35] In Cairo, the Church Missionary Society evangelists were likewise challenged to public dispute by Muslim opponents, which sometimes ended in rough disorder, though Thornton was undeterred because he had 'the spirit that enjoys a fight, and a good deal of the obstinacy that refuses to budge in a discussion'. Even in private conversations with sheiks, he 'would hit hard, and things often became, to say the least, lively'.[36] Yet the limitations of this style of apologetic engagement were recognized from the first. Martyn wrote, only a year after arriving in India, 'I lay not much stress upon *clear arguments*; the work of God is seldom wrought in this way.'[37] And again: 'I do use the means in a certain way, but frigid reasoning with men of perverse minds, seldom brings men to Christ. . . . How powerless are the best-directed arguments, till the Holy Ghost renders them effectual.'[38]

Towards the end of the nineteenth century, many evangelicals eschewed public dispute and rational argument in favour of new methods for converting Muslims, both philanthropic and literary. For example, Arthur Neve, medical missionary in Kashmir from the 1880s, emphasized that 'love' was the inspiration for his work, motivated by a desire to reach those lost in 'the loveless void of Islam . . . The stern intellectual barriers of Mohammedanism are to be attacked through the heart.'[39] His brother, Ernest Neve, agreed: 'Theological dialectics between opposing religions are of little value. Religious controversy is more apt to engender hatred than love. If men cannot be attracted by the love and sympathy of Christ, history and logic will not succeed.' Thus he advocated medical missions as the most 'potent agency' for reaching Muslims with the gospel.[40] There was also a decisive shift in the content and style of evangelistic literature. In 1906 Bishop George Lefroy warned a missionary conference at Cairo that Muslims would not be converted 'by throwing brick-bats at them, in the form of truth'. Most evangelistic tracts were 'very *hard* indeed', and he advocated a more winsome tone.[41] The Nile Mission Press in Egypt experimented with this new approach. One of Gairdner's friends, Yusef Effendi Tadros, remembered that 'No one else taught us as he did. Other teachers taught

---

34 Avril Powell, *Muslims and Missionaries in Pre-Mutiny India* (Richmond: Curzon, 1993).
35 Thomas Valpy French to Henry Venn, 2 May 1852, in Herbert Birks, *The Life and Correspondence of Thomas Valpy French, First Bishop of Lahore* (2 vols, London: John Murray, 1895), I: 66.
36 Gairdner, *Thornton*, p. 199.
37 Martyn Letter, 28 April 1807, in *Journals and Letters of the Rev. Henry Martyn*, edited by Samuel Wilberforce (2 vols, London: Seeley and Burnside, 1837), II: 55.
38 Martyn Letter, 8 September 1811, in *Journals and Letters*, II: 373.
39 Ernest Neve, *A Crusader in Kashmir: Being the Life of Dr Arthur Neve, with an Account of the Medical Missionary Work of Two Brothers and its Later Development Down to the Present Day* (London: Seeley, Service and Co., 1928), p. 34.
40 Neve, *Crusader in Kashmir*, p. 14, cited in Vander Werff, *Christian Mission*, pp. 77–8.
41 G. A. Lefroy, 'Preparation of Workers for Work Among Moslems', in *Methods of Mission Work Among Muslims: Being Those Papers Read at the First Missionary Conference on Behalf of the Mohammedan World* (New York: Fleming H. Revell, 1906), p. 225.

us how to refute Islam; he taught us how to love Muslims.'[42] Gairdner noticed, according to Padwick, that converts made via the older polemical literature were 'often born in its image – with the spirit of disputation rather than of worship and of love, and apt to hammer rather than to woo and win'.[43] Therefore his Arabic tracts aimed not so much at logic and argumentation, but rather taught theology through narrative and personal story, so that the message read by Muslims was 'not the dry cracked note of disputation, but the song note of joyous witness, tender invitation'.[44]

Zwemer concurred. He believed that older evangelical literature of 'the controversial type, destructively critical of Islam', remained useful as 'the plough-share for the sowing of the Truth', but 'a new era calls for a new program'. They must find 'new ways for presenting the one and only Gospel', especially tracts 'founded on first hand Oriental experience, not on translations of incidents and stories from the West'.[45] The church, Zwemer continued, must 'flood the world of Islam with a Christian literature that is apologetic without being too dogmatic, and captivating rather than polemic'. Rather than 'bombard the enemies' position', they must 'bridge the chasm and win captives'.[46] Lilias Trotter of the Algiers Mission Band hoped that 'the Eastern love of storytelling and story hearing' could be 'used for the Kingdom'.[47] She aimed to write parables in colloquial Arabic, artistically lithographed in Algerian script. The standard typeface of evangelical tracts, she observed, was 'cramped and banal to their beauty loving eyes, to say nothing of the infidel about it, and the doleful association with tax papers and police summons. We want to have it as Arab as possible.'[48] Rather than focus on the doctrinal differences between Christianity and Islam, Trotter's Arabic stories 'appealed first to the fundamental likenesses, the great human needs of all souls'.[49]

There were some parallels in Cragg's writings. Although he did not entirely reject Pfander's apologetic method, Cragg attempted, in the words of his biographer, 'to reorientate it in a completely new spirit of love, without the armour of political patronage, without the assumption of cultural superiority and without the expectation of destroying Islam by dialectical victory'.[50] In books such as *The Call of the Minaret* (1956) and *The Dome and the Rock* (1964), he urged the church to look for the best in Islam, not the worst, using 'the language of persuasion, almost of courtship, not the military vocabulary so often used in Christian missionary circles'.[51] Some Muslim commentators saw this as little better than 'a sugar-coated pill', however, a change of tactics not a change in proselytizing objectives.[52] Charismatic renewal also undermined evangelical reliance upon rationalistic argumentation. For example, when John and Ruthie Weed went to Egypt in 1984 with Mission to the World (the global mission agency of the Presbyterian Church in America) they deliberately eschewed an 'intellectual, apologetic approach' in favour of miraculous 'signs and wonders', as popularized by John Wimber and the Vineyard Movement.[53] After the collapse of the Soviet Union, the Weeds transferred to

---

42 Padwick, *Temple Gairdner*, p. 302.
43 Padwick, *Temple Gairdner*, p. 148.
44 Padwick, *Temple Gairdner*, p. 158.
45 Samuel Zwemer, 'The Printed Page', *Moslem World* vol. 8 (April 1918), 113–14.
46 Samuel Zwemer, 'The Chasm', *Moslem World* vol. 9 (April 1919), 113.
47 Trotter Journal, 29 December 1903, in Miriam Huffman Rockness, *A Passion for the Impossible: The Life of Lilias Trotter* (second edition, Grand Rapids, MI: Discovery House, 2003), p. 194.
48 Trotter Journal, 23 February 1904, in Rockness, *Passion for the Impossible*, p. 196.
49 Rockness, *Passion for the Impossible*, p. 327.
50 Christopher Lamb, *A Policy of Hope: Kenneth Cragg and Islam* (London: Melisende, 2014), p. 23.
51 Lamb, *Policy of Hope*, p. 151.
52 Lamb, *Policy of Hope*, p. 162.
53 John Weed, 'Signs and Wonders in Egypt', *Equipping the Saints* vol. 6 (Winter 1992), 26–8.

Kazakhstan in 1992 where they testified to 'the Holy Spirit falling mightily' in ways reminiscent of the Book of Acts, leading to hundreds of 'decisions for Christ'.[54]

The resurgence of interest in apologetics in the early twenty-first century led to fresh appreciation, in some quarters, for public debate as a fruitful evangelistic strategy. London's Pfander Centre for Apologetics distributed multi-media resources across the internet, and its founder Jay Smith (of Brethren in Christ World Missions) called for 'tough love' towards Muslims by 'confronting the very foundations of Islam' in order 'to destroy falsehood, and uphold the truth'. He frequently challenged Muslim opponents, both in formal debate and at Speakers' Corner in Hyde Park.[55] Colin Chapman, by contrast, advocated a more winsome approach. He counselled Christians to do 'their utmost to understand Islam as sympathetically as possible', and to avoid quarrels when evangelizing their Muslim neighbours, because 'Building a genuine relationship of trust and friendship is more important than defeating someone in an argument'.[56] Chapman rejected accusations from fellow evangelicals that this amounted to 'going soft on Islam'.[57]

The 'true face' of Islam

The ubiquity of hijabs and burqas within Islamic cultures provided a ready metaphor which proved irresistible to Christian authors, from Charles Forster's *Mahometanism Unveiled* (1829) to Phil and Julie Parshall's *Lifting the Veil* (2002). Historians, explorers and missionaries had an insatiable appetite to discover and debate the 'true nature' of Islam, hidden underneath its public presentation. Padwick, for example, studied Arabic devotional manuals on sale in cities across North Africa and the Middle East, believing these to reveal more about popular Islamic beliefs than formal theological treatises.[58] Likewise, Bill Musk argued that to evangelize Muslims effectively, Christians must appreciate the distinction between 'Qur'anic, institutionalized, orthodox and official Islam' and 'everyday, everyman, non-publicized, local and popular Islam'. They must reach behind the 'facade of established ritual worship' to engage with the folk-religion of ordinary Muslims.[59] Some authors distinguished between *islam* (personal surrender to God's will) and Islam (as a religious institution and ideology); or between Muslims and Islam; or between Islam and Islamism.[60] This acknowledgement of genuine diversity and complexity, between private and public spheres, or between personal and formal positions, enabled evangelicals to offer nuanced interactions. Islam took multiple forms, depending on the context. Nevertheless, some insisted that, properly understood, it was monolithic. For example, Alan Clifford, the outspoken pastor of Norwich Reformed Church, derided the British government

---

54 Bill Henderson, 'Letting God Break the Rules', *Equipping the Saints* (Second Quarter 1995), 2.
55 Jay Smith, 'The Case for Polemics', in *Between Naivety and Hostility: Uncovering the Best Christian Responses to Islam in Britain*, edited by Steve Bell and Colin Chapman (Milton Keynes: Authentic, 2011), pp. 241, 247.
56 Colin Chapman, *Cross and Crescent: Responding to the Challenges of Islam* (new edition, Nottingham: Inter-Varsity Press, 2007), pp. 213, 409.
57 Colin Chapman, 'Going Soft on Islam? Reflections on Some Evangelical Responses to Islam', *Vox Evangelica* vol. 19 (1989), 7–31; Colin Chapman, 'Christian Responses to Islamism and Violence in the Name of Islam', *Transformation: An International Journal of Holistic Mission Studies* vol. 34 (April 2017), 129.
58 Constance Padwick, *Muslim Devotions: A Study of Prayer-Manuals in Common Use* (London: SPCK, 1961).
59 Bill Musk, *The Unseen Face of Islam: Sharing the Gospel with Ordinary Muslims* (Eastbourne: Monarch, 1989), pp. 203–4.
60 Lamb, *Policy of Hope*, p. 28; Bell, *Grace for Muslims*, p. 7; Michael Nazir-Ali, *Triple Jeopardy for the West: Aggressive Secularism, Radical Islamism and Multiculturalism* (London: Bloomsbury, 2012), p. 79.

for 'playing dangerous games by ignorantly distinguishing between militant and moderate Islam. The only difference between moderates and militants is between those who keep their mouths shut, and those who don't!'[61]

One persistent refrain in evangelical commentary was a concern that Western audiences were being fed false portrayals of Islam by its apologists. *Mohammed and Mohammedanism* (1874), a positive appreciation by Harrow schoolmaster Reginald Bosworth Smith, was assailed by evangelical reviewers. *The Christian Observer*, for instance, wrote dismissively that first-hand knowledge of Islam among missionaries in Africa and India was far preferable to Smith's subversive theories derived merely 'from books', and queried his competence to teach in a Christian school.[62] In an article entitled 'Mohammed without Camouflage', Gairdner likewise complained that 'the works of modern Mohammedans and Islamophils are incorrigible in their glozing over of plain but uncongenial facts'. In particular he rebuked by the *Islamic Review*, the journal of the Woking Muslim Mission (founded 1913), for its 'Mohammed-cum-lavender-water' panegyrics, as if Mohammed was 'humanity's beau ideal and consummate example'.[63] Gairdner delineated multiple examples of Mohammed's brutality, from the Islamic sources, to counteract these 'Neo-Moslems who have assumed the task of dishing up the Biography to suit the taste of the Christian West'.[64] During the 1940s, *Evangelical Christendom*, the magazine of the Evangelical Alliance, carried regular reports from missionaries in Islamic contexts to counteract the 'apologists' in Britain who were trying to present Islam as 'a very different religion to what it really is'.[65] Sixty years later, Clifford Hill (founder in 1982 of Prophetic Word Ministries and its flagship magazine *Prophecy Today*) lamented that truth was 'sacrificed for expediency' in public debate about Islam, which was frequently portrayed by British politicians and church leaders, falsely according to Hill, as 'a religion of peace and compassion'.[66] The early twenty-first century saw a rapid multiplication of evangelical exposés, with titles such as *Secrets of the Koran* (2003), *The Mosque Exposed* (2006) and *Unmasking Islamic State* (2015).[67] The doctrine of *taqiyya*, which allowed Muslims to hide their religious allegiance in times of persecution, was prominent in some evangelical discourse as evidence that Muslims in the West were hiding their true agendas, guilty of 'outright lying' and 'deliberate deception'.[68] The doctrine of *hijra*, Muslim expansion by immigration, was likened to a 'modern day Trojan Horse'.[69]

These contrasting interpretations of Islam's 'true identity' resulted in a diverse array of evangelical perspectives. Some were notably sanguine. Henry Christmas, for example, told

---

61 Alan Clifford, *Christianity, Islam and British Politics: A Lecture* (Norwich: Charenton Reformed Publishing, 2006), pp. 19–20.
62 'Mohammed and Mohammedanism', *Christian Observer* no. 438 (June 1874), 434–48.
63 W. H. T. Gairdner, 'Mohammed without Camouflage: Ecce Homo Arabicus', *Moslem World* vol. 9 (January 1919), 26–7.
64 Gairdner, 'Mohammed without Camouflage', 57.
65 'The Moslems' Need of Christ', *Evangelical Christendom* (July–September 1942), 87.
66 Clifford Hill, 'Wake-Up Call!', *Prophecy Today* vol. 18 (March / April 2002), 4.
67 Don Richardson, *Secrets of the Koran* (Bloomington, MN: Bethany House, 2003); Sam Solomon and Elias al-Maqdisi, *The Mosque Exposed* (Charlottesville, VA: ANM Press, 2006); Patrick Sookhdeo, *Unmasking Islamic State: Revealing their Motivation, Theology and End Time Predictions* (McLean, VA: Isaac Publishing, 2015).
68 Patrick Sookhdeo, *Islam: The Challenge to the Church* (Pewsey: Isaac Publishing, 2006), pp. 33–5; Caroline Cox and John Marks, *The West, Islam and Islamism: Is Ideological Islam Compatible with Liberal Democracy?* (second edition, London: Civitas, 2006), pp. 97–9. In response, see Toby Howarth, '*Taqiyya* (Dissimulation) and Integrity', in *Between Naivety and Hostility*, edited by Bell and Chapman, pp. 218–36.
69 Sam Solomon and Elias al-Maqdisi, *Modern Day Trojan Horse: The Islamic Doctrine of Immigration* (Charlottesville, VA: ANM Press, 2009).

the Church of England Young Men's Society in 1854 that 'the principle of the Mohammedan religion is toleration', especially contrasted with religious persecution by the Church of Rome, and he praised Islamic virtues.[70] William Arthur, a Wesleyan missionary in India, likened the three major religions – Hinduism, Islam and Christianity – to the light provided respectively by the stars, moon and sun, arguing that Islam was a step towards the Christian gospel because it borrowed heavily from the Bible.[71] Keith-Falconer, in his final address in Scotland before departing for the mission field, declared that Islam to the Arabs was like the Old Testament law to the Jews, 'a schoolmaster to bring them to Christ'.[72] Bell also viewed Islam as 'an Arabized reflection of ancient Judaism', with the potential to 'pre-evangelize' Muslims and lead them part of the way down 'the right road towards Christ'.[73] Furthermore, he welcomed the moral influence of Muslims as 'a kind of spiritual reinforcement in the battle for biblical morality' in Western society where 'secularism is its biggest threat'.[74]

The weight of evangelical opinion, however, was overwhelmingly negative. Doctrinally, the two religions were said to be directly at odds. Zwemer argued that although Allah could not be categorized with the 'false gods', because he shared many of Jehovah's attributes, the Islamic conception of God was 'inadequate, incomplete, barren and grievously distorted'. No religious parliament could 'reconcile such fundamental and deep-rooted differences'.[75] W. A. Rice (an Anglican missionary in Persia) proclaimed that every 'cardinal fact' concerning the person and work of Jesus Christ was 'either denied, perverted, misrepresented or at least ignored in Muhammadan theology'.[76] Put simply, Islam was, in Gairdner view, 'the most formidable opponent of the Christian religion in the whole world'.[77] Evangelicals were quick to argue that the teaching of the Qur'an and the example of Muhammad led directly to immoral behaviour, especially violence and the degradation of women. For instance, at prestigious anniversary meetings of the Church Missionary Society, Thomas Scott denounced Islam's 'debauched prophet' and J. W. Cunningham delineated Islam's inherent 'errors', 'pollution', and 'cruelties'.[78] In the assessment of evangelical historian Henry Miers Elliot, the Islamic rulers of the Indian subcontinent were 'sunk in sloth and debauchery', guilty of injustice, corruption, violence and 'outrage', until overthrown in God's providence by the benevolent British Raj.[79] From Africa, Gwynne complained that Islam had turned womanhood into 'a toy, a drudge and a slave',[80] while Trotter lamented that 'an Arab woman always belongs to a man of some sort' – father, husband, brother, uncle – 'it is part of the iron yoke of Islam that will not snap but by the

---

70 Henry Christmas, 'The State and Prospects of Turkey and Mohammedanism', in *The Signs of the Times: Containing the Last Seven Lectures Delivered on Behalf of the Church of England Young Men's Society* (London: Wertheim and Macintosh, 1854), part 2, pp. 218, 231.
71 William Arthur, 'Mohammedanism', in *Lectures Delivered Before the Young Men's Christian Association, 1847–8* (London: Benjamin Green, 1848), p. 125.
72 Sinker, *Keith-Falconer*, p. 212.
73 Bell, *Grace for Muslims*, pp. 68, 86.
74 Bell, *Grace for Muslims*, p. 150.
75 Samuel Zwemer, *The Moslem Doctrine of God: An Essay on the Character and Attributes of Allah According to the Koran and Orthodox Tradition* (Edinburgh: Oliphant, Anderson and Ferrier, 1905), pp. 107, 120.
76 W. A. Rice, *Crusaders of the Twentieth Century; or The Christian Missionary and the Muslim: An Introduction to Work Among Muhammadans* (London: Church Missionary Society, 1910), p. 244.
77 Gairdner, *Thornton*, pp. vii–viii.
78 Bob Tennant, *Corporate Holiness: Pulpit Preaching and the Church of England Missionary Societies, 1760–1870* (Oxford: Oxford University Press, 2013), pp. 104, 184.
79 H. M. Elliot, *Bibliographical Index to the Historians of Muhammedan India* (Calcutta: Baptist Mission Press, 1849), p. xvi.
80 Gwynne to the parishioners of Emmanuel Church, Nottingham, 25 March 1900, in Jackson, *Pastor on the Nile*, p. 27.

touch of God's Hand'.[81] These negative verdicts showed no signs of abating by the twenty-first century. When Frog Orr-Ewing and Amy Kopsch, evangelical undergraduates at the University of Oxford, travelled to Afghanistan in April 1996 to interview the Taliban, they concluded that terrorism and the repression of women was 'profoundly theological', derived directly from the Qur'an, and must be acknowledged as an authentic expression of the Islamic religion.[82]

Nevertheless, evangelicals were often at the forefront of reconciliation ministry in the Middle East, like Andrew White, the so-called 'vicar of Baghdad'.[83] His namesake, Brother Andrew, coined a new mnemonic – ISLAM: 'I Sincerely Love All Muslims' – and provocatively declared that 'the best way to disarm a terrorist with a gun is to go up and hug him'.[84] As an act of remorse for historic animosities, Youth With A Mission (YWAM) organized a 'Reconciliation Walk' in the late 1990s, retracing the route of the Crusades from France, through the Balkans, and across Turkey, Syria, and Lebanon, to Jerusalem. About 3,000 people took part, mostly evangelicals from Britain and the United States, and their friendly interactions with local Muslims challenged negative preconceptions.[85] However, such acts of rapprochement divided evangelical opinion. Hostility to Islam, like anti-Catholicism in a previous generation, was so closely intertwined with evangelical identity that Bell, who advocated 'grace for Muslims', was accused of being 'either politically naïve, theologically liberal, or both'.[86]

A significant factor shaping evangelical attitudes was the rapid rise of the Muslim population in the West. When Martin Goldsmith was sent by the Overseas Missionary Fellowship to Singapore in 1960, he had never before met a Muslim in all his years in England.[87] Such Western isolationism was soon impossible as transnational migration transformed urban communities, which in turn led to cries of alarm at the imminent eclipse of Europe's Christian heritage by Islamic expansionism.[88] Yet it also provided evangelicals with abundant opportunities to meet Muslims face-to-face. For example, by 2013 at the Church of England primary school in Elswick, a deprived area of Newcastle upon Tyne, there were twenty-seven first languages spoken among the pupils, many of whose families came originally from Africa, India, Pakistan and Bangladesh. Thus the evangelical parish church, established in the mid-nineteenth century to reach Anglo-Saxon coalminers in the industrial slums, found itself in the midst of a new mission field among Muslim and Hindu communities.[89] On the other side of the Atlantic, David Goldmann (a former missionary in North Africa) observed that it was no longer necessary for evangelical churches to spend millions of dollars to send teams overseas to reach Muslims: 'Today the Muslim world is no longer "somewhere else"; instead, North America has become

---

81 Trotter Journal, 29 July 1908, in Rockness, *Passion for the Impossible*, p. 223.
82 Frog and Amy Orr-Ewing, *Holy Warriors: A Fresh Look at the Face of Extreme Islam* (Carlisle: Authentic, 2002), pp. 40, 71, 103–4.
83 Andrew White, *The Vicar of Baghdad: Fighting For Peace in the Middle East* (Oxford: Monarch, 2009); Andrew White, *My Journey So Far* (Oxford: Lion, 2015).
84 Brother Andrew with Al Janssen, *Secret Believers: What Happens When Muslims Turn to Christ?* (London: Hodder and Stoughton, 2007), pp. 236, 264.
85 Nick Megoran, 'Towards a Geography of Peace: Pacific Geopolitics and Evangelical Christian Crusade Apologies', *Transactions of the Institute of British Geographers* vol. 35 (July 2010), 382–98.
86 Bell, *Grace for Muslims*, p. 55.
87 Martin Goldsmith, *Beyond Beards and Burqas: Connecting with Muslims* (Nottingham: Inter-Varsity Press, 2009), p. 10.
88 Philip Jenkins, *God's Continent: Christianity, Islam, and Europe's Religious Crisis* (New York: Oxford University Press, 2007).
89 Alan Munden, *'A Beautiful Prospect': Elswick, Newcastle upon Tyne: St Paul's Chapel, Church and School* (Newcastle upon Tyne: Elswick Parish Church, 2013), pp. 141, 149–50.

part of the Muslim world'.[90] New evangelical literature taught culturally-sensitive outreach to Muslim next-door-neighbours, such as Bell's *Friendship First* consultancy to help 'ordinary Christians' discuss the gospel with 'ordinary Muslims', launched on 11 September 2002, the first anniversary of 9/11.[91] Personal interactions challenged evangelical preconceptions about Islam's true nature. After analysing a spectrum of early twenty-first-century approaches, Richard McCallum concluded that Western evangelicals who had lived in the Islamic world or who learned about Islam from contemporary Muslims tended to be more irenic than those who learned about Islam only from its religious texts and history. Yet he acknowledged also the counter-evidence that converts from Islam to Christianity, who had deep first-hand knowledge, tended to be among the most hostile to their old religion.[92]

Political prophecy and spiritual warfare

Islam's place in evangelical consciousness bore direct correlation to its political dominance. Since its zenith in the fifteenth century, Arthur announced in 1847, Islam had suffered constant reverses. 'No hero of Islam has arisen, no conquest of Islam been won. On all hands Christianity has gained upon the crescent.' He pointed to the success of Protestantism in India, Roman Catholicism in North Africa and Eastern Orthodoxy in Persia, under the flags of Britain, France and Russia. Thus in every part of the world 'a want of vigour marks the once impetuous Islam', and the only hero it had produced for many years was Abd al-Qadir who led the Algerian resistance to French invasion in the 1830s.[93] Bishop Daniel Wilson of Calcutta denounced Islam as a 'wretched imposture' but predicted its imminent demise, celebrating especially the Islâhat Fermâni of 1856 which granted religious liberty in Turkey as a result of British and French diplomatic pressure after the Crimean War.[94] At the turn of the new century, Zwemer could rejoice that 'The keys to every gateway in the Moslem world are today in the political grasp of Christian Powers, with the exception of Mecca and Constantinople.'[95] His 1915 Princeton lectures on *The Disintegration of Islam* asserted the 'utter collapse' of Islamic political power throughout Africa, Europe and Asia, and his confidence that 'when the crescent wanes the Cross will prove dominant'.[96] Thus in the 1908 edition of William Blackstone's best-selling tract *Jesus is Coming*, Islam was not even mentioned among the signs of the imminent parousia. Instead his focus was the rise of 'the atheistic Antichrist', revealed by 'the progress of Nihilism, Socialism, Communism and Anarchy'.[97] Blackstone's prescience seemed vindicated a decade later by the dissolution of the Ottoman Empire and the rise of the Bolsheviks. Soon the dominance of Hitler's Fascism was the chief threat to European Christianity, while the Cold

---

90 David Goldmann, *Islam and the Bible: Why Two Faiths Collide* (Chicago, IL: Moody Publishers, 2004), p. 13.
91 Steve Bell, *Friendship First, The Manual: Ordinary Christians Discussing Good News with Ordinary Muslims* (Market Rasen: Friendship First, 2003).
92 Richard McCallum, 'Rejection or Accommodation? Trends in Evangelical Christian Responses to Muslims', in *Religion and Knowledge: Sociological Perspectives*, edited by Mathew Guest and Elisabeth Arweck (Farnham: Ashgate, 2012), p. 127. See further, Richard McCallum, 'A Sociological Approach to Christian-Muslim Relations: British Evangelicals, Muslims and the Public Sphere' (unpublished PhD thesis, University of Exeter, 2011).
93 Arthur, 'Mohammedanism', pp. 124–5.
94 *The Journal of Bishop Daniel Wilson of Calcutta, 1845–1857*, edited by Andrew Atherstone (Woodbridge: Boydell, 2015), p. xxxii.
95 Zwemer, *Raymund Lull*, p. 153.
96 Samuel Zwemer, *The Disintegration of Islam* (New York: Fleming H. Revell, 1916), pp. 9–10.
97 William E. Blackstone, *Jesus is Coming* (third edition, Chicago: Fleming H. Revell, 1908), pp. 230–1.

War and fears of nuclear apocalypse kept Communism, not Islam, in the forefront of evangelical prophetic concerns.

There were occasional counterpoints. For example, when the British government in 1940 offered the gift of land near Regent's Park in London to build a mosque and Islamic cultural centre, *Evangelical Christendom* alerted its readers to 'The Moslem Problem' and urged them to resist 'the onward sweep of Mohammedanism'.[98] In the closing months of the Second World War, *The Record* (an Anglican evangelical newspaper) likewise declared 'the challenge of Islam' to be one of the most vital issues the church needed to confront in 'the new World Order'.[99] Yet it was not until the final decades of the century, especially after the escalation of the Arab-Israeli Crisis and the 1979 Iranian Revolution, that Islam came to dominate evangelical priorities and end-time predictions in the West.[100] The Evangelical Alliance magazine – renamed *Crusade*, apparently oblivious to the historic sensitivities of such a title – worried that Islam was 'vigorously on the march', with the oil-producing countries of the Middle East 'ploughing their profits into Islamic education and evangelism, as well as into western property'. It warned that 'highly trained' Muslim missionaries were at work in Africa, while in Europe the message was more subtly propagated by Islamic 'cultural centres' and festivals, such as that held in 1976 to mark the belated opening of the London Central Mosque.[101] Patrick Sookhdeo argued that Islam was entering 'a new era' as 'a potent social, economic and political force', partly due to widespread disillusionment with the dominant ideologies of Western secularism and Marxist materialism.[102] Brother Andrew, who made his name smuggling Bibles behind the Iron Curtain from the 1950s to the 1980s, turned his attention to the Middle East.[103] He concluded that Islam presented 'a far greater challenge' than Communism ever had, because Communism collapsed after seventy years but Islam had existed for 1,400 years.[104]

Islamic terrorism against Western targets – including New York and Washington in 2001, Madrid in 2004 and London in 2005 – heightened evangelical fears. While listening to an address by Sookhdeo in January 2002, Pawson was overwhelmed by a sudden premonition of 'an Islamic takeover' of Britain, which he believed to be 'a prophetic prediction from the Lord'.[105] He proclaimed that Islam was a Satanic deception and warned that it had 'infiltrated' the British education system, both in schools and universities, and been granted increasing political power.[106] In similar style, *Prophecy Today* announced a decisive battle: 'Either the Muslims will eventually take the West for Islam, or the church will take Islam for Christ'.[107] Hill maintained that extremists were plotting 'to make Britain into the first Muslim state in Europe as part of their plan for world domination', and unless the church took action 'the whole of the western world will be plunged into a new "dark ages" and the hard-won freedoms we have cherished will be lost. The Lord is sending an urgent wake-up call to his people. Blow

---

98 'The Moslem Problem' and 'The Challenge of Islam', *Evangelical Christendom* (October–December 1941), 145. See further, A. L. Tibawi, 'History of the London Central Mosque and the Islamic Cultural Centre, 1910–1980', *Die Welt des Islams* vol. 21 (1981), 193–208.
99 'Islam Today: A Challenge to the Christian Church', *The Record*, 29 December 1944, p. 539.
100 For analysis of the American apocalyptic literature, see especially Kidd, *American Christians and Islam*, Chs 5, 7–8.
101 'The New Face of Islam' and 'The Growth of Islam', *Crusade* vol. 25 (February 1980), 23, 26.
102 Patrick Sookhdeo, 'The Political Reality of Islam', *Crusade* vol. 25 (February 1980), 24.
103 Brother Andrew with Al Janssen, *Light Force: The Only Hope for the Middle East* (London: Hodder and Stoughton, 2005).
104 Brother Andrew, *Secret Believers*, p. 245.
105 Pawson, *Challenge of Islam*, pp. 6–7, 92–3.
106 Pawson, *Challenge of Islam*, pp. 30–2, 76–87.
107 Wong, 'The Harvest is Plentiful', 20.

the trumpet!'[108] These terrorist atrocities were interpreted as birth pangs before the return of Christ and as divine judgment to stir the church from its slumber. Fifty-two people were killed in the 7/7 attacks on London, but *Prophecy Today* warned that 'next time it could be 600 or 6,000, or more . . . *things are going to get worse* . . . God's purpose is to strengthen the remnant church – that's us!!'[109]

Ultimately, evangelicals agreed, it was not a human conflict. In a tract written for fellow missionaries in Muslim contexts, Trotter declared that 'the very air is full of the powers of darkness; and the enemy launches his fiery darts in showers on those who come to attack his strongholds'.[110] Brother Andrew suggested Islamic terrorism was 'a reflection of a spiritual war, an unseen conflict'.[111] Therefore he invited his readers to 'strap on your spiritual armour and join in the good jihad' by launching a major 'prayer offensive' for Muslims throughout the world. In particular they should pray for Hamas, Hezbollah, al-Qaeda and Osama bin Laden: 'Let's contest with the devil for the soul of the man, not with military might but with the gospel. . . . If our only response is to go out and destroy Muslim fundamentalists, we won't win a single soul'.[112] Hill concurred. Although the Second Gulf War might remove Saddam Hussein from power in Iraq, Islam could not be 'defeated by force of arms' because 'We are not dealing with "flesh and blood" but with a spiritual force or "principality" and the only way it can be opposed is through a more powerful spiritual force.'[113]

Counting converts

Evangelicals have a perennial desire for counting the number of converts, as evidence of the health of their congregations and missions. Accurate statistics for conversions from Islam are, however, notoriously elusive.[114] Some missionaries could not resist the temptation to inflate their success, like E. F. Baldwin, an American Baptist who published triumphant reports in the 1880s of many converts in Morocco. He was found to have been deceived by his Arabic interpreter into baptizing Muslims who submitted as a joke or for *bakhshish*, and was discredited.[115] Thornton in Egypt likewise wrote of 'many converts' where Gairdner believed it would be more accurate to write of 'many inquirers', though he excused his friend's exaggeration as a symptom of Thornton's optimistic nature and 'his readiness to *see possibilities*'.[116] Some Muslim leaders, paradoxically, also inflated the number of Christian converts in order to provoke a hostile reaction against the church, or to raise support for *da'wah* (Islamic proselytism). Furthermore, the phenomenon of 'secret believers' who keep their faith hidden for fear of persecution, and the 'insider movement' of Jesus followers who retain their Islamic identity and

---

108 Clifford Hill, 'PC Reigns! OK?', *Prophecy Today*, vol. 19 (March / April 2003), 6–8.
109 David and Catherine Lindsay, '"Read All About It" – In Your Bible!', *Prophecy Today* vol. 21 (November / December 2005), 20–1.
110 Rockness, *Passion for the Impossible*, p. 153.
111 Brother Andrew, *Secret Believers*, p. vii.
112 Brother Andrew, *Secret Believers*, pp. 262, 264.
113 Hill, 'PC Reigns! OK?', 8.
114 For the difficulties in estimating numbers of converts, see Duane Alexander Miller and Patrick Johnstone, 'Believers in Christ from a Muslim Background: A Global Census', *Interdisciplinary Journal of Research on Religion* vol. 11 (2015), 1–19.
115 Henry Harris Jessup, *Fifty-Three Years in Syria* (2 vols, New York: Fleming H. Revell, 1910), II: 546–48.
116 Gairdner, *Thornton*, pp. 124, 197.

mosque membership, make calculations especially contested. One sheik was quoted as saying that 'Many Christians will rise from Moslem graves in Syria.'[117]

A common evangelical refrain for most of the nineteenth and twentieth centuries was the particular difficulty of evangelizing Muslims, as more resistant than those from other religions or none. The American Mission in Egypt, established in 1854, had baptized only twenty-six converts from Islam by 1881. With a sudden flurry of twenty-two professions of faith during the next two years there was excitement at 'the stirring of a new life', which coincided with the British occupation of Egypt to suppress Arabi Pasha's rebellion. John Hogg wrote optimistically that 'If Egypt is given religious liberty worthy of the name, our success amongst the Mohammedans will soon surpass that amongst the Copts', yet the longed-for revival never materialized.[118] Henry Jessup in Syria refuted the suggestion that there were no converts from Islam: he knew of between forty and fifty, and had personally baptized at least thirty, most of whom had to flee the country for their own safety.[119] Nevertheless this was not a rapid rate of return for fifty years of evangelism. Likewise in Palestine, at the turn of the century, one optimistic clergyman reported to the Church Missionary Society that it seemed as if 'the day of grace were about to break', though he acknowledged that 'the red of dawn must not be mistaken for the full light of day'.[120] Bishop E. A. Knox was alarmed by 'the remarkable results of Mohammedan propagandism', especially the success of Wahhabism in Arabia, and the advance of Islam in Africa, China, the Malay archipelago, and southern Russia. He lamented that even if a million Muslims converted to Christianity every year, the statistics were unfavourable if in the same period 2 million pagans converted to Islam.[121] When Zwemer visited Java in 1922 he calculated that it was home to over 37,000 converts from Islam to Christianity, with an additional 8,000 on surrounding islands, more than anywhere else in the world; but a local Islamic newspaper was dismissive: 'After all what are these among thirty million Moslems on Java alone?'[122]

Soon after arriving in Algiers in 1888, Trotter wrote optimistically to the North Africa Mission that 'The whole place gives one the impression of being "White unto the harvest"', but with the benefit of hindsight she described those early years as 'knocking our heads against stone walls'.[123] When an American delegation visited the mission in 1907, she admitted that there was very little 'worth looking at or hearing about – no schools – no hospitals – no organizations – no results to speak of or to shew for our close on twenty years' fight in Algiers. Should we be able to help discouraging them!'[124] Trotter wrote in her journal that Jesus, the Good Shepherd, had 'such a very little flock in these Moslem Lands'.[125] In *A Thirsty Land and God's Channels* (1908) she compared Islam to the Sahara Desert, 'Dry as the dunes, hard as the

---

117 Jessup, *Fifty-Three Years*, I: 146.
118 Rena Hogg, *A Master-Builder on the Nile: Being a Record of the Life and Aims of John Hogg* (New York: Fleming H. Revell, 1914), p. 250, cited in Vander Werff, *Christian Mission*, p. 151. See further, Heather Sharkey, *American Evangelicals in Egypt: Missionary Encounters in an Age of Empire* (Princeton, NJ: Princeton University Press, 2008).
119 Jessup, *Fifty-Three Years*, II: 617.
120 Julius Richter, *A History of Protestant Missions in the Near East* (Edinburgh: Oliphant, Anderson and Ferrier, 1910), p. 254, cited in Vander Werff, *Christian Mission*, p. 161.
121 E. A. Knox, *The Crisis of Christendom and Islam: A Sermon Preached Before the Church Missionary Society in St Bride's Church, Fleet Street, London* (Manchester: John Heywood, 1910), pp. 4–6.
122 J. Christy Wilson, *Apostle to Islam: A Biography of Samuel M. Zwemer* (Grand Rapids, MI: Baker, 1952), pp. 119–20.
123 Rockness, *Passion for the Impossible*, pp. 116, 119.
124 Trotter Journal, 7 May 1907, in Rockness, *Passion for the Impossible*, p. 207.
125 Trotter Journal, 29 March 1908, in Rockness, *Passion for the Impossible*, p. 217.

gravel'.[126] It was a similar story in Morocco where Farnham St John served for thirty years, from 1945, as a missionary doctor in Tangier. He quickly discovered 'the crushing strength of Islam' and understood why so many missionaries had 'gone home in despair', because the Muslim population 'seem so unresponsive and there are complications wherever you turn'.[127] His sister Patricia – author of the evangelical children's classics *The Tanglewood's Secret* (1948) and *Treasures of the Snow* (1950) – joined him as a missionary nurse from 1949. She likewise spoke of 'the long, grinding and often disappointing years', painfully aware of 'the stranglehold of Islam and the spiritual warfare involved in the release of its followers'.[128] There were only a handful of conversions, as she wistfully recalled:

> How do we, who work among Moslems, measure the achievement of those years? A few bodies healed, for a few desolate children the memory that someone cared, and a few, so very few, who came to a living faith in Christ with all that means of suffering and family division. Only four remained openly avowed Christians in the years to come and no church formed. I believe there are some secret believers, but they are known only to God.[129]

Compared to such down-beat assessments, there was a remarkable shift in evangelical narratives towards the end of the twentieth century. The Indonesian 'revival', in the turbulent wake of the failed Communist coup in September 1965, was exceptional. Two million Javanese converts were baptized during the next six years, stimulated by the government's anti-Communist decree that every Indonesian must believe in God and choose a religion, or face the consequences.[130] A generation later there were reports from across the globe of Muslims turning in unprecedented numbers to Christianity (mostly to evangelicalism or Pentecostalism), in direct defiance of government pressure. Goldsmith had often likened mission among Muslims to a small boy ineffectually attacking the mighty walls of an old English castle with his toy bow and arrow, but the comparison was no longer appropriate because 'cracks' in the edifice were beginning to show.[131] Patricia St John heralded in 1990 a 'spiritual dawn' in Algeria, with hundreds, and perhaps thousands, of conversions.[132] The North Africa Mission – renamed Arab World Ministries – marked its 125th anniversary in 2006 with a volume celebrating conversion testimonies, which Trotter and her contemporaries had not lived to witness.[133] In Iran, there were perhaps only 500 Muslim-background believers in the Anglican and Presbyterian churches in 1979, despite a century of evangelical missions which came to an abrupt end when Ayatollah Khomeini seized power. Thirty-five years later there were said to be 370,000 converts in Iranian house churches and forecasts of over 1.2 million by 2020. There were quite simply, as Mark

---

126 Rockness, *Passion for the Impossible*, p. 221.
127 *Patricia St John Tells Her Own Story* (Carlisle: OM Publishing, 1995), p. 120.
128 *Patricia St John Tells Her Own Story*, pp. 119, 133.
129 *Patricia St John Tells Her Own Story*, p. 115.
130 Avery T. Willis, *Indonesian Revival: Why Two Million Came to Christ* (Pasadena, CA: William Carey Library, 1977). See further, 'The Spectacular Growth of the Third Stream: The Evangelicals and Pentecostals', in *A History of Christianity in Indonesia*, edited by Jan Aritonang and Karel Steenbrink (Leiden: Brill, 2008), pp. 867–902.
131 Goldsmith, *Beyond Beards and Burqas*, pp. 143, 149.
132 Patricia St John, *Until the Day Breaks: The Life and Work of Lilias Trotter, Pioneer Missionary to Muslim North Africa* (Bromley: OM Publishing, 1990), pp. 222–3.
133 David Lundy, Gary Corwin and Gail Martin, *The Desert is Alive: Streams of Living Water from Muscat to Marrakech* (Milton Keynes: Authentic, 2006).

Bradley put it, 'too many to jail'.[134] David Garrison investigated major 'movements' of Muslims to Christ, defined as 1,000 baptisms of new believers in a two-decade period, or the launch of 100 new churches. He calculated that there were eleven such 'movements' between 1980 and 2000, and another sixty-nine between 2000 and 2012, a dramatic rate of increase. 'Something is happening – something historic, something unprecedented', Garrison proclaimed. The church was standing, he announced, at 'a historic hinge moment in the spread of the gospel across the Muslim world'.[135] These widely-publicized reports of Christian revival among Muslims gave renewed confidence to evangelicals in the West who felt threatened by the advance of Islam in their own nations.

Scholarly analysis and media attention has focused especially upon the phenomenon of Western conversions to Islam, including autobiographical narratives like that of the German television presenter Kristiane Backer, *From MTV to Mecca* (2012).[136] There are multiple studies of Islam's appeal to Western women.[137] Also important are de-conversion narratives from Islam to secular humanism, notably *Why I am Not a Muslim* (1995) by the pseudonymous Ibn Warraq, and his edited collection, *Leaving Islam: Apostates Speak Out* (2003).[138] Among evangelicals in the West, there has always been a buoyant market for a rival set of testimonies, from Christian converts in the Muslim world.[139] Two of the best known in the nineteenth century were 'Abd al-Masih ('servant of the Messiah', the baptism name of Shaikh Salih), the only Muslim convert from Martyn's ministry, and 'Imad al-Din, an evangelist and tract-writer in the Punjab whose Urdu testimony went through multiple English editions as *A Mohammedan Brought to Christ* (1869).[140] A century later, *Design of My World* (1959) was widely circulated, the testimony of

---

134 Mark Bradley, *Too Many to Jail: The Story of Iran's New Christians* (Oxford: Monarch, 2014), pp. 36, 149.
135 David Garrison, *A Wind in the House of Islam: How God is Drawing Muslims Around the World to Faith in Jesus Christ* (Monument, CO: WIGTake Resources, 2014), pp. 18, 26.
136 Larry Poston, *Islamic Da'wah in the West: Muslim Missionary Activity and the Dynamics of Conversion to Islam* (New York: Oxford University Press, 1992); Jeffrey Lang, *Struggling to Surrender: Some Impressions of an American Convert to Islam* (Beltsville, MD: Amana Publications, 1994); Ali Köse, *Conversion to Islam: A Study of Native British Converts* (London: Kegan Paul, 1996); Kate Zebiri, *British Muslim Converts: Choosing Alternative Lives* (Oxford: Oneworld, 2008); Lucy Bushill-Matthews, *Welcome to Islam: A Convert's Tale* (London: Continuum, 2008); Kristiane Backer, *From MTV to Mecca: How Islam Inspired My Life* (Swansea: Arcadia, 2012); Jamie Gilham, *Loyal Enemies: British Converts to Islam, 1850–1950* (London: Hurst, 2014).
137 Carol Anway, 'American Women Choosing Islam', in *Muslims on the Americanization Path?*, edited by Yvonne Yazbeck Haddad and John Esposito (New York: Oxford University Press, 2000), pp. 145–60; Anna Mansson McGinty, *Becoming Muslim: Western Women's Conversions to Islam* (Basingstoke: Palgrave Macmillan, 2006); *Women Embracing Islam: Gender and Conversion in the West*, edited by Karin van Nieuwkerk (Austin, TX: University of Texas Press, 2006); Janet Testerman, *Transforming from Christianity to Islam: Eight Women's Journey* (Newcastle upon Tyne: Cambridge Scholars, 2014).
138 See further, Mohammad Hassan Khalil and Mucahit Bilici, 'Conversion Out of Islam: A Study of Conversion Narratives of Former Muslims', *Muslim World* vol. 97 (January 2007), 111–24.
139 Jean-Marie Gaudeul, *Called from Islam to Christ: Why Muslims Become Christians* (Crowborough: Monarch, 1999).
140 Avril Powell, 'Processes of Conversion to Christianity in Nineteenth-Century North-Western India', in *Religious Conversion Movements in South Asia: Continuities and Change, 1800–1900*, edited by Geoffrey Oddie (Richmond: Curzon, 1997), pp. 31–42; Avril Powell, '"Pillar of a New Faith": Christianity in Late-Nineteenth-Century Punjab from the Perspective of a Convert from Islam', in *Christians and Missionaries in India: Cross-Cultural Communication since 1500*, edited by Robert Eric Frykenberg (Grand Rapids, MI: Eerdmans, 2003), pp. 223–55.

Hassan Dehqani-Tafti who converted to Christianity as an Iranian teenager in the 1930s, and later served as an Anglican bishop.[141]

As conversions multiplied towards the end of the twentieth century, so did the number of evangelical paperbacks. Early best-sellers, both by female converts from Pakistan, were Bilquis Sheikh's *I Dared to Call Him Father* (1978) and Gulshan Esther's *The Torn Veil* (1984). Evangelical publishers were particularly interested in dramatic accounts by former Muslim 'fanatics', especially if they had been involved in terrorism, sometimes written in the style of a Hollywood blockbuster.[142] The autobiography of Mosab Hassan Yousef, *Son of Hamas* (2012), was subtitled, 'a gripping account of terror, betrayal, political intrigue, and unthinkable choices'. Likewise the story of Ali Husnain (a pseudonym), a Pakistani Muslim turned Christian evangelist, was marketed as a 'modern epic':

> Stabbed by a terrorist attacker – the blade narrowly missed his heart – Ali was left unconscious on the street. He was rushed to the hospital, and while he was lying on what the doctor declared would be his death bed, Jesus spoke to Ali for the second time. Throughout his ordeal – exile from home and family, a near-death experience, a miraculous healing, and a cross-continental chase as he fled for his life – Ali's faith compelled him to bring the gospel to Muslims. No matter the cost.[143]

The courage of converts facing persecution in Islamic nations was described for evangelical readers in Brother Andrew's *Secret Believers* (2007) and Tom Doyle's *Killing Christians* (2015),[144] while heroic women were especially popular. This genre included the autobiographies of Maryam Rostampour and Marziyeh Amirizadeh, imprisoned in Tehran in 2009 for distributing New Testaments,[145] and of Hannah Shah and Rifqa Bary who both fled their families, in Britain and the United States respectively, for fear of 'honour killings'.[146] In similar vein, narratives of Bible smuggling in the Arab world, or of two Texan women rescued by American special forces after being imprisoned for proselytism by the Taliban, became the twenty-first-century equivalent of the Victorian missionary adventure.[147] There were also modern missionary martyrs, like

---

141 H. B. Dehqani-Tafti, *Design of My World* (London: Lutterworth, 1959); H. B. Dehqani-Tafti, *The Unfolding Design of My World: A Pilgrim in Exile* (Norwich: Canterbury Press, 2000).
142 Steven Masood, *Into the Light: A Young Muslim's Search for Truth* (Eastbourne: Kingsway, 1986); Ghulam Masih Naaman with Vita Toon, *The Unexpected Enemy: A Muslim Freedom Fighter Encounters Christ* (London: Marshall Pickering, 1985); Reza Safa, *Blood of the Sword, Blood of the Cross: A Fanatical Muslim Tells His Story* (Chichester: Sovereign World, 1990); Christopher Alam, *Through the Blood and the Fire: A Muslim Fanatic Becomes a Fiery Evangelist for Jesus Christ* (Chichester: New Wine Press, 1994); Nabeel Qureshi, *Seeking Allah, Finding Jesus: A Devout Muslim Encounters Christianity* (Grand Rapids, MI: Zondervan, 2014).
143 Ali Husnain with J. Chester, *The Cost: My Life on a Terrorist Hit List* (Grand Rapids, MI: Zondervan, 2016), back cover.
144 Tom Doyle with Greg Webster, *Killing Christians: Living the Faith Where It's Not Safe to Believe* (Nashville, TN: Thomas Nelson, 2015). See also, Rupert Shortt, *Christianophobia: A Faith Under Attack* (London: Rider, 2012).
145 Maryam Rostampour and Marziyeh Amirizadeh, with John Perry, *Captive in Iran: A Remarkable True Story of Hope and Triumph Amid the Horror of Tehran's Brutal Evin Prison* (Carol Stream, IL: Tyndale, 2013).
146 Hannah Shah, *The Imam's Daughter: My Desperate Flight to Freedom* (Grand Rapids, MI: Zondervan, 2010); Rifqa Bary, *Hiding in the Light: Why I Risked Everything to Leave Islam and Follow Jesus* (Milton Keynes: Authentic, 2015).
147 Deborah Meroff, *Under Their Very Eyes: The Astonishing Life of Tom Hamblin, Bible Courier to Arab*

Stephen Foreman, murdered in North Africa in 2010 by al-Qaeda.[148] This abundant literature reinforced among a popular evangelical readership a widespread view of Islam's inherent brutality and misogyny, and of the ultimate triumphant victory of the Christian faith.

Converts and missionaries frequently recorded the significance of dreams and visions in bringing Muslims to Christian faith, though this troubled some evangelicals theologically. Trotter in 1898 wondered at its 'unorthodoxy', but justified revelatory dreams as appropriate for illiterate people groups because they were 'God's way of teaching just now those who are shut out by their ignorance from having the direct communication with Himself through His word'.[149] A century later, as reports of dreams multiplied in conversion testimonies, among literate and illiterate alike, evangelical missiologists struggled to integrate this with their axiomatic assumption that the normal means of conversion should be Bible reading and gospel preaching.[150] Nevertheless, Doyle asserted that dreams and visions were instrumental in the conversion of about a third of Muslim-background believers, and that 'God is happy to rescue people out of the darkness by means we more conservative types find unconventional'. He declared, with direct comparison to the eighteenth-century Evangelical Revival under Edwards and Whitefield, 'I believe we're seeing the Great Awakening of the Muslim world.'[151]

Conclusion

Over three centuries, evangelical interpretations of and engagements with Islam have taken multiple contrasting, and sometimes contradictory, forms. Popular rhetorical tropes about Mohammed and 'the Mussulmans' jostled with nuanced scholarly investigations, deep reading, and first-hand cross-cultural experience. Evangelistic methodologies fluctuated between forthright apologetics and friendship building, or between public debate in the *bazaars* and philanthropic medical and educational provision (such as the *zenana* missions, offering health care to women in India). Doctrinal treatises and parabolic story-telling flowed from mission presses, aimed at Muslim readers, while evangelical congregations in the West were inundated with exemplary missionary narratives or dramatic conversion testimonies. Evangelical attitudes often mirrored imperialistic confidence or anxieties concerning Islam's political and cultural strength, mixed with prophetic and apocalyptic fervour, stimulated by regime change, mass migration and international terrorism.

As this chapter has shown, evangelicals were sharply divided among themselves in their understanding of Islam's multiple identities, and the opportunities or threats that Islam and Islamism presented to the Christian church. By the twenty-first century, however, the rapid rise in the number of converts from Muslim backgrounds began to alter the balance of the debate. Evangelical opinions were no longer shaped predominantly by English-speakers from the West, but now by evangelical believers in Muslim-majority regions, numbering in their hundreds of

---

Nations (Oxford: Monarch, 2016); Dayna Curry and Heather Mercer, *Prisoners of Hope: The Story of our Captivity and Freedom in Afghanistan* (London: Hodder and Stoughton, 2002).

148 Emily Foreman, *We Died Before We Came Here: A True Story of Sacrifice and Hope* (Colorado Springs, CO: NavPress, 2016).

149 Trotter Journal, 28 May 1898, in Rockness, *Passion for the Impossible*, p. 169. For dreams of Algerian Muslims, recounted to Trotter, see Constance Padwick, 'Dream and Vision: Some Notes from a Diary', *International Review of Missions* vol. 28 (April 1939), 205–16.

150 George Martin, 'The God Who Reveals Mysteries: Dreams and World Evangelization', *Southern Baptist Journal of Theology* vol. 8 (Spring 2004), 60–72.

151 Tom Doyle with Greg Webster, *Dreams and Visions: Is Jesus Awakening the Muslim World?* (Nashville, TN: Thomas Nelson, 2012), pp. 127, 253.

thousands – from Ethiopia to Iran, Burkina Faso to Bangladesh, Cameroon to Kazakhstan, and many other lands. Although this chapter has examined exclusively Anglophone sources, many of the twenty-first-century texts engaging with Islamic doctrine and culture are produced by evangelicals within, for example, Farsi, Arabic, Hausa, Urdu or Javanese communities. The theological perspectives, missional methods and local narratives of these growing churches provide unexplored terrain, ripe for research by historians with the necessary linguistic abilities, to provide a fully global analysis of contemporary evangelical engagement with the Islamic world.

9

EVANGELICALS AND MISSION IN THE ATLANTIC NORTH

Martin Spence

Evangelicals are congenitally missional. The evangelical claim that individuals must decide personally to accept the saving grace of Christ, and the corollary that faithful believers must extend widely the offer of salvation, have been keynotes of evangelicalism since it emerged in the eighteenth century. The evangelical movement has flourished because it has transformed the potentially disastrous corrosion of culturally confessional Christianity into that which evangelicals have claimed to be the necessary prerequisite for the attainment of true faith: individual religious liberty. This astute adaptation of Reformation Protestantism to the world of modern North Atlantic liberalism has imposed a huge burden on evangelicals since it has required constant and ever more innovative attempts at persuading individuals to embrace the Gospel of Jesus Christ. Evangelicals have been entrepreneurial, strenuous and culturally-astute purveyors of redemption in an increasingly crowded religious free market. However, the demands of this often overwhelming task have exerted a subtle toll on the evangelical psyche, which has often been haunted by a fear that any slackening of the missionary task will lead to the haemorrhaging of Christianity. 'An evangelistic church is a flourishing church', wrote the celebrated Scottish missionary Alexander Duff (1806–1878) in 1839, 'and a church which drops the evangelistic character, speedily lapses into superannuation and decay'.[1]

There is no clearly demarcated historiographical corpus examining domestic mission comparable to the book series, journals, and study centres that have helped promote scrutiny of foreign mission. This historiographical neglect reflects an historical reality: foreign mission, replete with accounts of exotic cultures and romantic heroes, has always generated more attention among evangelicals themselves.[2] In 1822 the (British) Baptist Home Missionary Society income was ten times less that of the Baptist Missionary Society.[3] The voluminous scholarly literature on foreign mission is due also to the intersection of the topic with the historiographically-magnetic themes

---

1 Alexander Duff, *Missions the Chief End of the Christian Church* (London: J. Johnstone, 1839), p. 15.
2 Susan Thorne, *Congregational Missions and the Making of an Imperial Culture in Nineteenth-Century England* (Stanford, CA: Stanford University Press, 1999), p. 47.
3 Derek J. Tidball, 'English Nonconformist Home Missions, 1796–1901' (unpublished PhD thesis, Keele University, 1981), p. 127. Tidball's account is the most comprehensive treatment of English domestic mission in the nineteenth century and contains abundant information for future researchers, albeit focusing only on England and excluding Anglicans.

of political and cultural imperialism. By comparison, domestic mission has seemed parochial.[4] The study of domestic mission is also diffuse. Many studies of the evangelical movement contain valuable information about local and national missionary activity intertwined with the broader stories that their authors seek to narrate.[5]

These factors combine to make this survey necessarily, and no doubt sometimes inadvertently, selective. The chapter is divided into two parts. First, it explores the various resonances of the terms 'home' and 'domestic' mission, proposing that the words are freighted with historically-conditioned meaning that both complicates and stimulates historical investigation. Second, it provides a chronological survey of some of the ways in which evangelicals in Britain and North America have attempted to evangelize their local and national communities. This survey will adhere to the contours of existing historiography in order to map some of the relevant literature for future researchers.

Coming to terms with 'home' and 'domestic' mission

More than heuristic devices of the historian, the terms 'home mission' or 'domestic mission' are constructs of the evangelical imagination. It is well known that the formation of the Baptist Missionary Society in 1792 was triggered in part by William Carey's excited perusal of the Pacific travelogues of the British mariner James Cook. Such encounters with the 'foreign' transmogrified the immediate vicinity of evangelicals into a demarcated and denominated sphere of missionary activity. Of course, the eighteenth-century preaching endeavours of John Wesley, George Whitefield, Daniel Rowland, Gilbert Tennent, and Henry Alline were a kind of mission at home. The Methodist movement has a good claim to be the first 'home missionary' enterprise. 'We have hitherto taken the lead in Home missionary work', explained British Methodist Charles Prest (d.1875) in 1857, 'though we have not adopted the name. From the first ours was a Missionary system and our ministers were, and in most circuits still are, Home missionaries'.[6] Nevertheless, the deliberate classification of the local environment as a mission field did not begin until the last decade of the eighteenth century. One of the earliest uses of the term 'home mission' seems to have been in the British *Evangelical Magazine and Missionary Chronicle* in 1797.[7]

Sites of domestic missionary concern were often described using the subaltern codes generated by encounters with alien people groups.[8] 'Some of our market towns, and many of our villages, are yet destitute of that Gospel which is received with joy by the brutal Hottentot, and the bigotted Hindoo; and Otaheite is a well-watered garden compared with some of the districts at home', observed *The Missionary Magazine*.[9] Timothy Flint (1780–1840) of the Missionary Society of Connecticut opined similarly that 'Hindoostan is not more strictly heathen, than this country'.[10] Home mission thus relied on the foreign foil. 'The transition from the view of

---

4 Tidball, 'English Nonconformist Home Missions', p. 36.
5 David W. Bebbington, *The Dominance of Evangelicalism: The Age of Spurgeon and Moody* (Downers Grove, IL: InterVarsity Press, 2005).
6 Tidball, 'English Nonconformist Home Missions', p. 46.
7 *Evangelical Magazine* vol. 5 (1797), 473.
8 Richard Carwardine, 'The Evangelist System: Charles Roe, Thomas Pulford and the Baptist Home Missionary Society', *Baptist Quarterly* vol. 28 (1980), 209–10; Thorne, *Congregational Missions*, pp. 82–7.
9 *Missionary Magazine* vol. 34 (18 March 1799), 355.
10 Colin Brummitt Goodykoontz, *Home Missions on the American Frontier, with Particular Reference to the American Home Missionary Society* (New York: Octagon Books, 1971), p. 144.

the deplorable state of the heathen abroad to that of the heathen at home is easy and affecting', explained the London Itinerant Society.[11]

Despite the bifurcating rhetoric of 'home' and 'foreign', the two missionary enterprises were not hermetically-sealed enterprises. Early home mission endeavours were sponsored by foreign mission agencies,[12] and foreign missionaries often returned home and took up local missionary duties, thereby creating 'conduits by which influences from new movements of world Christianity circulated back' to the domestic sphere.[13] There was also a 'home front' of foreign mission.[14] Those concerned with raising money and support for overseas ventures were aware that multiplying the number of Christians at home was in their own self-interest. 'In order that this country might be a blessing to the world, it must be a blessing to itself', explained English Congregationalist John Angell James (1785–1859) in 1834.[15] 'The Homeland is . . . the familiar base of world-reaching operations', echoed Presbyterian Joseph E. McAfee (1870–1944) in 1909. 'A saved America holds the key to the world's saving'.[16]

Foreign mission triggered mission at home, but more than this, the globalization of mental horizons helped generate the very concept of 'home' in the first place. As Amy Kaplan has argued 'domestic and foreign are . . . not neutral legal and spatial descriptions, but heavily weighted metaphors'.[17] The rise of this 'domestic' metaphor among evangelicals flowed in part from the broader bifurcation of the world occurring in imperializing Anglophone states. In 1782, the British government reorganized its 'Southern' and 'Northern' departments into the 'Home' and 'Foreign' Offices. British evangelicalism mirrored the reach of governmental diplomacy both in globalizing its 'missions' and in the subsequent reconceptualization of a bounded 'home' zone.

A similar reorganization of geopolitical horizons occurred on the other side of the Atlantic as part of the very foundation of an independent American Anglophone polity. Despite being framed as a protest against tyrannical colonialism, the Declaration of Independence (1776) was in fact a hostile takeover bid of the southern region of the North American British colonial project by its resident agents. Rejecting their inferior constitutional position within the British imperial state, a large minority of British-American settlers domesticated their polity, turning a colony into a sovereign state, thereby refashioning the colonial periphery into a metropolitan 'home' in order to better subdue the 'foreign' – the coveted land west of the Appalachians – on terms favourable to their own interests. The Northwest Ordinance in 1787 announced that the new American state was intent on constructing an Anglophone empire through territorial annexation and subjection of the 'foreign' native populations. 'With the opening of the Northwest Territory', explained the early twentieth-century secretary of the Congregational Home Mission Society Joseph B. Clark, 'Home Missions received a new birth'.[18]

---

11 *Evangelical Magazine* vol. 7 (1799), 83.
12 Tidball, 'English Nonconformist Home Missions', pp. 120–1.
13 Jay Riley Case, *An Unpredictable Gospel: American Evangelicals and World Christianity, 1812–1920* (New York: Oxford University Press, 2012), p. 9.
14 *The Foreign Missionary Enterprise at Home: Explorations in North American Cultural History*, edited by Daniel H. Bays and Grant Wacker (Tuscaloosa, AL: University of Alabama Press, 2003).
15 John Angell James, 'The Conversion of the World', in *The British Pulpit: A Collection of Three Hundred and Fifty Original Sermons, by the Most Eminent Divines of the Present Day* (6 vols, London: G. Wightman, 1839), II: 364–5.
16 Joseph Ernest McAfee, *Missions Striking Home: A Group of Addresses on a Phase of the Missionary Enterprise* (London: Fleming H. Revell, 1908), pp. 9, 21.
17 Amy Kaplan, *The Anarchy of Empire in the Making of U.S. Culture* (Cambridge, MA: Harvard University Press, 2002), p. 3.
18 Joseph B. Clark, *Leavening the Nation: The Story of American Protestant Home Missions* (London: Fleming H. Revell, 1913), p. 52.

In the United States of America 'home' mission was therefore not simply a mission to a pre-existing homeland, but also a mission charged with helping to *create* and *sustain* a new domestic polity – a 'transformative endeavor to create a Christian nation'.[19] J. B. Lawrence, historian of the Southern Baptist Home Mission Board, explained that 'the history of domestic missions is an aspect of national expansion. It is the religious version of the geographical occupancy of the continent'.[20] The Christianization of the American 'West' has been the subject of study for a clutch of works focusing on particular regions, denominations or agencies.[21] On balance, this endeavour was probably less about conversionist evangelism and more about the replication of Christian institutions based on the putative religious culture of the old North-East.[22]

Domestic mission in the United States was thus also a *domesticating* mission, an attempt to bring the transforming virtues of white, Anglophone civilization to populations considered ethnically or culturally inferior, which included Native Americans, African Americans and non-Anglophone immigrant populations.[23] The high density of 'foreign' people groups in the 'domestic' sphere blurred boundaries between home and foreign in North America. 'It is Europe, it is Asia, it is Africa, it is all of these brought together upon our own continent', exclaimed the American Baptist Home Missionary Society in 1863.[24] This complexity created terminological ambiguity. In 1864, the Methodist Episcopal Church created a department for 'Domestic Foreign Missions'.[25] While American home mission was clearly shaped by 'manifest destiny', it is important to note that there was also a more inclusive, less nationalistic, vision of evangelism that often struggled against the hardening of racial categories in the nineteenth century.[26]

The Dominion of Canada, a confederation of British North American colonies granted autonomy under the British Crown in 1867, sought to unify the new domain through infrastructure, industry and ideological nationalism.[27] Home mission was tethered to a broader agenda to 'Canadianize and Christianize'.[28] Many Canadian evangelicals were committed to building a Christian Anglo-Saxon polity – 'his dominion' – through the dual conversion and civilization of native populations and by neutralizing the 'menace' of immigrant 'inferior

---

19 Derek Chang, *Citizens of a Christian Nation: Evangelical Missions and the Problem of Race in the Nineteenth Century* (Philadelphia, PA: University of Pennsylvania Press, 2010), p. 34.
20 J. B. Lawrence, *History of the Home Mission Board* (Nashville, TN: Broadman Press, 1958), p. 5.
21 Walter Brownlow Posey, *Frontier Mission: A History of Religion West of the Southern Appalachians to 1861* (Lexington, KY: University of Kentucky Press, 1966); Alice Cowan Cochran, *Miners, Merchants, and Missionaries: The Roles of Missionaries and Pioneer Churches in the Colorado Gold Rush and Its Aftermath, 1858–1870* (Metuchen, NJ: Scarecrow Press, 1980); Laurie F. Maffly-Kipp, *Religion and Society in Frontier California* (New Haven, CT: Yale University Press, 1994); Ferenc Morton Szasz, *The Protestant Clergy in the Great Plains and Mountain West, 1865–1915* (Lincoln, NE: University of Nebraska Press, 2004).
22 Jon Butler, *Awash in a Sea of Faith: Christianizing the American People* (Cambridge, MA: Harvard University Press, 1992), p. 276; Amy DeRogatis, *Moral Geography: Maps, Missionaries, and the American Frontier* (New York: Columbia University Press, 2003).
23 Clifford S. Griffin, 'Religious Benevolence as Social Control, 1815–1860', *The Mississippi Valley Historical Review* vol. 44 (1957), 423–44; Lois W. Banner, 'Religious Benevolence as Social Control: A Critique of an Interpretation', *Journal of American History* vol. 60 (1973), 23–41.
24 Chang, *Citizens of a Christian Nation*, p. 17.
25 Case, *Unpredictable Gospel*, p. 142.
26 Case, *Unpredictable Gospel*, pp. 97, 138–44; Chang, *Citizens of a Christian Nation*, pp. 29–30.
27 Robert Bothwell, *History of Canada Since 1867* (East Lansing, MI: Michigan State University Press, 1996), p. 22.
28 J. R. Robertson, 'The Home Mission Problem in Canada', *Missionary Review of the World* vol. 31 (1908), 833.

races'.[29] In terms of the former, E. H. Oliver, missionary to the Canadian West and Principal of the Presbyterian Theological College at the University of Saskatchewan, depicted the Canadian frontier as the catalyst for Christian mission, the place where the 'outriders of civilization do battle with the primitive and elemental'.[30] In terms of the latter, Canadian home missionaries sometimes outpaced their southern neighbour in utopian rhetoric: 'This is the last portion of the world to be settled', noted R. G. MacBeth of the Presbyterian Church in Canada Home Mission Board in 1912, 'and here some of the greatest problems will have to be solved . . . The star [of empire] will halt over Canada, and under it some great messianic achievement for the good of the world may be born', but only, he added, if the 'lower and degraded races' could be tamed through Christianity and civilizational uplift.[31] Here too, home mission was intended to provide connective tissue that united both churches and society across the polity.[32]

Although the language of domestication of the foreign was most readily deployed in relation to the ethnically alien within the sphere of white Anglophone hegemony, it also carried cultural and political freight within the Anglophone sphere. In the United States, the dominance of the Northeast meant that the domesticating, civilizing mission was in part concerned with taming the uncivilized West, which meant the inchoate Anglophone settlers as much as Native Americans.[33] The South was another *loci* for Northern evangelization, where Northern missionaries viewed both white and black communities as standing in need of fuller Christianization.[34] Britain also had its rural frontiers, populated by supposedly alien primitives who had long been compared to Native Americans and other 'uncivilized' tribes.[35] Methodist Thomas Coke (1747–1815) considered the Scottish Highlanders 'little better than the rudest Barbarians'.[36] After the Act of Union in 1801, Ireland provided a parallel to the American example of a foreign

---

29 N. K. Clifford, 'His Dominion: A Vision in Crisis', *Religion and Society* vol. 2 (1973), 314–26; Jiwu Wang, *'His Dominion' and the 'Yellow Peril': Protestant Missions to the Chinese Immigrants in Canada, 1859–1967* (Waterloo: Wilfrid Laurier University Press, 2006). Key studies of home mission on the Canadian frontier include: John Webster Grant, *Moon of Wintertime: Missionaries and the Indians of Canada in Encounter since 1534* (Toronto: University of Toronto Press, 1984); Peter Bush, *Western Challenge: The Presbyterian Church in Canada's Mission on the Prairies and North, 1885–1925* (Winnipeg: Watson Dwyer, 2000); Myra Rutherdale, *Women and the White Man's God: Gender and Race in the Canadian Mission Field* (Vancouver: UBC Press, 2002); *Canadian Missionaries, Indigenous Peoples: Representing Religion at Home and Abroad*, edited by Alvyn Austin and Jamie S. Scott (Toronto: University of Toronto Press, 2005); Jan Hare and Jean Barman, *Good Intentions Gone Awry: Emma Crosby and the Methodist Mission on the Northwest Coast* (Vancouver: UBC Press, 2006).
30 N. K. Clifford, 'Religion and the Development of Canadian Society: An Historiographical Analysis', *Church History* vol. 38 (1969), 508.
31 R. G. MacBeth, *Our Task in Canada* (Toronto: Westminster, 1912), pp. 21–5.
32 Phyliss D. Airhart, 'Ordering a New Nation and Reordering Protestantism', in *The Canadian Protestant Experience 1760 to 1990*, edited by George A. Rawlyk (Burlington: Welch, 1990), p. 99.
33 Goodykoontz, *Home Missions on the American Frontier*, p. 426.
34 John Wolffe, *The Expansion of Evangelicalism: The Age of Wilberforce, More, Chalmers and Finney* (Downers Grove, IL: InterVarsity Press, 2007), p. 179; Case, *Unpredictable Gospel*, p. 65; John Kuykendall, *Southern Enterprize: The Work of National Evangelical Societies in the Antebellum South* (Westport, CN: Praeger, 1982); Joe M. Richardson *Christian Reconstruction: The American Missionary Association and Southern Blacks, 1861–1890* (Athens, GA: University of Georgia Press, 1986).
35 Donald E. Meek, 'Protestant Missions and the Evangelization of the Scottish Highlands, 1700–1850', *International Bulletin of Missionary Research* vol. 21 (1997), 68; George Robb, 'Popular Religion and the Christianization of the Scottish Highlands in the Eighteenth and Nineteenth Centuries', *Journal of Religious History* vol. 16 (1990), 18–34.
36 Andrew Holmes, 'The Shaping of Irish Presbyterian Attitudes to Mission, 1790–1840', *Journal of Ecclesiastical History* vol. 57 (2006), 731–5.

zone targeted for incorporation into the domestic polity in which evangelical missionaries were, at least in part, adjuncts to a broader geopolitical project.[37]

Ireland is a reminder that across the North Atlantic world — from the immigrant communities of Liverpool, Glasgow and New York, to the French-speaking populations of Quebec, the South Louisianan Acadia, and the Hispanic populations of the South-West United States — Roman Catholicism was a sign of an alien and threatening religious-cultural synthesis, and thus an inspiration for Protestant domestic missionary endeavour.[38] Rival Catholic domestic missionary activity also incentivized Protestant home mission campaigns.[39]

During the nineteenth century, a further 'frontier' opened up in the great cities of the North Atlantic zone where the coagulating working-class populations alarmed and excited evangelicals in equal measure.[40] Here home mission tended to take a particularly 'domestic' turn. Evangelicals fretted about the islands of working-class neighbourhoods isolated from the benevolent guardianship of social superiors and bereft of the ministrations of the local church.[41] Endeavouring to weave a Christian presence back into the fabric of the city, from the 1820s they pursued an evangelistic strategy that was literally *domestic*, deploying lay agents to go door to door, one domicile at a time.[42] 'The readiest way of finding access to a man's heart is to go into his house', observed Scottish Presbyterian Thomas Chalmers (1780–1847) whose 'aggressive system' of domestic visitation was widely emulated.[43]

These mid-nineteenth-century city missionaries often ministered to women. While there were pragmatic reasons for this — it was women who tended to be at home during the visiting hours of the missionary[44] — there was also an ideological rationale. The redemption of women was viewed by many Victorians as the prerequisite to household godliness, and, since the household was presumed to be the foundation of social stability, the conversion of women was essential to inculcation of a peaceable, godly, and morally upright social order. Barbara Caine has demonstrated the frequency of an injunctive appeal to the 'domestic mission' with which women were charged in English literature of the 1830s and 1840s. Sarah Lewis' *Woman's Mission* (1839) is the *locus classicus*. This ideal of domestic mission comprehended both the female mandate to their literal home, but also to the broader 'domestic' social order. Women must always 'be conscious of their mission', advised Lewis. 'That mission contains, perhaps, the destinies of society'.[45] Charles Dickens' famous indictment of Mrs Jellyby for neglecting her household in favour of 'telescopic philanthropy' was in part a call for female evangelical

---

37 David Hempton and Myrtle Hill, *Evangelical Protestantism in Ulster Society 1740–1890* (London: Routledge, 1992).
38 Robert Merrill Black, 'Different Visions: The Multiplication of Protestant Missions to French-Canadian Roman Catholics, 1834–1855', in *Canadian Protestant and Catholic Missions, 1820s–1960s*, edited by John S. Moir and C. T. McIntire (New York: Peter Lang, 1988), pp. 49–74.
39 Ray A. Billington, 'Anti-Catholic Propaganda and the Home Missionary Movement, 1800–1860', *The Mississippi Valley Historical Review* vol. 22 (1935), 361–84.
40 Paul Boyer, *Urban Masses and Moral Order in America, 1820–1920* (Cambridge, MA: Harvard University Press, 1992), pp. 3–21; Callum G. Brown, *The Death of Christian Britain: Understanding Secularisation, 1800–2000* (London: Routledge, 2001), pp. 18–30.
41 Boyer, *Urban Masses and Moral Order in America*, p. 31; Brown, *Death of Christian Britain*, p. 25.
42 H. D. Rack, 'Domestic Visitation: A Chapter in Early Nineteenth Century Evangelism', *Journal of Ecclesiastical History* vol. 24 (1973), 357–76.
43 Brown, *Death of Christian Britain*, p. 46.
44 Donald M. Lewis, *Lighten Their Darkness: The Evangelical Mission to Working-Class London, 1828–1860* (New York: Greenwood Press, 1986), p. 123.
45 Sarah Lewis, *Woman's Mission* (London: John W. Parker, 1839), p. 149.

reformers to take the social maladies of domestic society as seriously as their concern for foreign lands.[46]

While the creation of godly households was itself a way to stabilize the domestic order, the logical consequence of a focus on women's 'domestic mission' was to invite Christian women into the domestic missionary field, 'to carry first into their homes and then into the wider society something of the religious zeal and fervour which other missionaries were taking to heathen in foreign lands'.[47] Women thus came to play an increasingly central role in domestic mission in the second half of the nineteenth century.[48] This development was not without paradox, since it involved women leaving the very household upon which rested their claim to moral authority, and entering a public sphere corrosive of female sanctity.[49] Dickens' Miss Wisk exemplified the potential problem, seemingly transgressing gendered boundaries by entering the masculine realm of public politics. 'Miss Wisk's mission, my guardian said, was to show the world that woman's mission was man's mission . . . [and that] such a mean mission as the domestic mission, was the very last thing to be endured among them'.[50]

To avoid this danger, female 'domestic mission' steered women toward public arenas that were presumed to preserve and reinforce the virtues of feminized domesticity, such as evangelism to other women, rescue missions, children's work, medical outreach and education – areas traditionally linked to the virtues of motherhood, domesticity and nurture. Ellen Ranyard's Bible and Domestic Female Mission (1857) was one of the most influential female mission movements, deploying poor women to evangelize and offer social services to other impoverished females. 'Having observed the power of NATIVE AGENCY in Foreign Missions, it also struck [Mrs Ranyard] that a good poor woman, chosen from among the classes she wished explored, would probably be the most welcome visitor'.[51] An appeal to the civilizing virtues of domesticity justified women's presence in the inhospitable frontier zones of North America, an outlook that Amy Kaplan has wittily dubbed 'manifest domesticity'.[52] Thus in both the urban and 'wilderness' regions, gendered 'domesticity', the construction of stable, Christian 'domestic' orders, and evangelical 'domestic mission' were linguistically and practically intertwined, and thus ripe for further fruitful historiographical investigations.

A survey of domestic mission

The religious enthusiasm of the evangelical revivals that characterized parts of the British and North American churches from the 1730s produced an undifferentiated combination of personal renewal, ecclesiastical revival and proselytizing evangelization. Eighteenth-century

---

46 Charles Dickens, *Bleak House* (London: Bradbury and Evans, 1853), p. 24; Thorne, *Congregational Missions*, p. 90.
47 Barbara Caine, *Victorian Feminists* (New York: Oxford University Press, 1992), pp. 85–6.
48 Bebbington, *The Dominance of Evangelicalism*, pp. 202–12; Airhart, 'Ordering a New Nation and Reordering Protestantism', 120–3.
49 Benjamin L. Hartley, *Evangelicals at a Crossroads: Revivalism and Social Reform in Boston, 1860–1910* (Durham, NH: University of New Hampshire Press, 2011), pp. 93–116; Priscilla Pope-Levison, *Building the Old Time Religion: Women Evangelists in the Progressive Era* (New York: New York University Press, 2014).
50 Dickens, *Bleak House*, p. 297.
51 Leslie Howsam, *Cheap Bibles: Nineteenth-Century Publishing and the British and Foreign Bible Society* (Cambridge: Cambridge University Press, 1991), p. 175.
52 Rutherdale, *Women and the White Man's God*; Brett Christophers, *Positioning the Missionary: John Booth Good and the Confluence of Cultures in Nineteenth-Century British Columbia* (Vancouver: UBC Press, 1998); Amy Kaplan, 'Manifest Domesticity', *American Literature* vol. 70 (1998), 581–606.

Methodism, evangelical Calvinism and Anglican evangelicalism hovered between an older tradition of intense pastoral rejuvenation and a newer tradition of staged, strategic and dramatic appeals to the unregenerate.

The eighteenth-century evangelical revival fuelled itinerant preachers – the first home missionaries – whose ministry reached into areas hitherto pastorally neglected. There was an element of competitive self-interest in this venture. American denominations competed to plant churches in frontier regions, while English Dissenters pursued their 'promiscuous scouring of the countryside' in part to opportunistically fill a gap in the religious marketplace left vacant by Anglican pastoral neglect.[53] In terms of the conversion of unreached peoples, the most significant results of the eighteenth-century itinerancy was among a 'domestic foreign' population: African American slaves. Baptist and Methodist itinerants energized African American evangelicalism in the 1760s.[54] From these revivals, emerged independent African American congregations and missionary-pastors, who evangelized both whites and blacks.[55]

In the 1790s, itinerancy became institutionalized. In Ireland, itinerant missionaries toured the north of the island under the auspices of the ecumenical Evangelical Society of Ulster (1798).[56] A constellation of Irish mission agencies followed.[57] In Scotland, Robert (1764–1842) and James Alexander Haldane (1768–1851) decided against going to India and turned instead to the Highlands, founding the Society for Propagating the Gospel at Home in 1797. In England, dissenting congregations affected by the evangelical revival, particularly Baptists and Congregationalists, created associations to organize and promote itinerant preaching. The most prominent were the Evangelical Association for the Propagation of the Gospel, known as the Village Itinerancy Society (1796), the Baptist Society in London for the Encouragement and Support of Itinerant and Village Preaching (1797), which in 1822 was renamed the Baptist Home Missionary Society, and the Congregational Society for Spreading the Gospel in England (1797), which evolved into the Congregational Home Missionary Society in 1819. In the United States regional mission agencies were founded as sponsoring agencies for itinerant preaching, including the Missionary Society of Connecticut (1798) and the Massachusetts Missionary Society (1799), both of which were Congregationalist, and the Massachusetts Baptist Missionary Society (1802).[58] American Methodism, employing iconic circuit riders such as Peter Cartwright (1785–1872), flourished from the 1780s. 'The whole system is a missionary system' wrote Nathan Bangs (1778–1862) in 1820.[59]

Between 1800 and 1830 an increasing number of large agencies dedicated to the evangelization of the domestic sphere were founded. This was an era of pan-evangelical co-operation, although individual societies often came to be dominated by a particular denomination.[60] Four

---

53 Deryck W. Lovegrove, *Established Church, Sectarian People: Itinerancy and the Transformation of English Dissent, 1780–1830* (Cambridge: Cambridge University Press, 1988), p. 150.
54 Sylvia R. Frey and Betty Wood, *Come Shouting to Zion: African American Protestantism in the American South and British Caribbean to 1830* (Chapel Hill, NC: University of North Carolina Press, 1998), pp. 96–106.
55 Frey and Wood, *Come Shouting to Zion*, p. 162; L. H. Whelchel, *The History and Heritage of African-American Churches: A Way out of No Way* (St Paul, MN: Paragon House, 2011), pp. 98–105; Case, *Unpredictable Gospel*, pp. 164–5.
56 Hempton and Hill, *Evangelical Protestantism*, pp. 37–8.
57 Hempton and Hill, *Evangelical Protestantism*, pp. 31–2.
58 Charles L. Chaney, *The Birth of Missions in America* (South Pasadena, CA: William Carey Library, 1976), pp. 161–2.
59 Goodykoontz, *Home Missions on the American Frontier*, p. 157.
60 Roger H. Martin, *Evangelicals United: Ecumenical Stirrings in Pre-Victorian Britain, 1795–1830* (Metuchen, NJ: Scarecrow Press, 1983); Chaney, *The Birth of Missions in America*, p. 157.

major types of agencies emerged: the home mission society, Sunday schools (often affiliated to a central denominational or ecumenical union), tract societies, and Bible societies.[61] These were the institutions described, in the American context, as a 'benevolent empire' – a 'vast moral machinery, which is designed, in its combined operation, to enlighten, and bless, and save the world'.[62] Flagship institutions included: the London Religious Tract Society (1799),[63] the (British) Sunday School Union (1803), American Sunday School Union (1824) and Sunday School Society of Canada (1824), the British and Foreign Bible Society (1804),[64] the American Bible Society (1816),[65] the American Tract Society (1825) and the American Home Mission Society (1826). Supported in general by middle-class sponsors, these agencies aimed to create and sustain Christian individuals and, in so doing, cultivate a Christian society. Denominations followed suit. American Methodists formed a dedicated home mission agency, the Missionary and Bible Society of the Methodist Episcopal Church in America in 1819, but there was no British Wesleyan Methodist home mission agency until 1857. The American Baptist Home Missionary Society was founded on the initiative of John Mason Peck (1789–1858) in 1832. Postmillennialism, a vision for the flourishing of godliness on earth before the return of Christ sustained by Christian activity and service, injected into these ventures an ebullient optimism.[66]

The 1830s were a period of considerable crisis among mission agencies. The American Home Missionary Society, an alliance of Congregational and Presbyterian churches, was strained by the objection of Old School Presbyterians to co-operation with Congregationalists. They walked out in 1837, also a year of financial disaster for the American economy that 'chastened' all of the institutions of the 'benevolent empire'.[67] In Britain, the emergence of an 'evangelical vigilante group' protested against the inclusion of the Apocrypha in Bibles and divided the Bible Society.[68] The rise of premillennialism strained British evangelical mission agencies since it seemed to call into question their optimism about human agency, although in the long term

61 Anne M. Boylan, *Sunday School: The Formation of an American Institution, 1790–1880* (New Haven, CT: Yale University Press, 1990); Thomas Walter Laqueur, *Religion and Respectability: Sunday Schools and Working Class Culture, 1780–1850* (New Haven, CT: Yale University Press, 1976); Philip B. Cliff, *The Rise and Development of the Sunday School Movement in England, 1780–1980* (Nutfield: National Christian Education Council, 1986).
62 Lawrence J. Friedman and Mark D. McGarvie, *Charity, Philanthropy, and Civility in American History* (Cambridge: Cambridge University Press, 2003), p. 187; Chaney, *Birth of Missions in America*, pp. 203–4. The classic works on the 'benevolent empire' are: Charles I. Foster, *An Errand of Mercy: The Evangelical United Front, 1790–1837* (Chapel Hill, NC: University of North Carolina Press, 1960); Clifford S. Griffin, *Their Brothers' Keepers: Moral Stewardship in the United States, 1800–1865* (Westport, CN: Greenwood Press, 1983). Both tend to over-state the homogeneity and the hegemony of their protagonists.
63 Aileen Fyfe, *Science and Salvation: Evangelical Popular Science Publishing in Victorian Britain* (Chicago, IL: University of Chicago Press, 2004).
64 *Sowing the Word: The Cultural Impact of the British and Foreign Bible Society, 1804–2004*, edited by Stephen K. Batalden, Kathleen Cann and John Dean (Sheffield: Sheffield Phoenix, 2004); Howsam, *Cheap Bibles*.
65 John Fea, *The Bible Cause: A History of the American Bible Society* (New York: Oxford University Press, 2016).
66 Martin Spence, *Heaven on Earth: Reimagining Time and Eternity in Nineteenth-Century British Evangelicalism* (Eugene, OR: Wipf and Stock, 2015), pp. 31–40.
67 Kuykendall, *Southern Enterprize*, p. 99. In 1861, the New School Presbyterians, feeling the agency privileged Congregational control, also left, although it was not until 1893 that the board admitted the reality of the situation, and adopted the name Congregational Home Missionary Society.
68 Timothy Stunt, *From Awakening to Secession: Radical Evangelicals in Switzerland and Britain 1815–1835* (Edinburgh: T. & T. Clark, 2000), p. 102.

it injected a new urgency to mission work to prepare the world for the imminent return of Christ – a pattern which was repeated when many American evangelicals embraced the doctrine after 1865. In the United States, the fissure of denominations over slavery in the 1840s put immense pressure on home mission agencies, no matter how hard they tried to remain neutral.[69] Denominational fracture led to the creation of the Southern Baptist Board of Domestic Mission (1845), which in time would become a leading home mission agency.[70]

A countervailing trend to such denominational strife was manifested in evangelical approaches to the new frontier zones of urban conurbations. In 1826, David Naismith (1799–1839) established the Glasgow City Mission on a nondenominational basis. Other city missions followed, including the Belfast Town Mission (1827),[71] the London City Mission (1835) and the Halifax City Mission (1852).[72] In 1828, New York businessman and philanthropist Arthur Tappan (1786–1865) helped reorganize the New York Religious Tract Society into a highly-organized mission agency drawing up detailed maps to systematically evangelize every part of the metropolis.[73]

A raft of new evangelical initiatives sprang up that attempted to contextualize the gospel to the diversity of urban life, including missions to particular professions, outdoor preaching, and the increasing utilization of male and female lay evangelists.[74] Individual churches, denominations, mission agencies and interdenominational enterprises all began constructing mission halls.[75] In England, evangelical Anglicans such as William Weldon Champneys (1807–85) and William Cadman (1835–91) established vast parochial machines for evangelism and social care.[76] The Church Pastoral Aid Society (1836) helped fortify evangelical Anglicans' parochial ministry for such home mission projects by funding ordained and lay workers. Mission to children also expanded as Sunday schools were supplemented with somewhat more jocund outreach initiatives, such as the beach missions undertaken by the British Children's Special Service Mission (1867).[77] In America and Canada immigrants were key targets for mission.[78]

Evangelicals increasingly wrestled with the bewildering range of social, economic, and environmental maladies of the urban sphere. City missions increasingly offered social support

---

69 Clifford S. Griffin, 'Cooperation and Conflict: The Schism in the American Home Missionary Society, 1837–1861', *Journal of the Presbyterian Historical Society* vol. 38 (1960), 89–105.
70 Arthur B. Rutledge and William Graydon Tanner, *Mission to America: A History of Southern Baptist Home Missions* (Nashville, TN: Broadman Press, 1983).
71 J. N. Ian Dickson, 'Evangelical Religion and Victorian Women: The Belfast Female Mission, 1859–1903', *Journal of Ecclesiastical History* vol. 55 (2004), 700–25.
72 Lewis, *Lighten Their Darkness*.
73 The society adopted the name New York City Mission and Tract Society in 1866. Carroll Smith Rosenberg, *Religion and the Rise of the American City: The New York City Mission Movement, 1812–1870* (Ithaca, NY: Cornell University Press, 1971).
74 D. W. Bebbington, *Evangelicalism in Modern Britain: A History from the 1730s to the 1980s* (London: Unwin Hyman, 1989), p. 120.
75 Rosenberg, *Religion and the Rise of the American City*, pp. 195–6; Jeffrey Cox, *The English Churches in a Secular Society: Lambeth, 1870–1930* (New York: Oxford University Press, 1982), pp. 57–8.
76 Kenneth Hylson-Smith, *Evangelicals in the Church of England 1734–1984* (London: T. & T. Clark, 1992), pp. 152–4.
77 John Pollock, *The Good Seed: The Story of the Children's Special Service Mission and the Scripture Union* (London: Hodder and Stoughton, 1959).
78 Boyer, *Urban Masses*, p. 80; Francesco Cordasco, *Protestant Evangelism among Italians in America* (New York: Arno Press, 1975); Wang 'His Dominion' and the 'Yellow Peril'; Daniel Liestman, '"To Win Redeemed Souls from Heathen Darkness": Protestant Response to the Chinese of the Pacific Northwest in the Late Nineteenth Century', *Western Historical Quarterly* vol. 24 (1993), 179–201.

mechanisms for the impoverished and destitute.[79] The Young Men's Christian Association, founded by George Williams (1821–1905) was an early example of a combined evangelistic and social service institution.[80] A distinct kind of 'rescue mission' emerged in the United States. The pioneer institution was the Water Street Mission (later renamed the New York City Rescue Mission), founded in 1872 by Jerry McAuley, while the Pacific Garden Mission (1877) was responsible for the conversions of evangelist Billy Sunday (1862–1935) and Mel Trotter (1870–1940). The latter founded his own influential rescue mission organization in Grand Rapids, Michigan.[81] Many rescue missions were run for, and by, women, such as Emma Whitemore's Door of Hope, founded in New York in 1890.[82] Belying a common perception that evangelicals were narrowing in their theology in the late nineteenth century, city evangelism was increasingly holistic. The Glasgow United Evangelistic Association (1874) combined mission halls and open air preaching, with medical centres, homes for the disabled, and care for impoverished children. In Canada, the Toronto Mission Union (1884) offered a similar range of social services.[83]

In an effort to reach the urban masses, large sections of British, American and Canadian evangelicals turned to an updated form of revivalism. Charles Finney's seminal *Lectures on Revivals of Religion* (1835) argued that God had provided humans with mechanisms to ensure that revivalist activity produced its desired outcomes, an idea that turned 'revival' into more of a rationally managed project than an expectant season of awaiting the Spirit's mysterious work.[84] The office of professional lay revivalist emerged in the middle decades of the nineteenth century. The archetype was D. L. Moody (1837–1899),[85] whose business-like urban revivals became a template for a form of evangelical domestic mission that was implemented by Canadian evangelist Hugh Thomas Crossley (1850–1934), American Billy Sunday,[86] and countless local imitators on both sides of the Atlantic.[87]

While the revivalist project was probably most popular among the middle classes, this socio-economic group was itself broadening in the *fin de siècle*, losing some of its strenuous pursuit of public virtue and instead preferring the pleasures of modern industrial life: sport,

---

79 Rosenberg, *Religion and the Rise of the American City*, pp. 182–5.
80 Clyde Binfield, *George Williams and the Young Men's Christian Association: A Study in Victorian Social Attitudes* (London: William Heinemann, 1973).
81 Norris Magnuson, *Salvation in the Slums: Evangelical Social Work, 1865–1920* (Eugene, OR: Wipf and Stock, 2004).
82 Pope-Levison, *Building the Old-Time Religion*, pp. 141, 150–71.
83 Ronald G. Sawatsky, 'Evangelicals, Civic Mission, and Prisoners' Aid in Toronto, 1874–1896', in *Canadian Protestant and Catholic Missions*, edited by Moir and McIntire, pp. 150–70.
84 Carwardine, 'The Evangelist System'.
85 Bruce J. Evensen, *God's Man for the Gilded Age: D. L. Moody and the Rise of Modern Mass Evangelism* (Oxford: Oxford University Press, 2003); Timothy George, *Mr Moody and the Evangelical Tradition* (London: T. & T. Clark, 2004).
86 Roger A. Bruns, *Preacher: Billy Sunday and Big-Time American Evangelism* (New York: W. W. Norton, 1992); L. Robert Francis Martin, *Hero of the Heartland: Billy Sunday and the Transformation of American Society, 1862–1935* (Bloomington, IN: Indiana University Press, 2002). For treatments of revivalist activities, see: Darrel M. Robertson, *The Chicago Revival, 1876: Society and Revivalism in a Nineteenth-Century City* (Metuchen, NJ: Scarecrow Press, 1989); Eric Robert Crouse, *Revival in the City: The Impact of American Evangelists in Canada, 1884–1914* (Montreal: McGill-Queen's University Press, 2005); Thekla Ellen Joiner, *Sin in the City: Chicago and Revivalism, 1880–1920* (Columbia, MO: University of Missouri Press, 2007).
87 Janice Holmes offers a unique survey of the working-class lay evangelists who emerged in this era. Janice Holmes, *Religious Revivals in Britain and Ireland, 1859–1905* (Dublin: Irish Academic Press, 2000), pp. 135–66.

Sears-Roebuck and seaside vacations. Evangelical mission in the revivalist tradition increasingly competed with other mass democratic pleasure pursuits, creating music-hall hymnody, urban parades and caravan missions – all increasingly promoted using the growing suite of tools associated with mass commercialism. 'Men are crying out for variety', Moody had proclaimed, 'Well let them have variety'.[88] While often funded by local business owners and organized by middle-class Christians, urban missionary endeavours in the revivalist tradition also helped create institutions that reached, and in some cases bequeathed ownership to, a subsection of the working classes.[89]

The new democratic ethos was best exemplified by the new Bible Training Institutes, such as the East London Training Institute (1873), the Bible Training Institute of Glasgow (1876), the Moody Bible Institute (1889) and the Toronto Bible School (1894), that aimed to equip a newly-enfranchised cohort of lay evangelists for demotic mission.[90] The 'faith mission' principle – a commitment to relying on God for financial provision and strategic guidance – also helped inspire lower-class evangelists. By eschewing the demands for funding and theological education laid on evangelists by denominations or some agencies, a lack of wealth and credentials was rendered a missiological virtue. Missionaries within the British Open Brethren (1848) and Faith Mission (1886) communities particularly exemplified the principle.[91]

Domestic mission was also energized in this period by the holiness movement, a prominent stream of spirituality that promised that every believer could receive a post-conversion blessing that opened up for him or her a 'higher' form of Christian life and service.[92] Holiness advocates were 'devoted to making the world a place where men might more readily choose the good path'.[93] Temperance was a key expression of this attitude, and the invitation to 'the pledge' absorbed some of the conversionist energy previously reserved for accepting Jesus. The most significant holiness network was the Salvation Army, initially founded in 1865 as the East London Christian Mission by Methodists William (1829–1912) and Catherine Booth (1829–1890).[94] Salvationists recognized the connection between spiritual and physical urban impoverishment, an attitude prominent in some other Holiness missionary-minded networks, such as A. B. Simpson's Christianity and Missionary Alliance (1887), which also adhered to the 'faith mission' principle.[95] 'The Gospel of practical religion [offers] . . . real help for human suffering as well as human sin', said Simpson.[96]

In the United States, the closing of the 'frontier' in 1890 marked the end of an era. Home

---

88 John Coffey, 'Democracy and Popular Religion: Moody and Sankey's Mission to Britain 1873–1875', in *Citizenship and Community: Liberals, Radicals and Collective Identities in the British Isles, 1865–1931*, edited by Eugenio F. Biagini (Cambridge: Cambridge University Press, 2002), p. 100.
89 Airhart, 'Ordering a New Nation and Reordering Protestantism', 119–20; Michael Gauvreau, 'Factories and Foreigners: Church Life in Working-Class Neighborhoods in Hamilton and Montreal, 1890–1930', in *The Churches and Social Order in Nineteenth- and Twentieth-Century Canada*, edited by Michael Gauvreau and Ollivier Hubert (Montreal: McGill-Queen's University Press, 2006), pp. 225–73.
90 Bebbington, *The Dominance of Evangelicalism*, p. 92.
91 Klaus Fiedler, *The Story of Faith Missions* (Carlisle: Regnum, 1994).
92 Melvin Dieter, *The Holiness Revival of the Nineteenth Century* (Metuchen, NJ: Scarecrow Press, 1980), p. 24.
93 Timothy L. Smith, *Revivalism and Social Reform: American Protestantism on the Eve of the Civil War* (Baltimore, MD: Johns Hopkins University Press, 1980), p. 94.
94 Pamela J. Walker, *Pulling the Devil's Kingdom Down: The Salvation Army in Victorian Britain* (Berkeley, CA: University of California Press, 2001); Diane H. Winston, *Red-Hot and Righteous: The Urban Religion of the Salvation Army* (Cambridge, MA: Harvard University Press, 1999).
95 Donald W. Dayton, *Discovering an Evangelical Heritage* (Grand Rapids, MI: Baker Academic, 1988).
96 Magnuson, *Salvation in the Slums*, p. 44.

mission subsequently reflected the progressive, liberal nationalism that dominated American politics and society in the first half of the twentieth century. Harlan Paul Douglass (1871–1953), Superintendent of Education for the American Missionary Association, captured the mood in his *The New Home Missions* (1914) which called for 'perfect realization of Christianity in America' by home mission emphasizing 'social redemption equally with individual salvation'.[97] This approach pervaded the Home Missions Council, an interdenominational co-ordinating body founded in 1908.[98] A similar pattern of Christian values through society suffused many British churches by the late nineteenth century. Our 'sole object is to do good', said the pastor of the Congregationalist Murphy Memorial Hall in Southwark. 'We avoid the "Come to Jesus" style'.[99]

'Functional differentiation' led to churches that opted for a social service role to be slowly eclipsed by other charitable, and then state, agencies as the century proceeded.[100] An exception to the rule was the black church in the post-bellum South. Segregation meant that the African American church was often the only venue for communal fraternity, and was thus more successful at creating the fusion of sociability and spirituality that often evaded other evangelical communities.[101] From black churches, particularly the African Methodist Episcopal Church, emerged thousands of lay preacher evangelists in the late nineteenth and early twentieth centuries.[102] African American domestic mission, especially in the urban centres evacuated by white evangelicals, may represent the greatest triumph of American evangelical mission in the twentieth century, according to historian Charles Chaney.[103]

As the liberal social gospel washed over mainline and liberal evangelicals, the older tradition of populist revivalism – a tradition increasingly inhabited of those who self-consciously adopted anti-modernist views – was still viewed by many as the key to converting the domestic order. The new-born Pentecostal movement's emphasis on the miraculous led to the growth of 'healing evangelism'. In Britain, George Jeffreys (1889–1962), one of many evangelists energized by the 1904–1905 Welsh Revival, trekked a revivalist circuit under the auspices of the Elim Evangelistic Band (1915).[104] In the United States, Canadian-born Aimee Semple McPherson (1890–1944) cultivated movie star name recognition and pursued her healing ministry in a purpose built auditorium, the Angelus Temple (1923).[105]

McPherson reflected a growing gimmickry within evangelical outreach in the twentieth century, exemplified also by the strange phenomenon of girl evangelists in the 1920s.[106] While Pentecostal and Holiness traditions were pioneers of these sensationalist techniques, by the

---

97 Harlan Paul Douglass, *The New Home Missions* (New York: Missionary Education Movement of the United States and Canada, 1914), pp. 227, 54.
98 L. C. Barnes, 'Church Union That Unites: II. The Home Missions Council', *The Biblical World* vol. 41 (1913), 390–2.
99 Cox, *The English Churches in a Secular Society*, p. 59.
100 Cox, *The English Churches in a Secular Society*, p. 182.
101 Paul Harvey, *Redeeming the South: Religious Cultures and Racial Identities Among Southern Baptists, 1865–1925* (Chapel Hill, NC: University of North Carolina Press, 1997), p. 59.
102 Case, *Unpredictable Gospel*, pp. 168–77.
103 Charles L. Chaney, 'The Near Demise of Domestic Mission in America in the Twentieth Century: Can We Learn Anything From It?', in *Between Past and Future: Evangelical Mission Entering the Twentieth Century*, edited by Jonathan J. Bonk (Pasadena, CA: William Carey Library, 2003), p. 110.
104 Ian M. Randall, *Evangelical Experiences: A Study in the Spirituality of English Evangelicalism 1918–1939* (Carlisle: Paternoster, 1999), pp. 211–4.
105 Edith L. Blumhofer, *Aimee Semple McPherson: Everybody's Sister* (Grand Rapids, MI: Eerdmans, 1993).
106 Thomas A. Robinson and Lanette R. Ruff, *Out of the Mouths of Babes: Girl Evangelists in the Flapper Era* (New York: Oxford University Press, 2012).

1930s, the allure of modern media and spectacle was shaping many evangelical missionary projects. Such gimmicks, more pronounced in the United States though not unknown in Canada or Britain, reflect what Thomas Bergler has called the 'juvenilization' of Christianity, a phenomenon that he argues derived from an obsession with the evangelization of the young by all denominations during the twentieth century.[107] The growing focus on youth reflected the growing social categorization of 'youth' as both problem and opportunity. In Britain the National Young Life Campaign founded in 1911 by Anglican evangelicals Frederick and Arthur Wood organized evangelistic rallies across Britain. Joel Carpenter has shown how American Fundamentalist churches were key to this development.[108] Percy Crawford's Young Person's Church of the Air (1930), an innovative radio broadcast, and New York evangelist Jack Wrytzen's flashy rallies pioneered a jovial, jazzy style that utilized new technology and marketing. Such sensationalist approaches became adopted as a strategy for evangelizing everyone. Canadian revivalist Oswald J. Smith (1889–1986) did 'anything to get a crowd' at his Toronto Peoples' Church in the 1930s,[109] and it was from the high-octane rallies of Youth for Christ (1944)[110] that sprang late twentieth century's most famous evangelist of adults, Billy Graham.[111] In his Youth for Christ days, Graham used to appear on stage with a horse that would kneel at the cross, and stamp its hoof three times to indicate the number of persons in the Trinity – a fact, claimed Graham, that proved even a horse knew more than theological liberals.[112] This was tame compared to some of the crass evangelistic techniques of the late twentieth century: 'Hell Houses', Sumo wrestling, and theme parks were all deployed by subgroups within the evangelical world.[113]

Billy Graham was the patron saint of post-Second World War American neo-evangelicalism. Invigorated by Cold War American Christian patriotism, the movement aspired to create a culturally-engaged evangelical coalition that would inculcate godliness across American society. In adopting this vision, neo-evangelicalism actually assumed the mantle of the early twentieth-century progressive elision of mission with Christian nationalism. Much American energy for domestic redemption was diverted into cultural and political campaigns to rescue the nation from moral decay, a campaign that construed its vision of domestic redemption as defending domestic 'family values'.[114] A more erudite version of redeeming the culture was pursued on both sides of the Atlantic in the proliferation of apologetics ministries, such as that of Francis Schaeffer (1912–1984), Josh McDowell (b.1939) and Ravi Zacharias (b.1946).[115]

In Britain, hopes for the re-Christianization of British society were raised in light of Billy

---

107 Thomas Bergler, *The Juvenilization of American Christianity* (Grand Rapids, MI: Eerdmans, 2012). For British evangelicalism, a parallel argument is implied in Pete Ward, *Growing Up Evangelical: Youthwork and the Making of an Evangelical Subculture* (Eugene, OR: Wipf and Stock, 2013).
108 Joel A. Carpenter, *Revive Us Again: The Reawakening of American Fundamentalism* (New York: Oxford University Press, 1997).
109 Carpenter, *Revive Us Again*, pp. 163–5; Kevin Kee, *Revivalists: Marketing the Gospel in English Canada, 1884–1957* (Montreal: McGill-Queen's Press 2006), pp. 53–95.
110 Carpenter, *Revive Us Again*, pp. 143–87.
111 Grant Wacker, *America's Pastor: Billy Graham and the Shaping of a Nation* (Cambridge, MA: Belknap Press, 2014).
112 William Martin, *A Prophet with Honor: The Billy Graham Story* (New York: Harper Perennial, 1992), p. 93.
113 Jason C. Bivins, *Religion of Fear: The Politics of Horror in Conservative Evangelicalism* (New York: Oxford University Press, 2008); Joiner, *Sin in the City*, p. 235.
114 Joiner, *Sin in the City*, pp. 234–6.
115 Harriet A. Harris, *Fundamentalism and Evangelicals* (Oxford: Oxford University Press, 1998), pp. 180–204.

Graham's celebrated visits to London and Glasgow in 1954–1955.[116] But as the cultural revolutions of the 1960s swept over the church, voices of critique were increasingly raised about this form of mass evangelization. The link between domesticity, gender and evangelicalism also collapsed in this decade, according to the thesis proposed by Callum Brown.[117] Dissent to older forms of outreach came especially from within the nascent charismatic movement. Charismatics favoured smaller, communal gatherings in which Spirit-inspired worship and *koinonia* – not Bev Shea and altar calls (nor Victorian-style tract and mission agencies, for that matter) – were the main tools of Christian witness. While large-scale evangelistic initiatives continued to be announced with great optimism, there were depressingly low returns.[118]

In the last decade of the century, a charismatic Anglican church, Holy Trinity Brompton (London) institutionalized such small group intimacy in the widely-adopted *Alpha* course, arguably the most successful domestic mission venture of the late twentieth century.[119] This was mission delivered in a comfortable (*faux* domestic?) context of a meal and an informal chat, although it was also, ironically, one of the most highly-branded enterprises of twentieth-century evangelism.

Recovering an emphasis on the local church as the locus of God's mission, church planting became a major outreach strategy in the twentieth century, and denominational home mission agencies tended to focus on nurturing church growth than on evangelism strictly defined. By the early twentieth century, energies were poured into creating contextually-embedded 'fresh expressions' and 'emergent' communities.[120] Such ventures were not, of course, as radical as some supporters claimed when set against the vast array of preaching stations, frontier churches, and urban mission halls, as well as the general cultural flexibility, that characterized evangelical history. *Ecclesia semper emergit*.

By the turn of the twenty-first century, the very language of 'home mission', carrying with it the supposed (or desired) homogeneity of the domestic sphere, had collapsed under the pluralism of late modernity. This collapse was undergirded by the post-colonial turn in evangelical missiology, signalled by the First International Congress on World Evangelization (the Lausanne Congress) in 1974. Along with broadening the notion of what constituted mission – laying an increasing stress on social justice and the everyday mission of God's people – Lausanne also hastened the dissolution of bifurcated concepts of 'home' and 'foreign'. Mission in the late twentieth century came to be described as a unitary and holistic activity pursued by all God's people 'from everywhere to everywhere'.[121]

This development has been hastened by growing awareness of the minority status of Christians in the Global North. 'Reverse missionaries' have inverted the old polarity of 'home' and 'foreign'. The largest African denomination in Britain is the Redeemed Christian Church

---

116 Alana Harris and Martin Spence, '"Disturbing the Complacency of Religion"? The Evangelical Crusades of Dr Billy Graham and Father Patrick Peyton in Britain, 1951–54', *Twentieth Century British History* vol. 18 (2007), 481–513.
117 Brown, *Death of Christian Britain*, esp. Ch. 7.
118 Rob Warner presents a damning portrait of over-blown evangelistic expectations met with bleak results in his *Reinventing English Evangelicalism, 1966–2001: A Theological and Sociological Study* (Carlisle: Paternoster, 2007).
119 James Heard, *Inside Alpha: Explorations in Evangelism* (Eugene, OR: Wipf and Stock, 2010).
120 Dan Kimball, *Emerging Church: Vintage Christianity for New Generations* (Grand Rapids, MI: Zondervan, 2003); *Church Growth in Britain 1980 to the Present*, edited by David Goodhew (Farnham: Ashgate, 2012).
121 Michael Nazir-Ali, *From Everywhere to Everywhere: A World View of Christian Witness* (London: Collins, 1991).

of God. By 2017 it had over 67,000 members, predominantly in urban centres.[122] The network aims to found a church within five minutes driving distance of every town and city in Great Britain, and, indeed, of the entire developed world.[123] Similar movements from among the African and Asian diaspora are evident in the United States and Canada.[124]

The end of home mission as a unified project means that historical study of the phenomenon will always centre on the long nineteenth century. Nonetheless, evangelicals are still highly activist Christians. A historiographical focus on religious decline and secularization in Britain and Canada, and on political Christianity in the United States, has distracted historians from exploring the intersection between evangelical mission and twentieth-century culture. There has been a particular neglect of those culturally or ecclesiastically marginal communities – such as lower-class lay evangelists, rescue missions or African American communities – who were successful at doing 'contextual mission' and 'fresh expressions', especially in urban settings, long before it became a fashionable imperative among larger (white) denominations.

Across the range of the evangelical movement, there are significant historiographical gaps to be filled. First, the huge contribution of women to domestic mission has received more attention among literary and social scholars than among religious historians. Second, a plethora of institutions and agencies concerned with home evangelism – of which only a handful have been referenced in this survey – await their historian. Even the 'benevolent empire' flagship agencies of the early nineteenth century have received little modern scholarly attention. Third, historiographical boundaries between foreign and domestic mission also need to become more porous. The division between home and foreign are culture metaphors of the era under study that should not be allowed artificially to constrain historical investigations. Finally, since the contemporary theological context stresses that Christian mission involves addressing both personal sin and structural injustice – the salvation of bodies as well as souls – contemporary historians should re-examine how tightly these now dissolved boundaries were ever drawn in the past. Despite caricatures, evangelical mission has never made absolute distinctions between individual and social redemption. While our modern preference might be more for the socially-sympathetic rescue missions of the late Victorian age than for the culturally-presumptuous civilizing missions of the early nineteenth century, in both instances – as in many others – evangelicals practised a 'missionality' that has often hoped for a wide-ranging transformation of the home environment.

---

122 Peter Brierley, *UK Church Statistics, No.3 (2018 Edition): 2012 to 2022* (Tonbridge: ADBC Publishers, 2017), §9.3, §9.8.
123 Richard Burgess, 'African Pentecostal Growth: The Redeemed Christian Church of God in Britain', in *Church Growth in Britain*, edited by Goodhew, p. 135.
124 Rebecca Y. Kim, *The Spirit Moves West: Korean Missionaries in America* (New York: Oxford University Press, 2015).

10
EVANGELICALS AND MISSION IN THE GLOBAL SOUTH

Michael Gladwin

The story of evangelicals and mission in the Global South is one of extraordinary expansion and transformation: from a movement with origins in eighteenth-century Europe and North America to a movement of immense dynamism and global reach that, since the nineteenth century, has played a key role in establishing Christianity as the most ubiquitous and culturally diverse religion on the planet. The Christian population of the world was estimated in 2010 at around 2.2 billion people. Of these an estimated 820 million could be described as evangelicals (defined here as including Pentecostals/Neo-Pentecostals, but excluding denominational charismatics). Of those 820 million, evangelicals in Asia, Africa and Latin America alone comprise around 690 million (nearly 85 per cent).[1] Since the eighteenth century, evangelicals have also demonstrated a profound ability to indigenize and adapt evangelical belief and practice to the diverse historical and geographical circumstances of the Global South.

The purpose of this chapter is to survey both the history and historiography of evangelicals and mission in the Global South. It is naturally impossible in a chapter of this size to assess adequately the historical development and influence of hundreds of diverse evangelical missions on a truly global stage over a span of nearly 300 years. This chapter will therefore approach the topic in two complementary ways: first, through an historical survey that follows the contours of the course and impact of evangelical missions in the Global South, from the eighteenth to the twenty-first centuries; and second, through a discussion of key themes and issues in the historiography of evangelicals and mission in these regions. Attention will be given in both cases to the broader cultural, social, intellectual and political contexts that have shaped – and been shaped by – the evangelical mission project.

The use of the term 'Global South' warrants brief comment. In recent years, the term has come to refer to countries that used to be thought of as the 'Third World', located mostly in the southern hemisphere and rated as medium and low according to the UN's human development index ('Global North' denotes countries rated as high according to the index). 'Global South' now tends to be the preferred term among political scientists, (global) policy scholars and the

---

1 'Table 8.3: Distribution of Evangelical Communities by Continent', in Mark Hutchinson and John Wolffe, *A Short History of Global Evangelicalism* (Cambridge: Cambridge University Press, 2012), p. 240. See also pp. 209–43 for a helpful discussion of difficulties regarding the quantification, definition and categorization of evangelicals.

UN, in part because it lacks the hegemonic and pejorative connotations of the previously used terms, 'Third World' and 'developing world'. In this chapter, 'Global South' is used in a broader, more general sense to refer to Africa, Asia, Latin America and Oceania (excepting Australia and New Zealand).[2]

Historical developments

The antecedents of evangelical missionary endeavour in the Global South lie in the seventeenth century. Newly Protestant nations such as England, now free from papal authorization of Portuguese and Spanish claims to control the non-European world, cast their gaze beyond Europe for the purposes of trading and planting colonies. Nevertheless, a few of the Protestant clergy attached to Dutch, English and German trading companies and military outposts looked outward to local indigenous populations in their regions. In North America, the Congregationalist pastor John Eliot commenced preaching and Bible translation among Native Americans in 1646. The German Protestant mission movement began later in the century when August Herman Francke drew pietists together at Halle, who, in turn, inspired Lutherans for mission in the Americas and India. German pietists arrived at Tranquebar, South India in 1706, under the patronage of the Danish crown, though without the consent of the Danish East India Company's governor.[3] British imperial overseers showed little enthusiasm for early British missionary efforts beyond European populations. The East India Company (EIC) ensured, for example, that its revised charter (1793) did not allow access to India by Christian missionaries, despite lobbying by evangelical William Wilberforce and well-connected evangelical missionary interests.[4] In eighteenth-century North America, Baptists, Congregationalists and Presbyterians showed little inclination – theologically or institutionally – to evangelize beyond white settlements. Where significant missions were established during the eighteenth century, such as those of the Moravians (1730s) and Methodists (1770s) among Caribbean slaves, they struggled due to a lack of effective leadership, decentralized authority and the absence of a coherent mission theology or strategy.[5]

After 1792, an explosion of missionary enthusiasm among evangelical Protestants issued in the creation of several voluntary lay missionary societies, few of which had close connections with established authorities in church and state: the Baptist Missionary Society (BMS; 1792); the London Missionary Society (LMS; 1795, initially non-denominational but eventually Congregational); and the Church Missionary Society (CMS; 1799), founded and patronized by Anglican evangelicals. The Edinburgh and Glasgow societies (1796) were followed by the Wesleyan Methodist Missionary Society (WMMS; 1818). Britain dominated missionary endeavour throughout the nineteenth century, but American and European missionary efforts were also significant, beginning with the American Board of Commissioners for Foreign Missions (ABCFM; 1810), the German Missionary Society (1816) and the Paris Evangelical Missionary

---

2 The term 'Global South' was coined in 1996. For a useful discussion of the term's semantic, political and geographical definition, see Andrea Hollington et al., 'Concepts of the Global South', *Voices from Around the World* (2015), Global South Studies Center, University of Cologne, Germany, http://voices.uni-koeln.de/2015-1/conceptsoftheglobalsouth (accessed 23 February 2018).
3 Dana Robert, *Christian Mission: How Christianity Became a World Religion* (Oxford: Wiley-Blackwell, 2009), p. 42.
4 Penelope Carson, *The East India Company and Religion, 1698–1858* (Woodbridge: Boydell, 2012), pp. 34–49.
5 Andrew Porter, 'An Overview, 1700–1914', in *Missions and Empire*, edited by Norman Etherington (Oxford: Oxford University Press, 2005), pp. 44–6.

Society (1822). Various factors converged to launch the movement: British maritime supremacy and imperial expansion; popular awareness of overseas cultures via recent explorations such as James Cook's epic Pacific voyages during 1768–1779; the impact of transatlantic evangelical 'revivals' and 'awakenings'; and the expansion of evangelical contacts and influences (transatlantic and continental) through religious, friendship, family, humanitarian and professional networks. Underpinning the missionary impulse was a shared stock of theological, philosophical and economic ideas that were subject to intense discussion and debate.[6] By the early nineteenth century, for example, most evangelicals were adopting a soft 'Moderate Calvinism' that eschewed fatalistic hyper-Calvinist excesses.[7] A late-eighteenth-century emphasis on human agency (often denoted as 'means') was applied to the fulfilment of Christ's Great Commission (Matt. 28: 16–20), perhaps most influentially articulated in the missionary manifesto of pioneer Baptist missionary to India, William Carey, entitled *An Enquiry into the Obligations of Christians to use Means for the Conversion of the Heathens* (1792).

Missionary energy and optimism was further galvanized by a doctrine of providence that stressed God's active government of the world and the historical process, whether through general providence (overall superintendence), or through particular providences (direct divine interventions in the course of events, displaying judgment or mercy). Providential thought also coloured missionary attitudes to colonialism and imperialism. Nineteenth-century Anglo-American evangelicals conceived Britain's Protestant character, empire, maritime supremacy, commercial power, political institutions and civilization as providential gifts for which Britain was accountable to God. This was fused with Burkean principles of trusteeship and Scottish Enlightenment notions of civilizing 'heathen' nations. The result was a vision of the empire and its colonies as a God-given trust for the furthering of the gospel and the provision of ancillary benefits such as Christian morality and civil rights to all imperial subjects. Slavery and religious intolerance (of Christian missions), in particular, were deemed national sins likely to attract divine judgment.[8]

Evangelical missionary effort was further fuelled by millennial beliefs, grounded in exegesis of Scripture passages that predicted a future outpouring of the Spirit in the 'latter days' or times near the end of world history. The mainstream postmillennialist eschatology of transatlantic Protestant missions after the seventeenth century – which envisioned Christ's second coming *after* the millennium – accommodated gradualist, Enlightenment-inflected notions of improvement and benevolence (or commerce and civilization), as churches and missions worked steadily to convert Gentile and Jew to usher in an era of peace and triumph prior to Christ's promised return.[9] As will be seen below, a more radical premillennial eschatology gained ground after the 1830s and influenced later faith missions.

These theological developments were accompanied by structural shifts in Western society that included accelerated population growth, the onset of the economic and social transfor-

---

6 Andrew Porter, *Religion Versus Empire? British Protestant Missionaries and Overseas Expansion, 1700–1914* (Manchester: Manchester University Press, 2004), pp. 40–1.

7 D. W. Bebbington, *Evangelicalism in Modern Britain: A History from the 1730s to the 1980s* (London: Unwin Hyman, 1989), pp. 2, 4–17; Nikolaus Ludwig von Zinzendorf, *Nine Public Lectures,* translated by George Forell (Iowa City, IA: University of Iowa Press, 1973).

8 The substance of the paragraphs in this section is drawn from Michael Gladwin, 'Missions and Colonialism in the Long Nineteenth Century', in *The Oxford Handbook of Nineteenth-Century Christian Thought,* edited by Joel Rasmussen, Judith Wolfe and Johannes Zachhuber (Oxford: Oxford University Press, 2017), pp. 282–304.

9 J. A. De Jong, *As the Waters Cover the Sea: Millennial Expectations in the Rise of Anglo-American Missions, 1640–1810* (Kampen: Kok, 1970), pp. 2–3, 228–9.

mation known as the 'Industrial Revolution', and the emergence of a commercial middle class, which further exposed the inability of traditional state churches to meet the people's spiritual needs. This created space for a transition from Christendom models to new voluntarist movements and associations, including the associational model of the joint stock company that provided a template for voluntary missionary societies.[10] Drawing on the model of the trading company, William Carey contended that voluntary societies be founded to which individuals would subscribe for the purpose of raising money for sending missionaries to the non-Christian world.[11] Also influential were the Anglican coteries around William Wilberforce and the Clapham Sect, who sought to bring Christian moral suasion to bear on the expanding British Empire. Their various projects included slavery abolition and the creation of a free colony (Sierra Leone), missionary access to India, and the channelling of forces of civilization and commerce for Christian mission.[12]

To the institutional Anglican Church and most *élites*, the evangelical missionary movement smacked initially of 'enthusiasm' (contemporary shorthand for fanaticism), propagated by men of relatively humble social and educational standing. Writing in the *Edinburgh Review* in 1808, Anglican clergyman Sydney Smith famously caricatured Baptist missionaries in Bengal as 'little detachments of maniacs'. More worrying for Smith and the imperial government was the potential of missionary meddling with indigenous cultures that might damage overseas commercial and political interests.[13] By the 1830s, however, missions were attracting widespread public acceptance (largely among the *petit bourgeois* and middle classes) and even official support. The LMS soon established a strong missionary presence in the Western Pacific (which eventually became one of the most rapidly Christianized regions in the world) and the Cape, the CMS in Sierra Leone and India, and Baptists in Bengal and the West Indies. Methodists and Presbyterians were poised for further expansion.[14]

A key continuing debate within the missionary movement before 1850 concerned the relative weight and priority that should be given to 'civilization' (the civilizing instruments of the Enlightenment such as literacy and education) and 'Christianity' (direct gospel proclamation) in bringing the 'heathen' to conversion. The majority position prioritized Christianity over civilization, but in practice most Protestant missions developed a pragmatic working partnership between gospel proclamation and civilization through educational or economic improvement.[15] This set the parameters for a new synthesis that achieved ascendancy between the 1830s and 1870s – that of 'civilization, commerce and Christianity', most famously articulated by evangelical humanitarian (and protege of Wilberforce), Thomas Fowell Buxton MP, and subsequently by missionary explorer David Livingstone. Such schemes sought to undercut Portuguese and Arab slave trade economies by founding African colonies that would open channels for civilization, 'legitimate commerce' and Christianity. In the longer term, however, Buxton and Livingstone's earnest hopes for African uplift were frustrated as slave raiders and Portuguese officials used Livingstone's well-publicized exploration accounts to expand their

---

10 Hutchinson and Wolffe, *Global Evangelicalism*, pp. 35, 56.
11 Carey, *An Enquiry*, pp. 81–4.
12 Gareth Atkins 'Wilberforce and his Milieux: The Worlds of Anglican Evangelicalism, c.1780–1830' (unpublished PhD thesis, Cambridge University, 2009), Chs 1, 6; John Wolffe, 'Clapham Sect (active 1792–1815)', *Oxford Dictionary of National Biography* (Oxford: Oxford University Press, 2004–11).
13 Sydney Smith, 'Indian Missions', *Edinburgh Review* vol. 12 (1808), 179–80.
14 Porter, 'An Overview', p. 47.
15 *Christian Missions and the Enlightenment*, edited by Brian Stanley (Grand Rapids, MI: Eerdmans, 2001), pp. 18–19, 182–4, 192.

reach, massacring inhabitants in the process. The emerging free markets also proved vulnerable to exploitation by powerful business, imperial and landowning interests.[16]

A crucial development by the mid-nineteenth century was a shift in focus towards creating indigenous national churches, which by definition were self-financing, self-governing and self-propagating (the 'three selfs'). Henry Venn (CMS secretary, 1841–1873) and Rufus Anderson (ABCFM secretary, 1826–1866) among others recalibrated the aim of missions towards the development of 'native' pastors who could prepare the way for the missionary eventually 'to resign all pastoral work into their hands' – Venn's famous notion of 'the euthanasia of a mission'.[17] Venn and Anderson's stress on indigenization offered a powerful corrective to the more ethnocentric approaches of some 'civilizing' missions such as those of the Scottish in India led by Alexander Duff.[18] The 'three-self' ideal was worked out in significant expansion of non-Western church leadership in places such as Africa, India and the South Pacific, Native Church Councils and the celebrated consecration in 1864 of Samuel Crowther as the first African Anglican bishop. From the 1860s until the late nineteenth century, the three-self theory became the stated policy of Anglo-American missions.[19]

The same period also witnessed the rise of 'faith mission' approaches. They adopted the 'indigenizing' ideal, but supercharged it with a premillennial eschatology that stressed the paramount concern of mission as the saving of souls from the present evil order. This imbued missionary efforts with an apocalyptic urgency and fostered impatience with the cumbersome bureaucracy of missionary societies and expensive civilizing adjuncts of schools, printing presses and hospitals.[20] A. N. Groves and George Müller pioneered primitivist mission strategies of unplanned dependence on 'the Spirit of God', which in turn inspired J. Hudson Taylor to establish the China Inland Mission (CIM) in 1865. Taylor and his missionaries targeted areas of inland China untouched by European influence, adopting simple vernacular gospel preaching and Chinese dress and habits to aid in establishing indigenous churches on an ecumenical basis of non-denominational evangelicalism. By the 1890s, the CIM was the second-largest British missionary venture (after the CMS), inspiring similar independent evangelical faith missions in Africa such as the Livingstone Inland Mission (1878) and Sudan Interior Mission (1893).[21]

Similarly dynamic impulses in the decades after 1875 issued from powerful transatlantic revivalist and holiness movements associated with the Keswick Conventions and North American revivalists such as Dwight L. Moody. Keswick Conventions aimed at the promotion of 'practical holiness' through consecration and sacrifice of one's whole life to God, and subsequent empowerment for mission by the Holy Spirit.[22] This holiness spirituality was cultivated in annual conventions that proved enormously popular among Anglo-American university students. Thousands were mobilized for cross-cultural missions through the Young Men's Christian Association and Young Women's Christian Association, the World Student

---

16 T. F. Buxton, *The African Slave Trade* (second edition, London: John Murray, 1839), pp. vi, xii; Andrew Ross, *David Livingstone: Mission and Empire* (London: Continuum, 2006), pp. 239–44; Robert, *Christian Mission*, pp. 84–5.
17 William Knight, *Memoir of the Rev. H. Venn* (London: Longmans, Green and Co., 1880), p. 307.
18 Alexander Duff, *India, and India Missions* (Edinburgh: J. Johnstone, 1839).
19 H. C. Tucker, *Conference on Missions* (London: James Nisbet, 1860), p. 311.
20 *The Collected Writings of Edward Irving*, edited by Gavin Carlyle (5 vols, London: Alexander Strahan, 1864-5), I: 431-3; De Jong, *As the Waters Cover the Sea*, pp. 2, 228–9.
21 J. Hudson Taylor, *A Retrospect* (Toronto: CIM, 1902); Porter, *Religion Versus Empire?*, pp. 191–224; Alvyn Austin, *China's Millions: The China Inland Mission and Late Qing Society, 1832–1905* (Grand Rapids, MI: Eerdmans, 2007).
22 Charles F. Harford-Battersby, *The Keswick Convention: Its Message, Its Method and Its Men* (London: Marshall Bros, 1907).

Christian Federation, and the interdenominational Student Volunteer Movement for Foreign Missions (SVM), founded in Massachusetts in 1888 and led by John R. Mott. The movement's 'watchword' neatly captures its bold, youthful optimism: 'the evangelization of the world in this generation'.[23] The result was a global evangelical missionary network. Although older missionary societies continued to invest in auxiliary activities, especially medical and welfare missions, they modified both methods and missionary qualifications to harness the new enthusiasm and spirituality.[24]

Missionary endeavour boomed across Asia, Africa and Oceania during the late nineteenth century, assisted by the British Empire's vast trade, communication, military and transport infrastructure, which included railroads, steamships, the telegraph and naval supremacy. Equally significant, however, was the energetic evangelism of indigenous Christians.[25]

Three-self and indigenizing aspirations nevertheless came under pressure from the expansion of colonial settlements as far afield as Australia, New Zealand, southern Africa and Kenya; and a shift from informal to formal empire in the British presence overseas after the 1870s, as Britain and other European colonies entered a 'high imperial' phase. The Berlin Conference of 1884–1885 heralded the 'Partition of Africa', whereby European countries parcelled out the continent into their own spheres of influence, including a recently united German nation that now sought its place in the imperial sun. Mid-century treaties with China had opened her interior to missions. Concerns about a resurgent Islam fuelled both millennial speculation and evangelical and Roman Catholic strategies for moving against Islam from African bases.[26]

A hardening of colonialist and racist *mentalités* during the high imperial period resisted the three-self logic of self-governing 'native' churches led by indigenous bishops and pastors. Some white settlers opposed the notion of working under non-white leaders, as did some white missionaries. Disaffection among some indigenous churches over settler racism and paternalism – most devastatingly exemplified in the *de facto* usurpation of Crowther's leadership of the Niger Mission by young Europeans who imposed their own standards of Keswick holiness on a church deemed to be lax and irregular – led to a proliferation of 'Ethiopian Churches' espousing an independent, indigenous African spirituality and moves away from white control by the 1880s (adumbrating the African Independent Churches of the 1920s and 1930s).[27] The National Church of India was established in Madras in 1886. Many missions faced agonizing choices regarding the separation of European and indigenous Christians (most notably in southern Africa) while they nevertheless opposed mounting injustice and racism that was taking a 'scientific' and 'biological' turn in the wake of Joseph-Arthur de Gobineau's *Essay on the inequality of human races* (1855), and a late-century 'religion of whiteness' that was drawing a global 'colour line'.[28]

The sheer diversity of missions, in terms of national background and arrangements with

---

23 John R. Mott, *The Evangelization of the World in this Generation* (New York: SVM, 1901).
24 Klaus Fiedler, *The Story of Faith Missions* (Oxford: Regnum, 1994).
25 Oceania is a case in point: Raeburn Lange, *Island Ministers: Indigenous Leadership in Nineteenth Century Pacific Islands Christianity* (Christchurch and Canberra: University of Canterbury and ANU, 2006).
26 Andrew Porter, 'Missions and Empire, c.1873–1914', in *The Cambridge History of Christianity, vol. 8: World Christianities, c.1815–c.1914*, edited by Sheridan Gilley and Brian Stanley (Cambridge: Cambridge University Press, 2006), p. 564.
27 Jehu Hanciles, *Euthanasia of a Mission: African Church Autonomy in a Colonial Context* (Westport, CT: Praeger, 2002).
28 The phrase was originally popularized by W. E. B. Du Bois. See Marilyn Lake and Henry Reynolds, *Drawing the Global Colour Line: White Men's Countries and the International Challenge of Racial Equality* (Cambridge: Cambridge University Press, 2008).

colonial governments and their dependent indigenous authorities, makes it difficult to offer neat generalizations about relationships with colonialism and empire between 1870 and 1914. Alongside the massive expansion of British, American, German and French missions were those, for example, of the Belgian, Danish, Norwegian and Swedish. Most missionaries affirmed the essential beneficence of empire, and where they agitated for colonial or imperial involvement it was primarily on grounds that were pragmatic, humanitarian and mission-oriented.[29] Nevertheless, many insisted on separating evangelization and the essentials of the faith from empire and Western culture. They recognized the limited value of imperial and colonial involvement and, by the early 1900s, had begun to welcome a renewed separation of missions and colonialism. Not a few missions, moreover, had attracted hostility from colonial officials for their advocacy and protest on behalf of indigenous peoples, especially in troubled places such as India and China.[30]

Colonial and imperial loyalty was further undercut among evangelicals by a powerful ideology of missionary internationalism and ecumenism – not unlike the internationalism emerging in contemporary Roman Catholicism, socialism and pan-Africanism. Missionary internationalism was fostered by regional, national and international networks of people, literature, missionary committees and conferences, which culminated in the massive World Missionary Conference in Edinburgh in 1910 (which, despite its lofty title, excluded Roman Catholics and Orthodox). Delegates at Edinburgh (who were mostly European) outlined plans for world evangelization and watered the seeds of a global ecumenical movement that later bore fruit in the creation of the World Council of Churches in 1947. Ingrained paternalist attitudes proved difficult to transcend, but there was a dawning realization that the future of Christian mission would be multi-directional, rather than flowing one-way from the Global North to the Global South.[31]

Early in the new century, a wave of simultaneous revivals in different parts of the world, coinciding with the emergence of Pentecostalism, unleashed powerful new movements in places as far afield as Korea, Brazil, India, China and East Africa. This contributed to the 'rapid emergence of a global evangelical culture', although there were growing divergences between Pentecostal movements and the ranks of both Keswick Conventions and conservative evangelicals.[32] Fundamentalist missions flourished in the wake of the Fundamentalist–Modernist debates of the 1910s and 1920s, expressing deeply conservative approaches to the historic faith over against engagement with Western intellectual and cultural life. Fundamentalists found their most potent missionary outlets within the ranks of faith missions.[33]

Global networks were maintained after the carnage of the First World War, and many mission-minded Protestants embraced internationalism as a means of forging a global community of nations, emphasizing social service (medicine, education and development) and friendship over conversion. By the mid-1920s, indigenizing priorities were once again gaining traction among both evangelicals and Roman Catholics, stressing the creation of vigorous national

---

29 Andrew Walls, 'British Missions', in *Missionary Ideologies in the Imperialist Era, 1880–1920*, edited by T. Christensen and W. R. Hutchison (Århus: Aros, 1982), pp. 164–5.
30 Porter, 'Missions and Empire', pp. 564–8.
31 Gladwin, 'Missons and Colonialism'; Brian Stanley, *The World Missionary Conference: Edinburgh 1910* (Grand Rapids, MI: Eerdmans, 2009).
32 Hutchinson and Wolffe, *Global Evangelicalism*, pp. 149–51; Allan Anderson, *Spreading Fires: The Missionary Nature of Early Pentecostalism* (Maryknoll, NY: Orbis, 2007).
33 Joel Carpenter, *Revive Us Again: The Reawakening of American Fundamentalism* (New York: Oxford University Press, 1997), pp. 178–84. George M. Marsden, *Fundamentalism and American Culture: The Shaping of Twentieth Century Evangelicalism, 1870–1925* (New York: Oxford University Press, 1980) provides context.

churches under indigenous leadership and incorporating indigenous cultures and worldviews into Christian theology and practice. New impetus for Bible translation was provided by the establishment of the Summer Institute of Linguistics (1934) and Wycliffe Bible Translators (1942).

In the aftermath of the Second World War's orgy of destruction, the notion of a 'world church' and 'world Christianity' emerged, one in which multi-cultural expressions of Christianity were seen to be crucial to a full expression of Christian witness. Europe's near destruction in that war ended four centuries of European expansion in other continents, reversing migration so that it now flowed from 'periphery' to 'centre'. Decolonizing nationalist movements across Asia and Africa, supported by the newly created UN, mushroomed in former colonial possessions and achieved independence in the postwar decades. With rejection of Western rule came rejection of missionaries and churches in places such as China, India and Indonesia. Accusations of missionary paternalism and neo-colonialist hegemony were complicated by many revolutionary Marxist regimes' Cold War allegiances. Yet an apparent paradox lay in the fact that it was mission schools who had educated and formed many nationalist leaders in post-colonial nations. European missionary agencies shifted their focus towards partnership and development aid, which they poured into the 'Third World' as reparation for colonialism. The growth of religious pluralism in the West after the 1960s accompanied declining church participation and the cultural marginalization of churches. A consequent climate of self-doubt led to diminishing missionary support and missionary numbers among Protestants and Catholics alike.[34]

Nevertheless, many evangelicals and Pentecostals rejected such uncertainties and fostered independent missionary movements focused largely on personal conversion and church planting. Returned servicemen, the Inter-Varsity Fellowship (1928) and evangelical and fundamentalist seminaries across the Western world contributed to a postwar 'missions surge'.[35] In the wake of the setbacks of the 1960s, a new global mission network was formed in 1974 when 2,300 evangelical leaders from 150 countries met in Lausanne to frame the Lausanne Covenant, a common framework and faith statement which served as a basis for church-planting and conversion-oriented missions. Evangelical missiologists had previously employed terms like 'adaptation', 'accommodation' and 'indigenization' to describe the relationship between gospel, church and culture. Terms such as 'contextualization', introduced in 1971, and 'inculturation', which emerged in Roman Catholic literature in 1974, were adopted as more dynamic and adequate terms to describe ideal evangelical mission paradigms in the post-colonial, post-Vatican II era. Such terms described attempts

> to establish the church in ways that make sense to people within their local cultural context, presenting Christianity in such a way that it meets people's deepest needs and penetrates their worldview, thus allowing them to follow Christ and remain within their own culture.[36]

Evangelical social concern, which Anglican leader and Lausanne architect John Stott affirmed as a Christian duty alongside evangelism, was given institutional form through organizations such as World Vision (1950) and Samaritan's Purse (1970), and was recognized as a priority at

---

34 Robert, *Christian Mission*, pp. 67–70. See also *Missions, Nationalism and the End of Empire*, edited by Brian Stanley (Grand Rapids, MI: Eerdmans, 2003).
35 Carpenter, *Revive Us Again*, pp. 178–84.
36 Darrell L. Whiteman, 'Contextualization: The Theory, the Gap, the Challenge', *International Bulletin of Missionary Research* vol. 21 (January 1997), 2.

Lausanne.[37] Evangelical scholarly reflection on missions – which had emerged as a sub-discipline of theology in its own right during the late nineteenth century under pietist Halle professor Gustav Warneck – was given a fillip by the creation of Fuller Theological Seminary's School of World Mission (1965). 'Neo-evangelical' missionary statesmen such as Max Warren, Lesslie Newbigin and John Stott distanced evangelicalism from Fundamentalism while embracing cross-cultural mission imperatives and creative partnerships with non-Western churches. As historian Dana Robert argues, Christianity's retreat under the forces of secularism and anti-colonialism was not the end of World Christianity, but rather 'the death rattle of European Christendom'.[38]

Lausanne had also forged awareness of powerful new growth and expressions of Christianity occurring from the 'bottom up' – and often despite European missionary activities and expectations – in Asia, sub-Saharan Africa, Oceania and Latin America, now freed in the post-colonial era from their dependence on the West to express Christianity in indigenous cultural forms. This spectacular expansion, in concert with religious revivals, indigenous leadership and evangelism, and rapid population growth in the fifty years after 1960, led to one of the largest geographical redistributions in the history of Christianity. The demography and 'centre of gravity' of Christianity shifted in this period from the European Global North to the Global South, as indicated by the numbers detailed in the introduction of this chapter. Crucial to this spectacular growth was the emergence of indigenous leadership and theologizing, coupled with the longstanding dynamic of indigenous agency in evangelism and church planting.

By the twenty-first century, the structure of missions had transformed into multi-cultural, multi-centred international networks. Vernacular translation of the Bible had also led to a greater diversity in expressions of evangelicalism in the Global South, fostering generally conservative approaches to theology and moral teaching, strongly supernaturalistic and charismatic religious sensibilities centring on the work of the Holy Spirit, progressive economic views and a wariness of both radical politics and secular states as a result of persecution.[39] Many former mission fields had by now birthed 'reverse mission' movements to the Global North ('south–north') and to other parts of the Global South ('south–south').[40] No case is more striking than that of Korea, which by 2006 had produced a missionary force of 13,000, drawn largely from Korea's 8.5 million evangelicals.[41] By the early twenty-first century, evangelical missions to the Global South had come full circle.

The historiography of evangelicals and mission in the Global South

From the eighteenth century until the 1950s, the historiography of evangelical mission in the Global South consisted largely of denominational, biographical or multi-volume surveys

---

37 John R. W. Stott, *Christian Mission in the Modern World* (London: Falcon, 1975).
38 Robert, *Christian Mission*, p. 69. See also, *Earthen Vessels: American Evangelicals and Foreign Missions, 1880–1980*, edited by Joel A. Carpenter and W. R. Shenk (Grand Rapids, MI: Eerdmans, 1990).
39 Philip Jenkins, *The New Faces of Christianity: Believing the Bible in the Global South* (New York: Oxford University Press, 2006); *Between Past and Future: Evangelical Mission Entering the Twenty-first Century*, edited by Jonathan Bonk (Pasadena, CA: William Carey Library, 2003); Joel Carpenter, 'Now What? Revivalist Christianity and Global South Politics', *Books and Culture* (March / April 2009), 34–38.
40 *Mission in the Twenty-First Century*, edited by A. F. Walls and Cathy Ross (Maryknoll, NY: Orbis, 2008); *Mission After Christendom*, edited by Ogbu Kalu et al (Louisville, KY: Westminster John Knox Press, 2010); *Religion Crossing Boundaries*, edited by Afe Adogame and James V. Spickared (Boston, MA: Brill, 2010).
41 Sangkeun Kim, 'Sheer Numbers Do Not Tell the Entire Story: The Challenges of the Korean Missionary Movement from an Ecumenical Perspective', *Ecumenical Review* vol. 57 (2005), 463–72.

authored by missionary leaders and activists. The focus was either celebratory (as an adjunct to promoting or fundraising for missions), apologetic or missiological (in attempts to assess the effectiveness of missionary strategy and to forge a robust theology of mission).[42] In their extensive publishing and fundraising efforts, missionary advocates were prone to offensive caricatures of the 'heathen' – the 'defamation of the other', as Jeffrey Cox puts it – yet they did so to highlight the capacity of the gospel to emancipate the 'heathen' from their barbarism, thereby uniting statements of extreme cultural difference with strong assertions of fundamental human unity.[43]

After the post-1945 dismemberment of European empires, but most obviously in the wake of massive decolonization worldwide after the 1960s, Christian missions were increasingly identified with Western oppression and the legacies of colonialism, neo-colonialism and globalization. This is not surprising, given that European colonial and capitalist expansion, beginning in the fifteenth century and reaching its apogee by 1914, provided the context for most evangelical missions. European powers' control of the earth's landmass grew from 35 per cent in 1800 to 85 per cent in 1914.[44] Since the beginning of the post-colonial era in the 1960s, therefore, few historical issues have been debated with as much fervour as the relationship of Christian missions to Western colonialism. This is partly because the concept of colonialism – derived from the Latin *colonus* for farmer – goes beyond the settling of territory and economic exploitation to processes of cultural and religious transformation. Evangelical missions became the object of strident scholarly critiques, largely from those working within nationalist, Marxist, secularist, post-structuralist and post-colonial intellectual frameworks. These literatures gave rise to popular and scholarly caricatures of missionaries as cultural imperialists, racist patriarchal colonizers or agents of a hegemonic globalizing capitalism.[45] The work of John and Jean Comaroff on missions to nineteenth-century South Africa has constituted one of the more influential recent critiques of evangelical missionaries as hegemonic 'colonizers of the consciousness' and midwives in the construction of colonial and neocolonial *mentalités*.[46] A significant 'Orientalist' literature has also implicated evangelical missionaries among Western creators of discourses that maintained Western hegemony through representations that essentialized and objectified the non-Western 'Other'.[47] Interdisciplinary lines of interpretation in anthropology, literary criticism and social and cultural history – as part of the so-called 'linguistic' and 'cultural' turns

---

42 See numerous nineteenth- and early twentieth-century histories (often published for anniversaries) of the CMS, BMS, LMS and USPG. The first scholarly survey of Christian missions from antiquity to the twentieth century was Kenneth Latourette's magisterial *A History of the Expansion of Christianity* (7 vols, New York: Harper, 1937–45).

43 Jeffrey Cox, *The British Missionary Enterprise Since 1700* (London: Routledge, 2008), pp. 144–5; Brian Stanley, 'Christian Missions, Antislavery and the Claims of Humanity, c.1813–1873', in *World Christianities*, edited by Gilley and Stanley, pp. 443–57.

44 Duncan Bell, 'Empire and Imperialism', in *The Cambridge History of Nineteenth-century Political Thought*, edited by Gareth Stedman-Jones and Gregory Claeys (Cambridge: Cambridge University Press, 2011), p. 865.

45 Important early critiques include Arthur Schlesinger Jr, 'The Missionary Enterprise and Theories of Imperialism', in *The Missionary Enterprise in China and America*, edited John K. Fairbank (Cambridge, MA: Harvard University Press, 1974); Arnold Temu and Bonaventure Swai, *Historians and Africanist History: A Critique. Post-colonial Historiography Examined* (London: Zed Press, 1981); William R. Hutchison, *Errand to the World: American Protestant Thought and Foreign Missions* (Chicago, IL: University of Chicago Press, 1987).

46 J. and J. A. Comaroff, *Of Revelation and Revolution* (2 vols, Chicago, IL: University of Chicago Press, 1991, 1997), I: 8–18.

47 Edward Said, *Orientalism* (London: Routledge, 1978); Edward Said, *Culture and Imperialism* (New York: Knopf, 1993).

– have more recently converged in the 'new imperial history'.[48] Here, evangelical missionaries have been scrutinized – often with a 'hermeneutic of suspicion' – through the conceptual lenses of race, class, gender and identity.[49] To some extent, this tradition of critical scholarship has reflected contemporary anxieties – accentuated by the 9/11 attacks in New York and 7/7 attacks in London – regarding national identity, immigration and social cohesion, imperial legacies and critiques of US 'imperialism'.

As a result of decolonization and an increasingly critical scholarship, missionaries and church leaders of the 1960s were forced to re-evaluate their posture in relation to indigenous states, churches and societies. Stephen Neill and Max Warren (both ordained missionary statesmen) provided the first modern assessments of these issues.[50] All were even-handed in their criticism of missionary endeavour and acknowledged the wounds of colonial contact, yet they also stressed positive results of missionary work such as the development of social institutions, amelioration of imperial and capitalist excesses, and missionaries' ambivalence regarding imperial authority, while recognizing the patchiness of research. Not until the late 1980s did there emerge a rigorous scholarly attempt to bring mission studies into dialogue with imperial and post-colonial history, principally in the work of Brian Stanley and Andrew Porter.[51] Several scholars have consolidated this early work, most notably through the 'Studies in the History of Christian Mission' monograph series.[52] These revisionist accounts of modern missionary history have challenged neo-Marxist, post-colonialist and post-structuralist accounts on both empirical and intellectual grounds. Numerous case studies have cast serious doubt on the 'cultural imperialist' thesis, highlighting the crucial role of indigenous agency in evangelical missions. The vast majority of Christian evangelists were indigenous – and hardly passive recipients – who selectively rejected, utilized or retranslated Christianity for their own ends and needs.[53] The mid-nineteenth-century formulation of 'Christianity, commerce and civilization' was, more-

---

48 *The New Imperial Histories Reader*, edited by Stephen Howe (Abingdon: Routledge, 2009).
49 'New imperial history' studies with a focus on evangelical missions include Susan Thorne, *Congregational Missions and the Making of an Imperial Culture in Nineteenth-century England* (Stanford, CA: Stanford University Press, 1999); Catherine Hall, *Civilising Subjects: Metropole and Colony in the English Imagination* (Cambridge: Polity Press, 2002); Esme Cleall, *Missionary Discourse: Negotiating Difference in the British Empire, c.1840–95* (Basingstoke: Palgrave Macmillan, 2012).
50 Max Warren, *The Missionary Movement from Britain in Modern History* (London: SCM, 1965); Stephen Neill, *Colonialism and Christian Missions* (London: Lutterworth Press, 1966).
51 Brian Stanley, '"Commerce and Christianity": Providence Theory, the Missionary Movement, and the Imperialism of Free Trade, 1842–1860', *Historical Journal* vol. 26 (1983), 71–94; Brian Stanley, *The Bible and the Flag: Protestant Missions and British Imperialism in the Nineteenth and Twentieth Centuries* (Leicester: Apollos, 1990); Andrew Porter, 'Religion and Empire: British Expansion in the Long Nineteenth Century', *Journal of Imperial and Commonwealth History* vol. 20 (1992), 370–90; Porter, *Religion Versus Empire?*.
52 At the time of writing there are twenty-one books in the series, published by Eerdmans under the editorship of Robert Eric Frykenberg and Brian Stanley. See also James M. Greenlee and Charles M. Johnston, *Good Citizens: British Missionaries and Imperial States, 1780–1918* (Ontario: McGill-Queen's University Press, 1999); Jeffrey Cox, *Imperial Fault Lines: Christianity and Colonial Power in India, 1818–1940* (Stanford, CA: Stanford University Press, 2002); Cox, *The British Missionary Enterprise*; *Missions and Empire*, edited by Norman Etherington (Oxford: Oxford University Press, 2005); Tony Ballantyne, 'Religion, Difference and the Limits of British Imperial History', *Victorian Studies* vol. 47 (2005), 427–55.
53 Richard Gray, *Black Christians and White Missionaries* (New Haven, CT: Yale University Press, 1990); Leon De Kock, *Civilising Barbarians* (Johannesburg: Witwatersrand University Press, 1996); Lamin Sanneh, *West African Christianity: The Religious Impact* (Maryknoll, NY: Orbis, 1983); Porter, *Religion Versus Empire?*, pp. 316–30; Ogbu Kalu. *Power, Poverty and Prayer: The Challenges of Poverty and Pluralism in African Christianity, 1960–1996* (Trenton, NJ: Africa World Press, 2006).

over, driven significantly by missionary–humanitarian campaigns against slavery and is more reflective of modern development theory than merely an attempt to impose economic dependency.[54] Other research has questioned the correlation between missions and the economic peak of British imperialism, or any simple correlation between missions and colonial reach.[55] The modern missionary emphasis on literacy, education and vernacular translation of the Christian message helped preserve indigenous languages and cultures, and created nurseries for nationalist leaders and movements – what Horst Gründer has termed the 'dialectic of Christianisation'.[56] Influential sociological studies have also correlated the expansion of evangelicalism (defined as 'conversionary Protestantism') with the rise and spread of stable democracy around the world, demonstrating that conversionary Protestants were a 'crucial catalyst initiating the development and spread of religious liberty, mass education, mass printing, newspapers, voluntary organizations, and colonial reforms, thereby creating the conditions that made stable democracy more likely'.[57]

Some post-colonialist scholarship has drawn criticism for being in danger of becoming 'yet another totalising method and theory' like the colonialist and neo-colonialist discourses it critiques.[58] Saidian orientalist critiques have been accused of a tendency to utilize the same Enlightenment 'malpractices' which Edward Said criticized with regard to 'the East', namely representing European culture (and evangelical mission as a subset of that) in ways which 'essentialise, objectify, demean, de-rationalise, and de-historicise it' – an 'occidentalist' representation of 'the West'.[59] A concomitant weakness of many 'missionary as colonialist' critiques has been a tendency to de-historicize and essentialize missionary visions and endeavours.

Recent models of intercultural 'dialogue', 'hybridity' and missions 'from below' have recognized the importance of indigenous agency and have offered more nuanced ways of understanding the complex creation of identities and worldviews in the encounter between missionary and convert, as have conceptual frameworks of 'translation' and 'constructive conversation'.[60]

A recurrent theme in critical modern studies of evangelical missions, therefore, has been a tendency to overlook the fundamental ambiguity and multiformity of evangelical missionary attitudes towards colonial and imperial endeavour, as well as evangelicals' insistence on fundamental human unity and racial egalitarianism, grounded in the *imago dei* and a belief in fallen humanity; belief in the universalizing logic of the Christian gospel; notions of colonial and

---

54 Stanley, 'Christian Missions', pp. 451–2. See also Elizabeth Elbourne, 'Word Made Flesh: Christianity, Modernity, and Cultural Colonialism in the Work of Jean and John Comaroff', *American Historical Review* vol. 108 (2003), 435–59.
55 See, for example, Stanley, *Bible and the Flag*; Porter, *Religion Versus Empire?*; Cox, *British Missionary Enterprise*.
56 Horst Gründer, *Welteroberung und Christentum* (Gütersloh: Gütersloher Verl.-Haus Mohn, 1992), p. 580.
57 Robert D. Woodberry, 'The Missionary Roots of Liberal Democracy', *American Political Science Review* vol. 106 (2012), 244–74.
58 Leela Gandhi, *Postcolonial Theory: A Critical Introduction* (Edinburgh: Edinburgh University Press, 1998), p. 167.
59 D. A. Washbrook, 'Orients and Occidents: Colonial Discourse Theory and the Historiography of the British Empire', in *Oxford History of the British Empire. vol. 5: Historiography*, edited by Robin Winks (Oxford: Oxford University Press, 1999), pp. 606, 609–10.
60 See Lamin Sanneh, *Translating the Message: The Missionary Impact on Culture* (Maryknoll, NY: Orbis, 1989); Andrew F. Walls, *The Missionary Movement in Christian History: Studies in the Transmission of Faith* (Edinburgh: T. & T. Clark, 1996); David Maxwell, *Christians and Chiefs in Zimbabwe: A Social History of the Hwesa People* (Edinburgh: Edinburgh University Press, 1999); Elizabeth Elbourne, *Blood Ground: Colonialism, Missions, and the Contest for Christianity in the Cape Colony and Britain, 1799–1853* (Montreal: McGill-Queen's University Press, 2002).

imperial influence as a providentially bestowed trust; and an internationalist character which fostered a *mentalité* that subordinated and relativized all other allegiances, whether national, colonial or imperial. Like most of their contemporaries, few missionary leaders and thinkers before the 1960s opposed colonial rule on principle, but they did seek to civilize it.[61] But perhaps more fundamentally, as Dana Robert suggests, they sought to convert it.[62]

Beyond the question of complicity with imperial and colonial projects, the 'cultural turn' in historiography has yielded rich insights into evangelical mission in the Global South. In addition to the familiar questions of whether some southern churches' emphases reflect syncretism rather than pristine New Testaments beliefs and practices, themes relating to gender, family and sexuality in mission history have generated significant scholarly interest since the 1980s, particularly where they have intersected with social fault-lines of class, race and ethnicity. After all, late nineteenth-century women constituted the majority of evangelical foreign mission personnel. Initially scholars focused on nineteenth-century European evangelical missionaries, particularly their 'civilizing' and 'modernizing' influence on indigenous peoples, and their work in the 'feminine' domestic sphere as doctors and teachers among women and children. The latter reflected Victorian notions of 'separate spheres' for men and women's work, as well as evangelistic strategy within patriarchal societies. Increasing professionalism of women missionaries in medicine, education and social work fostered new outlets beyond domestic life and a renegotiation of their typically subordinate roles in metropolitan churches and missionary societies, in contrast with their more dominant positions among indigenous women and children. More recent work has considered gender and family dynamics among both indigenous missionaries and indigenous peoples themselves, where gender roles, identities and sexual practices were being re-evaluated and negotiated in complex ways.[63] Scholars have only recently turned attention to the issue of evangelical missionaries and masculinity, in contrast with a large literature on the 'muscular Christianity' that gained prominence after the mid-nineteenth century.[64]

Cultural historians have begun to explore the interplay between the 'textuality' and 'materiality' of missions. Here the focus has been on ways in which missionaries carried, performed and translated their messages in the material clothing of bodies, medicine and architecture; the semiotic role of material items; and corresponding ways in which this materiality shaped cultural interactions and the practices of lived religion, while providing an index of the processes of indigenization.[65] Related avenues of research have focused on the interplay between evangelical

---

61 Gladwin, 'Missions and Colonialism'.
62 Dana Robert, *Converting Colonialism: Visions and Realities in Mission History, 1706–1914* (Grand Rapids, MI: Eerdmans, 2008), p. 20.
63 See *Women and Missions: Past and Present Anthropological Perspectives*, edited by F. Bowie, D. Kirkwood and S. Ardener (Oxford: Berg, 1993); Dana Robert, *American Women in Mission: A Social History of their Thought and Practice* (Macon, GA: Mercer University Press, 1996); Rhonda Ann Semple, *Missionary Women: Gender, Professionalism and the Victorian Idea of Christian Mission* (Woodbridge: Boydell and Brewer, 2003); Emily Manktelow, *Missionary Families: Race, Gender and Generation on the Spiritual Frontier* (Manchester: Manchester University Press, 2013); 'Gender and Family in the History of Christian Missions' (special issue), *Studies in World Christianity* vol. 21 (2015), 1–85. For influential 'Zenana' missions to Indian women, see Antoinette M. Burton, 'Contesting the Zenana: The Mission to Make "Lady Doctors for India", 1874–1885', *Journal of British Studies* vol. 35 (1996), 368–97; Bināya Bhūshaṇa Rāya and Pranati Ray, *Zenana Mission* (Delhi: ISPCK, 1998).
64 See, however, Rhonda Ann Semple, 'Missionary Manhood: Professionalism, Belief and Masculinity in the Nineteenth-Century British Imperial Field', *Journal of Imperial and Commonwealth History* vol. 36 (2008), 397; José Leonardo Santos, *Evangelicalism and Masculinity: Faith and Gender in El Salvador* (Lanham, MD: Lexington Books, 2012).
65 For a helpful introduction see *Mixed Messages: Materiality, Textuality, Missions*, edited by James S. Scott and Gareth Griffiths (Basingstoke: Palgrave Macmillan, 2005), Chs 1–7, 12; David Morgan, *The Sacred*

missions and medicine, both at home and on the mission field.[66] Likewise the extensive interests of evangelical missionaries in anthropology and science have attracted growing scholarly attention.[67] In keeping with the prominence of 'conversionism' within evangelical belief and practice, a large literature has examined the importance of missionaries as agents of religious and cultural change, and the varying patterns and processes of conversion that are further shaped by cultural and historical contexts.[68]

The historical span and scope of evangelical mission historiography has also expanded dramatically in recent decades. Evangelicals' prominence within global humanitarian networks has garnered significant attention.[69] Likewise regional (Africa, Asia, Latin America, Oceania) and national histories have offered important avenues through which to explore the place of evangelicals and mission in the Global South. Increasingly these histories are being written by scholars with origins in the Global South, rather than by Western historians.[70] Since the late 1990s, historians have been writing the history of modern Christianity – including evangelicalism and Pentecostalism as some of its key components – with a scope that has been global and a chronological span that may be described as a *longue durée*. Histories of 'world Christianity' and 'global Christianity' have proliferated in monographs, academic journals and seminary course offerings, in part due to an increasing awareness among scholars of the seismic shift of Christianity's 'centre of gravity' from the Global North to the Global South, and in part due to a broader interest among academic historians in globalization and corresponding conceptual frameworks of 'world history' and 'global history'.[71] An adjunct to these broader histories of

Gaze: Religious Visual Culture in Theory and Practice (Berkeley, CA: University of California Press, 2005).

66 A. F. Walls, '"The Heavy Artillery of the Missionary Army": The Domestic Importance of the Nineteenth-century Medical Missionary', in *The Church and Healing*, edited by W. J. Shiels (Oxford: Blackwell, 1982), pp. 287–97.

67 Sujit Sivasundaram, *Nature and the Godly Empire: Science and Evangelical Mission in the Pacific, 1795–1850* (Cambridge: Cambridge University Press, 2005).

68 See Sanneh, *Missionary Impact*; Walls, *Missionary Movement*; *The Oxford Handbook of Religious Conversion*, edited by Lewis R. Rambo and C. E. Farhadian (New York: Oxford University Press, 2014).

69 Andrew Porter, 'Trusteeship, Anti-Slavery, and Humanitarianism', in *Oxford History of the British Empire, vol. 3: The Nineteenth Century*, edited by Andrew Porter and William Roger Louis (Oxford: Oxford University Press, 1999); Stanley, 'Claims of Humanity'; Alan Lester and Rob Skinner, 'Humanitarianism and Empire: New Research Agendas', *Journal of Imperial and Commonwealth History* vol. 40 (2012), 729–47.

70 The following represent introductions to large and growing literatures in each region. For Asia generally see Scott W. Sunquist, *A Dictionary of Asian Christianity* (Grand Rapids, MI: Eerdmans, 2001); *Christianities in Asia*, edited by Peter Phan (Oxford: Wiley-Blackwell, 2011). For China, see Lian Xi, *Redeemed by Fire: the Rise of Popular Christianity in Modern China* (New Haven, CT: Yale University Press, 2010); Daniel H. Bays, *A New History of Christianity in China* (Oxford: Wiley-Blackwell, 2012). For India, see Robert Frykenberg, *Christianity in India: From Beginnings to the Present* (Oxford: Oxford University Press, 2010). For Africa, see Bengt Sundkler and Christopher Steed, *A History of the Church in Africa* (Cambridge: Cambridge University Press, 2000); *African Christianity: An African Story*, edited by Ogbu Kalu (Pretoria: University of Pretoria, 2005); *Christianity in Africa and the African Diaspora: The Appropriation of a Scattered Heritage*, edited by Afe Adogame (New York, Continuum, 2011). For Latin America see Samuel Escobar, *The New Global Mission: The Gospel from Everywhere to Everyone* (Downers Grove, IL: InterVarsity Press, 2003); David Martin, *Tongues of Fire: The Explosion of Protestantism in Latin America* (Oxford: Blackwell, 2008); *Evangelical Christianity and Democracy in Latin America*, edited by Paul Freston (Oxford: Oxford University Press, 2008). For Oceania, see Ian Breward, *A History of the Churches in Australasia* (Oxford: Oxford University Press, 2001); Raeburn, *Island Ministers*.

71 Key histories of 'world' or 'global' Christianity include Walls, *Missionary Movement*; *A World History of Christianity*, edited by Adrian Hastings (Grand Rapids, MI: Eerdmans, 1999); *The Changing Face of Christianity: Africa, the West, and the World*, edited by Lamin Sanneh and Joel A. Carpenter (Oxford:

Christianity has been scholarly study of evangelicalism (often including Pentecostalism) as a global movement, profoundly shaped by – and shaping – converging forces of urbanization and globalization.[72] Perhaps the most provocative study within this emerging genre has been Philip Jenkins' *The Next Christendom* (2002), now in its third edition. Jenkins charted the shifting centre of gravity of Christianity towards Latin America, Africa and Asia, suggesting the challenges that conservative, non-Western forms of Christianity pose to Western liberal values, Enlightenment ideas and liberal theologies (on issues such as homosexuality in the Anglican Church, for example). More controversially, Jenkins invoked political scientist Samuel Huntingdon's contested 'clash of civilizations' theory to posit the potential for religio-cultural conflict between Islam and 'a new Christendom, based in Africa, Asia and Latin America'.[73] A striking theme in all of these literatures is the importance of Christianity – and evangelicalism as one of its most dynamic manifestations – for the future of the Global South.

Conclusions

In many ways the historiography of evangelicals and mission in the Global South has followed the contours of the movement's historical trajectory. The southward shift in Christianity's 'centre of gravity' and its decoupling from empires during the twentieth century has paralleled southward emphases and post-colonial reassessments in its history writing. The recent efflorescence of global histories of evangelicalism, in the context of non-Western and global histories of Christianity, reflects the changing reality on the ground in Asia, Africa, Latin America and Oceania. This historiography also reflects wider shifts in the Western academy towards understanding the forces of globalization in harness with post-colonial, transnational (rather than merely national) and world histories. In a globalized world, church historians, religious historians and secular historians alike are finding it increasingly difficult to write credible modern histories of Christianity without reference to the global context generally, and evangelicalism specifically. Profound interest in Christianity has also reflected scholarly recognition of the utter inadequacy of the post-1960s 'secularization thesis' and the enduring importance of religious

---

Oxford University Press, 2005); *World Christianities*, edited by Gilley and Stanley; *The Cambridge History of Christianity, vol. 9: World Christianities, c.1914–c.2000*, edited by Hugh McLeod (Cambridge: Cambridge University Press, 2006); Sebastian Kim, *Christianity as a World Religion* (London: Continuum, 2008); Lamin Sanneh, *Disciples of all Nations: Pillars of World Christianity* (Oxford: Oxford University Press, 2008); Robert, *Christian Mission*. Key journals include *The Journal of World Christianity* and *Studies in World Christianity*.

72 The best single-volume introduction is Wolffe and Hutchinson, *Global Evangelicalism*. Other key scholarly studies include Donald M. Lewis, *Christianity Reborn: Evangelicalism's Global Expansion in the Twentieth Century* (Grand Rapids, MI: Eerdmans, 2004); David Hempton, *Methodism: Empire of the Spirit* (New Haven, CT: Yale University Press, 2006); Mark A. Noll, *The New Shape of World Christianity: How American Experience Reflects Global Faith* (Downers Grove, IL: InterVarsity Press, 2009); Brian Stanley, *The Global Diffusion of Evangelicalism: The Age of Billy Graham and John Stott* (Nottingham: InterVarsity Press, 2013); Allan Anderson, *An Introduction to Pentecostalism: Global Charismatic Christianity* (Cambridge: Cambridge University Press, 2014); Donald M. Lewis and Richard V. Pierard, *Global Evangelicalism: Theology, History and Culture in Regional Perspective* (Downers Grove, IL: InterVarsity Press, 2014). For processes of urbanization and globalization, see *A Global Faith: Essays on Evangelicalism and Globalization*, edited by Mark Hutchinson and Ogbu Kalu (Sydney: Centre for the Study of Australian Christianity, 1998); Dale T. Irvin, 'The Church, the Urban, and the Global: Mission in an Age of Global Cities', *International Bulletin of Missionary Research* vol. 33 (October 2009), 177–82.

73 Philip Jenkins, *The Next Christendom: The Coming of Global Christianity* (New York: Oxford University Press, 2011), pp. 9–20. For a critique, see *Global Christianity: Contested Claims*, edited by Frans Wijsen and Robert J. Schreiter (Amsterdam: Rodopi, 2007).

faith (including its fundamentalist manifestations) for the vast majority of the world's population, both historically and in the context of a post-Cold War, post-9/11 global order.

As we have seen, modern histories of evangelicalism and mission in the Global South since the 1960s have produced two recognizable (but sometimes overlapping) literatures. The first literature, grounded in nationalist, Marxist, post-colonial or post-structuralist modes of analysis (including the 'new imperial history'), has produced stridently critical assessments, sometimes at the expense of intellectual and empirical nuance. A second literature, which might be labelled 'modern missions history', has revised longstanding caricatures of Western missionaries as political or cultural imperialists. Not a few of the latter group of scholars have espoused evangelical beliefs or at least sympathies. In turn, their scholarship has reflected two aspects of Western evangelicals' experience since the 1960s: first, a need for post-colonial introspection and consequent recalibration of mission approaches and priorities; and second, a growing maturity and confidence among evangelicals in engaging both culture and the secular academy. A 'renaissance' in evangelical theology, philosophy and history writing has ensured that evangelical scholars – not least historians – now routinely write for two audiences: the church and the academy, rather than the church alone. Universities and educational resources for evangelicals are still located disproportionately in the Global North. Nevertheless, just as southern evangelical Christianities are emerging and evolving at a prodigious rate, so they are beginning to write their own histories.

Another striking feature of the historiography of evangelicalism and missions has been its interdisciplinary character. Anthropology, sociology and the 'cultural' and 'imperial' turns in history have produced richly textured insights and accounts of the movement. The most nuanced, methodologically sophisticated and enlightening studies have been those that have drawn critically from many of these various literatures and approaches. This should not be surprising, given the historical complexity, diversity and dynamism of evangelicals and mission in the Global South.

11

EVANGELICALS AND THE END OF THE WORLD

Mark S. Sweetnam

'"The future" is big business'.[1] This observation, contained in Hal Lindsey's phenomenonally successful bestseller, *The Late Great Planet Earth* (1970), seems to sum up, in an economical phrase of five words, the crucial elements of Lindsey's idiosyncratic approach to the interpretation of prophetic Scripture. Lindsey's facility for turning a memorable phrase, his tendency to reduce theological detail to a soundbite, and the overwhelming commercial success of his approach are all here captured in essence – which may help to explain why it has caught the eyes, and attracted the ire, of some of his critics.[2] But, though they may not have expressed it in quite the same way, the future has always been 'big business' for evangelicals. The interpretation and application of prophetic Scripture has played an important role in the thought and praxis of evangelical believers since the emergence of evangelicalism as a distinctive movement.

It is not, perhaps, surprising that this should be the case. David Bebbington has demonstrated the central importance of Biblicism (which he defines as 'a particular regard for the Bible') to evangelical identity.[3] Given how much of the Bible is devoted to prophecy, any movement that is heavily invested in the authority and importance of Scripture will, of necessity, have to reflect on its understanding of prophetic Scripture and take a stance on how these Scriptures are to be understood. Evangelicals have varied widely in their understanding of these details, but have been united by a shared understanding of the importance of prophecy. What is less readily explicable is a widespread failure in the historiography of the evangelical movement to recognize the importance of this issue. The historiography of evangelicalism is, of course, itself rather a recent phenomenon – David Bebbington's *Evangelicalism in Modern Britain: A History from the 1730s to the 1980s*, published in 1989, can lay good claim to kick-starting a new field of historical research. It is, nonetheless, striking that only recently have scholars begun to look in sustained detail at the eschatology of evangelicalism.

Before commencing our own consideration of that eschatology (or, perhaps more accurately,

---

1 Hal Lindsey, *The Late Great Planet Earth* (Grand Rapids, MI: Zondervan, 1970), p. 16.
2 Gary DeMar, *Why the End of the World is Not in Your Future* (Braselton, GA: American Vision Press, 2010), p. 13; Philip Jenkins, *Decade of Nightmares: The End of the Sixties and the Making of the Eighties in America* (New York: Oxford University Press, 2006), p. 84.
3 David W. Bebbington, *Evangelicalism in Modern Britain: A History from the 1730s to the 1980s* (London: Unwin Hyman, 1989), p. 3.

those eschatologies) it will be useful to define the terminology used in this chapter. 'Eschatology' itself is a good place to start. In the Christian tradition, this term was classically used to speak of doctrine concerning the 'four last things' – death, judgment, heaven and hell. In more recent usage, however, the term has been used more loosely to refer to beliefs about the end of the world (or, more loosely still, given that the eschatology of many evangelicals begins, as we shall see, at a minimum distance of 1,007 years from the end of the world, simply beliefs about the future). Evangelical eschatology comes in a variety of forms, which differ in emphasis, chronology and in exegetical basis.

In terms of emphasis, evangelical eschatology typically combines elements of millennialism and apocalypticism. Like eschatology, the term 'apocalyptic' has both theological and popular meanings. Strictly, apocalyptic is a biblical 'genre, of revelatory literature with a narrative framework, in which revelation is mediated by an otherworldly being to a human recipient, disclosing a transcendent reality which is both temporal, insofar as it envisages eschatological salvation, and spatial, insofar as it involves another, supernatural world'.[4] In popular usage, 'apocalyptic' focuses on one element of these texts – their denouncement of catastrophic global judgment on the world, leading, ultimately to its destruction and dissolution. By contrast, 'millennialism' refers to the expectation of a future golden age, as described in Revelation 20: 1–10. Based on this passage, this period will involve the binding of Satan, the limitation of evil and the outpouring of Divine blessing on earth. Apocalypticism and millennialism, therefore, exist in tension with each other. It is important, however, to understand that they are by no means mutually exclusive and that, in an evangelical context at least, eschatology almost always involves a mixture of apocalyptic and millennial expectation. The balance between these emphases differs from interpretative system to interpretative system, and from individual interpreter to individual interpreter, but almost always, pessimism and optimism about the future fate of the world will be found co-mingled.

Evangelical eschatology, then, varies by the emphasis that is accorded to millennial and apocalyptic elements. But an even more significant source of variation is the question of chronology or, in more overtly theological terms, the choice between pre-, post-, and amillennial understandings of prophetic Scripture. These interpretations of prophetic Scripture differ in their understanding of the relationship between the second coming of Jesus Christ and the instantiation and course of the millennial kingdom. As its name suggests, premillennialism expects the second coming of Christ before the commencement of the millennial age. Christ's return to earth will be attended by cataclysmic judgment, in particular the seven-year period referred to as the Tribulation or, in a reference to Daniel 9, 'Daniel's seventieth week'. The judgments of the Tribulation and the return of Christ will obliterate the existing social, political and ecological order, providing a *tabula rasa* for the establishment of Christ's kingdom and the outpouring of millennial bliss.

Premillennialism can be divided into two significant variants. 'Historic' premillennialism posits a return of Christ after the Tribulation (for which reason it is often referred to as 'post-tribulationism'). By contrast, 'dispensational' premillennialism (or, simply, 'dispensationalism') anticipates a two-stage return of Christ: a pre-Tribulation 'secret rapture', when he returns in the air to rapture, or snatch up, true believers, living and dead, and a 'glorious appearing' at the end of the Tribulation to put down all human and satanic rebellion, and set up his kingdom. Premillennialism inevitably stresses the apocalyptic aspect of prophetic expectation, for it expects the imminent dissolution of the world as it now is. Its critics, indeed, have often depicted it as a wholly pessimistic mindset. However, premillennialism also stresses millennial

---

4 John J. Collins, 'Apocalypse: The Morphology of a Genre', *Semeia* vol. 14 (1979), 9.

expectation, because that dissolution is the preliminary to the commencement of Christ's reign. This implication of premillennial teaching has not always been given equal attention to the lurid horrors of the Tribulation period, but it is reductive – though relatively common – to deny the role played by millennial expectation in premillennial thought.[5]

By contrast, postmillennialism is the belief that human progress, and particularly the global spread and prosperity of the gospel, will gradually transform society to the extent that millennial conditions will be enjoyed on earth without the radical irruption of Christ into history. Rather, his second coming will take place at the end of the millennium, and at that stage, the last judgment and the end of the world will take place. Postmillennialism manifestly implies a very different reading of history from that espoused by premillennialism. Its narrative is one of progress, rather than deterioration, and emphasizes the potential of Christian engagement with society and its institutions, rather than the withdrawal promoted by a premillennial understanding of history.

Finally, amillennialism rejects the concept of a literal, 1,000 year reign of Christ altogether. Instead, amillennialists see Revelation 20: 1–10 as a metaphor for some or all of the time between Christ's ascension and his return. They apply a spiritualizing hermeneutic, which adopts a non-literal, allegorical interpretation of the Old Testament prophecies referring to the millennium. Amillennialism emerged from Augustine's teaching, which, in turn, was based on Origen's allegorical approach to the interpretation of Scripture. It was, and remains, the dominant position of the Roman Catholic Church, and continued to be the position espoused by the magisterial reformers. In the context of evangelicalism, amillennialism was displaced by the emergence of postmillennial expectation, and it has remained of marginal importance, though it increased in popularity towards the end of the twentieth century, with the resurgence of reformed theology.

The relevance of the exegetical approach to amillennialism is obvious, but it is worth noting that pre- and postmillennialism, too, are the result of the hermeneutical positions that inform the reading of prophetic Scripture and, especially, of the book of Revelation. Evangelicals have adopted four interpretative methods: idealism, preterism, historicism and futurism. Idealism, which tends to be a feature of amillennial exegesis, rejects the idea that Revelation has any specific historical application, and argues, instead, that the book is intended to communicate a series of timeless truths, which are applicable to all ages and social contexts. Preterists, by contrast, see the prophecies of Revelation as having a very specific historical application, as descriptions of the destruction of Jerusalem by the Roman armies of Titus in AD 70. Historicism (which must not be confused with historical premillennialism, as described above) sees in Revelation prophetic reference to a range of events throughout the history of the Church. This position was adopted by many of the Protestant reformers and is most notoriously exemplified in the widespread identification of the Pope as the Antichrist. Finally, futurism (which is common amongst both pre- and amillennialists, and which is an integral part of dispensationalism) sees Revelation 5–22 as prophetic, referring not to the past or the present, but to the future, and particularly to the events that will take place during the seven year Tribulation period that precedes the return of Christ and the establishment of his kingdom.

There has been, and continues to be, a good deal of variety in the ways in which evangelicals have understood prophetic Scripture. It is probably fair to say that all of these views have been held by evangelicals throughout the history of the movement. It is, however, also the case that

---

5 See for a fuller discussion of this tension Mark S. Sweetnam, 'Tensions in Dispensational Eschatology', in *Expecting the End: Millennialism in Social and Historical Context*, edited by Kenneth G. C. Newport and Crawford Gribben (Waco, TX: Baylor University Press, 2006), pp. 173–92.

each position has not been of equal importance. In the balance of this chapter, we will look in some detail at the ways in which the dominant emphasis of prophetic interpretation has shifted. Before doing so, two caveats must be noted. First, we need to be aware that the appeal of the neat trajectory does not seduce us into oversimplifying the picture of evangelical eschatology that emerges from our consideration. That a trajectory exists is difficult to deny. It is easy to trace a development from amillennialism in the seventeenth century, to postmillennialism in the eighteenth century, from premillennialism in the nineteenth and twentieth, to an increasing breakdown of eschatological consensus in the latter half of the twentieth century. It would, however, do poor service to our understanding of the evangelical movement, and to its approach to prophetic issues, if we allow the existence of this trajectory to blind us to the continuous and continuing existence of alternative viewpoints in each century of the movement's history.

The second danger also stems from the lure of over-simplification and the temptation to adopt an excessively rigid and essentialized view of theological positions. As Smolinski has suggested:

> The study of late Reformation eschatology is frequently bogged down in a quagmire or terminology which can be as puzzling to novices as it is to those who plumb its depth. All too often modern assumptions about, and definitions of, the terms 'premillennialism' . . . and 'postmillennialism' . . . are rigidly superimposed upon the developing historical context in the early modern era.[6]

Especially in the early decades of the history of the evangelical movement, there is evidence of far more fluidity than the definitions of pre-, post- and amillennialism might lead us to suppose. This fact can lead scholars to some strangely contradictory conclusions. To take but one instance, Crawford Gribben points out that the Westminister Confession of Faith (1647) has been described as clearly amillennial, as 'the strongest premillennialist symbol of Protestantism', and as an expression of 'mild, unsystemized, postmillennial expectations'.[7] That this phenomenon is not limited to early expressions of millennialism is demonstrated by the example of Thomas Kelly (1769–1855).[8] Kelly was one of the Dublin ministers of the Church of Ireland who grew frustrated with the limitations that the Established Church placed upon their evangelical zeal and seceded in order to form their own evangelical 'connexions'. Kelly was a prolific hymnwriter and editor of hymnbooks. Having left the Church of Ireland, and established a number of chapels, he engaged in a programme of anthologizing the hymns of others, and writing individual compositions of his own. His first collection was published in 1804 and, by the publication of his final collection in 1853, he had written no less than 765 original hymns. These hymns covered a wide range of subjects, but prophecy, specifically the return of Christ, featured heavily. However, in spite of the amount of available evidence, attempts to use Kelly's hymns to pin him down to a clearly defined pre- or postmillennial position or to demonstrate a clear trajectory of theological development from one position to the other are destined to fail. Kelly makes frequent use of millennial tropes and figures, but he does

---

6 R. Smolinski, 'Caveat Emptor: Pre- and Postmillennialism in the Late Reformation Period', in *Millenarianism and Messianism in Early Modern European Culture*, edited by James E. Force and Richard H. Popkin (New York: Springer, 2001), pp. 145–69.

7 Crawford Gribben, *Evangelical Millennialism in the Trans-Atlantic World, 1500–2000* (Basingstoke: Palgrave Macmillan, 2011), pp. 48–9.

8 Mark S. Sweetnam, 'Canonicity and Radical Evangelicalism: The Case of Thomas Kelly', in *United Islands? The Languages of Resistance*, edited by John Kirk, Andrew Noble and Michael Brown (London: Pickering & Chatto, 2012), pp. 77–94.

not do so to advance any single reading of prophecy. It may be for this reason that his hymns remain popular with committed premillennialists and ardent postmillennialists alike. In any case, his example – along with many others – does caution us about too hermetically dividing our categories of prophetic belief.

The development of a postmillennial consensus

With these caveats in mind, we can identify the emergence of a broad postmillennial consensus as the first outcome of the evangelical engagement with prophetic Scripture. This consensus emerged against a background of amillennialism. To a man, the magisterial reformers had denied the possibility of a literal millennialism, and denounced those so foolish as to cherish 'Jewish dreams' on the subject. This attitude was the result, in part, of lingering doubts about the canonical status of the book of Revelation,[9] but also a reaction to the political and social upheaval that had resulted from the more extreme fringes of the Reformation movement. Events like those that unfolded in the Anabaptist rebellion at Münster seemed to the reformers to exemplify and underscore the dangers of unrestrained engagement with the text of Scripture and the perils of too ardent and unrestrained a millennial expectation.[10] Hermeneutical and social concerns, alike, seemed to make millennialism an unacceptable option, and it was pushed out of the mainstream of the Protestant Reformation to the sometimes extreme, and often persecuted, margin. In the context of England, Ireland and Scotland, the civil wars and interregnum offered new opportunity for those on the extremes to practice and propagate their beliefs, and the apparently apocalyptic events unfolding all around gave fresh relevance and legitimacy to eschatological concerns. In this area, as in many others, however, the Restoration had a chilling effect on doctrinal speculation. The 'Great Ejection', which followed the passing the Act of Uniformity in 1662, saw the separation of non-subscribing clergy from the Established Church, and 'as latitudinarian and moderate clergy dominated within the English establishment and as apocalyptic speculation was increasingly associated with the horror of the civil wars, it became clear that the intellectual trends of the Enlightenment had so generally "diminished" the significance of eschatology in the "mainstream Christian thought" that its most natural home was now in evangelical dissent'.[11]

Within evangelical dissent, eschatology would take a markedly – though not universally – postmillennial shape. There were a number of factors that helped to give evangelical eschatology this dominant shape. The implications of Enlightenment thought encouraged a renewed optimism about human potential, and seemed to lend credence to the notion that human agency could, and did, have a role to play in preparing the planet for Christ's return. This emphasis was, perhaps, especially marked in the North American context. Millennial thinking had played an important role in puritan emigration to the new world, and the rhetoric of millennialism continued to play a vital role in the American narrative. The representation of the American colonies as a 'city set upon a hill', and the seemingly limitless potential of the new society that was being pioneered on the North American continent offered a secularized narrative of human progress and perfectability, even as the widespread religious revivals of the first and second Great

---

9 On Luther's views on the canonicity of Revelation, see Irena Backus, *Reformation Readings of the Apocalypse: Geneva, Zurich, and Wittenberg* (Oxford: Oxford University Press, 2000), pp. 6–11.
10 See Franklin Hamlin Littell, *The Origins of Sectarian Protestantism: A Study of the Anabaptist View of the Church* (New York: Macmillan, 1964), pp. 27–32. On earlier radical sects see Norman Cohn, *The Pursuit of the Millennium*, revised and expanded edition (London: Temple Smith, 1970), pp. 252–78.
11 W. J. van Asselt, 'Chiliasm and Reformed Eschatology in the Seventeenth and Eighteenth Centuries', *Studies in Reformed Theology* vol. 4 (2001), 12.

Awakenings seemed to offer confirmation that religious progress was keeping pace with social developments. Indeed, Jonathan Edwards, who played a prominent role in the first Awakening, is often identified as one of the most important influences upon the emergence of evangelical postmillennialism.[12]

On the other side of the Atlantic, too, the widespread conversions that attended the preaching of Whitefield and Wesley seemed to offer the genuine prospect of the sort of wholesale transformation of society that would provide the ideal conditions to presage Christ's return. This expectation became a powerful driver of missionary activity. On the basis of Scripture passages like Matthew 24: 14 ('And this gospel of the kingdom shall be preached in all the world for a witness unto all nations; and then shall the end come') the preaching of the gospel to all peoples was seen as a vital step in preparing for the return of Christ. The efflorescence of missionary societies at the beginning of the nineteenth century, and the progress that was made in opening up the African and Asian continents to the gospel were both the causes and the consequences of a new optimism about the prospects for global evangelicalism. An expectation that the Jews would be regathered lent a particular focus to efforts to preach the gospel amongst them. This fusion of social, technological and religious progress was a heady mix, which seemed to provide ample assurance that the optimism of postmillennialists was justified, and that history was, in fact, on an upward trajectory.[13]

But while postmillennial expectation did dominate eschatological discourse through the eighteenth and nineteenth centuries, it is important, as Crawford Gribben, amongst others, has pointed out, not to overstate the extent of its dominance. A number of prominent evangelical figures rejected the optimistic implications of the postmillennial framework, even as they participated in the very success that energized postmillennial expectation. An important figure in this connection is John Gill (1697–1771), 'the most influential Baptist theologian of the eighteenth century'.[14] Although Gill's 'eschatology has not received the attention it has deserved',[15] Gribben has identified his efforts 'to reclaim the premillennial hope' as a significant expression of an alternative understanding of prophecy in this period. Gill adopted and adapted the methods of earlier students of prophecy to chart 'the premillennial fulfilment of biblical prophecy in robustly optimistic terms'.[16] He went so far as to propose – without any dogmatism – a number of significant dates, suggesting that the reign of the Antichrist (which he argued had begun in AD 606) would end in 1866, the Jews would be converted and resettled in 1896, and the Islamic empire would be destroyed and the gospel universally preached by 1941. Subsequent to these

---

12 See C. C. Goen, 'Jonathan Edwards: A New Departure in Eschatology', *Church History* vol. 28 (March 1959), 25–40; Ernest Lee Tuveson, *Redeemer Nation: The Idea of America's Millennial Role* (Chicago, IL: University of Chicago Press, 1968); Alan Heimert, *Religion and the American Mind* (Cambridge, MA: Harvard University Press, 1966); pp. 59–66; Stephen J. Stein, 'Introduction', in *The Works of Jonathan Edwards, vol. 5: Apocalyptic Writings* (New Haven, CT: Yale University Press, 1977), 7–19 and 40–59; and Robert W. Jenson, *America's Theologian: A Recommendation of Jonathan Edwards* (New York: Oxford University Press, 1988), pp. 133–4. See also James West Davidson, *The Logic of Millennial Thought* (New Haven, CT: Yale University Press, 1977), pp. 25–36; John F. Wilson, 'History, Redemption, and the Millennium', in *Jonathan Edwards and the American Experience*, edited by Nathan O. Hatch and Harry S. Stout (New York: Oxford University Press, 1988), pp. 133–41, and Gribben, *Evangelical Millennialism*, pp. 58–62.
13 See Iain H. Murray, *The Puritan Hope: Revival and the Interpretation of Prophecy* (Edinburgh: Banner of Truth Trust, 1971).
14 Gribben, *Evangelical Millennialism*, p. 62.
15 Gribben, *Evangelical Millennialism*, p. 62.
16 Gribben, *Evangelical Millennialism*, p. 65.

events, the 'spiritual reign' of Christ would begin 'after which will be the personal appearance of Christ to reign in a still more glorious manner'.[17]

Not everyone who expected the premillennial return of Christ shared Gill's optimism. Charles Wesley was a particularly notable instance. In spite of the success of the burgeoning evangelical movement on both sides of the Atlantic, Wesley developed a 'historicist, pre-millennial, and anti-Catholic' eschatology, which 'robustly contradicted the possibility of worldwide blessing towards the end of the church age'.[18] In this regard, he stands as a useful counter example to the thesis that prophetic expectation can be explained as a response to the prevailing social and religious climate. Large-scale conversion did not dispose Wesley to an optimistically postmillennial reading of history.

The rise of premillennialism and the role of J. N. Darby

In the event, the pessimism of Wesley's eschatology set the tone for the re-energized engagement with premillennialism that emerged in the prophetic ferment of the eighteenth-century *fin de siècle*.[19] Samuel Taylor Coleridge described the turn of the nineteenth century as 'an age of anxiety from the crown to the hovel, from the cradle to the coffin',[20] and his words accurately capture the pervasiveness of social uncertainty and upheaval as revolution overthrew established social orders in America and France. In this ferment, speculation about the future of the world increased the urgency of understanding prophetic Scripture, and prompted a thoroughgoing re-evaluation of the postmillennial optimism that had previously dominated evangelical prophetic discourse. In Ireland concern over global events was married with the increasing pessimism of an Anglo-Irish ascendency reeling from the horrors of the 1798 rebellion, and feeling ever more besieged.[21] It is this context that provided a background for the development of John Nelson Darby's ideas, which had a profound impact on the ways in which evangelicals would interpret and understand biblical prophecy.

John Nelson Darby (1800–1882) is a figure of towering significance in the development of evangelical eschatology.[22] During his life, his influence and ideas spread by means of his prolific

---

17 Gribben, *Evangelical Millennialism*, p. 66.
18 Kenneth G. C. Newport, *Apocalypse and Millennium: Studies in Biblical Eisegesis* (Cambridge: Cambridge University Press, 2000), p. 120.
19 For discussions of the relationship between Darby's theology, and later dispensationalism, see Michael Williams, *This World is Not My Home: The Origins and Development of Dispensationalism* (Fearn: Mentor, 2003); Stewart G. Cole, *The History of Fundamentalism* (New York: Richard R. Smith, 1931); Norman F. Furniss, *The Fundamentalist Controversy, 1918–1931* (New Haven, CT: Yale University Press, 1954); Ernest R. Sandeen, *The Roots of Fundamentalism: British and American Millenarianism, 1800–1930* (Chicago, IL: University of Chicago, 1970); George M. Marsden, *Fundamentalism and American Culture: The Shaping of Twentieth-Century Evangelicalism, 1870–1925* (New York: Oxford University Press, 1980).
20 Samuel Taylor Coleridge, *A Book I Value: Selected Marginalia*, edited by H. J. Jackson (Princeton, NJ: Princeton University Press, 2003), p. 172.
21 For discussions of this context, see the essays collected in, *Prisoners of Hope? Aspects of Evangelical Millennialism in Britain and Ireland, 1800–1880*, edited by Crawford Gribben and Timothy Stunt (Milton Keynes: Paternoster, 2004); *Protestant Millennialism, Evangelicalism and Irish Society, 1790–2005*, edited by Crawford Gribben and Andrew Holmes (Basingstoke: Palgrave, 2006).
22 There is no published scholarly biography of J. N. Darby. Two biographies are available: W. G. Turner and Edwin Cross, *Unknown and Well Known: A Biography of John Nelson Darby* (London: Chapter Two, 1990) is a new edition, with additional material, of a laudatory biography by a contemporary of Darby. Max Weremchuk, *John Nelson Darby*, (Neptune, NJ: Loizeaux, 1992) is a more recent work. A more scholarly, unpublished treatment can be found in Robert Henry Krapohl, 'A Search for Purity: The

writing of commentaries, pamphlets and letters, and through his travels, which covered large parts of Europe and North America. But his ideas and their influence lasted well beyond Darby's lifetime, and their impact would be felt in parts of the globe that Darby himself never visited. Darby's principal legacy remains the system of biblical interpretation known as dispensationalism.

Darby's approach to the interpretation of prophecy was both original and far-reaching. The dispensationalism that he taught outlined an idiosyncratic version of the prophetic calendar, but its hermeneutical implications were far wider than that – while its eschatological aspects have attracted most attention, it is important not to lose sight of the fact that dispensationalism posited a distinctive way of reading all of Scripture and understanding the whole of history. Darby's approach to Scripture was underpinned by his concept of the two peoples of God. In contrast to most biblical interpreters, who had tended to see continuity between Israel in the Old Testament, and the Church in the New, Darby argued that Israel was always distinct from the Church – an earthly people with an earthly hope, in contrast to the Church, whose hope and destiny were heavenly. Later dispensationalists would insist that literal interpretation was 'the "bottom line" of Dispensationalism'.[23] However, there is some evidence that, for Darby, the distinction between Israel and the Church was the real bottom line.[24]

From this foundation, Darby elaborated a series of dispensations – distinctive periods in human history. Darby was by no means the first to recognize different periods in salvation history – to a greater or lesser degree, the existence of distinct eras in God's dealing with mankind was, and is, acknowledged by all Christians. Nor did Darby work out his dispensational schema as clearly as his later interpreters would. But his insistence on the distinctness of Israel and the Church, and their shared importance in prophetic history were unusual, if not unique. The implications of these views for the interpretation of prophecy were equally idiosyncratic. In a sense, Darby's system of prophetic interpretation might be said to involve two eschatologies – one for Israel, and the other for the Church. The future for Israel would be both apocalyptic and millennial – the nation would pass through seven years of Tribulation, which would affect the whole world, but whose sufferings would be especially intense for Israel. At the end of the Tribulation, Christ would return, inaugurating the millennium. But before any of this could happen, the 'secret rapture' of the Church would take place – Christ would come in the air to summon the believers of the Church age ('the dispensation of grace') to be with himself in the air. There, they would not only be preserved from the tumult of the Tribulation, but would be semi-detached from the events of the millennium, taken up, instead, with the enjoyment of Christ and his presence.[25] Dispensationalism was to have a profound impact on evangelicalism, especially in an American context, but its most visible elements, certainly in the

---

Controversial Life of John Nelson Darby' (unpublished PhD thesis, Baylor University, 1988). More recently, Timothy C. F Stunt, *From Awakening to Secession* (Edinburgh: T. & T. Clark, 2000), has set him in a wider context, with relevance to this chapter. See also Mark S. Sweetnam and Crawford Gribben, 'J. N. Darby and the Irish Origins of Dispensationalism', *Journal of the Evangelical Theological Society* vol. 52 (2009), 569–77.

23 Earl D. Radmacher, 'The Current Status of Dispensationalism and its Eschatology', in *Perspectives on Evangelical Theology*, edited by Kenneth S. Kantzer and Stanley N. Gundry (Grand Rapids, MI: Baker, 1979), p. 171. Charles Ryrie and Mark Sweetnam both include a literal approach to the interpretation of Scripture as crucial elements of dispensationalism. See Charles Ryrie, *Dispensationalism* (Chicago, IL: Moody, 1995), pp. 33–40, and Mark S. Sweetnam, 'Defining Dispensationalism: A Cultural Studies Perspective', *Journal of Religious History* vol. 34 (2010), 191-212.

24 Martin Spence, *Heaven on Earth: Reimagining Time and Eternity in Nineteenth-Century British Evangelicalism* (Eugene, OR: Pickwick Publications, 2015), p. 119.

25 Gary L. Nebeker, '"The Ecstasy of Perfected Love": The Eschatological Mysticism of J. N. Darby', in *Prisoners of Hope?*, edited by Gribben and Stunt, pp. 69–94.

twentieth and twenty-first centuries, have been the importance that it attaches to the destiny of Israel and the Rapture – both of which feature prominently in the later history of the origins of dispensationalism.[26]

For all its importance, the origins continue to be poorly understood. Despite the scale of Darby's legacy, and the complexity and originality of his thought, he has been poorly served by modern scholarship. It is telling, for example, that no scholarly intellectual biography of Darby exists. And, in spite of the romantic details of his life the number of popular-level biographical treatments is very small.[27] Because of the important role that Darby played in the early history of the so-called 'Plymouth Brethren', his contribution has most often been discussed in the context of histories of that movement. Early accounts of the emergence of the Brethren movement tended to advance a heavily supernaturalist historiography, which read the development of the Brethren and their distinctive teachings as the direct result of a Spirit-led revival and which, consequently, were uninterested in attempting to identify the contemporary influences that shaped Darby's teaching.[28]

More recent accounts have attempted to address this deficit – with varying degrees of success. Darby was a controversial figure in his own lifetime, and has continued to attract controversy, and to provoke a profoundly partisan response since. This is abundantly illustrated by the work of Dave MacPherson, who has made a long career of suggesting that Darby and his followers were guilty of perpetrating a 'Rapture Hoax', successfully repackaging the ecstatic utterances of a young, Scottish, Irvingite girl called Margaret Macdonald as dispensational theology.[29] Other, less polemically invested contributions have questioned the existence of any such relationship. So, for instance, F. F. Bruce argued simply that the material that shaped Darby's prophetic ideas 'was in the air in the 1820s and 1830s among eager students of unfulfilled prophecy ... direct dependence by Darby on Margaret Macdonald is unlikely'.[30] More recently, Timothy C. F. Stunt, in addition to effectively addressing MacPherson's accusations, has pointed to the premillennial writing of the Dominican Jansenist theologian Bernard Lambert, an important influence both on Edward Irving and J. N. Darby.[31]

In contrast to the context-free narratives offered by the supernaturalist accounts of the

---

26 Paul Wilkinson, *For Zion's Sake: Christian Zionism and the Role of John Nelson Darby* (Eugene, OR: Wipf and Stock, 2008).
27 Most recently, see Marion Field, *John Nelson Darby: Prophetic Pioneer* (Godalming: Highland Books, 2008).
28 See, for example, Andrew Miller, *Miller's Church History* (London: Pickering and Inglis, 1967) and E. H. Broadbent, *The Pilgrim Church* (London: Pickering and Inglis, 1974).
29 See the books by Dave MacPherson: *The Rapture Plot* (Simpsonville, SC: Millennium III Publishers, 1994); *The Unbelievable Pre-Trib Origin* (Kansas, KS: Heart of America Bible Society, 1973); *The Three R's: Rapture, Revisionism, Robbery* (Monticello, Utah: P.O.S.T., 1998); *The Great Rapture Hoax* (Fletcher, NC: New Puritan Library, 1983); *Rapture?* (Fletcher, NC: New Puritan Library, 1987); *The Incredible Cover-Up* (Plainfield, NJ: Logos International, 1975), and *The Late Great Pre-Trib Rapture* (Kansas, KS: Heart of America Bible Society, 1974). For some responses see R. A. Huebner, *The Truth of the Pre-Tribulation Rapture Recovered* (Millington, NJ: Present Truth Publishers, 1976); R. A. Huebner, *Precious Truths Revived and Defended Through J. N. Darby*, vol. 1 (Morganville, NJ: Present Truth Publishers, 1991); Thomas Ice, 'Why the Doctrine of the Pretribulational Rapture did not Begin with Margaret Macdonald', *Bibliotheca Sacra* vol. 147 (1990), 155–68; Gerald Stanton, *Kept From The Hour* (fourth edition, Miami Springs, FL: Schoettle Publishing, 1991), and most recently, Timothy C. F. Stunt, 'The Tribulation of Controversy: A Review Article', *Brethren Archivists and Historians Network Review* vol. 2 (2003), 91–8.
30 F. F. Bruce, review of *The Unbelievable Pre-Trib Origin*, in *Evangelical Quarterly* vol. 47 (1975), 58.
31 Stunt, 'Influences in the Early Development of J. N. Darby', in *Prisoners of Hope?*, edited by Gribben and Stunt, pp. 44-68

emergence of dispensationalism, a number of recent historians have emphasized the significance of the time and the place at which dispensationalism emerged. This has resulted in an increased focus on the relevance of Darby's Irish context and specifically on the role of Trinity College, Dublin, in shaping the views of Darby and the other premillennialists who emerged in the city at around the same time.[32] So, for example, Ernest Sandeen acknowledges that 'if more were known about early nineteenth-century Irish Protestantism and, particularly, the intellectual history of Trinity College, Dublin, a clearer light might be thrown upon these puzzling and difficult points' concerning Darby's development and influence.[33] Similarly, David Hempton concludes that 'without knowing the intellectual history of Trinity College in the first quarter of the century it is difficult to be certain about the relationship between anti-Catholicism and premillennialism'.[34] More recently, Floyd Elmore and Gary Nebeker have addressed the question: 'Why did Trinity College, Dublin, become such a centre of millenarian ferment in the late eighteenth- and early nineteenth-century Ireland?'[35] Elmore draws attention to the overwhelmingly postmillennial orientation of the early influences on Darby's thought and finds in the postmillennial teaching of Richard Graves, Edward Hincks and Thomas Elrington 'the theological grist for Darby's later synthesis'.[36] Nebeker, too, foregrounds the contrast between the optimistic postmillennialism espoused by his tutors at Trinity, and Darby's pessimistic premillennialism to argue that he was reacting against, as much as responding to, the intellectual formation that he had received.

More recently, and with an unprecedented level of detailed historical investigation, Donald Harman Akenson has investigated the pertinence of Darby's Irish context in *Discovering the End of Time: Irish Evangelicals in the Age of Daniel O'Connell* (2016). Akenson has painstakingly reconstructed the social and intellectual *milieu* that he terms 'Dalyland' – the parishes of Wicklow and South Dublin, where an intricate web of family connections bound together a group of aristocratic and upper-class evangelicals. For Akenson, Darby cannot be properly understood apart from this context:

> Possibly, John Nelson Darby could have formed his distinctive views of the Bible and the way God's hand was about to press out the dross from humankind if he had been something other than an evangelical Anglican curate someplace other than Ireland, but I doubt it.[37]

However, Akenson differs from most of the historians who have written about Darby's Irishness by the way he interprets the importance of Trinity College, Dublin, to the development of Darby's thought. He dismisses the suggestion that Trinity was 'directly causal in producing ... the religious mind of John Nelson Darby' as 'a clear instance of what should be called the

---

32 See Stunt, *Awakening to Secession*; Grayson Carter, *Anglican Evangelicals: Protestant Secessions from the Via Media, c.1800–1850* (Oxford: Oxford University Press, 2000), pp. 58–104.
33 Sandeen, *The Roots of Fundamentalism*, p. 90.
34 D. N. Hempton, 'Evangelicalism and Eschatology', *Journal of Ecclesiastical History* vol. 31 (1980), 185.
35 Floyd Saunders Elmore, 'A Critical Examination of the Doctrine of the Two Peoples of God in John Nelson Darby' (unpublished ThD thesis, Dallas Theological Seminary, 1990); Gary L. Nebeker, 'John Nelson Darby and Trinity College, Dublin: A Study in Eschatological Contrasts', *Fides et Historia* vol. 34 (2002), 87.
36 Elmore, 'A Critical Examination', p. 73.
37 Donald Harman Akenson, *Discovering the End of Time: Irish Evangelicals in the Age of Daniel O'Connell* (Montreal: McGill-Queen's University Press, 2016), p. 7.

Professorial Fallacy, the ill-founded assumption that most of the important beliefs, attitudes, and knowledge that students acquire at university come from the curriculum and the faculty'.[38] By contrast, he argues, 'John Nelson Darby's own behavior confirms that his four years at TCD did not move him from his pre-admission commitment to a career in law'.[39] Akenson's re-evaluation of Darby is rigorous and radical, and he leaves a trail of sacred cows bleeding in his wake. However, he has provided the most thoroughly documented account of the Irish origins of dispensational premillennialism to date and, while repeatedly disclaiming any aspiration to provide a biography of Darby, has done a good deal to emphasize the importance of, lay the foundations for, and highlight the challenges of such a project.

The other premillennialism

The narrative of the origins of premillennialism in a context of societal unrest and pessimism is a powerful and well-established one. Recently, however, it has been challenged by Martin Spence, in his important study *Heaven on Earth: Reimagining Time and Eternity in Nineteenth-Century British Evangelicalism* (2015). Spence protests that the eventual success and global dominance of Darby's futurist premillennialism has eclipsed another important form of premillennialism which had emerged as a very different sort of response to the *fin de siècle*. Historicist premillennialism, as expressed in the works of writers like Edward Bickersteth and Thomas Rawson Birks, was a more optimistic affair than the futurist approach. It located the terrors of Daniel and Revelation safely in the first century, and so contemplated a return of Christ unalloyed by the suffering and Tribulation anticipated by futurists. The expectation of that return, and the millennium which it would inaugurate, helped to reshape evangelical understanding of creation, the body, death, and time itself:

> Far from abandoning the positive view of the world held by the Hanoverian postmillennialists, these mid-nineteenth-century Evangelicals were robustly positive about the created order. In fact, they were *far more* positive about time and space than their postmillennial forbears.[40]

Spence argues that this spirit of optimism and transformed view of time were both shaped by and helped to shape the temper of the Victorian age, with its emphasis on progress, development and renewal. Ultimately, however, this brand of premillennialism never achieved the degree of success and popularity that dispensationalism enjoyed, and ultimately, Spence argues, a

> focus on a desire for a personal experience of the Holy Spirit [became] increasingly intertwined with the premillennial movement. In time, it would change the temperament of eschatological speculation, and of Evangelicalism as a whole. Its rise both signalled and precipitated the end of the historicist premillennialist project.[41]

---

38 Akenson, *Discovering the End of Time*, p. 132.
39 Akenson, *Discovering the End of Time*, p. 133.
40 Spence, *Heaven and Earth*, p. 62.
41 Spence, *Heaven and Earth*, p. 251.

From Darby to dispensationalism

While historicist premillennialism waned, futurist premillennialism waxed. Over the second half of the nineteenth century, and into the opening decades of the twentieth, the dispensational premillennialism that developed from Darby's interpretation of Scripture was to become the dominant evangelical eschatology.[42] The text that catapulted it to that position was the *Scofield Reference Bible*.[43] C. I. Scofield's ground-breaking Study Bible, which accompanied the text of Scripture with marginal notes setting out a dispensational exegesis of the text, was published by Oxford University Press in 1909, with a revision in 1917. A more wide-ranging revision, by a team of dispensational scholars, was published in 1967 as *The New Scofield Reference Bible*. Within twenty years of its initial release, it became the first Oxford University Press publication to garner a million sales, and played an important role in helping the publisher to survive the economic rigours of the Great War. Remarkably, sales continued to climb even through the Great Depression in the 1930s, and the Scofield Reference Bible continues to sell strongly, in a variety of formats and bindings. Scofield's Bible was to play a crucial role in ensuring the spread of dispensational premillennialism, especially in North America. It was not the only factor in the success of dispensationalism – a lively 'Bible conference' movement, and the establishment of a number of dispensational seminaries also played a part, but, to judge by the numbers of Bibles sold, many evangelicals were receiving their instruction in dispensational truth direct from Scofield's notes.

It is worth noting that Scofield was not a theological innovator. In his preface to the 1917 edition of his Bible, he vigorously denied any claim to original theological thinking:

> The Editor disclaims originality. . . . The Editor has proposed to himself the modest if laborious task of summarizing, arranging, and condensing this mass of material [of biblical scholarship of the last 50 years].[44]

And this was not the only indication that Scofield was giving expression to an existing consensus, rather than blazing an independent trail of his own. The title page of the 1909 and 1917 editions listed eight consulting editors, including such prominent dispensational teachers as Arno Gaebelein, James M. Gray and Arthur T. Pierson. The *Scofield Reference Bible*, then, was a brilliantly conceived exercise in popularization, which juxtaposed dispensational exegesis with the text of Scripture, presenting it as the obvious, inevitable, and correct reading.

If *The Scofield Reference Bible* codified dispensationalism, it did not ossify it. A comparison of the 1967 *New Scofield Reference Bible* with earlier editions reveals a variety of slight but significant changes to the dispensational paradigm. These changes represented an evolution of dispensationalism from the 'classical dispensationalism' of the original Scofield Bible, to the 'revised' or 'essentialist' dispensationalism that had emerged under the influence of Charles Ryrie and others in the early 1960s, in response to criticism of some aspects of dispensational teaching. This system was eventually embodied extensively in Lewis Sperry Chafer's *Systematic Theology* (1948) and J. Dwight Pentecost's *Things to Come* (1964), and was summarized in Charles Ryrie's

---

42 Sweetnam, 'Defining Dispensationalism'.
43 R. Todd Mangum and Mark S. Sweetnam, *The Scofield Bible: Its History and Impact on the Evangelical Church* (Colorado Springs, CO: Paternoster, 2009).
44 *The Scofield Reference Bible*, edited C. I. Scofield (New York: Oxford University Press, 1909), p. v.

Dispensationalism Today (1965).[45] The emergence of essentialist dispensationalism is significant, for it is indicative both of an increased academicization of the dispensationalist movement, and of the role of non-dispensationalist critique in prompting the movement to define and defend its position. But the actual differences between classical and essentialist dispensationalism are differences of detail – it represents a theological fine-tuning, rather than any sort of revolutionary re-evaluation. So, while Michael Williams is stretching the point too far by suggesting that dispensationalism 'has been an essentially monolithic system of theology',[46] it is fair to say, with Charles Bass, that 'the lines of continuity from Darby to the present can be traced unbroken'.[47]

Pop-dispensationalism: the cultural mainstreaming of dispensationalism

Certainly, the differences of tone and theology between the work of Scofield and Chafer pales by comparison with the differences between either of these dispensationalist voices, and the strident populism of the way in which the core ideas of dispensationalism were adapted and developed by Hal Lindsey. The scale of Lindsey's transformation of earlier forms of dispensationalism has not always been recognized – in part, perhaps, because he serves as such a convenient lightning rod for the critics of dispensationalism. The brashness of Lindsey's approach is such that there is polemical mileage in depicting him as merely an expression of dispensational norms. In reality, however, there are clear – and very significant – differences between Lindsey's pop-dispensationalism (or, to use Gary North's admirable phrase, his 'dispen-sensationalism')[48] and the teachings of either classical or essentialist dispensationalism.

Lindsey was born in Houston, Texas, in 1929. His early family life was marked by 'ups and downs',[49] but by the time he reached the age of fifteen he had become 'extremely frustrated' as a result of 'conflict in [his] home life and in [his] personal life'.[50] His late teens were also marked by an increasing disillusionment about the evangelical Christianity to which he had made several commitments. After two years at the University of Houston he joined the United States Coastguard, hoping, by his own admission, to avoid service in Korea. Lindsey's years of service with the Coast Guard were marked by increasingly profligate behaviour until he experienced evangelical conversion while stationed in New Orleans. Subsequently he left the Coast Guard, and returned to Houston. Believing that God was calling him to be a preacher he applied for and was accepted as a student at the Dallas Theological Seminary, where he spent four years from 1958 to 1962. While Lindsey gives no account of the reasons that led him to Dallas, his choice was a significant one. The seminary had been one of the most notable strongholds of dispensational teaching, and it included among its students and faculty such names as J. Dwight Pentecost and John F. Walvoord.[51] Lindsey graduated successfully from Dallas, and embarked on a new career as a student evangelist, working with the Campus Crusade for Christ, alongside

---

45 J. Dwight Pentecost, *Things to Come: A Study in Biblical Eschatology* (Grand Rapids, MI: Zondervan, 1964); Lewis Sperry Chafer, *Systematic Theology, volume IV: Ecclesiology, Eschatology* (Dallas, TX: Dallas Seminary Press, 1948); Charles Ryrie, *Dispensationalism Today* (Chicago, IL: Moody, 1965).
46 Williams, *This World is Not My Home*, p. 11.
47 Clarence B. Bass, *Backgrounds to Dispensationalism* (Grand Rapids, MI: Eerdmans, 1960), p. 17.
48 Gary North, 'Publisher's Preface', in Dwight Wilson, *Armageddon Now! The Pre-millenarian Response to Russia and Israel since 1917* (second edition 1977, Tyler, TX: Institute for Christian Economics, 1991), p. x.
49 Hal Lindsey, *The Liberation of Planet Earth* (New York: Bantam Books, 1976), p. 1.
50 Lindsey, *Liberation of Planet Earth*, p. 2.
51 See, for a discussion of the history and influence of this institution, John D. Hannah, *An Uncommon Union: Dallas Theological Seminary and American Evangelicalism* (Grand Rapids, MI: Zondervan, 2009).

his second wife Jan, whom he met at Dallas. Subsequently, he left the Campus Crusade and established the Jesus Christ Light and Power Company, an enterprise directed at similar ends of student evangelization, mostly on the campus of the University of California (Los Angeles).

Lindsey's ministry with these two agencies had a strong prophetic content.[52] The popularity of prophetic teaching with his audience encouraged him to publish 'a direct account of the most thrilling, optimistic view of what the future could hold for any individual'.[53] That account, based on his campus ministry, and co-written with Carole Carlson, was *The Late Great Planet Earth* (1970). The phenomenal success of this book catapulted Lindsey to a position of prominence as an interpreter of biblical prophecy and contemporary geopolitics. *The Late Great Planet Earth* was the best selling American non-fiction book of the 1970s, outsold only by the Bible.[54] The book has gone through more than 108 printings with sales, by 1993, of more than 18 million copies in English, and between 18–20 million further copies in fifty-four foreign languages.[55] In 1977, a film version of the book was produced, narrated by Orson Welles. Subsequently Lindsey published over twenty books, refining and adjusting his ideas, claiming credit for accurate predictions, and rewriting those that had failed to come true. So, for example, *The Final Battle* (1994) is essentially an unacknowledged rewrite of *Late Great Planet Earth* (1970), *Apocalypse Code* (1997) is a rewrite of *There's a New World Coming* (1973), and *Planet Earth 2000 A.D.* (1994, 1996) are revisions of *The 1980's Countdown to Armageddon* (1980). *Planet Earth: The Final Chapter* (1998) is the most recent version of the *Planet Earth* books, with the date removed from the title. In parallel with these series, Lindsey aligned his prophetic interpretations more closely with Scripture in a number of commentaries on biblical prophecy. In addition, the love of geopolitical surmise and military speculation that underwrite all of Lindsey's books is given more explicit expression in volumes like *The Road to Holocaust* (1990), a volume that engaged vigorously with replacement theology, *The Final Battle* (1995), and *The Everlasting Hatred: The Roots of Jihad* (2002). The popularity of Rapture fiction, as represented by the success of the 'Left Behind' series, was not lost on Lindsey, and in 1995 he made his first foray into prophetic fiction, with *Blood Moon*.

To some extent, Lindsey's work is simply a popularization of a fairly barebones dispensational outline, shorn of any sustained attempt at biblical exegesis. If we restrict ourselves to the broadest of overviews, the prophetic schema outlined by Lindsey closely resembles the programme outlined by generations of classical dispensationalists. However, Lindsey added to this outline in a number of ways that claimed a far greater contemporary geopolitical relevance for his interpretations.

Perhaps Lindsey's most significant departure from earlier dispensationalism lay in his response to the founding of the State of Israel in 1948. One of the key tenets of dispensationalism has been the distinctness of the present dispensation – the 'Church Age' or the 'Dispensation of Grace'. This period is, for dispensationalists, a 'prophetic parenthesis', a period of time that was not foreseen by Old Testament prophets – who saw no gap between the first and second advents of Jesus Christ. As such, the dawning of the dispensation of grace had 'stopped the prophetic clock', and God's prophetic programme would only begin to tick again once the Rapture had

---

52 Lindsey, *Late Great Planet Earth*, p. 8.
53 Lindsey, *Late Great Planet Earth*, p. 7.
54 Grace Halsell, *Prophecy and Politics: Militant Evangelists on the Road to Nuclear War* (Westport, CT: Lawrence Hill, 1986), p. 4.
55 Hal Lindsey, *Road to Holocaust* (New York: Bantam Books, 1989), p. 195. See also George Marsden, *Understanding Fundamentalism and Evangelicalism* (Grand Rapids, MI: Eerdmans, 1991), p. 77, and Michael Lienesch, *Redeeming America: Piety and Politics in the New Christian Right* (Chapel Hill, NC: University of North Carolina Press, 1993), p. 311.

removed the Church, concluding that strand of God's purpose, and clearing the stage for the resumption of his dealings with Israel. This understanding of Scripture explains another key teaching of dispensationalism – the imminence of the Rapture. If we have no prophecy for this age, then Christ's return can happen at any point – it is the next event on the prophetic calendar.

In *The Late Great Planet Earth*, Lindsey makes a definitive break with this approach. He argues that Christ's words about the fig tree in Matthew 24: 32–3 had been fulfilled in the foundation of the State of Israel:

> Even the figure of speech 'fig tree' has been a historic symbol of national Israel. When the Jewish people, after nearly 2,000 years of exile, under relentless persecution, became a nation again on 14 May 1948 the 'fig tree' put forth its first leaves.
>
> Jesus said that this would indicate that He was 'at the door,' ready to return. Then He said, 'Truly I say to you, *this generation* will not pass away until all these things take place.' (Matthew 24: 34 NASB)
>
> What generation? Obviously, in context, the generation that would see the signs – chief among them the rebirth of Israel. A generation in the Bible is something like forty years. If this is a correct deduction, then within forty years or so of 1948, all these things should take place.[56]

This interpretation of the passage is entirely inconsistent with most dispensational exegesis. The mainstream dispensational reading of the passage identifies the coming referred to as Christ's return to establish his millennial kingdom (in an apparent bid to have his exegetical cake and eat it, Lindsey glosses the passage later in his book in this way).[57] But more fundamentally, Lindsey's interpretation undermined the dispensationalist insistence on the uniqueness of the Church age and the imminence of the Rapture. By identifying the fulfilment of prophecy during the course of the 'dispensation of grace', and by using that identification to predict the timing of the Rapture, Lindsey was moving in the direction of historicist premillennialism – and sharing the perils of date-setting.

The failure of his teaching to align with the norms of dispensationalism was, perhaps, the least of Lindsey's problems – after 1988, it was in evident discord with history as well. To be sure, Lindsey had built a little 'wriggle-room' into his prediction. In this regard, he proved wiser than some of those who followed his date-setting, including, most prominently, Edgar Whisenant, whose *88 Reasons Why the Rapture Will Be in 1988* (1988) was the most obvious casualty of a rapture-less 1988. This deniability notwithstanding, Lindsey went on to base his entire argument upon the importance of the establishment of the State of Israel as a sign. With the passing of 1988, the required room for manoeuvre was found in varying the length of a generation, rather than revising the basic methodology.

This willingness to identify the fulfilment of prophecy in the period before the Rapture is not limited to Lindsey's treatment of the role of Israel. At the core of Lindsey's methodology is a belief in his ability to identify the biblical players in this great end-time drama with the national and international power brokers of the late twentieth (and now the twenty-first) century. So, for example, the re-energized Roman empire, which dispensationalists expect to see at the time of the Tribulation, was identified with the nascent European Common Market, the precursor of the European Union. This identification was clinched, for Lindsey, by virtue of the foundational importance of the 'Treaty of Rome' (1957) to the European project, and by the

---

56 Lindsey, *Late Great Planet Earth*, pp. 53–4.
57 Lindsey, *Late Great Planet Earth*, p. 173.

involvement of ten member states, which were self-evidently the ten nations foretold in Daniel 7: 24. Antichrist would emerge, then, as a European leader. A child of the Cold War, Lindsey had no doubt that the king of the North was a biblical reference to the power of the USSR and its Soviet satellite states, a conclusion summarized in his punning chapter title 'Russia is a Gog'. The king of the South would be a leader who would marshal a force from Islamic North Africa, in which Egypt would play a prominent role. Finally, the 'kings of the East' were revealed as the 'Yellow Peril' (to quote Lindsey's title to the relevant chapter), the forces of Communist China. This approach to biblical prophecy was not new – all sorts of identifications of the end-time nations and rulers outlined in Daniel and Ezekiel had been attempted by interpreters of prophecy over the centuries. But the injection of this approach into a dispensationalist structure that had insisted that biblical prophecy was not, and could not be, fulfilled during the 'dispensation of grace' was something new. It had the effect of dragging prophetic discourse into the present, and allowed the geopolitical upheavals of the second half of the twentieth century to be read in overtly apocalyptic terms. This was, as Lindsey acknowledged, a risky strategy:

> Now I am about to walk into the Lion's Den. Perhaps it would be wise to follow Churchill's tactic when he said, 'You know I always avoid prophesying beforehand, it is a much better policy to prophesy after the events have taken place'.[58]

The on-going need for the revision and rewriting of Lindsey's predictions in the light of subsequent events gives point to this observation. The expansion of the European Union to twenty-seven states, the demise of Communism and the rise of militant Islam all necessitated the reworking of Lindsey's prophetic panorama. Nonetheless, Lindsey retained his basic paradigm for understanding prophecy and his confidence in his own ability accurately to decipher the eschatological significance of contemporary geopolitics.

In spite of its rather swashbuckling approach to exegesis and its need for repeated readjustment, Lindsey's approach to prophetic Scripture was enormously successful and left its mark across popular culture, from the re-emergence of the Rapture novel and the Rapture film, most notably Russell S. Doughten's four-part series: *A Thief in the Night* (1972), *A Distant Thunder* (1978), *Image of the Beast* (1981), and *The Prodigal Planet* (1983). Lindsey's views have also impacted popular music. Larry Norman's 'I wish we'd all been ready', which featured on the soundtrack of *A Thief in the Night*, was written at Lindsey's request. Closer to the musical mainstream, the impact of pop-dispensationalism can also be seen in some of the lyrics written and recorded by Johnny Cash during this period, including 'Over the Next Hill We'll be Home' (recorded 1973), 'Matthew 24 (is knocking at the door)', co-written with June Carter Cash in 1973, and 'Look unto the East' (1974).[59]

As is so often the case, the response of British evangelicalism contrasted with that of its American counterpart in a way that seemed to reinforce national stereotypes. Britain's closest approach to pop-dispensationalism came from F. A. Tatford, a civil servant who ended his career with the United Kingdom's Atomic Energy Authority. He was a prolific author of commentaries on prophetic Scripture and a number of works that focused on geopolitics and prophecy, including: *The Rapture and the Tribulation* (1957), *The Middle East: War Theatre of Prophecy* (1959), *A One World Church and Prophecy* (1967), *China and Prophecy* (1968), *Russia and*

---

58 Lindsey, *Late Great Planet Earth*, p. 181.
59 Mark S. Sweetnam, 'Evangelical Millennialism in the Lyrics of Johnny Cash', in *Anthems of Apocalypse: Popular Music and Apocalyptic Thought*, edited by Christopher Partridge (Sheffield: Sheffield Phoenix Press, 2012), pp. 13–26.

Prophecy (1968), *Egypt and Prophecy* (1968), *The Jew and Prophecy* (1969), *Middle East Cauldron* (1971), *Going into Europe: The Common Market and Prophecy* (1971) and *Israel and her Future* (1971). In addition, he produced *The Clock Strikes* (1971), one of a very few British Rapture novels.[60] Tatford's publications reveal the same sort of sense about the need to view the unfolding global situation in prophetic terms, which we find in Lindsey's work. But Tatford's response to these events was markedly different from Lindsey's, and was characterized by caution as to speculation and a careful insistence upon the detail of dispensational teaching. Tatford was an admirably clear communicator, but his books were the antithesis of Lindsey's catchy, slangy approach, and it is difficult to imagine any of them ever disturbing the bestseller list, still less topping it in the way in which Lindsey's books did.

Lindsey's success was the product of a confluence of factors — the heightened tensions of Cold War geopolitics, an increased sense of concern and foreboding about the future, and a popularizing approach that seemed to offer certainty and clarity based on its racy repackaging of prophetic Scripture. In the event, the mixture, while heady, proved to have a limited shelf life, and Lindsey's teaching receded from the cultural mainstream, and lost any appeal it had once held for a dispensational movement increasingly concerned with academic respectability.

Pop-dispensationalism did enjoy another moment of crossover cultural success, in the uncertainty and millennial excitement that marked the end of the twentieth century, and in the aftermath of the events of 11 September 2001. The 'Left Behind' franchise that would ultimately embrace sixteen novels, four films, a range of graphic novels targeted at children, a controversial computer game, and a para-textual culture including 'Left Behind' prophecy guides and narratives of those who experienced conversion under the influence of the series. In 2004, total sales of all the novels, including a separate series for younger readers, exceeded 60 million and appeared on, and sometimes even topped, the *New York Times* bestsellers list.[61]

The prodigious popular cultural success of the 'Left Behind' novels resulted in a corresponding upsurge of scholarly interest in the novels, and what they might reveal about the condition of contemporary evangelicalism. Crawford Gribben was one of the first scholars to read 'Left Behind' in this way, in a series of articles and chapters that culminated in his *Writing the Rapture: Prophecy Fiction in Evangelical America* (2009). Gribben has placed 'Left Behind' in its historical context, tracing the genre history of the rapture novel back to the end of the nineteenth century, and has highlighted a surprising degree of consistency in the tropes that recur throughout the genre. Gribben is not the only critic to find 'Left Behind' a useful lens through which to examine contemporary evangelicalism. Glenn Shuck,[62] Amy Frykholm,[63] Jennie Chapman[64] and Jason C. Bivins[65], among others,[66] have read the 'Left Behind' phenomena in this way, and

---

60 Crawford Gribben, 'Novel Doctrines, Doctrinal Novels: F. A. Tatford and Brethren Prophecy Fiction', in *Culture, Spirituality, and the Brethren*, edited by Neil T. R. Dickson and T. J. Marinello (Troon, Ayrshire: Brethren Archivists and Historians Network, 2014), pp. 159–72.

61 See Bruce David Forbes, 'How Popular are the Left Behind Books ... and Why?', in *Rapture, Revelation, and the End of Times: Exploring the Left Behind Series*, edited by Bruce David Forbes and Jeanne Halgren Kilde (New York: Palgrave Macmillan, 2004).

62 Glenn W. Shuck, *Marks of the Beast: The Left Behind Novels and the Struggle for Evangelical Identity* (New York: New York University Press, 2005).

63 Amy Frykholm, *Rapture Culture: 'Left Behind' in Evangelical America* (New York: Oxford University Press, 2004).

64 Jennie Chapman, *Plotting Apocalypse: Reading, Agency, and Identity in the 'Left Behind' Series* (Jackson, MS: University Press of Mississippi, 2013).

65 Jason C. Bivins, *Religion of Fear: The Politics of Horror in Conservative Evangelicalism* (New York: Oxford University Press, 2008).

66 See the essays collected in *Left Behind and the Evangelical Imagination*, edited by Crawford Gribben and

John Walliss has examined the related 'Rapture film' mini-industry.[67] The approach adopted by most of these scholars has been critiqued by Mathew Guest, who complains that:

> both supporters and critics alike treat the novels as carriers of propositional truth claims; however clothed they may be in the subtleties of narrative, observers are keen to highlight what lies beneath, what they are really about, whether they approve or not. This engenders an oversimplification of the relationship between religious ideas and their human expression, and is a tendency that extends beyond popular discourse into more serious treatments of the Left Behind phenomenon.[68]

Guest's thesis is unlikely to be accepted without challenge by those who have worked on the novels, but the concerns that he highlights do raise important issues about the didactic function of religious literature.

There is evidence, however, that Left Behind's moment of cultural impact passed relatively quickly – perhaps because the 'Left Behind' paradigm was poorly adapted to reflect the geo-political scenery that emerged following 9/11 and the war on terror. Though the franchise has continued to churn out books and has produced a 2014 movie starring Nicolas Cage, the rapture genre appears to have retreated, once again, to the cultural margins.

Evangelical expectation at the end of the twentieth century

The success of Lindsey and, later, of 'Left Behind', make it easy to overstate the dominance of dispensationalism in American evangelicalism in the second half of the twentieth century, especially as claims about the numbers of people subscribing to a particular doctrinal position are notoriously difficult to substantiate. Dispensationalism has certainly exerted an enormous influence on evangelicalism, though that influence has been dramatically less on the eastern side of the Atlantic. But even in America, its hegemony was never total, and towards the end of the twentieth century, began increasingly to be challenged by other views of prophetic Scripture.

One such view was an idiosyncratic American variant of postmillennialism – Christian Reconstructionism, or theonomic postmillennialism. This position was adumbrated by, among others, Rousas John Rushdoony's *The Institutes of Biblical Law* (1973), Gary North's *Unconditional Surrender: God's Program for Victory* (1983), David Chilton's *Paradise Restored: A Biblical Theology of Dominion* (1985), Gary DeMar's *Something Greater is Here: Christian Reconstructionism in Biblical Perspective* (1988), and Kenneth L. Gentry's *The Beast of Revelation* (1989). As the name suggests, Christian Reconstructionism calls for the radical reconstruction of society, including the introduction of theocratic government, the enforcement of the Mosaic Law, and the implementation of egalitarian principles. The movement enjoyed its high point in the late 1980s, though it declined in popularity throughout the 1990s. The scale and enduring significance of its wider

---

Mark Sweetnam (Sheffield: Sheffield Phoenix, 2011); Melani McAlister, 'Prophecy, Politics, and the Popular: The *Left Behind* Series and Christian Fundamentalism's New World Order', *South Atlantic Quarterly* vol. 102 (Fall 2003), 773–98; Darryl Jones, 'The Liberal Antichrist – Left Behind in America', in *Expecting the End*, edited by Newport and Gribben, pp. 97–112.

67 John Walliss, 'Celling the End Times: The Contours of Contemporary Rapture Films', *Journal of Religion and Popular Culture* vol. 19 (Summer 2008), 1–15.

68 Mathew Guest, 'Keeping the End in Mind: Left Behind, the Apocalypse and the Evangelical Imagination', *Literature and Theology* vol. 26 (2012), 477.

impact continues to be the subject of some debate, though it is generally acknowledged to have remained a niche movement within American evangelicalism.[69]

Although amillennialism had not been especially visible as an eschatological option, it has continued to exist, and enjoyed renewed popularity with the resurgence of Reformed theology from the mid-twentieth century. However, within the span of amillennialism, there has been space for significant disagreement about the details of the eschatological programme, especially as it relates to the future of Israel. Some amillennialists, like O. Palmer Robertson, deny any distinct future for ethnic Israel.[70] Others, like Martyn Lloyd-Jones, believe that Romans 11 teaches a future blessing for Israel in an outpouring of evangelistic blessing before the second coming of Christ.[71] Yet others, like Vern Poythress, argue that there will be a literal fulfilment of God's promises to Israel, but that this fulfilment will take place in the eternal state, rather than in the millennium.[72] Poythress acknowledges the similarity of his position with that held by premillennialists, and goes so far as to describe himself as an 'optimistic premillennialist'. However, the resurgence of Calvinism within American evangelicalism has not entailed an inevitable resurgence of amillennialism. 'New Calvinism' has tended to endorse a premillennial approach, and John MacArthur, one of the figureheads of 'New Calvinism', has courted controversy by suggesting that Calvinists should, *de facto*, adhere to a dispensational premillennialism.[73] Similarly, postmillennialism has continued to attract adherents. In the United Kingdom, Iain H. Murray's *The Puritan Hope* (1990), was a significant intervention, designed to position a postmillennial approach to Scripture as the historical Calvinist norm, and in the United States, theologians like Keith A. Mathison, Loraine Boettner and Greg L. Bahnsen have defended postmillennialism from within the Reformed tradition. It may well be a fiction of hindsight to think that a dominant evangelical approach to prophecy could ever have been identified; any attempt to do so in the twenty-first century certainly faces formidable obstacles.

Conclusion

As has been seen in this chapter, evangelical thinking about the end of the world has been decisively influenced at a number of significant points by the ideas of prominent prophetic interpreters. We have seen how prevailing political, social and cultural conditions lent credibility and credence to particular approaches to prophecy. So, the optimism of the Enlightenment fostered an optimistic postmillennialism, just as the uncertainty and fear that marked the turn of the nineteenth century proved to be a fertile ground for the teaching of John Nelson Darby, and the dispensationalists who popularized his ideas. The success of Lindsey in the 1970s, and of the 'Left Behind' project in the 1990s similarly coincided with a moment of cultural angst, fuelled by the secular concerns of Y2K (the year 2000), and the rise of militant Islam. However, it has

---

69 See Michael Joseph McVicar, *Christian Reconstruction: R. J. Rushdoony and American Religious Conservatism* (Chapel Hill, NC: University of North Carolina Press, 2015). For a discussion of the influence and 'death' of Christian Reconstructionism, see Molly Worthen 'The Chalcedon Problem: Rousas John Rushdoony and the Origins of Christian Reconstructionism', *Church History* vol. 77/2 (June 2008), 399–437.
70 O. Palmer Robertson, *The Israel of God: Yesterday, Today, and Tomorrow* (Phillipsburg, NJ: P&R Publishing, 2000).
71 D. M. Lloyd-Jones, *Romans: An Exposition of Chapter 11: To God's Glory* (Carlisle, PA: Banner of Truth Trust, 1998).
72 Vern Sheridan Poythress, 'Currents within Amillennialism', *Presbyterion* vol. 26 (2000), 21-5.
73 John MacArthur, 'Why Every Self-Respecting Calvinist Must Be a Premillennialist' (2007), in *The Shepherd as Theologian: Accurately Interpreting and Applying God's Word*, edited by John MacArthur (Eugene, OR: Harvest House, 2017), pp. 179-99.

also been seen that any attempt to explain evangelical expectation as simply a function of the prevailing social and religious environment is doomed to fail as a reductive over-simplification of a much more complex issue, which involves hermeneutics as well as history, and which at all times embraces more than one approach to prophecy. Above all, we have seen that, for evangelicals, prophecy has always been 'big business', a vital element of their response to Scripture and a key element of their response to the world in which they have lived. We cannot understand evangelicals without understanding the role of prophetic expectation in their theology, thought and life.

A glance through the footnotes to this chapter provides real encouragement that scholars are making a sustained effort to engage with and understand the nature of evangelical eschatology. In the past decade or so, there has been a remarkable efflorescence of detailed scholarship in the area. Partly this related to the lightning rod prominence of 'Left Behind', and partly to the generally increased interest in millennialism, broadly defined, which marked scholarly discourse at the turn of the twenty-first century. But it has also emerged from a renewed interest in the origins of evangelicalism, and has benefited from new multi-disciplinary approaches and a trend away from the grand narrative and towards micro-studies. There continues to be a good deal of work to be done. Some of the wider implications of the important recent studies by Spence and Akenson will need to be examined by scholars, and will require a reappraisal of existing work and assumptions. Akenson's work has also highlighted once again one of the most obvious lacunae in the study of evangelicalism in the fact that no scholarly biography of John Nelson Darby exists. For all the reasons that Akenson points out, it is unlikely that this gap will soon be filled. It is to be hoped that scholarly courage will make a liar of him.

More work also needs to be done on the history of dispensationalism in the decades following Darby's death. We have the broad brushstrokes, but not the fine detail of how dispensationalism became dominant in the United States. Equally, work needs to be done on the British context, to account for the very different trajectory of prophetic expectation on the east of the Atlantic. Timothy Stunt's important work on European evangelicalism needs to be built upon, in order to expand the study of these issues beyond the Anglophone world. Beyond the European context, there is boundless scope for work on the history of global evangelicalism generally, and of evangelical prophetic expectation specifically. There is also a need for work on twentieth-century prophetic expectation. Reconstructionism is one particularly interesting area that has yet to receive the attention it deserves,[74] but research is also needed to examine the changing fortunes of pre-, post- and amillennialism from a scholarly and historical, rather than a theological or polemical perspective. The scholar embarking on the study of evangelical eschatology today has access to a far wider range and a far greater depth of relevant scholarly work than would have fallen to hand twenty years ago, but the scope for further work has increased, rather than diminished in the process.

---

74 See, however, McVicar, *Christian Reconstruction* for an important contribution to the subject.

12

EVANGELICALS AND RACE

John Coffey and Stephen Tuck

On 20 June 1995, in Atlanta, Georgia, delegates to the Southern Baptist Convention approved a resolution to 'repent of racism of which we have been guilty'. The Convention confessed: 'Many of our Southern Baptist forbears defended the right to own slaves', and 'In later years Southern Baptists failed, in many cases, to support, and in some cases opposed, legitimate initiatives to secure the civil rights of African-Americans'. The Convention asked for 'forgiveness from our African-American brothers and sisters'. The Southern Baptist Convention – which had formed 150 years previously to defend slavery – was but one of many evangelical denominations, in the United States and around the world, to repent of past racism in the late twentieth century.[1]

The history of evangelicals and race, then, is a history – by evangelicals' own admission – that includes discrimination and oppression. Following the SBC's highlighting of slavery and the civil rights movement, this chapter will focus on the age of William Wilberforce and the age of Martin Luther King, and explore the evangelical role in both eras.[2] A focus on the history of racism, though, only tells part of the story of evangelicalism and race. It ignores those within white churches who challenged racism. And it ignores black evangelicals.

In recent years, scholars have begun to recover black evangelical voices.[3] Such voices had previously been ignored, in part because of assumptions that black religion was about protest and that black evangelicalism was merely derivative of white evangelicalism, and because black evangelicals did not identify themselves as part of an evangelical movement – not least because

---

1 'Resolution on Racial Reconciliation on the 150th Anniversary of the Southern Baptist Convention, Atlanta, Georgia, 1995', www.sbc.net/resolutions/899/resolution-on-racial-reconciliation-on-the-150th-anniversary-of-the-southern-baptist-convention (accessed 23 February 2018); Gustav Niebuhr, 'Baptist Group Votes to Repent Stand on Slaves', *New York Times* (21 June 1995).
2 Space constraints preclude a broader discussion of imperialism, other parts of the world and other types of racism (including the experience of other minority groups) – which raise many of the same issues.
3 William C. Turner noted 'the amazing lack of attention given to black religion under the heading of evangelicalism'. William C. Turner, 'Black Evangelicalism: Theology, Politics and Race', *Journal of Religious Thought* vol. 45 (1989), 42. For a more recent addition to the literature, see Mary Beth Swetnam Mathews, *Doctrine and Race: African American Evangelicals and Fundamentalism between the Wars* (Tuscaloosa, AL: University of Alabama Press, 2017). In Britain, see *Black Voices: The Shaping of our Christian Experience*, edited by David Killingray and Joel Edwards (Nottingham: Inter-Varsity Press, 2007).

they were ignored (or shunned) by white evangelical leaders.[4] Even today, as historian of African American religion Anthea Butler, pointed out in 2015, 'Mainstream media outlets seldom use the word "evangelical" to describe African Americans with conservative viewpoints, despite the fact that they fit neatly into the evangelical definition'.[5] But the very fact that black evangelicals were, and are, a group apart meant that theirs was a distinctive history, with separate structures and priorities, including a commitment to equality and a critique of white evangelicalism. For all the diversity within black evangelicalism,[6] as William C. Turner noted in a 1989 article on black evangelicalism in the United States, 'The fairly consistent position taken within the Black Church is that evangelical faith rooted in the gospel of Jesus Christ neither requires denial of blackness nor reduces a commitment to social justice'.[7] This chapter, then, will foreground the distinctiveness and importance of black evangelicalism as part of a broader discussion of evangelicalism and racism, reform and repentance.

The age of Wilberforce

On 1 August 1838, celebrations were held across Jamaica to greet the end of apprenticeship and final emancipation from West Indian slavery. In Falmouth, the Baptist missionary, William Knibb, and his black deacons, organized a great procession. Portraits of the liberators – Thomas Clarkson, William Wilberforce and Thomas Fowell Buxton – were paraded through the streets, and an hour before midnight, crowds gathered around the coffin of slavery, inscribed 'Colonial Slavery, died July 31st 1838'. At midnight, as the clock struck, Knibb cried 'THE MONSTER IS DEAD! THE NEGRO IS FREE! THREE CHEERS FOR THE QUEEN!' Services were held at the town's chapels, followed by a public meeting in which all the speakers except the missionary were of African descent.[8]

To begin with this Jamaican vignette might suggest a triumphalist history of evangelicalism and race, one in which black and white believers joined hands to abolish the Atlantic slave trade, and eradicate racial slavery. The full story, of course, was far more ambiguous, revealing some of the failures, ironies and tragedies of evangelical history. Yet West Indian emancipation was an unprecedented achievement. The activism of British evangelicals, combined with the uprisings of missionary congregations in Demerara and Jamaica, had pushed Parliament into freeing 800,000 people from slavery. For the American abolitionist, William Lloyd Garrison,

---

4 See, for example, George Marsden, *Fundamentalism and American Culture* (New York: Oxford University Press, 2006), p. 324, n. 11; David Bebbington, 'Evangelicalism in its Settings: The British and American Movements since 1940', in *Evangelicalism: Comparative Studies of Popular Protestantism in North America, the British Isles, and Beyond, 1700–1990*, edited by Mark A. Noll, David Bebbington and George A. Rawlyk (New York: Oxford University Press, 1994), p. 367; Milton Sernett, 'Black Religion and the Question of Evangelical Identity', in *The Variety of American Evangelicalism*, edited by Donald W. Dayton and Robert K. Johnston (Knoxville, TN: University of Tennessee Press, 1991), p. 143.

5 Anthea Butler, 'African American Religious Conservatives in the New Millennium', in *Faith in the New Millennium: The Future of Religion and American Politics*, edited by Matthew Avery Sutton and Darren Dochuk (New York: Oxford University Press, 2015), p. 61.

6 Black evangelicals – like their white counterparts – have been based in mainline Protestant denominations, Pentecostal denominations and, more recently, in non-denominational churches.

7 Turner, 'Black Evangelicalism', 56. Mary Beth Swetnam Mathews also writes that 'African Americans created their own traditionalist conservative evangelicalism. It drew heavily from what they perceived as traditional Protestant doctrines but could also include more progressive notions as well'. Mathews, *Doctrine and Race*, p. 2

8 Catherine Hall, *Civilising Subjects: Metropole and Colony in the English Imagination, 1830–1867* (Cambridge: Polity, 2002), pp. 117–8.

this was 'the most thrilling event of the nineteenth century'.[9] Within half a century, slavery was outlawed across the Western hemisphere. Before reckoning with the shortcomings of the evangelical tradition, we should register the major contribution made by black and white evangelicals to British and American abolitionism.

Modern evangelicalism was forged in the revivals of the mid-eighteenth century, and emerged into an Atlantic world that already bore the imprint of the slave trade and the slave plantation. Having been pioneered by the Portuguese, the business of the slave trade came to be dominated by the British. By the later decades of the century, the slave ships of Liverpool and Bristol were purchasing and transporting 30–40,000 new captives each year to New World plantations. Most went to the Caribbean, where the British sugar colonies produced handsome profits for local planters and metropolitan merchants. In North America too, Britain's Southern colonies became slave societies, not merely societies with slaves (as were the Middle Colonies and New England).

The Anglican Society for the Propagation of the Gospel had made some effort to evangelize enslaved people of African descent, but with little success, and it was the missionary zeal of pietist and evangelical movements that would drive preachers to reach the most despised and downtrodden peoples of the colonial world. The emergence of black evangelicalism can be dated to the 1730s, and located quite precisely in the Danish island colony of St Thomas.[10] It was here that Moravian missionaries formed the first black Protestant congregations in the North Atlantic. Their success owed much to local converts like Rebecca, who acted as catechists and evangelists. As a free person of mixed European and African descent, Rebecca proved remarkably effective in spreading the gospel among African slaves. The Moravians connected her to a religious network that criss-crossed the Atlantic world. Sent to the church's headquarters in Herrnhut, Saxony, in 1742, she married the missionary Christian Protten, himself of mixed African and European descent. In the 1750s, the couple travelled to Christiansborg, a fort on the Danish Gold Coast, where Rebecca taught African children until her death in 1780.

In North America too, evangelicals were winning significant numbers of black converts. Revivalists like the Anglican itinerant George Whitefield and the Presbyterian Samuel Davies preached with missionary intent, emotional power and populist appeal. Subsequent waves of awakening, like the 'Great Revival' of 1785–1792 in Virginia, swept many more African Americans into Baptist and Methodist churches.[11]

Historians have puzzled over why revivalist Protestantism proved so compelling to people of African descent across the Anglophone Atlantic world.[12] It is significant that revivalist itinerants came to save souls rather than exploit bodies, in striking contrast to the predatory attentions of slave traders and planters. Blacks who had been bought and sold in slave markets, now heard that they mattered to God, that God's incarnate Son had shed his own blood for them. In an era of

---

9 *The Letters of William Lloyd Garrison*, edited by Walter Merrill and Louis Ruchames (6 vols, Cambridge, MA: Harvard University Press, 1971–81), III: 642.
10 Jon Sensbach, *Rebecca's Revival: Creating Black Christianity in the Atlantic World* (Cambridge, MA: Harvard University Press, 2005).
11 Sylvia R. Frey and Betty Wood, *Come Shouting to Zion: African American Protestantism in the American South and British Caribbean to 1830* (Chapel Hill, NC: University of North Carolina Press, 1998), Chs 4–5.
12 Douglas Ambrose, 'Religion and Slavery', in *The Oxford Handbook of Slavery in the Americas*, edited by Robert L. Paquette and Mark M. Smith (Oxford: Oxford University Press, 2010), Ch. 17. Classic accounts include Eugene Genovese, *Roll, Jordan, Roll: The World the Slaves Made* (New York: Random House, 1972), pp. 161–284; Albert Raboteau, *Slave Religion: The 'Invisible Institution' in the Antebellum South* (Oxford: Oxford University Press, 1978); Frey and Wood, *Come Shouting to Zion*.

polite, decorous and rather anodyne Enlightenment Protestantism, the 'New Lights' preached with passion about sin, guilt, redemption, blood sacrifice and the power of the Holy Spirit. This visceral message spoke to the existential experience of an enslaved population whose life was marked by blood, sweat, toil and tears. It seems likely that the evangelical style also resonated with traditional religious beliefs carried over from Africa. The dramatic rite of adult baptism, for example, conducted by Baptists in the rivers of Virginia and other colonies, may have reminded Africans of traditional rituals of cleansing. At the same time, evangelicalism offered community, fostered literacy and empowered a new cohort of indigenous evangelists. In 1782, ten years before William Carey and the 'birth' of the evangelical missionary movement, the black Virginian George Liele inaugurated Baptist missions by sailing for Kingston, Jamaica; by 1814, when the first English Baptist missionaries arrived, Jamaica already had 8,000 black Baptists.[13]

White evangelicals gloried in the power of the gospel to convert the heathen, and saw African and Native American converts as valuable witnesses to the authenticity of their preaching. Indeed, the conversion of Africans was taken to be a fulfilment of the Old Testament prophecy that 'Ethiopia shall soon stretch out her hands unto God' (Psalm 68: 31). Accordingly, black converts enjoyed a certain prestige, and attracted the patronage of evangelical leaders like the Countess of Huntingdon, whose Connexion sponsored a remarkable number of the first generation of Anglophone black authors – Briton Hammon, whose 1760 captivity narrative was the first published African American (or Afro-British) prose text; Jupiter Hammon, author of the first published work of poetry in English by a black author; James Gronniosaw, whose 1772 autobiography initiated the Anglophone tradition of slave narrative; Phillis Wheatley, the first published woman of African descent, and only the second American woman to publish a book of poems; John Marrant, who was ordained as a minister in the Countess of Huntingdon's Connexion, ministered among the Cherokee, the black refugees of Nova Scotia, and in London, and published an autobiography, a journal and several sermons; Ottobah Cugoano, whose *Thoughts and Sentiments* (1787) was the first abolitionist tract published by a former slave; and Olaudah Equiano, whose 1789 autobiography was part slave narrative, part conversion narrative, and made him the first black Atlantic author to make a living from his royalties.[14] The book's subscribers included some of Britain's most eminent evangelicals: the Earl of Dartmouth, Hannah More, Henry Thornton, John Erskine, and John Wesley who read Equiano's *Interesting Narrative* on his deathbed.[15]

Like Wesley, Equiano and Cugoano were eloquent critics of racial slavery, and by the late 1780s many evangelicals had thrown their weight behind the campaigns to abolish the Atlantic slave trade. There were two critical factors here. The first was the agitation of the Pennsylvania Quaker, Anthony Benezet, who expressly challenged leading evangelicals to take up the cause. By the 1770s, his efforts were gaining traction, prompting landmark anti-slavery pamphlets by Wesley and the American Presbyterian intellectual Benjamin Rush.[16] When a Society for the Abolition of the Slave Trade was established in 1787 it brought together Quakers and devout Anglicans, with Wilberforce as their parliamentary spokesman. As Christopher Leslie Brown

---

13 Doreen Robinson, *Slavery's Heroes: George Liele and the Ethiopian Baptists of Jamaica, 1783–1865* (n.p.: Liele Books, 2014).
14 *Unchained Voices: An Anthology of Black Authors in the English-Speaking World of the 18th Century*, edited by Vincent Carretta (Lexington, KY: University Press of Kentucky, 1996).
15 Olaudah Equiano, *The Interesting Narrative and Other Writings*, edited by Vincent Carretta (London: Penguin, 2003), pp. 15–8.
16 Maurice Jackson, *Let This Voice be Heard: Anthony Benezet, Father of Atlantic Abolitionism* (Philadelphia, PA: University of Pennsylvania Press, 2009).

explains, 'The British antislavery movement emerged from a religious reaction against what its evangelical and Quaker founders derided as nominal Christianity'.[17]

The second factor was the American Revolution. The Patriots depicted themselves as political slaves under the arbitrary rule of the British Parliament, but that highlighted the glaring mismatch between libertarian rhetoric and American slaveholding. It is no coincidence that on the eve of the American revolutionary war, the heirs of Jonathan Edwards – including Samuel Hopkins of Rhode Island, and Jonathan Edwards Jr. – began to denounce black slavery, or that black evangelicals like Wheatley, Lemuel Haynes and David Margrett began to do the same, moving beyond the apolitical stance that had hitherto characterized Calvinistic Methodism.[18] On the other side of the Atlantic, Britain's calamitous loss of her American colonies prompted considerable soul-searching; evangelicals were not the only ones to conclude that the slave trade was a national crime that had provoked a national punishment.[19]

A chorus of evangelical voices now spoke out against the slave trade, and even slavery itself. In the newly independent United States, the Methodist Conference of 1784 (under the influence of Francis Asbury and Thomas Coke) declared that slavery was contrary to 'the unalienable rights of Mankind' 'capable of the Image of God'; it gave Methodist slaveholders twelve months to execute a legal deed of emancipation.[20] For the first time in history, anti-slavery societies were established in a slave society, as evangelicals in Southern states spoke out against the enslavement of blacks, and participated in a wave of manumissions. Among the beneficiaries was Richard Allen, later the founder of the African Methodist Episcopal Church (the AME), whose owner emancipated him after experiencing an evangelical conversion.[21]

In Britain, the circle around Wilberforce (including Zachary Macaulay and James Stephen) played a critical role in keeping abolition on the agenda during the reaction against the French Revolution, and they helped devise the strategy that would see Parliament abolish the British Atlantic slave trade in 1807.[22] In the following years, they refused to slacken their pace, campaigning for suppression of the trade by the Royal Navy, an international ban secured through diplomatic treaties, the registration of West Indian slaves and the amelioration of their conditions. Although the abolitionists were idolized by many, they were also subjected to vilification, not least in George Cruickshank's grotesquely racist cartoon, *The New Union Club* (1819), depicting Wilberforce, Stephen and Macaulay cavorting with blacks at a drunken and debauched dinner held by the African Institution.

Black and white evangelicals collaborated in attempts to establish model societies of free blacks in Sierra Leone, Liberia and even Haiti, whose 'black king' Henri Christophe corresponded with Wilberforce and Clarkson. African American evangelicals played an important role in each of these enterprises. Pastors like David George and Boston King were civic leaders in Sierra Leone, having taken their flock of black loyalists from New York via Nova Scotia;

---

17 Christopher Leslie Brown, *Moral Capital: Foundations of British Abolitionism* (Chapel Hill, NC: University of North Carolina Press, 2006), p. 28.
18 See John Coffey, *Exodus and Liberation: Deliverance Politics from John Calvin to Martin Luther King Jr.* (New York: Oxford University Press, 2014), Ch. 3.
19 See John Coffey, 'Tremble Britannia: Fear, Providence and the Abolition of the Slave Trade, 1758–1807', *English Historical Review* vol. 127 (2012), 853–9.
20 John Wigger, *American Saint: Francis Asbury and the Methodists* (New York: Oxford University Press, 2009), pp. 122–5, 148–55.
21 See Richard Newman, *Freedom's Prophet: Bishop Richard Allen, the AME Church, and the Black Founding Fathers* (New York: New York University Press, 2008).
22 Roger Anstey, *The Atlantic Slave Trade and British Abolition, 1760–1810* (Atlantic Highlands, NJ: Humanities Press, 1975).

Daniel Coker, a co-founder of the AME, promoted migration to Liberia; and Prince Saunders, a graduate of Dartmouth College, was sent to Haiti by Wilberforce and Clarkson to promote the new nation's education.[23] For a time, Wilberforce's own children were educated in Clapham alongside the children of Sierra Leone's black settlers.[24] Fittingly, perhaps, America's first black university (founded in 1856) would be named after Wilberforce.

In 1823, British abolitionists established a new Anti-Slavery Society, led by Wilberforce's successor, Thomas Fowell Buxton, an evangelical Anglican with strong Quaker connections. The Society was committed to 'gradual emancipation', but two major slave rebellions in the Caribbean radicalized the British anti-slavery movement. Both broke out from missionary chapels. In Demerara, leading members of Bethel Chapel, pastored by John Smith of the London Missionary Society, rose up in protest after hearing rumours that the governor was refusing to comply with reforms mandated by king and parliament (and 'Mr Wilberforce'). Their leader, Jack Gladstone, bore the surname of his plantation's owner, the Liverpool MP John Gladstone (a keen supporter of the Bible Society and father of the future prime minister). Jack's father, Quamina, was the Chapel's head deacon, and the rebels drew inspiration from Scripture, including the Exodus story. As a consequence, the missionary was charged with 'inciting the negroes to rebellion'. Found guilty by a court martial, and dying of consumption while under arrest, Smith was acclaimed a martyr back in England, where some abolitionists now began to call for 'immediate emancipation'.[25] Immediatism gathered pace after another slave revolt in Jamaica, led by the Baptist deacon, Sam Sharpe, and known as 'the Baptist war'.[26] Here too, an apparently calamitous rebellion galvanized British abolitionists. The missionary William Knibb denounced slavery in a barnstorming tour of Britain, and Baptists, Methodists and Congregationalists inundated Parliament with massive petitions. The agitation led directly to the Emancipation Act of 1833, and the liberation of Britain's West Indian slaves by 1838.

West Indian emancipation was a powerful inspiration to American abolitionists. The 1830s witnessed a second wave of American abolitionism fuelled by the millennial fervour of the Second Great Awakening. The evangelist Charles G. Finney attacked racial slavery with the same zeal as Wesley before him, and his converts like Theodore Dwight Weld and the students of Lane College, Cincinnati, became powerful activists in the abolitionist movement. At Oberlin College, near Cleveland, Finneyite evangelicals created the first interracial and co-educational college in America, training women and African Americans as equals with white men. Indeed, Oberlin 'educated more black students before the Civil War than all other American colleges combined'. In the judgment of its most recent historian, it was 'the most progressive academic environment in the nation, perhaps the world'.[27] In New York, the wealthy businessmen Arthur and Lewis Tappan bankrolled revivalism and abolitionism, displaying great personal

---

23 Manisha Sinha, *The Slave's Cause: A History of Abolition* (New Haven, CT: Yale University Press, 2016), pp. 51–3, 166–70.
24 Bruce Mouser, 'African Academy: Clapham, 1799–1806', *History of Education* vol. 33 (2004), 87–103.
25 John Coffey, '"A Bad and Dangerous Book": Biblical Identity Politics and the Demerara Slave Rebellion', in *Chosen Peoples, Promised Lands: The Bible, Race and Empire in the Long Nineteenth Century*, edited by Gareth Atkins, Shinjini Das and Brian Murray (Cambridge: Cambridge University Press, forthcoming).
26 Mary Turner, *Slaves and Missionaries: The Disintegration of Jamaican Slave Society, 1787–1834* (Barbados: The Press University of the West Indies, 1982); Larry Kreitzer, *'Kissing the Book': The Story of Sam Sharpe as Revealed in the Records of the National Archives at Kew* (Oxford: Centre for Baptist History and Heritage Studies Occasional Papers, 2013).
27 J. Brent Morris, *Oberlin: Hotbed of Abolitionism* (Chapel Hill, NC: University of North Carolina Press, 2014), pp. 2–4. See also Donald Dayton with Douglas M. Strong, *Rediscovering an Evangelical Heritage* (Grand Rapids, MI: Baker, 2014).

courage and sacrifice in the face of a rising tide of white supremacy. Most famously, they leapt to the defence of the Africans who had revolted on board the slave ship *Amistad*, working with John Quincy Adams to secure their release. And by supporting the Liberty Party, with fellow evangelical James G. Birney as its Presidential candidate, the Tappans facilitated the birth of abolitionism's political wing.[28]

American abolitionism owed much to black activists. The Presbyterian pastor, Samuel Cornish, pioneered the first black newspaper, the *Freeman's Journal* in 1828, and the following year, the Methodist David Walker wrote his *Appeal to the Colored Citizens of the World*, calling white Christians to repent of their racism and enact immediate emancipation. The black Congregationalist pastor, Hosea Easton, whose church was burned down by a mob in 1836, published one of 'the first full-blown analyses of American racism': *A Treatise On the Intellectual Character, and Civil and Political Condition of the Colored People of the U[nited] States; And the Prejudice Exercised Towards Them; With A Sermon on the Duty of the Church To Them* (1837). Another black pastor, the Presbyterian James Pennington, took up his pen against the new pseudoscience of race, setting biblical monogenesis against 'absurd' notions of racial 'inferiority'. Black evangelicals attacked 'colorphobia' with Scripture: God had created all people 'of one blood'. As the Presbyterian Henry Highland Garnet put it, the language of 'races' was one of 'the improper terms of our times' – 'in fact there is but one race, as there was one Adam'. African American clergy and other free blacks in the North campaigned for black suffrage and for desegregation of public transport and public schools. In 1843, their lobbying contributed to the repeal of the law against interracial marriage in Massachusetts.[29]

Yet for all their heroic activism, American abolitionists failed to win over the churches. Only a small minority of American evangelicals embraced immediatism, while a much greater proportion defended the institution of slavery. Evangelical colonizationists often supported the Liberian project as a means of exporting free blacks from America. Even in the North, racial prejudice was rife, and segregation was commonplace on public transport and in churches. In the South, evangelical divines developed a robust proslavery theology, arguing that slavery was biblical. By emphasizing that neither Old nor New Testament demanded the eradication of slavery, and sidestepping the specific problem of justifying American racial slavery, they may have won the exegetical argument. Having failed to resolve the theological dispute over slavery, Americans were forced to resolve it in a brutal civil war.[30]

No one spoke more powerfully about this failure than Frederick Douglass, America's most famous former slave. He turned the evangelical critique of nominal Christianity against evangelicals themselves, declaring that 'Revivals of religion and revivals in the slave-trade go hand in hand together'.[31] Divines had made the American church 'the bulwark of American slavery, and the shield of American slave-hunters', and 'have shamelessly given the sanction of religion and the Bible to the whole slave system'. Douglass observed that things were different in Britain. The British anti-slavery movement 'was not an anti-church movement', because there 'the question of emancipation' was 'a high religious question', a cause supported by men famous for

---

28 Bertram Wyatt-Brown, *Lewis Tappan and the Evangelical War on Slavery* (Cleveland, OH: Case Western Reserve, 1980).
29 Sinha, *The Slave's Cause*, pp. 308, 309, 313.
30 Mark Noll, 'The Bible and Slavery', in *Religion and the American Civil War*, edited by Randall Miller, Harry Stout and Charles Wilson (New York: Oxford University Press, 1998), pp. 43–73; Mark A. Noll, *The Civil War as a Theological Crisis* (Chapel Hill, NC: University of North Carolina Press, 2006).
31 Frederick Douglass, *Autobiographies* (New York: Library of America, 1994), p. 98.

their piety – 'The Sharps, the Clarksons, the Wilberforces, the Buxtons, the Burchells, and the Knibbs'.[32]

The irony was that British and American evangelicals read the same Bible, and taught the same soteriology. What divided them was geographical context and social location. Britain's slaves were 3,000 miles away in Caribbean colonies; America's slaves were an ever-present reality, especially in the slave society of the South. While slavery benefited the British economy, it was far less integral to it than American slavery was to the economy of the United States. The British had greater distance on the problem of racial slavery, and were unthreatened by the prospect of a domestic slave revolt. In Britain, abolitionism enjoyed mass popular support; in America, it was a more marginal cause. Ultimately, regional location and ethnic identity were better predictors of attitudes to slavery than was evangelical religion. Place and race exercised a powerful influence on how particular groups of evangelicals read their Bible and applied their faith.

Tempting as it might be to see American proslavery as an aberration, it was not out of line with the early history of evangelicalism. The German pietist Count von Zinzendorf had instructed an assembly of 300 black slaves on St Thomas that 'God has punished the first Negroes with slavery';[33] Whitefield had imported African slaves to labour on his Georgia orphanage;[34] Jonathan Edwards had purchased a domestic slave at auction; the Countess of Huntingdon had resisted the attempt of Benezet to press her into taking an anti-slavery stand. Most dramatically of all, the Anglican evangelical leader John Newton had first turned to serious religion while captaining a slave ship, and when he published his conversion narrative in 1764, he lamented his sins of blasphemy, drunkenness and licentiousness, without questioning the ethics of the slave trade. 'I never had a scruple upon this head', he later admitted, 'nor was such a thought once suggested to me, by any friend'.[35] British evangelicals in the 1750s and 1760s, were largely oblivious to the evils of the slave trade. It was only many years later, perhaps at Benezet's prompting, that Newton began to see the Atlantic slave trade as a great national sin.[36]

The powerful surge in anti-slavery sentiment during the era of the American Revolution was without historical precedent, but it had its limitations. Initially, at least, most abolitionists targeted the slave trade rather than the institution of racial slavery itself. Even Wilberforce believed that enslaved blacks were not ready for freedom – amelioration and gradual emancipation were the goals. While evangelical egalitarianism made remarkable inroads in the slave societies of the American South, 'white evangelicals in the South never seriously threatened slavery'.[37] Historians have often told a story of declension, in which Southern evangelicals traded their radical anti-slavery convictions for cultural dominance and cultural captivity. According to

---

32 Frederick Douglass, *Selected Speeches and Writings*, edited by Philip Foner (Chicago, IL: Lawrence Hill Books, 1999), pp. 200, 202.
33 Jon Sensbach, '"Don't Teach My Negroes to be Pietists": Pietism and the Roots of the Black Protestant Church', in *Pietism in Germany and North America, 1680–1820*, edited by Jonathan Strom, Hartmut Lehmann and James van Horn Melton (Farnham: Ashgate, 2009), p. 194.
34 Carla Gardina Pestana, 'Whitefield and Empire', in *George Whitefield: Life, Context, and Legacy*, edited by Geordan Hammond and David Ceri Jones (Oxford: Oxford University Press, 2016), pp. 94–7.
35 John Newton, *Thoughts upon the African Slave Trade* (London, 1788), p. 4. See also John Newton, *An Authentic Narrative* (London, 1764), pp. 192–3.
36 Newton was almost certainly the slave ship captain whose anonymous testimony was printed in [Anthony Benezet], *Considerations on Several Important Subjects* (Philadelphia, PA, 1778), pp. 33–5 footnote. Like Newton, this witness had sailed from Liverpool to the coast of Guinea 'About the Year 1749', and had foiled a slave revolt on board his ship. He now wished to 'atone' for his sins.
37 Charles Irons, *The Origins of Proslavery Christianity: White and Black Evangelicals in Colonial and Antebellum Virginia* (Chapel Hill, NC: University of North Carolina Press, 2008), p. 13.

Henry May, 'the collapse of evangelical antislavery is the most lamentable fact in American religious history'.[38] There is some truth to this tale – figures like the Baptist John Leland and the Methodist Francis Asbury did shift from prophetic critique of slavery to a more accommodating stance.[39] But the declension story oversimplifies.

In his exemplary study of Virginia, Charles Irons offers a more nuanced account. He emphasizes that 'From the beginning, evangelicalism was a biracial enterprise'. Although there were some independent black churches in the cities, and clandestine gatherings of black Christians on the plantations, the state's Baptist and Methodist churches were often mixed. But whereas black evangelicals pushed for racial equality, whites typically took a paternalist view of both churches and slaveholding. In the 1810s and 1820s, Virginian evangelicals played a major role in launching the American Colonization Society; a few hundred white slaveholders even manumitted slaves and funded their migration to Liberia. But whites had trouble imagining an America in which blacks and whites lived side by side as equals. Nat Turner's violent slave rebellion in 1831 caused a wave of panic among white Virginians that resulted in a determination to supervise and police black religious worship. White evangelicals redoubled their commitment to mission among slaves, 'but the new objective was not fellowship; it was security'. A number of black churches were shut down, and some black preachers were even defrocked, as whites sought to gather black evangelicals into churches supervised by whites, creating 'a safe brand of biracial evangelicalism'. Typically, blacks sat in the galleries, and took communion after whites – Harriet Jacobs remembered a white pastor saying 'Come down, now, my coloured friends'.[40]

The mission to slaves enjoyed real success, with the number of blacks in evangelical churches doubling between 1830 and 1850. Whites concluded that slavery was working as 'a benign vehicle for Christianisation'. In this way, argues Irons, 'Evangelical blacks inadvertently abetted the development of proslavery evangelicalism'. As Northern abolitionists intensified their campaign against slavery, the Southern churches became more entrenched in their defence of the institution. Blacks did push successfully for greater freedom for their preachers, for literacy and access to the Bible, and for semi-autonomous churches under the nominal supervision of a white clergyman. But the flourishing state of Southern black evangelicalism was used as an argument against abolitionists, who were increasingly depicted as political agitators who put utopian projects ahead of the gospel. In 1837, 'Old School' Presbyterians, dominant in the South, separated from the Finneyite 'New School', who were associated with immediatism. In the mid-1840s, the Baptists and Methodists also experienced sectional schisms, with slavery as the presenting issue.[41]

These American divisions posed a major problem for the Evangelical Alliance founded in 1846. At its founding conference in London, there were seventy-four Americans among the 910 participants, though only one African American, Molliston Madison Clark of the AME. Although there were tensions over certain doctrinal matters, the bitterest divisions emerged over slavery, when some British delegates insisted that 'Slaveholders' should be excluded from membership. The Americans resented British moralizing, and opposed the adoption of an abolitionist stance on the grounds that it would undermine evangelical unity over a secondary

---

38 Henry May, *The Enlightenment in America* (New York: Oxford United Press, 1976), p. 328. See also Christine Heyrman, *Southern Cross: The Beginnings of the Bible Belt* (Chapel Hill, NC: University of North Carolina Press, 1997).
39 Wigger, *American Saint*, pp. 384–5.
40 Irons, *The Origins of Proslavery Christianity*, pp. 18, 153, 168, 159.
41 Irons, *The Origins of Proslavery Christianity*, pp. 190, 170.

issue. Plans for a 'General Alliance' were shelved in favour of a set of separate national organizations.[42]

In the United States, there was a growing rift between abolitionism and the churches. William Lloyd Garrison widened it by linking anti-slavery to women's rights and universal reform, and joining with Unitarians in attacking evangelical biblicism. In 1840, with the Garrisonian takeover of the American Anti-Slavery Society, evangelicals like Tappan, Birney and Weld founded the American and Foreign Anti-Slavery Society, designed to foster a more collaborative relationship with churches and missionary societies. But as Timothy Smith once noted, 'only sects confined to the northernmost portions of free territory – Congregationalists, Unitarians, Universalists and smaller groups like the Freewill Baptists and Wesleyan Methodists – could take a stand without offending major sections of their membership'.[43]

Meanwhile, Southern evangelicals were increasingly emphatic in defending slavery from the Bible, contrasting their biblical and missionary faith with impiety of Northern abolitionists like Garrison. Garrison continued to cite the Bible's prophetic denunciations of injustice, but he repudiated biblical infallibility, sparking an exchange of letters with Harriet Beecher Stowe. The daughter of a famous evangelical preacher, and author of the bestselling anti-slavery novel, *Uncle Tom's Cabin* (1852), Stowe accused Garrison of depriving Uncle Tom of the Bible.[44] But in trying to reclaim the Bible, 'antislavery moderates never put race at the center of their antislavery appeals'.[45] By arguing against slavery in the abstract, and failing to foreground the racial character of American slavery, they weakened their case – it was one thing to argue that Christianity provided no grounds for white supremacy, but much harder to show that the Old and New Testaments condemned slaveholding *per se*. In the face of relentless proof-texting by proslavery evangelicals, growing numbers of Northern Protestants turned to the notion of progressive revelation, preparing the way for liberal Protestantism. The failure to win the exegetical war, and to win over the churches, meant that abolitionist disillusionment with evangelicalism ran deep. It would contribute to a crisis of faith among leading activists, including Theodore Dwight Weld, Sarah Grimke and Gerrit Smith, who each broke with evangelicalism and conventional Christianity.[46] The days in which Wilberforce and Buxton had rallied evangelicals around the abolitionist flag seemed like a distant memory.

Yet even the heroic ventures of Britain's evangelical abolitionists had often ended in disappointment. The great expectations for Sierra Leone, the British West Indies, the Khoi Khoi, and Buxton's Niger Expedition were not fulfilled. By the 1850s, missionary or humanitarian imperialism was losing ground to visions of empire based on racial superiority.[47] Evangelicals in the age of Wilberforce had been buoyed by post-millennialism, the expectation that Christ's coming reign of justice and peace would gradually transform the world. That hope dimmed as the nineteenth century wore on, though it was kept alive by the social gospel. African American evangelicals continued to draw on the millennialist tradition to critique contemporary society

---

42 John Wolffe, *The Expansion of Evangelicalism: The Age of Wilberforce, More, Chalmers and Finney* (Leicester: Inter-Varsity Press, 2006), pp. 231–4.
43 Timothy L. Smith, *Revivalism and Social Reform: American Protestantism on the Eve of the Civil War* (1957; reprinted Baltimore, MD: Johns Hopkins University Press, 1980), p. 190.
44 *The Letters of William Lloyd Garrison*, edited by Merrell and Ruchames, IV: 280–8.
45 Molly Oshatz, *Slavery and Sin: The Fight against Slavery and the Rise of Liberal Protestantism* (New York: Oxford University Press, 2012), p. 73.
46 David Hempton, *Evangelical Disenchantment: Nine Portraits of Faith and Doubt* (New Haven, CT: Yale University Press, 2008), Chs 4–5.
47 Zoe Laidlaw, 'Slavery, Settlers, and Indigenous Dispossession: Britain's Empire through the Lens of Liberia', *Journal of Colonialism and Colonial History* vol. 13 (Spring 2012).

and sustain their hopes for a better world.[48] Among conservative white evangelicals, however, the rise of premillennialism reflected and reinforced a more pessimistic outlook, undercutting the motivation for social reform.[49]

Indeed, by the late nineteenth century, American churches were more divided by race than ever before. After Emancipation, many African Americans voted with their feet, leaving white-led churches to form their own congregations and denominations. Black Baptist and Methodist churches enjoyed explosive growth, amounting to an 'African American Great Awakening'.[50] White evangelicals, who saw themselves as benevolent paternalists, were shocked at this ecclesiastical exodus. The Presbyterian theologian, Robert Dabney, complained that blacks had 'deserted their true friends', and failed to recognize that they were 'a subservient race'. According to Charles Irons, 'the fragmentation of spiritual community in the late 1860s removed the most significant check on white antagonism and left only the impulse for racial control'.[51]

African Americans had asserted their religious independence; they would now face a white supremacist backlash. During the late nineteenth century in the United States, the so-called Jim Crow system established white supremacy in the American South through the law and violence. This was no anomaly. The turn of the century saw rising racism across the United States and throughout the European empires – a structure that would be challenged, in the mid-twentieth century, by nationalism, and in the case of American Jim Crow, by a civil rights movement associated with a Baptist minister.

The age of King

On the 16 April 1963, Martin Luther King Jr wrote a letter from jail in Birmingham, Alabama. The black Baptist minister had been arrested for protesting against segregation. His letter, which was widely published, was addressed to eight local white clergymen, including a leading Baptist pastor. The clergymen, who had written a letter earlier in the year denouncing the state governor's white supremacist rhetoric, had called on King to delay civil rights demonstrations in the city.[52] In response, King said he was 'gravely disappointed' by Christian moderates, including one who had told him 'The teachings of Christ take time to come to earth'. He pointed to the example of Old and New Testament heroes of the faith who defied unjust laws, and asked, 'Was not Jesus an extremist for love?' King concluded, 'I must honestly reiterate that I have been disappointed with the church', but he was 'grateful to God' for 'the influence of the Negro church' in the struggle.[53]

King's invocation of a Christian protest heritage is a reminder, if one were needed, of the Christian dimensions of the civil rights movement. From the perspective of Christian activists,

48 Timothy Fulop, '"The Future Golden Day of the Race": Millennialism and Black Americans in the Nadir, 1877–1901', in *African-American Religion: Interpretive Essays in History and Culture*, edited by Timothy E. Fulop and Albert J. Raboteau (New York: Routledge, 1997), pp. 227–54.
49 David W. Bebbington, *The Dominance of Evangelicalism: The Age of Spurgeon and Moody* (Leicester: Inter-Varsity Press, 2005), pp. 179–88.
50 Jay R. Case, 'The African American Great Awakening and Modernity', in *American Evangelicalism: George Marsden and the State of American Religious History*, edited by Darren Dochuk, Thomas Kidd and Kurt Petersen (Notre Dame, IN; University of Notre Dame Press, 2014), Ch. 6.
51 Irons, *The Origins of Proslavery Christianity*, pp. 259–60.
52 S. Jonathan Bass, *Blessed Are the Peacemakers: Martin Luther King, Jr., Eight White Religious Leaders, and the 'Letter from Birmingham Jail'* (Baton Rouge, LA: Louisiana State University Press, 2002).
53 Martin Luther King, 'Letter from Birmingham Jail', 16 April 1963, https://kinginstitute.stanford.edu/king-papers/documents/letter-birmingham-jail (accessed 23 February 2018).

to quote student leader, Baptist seminarian and future Congressman, John Lewis, the movement was a 'holy crusade'. King insisted, 'God is with the movement'. Rosa Parks, who famously refused to give up her seat in a segregated Montgomery, Alabama bus, was a devout Christian and member of the African Methodist Episcopal Church. King's organization was called the Southern Christian Leadership Conference, his rhetoric was from the black Baptist pulpit, and his sacrificial death earned him a place in popular memory as a Christian martyr. Mass meetings took on the fever of revivals, with prayer, the singing of spirituals and calls to commitment to the cause, ahead of the testing of faith in the days to come.[54]

King's praise of the 'influence of the Negro church' is a reminder, too, that black churches were a bedrock of the civil rights movement. The first separate black churches were founded in the Northern, non-slave states in the late eighteenth century, but the main growth of black churches occurred after emancipation, in the later nineteenth century. In 1926, at the height of the segregation era, there were 5 million black church members; by the time of the civil rights movement, 10 million – half the total African American population, and a higher proportion of churchgoers than in white communities. The vast majority of black churches fit the description of evangelical.

But the 'Letter from Birmingham Jail' also reminds us that the civil rights movement was not a simple story of the Christian Church facing down a racist world. Rather, the battle over race was within the church, too. In his letter, King told the clergymen, 'In deep disappointment I have wept over the laxity of the church'. Though noting honourable exceptions, his hopes of support from white clergy had ended up as 'shattered dreams', since 'some have been outright opponents' and 'all too many others have been more cautious than courageous and have remained silent behind the anesthetizing security of stained-glass windows'.[55] Churches were invariably segregated (in the North as well as the South) – and white-only churches became one of the main targets of civil rights protest. During the spring of 1961, black men and women conducted 'kneel-ins' at some 200 white churches – a majority of churches turned them away. As the liberal *Christian Century* wryly observed, 'bread served at a lunch counter is one thing: bread shared in church is another'.[56]

Ironically, it was discrimination and racism within the white church that had led to the establishment of separate black churches in the first place, churches that would, in turn, challenge discrimination and racism. From the outset, many black churches stood against white supremacy. In the antebellum era, black clergy denounced slavery and black churches supported the underground railroad. At the height of the segregation era, at the turn of the twentieth century, black clergy denounced lynchings and some supported the creation of civil rights organizations. By the time of the civil rights movement, the black church had become the leading institution in many communities, so clergy often joined the leadership of local protest movements. For example, King did not initiate the Montgomery bus boycott – that was done by a local women's committee. But the first mass meeting was held in church, and the organizing committee asked the young charismatic pastor to speak.[57]

Black clergy stood against racism within the church, too. At the turn of the twentieth century, they challenged a theology that denied their humanity or equality. As African Methodist Bishop

---

54 Rosa Parks, *Quiet Strength: The Faith, the Hope, and the Heart of a Woman Who Changed a Nation* (New York: Zondervan, 1994).
55 King, 'Letter from Birmingham Jail'.
56 Stephen R. Haynes, *The Last Segregated Hour: The Memphis Kneel-Ins and the Campaign for Southern Church Desegregation* (New York: Oxford University Press, 2012), p. 14.
57 See, for example, Aldon Morris, *The Origins of the Civil Rights Movement: Black Communities Organizing for Change* (New York: The Free Press, 1984).

Levi Coppin put it, 'others have written for us, we must now write for ourselves ... much of the theological work extant needs reconstruction'.[58] Drawing on biblical genealogies, black religious writers traced their heritage to Noah, and refuted claims that Noah's curse on Canaan meant that their destiny was servitude. Pointing to high levels of African American (and African) religiosity, black apologists asserted that God had used black suffering to foster a deeper faith, and citing the 'Ethiopian prophecy' of Psalm 68: 13, they looked to justice in America and the redemption of Africa. They noted that God's chosen people in the Bible had been slaves, and that God's own Son – like many thousands of lynch victims – had been murdered by the mob.[59] As the renowned black theologian James Cone observed in 2011, 'Black Christians ... sang more songs and preached more sermons about the cross than any other aspect of Jesus' ministry'.[60]

Black evangelicals denounced racist practices as well as white supremacist theology. Leading black churchwoman Fannie Barrier Williams told the World Parliament of Religions in 1893, 'It is a monstrous thing that nearly one-half of the so-called evangelical churches of this country, those situated in the South, repudiate fellowship to every Christian man and woman who happens to be of African descent'.[61] Time and again, black ministers pointed out that Jesus, on account of his Palestinian origins, would not have been welcomed in a white church. In 1935, in a widely publicized speech *The Negro: The Hope or The Despair of Christianity*, Methodist Bishop Reverdy Ransom made the treatment of black people the litmus test of genuine faith and the viability of Christianity in a changing world.[62] So when Martin Luther King questioned the authenticity of white church leaders in his letter from Birmingham jail, he was standing in a long tradition.

Black churches should not be stereotyped, let alone romanticized, as civil rights protest organizations. Clergy received plenty of criticism from civil rights leaders for hyper-emotionalism, preaching other-worldly religion, or using precious resources on building their institutions. One of the reasons Martin Luther King established his own Southern Christian Leadership Conference was because the main National Baptist Convention refused to approve direct action protest. In Birmingham, only a minority of black clergy joined King's campaign. Moreover, black evangelicals were concerned with many issues of Christian living and Bible teaching beyond racism. For example, like his white counterparts, many of the sermons of the leading black pastor in Washington DC in the early twentieth century, the Presbyterian Francis Grimke, focused on marriage and family life – even though he was a forthright critic of segregation.[63] Unlike their white counterparts, though, black evangelicals tended to be quick to embrace the social gospel, opposed to the idea of America as God's promised nation, and sought to avoid doctrinal squabbles.[64]

58 Levi Coppin, 'Editorial', *African Methodist Episcopal Review* vol. 11 (October 1894), 316.
59 See, for example, Benjamin Arnett, 'Africa and the Descendants of Africa', *African Methodist Episcopal Review* vol. 11 (October 1894), 231–8; James Holly, 'The Divine Plan of Human Redemption in its Ethnological Development', *African Methodist Episcopal Review* vol. 1 (1884), 82; Benjamin Tanner, 'The Hamitic Origin of the Negro', *African Methodist Episcopal Review* vol. 4 (1888), 550.
60 James Cone, *The Cross and the Lynching Tree* (Maryknoll NJ: Orbis Books, 2011), p. 25.
61 Fannie Barrier Williams, 'What Religion Can Do to Advance the Condition of the American Negro', in *The Dawn of Religious Pluralism: Voices from the World's Parliament of Religions, 1893*, edited by Richard Hughes Seager (Lasalle, IL: Open Court Press, 1993), p. 149.
62 Reverdy Ransom, *The Negro: The Hope or the Despair of Christianity* (Boston, MA: Ruth Hill, 1935).
63 *The Works of Francis J. Grimke*, edited by Carter Woodson (Washington, DC: The Associated Press, 1942).
64 On the black social gospel, see Gary Dorrien, *The New Abolition: W. E. B. Du Bois and the Black Social Gospel* (New Haven, CT: Yale University Press, 2015).

White opponents of the civil rights movement were also part of a longer tradition. It was a former Methodist circuit rider, William Simmons, who led the revival of the Ku Klux Klan in the early twentieth century. The book that helped inspire that revival, *The Clansman* (1905), was written by a Baptist preacher, Thomas Dixon. The novel had a Presbyterian preacher as chaplain for a local branch of the first Klan, defending the 'Christian Southland' after the Civil War.[65] At the height of the segregation era, many evangelical preachers in the Southern states defended segregation as God's natural order. Some claimed biblical backing for white supremacy. In 1948, on the eve of the civil rights movement, Frank S. Loescher, concluded a survey into Protestant church congregations: 'Protestantism, by its policies and practices, far from helping to integrate the Negro in American life, is actually contributing to the segregation of Negro Americans'.[66]

There were progressive white evangelicals in the South, but they usually talked of fair treatment rather than of integration. Likewise white evangelicals from Northern states, who tended to be more moderate than their Southern segregationist counterparts, rarely sought to challenge the social order. D. L. Moody, for example, accepted segregated audiences when visiting the South in order to fit in with local custom and have the opportunity to preach the gospel. The devout black Methodist anti-lynching campaigner, Ida B. Wells, complained of Moody, 'Our American Christians are too busy saving the souls of white Christians from burning in hellfire to save the lives of black ones from present burning in fires kindled by white Christians'.[67] Clergy who pushed for interracial actions tended to be liberal theologically – the Federal Council of Churches, for example, formed a Commission on Race Relations in 1921. But even the Commission tended to promote limited interaction at most – such as Race Relations Sundays, where black and white preachers swapped pulpits – rather than congregational integration. Moreover, the fact that such tentative moves came from liberal sources meant that evangelicals tended to stay aloof from race relations initiatives.

The seminal 1954 Supreme Court decision, *Brown vs Board of Education*, which declared segregation in schools unconstitutional, changed the theological terrain for white evangelicals. No longer could defence of segregation be couched in terms of submission to authority or support for the social order. Evangelical (and liberal) denominations swiftly endorsed *Brown*, with the Southern Baptist Convention describing it as 'in harmony . . . with the Christian principles of equal justice and love for all men'. The *Christian Century* acknowledged editorially soon afterwards that the Southern Baptists had done 'more than any other group in the country could to secure cooperation of the South with the Court's verdict'.[68] There was a practical benefit, too, because previous support for segregation had undermined evangelical missionary work in Africa. Examples of Africans coming to America and being denied entry into the very churches that had sent out the missionaries who had converted them caused great embarrassment.[69] However, as Southern resistance to school integration grew (and often grew violent), white evangelical churches were conspicuous by their silence. An internal survey of 1,200 congregations by the

---

65 Thomas Dixon, *The Clansman: An Historical Romance of the Ku Klux Klan* (New York: Grosset and Dunlap, 1905).
66 Frank Loescher, *The Protestant Church and the Negro: A Pattern of Segregation* (New York: Association Press, 1948), p. 13.
67 *Crusade for Justice: The Autobiography of Ida B. Wells*, edited by Alfreda M. Duster (Chicago, IL: University of Chicago Press, 1970), p. 154. See also, Edward J. Blum, *Reforging the White Republic: Race, Religion, and American Nationalism, 1865–1898* (Baton Rouge, LA: Louisiana State University Press, 2005).
68 'Southern Baptists Support Court', *Christian Century* (16 June 1954), 723.
69 See, for example, Stephen Tuck, *Beyond Atlanta: The Struggle for Civil Rights in Georgia, 1940–1980* (Athens, GA: University of Georgia Press, 2001), p. 142.

Presbyterian Church (US) in 1963 found that only 63 per cent of congregations were willing to accept black members, and only twenty-eight congregations (barely 2 per cent) had actually done so,[70] despite the PCUS being the first Protestant denomination formally to endorse the *Brown* decision.

Again, there were exceptions.[71] In 1962 in Albany, Georgia, in the heart of the so-called Deep South, black activists tried to visit the deeply segregated city's First Baptist Church during a mass movement involving Martin Luther King. 'This is Christ's Church', declared the pastor, Brooks Ramsey, 'And I can't build any walls around it that Christ did not build. And Christ did not build any racial walls'. The activists were arrested, but the church board backed their pastor, and Baptist missionaries in Southern Africa wrote to thank him.[72] Still, Ramsey was an exception rather than the rule. As historian of Southern religion Paul Harvey concluded, 'most pastors were silent, or silenced'.[73]

Beyond the segregated South, evangelicals tended to be lukewarm, at best, about the civil rights movement. The leading evangelical magazine of the 1960s, *Christianity Today*, was mostly critical of Martin Luther King – if it mentioned him at all. From its founding in 1957, soon after the Montgomery bus boycott that launched King to prominence, through to 1965, the year of King's final major Southern campaign, in Selma, *Christianity Today* published fewer than two articles per year on race. 'On the whole', concluded Michael Emerson and Christian Smith in their survey of white evangelicalism, 'in comparison to the thought and activities of contemporary black evangelicals, this mainly white evangelical periodical spoke little and, when it did speak, did so hesitantly'.[74]

Why so many white evangelicals were silent, or hesitant, at best, has been the subject of historical debate. Initially scholars suggested cultural captivity, where evangelical thought on race was imprisoned by the prevailing white supremacy, especially in the Southern states. It is true that, as in the case with the response to slavery, there were regional patterns in evangelical responses, with outright hostility concentrated in Deep South states where politicians, such as Georgia's governor Herman Talmadge in 1955, justified racial segregation as an act of obedience to God.[75]

In recent years, though, historians have suggested reasons that place the responsibility more squarely on the evangelical tradition as a cause, rather than simply a reflection, of wider racist attitudes or practice. Most importantly, Southern segregationist preachers thundered that the Bible condemned interracial marriage. White clergy also denounced Communism – which segregationist propagandists had linked to the civil rights movement – as a godless adversary. White evangelical leaders also opposed the interference of the federal government in regional affairs, including interference in Southern race relations.[76]

---

70 Haynes, *Last Segregated Hour*, p. 91.
71 See, for example, Brantley Gasaway, 'Glimmers of Hope: Progressive Evangelicals and Racism, 1965–2000', in *Christians and the Color Line: Race and Religion After Divided by Faith*, edited by J. Russell Hawkins and Philip Luke Sinitiere (New York: Oxford University Press, 2014), pp. 72–99.
72 Haynes, *Last Segregated Hour*, p. 31.
73 Paul Harvey, *Freedom's Coming: Religious Culture and the Shaping of the South from the Civil War through the Civil Rights Era* (Chapel Hill, NC: University of North Carolina Press, 2012), p. 235.
74 Michael Emerson and Christian Smith, *Divided by Faith: Evangelical Religion and the Problem of Race in America* (New York: Oxford University Press, 2001), p. 46. See also, Curtis Evans, 'White Evangelical Protestant Responses to the Civil Rights Movement', *Harvard Theological Review* vol. 102 (2009), 269.
75 Tuck, *Beyond Atlanta*, p. 193. See too Herman Talmadge, *You and Segregation* (Birmingham, AL: Vulcan Press, 1955).
76 Jane Dailey, 'Sex, Segregation, and the Sacred after *Brown*', *Journal of American History* vol. 91 (2004), 119–44. Note that David Chappell argues that the theological support for segregation was unsophisti-

For many evangelicals, though, their complaint was not the aims of the civil rights movement, but the means. The clergy to whom Martin Luther King had written his Birmingham letter, many of whom had a reputation for being moderate or progressive on race, had not opposed King's aims, but criticized his actions as 'unwise and untimely'. The National Association of Evangelicals, which had made statements against segregation, responded to King's call for ministerial support by stating that the Association 'has a policy of not becoming involved in political or sociological affairs that do not affect the function of the church or those involved in the propagation of the gospel'. Those ministers, mostly from Northern states, who did get involved, some of whom suffered and were killed, tended to be from the liberal wing of the church.[77]

Underpinning a reluctance to support King was an evangelical theology that saw salvation as a matter for the individual rather than society. Billy Graham, for example, the most prominent white evangelical of the period, argued that 'social sins' were 'merely a large-scale projection of individual sins'. There was optimism in this view, with the assumption that mass conversion would lead to the transformation of many individual lives, which, when aggregated, would change society as a whole.[78] But it was also a reason – civil rights activists said an excuse – to avoid involvement in the civil rights movement. Although Graham preached that 'faith without works is dead', condemned racism as the world's 'foremost social problem', invited Martin Luther King to give the opening prayer at a New York Crusade, and even before *Brown* removed ropes that separated white and black members of a crowd, he did not support protest to force a change in the law. 'Only when Christ comes again will little white children of Alabama walk hand in hand with little black children', Graham wrote.[79] King was unimpressed. As he put it in his 'Letter from Birmingham Jail': 'In the midst of a mighty struggle to rid our nation of racial and economic injustice, I have heard so many ministers says, "Those are social issues with which the gospel has no real concern"'.

The limits and legacy of such a view remained apparent in the decades after the civil rights movement. It is an oft quoted American saying that Sunday morning at 11 is the most segregated hour in the week, and polls suggest that churchgoers had no inclination to seek change. In one survey in 2015, nearly two-thirds of white conservative Protestants said that African Americans were poor because they lacked sufficient motivation - rather than, for example, having fewer resources, far higher chances of incarceration, or inferior education, housing and employment opportunities. This is not an easily explicable case of cultural captivity, since only half of white Americans in general thought the same.[80]

In turn, black evangelicals have also grappled with issues of disproportionate levels of black poverty. In the early twentieth century, some evangelical black leaders spoke of 'uplifting the race' by teaching morals and thrift, while others supported the social gospel, despite its association with theological liberalism. In more recent years, a disproportionately high number of African Americans (and other minority groups) have joined the prosperity gospel movement. 'For the groundswell of African American pentecostals, locked out of the boom years by

---

cated, and could not stand up to the scrutiny, and the opposing biblical arguments, of the civil rights movement. David L. Chappell, *A Stone of Hope: Prophetic Religion and the Death of Jim Crow* (New York: Oxford University Press, 2005).

77 'Jim Crow, Civil Rights and Southern White Evangelicals: A Historians Forum' (February 2015), www.thegospelcoalition.org (accessed 24 February 2018).
78 Billy Graham, 'Postwar Revivalism', in *A Documentary History of Religion in America since 1877*, edited by Edwin Gaustad and Mark Noll (Grand Rapids, MI: Eerdmans, 2003), p. 562.
79 Emerson and Smith, *Divided By Faith*, p. 47.
80 Bob Smietana, 'Sunday Morning Segregation: Most Worshippers Feel their Church has Enough Diversity', *Christianity Today* (January 2015).

segregated housing and a discriminatory labor market', noted historian of the prosperity gospel, Kate Bowler, 'divine prosperity promised an end-run around the political, economic, and social forces of oppression'. For example, by 2010, the Redeemed Christian Church of God (RCCG), founded in 1952 by Nigerian Josiah Akindayomi, had established 359 congregations across the United States. Bowler also observed that contemporary prosperity megachurches claim some of the highest rates of multicultural congregations.[81]

The modern American story may be distinctive, but there are clear echoes beyond in the history of evangelicals and racism. Within the British Empire the Jamaican born Robert Gordon, who had been denied the opportunity to be an Anglican priest by the white planter dominated island church, ended up as a curate in London during the 1870s. Writing to Britain's Colonial Secretary, Gordon charged: the 'hateful policy of the Jamaican Church, persistently carried out by the Bishop of Kingston, has ever been to make an invidious distinction between the white and coloured subjects of Her Majesty'. Discrimination in the church was prevalent in Britain, too. The early twentieth-century black British activist Dr Harold Moody, a Congregationalist, was outraged that the 'economic condition of our people in Cardiff is simply appalling'. To Moody's dismay, 'I have tried, so far without avail, to awaken the Christian conscience of our organized religion to tackle this human problem'.[82]

In Britain, there were similarities in the belated, but limited, engagement with the issue of racism, too. A 1985 Church of England report, *Faith in the City*, found that black Christians felt excluded or unwelcome by the church, whereas white Anglicans thought there were no such problems. This was an institutional challenge and not just a local one. *Faith in the City* noted that there were fewer than 100 black clergy and not a single black bishop, archdeacon or cathedral dean. *Faith in the City* recommended that the Church of England create a Commission on Black Anglican Concerns.[83] It was the only one of sixty-three recommendations to be rejected by the General Synod. The Synod also rejected a proposal that a minimum of twenty-four out of its 600 members should be black. Reflecting on those votes, Bishop Wilfred Wood concluded: 'It was clear to me that as expressed by Synod's behaviour, Church of England members saw Christianity not as the local expression of an universal faith, but as the religious expression of their national identity – and this was white'.[84]

Little wonder that in Britain, there has been a rise of Black Majority Churches during the later twentieth century, a diverse group of churches both within and outside existing denominations. A MARC Europe survey recorded a 20 per cent growth in Caribbean Churches between 1975 and 1979, despite immigration restrictions in these years. Joel Edwards observed that the churches did not form in response to racism, but at the same time, they did focus on serving black needs in a society that could produce 'lethal doses of economic deprivation, marginalization, institutional and personal racism'. Black evangelicals who remained within the Church of England also tended to support the social gospel. Though 'their attitude to the Bible is conservative', *Faith in the City* observed, 'There is increasing concern for the social and political implications of the Gospel as well as for the salvation of individuals'.[85]

Similarly in South Africa in 1997, three years after Nelson Mandela became president, the Nederduitse Gereformeerde Kerk ('Dutch Reformed Church') took responsibility for

---

81 Kate Bowler, *Blessed: A History of the American Prosperity Gospel* (New York: Oxford University Press, 2013), pp. 53, 231, 207.
82 *Black Voices*, edited by Killingray and Edwards, pp. 90, 134.
83 *Faith in the City: A Call for Action by Church and Nation* (London: Church House Publishing, 1985).
84 Glynne Gordon-Carter, *An Amazing Journey: The Church of England's Response to Institutional Racism* (London: Church House Publishing, 2003), p. xi.
85 *Faith in the City*, p. 43.

'great wrongs' and 'spiritual and structural injustices' before the Truth and Reconciliation Commission. It was a highly symbolic moment: Freek Swanepoel, moderator of the church, and Archbishop Desmond Tutu, chairman of the Commission, embraced. But the apology was carefully crafted. Until three weeks previously, the NGK had not intended to testify, insisting that it had not been an 'accomplice' to violent apartheid, just to segregation within the church. Owing to pressure from some members who wanted far-reaching repentance, there was recognition that the church 'had not always heard the word of God correctly'. But there was no acknowledgement that such mishearing in the church had underpinned apartheid, including violence and subjugation, in the state.[86]

Conclusion

In 1997, a front-page article in *The Wall Street Journal* claimed that 'the most energetic element of society addressing racial divisions may also seem the most unlikely: the religious right'.[87] Denominations, such as the Southern Baptists, had repented of their past racism. Inter-Varsity Christian Fellowship promoted racial reconciliation on campus. In 1994, Billy Graham had welcomed Coretta Scott King onto the stage at a rally in her hometown of Atlanta. That same year, black and white Pentecostal and charismatic denominations joined together in the so-called 'Miracle of Memphis'. In 1996, Promise Keepers, an evangelical mission group to men, made racial integration one of its fundamental seven promises during a series of mass rallies.[88]

Such statements continued into the twenty-first century. In 2015, Russell Moore, president of the Southern Baptist Convention's Ethics and Religious Liberty Commission accepted that: 'Our heritage comes to us through a trail of blood, but not all of it is Christ's blood, and some of it cries out from the ground right now'.[89] Inter-Varsity Christian Fellowship, having not taken a stance during the civil rights movement, came out in support of Black Lives Matter, and invited a black supporter of BLM, Presbyterian Church in America minister Michelle Higgins, to be a keynote speaker at their annual conference. It was a controversial move. The *New York Times* noted, in a comment that could have been applied to many moments in the history of evangelicals and race; 'The discomfort of evangelicals about Black Lives Matter goes beyond specific policies. Many believe that the church should not be intimately involved with politics'. We 'got blowback from just about every side', admitted one of Inter-Varsity's leaders, Greg Jao. 'Certainly we have donors and friends who have raised concerns and questions. They want to know how to interpret this. And we've had friends and donors say, "Bravo, that was brave and courageous".'[90]

Given the tensions and inequalities of the present, the past history of evangelicalism and race

---

86 Mary Braid, 'South Africa: Apartheid's Priests Don Sackcloth and Seek Forgiveness', *Independent* (20 November 1997). See too Piet Meiring, 'The Dutch Reformed Church and the Truth and Reconciliation Commission', *Scriptura* vol. 83 (2003), 250–7; Johan van der Merwe, 'Between War and Peace: The Dutch Reformed Church Agent for Peace, 1990–1994', *Studia Historiae Ecclesiasticae* vol. 40 (2014), 85–103; Megan Shore, *Religion and Conflict Resolution: Christianity and South Africa's Truth and Reconciliation Commission* (Farnham: Ashgate, 2009).
87 Douglas A. Blackmon, 'Racial Reconciliation Becomes a Priority for the Religious Right', *Wall Street Journal* (23 June 1997).
88 On the wider trend of churches to repent of racism, see Jeremy M. Bergen, *Ecclesial Repentance: The Churches Confront Their Sinful Pasts* (London: T. & T. Clark, 2011), Ch. 2.
89 Heidi Hall, 'Southern Baptists Address Church's Racist Past, Focus on Reconciliation', *Huffington Post* (27 March 2015), www.huffingtonpost.co.uk (accessed 23 February 2018).
90 Mark Oppenheimer, 'Some Evangelicals Struggle with Black Lives Matter Movement', *New York Times* (22 January 2016).

has a vital relevance. Many contemporary evangelicals have seized on Wilberforce as an inspiring and reassuring icon, his profile enhanced by the Hollywood biopic *Amazing Grace* (2006). Similarly many white evangelicals now pay tribute to the civil rights movement and hold up King as a Christian hero. John Piper, head of Desiring God ministries, has written in praise of Wilberforce, and in 2013 he reflected on King's influence on the segregated American South in which Piper grew up: 'Between that racially appalling world and this racially imperfect one strode Martin Luther King'; 'Leave aside his theology and his moral flaws. He was used in the mighty hand of Providence to change the world . . . and I am thankful'.[91] The following year, Rick Warren, head of Purpose-Driven ministries, who delivered the invocation at President Obama's first inauguration, praised King: 'a Baptist minister of the Gospel, and a pastor of a local church . . . Everything he did to promote freedom, justice, and racial equality flowed out of his understanding of God's Word'.[92]

The history of black evangelicalism, so long ignored, is now being excavated and made available to the church.[93] Academic studies of evangelicalism increasingly recognize the seminal role of figures like Rebecca Protten and David George.[94] African American theologians like Kameron Carter and Willie Jennings have articulated a theological account of race forged in dialogue with the Western theological tradition and with black voices like Briton Hammon, Olaudah Equiano, Frederick Douglass and Jarena Lee.[95] Others have sought to bring Martin Luther King into dialogue with white evangelical theologians like the neo-evangelical Carl Henry.[96]

Thus it has become increasingly clear that the history of modern evangelicalism is thoroughly intertwined with the history of race, and the long struggle over slavery and segregation. Evangelical history has often been told as the story of Whitefield, Wesley, Edwards, Newton, Wilberforce, Finney, Moody and Graham. Yet the racial politics of each of these figures points us to a wider story, and to the rise and challenge of black evangelicalism. Retrieving that history and making it more widely known is an urgent task.

---

91 John Piper, 'Martin Luther King Changed My World and I Am Thankful' (21 January 2013), www.desiringgod.org (accessed 24 February 2018).
92 Rick Warren, 'My Ten Favorite Martin Luther King Quotes' (19 January 2015), www.facebook.com/pastorrickwarren (accessed 24 February 2018).
93 See for example, *Black Voices*, edited by Killingray and Edwards; Thabiti Anyabwile, *The Faithful Preacher: Recapturing the Vision of Three Pioneering African-American Pastors* (Wheaton, IL: Crossway, 2007); *Preaching with Sacred Fire: An Anthology of African American Sermons, 1650 to the Present*, edited by Martha Simmons (New York: Norton, 2010).
94 See, for example, David Hempton, *The Church in the Long Eighteenth Century* (London: I. B. Tauris, 2011), pp. 82–99.
95 J. Kameron Carter, *Race: A Theological Account* (New York: Oxford University Press, 2008); Willie Jennings, *The Christian Imagination: Theology and the Origins of Race* (New Haven, CT: Yale University Press, 2010).
96 Peter Heltzel, *Jesus and Justice: Evangelicals, Race and American Politics* (New Haven, CT: Yale University Press, 2009).

13

EVANGELICALS AND GENDER

Linda Wilson

Gender may be defined as 'the way any given society believes women and men ought to be and should behave, that is, what is properly feminine and masculine',[1] whereas 'sex' refers to physical characteristics. Implicit in this definition is the assumption that gender is socially constructed and that what it means to be female or male varies in different cultures and over time. If people believe that the woman should be a homemaker, for instance, there is usually a parallel assumption that the man should be the breadwinner: thus both of their lives are shaped by the expectations of church or society, which may or may not suit either of them personally. In recent years, following the suggestion of Joan Scott, gender has come to be accepted as a category of historical analysis.[2] Although initially rather slow to make gender an integral part of its investigations and discussion, religious history has now made up for this deficiency with several useful studies.[3] This chapter, drawing on these studies and supplementing them with new research, will explore some aspects of evangelical attitudes in this area.

Gender history is not identical with women's history, but has developed alongside it, including consideration of the roles of both sexes as they have been shaped by history and culture. It should be noted, however, that because most of the attention of scholars until recent years has been focused on the experiences of men, in discussing gender it is often women's lives that are given more prominence, in order to redress the balance: an issue of gender justice.[4] This is to some extent the case here. For instance, in discussing questions of who is entitled to preach or to lead churches, the emphasis is on women, who were often discriminated against, yet found opportunities to flourish within evangelicalism. Whilst much of the material in this chapter relates to British and to a lesser extent American evangelicalism, there has been some integration

---

1 Fran Porter, *Changing Women, Changing Worlds: Evangelical Women in Church, Community and Politics* (Belfast: Blackstaff Press, 2002), p. 3.
2 The classic paper on this is Joan Scott, 'Gender: A Useful Category of Historical Analysis', *American Historical Review* vol. 91 (December 1986), 1053–75.
3 See Sue Morgan, 'Introduction: Women, Religion and Feminism: Past, Present and Future Perspectives', in *Women, Religion and Feminism in Britain, 1759–1900*, edited by Sue Morgan (Basingstoke: Palgrave Macmillan, 2002), pp. 1–19. Callum G. Brown, *The Death of Christian Britain: Understanding Secularisation, 1800–2000* (London: Routledge, 2001) is a good example of a recent religious history which incorporates gender into its analysis.
4 Porter, *Changing Women, Changing Worlds*, p. 3.

of examples from other parts of the evangelical world, and in particular a study of a network of churches in contemporary India. Despite being of necessity a limited exploration, this chapter aims to highlight the key issues and point the way to opportunities for further research.

Over the years, there has been a surprisingly broad spectrum of theology and practice regarding being female and male within evangelical denominations and churches. At one end of the spectrum is a conservative definition of female and male roles, restricting the opportunities available for women. This has sometimes reflected, and even helped to shape, society's notions of correct gender behaviour, as in sections of nineteenth-century Britain and America, whilst at other times it led to conservative attitudes opposed to trends in society, as in fundamentalist churches in parts of the United States in the late twentieth century. The other end of the spectrum is a deliberate challenge to established ideas of female and male in society as well as church, seen especially in Biblical Feminism since the 1970s. In between these two extremes a wide range of evangelical understandings of what it means to be female or male is found.

Separate spheres and the domestication of evangelicalism

Towards the conservative end of the spectrum, we find the idea of 'separate spheres', often associated with the nineteenth century, in which women occupied the private, and men the public sphere. During this period, women were frequently regarded as comparatively weak physically and intellectually, expressive emotionally and superior spiritually, with 'a fibre more in her heart and a cell less in her brain', a common phrase denounced by Catherine Booth in correspondence with her future husband William.[5] Evangelicalism has been implicated in England in the development of the middle classes and its accompanying domestic ideology. Davidoff and Hall explored these ideas in their seminal book, *Family Fortunes* (1987), on the Victorian middle classes.[6] During this period, increased industrialization and the separation of workplace and living accommodation accelerated the process of separation. Some historians, for instance Amanda Vickery, have challenged this thesis and argued that the origins of separate spheres were earlier.[7] Others such as Robert Shoemaker take a middle line, noting 'an increasing stress on the moral importance of women's domestic role' between 1750 and 1850.[8] Despite the difficulties over the concept, it is a useful tool for considering evangelical identity at this time.[9]

The Anglican writer and founder of Sunday schools, Hannah More, linked in friendship to the Clapham Sect, an evangelical group which included William Wilberforce, wrote tracts to reinforce specific class and gender roles[10] as did Congregationalist Sarah Ellis in her writings including *Women of England* (1839).[11] These female evangelicals helped to influence and shape the ideal of women as the spiritual guardians of the home, and ultimately of the nation, with men as providers and protectors. In a parallel development in nineteenth-century America,

---

5 Quoted in F. de L. Booth-Tucker, *The Short Life of Catherine Booth the Mother of the Salvation Army* (London: Forgotten Books, 2013), p. 44.
6 Leonore Davidoff and Catherine Hall, *Family Fortunes: Men and Women of the English Middle Class, 1780–1850* (London: Routledge, 1987).
7 Amanda Vickery, 'Golden Age to Separate Spheres? A Review of the Categories and Chronology of Women's History', *Historical Journal* vol. 36 (1993), 383–414.
8 Robert B. Shoemaker, *Gender in English Society 1650–1850: The Emergence of Separate Spheres?* (London: Longman, 1998), p. 32.
9 See Linda Wilson, *Constrained by Zeal: Female Spirituality amongst Nonconformists, 1825–75* (Carlisle: Paternoster, 2000).
10 Anne Stott, *Hannah More: The First Victorian* (Oxford: Oxford University Press, 2003).
11 Sarah Ellis, *The Women of England* (London: Fisher, 1839).

there was an increasing tendency to see religion as part of the private, female realm, with women being more spiritual than men. According to Ruether and Keller, in America during this period 'Christian categories – sacrificial love, servanthood, altruism and even redemptive grace – came to be identified as characteristically feminine. Piety, domesticity and submissiveness were also seen as essential to woman's nature and contrary to man's'.[12] This process, they argued, strengthened the dominant social ideology and constrictive gender roles.

People who held to this conservative understanding believed that Christianity was equally beneficial to women as well as men: this was rarely a conscious patriarchy. For instance, in a series of sermons on 'Female Piety', published in 1852, John Angell James, the Congregational minister of Carrs Lane, Birmingham, reinforced an evangelical version of Coventry Patmore's famous poem, 'The Angel in the House'.[13] His sermons were influential in America as well as his home country of England.[14] James argued that Christianity was beneficial to women, with Jesus being their 'Emancipator for this present world, as well as their Saviour for the next' and that the Bible should be loved by women 'as the charter of thy liberty'.[15] Evangelical marriage, he argued, should be a companionate marriage, in which the wife is the husband's 'constant companion'[16]. Yet her role is merely supportive: 'man shines as the primary planet, reflecting the glory of God, who is the orb of the moral universe; and woman shines as the satellite of man', her role being subjection to her husband, living 'to repair the wrong she has inflicted on man' through the fall.[17] Her area of influence is limited: 'HOME is the proper scene of woman's action and influence'.[18] This statement reflected the mixed message that many evangelicals lived with and the gender roles that, for the most part, they unthinkingly accepted.

In this evangelical understanding of male and female, women were both more culpable for the fall than men and yet more spiritual than they were. James believed that the larger numbers of women in evangelical congregations was evidence of this greater sensitivity to spiritual things.[19] This framework at once elevated women and limited them to a specific, nurturing role. James was very clear that it was wrong to remove the 'line of demarcation' between male and female roles, arguing that neither 'reason nor Christianity invites woman to the professor's chair, nor conducts her to the bar, nor makes her welcome to the pulpit'.[20] These beliefs were rooted in his understanding of Scripture, including the Pauline injunctions about the role of women in church and in home. He did, however, encourage women to be active in the third sphere of church, undertaking tasks such as distributing tracts and visiting the sick, as long as this did not conflict with their home duties.[21] Despite what James believed about freedom, his was a restrictive view of gender identity. He did not develop his understanding of women's role, unlike the Baptist writer William Landels, who between two publications, one in 1859 and the second in 1871, changed his attitude. Although Landels still expected women to become wives

---

12 *Women and Religion in America, volume 1: The Nineteenth Century*, edited by Rosemary Radford Ruether and Rosemary Skinner Keller (San Francisco, CA: Harper & Row, 1981), p. ix.
13 John Angell James, *Female Piety: or, The Young Woman's Friend and Guide Through Life to Immortality* (London: Hamilton, Adams, 1852); 'The Angel in the House', in *The Poems of Coventry Patmore*, edited by Frederick Page (London, 1949), p. 89.
14 David W. Bebbington, *The Dominance of Evangelicalism: The Age of Spurgeon and Moody* (Leicester: Inter-Varsity Press, 2005), p. 202.
15 James, *Female Piety*, p. 23.
16 James, *Female Piety*, p. 56.
17 James, *Female Piety*, p. 55.
18 James, *Female Piety*, p. 58.
19 James, *Female Piety*, pp. 16–17.
20 James, *Female Piety*, pp. 61–2.
21 James, *Female Piety*, pp. 126, 129, 133–4.

and mothers, in the later publication he supported the Married Women's Property Act and suffrage for female heads of households.[22] Evangelical views of the respective roles of women and men were slowly shifting.

The home and male evangelical identity

To divide public and private clearly into male and female domains, however, is too crude a separation. As John Tosh has asserted, during the Victorian period in England, evangelicalism was 'essentially a *domestic* religion' in which evangelical male identity, too, was rooted in the home.[23] During the mid-nineteenth century in England, Tosh argued, domesticity was 'central to masculinity' in a way that was not true to the same extent before or since.[24] He noted that the middle decades of the nineteenth century were years of peace, and that men no longer expected to 'be called to a life of adventure as soldier, sailor, emigrant or frontiersman'.[25] Instead their identity was linked to domesticity, professional or entrepreneurial success, and one could add for evangelicals, active church involvement. Even before this period, a love of domesticity was demonstrated by evangelical men, notably seen in the study by Anne Stott of William Wilberforce, his family and the other key families of the Clapham Sect. Stott noted that these men 'drew their emotional sustenance from family intimacy and close friendships'.[26] Davidoff and Hall, too, discovered that men's lives during these years were built on domestic foundations, noting that 'Evangelical manhood, with its stress on self-sacrifice and influence, came dangerously close to embracing "feminine" qualities'.[27] Men, as portrayed in Patmore's poem 'The Angel in the House', were second-class citizens spiritually.[28] It has been argued convincingly that this famous poem reflected a contemporary crisis of masculinity as well as commenting on the nature of femininity.[29] Research into evangelical obituaries has revealed that despite the claim that women were more spiritual during this period, accounts of personal devotions were largely undifferentiated by gender.[30] Both men and women's lives were shaped and restricted by this discourse.

After 1880, an expanding British empire opened fresh opportunities for men and they increasingly delayed marriage in favour of the experiences this provided, a situation reflected in a new form of literature, adventure stories, which appeared in the 1880s.[31] As Tosh has argued, in this period 'Empire was actively embraced by young men as a *means* of evading or postponing the claims of domesticity'.[32] One evangelical version of masculinity from this period is found in a series of biographies by the Baptist Marianne Farningham, who under the pseudonym of Eva Hope, wrote about men as varied as General Gordon, Charles Spurgeon and Abraham Lincoln.

---

22 Jennifer Lloyd, *Women and the Shaping of British Methodism: Persistent Preachers, 1807–1907* (Manchester: Manchester University Press, 2009), p. 200.
23 John Tosh, *A Man's Place: Masculinity and the Middle-Class Home in Victorian England* (New Haven, CT: Yale University Press, 2007), p. 5.
24 Tosh, *A Man's Place*, p. 1.
25 Tosh, *A Man's Place*, p. 7.
26 Anne Stott, *Wilberforce: Family and Friends* (Oxford: Oxford University Press, 2012), p. 4.
27 Davidoff and Hall, *Family Fortunes*, p. 111.
28 Patmore, 'Angel in the House', pp. 89–90.
29 Carol Christ, 'Victorian Masculinity and the Angel in the House', in *A Widening Sphere: Changing Roles of Victorian Women*, edited by Martha Vicinus (London, IN: Indiana University Press, 1977), pp. 146–62.
30 Wilson, *Constrained by Zeal*, Ch. 5.
31 Tosh, *A Man's Place*, p. 174.
32 Tosh, *A Man's Place*, p. 177.

The version of masculinity she hoped her male readers would emulate included singleness of purpose; diligence and self-help; a strong common sense; kindness and love to others, and godliness. These, she asserted, were the ingredients 'out of which all heroes are made'.[33] She approved of Gordon when he wrote: 'I prefer life amidst sorrows, if those sorrows are inevitable, to a life spent in inaction'.[34] This was not just a male characteristic, however. Both her biographies and her journalistic writing reveal that Farningham had a strong view about the necessity of work, whether paid or unpaid, as the primary way of serving God.[35] Identifying characteristics specific to evangelical masculinity is complex, and much remains to be discovered.

Opportunities for women within the 'third sphere'

Within this limited framework of separate spheres, many lay people, particularly women, found opportunities in the 'third sphere' of churches which were denied them in society at large,[36] for instance through Sunday-school teaching, fund-raising for missions or church buildings, participating in prayer meetings or leading Methodist classes.[37] In a study of English evangelical obituaries, it was discovered that as many as 60 per cent of the Congregationalist women and 33 per cent of the Baptist women studied had taught Sunday school at some stage in their lives.[38] In New Zealand, some missionary wives 'were able to manipulate the "separate spheres" ideology for their own purposes'.[39] Elizabeth Colenso (1821–1904) is one such example. Born and brought up in New Zealand, by the age of nineteen she was running her own school. Her marriage to William Colenso who worked for the Church Missionary Society (CMS) was unhappy, but she continued to teach and after separating from her husband was appointed by the Society as a teacher in Taupiri.[40] It seems that in a missionary situation separate spheres were subverted more readily. In the second half of the nineteenth century, faith missions such as the China Inland Mission provided opportunities for the first time for single women to go abroad in their own right, evangelizing and church planting.[41] By the late nineteenth century, 60 per cent of US missionaries were women.[42] At the same time, within America there was 'an explosion of women's religious involvement'[43] which for some women led to opportunities to break out from traditional roles. Women were converted through the revivals and in turn sought to convert others, partly through prayer meetings linked to revival campaigns.[44] In Baptist churches affected by revival, and which believed in congregational independence, women could find new opportunities including speaking, whilst men 'found a depth of caring relationships that

---

33 Eva Hope, *Life of General Gordon* (London: Walter Scott, 1901), p. 362.
34 Hope, *Life of General Gordon*, p. 172.
35 Eva Hope, *Grace Darling, Heroine of the Farne Islands* (London: Walter Scott, 1875), pp. 1–15; Marianne Farningham, *Life Sketches and Echoes from the Valley* (London: James Clarke, 1861), p. 66.
36 Wilson, *Constrained by Zeal*, pp. 210–11.
37 Wilson, *Constrained by Zeal*, Ch. 7.
38 Wilson, *Constrained by Zeal*, pp. 190–1.
39 Cathy Ross, 'Separate Spheres or Shared Dominions?', *Transformation* vol. 23 (2006), 228–35.
40 Ross, 'Separate Spheres', 230–2.
41 Bebbington, *The Dominance of Evangelicalism*, p. 178.
42 Mark Noll, *A History of Christianity in the United States and Canada* (Grand Rapids, MI: Eerdmans, 1992), p. 294.
43 *Women and Religion*, edited by Ruether and Keller, p. viii.
44 Martha Tomhave Blauvelt, 'Women and Revivalism', in *Women and Religion*, edited by Ruether and Keller, p. 7.

had previously been the preserve of women'.[45] Occasionally, women such as Margaret Newton Van Cott, or Sojourner Truth, became directly concerned in preaching revival.[46]

There were also major developments in philanthropy, as middle-class women needed projects on which to focus their energy and paid work was out of the question for most of them.[47] However, although philanthropic work in their local communities took women outside the private sphere, there was rarely any challenge to the accepted primarily domestic understanding of women's identity. The designation of these women as 'Angels out of the House' is largely accurate.[48] Shoemaker notes 'in its heightened estimate of feminine worth and its introduction of traditionally feminine concerns into the public sphere, evangelicalism was an important development'.[49]

Women preachers

Because the Bible is central to evangelical identity, biblical interpretation is also part of the story of gender relations. Scriptural interpretation became more pertinent when women sensed a calling to lead and to preach, within church cultures which valued close interpretation of the biblical text and justified actions from that text. Mark Noll has suggested that conservative understandings of Scripture, combined with an experiential faith, could clash with patriarchy and open up possibilities to women, if, for instance, texts like Galatians 3: 28 ('there is neither male nor female') were taken literally[50] and privileged over other, restrictive texts, such as those on which John Angell James based his arguments. Often, however, the apparently restrictive Pauline texts were either ignored or re-interpreted by women preachers and their male supporters. For instance, Ann Swales (1814–1895), a Primitive Methodist local preacher, wrote in her private notebook:

> Tell me that it is wrong for a woman to preach and I will say it is right. God has told me hundreds of times. If a man was drowning and a female threw the rope, would he not seize it to save his life because it was a female? . . . Come then men of God and women, come with all your faith and pray. Preach the gospel females. Preach if you can be the means of one soul being saved.[51]

She made no reference to 'women should remain silent' (1 Corinthians 14: 34) or 'a woman should learn in quietness' (1 Timothy 2: 11); merely sidestepping these problematic texts. When Swales wrote these words in 1875, she had been preaching for about twenty years. The Primitives did have a theology that allowed this, although by this stage in the century there were no female itinerant preachers, only unpaid local ones.[52] The Primitives, along with the Bible

---

45 Mark Noll, *American Evangelical Christianity: An Introduction* (Oxford: Blackwell, 2001), p. 84.
46 Blauvelt, 'Women and Revivalism', pp. 8–11.
47 Frank Prochaska, *Women and Philanthropy in Nineteenth-Century England* (Oxford: Clarendon Press, 1980).
48 Elizabeth K. Helsinger, Robert L. Sheets and William Veeder, *The Woman Question* (Chicago, IL: University of Chicago Press, 1983), pp. xiv–xv.
49 Shoemaker, *Gender in English Society*, p. 50.
50 Noll, *American Evangelical Christianity*, p. 82.
51 Manuscript notebook of Ann Swales edited by her great-granddaughter Marjorie Waine, p. 2. Oxford, Wesley Historical Society Library: B/SWALES/Waine.
52 Wesley Swift traced forty women itinerant preachers in the denomination, but all started their ministry prior to 1844. See his article, 'The Women Itinerant Preachers of Early Methodism', *Proceedings of the*

Christians, were the only Methodist denominations after John Wesley's death to encourage female preaching. The whole situation was complicated by Wesley's ambiguity over the issue. Despite believing that the Bible taught that women should not be preachers, or 'usurp authority over a man' (1 Timothy 2: 12), Wesley came to believe that some women had 'an extraordinary call'. Thus in 1787 he sent Sarah Mallet 'a note giving her authorization to preach by order of the Conference: "We ... have no objection to her being a preacher in our connexion, so long as she preaches the Methodist doctrines, and attends to our discipline." '[53] However, such opportunities did not last long after Wesley's death, and in 1803 and 1804 the Methodist Conference passed resolutions which effectively banned women preaching. Ann Swales knew that by preaching she was challenging established gender roles within Christian ministry. It is interesting that her husband drove her to her preaching appointments: clearly he supported her. There is also no indication that she wanted to upset gender relations between men and women in other spheres of life: like other Methodist women preachers, she was primarily concerned with conversion.

Challenging the gender norms: limited subversion

There was a clearer challenge to gender roles in the life of Sarah Terrett, a local preacher with the Bible Christian Church in Bedminster, Bristol, whose marriage to William, a butcher, provides an interesting study of gender relations.[54] Sarah was an activist who launched a temperance movement, the White Ribbon Army, in 1878. She became known as its general while her husband William acted as lieutenant-general, her second-in-command. At the yearly anniversary meetings held from 1882 onwards in the Colston Hall,[55] a sizeable Bristol concert hall, Sarah presided and gave the motivational speech whilst William had the role of reading a report on the previous year's activities and developments.[56] Their relationship and respective roles are complex: as well as being 'general', Sarah was a homemaker, a mother and a provider of hospitality, but like many with working-class origins, she was also involved in the family business. As her father was also a butcher, she would have known the business well. In their marriage Sarah appears to have been the stronger character, with a final say in some financial transactions. She committed her organization to buy the old Bible Christian chapel in Bedminster to use as a Mission Hall for her temperance movement, only informing William a few days later.[57] Yet William was a significant man in his own right, running a successful business and becoming a city councillor.[58] Sarah and William Terrett are an example of what might be called 'limited subversion' of gender norms in which, by their behaviour or beliefs, women and men challenge the accepted standards of female and male behaviour.

Wesley Historical Society vol. 28 (March 1952), 89–94; vol. 29 (December 1953), 76–83. Also see Lloyd, *Women and the Shaping of British Methodism*, p. 121.

53 Lloyd, *Women and the Shaping of British Methodism*, p. 36.
54 See Linda Wilson, 'Sarah Terrett, Katherine Robinson and Edith Pearce: Three Nonconformist Women and Public Life in Bristol, 1870–1910', in *Grounded in Grace: Essays to Honour Ian M. Randall*, edited by Pieter L. Lalleman, Peter J. Morden and Anthony R. Cross (London and Oxford: Spurgeon's College and the Baptist Historical Society, 2013), pp. 118–32.
55 F. W. Bourne, *Ready in Life and Death: Brief Memorials of Mrs S. M. Terrett* (London: Bible Christian Book Room, 1893), pp. 78–9.
56 For example, *Bristol Mercury*, 28 November 1882.
57 Bourne, *Ready in Life and Death*, pp. 54, 153.
58 M. J. Crossley Evans, 'Christian Missionary Work Among the Seamen and Dock Workers of Bristol, 1820–1914', in *Historic Churches and Church Life in Bristol*, edited by Joseph Bettey (Bristol: Bristol and Gloucestershire Archaeological Society, 2001), p. 178; *Bristol Mercury*, 2 November 1882.

Others challenged the existing situation more directly. Around the same time as Ann Swales was writing in her notebooks and Sarah Terrett was developing her temperance campaign, Catherine and William Booth were launching the Salvation Army, in which there were opportunities for women as well as laymen to be actively involved. Based on Catherine Booth's pioneering arguments from Scripture for the ministry of women, the 'lasses' of the Salvation Army were involved in the work of the Mission from the start and continued to preach and hold leadership roles as it developed. In 1881 a small book authored by William Booth, with arguments based on exegesis from Catherine and others, dealt with the difficult text in St Paul's first letter to the Corinthians, that women should keep silent in church (1 Corinthians 14: 34), by arguing that it referred to debates, not preaching. He then discussed examples of women leaders and preachers in the Bible, before quoting Galatians 3: 28 'there is neither male nor female, but all are one in Christ Jesus'.[59] They were not as equal as has sometimes been claimed, with General Booth always having some ambiguity towards the practical equality of women, and women who held leadership roles in the Army still being expected to fulfil their domestic duties.[60] However, the opportunities for women within the movement were still remarkable. Today the Army is notable for its consistent evangelical beliefs alongside an encouragement of women's ministry. The world leader of the Army from 1986 to 1993 was a woman, Eva Burroughs, and the British-based website explicitly states that the movement is gender-inclusive in leadership.[61]

This strand can also be traced in the twentieth century. Within the new Pentecostal churches and missions there were often ample opportunities for women to develop ministry, whether pastoring churches or becoming evangelists, although there could often still be expectations around traditional male/female roles. Pentecostalism, with its stress on the anointing of the Spirit as the main qualification for leadership, naturally lent itself to opportunities for women. The first Scandinavian Pentecostal missionaries were women, for instance.[62] Meanwhile in America, Aimee Semple McPherson (1890–1944) established and led a successful denomination, the Church of the Foursquare Gospel.[63] Kathryn Kuhlman (1907–1976) was another Pentecostal who came to prominence through a widespread healing ministry.[64] Anderson has noted that within Pentecostalism in the Global South there were opportunities for women, which 'accorded well with the prominence of women in many traditional religious rituals' in these countries.[65] For instance, Pandita Mary Ramabai, a prominent Indian reformer, helped to lead a Pentecostal revival in her country which took place before the famous events of Azusa Street.[66] Ramabai was a complex character, who kept her Brahmin identity after her conversion, and who had earlier formed a female religious community which 'experimented with new and enabling models of femininity'.[67] Women, like men, do not always fit neatly into categories in terms of their belief and practice.

---

59 Mark Eason, *Women in God's Army: Gender and Equality in the Early Salvation Army* (Waterloo: Wilfrid Laurier University Press, 2003), pp. 48–9.
60 Eason, *Women in God's Army*, pp. 54–5.
61 www.salvationarmy.org.uk/inclusion (accessed 24 February 2018).
62 Allan Anderson, 'The Vision of the Apostolic Faith: Early Pentecostalism and World Mission', *Svensk Missionstidskrift* vol. 97 (2009), 304.
63 Allan Anderson, *An Introduction to Pentecostalism: Global Charismatic Christianity* (Cambridge: Cambridge University Press, 2004), pp. 56–7.
64 See Edith L. Blumhofer, *Aimee Semple McPherson: Everybody's Sister* (Grand Rapids, MI: Eerdmans, 1993).
65 Anderson, *An Introduction to Pentecostalism*, p. 273.
66 Anderson, *An Introduction to Pentecostalism*, p. 173.
67 Parinitha Shetty, 'Christianity, Reform, and the Reconstitution of Gender: the Case of Pandita Mary

Within early fundamentalism, too, it is interesting to note that a conservative understanding of the Christian faith allowed challenges to gender roles. Christabel Pankhurst, for instance, never stopped being a feminist when she became a fundamentalist preacher.[68] However, a study of British fundamentalist publications revealed that whilst fundamentalism, like nineteenth-century evangelical churches, provided women with a 'third sphere', in which they 'facilitated prayer groups, participated in Bible schools ... organised meetings to promote the fundamentalist viewpoint, and sometimes spoke at such gatherings',[69] gender issues were of little interest to either female or male fundamentalists. The fight against modernism always took centre stage. These early opportunities tended to be in tension with a fundamentalist approach to the interpretation of Scripture, and it is perhaps unsurprising that more recently United States fundamentalism has retreated and supported conventional gender identities.

Hermeneutics and gender in the late twentieth century

The final decades of the twentieth century saw a significant change within evangelicalism in the West, reflecting and responding to wider shifts in society at large, including attitudes to gender roles. Part of this response was a new movement known as Biblical Feminism. By the early 1970s, there was some openness within evangelicalism to new ideas emerging from the challenges of the 1960s. As Brian Stanley has helpfully outlined, changes in attitudes to the roles of women and men were intertwined with developments in understanding and applying the Bible, and in particular a move from traditional interpretation to the use of hermeneutics as a tool for understanding.[70] Pamela Cochran has noted of American Biblical Feminists, they 'have used modern hermeneutical methods based on a modified definition of inerrancy' in order to reinterpret biblical passages concerning women.[71] This can probably be dated from the Chicago Declaration of Evangelical Social Concern in 1973, which although primarily about social action, included a statement that: 'We acknowledge that we have encouraged men to prideful domination and women to irresponsible passivity. So we call both men and women to mutual submission and active discipleship'.[72]

While some of the debate was focused on the question of women's ordination in various denominations, there were broader issues to do with spheres of life. In America the Evangelical Women's Caucus was formed in January 1975, drawing support from several denominations in the US and Canada, committed to seeking what they believed was biblical equality. By the following year the influence of this Biblical Feminism movement within evangelicalism was being felt across many churches. Key leaders included Nancy Hardesty and Letha Scanzoni. Ten years later in Britain, the evangelical academic Elaine Storkey published a thoughtful and influential analysis called *What's Right with Feminism* (1985).[73] Women and men who believed

---

Ramabai', *Journal of Feminist Studies in Religion* vol. 28 (Spring 2012), 27. 'Pandita' is a title relating to her mastery of Sanskrit texts.
68 Timothy Larsen, *Christabel Pankhurst: Fundamentalism in Coalition* (Woodbridge: Boydell Press, 2002).
69 Linda Wilson, 'Women, Men and Fundamentalism in England during the 1920s and 30s', in *Evangelicalism and Fundamentalism in the United Kingdom during the Twentieth Century*, edited by David W. Bebbington and David Ceri Jones (Oxford: Oxford University Press, 2013), pp. 132–50.
70 Brian Stanley, *The Global Diffusion of Evangelicalism: The Age of Billy Graham and John Stott* (Leicester: Inter-Varsity Press, 2013), p. 212.
71 Pamela D. H. Cochran, *Evangelical Feminism: A History* (New York: New York University Press, 2005), p. 191.
72 Quoted in Cochran, *Evangelical Feminism*, p. 14.
73 Elaine Storkey, *What's Right with Feminism* (London: SPCK, 1985).

that women should be encouraged to develop their gifts and abilities and that men should actively encourage them, sharing domestic duties to enable this, based their understanding on certain understandings of biblical texts.[74] Conservative Biblical Feminists focused their attention on re-interpreting the key texts about women, using a hermeneutical approach which paid attention to the culture of the time and the specific audience addressed.[75]

A study of gender in Christian magazines

Such discussions about the roles of women and men in the light of changes in society and fresh understandings of Scripture played out in Christian magazines. A study of two representative publications from 1976, when much of the discussion was going on, is illuminating. *Christianity Today* is an American evangelical magazine, published fortnightly, including a variety of articles about topics of interest to evangelicals, book reviews, news and letters, whilst *Renewal* was a British magazine which reached the new charismatic constituency in the country, eventually being absorbed into *Premier Christianity,* now a major British evangelical publication. In 1976, before the words 'charismatic evangelical' were usually paired together, *Renewal* included contributors from Roman Catholic and High Anglican backgrounds, but it was predominantly evangelical. These two magazines provide a useful comparison. It is interesting to note that in 1976 *Christianity Today* had more articles by women than *Renewal*, although men were still in the majority. Amongst the female contributions to *Christianity Today* was a regular column by Edith Schaeffer, wife of evangelical thinker Francis Schaeffer and co-founder of L'Abri. There were also frequent pieces on literature by Cheryl Forbes, editorial associate.[76] An edition focusing on children's books had a higher percentage of female contributors, as might be expected, and there were letters and occasional book reviews by other women. Another edition carried articles related to the debate around women's roles, primarily in home, society and marriage, rather than about ordination. There was reporting on the Evangelical Women's Caucus, which included articles from people involved in evangelical feminism, Letha and John Scanzoni. These, and a book co-authored by Scanzoni and Nancy Hardesty, provoked further letters and articles.

In *Renewal*, however, only two articles were by women, and only one of those was related to gender issues. Most of the focus in this magazine was on the charismatic movement, and there was much less on literature, politics and biblical interpretation than in *Christianity Today*. Of the two articles, one was about reinvigorating dying churches,[77] and only one, 'Work, women and God' by Jenny Cooke, dealt with gender issues, although Frank Lake discussed the question of 'Same-sex loving' (April / May and June / July) and the topic of marriage in August / September. *Renewal* was clearly not as interested in feminism as the American magazine, perhaps reflecting the issues of significance to the Christian reading public in the two countries at the time. Most of the articles were about the spread of the renewal movement, which not surprisingly was the clear focus of all the issues. Yet the language in *Renewal* was occasionally surprisingly inclusive, referring to both men and women.[78] Jenny Cooke's article on 'Work, women and God' in *Renewal*, whilst insisting on the importance of listening to the Spirit,

---

74 Cochran has explored the history of this movement in *Evangelical Feminism*, p. 191. The movement eventually split over a variety of issues including attitudes to homosexuality.
75 Cochran, *Evangelical Feminism*, p. 49.
76 Cochran, *Evangelical Feminism*, p. 14.
77 Gillian Newton, 'Raise the Dead', *Renewal* (December 1976 / January 1977), 23–4.
78 *Renewal* (June / July 1976), 23.

was biased towards the wife staying at home rather than working. In this, as well as reflecting middle-class values, her article was very much of its time. Families where the wife had to work to make ends meet were dismissed in a sentence.[79]

Christianity Today's stated approach to Scripture was infallibility and inerrancy, and in various articles the editor, Harold Lindsell (who in 1976 published *The Battle for the Bible* in support of his position) and contributors were anxious to preserve these aspects of evangelical faith, whilst encouraging dialogue with evangelicals who took slightly different views. This open approach led to articles from varying perspectives including, in June 1976, one by Letha Scanzoni entitled 'How to live with a liberated wife' and another by her husband John on the topic of 'Assertiveness for Christian Women'.[80] The June editorial urged people to 'ponder their words' and the August edition carried two letters responding to the articles from people who had done just that, a male correspondent who wrote 'I agree with its main thesis' and a female one who clearly did not.[81] The debate has continued in various forms in the decades since, leading to a polarization between evangelicals whose reinterpretation of Scripture has led to a new understanding of the gender balance between women and men, and others who have maintained a conservative interpretation. These two camps are usually known respectively as egalitarian and complementarian. Christian magazines provide a useful insight into the understandings of the time.

A direct challenge to the status quo was echoed some years later in the British evangelical magazine *Premier Childrenswork*, in an article entitled 'Neither Male nor Female' in which Margaret Pritchard Houston, a children's and youth worker, presented 'a case for gender neutrality in children's ministry'. She argued against the simple stereotyping of girls and boys, suggesting that even in the patriarchal society in which the Bible was written, women and men were 'complex and multifaceted, and [Scripture] used both masculine and feminine imagery to describe everything from God to his people'. Houston suggested that, rather than stereotyping the sexes, the aim of Christians should be to create a church 'in which everyone is free to grow into their individual, complex selves, whatever combination of kindness and strength, stillness and noise that may be'. She hoped that evangelicals would be able to develop new forms of femininity and masculinity.[82]

Evangelical masculinity in the late twentieth and early twenty-first centuries

The increasing awareness of the need for gender justice for women has contributed to a perceived 'feminization' of the church, spirituality and discipleship, leading to a backlash in favour of a more masculine spirituality. Since the 1990s, various groups and movements have developed with a focus on specific masculine identities. One of these is Promise Keepers (PK), primarily in America and Canada although it has had a smaller following in other countries. PK was for a while the 'dominant evangelical men's movement' in America, with a numerical highpoint in 1996.[83] Operating through large gatherings, PK championed responsible manhood and encouraged men to take up leadership in their families and communities and be faithful

---

79 *Renewal* (October / November 1976), 22–4.
80 *Christianity Today* no. 18 (4 June 1976), 16–8.
81 *Christianity Today* no. 22 (6 August 1976), 22–3.
82 Margaret Pritchard Houston, 'Neither Male nor Female', *Premier Childrenswork* vol. 1 (April / May 2015), 17-19.
83 Sally K. Gallagher and Sabria L. Wood, 'Godly Manhood Going Wild? Transformations in Conservative Protestant Masculinity', *Sociology of Religion* vol. 66 (2005), 136.

husbands in obedience to Jesus.[84] Linked with a particular kind of hierarchical marriage, it also represented a domesticated masculinity. Others have responded more directly to the concept of Biblical Feminism, including John Piper and Wayne Grudem, who edited *Recovering Biblical Manhood and Womanhood: A Response to Evangelical Feminism* (1991), the title itself declaring that they believed the approach of Cochran and others was, despite their claim, not biblical.[85] Indeed, the various contributors to the book were seeking to reclaim the conservative stance on women's role and identity as the only biblical view. D. A. Carson, in a chapter called 'Silent in the Churches' analysed in detail various interpretations of 1 Corinthians 14: 33–6, where Paul stated that women should 'keep silent', coming to the conclusion that 'a strong case can be made for the view that Paul refused to permit any woman to enjoy a church-recognized teaching authority over men'.[86] In turn, moderate evangelicals responded to this book, such as Ronald Pierce, Rebecca Groothuis and Gordon Fee in *Discovering Biblical Equality* (2004).[87] This serves to highlight the fact that given the variety of interpretive approaches to this and other texts by evangelicals, there is unlikely ever to be agreement either over the meaning of these difficult passages, or over their significance.

Another approach is linked with the book *Wild at Heart* (2001) by American John Eldredge. His vision of masculinity, partly shaped in opposition to PK is, as Gallagher and Wood point out, 'most emphatically not domestic', but is about being a warrior and having wilderness experiences.[88] 'Ransomed Heart', Eldredge's website, offers men 'Battle, Beauty, Adventure'. Women, by contrast, are seen as passive and in need of rescuing and being given the opportunity 'to be Romanced'.[89] Gender identity here is polarized, with little middle ground. Eldredge's book sold over 200,000 copies the year after publication but has been criticized on several grounds. Gallagher and Wood undertook a survey of the responses of a cross-section of church members to *Wild at Heart*, which illustrates some of these objections. While some men found the book helpful, several respondents noted that it was aimed at white, middle-class men who have the opportunity and resources to pursue wilderness adventures.[90] In addition, it was suggested that Eldredge paid too little attention to the need for transformation and redemption. After assessing their interviews, Gallagher and Wood concluded that 'the range of masculinities and femininities among ordinary believers is much broader than those presented in most conservative Protestant family advice literature', a similar conclusion to that reached by studying gender and evangelicalism in the nineteenth century.[91]

Other evangelical groups aimed at men include, in South Africa and Australia the 'Mighty Men Movement' started by Angus Buchan; in America, 'Church for men' founded by David Murrow and 'Godmen' by Brad Stine; and in Britain, 'Christian Vision for Men' (CVM), which aims to equip churches to specifically evangelize men. An article by Carl Beech, until February 2015 the director of CVM, claimed that: 'Men seek adventure and challenge and whilst love and compassion are important traits for men, the wild and adventurous aspects of their personalities can

---

84 https://promisekeepers.org (accessed 24 February 2018).
85 *Recovering Biblical Manhood and Womanhood: A Response to Evangelical Feminism*, edited by John Piper and Wayne Grudem (Wheaton, IL: Crossway Books, 1991).
86 D. A. Carson, 'Silent in the Churches: On the Role of Women in 1 Corinthians 14:33B–36', in *Biblical Manhood and Womanhood*, edited by Piper and Grudem, pp. 133–44.
87 *Discovering Biblical Equality: Complementarity without Hierarchy*, edited by Ronald W. Pierce and Rebecca Merrill Groothuis (Leicester: Inter-Varsity Press, 2004).
88 Gallagher and Wood, 'Godly Manhood Going Wild?', 140.
89 http://www.ransomedheart.com (accessed 24 February 2018).
90 Gallagher and Wood, 'Godly Manhood Going Wild?', 146.
91 Gallagher and Wood, 'Godly Manhood Going Wild?', 156.

Evangelicals and gender

be completely starved in church'.[92] A male critique of the masculinity encouraged in these various organizations was made by Brandon O'Brien who argued that these movements do not take enough account of the need to be transformed, something which affects men as well as women, and that they leave women without the option to be full disciples. O'Brien observed that: 'We are most like Christ not when we win a fight, but when we suffer for righteousness' sake'.[93] The nature of evangelical masculinity, like femininity, is contested and fluid in the early twenty-first century.

Outside the West, it has been suggested that African churches, especially Pentecostal ones, work largely within a patriarchal framework. One church in Zambia, for instance, focuses on 'Biblical manhood' including 'male responsibility, male headship and self-control' in order to combat HIV, rather than aiming at 'a transformation of masculinities beyond patriarchy towards gender justice'.[94] The same phrase, 'gender justice', was used by an Indian woman writing about the need for change in her own country.[95] A study of one group of Indian churches demonstrates that some evangelicals there are working towards limited change in this area.

Beyond the West: an Indian study

As noted earlier, different understandings of gender may overlap and this is evident in a recent study of the Victory Churches of India (VCI) network, an 'apostolic and prophetic church planting movement'.[96] It has been asserted that in general, 'the Indian Church is a patriarchal church', despite the presence of some significant female leaders. The same can be said of Indian society as a whole.[97] Given this context, the VCI website carries a significant statement: 'The strongest point in the Victory Churches is the empowerment of the women folk. Women play a vital role in the building up of any society, ethnic group or nation'.[98] VCI, which has recognizably evangelical and Pentecostal beliefs and practice, started with one church in Agra in the 1970s and is now active in eleven regions, including in social care,[99] with over 125 churches.[100] The founders and leaders of the network, Dr Jey and Pastor Lizy Jeyaseelan are the senior leaders, with Dr Jey the overall leader.[101] Churches are grouped in clusters under the leadership of regional overseers, all of whom are male.

How does the claim to female empowerment within these churches work out in practice? A survey was undertaken at the annual VCI leadership conference in February 2015, and resulted in fifty-four useable questionnaires, thirty-five men and nineteen women, a healthy representation of a cross-section of the conference. Out of the thirty-five men, four were regional overseers, fourteen pastors, two evangelists (trainee pastors), and the rest had a variety

---

92 https://www.cvm.org.uk/why-mens-ministry (accessed 24 February 2018).
93 Brandon O'Brien, 'A Jesus for Real Men: What the New Masculinity Movement Got Wrong', *Christianity Today* vol. 52 (April 2008), 52-3.
94 Adriaan S. van Klinken, 'Theology, Gender Ideology and Masculinity Politics: A Discussion on the Transformation of Masculinities as Envisioned by African Theologians and a Local Pentecostal Church', *Journal of Theology for Southern Africa* vol. 138 (November 2010), 3.
95 Evangeline Anderson-Rajkumar, 'Practicing Gender Justice as a Faith Mandate in India', *Studies in World Christianity* vol. 13 (2007), 47.
96 They are linked to Victory Churches International which is based in Canada, https://victoryint.org/ (accessed 24 February 2018).
97 Anderson-Rajkumar, 'Practicing Gender Justice as a Faith Mandate in India', 35, 37.
98 www.victorychurchesofindia.com/ministries.html (accessed 24 February 2018).
99 The social care is in partnership with The Bridge Trust Ltd, Bristol, thebridgetrustltd.org (accessed 24 February 2018).
100 Personal email from Dr Jey Jeyaseelan, 25 March 2015.
101 www.victorychurchesofindia.com/index.html (accessed 24 February 2018).

of roles, including worship leaders, musicians and a projector operator. A few just called themselves 'student' or 'believer'. Not all women married to pastors were themselves pastors: out of the sixteen female respondents who gave their role or job title, fourteen were leaders of some kind, four called themselves 'pastor', two 'assistant pastor', three 'leader', with one being a teacher, one a church administrator and pastor's wife, two worship leaders and three merely self-identifying as 'pastor's wife'.

Asked whether women should be encouraged to lead worship (which in this context means not leading a service, but leading the singing), 100 per cent of both sexes responded positively, with 47 per cent of the female respondents regularly leading worship, while 40 per cent of the men said women led worship at least once a month in their church. Similarly 93 per cent of respondents, 100 per cent of women and 89 per cent of men, thought women should be encouraged to preach, with 80 per cent of respondents saying that women regularly preached at their meetings, although in some cases this meant women's meetings or cell groups rather than Sunday services. One man said: 'Any anointed or gifted' woman could preach. Opportunities are clearly available for appropriately gifted women.

The pattern in VCI churches is for women who want and are able, to work with their husbands as co-pastor, with the man as senior pastor. One woman wrote: 'Yes! Because woman [sic] can do this. I have seen women pastors are doing well in their churches', whilst a male respondent stated clearly that: 'God has given the same anointing and also pastoral gift/calling to women as to men'. Women who work in this capacity within the VCI churches are ordained, just as the men are, supporting their claim to empower women.[102] The survey results indicated that this practice was accepted and supported within the churches: 95 per cent of the women and 91 per cent of the men, 93 per cent overall, believed that a woman could be a pastor. More than one used the biblical example of Deborah to support women's leadership roles. Interestingly, some of the comments made use of gender stereotypes to argue in favour of women taking up this caring, leadership role. One pastor said: 'Yes, women can be pastor if they are trained in the role. Because women are more caring and relational. Because women are more sensitive towards God's intuitions. And women are strong leader, they take care of House and can take care of House of God too [sic]'. Another man commented: 'Yes, in Jesus Christ no man or woman according to Gal 3: 28'. There is a clear belief in opportunities for women, despite the presence of some patriarchal assumptions and practices.

One woman's comment represents this situation: 'Woman can teach, pray, serve as usher or volunteer, and do all in church except be a senior most leader'. Surprisingly, despite this, 23 per cent of the men thought that a woman could be a pastor even if her husband was not. This open attitude to women's ministry was also reflected in attitudes to education and jobs, as would be expected from a largely middle-class Indian group, to whom education is extremely important, reflecting the surrounding culture. Asked whether education was equally important for women and men, 86 per cent of men and 89 per cent of the women replied that it was and many (although not all) of the respondents felt that it was important for a woman to have a good job and share in the financial provision for their family. Yet both these attitudes co-existed alongside a belief on the part of many respondents of specific, fairly conservative attitudes within the home and family. This is a church culture in which everyone marries – a man cannot become a VCI pastor until he is married, and marriages are arranged if necessary. The understanding of marriage is more complementarian than egalitarian. For instance, when asked: 'Is it acceptable for a man to be the main carer for the children while his wife earns?', 60 per cent of men and

---

102 Personal email from Dr Jey Jeyaseelan, 25 March 2015.

29 per cent of women, 57 per cent in total, said no and of those who said yes or 'depends', the majority applied it to specific circumstances such as illness or unemployment.

Thus, on the one hand there was a belief in equality when it came to spiritual gifts, roles in church and education, yet within the home gender roles were often differentiated: 'Husband: leadership. Wife: taking care' was one woman's response. Other comments reinforced this belief that the woman was usually seen as the main carer, with responsibility for cooking and housework (often employing others). These churches encourage a partnership in which there are often different roles, which are perceived to be the biblical norms. In the context of the current situation in India, women are well treated in these churches. Female infanticide is named and rejected,[103] and one VCI leader recently joined a protest march on behalf of women in his home city.[104] Within most of the VCI churches, therefore, women are encouraged to take roles including leading worship, pastoring other women and women's groups and where appropriate, working in partnership with their husbands in leading the church, although they are still expected to take the primary domestic role. Given the situation in India in general, whilst clearly more could be done to challenge some gender assumptions, the claim to 'empowerment' of women does have some substance.

Conclusion

It has been suggested that evangelicalism provides an ambiguous heritage for those wanting to challenge gender roles.[105] The call to activism and the imperative to seek conversions opened up opportunities for women, yet evangelicals were frequently influenced by an interpretation of Scripture perceiving women as dependent on men.[106] It is certainly the case that many evangelicals have believed, on biblical grounds, in a restricted role for women compared to that of men. At times conservative evangelicals have encouraged women in higher education and in substantial jobs, whilst restricting their roles within the church, and still keeping to a hierarchical view of marriage. Other evangelicals, however, especially since 1970, have believed that gender roles have been constrained by culture, and that a truer and more appropriate hermeneutic would allow women to take part in churches in an equal way to men.

It can, therefore, be seen from this study that there has been and still remains a wide spectrum of belief and practice within evangelicalism relating to gender roles. It has been suggested that 'gender justice should be the starting point for the church to be truly a church after the calling of Jesus Christ',[107] but not everyone understands the issues in that way. The ambiguity found in the early decades of the evangelical revival in Wesley's attitude to the roles of women and men can still be seen in the early decades of the twenty-first century, with even more diversity and variety. From so-called 'traditional' roles for men and women, and conservative/fundamentalist interpretation of biblical teaching, through to an inclusive evangelical feminism, it is clear that there are multiple evangelical approaches to gender. What they all share is the desire to root their beliefs and practices in the Bible, yet even here differing methods of interpretation and a wide range of hermeneutical understandings mean that agreement on how to do that, and what the results might mean, is still varied. Meanwhile, much research remains to be done into the lives of women and men within religious communities in general and evangelical ones in particular.

103 Personal conversation with church leaders in Gwalior, November 2008.
104 Personal information, March 2015.
105 Eason, *Women in God's Army*, pp. 21–31.
106 Eason, *Women in God's Army*, pp. 22, 28.
107 Anderson-Rajkumar, 'Practicing Gender Justice as a Faith Mandate in India', 47.

14
EVANGELICALS, CULTURE AND THE ARTS

Peter Webster

One evening in the early 1960s, Michael Saward, curate of St Margaret's Edgware, a thriving evangelical Anglican parish in north London, went to the Royal Festival Hall to hear the aged Otto Klemperer conduct Beethoven. As the Polish violinist Henryk Szeryng played the violin concerto, Saward unexpectedly found himself 'sitting (or so it seemed) a yard above my seat and experiencing what I can only describe as perhaps twenty minutes of orgasmic ecstasy. . . . Heaven had touched earth in the Royal Festival Hall'. Saward later came to view the experience as the third instalment in a 'trinity of revelation . . . a taste of [God's] work as creator of all that is beautiful, dynamic and worthy of praise . . . speaking of his majesty in the universe which he has made, goes on sustaining, and fills with his life force, the Holy Spirit, who draws out of humanity an infinite range of talent, skill and glorious creativity in artistic works'.[1]

Saward's words were part of a memoir and not a work of theology, but they challenge many received views of the relationship between evangelicals and the arts. Here was a graduate of the conservative theological college Tyndale Hall, Bristol, sitting in a concert hall, listening to a German Jew conduct a Polish Jew in a piece of secular music, wordless and without any explicit programmatic meaning, and yet attaching such significance to the experience. Even though, as we shall see, music was the art form most likely to be appreciated within the evangelical constituency, rarely does the historian find such a positive evaluation of the arts, their effects and their place in the theology of creation and of the work of the Holy Spirit.

The historian thinking about the relationship between evangelicals and culture must begin with finding stable definitions of both 'evangelical' and 'culture'. On the former, this chapter adopts the now famous 'Bebbington Quadrilateral', which identifies the four key features of evangelicalism as its activism, biblicism, conversionism and crucicentrism.[2] In the latter case, this chapter takes a catholic definition of culture, akin to that of the New Cultural History of recent years, which defines culture as the whole gamut of thought, feeling, practices and objects that humans produce, enact and consume collectively as a means of making sense of

---

1 Michael Saward, *A Faint Streak of Humility: An Autobiography* (Carlisle: Paternoster, 1999), pp. 183–4.
2 David Bebbington, *Evangelicalism in Modern Britain: A History from the 1730s to the 1980s* (London: Unwin Hyman, 1989), pp. 4–17.

themselves and their social surroundings.[3] Although the chapter is concerned primarily with the production, reception and performance of works of art among evangelicals, this cannot be understood outside the broader contours of their understanding of culture in the wider sense. In addition, this inclusive definition of culture clears the way for the consideration of forms of artistic production, such as heavy metal music or the 'Left Behind' novels, which are excluded by higher-pitched definitions of art.

Evangelical theologies of culture have at root been theologies of the Fall. A contrast may be drawn between evangelical understandings of the status of the created physical order which have been generally positive, and more pessimistic estimates of human potential. Whilst some have centred upon Paul's description of creation as frustrated by sin and groaning in anticipation of its redemption (Romans 8), the more resonant note has been that struck by the Psalmist, of the heavens telling the glory of God (Psalm 19). Creation was not so completely marred and defaced by sin that it could not be read as evidence of both God's creative work and his judgment on sin (in the form of natural disasters). Although this kind of natural theology was a poor relation to God's revelation through his Word, it was part of the family nonetheless.[4]

Evangelical understandings of humanity after the Fall may be contrasted with the catholic sense of human capability. Anglican Catholics in England in the twentieth century began to recover a much older incarnational sense, thought to have been lost since the Reformation, of human activity of all kinds as subordinate participation in the work of creation. Not only could the maker of a work of art communicate something to the viewer about the aspect of creation that he or she was representing; the act of making could also in some sense be co-operating with God.[5]

In contrast, the characteristic evangelical view of human capability has tended to be more pessimistic. Put most strongly, sin so defaced the divine image in human beings and so clouded their perception that their unaided attempts at understanding God and creation would be at best partial and incomplete, if not indeed corrupted and thus useless. Any attainment of virtue would be accidental, the product of external influence rather than any effort on the part of the individual. To attempt to create anything of beauty would be futile, and all participation in secular activity prone to the corruption of pride and self-interest.[6]

At base, this is the centre of gravity in what remains the most sustained historical treatment of the question of evangelicalism and culture in Britain, *Evangelicals and Culture* (1984) by Doreen Rosman. In the early nineteenth century, Rosman argued, many individual evangelicals were able to engage in the arts in positive ways, and indeed to delight in their performance. However, evangelical theology was never able to develop its instinctive rhetorical claim on the whole of human life into a framework that could comfortably encompass the arts. Unable to sanctify the senses, it was often forced instead to seek to subjugate them. Evangelicals 'were never confident to assimilate such worldly activities within the framework of their world-denying theology'.[7]

Rosman's study laid to rest lingering stereotypes of the evangelical as philistine and kill-joy – characterizations which owed much to the historiography of puritanism – and this chapter will

---

3 Lynn Hunt, 'Introduction: History, Culture and Text', in *The New Cultural History*, edited by Lynn Hunt (Berkeley, CA: University of California Press, 1989), pp. 1–22.
4 Doreen Rosman, *Evangelicals and Culture* (London: Croom Helm, 1984), pp. 44–7.
5 For an example, see Dorothy L. Sayers, *The Mind of the Maker* (London: Methuen, 1941); Peter Webster, 'The "Revival" in the Visual Arts in the Church of England, c.1935–c.1956', in *Revival and Resurgence in Christian History*, edited by Kate Cooper and Jeremy Gregory (Woodbridge: Boydell, 2008), pp. 301–5.
6 Rosman, *Evangelicals and Culture*, pp. 47–50.
7 Rosman, *Evangelicals and Culture*, pp. 59, 178.

not seek to bury them again.[8] It will instead extend the analysis beyond Rosman's chronological and geographical parameters. It will observe evangelical encounters with the arts in each of the possible modes: as both consumer and performer in the apparently 'neutral' sphere of the home and in private recreation; as user of the arts in the context of public worship; as user of the arts as tools for evangelism, and as moralist and reformer of the artistic pursuits of others. It concerns itself mainly with music, literature, the visual arts and drama, although none of these will receive an exhaustive treatment in its own terms. Its examples are drawn chiefly from Britain and the United States, and from the nineteenth and twentieth centuries, which distribution represents the weight of the scholarship to date. That said, its overall analysis makes a claim to be applicable to the evangelical movement in all its geographical diversity and temporal spread.

The arts and private leisure

We begin in the evangelical home, since it was here that priorities could most easily and safely be worked out away from the tension of confrontation with the 'world'. The typical puritan home of an earlier period has been caricatured as one of diligent labour and strenuous godly exercise, with little time left over for much except eating and sleep. Some traces of the same unease about an unreserved delight in the arts may be found in evangelical theology and practice. There was a continuity between the agonies of the spiritual diaries of the puritans and that of the eighteen-year-old New England Congregationalist Susanna Anthony (1726–1791). On reaching adulthood, she asked, should she now 'forsake strict and solid religion, and run with the young, giddy multitude, into the excesses of vanity?' No: it was right for her to choose 'the sorrows of religion' over 'the world in all its pomp and splendor, with ten thousand enjoyments'.[9]

Despite this, it is abundantly clear that evangelical households were places in which the arts could be received and enjoyed. Many in the nineteenth century were keen private readers. The young Thomas Babington Macaulay, within the orbit of the Clapham Sect, read such edifying literature as Foxe's 'Book of Martyrs' and Bunyan's *Pilgrim's Progress*; Foxe was also part of the childhood reading of the hymn writer Frances Ridley Havergal. In the same circle as Macaulay, the teenage Jane Catherine Venn read the poetry of Walter Scott and works of history as well as William Wilberforce's *Practical View* (1797). Among the poets, Havergal read John Milton, George Herbert and Robert Browning; for Venn it was Milton and Dryden. Classic imaginative literature of earlier ages was also in view. The young Macaulay read Alexander Pope's 'Homer' and Dryden's 'Virgil'; in the case of John Wesley, it was Horace.[10] To a large extent, evangelicals shared the taste of the educated middle class in the early nineteenth century.[11]

The novel, a newer artistic form in the eighteenth century, was regarded with greater caution initially. The young Edmund Knox, later bishop of Manchester and leader of the evangelical opposition in the Church of England between the two world wars, grew up in a household in the 1850s where novels were disallowed entirely.[12] A similar prohibition had held

---

8 On puritanism and culture, see the diverse chapters in *The Culture of English Puritanism*, edited by Christopher Durston and Jacqueline Eales (London: Macmillan, 1996).
9 'The Life and Character of Miss Susanna Anthony' (1796), in *Early Evangelicalism: A Reader*, edited by Jonathan Yeager (New York: Oxford University Press, 2013), pp. 103, 105.
10 Bebbington, *Evangelicalism*, p. 67; Christopher Tolley, *Domestic Biography: The Legacy of Evangelicalism in Four Nineteenth-century Families* (Oxford: Clarendon, 1997), p. 13; Janet Grierson, *Frances Ridley Havergal: Worcestershire Hymnwriter* (Bromsgrove: Havergal Society, 1979), pp. 5, 76.
11 Rosman, *Evangelicals and Culture*, pp. 121, 125.
12 Penelope Fitzgerald, *The Knox Brothers* (London: Macmillan, 1977), p. 19.

in the Havergal household a decade or so earlier.[13] Objections were raised to the format in principle: that the reading of them was seductively easy and spoiled the reader for more exacting fare; and that history and biography, dealing as they did in facts, were inherently a better means of conveying truth than mere stories. If the medium was to be allowed at all, particular novels might over-familiarize the mind to vice, even if it were made repellent. They might inflame the passions and sensual desire, or overvalue excitement and adventure at the expense of contentment with mundane reality.[14] Frances Havergal's sister Maria was grateful for her father's prohibition, but later as an adult tried reading a novel by way of an experiment, 'to see if I could close the book and go with appetite to other studies. No. I felt the whirlpool of imagination stirred, but the dreamy mawkishness and unreality disgusted me'.[15]

However, the evangelical scruple at fictional writing was neither universal in the early nineteenth century, nor durable over time. The popularity of the novels of writers such as Hannah More at the beginning of the nineteenth century or the brothers Silas and Joseph Hocking at its end show that many evangelicals were keen readers of at least some novels.[16] More recently, Alister McGrath has drawn attention to the recovery of C. S. Lewis particularly among American evangelicals since the 1970s, and as much for Narnia as for *Mere Christianity*.[17] Remarkably popular, in the United States at least, was the genre of evangelical romance fiction, finding its inception in the work of Grace Livingston Hill (1865–1947) and subsequently burgeoning from the 1970s onwards.[18] Crawford Gribben has documented the remarkable commercial success of rapture fiction, and in particular the 'Left Behind' books by Tim LaHaye and Jerry B. Jenkins.[19] Evangelicals have found much to delight them in a wide variety of literary forms.

Examples also abound of evangelical households that took delight in artistic performance. Chief among them was music, perhaps the most communal of the arts. The palace of Francis Chavasse, bishop of Liverpool, resounded to the efforts of the 'Chavasse concert party', as Christopher, future bishop of Rochester, played the concertina alongside his siblings in the years before the First World War.[20] In an earlier generation, the Anglican Richenda Cunningham's recreation was her piano. Drawing on a much older puritan tradition of domestic psalm singing, evangelical families were to be found singing religious music in a domestic setting. John Jowett, evangelical layman of Newington in Surrey and founder of the Church Missionary Society, often took the tenor part in home performances of choruses of Handel oratorios with his brothers and children.[21] Mrs Chavasse was piano accompanist to domestic worship in Liverpool.[22] On

---

13 Grierson, *Frances Ridley Havergal*, p. 75.
14 David John Sandifer, '"The Most Dangerous of Allies": Evangelicals and the Novel, 1790–1840', *Christianity and History Forum Bulletin* vol. 6 (2010), 26–7.
15 Grierson, *Frances Ridley Havergal*, p. 75.
16 Martin Wellings, '"Pulp Methodism" Revisited: The Literature and Significance of Silas and Joseph Hocking', in *The Church and Literature*, edited by Peter Clark and Charlotte Methuen (Woodbridge: Boydell and Brewer, 2012), pp. 362–73.
17 Alister McGrath, *C. S. Lewis: A Life* (London: Hodder and Stoughton, 2013), pp. 371–8.
18 Lynn S. Neal, *Romancing God: Evangelical Women and Inspirational Fiction* (Chapel Hill, NC: University of North Carolina Press, 2006), pp. 16–24.
19 Crawford Gribben, *Writing the Rapture: Prophecy Fiction in Evangelical America* (Oxford: Oxford University Press, 2009).
20 Selwyn Gummer, *The Chavasse Twins* (London: Hodder and Stoughton, 1963), p. 45.
21 Rosman, *Evangelicals and Culture*, pp. 97–8. His son William was the first Anglican clergyman to serve overseas with the CMS. See, 'William Jowett, 1787–1855', *Oxford Dictionary of National Biography* (Oxford: Oxford University Press, 2004).
22 Gummer, *Chavasse Twins*, p. 31.

a Sunday evening, Frances Havergal sang hymns as a young child to the keyboard accompaniment of her father, William Henry Havergal, rector of Astley in Worcestershire.[23]

Despite this apparent enthusiasm for domestic consumption and performance of the arts, there was an ever-present note of concern about the right use of time. Could any enjoyment of the arts really be justified on its own terms when time on earth was short and the business of devotion and mission so pressing? Richard Cecil, prominent Anglican evangelical in the early years of the nineteenth century, attempted to find fifteen minutes every day for his violin, but found the temptation to play longer too much to resist, and so gave it up entirely.[24] In Oxford in the 1940s, the young James I. Packer allowed his friends in the university Christian Union to persuade him that playing the clarinet in a local dance band ought to give way to the Saturday evening Bible readings, although he evidently continued as a keen listener to recorded jazz.[25]

The most longstanding and widespread evangelical objection to a whole art form concerned drama. Frances Ridley Havergal, often a contralto soloist on the oratorio stage, apparently never set foot in a theatre.[26] Charles Simeon advised one lady that to disobey her husband was a better course than to accompany him to a play; the evil of the theatre was intrinsic, not merely circumstantial.[27] For some, acting itself placed the player in danger of vain ostentation, a temptation to pride. Even though for Frances Havergal the semi-staged nature of the oratorio was acceptable in a way the theatre was not, there were still scruples at the 'wild intoxication of public applause', a 'delicious delusion'. The very act of dissimulation – of appearing to be what one was not – was also a source of discomfort. Havergal at one point consented to perform the part of Jezebel in Mendelssohn's oratorio *Elijah*, but was persuaded that a 'Christian girl' could not safely personate such a character.[28] The Regency theatre also often seemed to lionize the very values of which evangelicals disapproved: honour, romance, adventure and conflict. Even a play that eventually showed the consequences of sin could do harm in familiarizing the viewer with that sin in the first place.[29]

However, even this most strong of taboos showed some signs of relaxation in later periods, at least in Britain. Attitudes to the theatre were relaxed among the Oxford Group between the wars, and by 1947 John Wenham was urging members of the Inter-Varsity Fellowship to drop the blanket prohibition.[30] In the early 1960s, Michael Saward was daring enough to see the controversial satire 'Beyond the Fringe'.[31] By the 1980s, the British charismatic Gerald Coates was to wear his love of cinema and theatre as a badge of the movement's new-found freedom.[32]

This change can surely be attributed in part to the changing status of the theatre amongst the respectable middle class. The atmosphere and social connotation of the London stage of the Regency period – bawdy, unruly and shunned by the better sort – was very different from that of the new National Theatre in London after 1945. In this, the evangelical objection voiced by William Wilberforce or Hannah More can be seen as a product of a social context. However,

---

23 Grierson, *Frances Ridley Havergal*, p.11.
24 Rosman, *Evangelicals and Culture*, p. 98.
25 Alister McGrath, *To Know and Serve God: A Biography of James I. Packer* (London: Hodder and Stoughton, 1997), p. 21.
26 Grierson, *Frances Ridley Havergal*, p. 75.
27 Rosman, *Evangelicals and Culture*, p. 56.
28 Grierson, *Frances Ridley Havergal*, pp. 85, 110.
29 Rosman, *Evangelicals and Culture*, pp. 56–8.
30 Bebbington, *Evangelicalism*, pp. 238, 263.
31 Saward, *Faint Streak of Humility*, p. 207.
32 Bebbington, *Evangelicalism*, p. 244.

it is also noteworthy that there was greater openness to the private reading of plays amongst those who would not contemplate visiting a theatre. Away from suspect company, and from the seductive power of the spectacle itself, a play was rendered safe, and could be subjected to the same disciplined attention and critique that evangelicals applied to all their reading.[33]

The arts in evangelical worship

Evangelical meeting places have generally been relatively plain, at least in comparison to Roman Catholic or Orthodox churches: neat, well kept, but with a minimum of ornament. As Patrick Collinson observed of the Reformation period, this was not merely a matter of inattention, but at one level an aesthetic statement in itself.[34] While other Christians might understand the beauty of holiness of the Psalmist in material terms, in reference to the worship space, the aesthetic of Protestant worship has been one in which to worship in spirit and truth required no trappings. There was beauty in the truth, and in true worship. At the same time, Donald Davie has rightly observed that to demand of the worship space such qualities of 'simplicity, sobriety, and measure' is not a denial of the senses as is often supposed, but 'sensuous pleasure deployed with an unusually frugal, and therefore exquisite, fastidiousness'.[35]

This plainness was not only a positive statement, but an insurance. Encoded in the Protestant DNA that evangelicals shared was a fear of idolatry: of the misuse of the visual image, particularly in church buildings. While in the modern period few really feared that the ignorant might mistake the image for the thing it represented – the fear that had prompted the iconoclasm of the Reformation period – a residual unease with the visual image often persisted. This point should not be overstressed: recent work on Protestant and evangelical visual culture by John Harvey and David Morgan among others has shown the complex ways in which word and image have interacted.[36] E. J. H. Nash (or 'Bash', whose influence may be traced throughout the recent history of British evangelicalism) was given to using Holman Hunt's painting 'The Light of the World' as a visual aid in evangelistic preaching.[37] However, until the late twentieth century, it was an uncommon evangelical church that used sculpted or painted images as the central focus of contemplation in public worship without a protective covering of orthodox words.[38]

The art form used most in evangelical worship was of course music. Although there was a strain in Reformation thought, associated with Calvin but most particularly with Zwingli in Zurich, that sought to restrict or disallow music for very fear of its persuasive power, this has rarely been dominant. The literature on church music is very extensive, much more so than for the other arts, and particularly for the nineteenth century, and it is in hymnody rather than

---

33 Rosman, *Evangelicals and Culture*, pp. 55–6, 129–30.
34 Patrick Collinson, *The Reformation* (London: Weidenfeld and Nicolson, 2003), p. 154.
35 Donald Davie, *A Gathered Church: The Literature of the English Dissenting Interest, 1700–1930* (London: Routledge and Kegan Paul, 1978), pp. 25–6.
36 John Harvey, 'Seen to be Remembered: Representation and Recollection in Contemporary British Evangelicalism', in *British Evangelical Identities: Past and Present*, edited by Mark Smith (Carlisle: Paternoster, 2008), pp. 180–200; David Morgan, 'Seeing Protestant Icons: The Popular Reception of Visual Media in Nineteenth- and Twentieth-century America', in *Elite and Popular Religion*, edited by Kate Cooper and Jeremy Gregory (Woodbridge: Boydell, 2006), pp. 406–28.
37 Dick Knight, 'The Speaker', in *Bash: A Study in Spiritual Power*, edited by John Eddison (Basingstoke: Marshall, Morgan and Scott, 1983), p. 51.
38 Recent years have seen the widespread adoption of overhead projection equipment. Even then, it might be argued that, when these are used to project visual images (rather than the texts of songs for singing), those images are rarely used as a primary focus of attention.

the choral and instrumental tradition that evangelicals have featured most prominently.[39] Music, unlike any other art form, was directly sanctioned for use in worship by Scripture itself: at every turn by the Psalmist; by Paul and apparently by Christ himself.[40] As a result, the hymns of Charles Wesley are only the best known of the many hymns produced by evangelicals for their own use in worship, to which we must add those of John Newton, William Cowper and others.

But there were limits on the kinds of music that could be so welcomed. There was a very clear line of descent from the Reformation critique of medieval polyphony on grounds that the text was unintelligible, to later evangelical rejection of forms of church music that similarly obscured the words sung. This in part explains the lack of engagement by evangelicals with the elaborate cathedral musical tradition that reached its acme in England in the period under discussion and was transplanted all over the Anglican world. It also frames the enthusiasm with which a godly family such as that of John Jowett had embraced the oratorios of Handel, which combined musical invention with clarity of word setting.[41] To allow music that merely delighted the hearer without instructing them was to miss the purpose of public worship.

Distinct but closely related was evangelical concern about the performer, as well as the music itself. The victory of the organ over the English parish band as the means of accompaniment to singing was welcomed by some evangelicals, since the organ, being in the hands of a single player, tended to curb ostentatious excess.[42] In some Methodist chapels in the early nineteenth century, some band players had introduced 'almost every variety of musical instrument, destroying the simplicity and devotional character of the singing'. Even if some in the congregation may have delighted in such elaboration, it was the edification of 'the more sober part of the congregation' which was paramount.[43]

Key to differentiating evangelical enthusiasm for music in church from that of others is a distinctive understanding of the nature of a 'sacrifice of praise' (Hebrews 13: 15). Catholic thinkers have tended to stress the offering of the work of art itself as the key transaction. In musical terms, a well-wrought composition expertly performed could in and of itself constitute an offering.[44] As a result, many of the critiques of pop church music in its early days were both of the standard of the composition, and the inexpert nature of some early performances. Few evangelicals have been able to accept such an understanding without wishing also to stress the importance of the intention of the performer. A bad song inexpertly sung but with the right intention would nonetheless be acceptable to God.

This concentration on the singer and not the song has also meant that evangelicals have

---

39 Older but still useful studies include Horton Davies, *Worship and Theology in England: From Watts and Wesley to Martineau, 1690–1900* (Grand Rapids, MI: Eerdmans, 1996), pp. 201–4, 210–40; see also Erik Routley, *The Musical Wesleys* (London: Herbert Jenkins, 1968). More recently, see the two volumes by Lionel Adey: *Hymns and the Christian Myth* (Vancouver: University of British Columbia Press, 1986), pp. 99–149; *Class and Idol in the English Hymn* (Vancouver: University of British Columbia Press, 1988). For the United States, see Donald P. Hustad, *Jubilate! Church Music in the Evangelical Tradition* (Carol Stream, IL: Hope, 1981).
40 The key passages from Paul were Colossians 3: 16 and Ephesians 5: 19, and (in the Gospels) Matthew 26: 30.
41 Rosman, *Evangelicals and Culture*, p. 98.
42 On evangelical use of the organ in the early nineteenth century, see Nicholas Temperley, *The Music of the English Parish Church* (2 vols, Cambridge: Cambridge University Press, 1979), I: 214–8.
43 The recollection of Thomas Jackson in 1873, as quoted by Rosman, *Evangelicals and Culture*, p. 100.
44 On the debate about 'authenticity' in contemporary church music, see Ian Jones with Peter Webster, 'Expressions of Authenticity: Music for Worship', in *Redefining Christian Britain: Post-1945 Perspectives*, edited by Jane Garnett, Matthew Grimley, Alana Harris, William Whyte and Sarah Williams (London: SCM, 2006), pp. 50–62.

often been, in the words of a sympathetic outsider, prepared to 'embrace bad taste for the sake of the gospel'.[45] By no means all evangelicals were prepared to use popular tunes and musical styles, fearing the effects on the listener of pre-existing secular associations that such melodies and styles carried.[46] However, three well-known examples will suffice to show evangelicals making use of popular styles in evangelistic services and (latterly) in regular worship. The Salvation Army, founded in 1865, overcame scruples about vigorous use of the full panoply of musical instruments; the bands 'broke through the cordons of reserve and decorum in a riot of joyous righteousness', thus (to use William Booth's most famous saying) 'robbing the Devil of his choice tunes'.[47] Originating in songs written for use in American Sunday schools, the gospel song genre – simple, direct, tuneful verse-refrain songs with uncomplicated harmony – was popularized both in America and Britain by Dwight L. Moody and his singing partner Ira D. Sankey in the later nineteenth century. Spreading beyond the narrow confines of public worship by means of concert appearances by principal singers as well as radio and recorded distribution, the genre became what one observer has called 'the folksong of American religious life'.[48] Cliff Barrows, leader of the music in Billy Graham's London crusade of 1954, blended traditional hymnody with such popular gospel songs as 'Blessed assurance' and 'What a friend we have in Jesus'.[49]

It remains to be established how quickly the gospel song repertoire was incorporated into authoritative hymnals, or found its way into the repertoire by other means. However, by the end of the twentieth century, in many churches it was no longer gospel songs that were found amongst the larger body of hymns, but a handful of hymns that jostled for space amongst a standard repertoire of songs in popular style. Even though British evangelicals came later to experimentation with pop church music than other sections of the churches, by the 1970s they were firmly in the lead, and by the 1990s popular songs played by guitar bands had become one of the visual markers of Anglo-American evangelicalism.[50] Only a minority of critics still voiced the same principled criticisms of the use of non-sacred styles of music. Evangelicals had adopted the musical language of the world, whilst emptying it of its notes of rebellion and unregulated sexuality.[51]

The arts as evangelism

Evangelicals were at certain times and places assiduous producers of the arts for those outside the fold. However, the underlying motivation to do so was fundamentally different from many other artists, although the difference only came into relief (in Britain, at least) in the later nineteenth and early twentieth century. Before that time, as David Sandifer has pointed out,

---

45 Richard Holloway, 'Evangelicalism: An Outsider's Perspective', in *Evangelical Anglicans: Their Role and Influence in the Church Today*, edited by R. T. France and A. E. McGrath (London: SPCK, 1993), p. 182.
46 Rosman, *Evangelicals and Culture*, p. 99; Hustad, *Jubilate!*, pp. 26–32.
47 Davies, *Worship and Theology in England*, p. 169.
48 Mel R. Wilhoit, 'Gospel Songs / Gospel Hymns', in *The Guide to United States Popular Culture*, edited by Ray Broadus Browne and Pat Browne (Madison, WI: University of Wisconsin Press, 2001), pp. 333–4; Hustad, *Jubilate!*, pp. 130–2, 248–51.
49 Frank Colquhoun, *Harringay Story: The Official Record of the Billy Graham Greater London Crusade 1954* (London: Hodder and Stoughton, 1955), pp. 100–2.
50 On the key influence of the charismatic movement in this transition, see James Steven, *Worship in the Spirit: Charismatic Worship in the Church of England* (Carlisle: Paternoster, 2002).
51 Peter Webster and Ian Jones, 'New Music and the "Evangelical Style" in the Church of England, c.1958–1991', in *British Evangelical Identities*, edited by Smith, pp. 167–79.

there were very considerable affinities between an evangelical view of the real purpose of art, and assumptions made more generally. It was widely held that 'human beings exist for moral and spiritual excellence; [that] this excellence is progressive [and] every action must be judged on the basis of how it contributes or does not contribute to this growth in excellence'.[52] The evangelical concern that cultural products should be judged by their effects on the receiver was thus aligned with assumptions common to many others. It was only as artists, philosophers and critics asserted the independence of art from any criterion other than its own beauty, that the evangelical insistence on wider and older criteria began to appear counter-cultural.

Readers may pause over the treatment here of almost all evangelical artistic work outside public worship as a form of evangelism, but evangelism it overwhelmingly was, in one important sense. Few intended that these works of art should merely be a source of delight to the receiver, although delight was a welcome side-effect, which in itself aided the main purpose. The arts were a means of aiding private devotion; of convincing the reader or viewer of a theological argument; of convicting the reader of their sinfulness and need of grace; of calling the reader to amendment of life and reformation of conduct. Seldom were they an end in themselves.

One early and highly self-conscious deployment of a literary form for these polemical ends was *Theron and Aspasio* (1755) by the Anglican evangelical James Hervey (1714–1758). Looking to deliver a message in a form acceptable to elite taste, Hervey cast the work in the form of a series of dialogues in which Aspasio gradually leads his friend towards an acceptance of the gospel. That Hervey expected his readers to object is apparent at the very beginning. Before Aspasio can embark on his exposition of imputed righteousness, Hervey makes him justify the introduction of '*edifying* Talk into our *fashionable* Assemblies', an 'outrageous Violation of the Mode [of polite conversation]' which might arouse 'the Suspicion of *Enthusiasm*'.[53]

Early evangelicalism was also not without its poets, perhaps the most significant of whom was William Cowper (1731–1800). Although now better known for hymns such as 'O for a closer walk with God', Cowper's poetry was frequently reprinted and included in anthologies throughout the nineteenth century before falling from critical favour in the twentieth.[54] The poems of the Particular Baptist Anne Steele (1717–1778) were published by her family for public use. In the United States, Phillis Wheatley was bought as a slave by an evangelical Boston merchant, and through his connections was to publish *Poems on Various Subjects, Religious and Moral* (1773) under the powerful patronage of the Countess of Huntingdon. These poems were not simply private devotional exercises, but public offerings for edification and influence.

Phillis Wheatley's works achieved very considerable success in terms of sales, but even wider reach was achieved by the group of British writers working around the turn of the nineteenth century. The *Annals of the Poor* (1809–10) by Legh Richmond, a literary recounting of tales of the rural poor and their edifying deaths, achieved a readership not only among the evangelical middle classes but also among those whom it depicted.[55] Hannah More, evangelical royalty from the centre of the Clapham Sect, achieved even greater success, in more than one genre. Like *The Annals of the Poor*, More's *Cheap Repository Tracts* (1795–1798) were examples of the genre of the 'moral tale' described by Tim Killick, the production of which was by no means only

---

[52] Sandifer, 'The Most Dangerous of Allies', 28.
[53] Hervey, *Theron and Aspasio* (1755), in *Early Evangelicalism*, edited by Yeager, pp. 189, 192–3.
[54] John D. Baird, 'William Cowper', in *Oxford Dictionary of National Biography*; on the complex relationship between Cowper's work, faith and mental health, see Diane Buie, 'William Cowper: a Religious Melancholic?', *Journal for Eighteenth Century Studies* vol. 36 (2013), 103–19.
[55] A. G. Newell, 'Early Evangelical Fiction', *Evangelical Quarterly* vol. 38 (1966), 81–5.

by evangelicals.[56] Fictionalized tales of the poor from town and country (whereas Richmond's were based on real events), an estimated 2 million copies were in circulation by 1796. Nearly forty years later, they were thought to be 'a principal part of the English cottagers' library'.[57] Modern critics have charged the *Tracts* with being an attack on popular culture, which in one sense they were, in that More very clearly intended to influence behaviour for the better. Neither were the *Tracts* artistic failures. More showed considerable skill in employing existing genres – 'moral tales', ballads, allegories – to a self-conscious and sustained educational and moral purpose. Despite some unease amongst the evangelical press, More achieved similar success with the anonymous novel *Coelebs in Search of a Wife* (1809). Reviewed very favourably in literary periodicals, it went through nine editions in nine months, as well as thirty in the United States, and German and French editions, and remained in print twenty years later.[58]

Other British evangelical writers were equally successful but without achieving the same fusion of literary achievement and seriousness of purpose. Emma Jane Worboise published some fifty works between 1846 and 1887, an explicit attempt to 'provide something purer' to replace the popular literature of her time. However, in the words of Elisabeth Jay, 'the combination of her devotion to fact and the paramount desire to provide an Evangelical witness were Mrs Worboise's downfall'. In *Thornycroft Hall*, her answer to *Jane Eyre*, Worboise was prepared to sacrifice psychological plausibility in order to force all her characters, however bad, to accept the gospel before their final demise. It was this kind of instrumentalization of the arts that discredited evangelical artistic work in the eyes of critics and artists from outside the evangelical fold.[59]

The evangelistic importance of the music of Ira D. Sankey was noted earlier, but in the United States we might add the names of Charles Alexander and Homer Rodeheaver as the musical partners of prominent evangelists.[60] In England, Frances Ridley Havergal regarded her life's work as proclaiming the gospel. As well as being an oratorio soloist and trainer of her church choir, Havergal was ever alert to the opportunity to share the gospel in song. At a mission among the urban working class in Liverpool, she took rehearsals of the hymns for the main mission services, interspersed with her own songs. 'The silence and breathless attention would have been remarkable anywhere' she reported, 'but fancy these poor wretches, who certainly never heard anything but the lowest songs before'. At a YWCA mission in Swansea, there was distributed a card with her own hymn 'Take my life and let it be' printed on it, with a space for a written response by the recipient; her sister recalled the occasion as 'a great night of decision for many present'. Even her music tuition classes were 'a grappling-iron to draw many drifting vessels close to our side, bringing them within hearing of loving and sympathizing words, and of the One name which is sweeter than music'.[61]

It was also the case that whole art forms were at times suspect, yet embraced at other times as a means of evangelism. Such was the case with drama. Not only was attendance at the secular theatre suspect to the majority of British evangelicals in the eighteenth and nineteenth

---

56 Tim Killick, *British Short Fiction in the Early Nineteenth Century: The Rise of the Tale* (Farnham: Ashgate, 2008), pp. 73–115.
57 Julia Saunders, 'Putting the Reader Right: Reassessing Hannah More's *Cheap Repository Tracts*', *Romanticism on the Net*, no. 16 (November 1999), para 6: http://id.erudit.org/iderudit/005881ar (accessed 24 February 2018).
58 Sandifer, 'The Most Dangerous of Allies', 23.
59 Elisabeth Jay, *The Religion of the Heart: Anglican Evangelicalism and the Nineteenth-Century Novel* (Oxford: Clarendon, 1979), pp. 244–5.
60 Hustad, *Jubilate!*, pp. 132–7.
61 Grierson, *Frances Ridley Havergal*, pp. 130, 132, 86.

centuries, for reasons already examined; the idea of dramatic presentations of the gospel was also hard to comprehend for some. In 1795, Rowland Hill asserted the 'illegitimacy of plays, in any circumstances'.[62] In 1928, when the chapter of Canterbury cathedral staged what was (wrongly) thought to be the first play in a cathedral since the Reformation, a similar objection was raised by the National Church League over the signature of E. A. Knox. Such 'pagan methods of imparting religious teaching' had no warrant in Scripture and were a poor substitute for a clear verbal apprehension of the truth. In the jazz age, when 'the pursuit of pleasure and love of vain display' were blinding people to the reality of sin, any 'frivolous accommodation to that craze for amusement' was not to be countenanced.[63]

However, the evangelical objection to the use of drama waned as did the taboo on the secular theatre. John Masefield's play for Canterbury marked the beginning of a remarkable flowering of religious drama in England, most associated with the catholic wing of the Church of England. Less well understood is evangelical experimentation with drama at much the same time, such as the plays written by G. R. Balleine for his London parish in the 1930s.[64] The Riding Lights Theatre Company traces its origins to the evangelistic ministry of David Watson at the church of St Michael-le-Belfrey in York in the late 1970s.[65] Once again, evangelical attitudes to the arts could and did shift depending on the context in which they found themselves.

Evangelicals against the arts

Evangelicals had also to engage with artistic production and consumption outside their control: amongst their neighbours, in local theatres, concert and music halls, in print, and (in the twentieth century) on national and local broadcast media. The assumptions that drove evangelical involvement in campaigns against the arts have remained relatively consistent, and relate to those that governed their own use of the arts. The arts could certainly conduce to vice if incorrectly handled, and the activism and conversionism that defined the evangelical meant that unsaved souls could not simply be left to their corruption. The correct use of the arts was part of a broader concern for public morality, in which the Christian standard was held to be normative, and which was the duty of the state to enforce. Any artistic output that caused the deterioration of that Christian moral standard was subject to intervention.

One common impulse among evangelicals when faced with the kind of cultural production they disliked was to attempt to displace it. It was key that evangelicals themselves had these alternatives to choose for their own use. Benjamin L. Fischer has noted the development of separate journals and magazines for evangelicals in the early nineteenth century. Titles such as the *Evangelical Magazine* or the *Eclectic Review* offered an alternative to the pernicious influence of secular magazines such as the *Edinburgh Review*. As well as offering more acceptable interpretations of contemporary politics and current affairs, these journals sought to provide alternative

---

62 Rosman, *Evangelicals and Culture*, p. 55.
63 A remonstrance presented to the Dean and Chapter in July 1928, as quoted in Peter Webster, 'George Bell, John Masefield and *The Coming of Christ*: Context and Significance', in *The Church and Humanity: The Life and Work of George Bell, 1883–1958*, edited by Andrew Chandler (Farnham: Ashgate, 2012), pp. 51–3.
64 Andrew Atherstone, 'George Reginald Balleine: Historian of Anglican Evangelicalism', *Journal of Anglican Studies* vol. 12 (2014), 98–9.
65 *The Charismatic Movement in the Church of England* (London: CIO, 1981), p. 25; Mathew Guest, *Evangelical Identity and Contemporary Culture: A Congregational Study in Innovation* (Carlisle: Paternoster, 2007), p. 58.

material for recreational reading as well. Evangelicals (it was thought) ought to prefer the truth over fiction, and this need was well served by a new genre of narratives of daring and dangerous missionary journeys in far-off lands: factual, edifying, yet still a stimulation to the imagination, and thus to be read with pleasure.[66] In 1995, Dave Tomlinson noted a Christian alternativism that sought to replace all the enticing pleasures of the world with Christianized alternatives: 'It is like a parallel universe: Christian festivals, Christian records, Christian holidays, Christian social events, Christian dating agencies, Christian theatre, Christian comedy, Christian television, Christian aerobics set to Christian music – it seems like the resourcefulness of "Christian" imitation knows no bounds'.[67]

It is in the light of this conscious or unconscious impulse towards the replacement of unwholesome with wholesome that evangelical domestic music-making can also be read. As well as being a source of delight, the music played and sung in the homes of Francis Chavasse and John Jowett kept closed any space that might otherwise have been filled with more frivolous or lascivious fare. In the late twentieth century, the phenomenon of Contemporary Christian Music, as well as being music for a specific use in worship, also showed some signs of having the same effect. Studio recordings of music by prominent worship leaders have come to be music for recreation and private consumption, displacing secular alternatives. While not unprecedented in evangelical history, this trend has arguably accelerated in the early twenty-first century. It is also notable that live recordings of worship services have also crossed into the home, to be listened to while engaged in other activities: a blurring of the spheres of religious activity impossible before the age of the Walkman and the iPod.[68]

The impulse to replacement was not confined within the evangelical constituency but spilled over into society at large. The year 1995 saw the appearance of the first title in the phenomenally successful 'Left Behind' series of novels, and Gribben has shown the degree to which 'prophecy fiction' broke out from within evangelical circles to find a wider readership, such that 'the evangelical imagination has entered the cultural mainstream'. However, the dispersed and independent nature of both the writing and publication of prophecy fiction has resulted in a theologically unruly genre which itself demonstrated the degree to which '[American] evangelicalism has lost its theological coherence'.[69] Allowing the cultural products of evangelicalism to spread and develop freely outside the constituency is not without its risks.

On occasions, evangelicals have sought very directly to place an alternative cultural product in the secular marketplace, in order to supplant the secular choice. One such intervention was in that most competitive of markets, the theatres of London's West End. In 1946 a group associated with Moral Re-Armament, the political wing of Frank Buchman's Oxford Group, bought the Westminster Theatre (itself formerly the Charlotte Chapel) to provide the venue for a theatre of 'not only entertainment but a constructive drama of ideas, relevant to the post-war world, and based on Christian faith and moral values'.[70] The theatre provided a base from which Peter Howard, playwright and MRA leader, could put forward what he himself described as his 'propaganda plays'. Howard was explicit that matter presented on stage had a direct effect on

---

66 Benjamin L. Fischer, 'A Novel Resistance: Mission Narrative as the Anti-novel in the Evangelical Assault on British Culture', in *The Church and Literature*, edited by Clarke and Methuen, pp. 232–45.
67 Dave Tomlinson, *The Post-Evangelical* (London: SPCK, 1995), p. 124.
68 Much more research is required on the degree to which this trend represents the consumerisation of religious practice, as outlined at large in Vincent J. Miller, *Consuming Religion: Christian Faith and Practice in a Consumer Culture* (New York: Continuum, 2003).
69 Gribben, *Writing the Rapture*, p. 170.
70 K. D. Belden, *The Story of the Westminster Theatre* (London: Westminster Theatre, 1965), p. 23.

the viewer's subsequent behaviour, and so the theatre had a part to play in 'restoring honour to homes, unity between colours and classes, and to all men faith in God'.[71]

But sometimes displacement was not enough, and the only appropriate evangelical response to a particular work of art was to fight it. Just as before the twentieth century, evangelicals shared many elite assumptions about the purposes of art, so too were there common assumptions about state and voluntary intervention in public morality. On the voluntary side, a great deal of research remains to be done on the extent of evangelical involvement in campaigning movements about public morals. In the United States, the career of Anthony Comstock illustrates the difficulties for the historian in untangling the threads of evangelical piety and what could still be described in late nineteenth-century America as puritanism. In his assiduous churchgoing and intense private examination of his conscience, Comstock was like a puritan in the classical seventeenth-century sense, but his decades-long campaign against obscenity in literature could carry with it many what might be called 'social puritans' who would not have shared his style of piety.[72] Comstock's New York Society for the Suppression of Vice bore some similarities with British organizations, such as the London Council for the Promotion of Public Morality, which between 1899 and 1967 concerned itself with sexual behaviour in the city, along with the capital's music halls, theatre performance and latterly radio and television broadcasts.[73] It remains to be seen how far evangelicals were prepared to lend their support to broader-based campaigns of this sort. Evangelicals were certainly very often morally conservative, but such conservatism was not unique to them.[74]

However, as the twentieth century wore on, and public (or at least elite) consensus about the shape of public morality was weakened, evangelical concerns became both sharper and more clearly distinctive. In 1929, William Joynson-Hicks, former Conservative politician and Protestant leader, was able to assert that the bulk of Christian opinion in Britain still supported the censorship that was then operative in the United Kingdom.[75] The postwar period however saw a series of significant moments in the loosening of state control of the arts in Britain. The Obscene Publications Act of 1959, whilst maintaining the offence of obscenity, introduced a defence of being in the public good (that is, having artistic merit). The Theatres Act of 1968 ended the censorship of the British stage that had been exercised by the Lord Chamberlain. While there was vigorous conservative opposition to these perceived relaxations of the safeguards against literature and drama that might deprave the reader or viewer, they were by no means universally opposed by the churches.[76]

There were moments in this process in which evangelicals were involved. The year 1967 saw what turned out to be the last significant obscenity trial of a work of fiction under the 1959 Act: *Last Exit to Brooklyn*, by Hubert Selby Jr. The test of obscenity was whether the work had a tendency to 'deprave and corrupt' the reader, which could be offset if the work could be

---

71 Philip Boobbyer, 'The Cold War in the Plays of Peter Howard', *Contemporary British History* vol. 19 (2005), 210.
72 Heywood Broun and Margaret Leech, *Anthony Comstock: Roundsman of the Lord* (London: Wishart, 1928), pp. 24–32
73 On the attention paid by the Council to the censorship of stage plays, see Peter Webster, 'The Archbishop of Canterbury, the Lord Chamberlain and the Censorship of the Theatre', in *The Church and Literature*, edited by Clark and Methuen, p. 439.
74 On the various campaigns against 'obscene' literature in Britain, see Celia Marshik, *British Modernism and Censorship* (Cambridge: Cambridge University Press, 2006).
75 Viscount Brentford [William Joynson-Hicks], *Do we Need a Censor?* (London: Faber, 1929), p. 23.
76 On the churches' involvement in the reform of the law on the theatre, see Peter Webster, *Archbishop Ramsey: The Shape of the Church* (Farnham: Ashgate, 2015), pp. 74–7.

shown to have significant artistic merit. Whilst the defence counsel for the publisher lined up several critics to establish the latter point, one of the prosecution witnesses was David Sheppard, later Anglican bishop of Liverpool, but at the time a priest-cum-social worker at the Mayflower Centre in Canning Town in east London. Sheppard later recalled his view, a view similar to that of much evangelical opinion (and indeed wider conservative Christian opinion) in the late 1960s: that 'though censorship should be a weapon sparingly used, there were times when it made for health'. [77]

There were many aspects of the arts that were not subject to this kind of statutory and systematized censorship. In these cases, if evangelicals wanted to counter them, different methods were required. One such matter was the suspected effects of popular music, particularly in the twentieth century. Popular forms of music-making had for long been a source of worry, due to a tight knot of concerns. Uncontrolled music-making and listening had often betokened a lack of restraint: an invitation to dancing and associated licentiousness. When dealing with music with sung words, the most common concern amongst evangelicals was with covert or overt references to sex or violence or the questioning of legitimate authority that might be an occasion to sin. With the advent first of jazz, and supremely of rock and roll after 1945, these longstanding concerns were both heightened and broadened in scope. In the British context, once the indigenous music styles of folk song and the music hall began to be supplanted by such 'foreign' styles, concern mounted (and not only amongst evangelicals) about the supposedly 'primal' nature of the music.[78] These concerns reached a particular height in the United States from the early 1970s onwards in relation to heavy metal (which added occultic references to the older themes of sex and violence).[79] Some of the same concerns have been observed being played out in relation to rap music in the last few decades.[80]

In America, evangelical ministers such as Bob Larson wrote and preached energetically against rock music in all its forms, and organized a new form of conversion ritual, the record burning, in which heavy metal fans destroyed the objects of their sinfulness as a sign of a turning from temptation. Morality campaigns against popular music have tended to focus on lyrics, since these may be tested and assessed in ways in which the style of music, the personal image of the musician and the fan culture that surrounds him or her may not. The greatest national success of the movement in the United States, although indirect, was the 'Tipper sticker': labels placed on records advising parents of sexually explicit or violent content, named after Tipper Gore, leader of the group of so-called 'Washington Wives' that pressed for the legislation. It was an evangelical, Pastor Jeff Ling of Clear River Community Church in Virginia, who briefed a Senate hearing on the matter in September 1985.[81]

In Britain, while the theatre and literature remained subject to censorship backed by law, the national broadcaster was not. It was the BBC that provoked the first entry into public life

---

77 David Sheppard, *Steps Along Hope Street* (London: Hodder and Stoughton, 2002), pp. 137–8; John Sutherland, *Offensive Literature: Decensorship in Britain, 1960–1982* (London: Junction, 1982), p. 69; John Mortimer, *Clinging to the Wreckage* (London: Penguin, 2010), pp. 200–4.
78 Ian Jones and Peter Webster, 'Anglican "Establishment" Reactions to "Pop" Church Music in England, c.1956–1991', in *Elite and Popular Religion*, edited by Cooper and Gregory, pp. 433–4.
79 Jason C. Bivins, *Religion of Fear: The Politics of Horror in Conservative Evangelicalism* (Oxford: Oxford University Press, 2008).
80 Sandra L. Barnes, 'Religion and Rap Music: An Analysis of Black Church Usage', *Review of Religious Research* vol. 49 (2008), 319–38.
81 ABC News clip, 19 September 1985, www.gettyimages.co.uk/detail/video/pastor-jeff-ling-of-virginia-gives-a-slideshow-detailing-news-footage/450014078 (accessed 24 February 2018). On the Parents Music Resource Center, and on Ling, see Bivins, *Religion of Fear*, pp. 96–7.

of Mary Whitehouse with her Clean-Up TV campaign of 1964. This soon led to the formation of the National Viewers' and Listeners' Association, which in turn influenced the shape of the Nationwide Festival of Light (NFOL), inaugurated in 1971. Whitehouse, who was also involved with the NFOL, had been influenced in earlier life by Moral Re-Armament, and Matthew Grimley has shown that the NFOL was strongly influenced by evangelicals from its outset. Although Whitehouse's work began with television and radio, the scope was soon widened to cover several of the other arts. The NFOL's opening statement of intent named as its targets films such as Ken Russell's *The Devils*, with its mixture of sex, religion and brutality; the group was to derail the proposed ending of film censorship in London in 1975.[82] Mary Whitehouse successfully sued the periodical *Gay News* in 1977 over the content of a blasphemous poem; her case against the production of *The Romans in Britain* at the National Theatre in 1982 was to end inconclusively.[83]

The campaigns of Mary Whitehouse may be seen as a component part of a wider response to a perceived moral crisis. That this sense of crisis was not unique to the United States has been shown by Hugh McLeod and others, and a parallel movement may be seen among evangelicals elsewhere in the same period.[84] To conservative observers, it seemed that most Western countries were witnessing a decline in traditional religious observance simultaneous with increased permissiveness, which were both reflected in and fostered by the media and the liberal artistic establishment. While evangelicals were involved in campaigns against the arts before the middle of the twentieth century, they were less prominent simply because the consensus of the respectable was with them. By the end of the century, evangelicals stood out as that consensus had disintegrated around them.

Conclusion

This chapter has examined evangelical attitudes to and participation in the arts in four main contexts: in domestic settings, in public worship, in evangelism, and when created and consumed by others in society at large. In certain cases, there were evangelical principles that went to the very basis of the art form concerned, such as the stress on the intelligibility of words sung to music, which as a result were both widespread and persistent. It has also shown that there were other evangelical shibboleths, such as the taboo on attendance at the theatre, which were not so much issues with the medium itself, but a particular social context in which it was produced. As a result such prohibitions could be, and were, relaxed at other times and in other places.

Implicit in much of the chapter is a wider question which still awaits a full historico-theological treatment: the degree to which evangelical engagement with the arts was conditioned by the cultural power that evangelicals were able to exercise in general, and the extent to which their cultural presuppositions were shared with others. At the height of the influence of British evangelicalism in the mid-nineteenth century, evangelicals shared many presumptions with their neighbours about the moral purpose of the arts, and about the conditions that should surround their production and reception. As Elisabeth Jay has shown, this cultural closeness was mirrored in the degree to which evangelical life itself was the subject of the Victorian novel;

---

82 Matthew Grimley, 'Anglican Evangelicals and Anti-permissiveness: The Nationwide Festival of Light, 1971–1983', in *Evangelicalism and the Church of England in the Twentieth Century: Reform, Resistance, and Renewal*, edited by Andrew Atherstone and John Maiden (Woodbridge: Boydell, 2014), pp. 186–8.
83 On the *Gay News* case, see David Nash, *Blasphemy in Modern Britain: 1789 to the Present* (Aldershot: Ashgate, 1999), pp. 239–57. On *The Romans in Britain*, see Mary Whitehouse, *A Most Dangerous Woman?* (Tring: Lion, 1982), pp. 232–49.
84 Hugh McLeod, *The Religious Crisis of the 1960s* (Oxford: Oxford University Press, 2007).

an interest which waned as did evangelical influence in society, reaching a terminal point in Samuel Butler.[85]

In contrast, evangelicals in late twentieth-century Britain and America found themselves marooned by the processes of secularization in societies in which any consensus amongst the respectable on the purpose of art had fractured, and in which middle-class consensus on morality (the consensus that mattered) had disintegrated. It is no coincidence that this period saw a spate of evangelical writing on the supposed death of Christian culture in the West as reflected in the arts, by figures such as Francis Schaeffer and H. R. Rookmaaker.[86] In this context of perceived cultural and moral crisis, the paradox was that evangelicals were in confrontation with secular artistic production for its godlessness, while domesticating its forms for their own purposes – in popular church music, or in religious drama – to a greater extent than ever.

---

85 Jay, *Religion of the Heart*, pp. 11, 260.
86 Francis A. Schaeffer, *Escape from Reason* (Leicester: Inter-Varsity Press, 1968); H. R. Rookmaaker, *Modern Art and the Death of a Culture* (Leicester: Inter-Varsity Press, 1970).

15

EVANGELICALS, MONEY AND BUSINESS

Richard Turnbull

The relationship between evangelicalism, money and business is as complex as the phenomenon of evangelicalism itself. Indeed, in a number of ways the two are related. The way in which the prevailing intellectual culture has formed and shaped evangelicalism is a widely accepted theme of evangelical studies following David Bebbington's *Evangelicalism in Modern Britain* (1989).[1] The application of this thesis to the economy is masterfully expounded by Boyd Hilton in *The Age of Atonement* (1988).[2] The debate is not straightforward and Hilton, as will be seen, conflates evangelicalism and political economy in a way that obscures rather than explicates some of the nuances. Evangelicalism, however, is also an essentially pragmatic expression of faith. Many evangelicals entered business. In doing so, they faced numerous practical dilemmas. They knew that evangelicals were against sin, but how did this relate to the particular temptations of the market? George Eliot noted that 'duty' was an essential element of evangelicalism.[3] This duty, of course, extended from the home to society, from personal behaviour to the market, a point often missed in discussions of evangelical social and economic concern. Indeed, evangelicals regarded the marketplace rather like life, as 'a school of moral discipline'.[4]

The assessment of the evangelical moral response to money and business is all the more important, not only because some evangelicals became very wealthy, but also because, as Jane Garnett points out, 'Britain's increasing prosperity', in the first half of the nineteenth century, was 'a focus for Protestant pride'.[5] Evangelicals had a sense of inner conflict in their dealings with money. Success in business was seen as an act of providence; bankruptcy as divine judgment. The Quakers – founders of many businesses – were particularly severe on failure, though that was as much a reflection of Quaker culture as of theological conviction. Evangelicals were

---

1 D. W. Bebbington, *Evangelicalism in Modern Britain: A History from the 1730s to the 1980s* (London: Unwin Hyman, 1989).
2 Boyd Hilton, *The Age of Atonement: The Influence of Evangelicalism on Social and Economic Thought, 1795–1865* (Oxford: Clarendon Press, 1988).
3 Quoted in *Evangelical Faith and Public Zeal: Evangelicals and Society, 1780–1980*, edited by John Wolffe (London: SPCK, 1995), p. 1.
4 J. Baldwin Brown, 'The Young Man's Entrance into Life, and Commencement of Business', in *Christianity in the Business of Life: Four Lectures* (London: John F. Shaw, 1858), p. 23.
5 Jane Garnett, '"Gold and the Gospel": Systematic Beneficence in Mid-Nineteenth-Century England', in *The Church and Wealth*, edited by W. J. Shiels and Diana Wood (Oxford: Blackwell, 1987), p. 347.

not only to act properly in the conduct of the acquisition of wealth but once it was in their hands, wealth carried many dangers and deep responsibilities. Philanthropic enterprise carried such expectation that the doctrine of salvation by faith alone could easily become confused with salvation by good works. Evangelical business leaders may have been essentially paternalistic in their social outlook – they built model villages, sang hymns and organized the voluntary clubs and societies which could almost be characterized as a distinguishing mark of evangelical faith – but they also applied their business minds to the achieving of social good. The houses in the Bournville model village were not given away, but sold with a 999-year lease on a mortgage at 2.5 per cent with a deposit of up to 50 per cent.[6] Questions of the treatment of employees, profit-sharing, advertising, and limited liability also exercised evangelical minds. God had certainly, in his providence, provided the iron laws of economics; the task for evangelicals was how to reconcile commerce and conscience when the laws of economics produced decidedly unpalatable consequences.

'Earn all you can, save all you can, give all you can'

John Wesley first preached his sermon on 'The Use of Money' in 1744, in the early pioneering years of the revival.[7] Perhaps the fact that he felt the need to preach such a sermon so early on in the history of the evangelical movement, and indeed to repeat it often (twenty-three times in his sermon register), is an indication that Wesley observed the complexities and challenges which money and wealth brought to disciples. He certainly made clear that followers of Christ gave insufficient importance and attention to the subject, although the sermon itself was not published until 1760. Perhaps the sermon was indicative of the journey that Wesley himself had travelled.

Henry Rack has pointed out the nature of the apparent contradictions in Wesley's teaching which have led some to align him with Adam Smith, others with the restrictive practices of mercantilism and yet others to place him in a communitarian or social gospel trajectory. Wesley seems to have experimented, at least intellectually, with the idea of 'holding all things in common', but any attachment to the idea was short lived.[8]

He was clear in his sermon that the problem of money rested not in the medium itself, but 'in them that use it'. Money itself 'is of unspeakable service to all civilized nations in all the common affairs of life', and 'is an excellent gift of God, answering the noblest ends'.[9] There is little economics here; the admonitions are those of a preacher.

Although Wesley constructed his sermon around the three well-known expressions, 'gain all you can', 'save all you can' and 'give all you can', these were not unrestricted injunctions. So, to gain all you can was not to come at the expense of either our physical or mental health or indeed to damage our neighbours. Trade deemed 'sinful' was to be avoided. Wesley showed at least some awareness of the operations of the market in a more detailed comment concerning undercutting a competitor's price or his business.

---

6 Richard Turnbull, *Quaker Capitalism* (Oxford: Centre for Enterprise, Markets and Ethics, 2014), p. 54.
7 Ralph Waller, *John Wesley: A Personal Portrait* (London: SPCK, 2003), p. 104.
8 Henry D. Rack, *Reasonable Enthusiast: John Wesley and the Rise of Methodism* (London: Epworth Press, 1989), pp. 364–5. See further, W. R. Ward, 'Methodism and Wealth, 1740–1860', in *Religion, Business and Wealth in Modern Britain*, edited by David J. Jeremy (London: Routledge, 1998), pp. 63–70.
9 'Sermon 50: The Use of Money', in *The Works of John Wesley*, vol. 2: *Sermons II, 34–70*, edited by Albert C. Oulter (Nashville, TN: Abingdon Press, 1985), p. 268.

> We cannot, consistent with brotherly love, sell our goods below the market price. We cannot study to ruin our neighbour's trade in order to advance our own. Much less can we entice away or receive any of his servants or workmen whom he has need of.[10]

Wesley may indeed have rapidly travelled away from the community of goods, but the market was not a place for either destructive or unfair behaviour. So, he argued that whilst to gain all you can 'is the bounden duty of all who are engaged in worldly business', the injunction was only to be discharged by 'honest industry'.[11]

Wesley's second injunction in the sermon ('save all you can') was largely aimed at excess – a theme which would remain a common refrain in later evangelicalism. He warned against wasting money on idle expenses or in 'curiously adorning your houses in superfluous or expensive furniture; in costly pictures, painting, gilding, books; in elegant (rather than useful) gardens'.[12] In his sermon on 'The Danger of Riches', Wesley warned those in business against covetousness, excessive consumption and acquisition.[13] To acquire more than was required for necessity, the business itself, the family and the avoiding of indebtedness, was clearly forbidden, according to Wesley. Similarly in a later sermon, 'On Riches', Wesley defined a rich person as not only 'a man that has immense treasures' but also as 'anyone that possesses more than the necessaries and conveniences of life'.[14]

Wesley seems to have established a position somewhat different from his early communitarianism with some endorsement given to honest gain albeit tempered by warnings against luxurious excess. However, he did not leave matters there and the third part of his sermon on 'The Use of Money' acted as a powerful counter-balance to any complacency. The theme was 'give all you can'. Wesley was clear that after the provision of food, clothing and shelter for the self and wider provision for the family, the good steward's responsibilities extended first of all to the household of faith and then to doing good to all of humanity.

According to Rack, Wesley is disappointing as an encourager of capitalism. There is certainly little sophistication or intellectual argument in Wesley's exposition, although in his *Thoughts on the Present Scarcity of Provisions* (1773), he showed some understanding of market mechanisms. Rack is surely correct here to observe that to interpret this particular treatise as support for liberal approaches to economics amounts to selective reading. Nevertheless, Rack also suggests that there is no doubt that 'some of his readers were comforted by his injunctions to gain and save and failed to take his concluding advice'.[15]

'No more sloth!' pleaded Wesley, 'Whatsoever your hand findeth to do, do it with your might'. He added, 'No more waste! . . . No more covetousness!'[16] Wesley tells us nothing about how the teachings of Adam Smith were adopted into evangelical thought. In some ways Wesley represents the classic evangelical response to money, business and social need. Despite his occasional radical thoughts Wesley stood in the mainstream tradition; he accepted the basic role of the market, offered strictures against excess and looked to the voluntary principle as a response to social need. However, for all that, we should not underestimate the power of his critique of wealth and money. David Hempton observes that Wesley's flirtation with the community of

---

10 'The Use of Money', p. 271.
11 'The Use of Money', pp. 272–3.
12 'The Use of Money', p. 274.
13 'Sermon 87: The Danger of Riches', in *The Works of John Wesley*, vol. 3: *Sermons III, 71–114*, edited by Albert C. Oulter (Nashville, TN: Abingdon Press, 1986), pp. 227–46.
14 'Sermon 108: On Riches', in *The Works of John Wesley*, III: 520.
15 Rack, *Reasonable Enthusiast*, p. 367.
16 'The Use of Money', p. 279.

goods may not have lasted, but it did mean that 'he never lost his deep-seated mistrust of the corrupting power of money on the spiritual life'.[17] Of course, in some ways, Wesley was the classic entrepreneur and like the best examples of the entrepreneurial spirit, his own disciplined and frugal life matched that of the Quaker entrepreneurs of the next century. Whether the return was spiritual or economic, discipline was required.

The evangelical revival was, at least in part, a reaction against worldliness. In that respect Wesley's strictures against excess are unremarkable. However, if some strands of the evangelical tradition emphasize separation from the world, the mainstream, in the immediate next generation after Wesley, appeared to be disproportionately represented in the professions of 'this world', namely, commerce, politics, government service and the military.[18] As we examine the reasons for this, we will see some aspects of Wesley's critique repeated in greater depth, but also a greater articulation of the place of money, business and wealth within the evangelical scheme. Methodism itself experienced the effect of 'aspiration', upon both its members and its attitudes. Adam Smith published *The Wealth of Nations* in 1776 at the height of the Wesleyan revival. Somewhat surprisingly, there is little mention of Smith in the Wesleyan corpus, and certainly no engagement in depth with the issues he raised. Yet, within a few decades of Wesley's death, the evangelical Thomas Chalmers, among others, was seeking to apply the Smithian model to both economic and social thought from an explicitly evangelical position. The sermons and treatises against excess continued, but some elements of Smithian economics were adopted by evangelicals, as will be seen.

Evangelical responses to Adam Smith

Wesley's ambiguity was swept away by Chalmers, who wrote:

> The philosophy of free trade is grounded on the principle, that society is most enriched or best served, when commerce is left to its own spontaneous evolutions; and is neither fostered by the artificial encouragements, nor fettered by the artificial restraints of human policy. The greatest economic good ... or, in other words, a more prosperous result is obtained by the spontaneous play and busy competition of many thousand wills, each bent on the prosecution of its own selfishness, than by the anxious superintendence of a government, vainly attempting to medicate the fancied imperfections of nature, or to improve on the arrangements of her previous and better mechanism. It is when each man is left to seek, with concentrated and exclusive aim, his own individual benefit – it is then, that markets are best supplied.[19]

This alignment of evangelicalism and political economy comes about through the interplay of natural theology, the doctrine of providence, the influence of the prevailing culture upon the development of evangelicalism (the classic Bebbington thesis) and two crucial publications of Adam Smith – not only *The Wealth of Nations* (1776), but also *The Theory of Moral Sentiments* (1759). As Anthony Waterman put it: 'The process by which this took place arose from the

---

17 David Hempton, 'A Tale of Preachers and Beggars: Methodism and Money in the Great Age of Transatlantic Expansion, 1780–1830', in *God and Mammon: Protestants, Money, and the Market, 1790–1860*, edited by Mark A. Noll (New York: Oxford University Press, 2002), p. 124.
18 Ian Bradley, *The Call to Seriousness: The Evangelical Impact of the Victorians* (London: Jonathan Cape, 1976), p. 156.
19 'On Natural Theology IV.iv.15', in *The Works of Thomas Chalmers* (25 vols, Glasgow: William Collins, 1835–42), II: 136–7.

confrontation between and interaction of the "new learning" of political economy and the "old learning" of Christian theology'.[20]

Smith's *Wealth of Nations* has been described as 'the fountainhead of classical economics'[21] which 'launched the classical tradition in economic thought'.[22] His model was essentially one of growth in an agrarian economy. He defined the foundational elements of a market economy as value, price, cost and exchange. The place of capital and capital accumulation was central to the concept of economic growth implicit in the model. Money was neutral; its role was not to determine prices, but to enable transactions. Smith's theoretical model was not a coherent whole and was subject to development and adjustment by many subsequent economists including David Ricardo, John Stuart Mill and Thomas Malthus. However, at the heart of the model lay not a mechanistic or mathematical identity, but a philosophical proposition. The essence of Smith's economic theory was the paradox that by the individual pursuit of self-interest (as implanted by nature) not only were the needs of others in society met, but greater public good was achieved. This is the famous 'invisible hand' bringing buyers and sellers together, setting market prices through competition and the reconciliation of supply and demand. Smith left the identity of the hand open; to Chalmers and others, it was the hand of the Almighty.

The classical model can only be evaluated within the framework of how Smith understood the world. This view was essentially one analogous to Newtonian mechanics applied to the economic universe,[23] a worldview of natural law, reflected both in humanity's innate nature and in the economic laws that governed the universe. Order and harmony were the key characteristics. However, it is a mistake to understand Smith's economic theories simply in mechanistic terms. His prior work, *The Theory of Moral Sentiments* (1759), saw humanity as compelled by three sets of motives; self-love and sympathy, freedom and propriety, and labour and exchange. The interaction of these motives produced both the classic economic model, and moral and social sympathy.

From these motives derived 'a certain propensity in human nature', that is, 'the propensity to truck, barter, and exchange one thing for another'.[24] Bargains were struck in the economic field through self-love accompanied by comparative advantage gained from trade. Paradoxically, the invisible hand of the economic mechanism allowed for the satisfaction of others by each serving their own needs. Smith added that the same natural law which had implanted in each person the propensity to barter for his own advantage had also implanted principles, 'which interest him in the welfare of others and make their happiness necessary to him'.[25] The Smithian position can be summarized:

> Smithian man, then, is roughly equal by natural abilities and equipped with a propensity to exchange; he is also motivated principally by self-interest in his economic dealings, and he is provided by nature, slowly and spontaneously, with a system which perfectly suits him and one which naturally makes his inherent self-seeking fit him for

---

20 A. M. C. Waterman, 'The Ideological Alliance of Political Economy and Christian Theology, 1798–1833', *Journal of Ecclesiastical History* vol. 34 (April 1983), 232.
21 B. A. Corry, *Money, Saving and Investment in English Economics 1800–1850* (London: Macmillan, 1962), p. 1.
22 William J. Barber, *A History of Economic Thought* (London: Penguin, 1967), p. 17.
23 Barber, *A History of Economic Thought*, p. 21.
24 Adam Smith, *An Inquiry into the Nature and Causes of the Wealth of Nations* (new edition, 3 vols, London: Cadell and Davies, 1812), I: 20.
25 E. L. Paul, *Moral Revolution and Economic Science: The Demise of Laissez-Faire in Nineteenth-Century British Political Economy* (Westport, CT: Greenwood, 1979), p. 5.

society. And from this desire of every man to seek his own advantage and to improve his condition arises all public and private wealth.[26]

The link between this and evangelical faith was not made by all. Chalmers saw that this outlook 'strongly bespeaks a higher agent, by whose transcendental wisdom it is, that all is made to conspire so harmoniously and to terminate so beneficially'.[27] According to Chalmers, the idea that public good could be obtained from the exercise of individual self-interest required a presiding wisdom. For others, however, it amounted to 'a supplementary revelation', or 'a repugnant perversion of traditional Christian values'.[28] Hilton's *The Age of Atonement* comprehensively demonstrated the link between Christian theology and political economy, although he overplayed the concept of 'evangelical economics' and underplayed the diversity of economic opinion within the evangelical movement.[29]

There are two theological links between economic thought and evangelical belief – natural theology and the doctrine of providence. Jacob Viner has pointed out that the natural sentiments within human beings as described by Adam Smith were endowed by divine providence and indeed that Smith's whole argument was a significant application of the providential and teleological argument to human behaviour. Thus, 'all of this psychological apparatus is providential; it is designed by God for the benefit of mankind, and it is presumptuous for man, even if he be a moral philosopher ... to find flaws in it'.[30] The paradox in the classical model between the pursuit of individual self-interest and the overall achievement of the public good could only be explained by the providential design of the laws of political economy and competition. This same doctrine of providence also explains why it seemed to so many that 'the imperialism of the Gospel and of Free Trade went hand in hand'.[31] Industry and commerce would bring about moral and religious improvement; even the slave trade would succumb to the forces of competition.[32]

Evangelicalism has been more dependent on the natural theology tradition than is sometimes allowed. Chalmers wrote several important works, including not only *On Political Economy* (1832) and *On the Christian and Economic Polity of a Nation* (1836–1842), but also two volumes *On Natural Theology* (1836). He considered in detail how the natural order affected both the economic and political well-being of society. Chalmers asserted a natural law of property and built upon Smith's philosophical basis. So he appealed to a law of self-preservation which led to industry, and a law of relative affection which was implanted by nature and led to compassion for the distress of others. Indeed Chalmers rejected the notion of state intervention on the grounds of the violation of the natural order: 'We cannot translate beneficence into the statute-book of law, without expunging it from the statute-book of the heart'.[33] So Chalmers concluded that political economy had been established by God to bring together prudence,

---

26 Paul, *Moral Revolution and Economic Science*, p. 20.
27 'On Natural Theology IV.iv.15', in *The Works of Thomas Chalmers*, II: 137.
28 R. A. Soloway, *Prelates and People: Ecclesiastical Social Thought in England, 1783–1852* (London: Routledge, 1969), p. 93.
29 For comparison with North America, see Stewart Davenport, *Friends of the Unrighteous Mammon: Northern Christians and Market Capitalism, 1815–1860* (Chicago, IL: University of Chicago Press, 2008).
30 Jacob Viner, *The Role of Providence in the Social Order: An Essay in Intellectual History* (Princeton, NJ: Princeton University Press, 1976), p. 81.
31 Andrew Porter, 'Commerce and Christianity: The Rise and Fall of a Nineteenth-Century Missionary Slogan', *Historical Journal* vol. 28 (1985), 613.
32 Porter, 'Commerce and Christianity', 613–4.
33 'On Natural Theology IV.iv.10', in *The Works of Thomas Chalmers*, II: 128.

moral principle and physical comfort.[34] This close link between providence, natural theology and political economy was not restricted to evangelicalism, but did embrace the tradition. Waterman names six Christian theologians who made significant contributions to economics: Edward Copleston, Thomas Malthus, William Paley and Richard Whately, plus two prominent evangelicals, Chalmers and J. B. Sumner.[35]

This essentially optimistic viewpoint reflected both the early streams of evangelical opinion until about 1830 and, of course, the influence upon evangelical opinion of the prevailing intellectual culture. However, both Porter and Viner note ambiguity in evangelical attitudes.[36] Porter argues that post-1870 'the greater difficulty by far lies in finding evangelicals who had confidence in the beneficial association of Christianity and commerce',[37] although he denies that theology had anything to do with that change in the prevailing viewpoint. On the contrary, it was central. Economic competition resulted inevitably in inequality, which fitted well with the classic evangelical interpretation of life on earth as a time of probation and discipleship. The rewards and punishments of the market – from wealth to bankruptcy – were inherent in this view.

Trade, business and sin

The preceding analysis goes some way towards explaining the inherent attractiveness of business and commerce for evangelicals. Nevertheless many were aware of the ambiguities and continued throughout the nineteenth century to critique business practice and the dangers of wealth. Even if the sociological thesis of Max Weber's *The Protestant Ethic and the Spirit of Capitalism* (1905) is not accepted, the link of capitalism and evangelicalism is undeniable. Indeed, there is a strong argument that it was theology – and especially the notion of providence and the evangelical embrace of natural theology – alongside the essential discipline of evangelical spirituality which lay at the heart of the evangelical understanding of the business enterprise. Ian Bradley summarized succinctly W. E. Gladstone's observation on the natural harmony between evangelicals and commerce. 'Evangelicalism', Bradley notes, 'rationalized and justified worldly success'.[38]

Many commentators articulated the principles of commerce, business and wealth creation. Henry Boardman affirmed commerce because it 'stimulates skill, rewards enterprise, diffuses knowledge'.[39] Thomas Gisborne, a Clapham evangelical, in *An Enquiry into the Duties of Men* (1794) argued that the purpose of business was 'to promote the cultivation of the earth; to call forth into use its hidden treasures; to excite and sharpen the inventive industry of man'.[40] Thus natural theology and the doctrine of divine providence interacted together to produce a rationale for business and commerce; the Lord has provided and the Lord has endowed. In 1874, W. H. Lyttelton (an evangelical clergyman in Worcestershire) took a view which might be regarded as 'negative assurance':

---

34 'On Natural Theology IV.iv.18', in *The Works of Thomas Chalmers*, II: 142.
35 Waterman, 'The Ideological Alliance of Political Economy and Christian Theology, 1798–1833', 232.
36 Viner, *Role of Providence*, p. 45; Porter, 'Commerce and Christianity', 618.
37 Porter, 'Commerce and Christianity', 619.
38 Bradley, *Call to Seriousness*, p. 157.
39 H. A. Boardman, *The Bible in the Counting House: A Course of Lectures to Merchants* (London: Thomas Bosworth, 1854), p. 53.
40 Thomas Gisborne, *An Enquiry into the Duties of Men in the Higher and Middles Classes of Society in Great Britain: Resulting from Their Respective Stations, Professions, and Employments* (London: B. and J. White, 1794), p. 368.

> It is most important that we should clearly understand that a business-life and the deliberate adoption of money-making as the leading practical operation of life, is not, in itself, or necessarily, contrary to the mind of Christ.[41]

Perhaps Lyttelton understood that even if business and commerce had divine endorsement, it could not be an unlimited one. Herbert Spencer followed Wesley in noting 'that which we condemn as the chief cause of commercial dishonesty, is the *indiscriminate* admiration of wealth'.[42] In other words, the love of money rather than the medium itself. The point was reinforced by Montagu Villiers (later bishop of Durham) speaking to the Young Men's Christian Association (YMCA):

> Wealth, by itself, is neither good nor evil. In seeking gold, in a measure, we do our duty. Our families are supported by it, commerce requires it, and man is taught, indeed, that he must earn his bread by the sweat of his brow.[43]

Villiers added that the Bible was not opposed to political economy and is a moral force to help the poor by encouraging industry and trade.

However, despite this affirmation of business it was clear that there were problems at both the conceptual and practical levels. Jane Garnett has shown that the increase in the number of companies, indeed limited liability companies, from the 1830s onwards, was matched by an increased prevalence of fraud and unfair trade practices.[44] The financial journalist David Morier Evans was scathing:

> Eminently characteristic of the period is the extraordinarily large scale on which ordinary crimes are planned, and, for the moment, successfully carried out. From time immemorial clerks have been discovered embezzling the property of their employers but when, save in the middle of the nineteenth century, could it be supposed a case such as that of Walter Watts would occur, who, not content with trifling peccadilloes successively opened two theatres with money surreptitiously obtained from the Globe Insurance Company.

He described Watts's career as 'a symbol of that taste for luxury, and that recklessness . . . which so singularly distinguish the present age'.[45] The problem was two-way – individual behaviour and unfair trade practice. Evangelicalism was more interested in the former but the latter could not be ignored. So Gisborne, while noting Adam Smith's 'force and acuteness of reasoning', and accepting most of his conclusions, also added that 'some of them seem at any rate to require considerable limitations'.[46] Perhaps this was due to what Lyttelton referred to as 'immoderate eagerness' for speculation and making money, or, in case his readers had not appreciated his nuanced approach, 'this ravenous, and insatiable, and ever-hurrying greediness of pursuit of it,

---

41 W. H. Lyttelton, *Sins of Trade and Business: A Sermon* (London: Isbister, 1874), pp. 4–5.
42 Herbert Spencer, *The Morals of Trade*, p. 81, attached to Lyttelton, *Sins of Trade and Business*.
43 H. M. Villiers, 'Gold and Gold-Seekers', in *Lectures Delivered Before the Young Men's Christian Association, in Exeter Hall, from November 1852, to February 1853* (London: James Nisbet, 1853), p. 141.
44 Jane Garnett, 'Evangelicalism and Business in Mid-Victorian Britain', in *Evangelical Zeal and Public Faith*, edited by Wolffe, p. 60.
45 D. Morier Evans, *Facts, Failures and Frauds: Revelations, Financial, Mercantile, Criminal* (London: Groombridge and Sons, 1859), p. 3.
46 Gisborne, *An Enquiry into the Duties of Men*, p. 372.

this intoxication of love of it'.[47] Villiers noted that 'in the search for gold, the golden rule itself is forgotten'.[48] Boardman criticized luxury and extravagance noting that the 'money which is hurriedly made, is wastefully expended', and adding that the 'contest for gain in the arena of business is carried forward as a race for ostentation in social life'.[49] The evangelical clergyman, Hugh Stowell, lecturing to the YMCA in Manchester in the mid-1850s on 'The Christian Man in the Business of Life', noted how 'fatally is wealth set up as a standard, as though it were the measure of right and wrong, greatness and meanness, virtue and vice!'[50] His colleague in Anglican ministry, George Fisk, summed it up elsewhere: 'And when I contemplate the character of the commercial spirit of the day, I sometimes tremble while I mark the progress of the making haste to be rich, which dares not look up to heaven'.[51]

It is clear there was a problem. The evangelicals of the nineteenth century stood four-square with Wesley in their criticisms of excess, luxury and overly ostentatious lifestyles. However, the extent of the evangelical dissension, not with business, but with commercial practice, extended further. The sins of trade were regularly enumerated by evangelical commentators and preachers. Gisborne argued that the 'origin of almost all the unjustifiable proceedings in trade, is a spirit of covetousness'.[52] In his introduction to Boardman's lectures given to merchants in America, Robert Bickersteth suggested that the author's conclusion was that 'the dealings and speculations of commerce . . . will not bear investigation by the light of God's Word'.[53] What had changed from the early evangelical movement was not the critique of wealth's dangers, not even the basic affirmation of business, but a significantly more detailed understanding of how evangelical concepts of sin extended to business practice. Stowell said that the level of 'manifold and intricate fraud' in business dealings meant that 'I cannot but tremble for young men' entering into business.[54]

There were a number of areas of concern: first, a lack of honesty in business practice. Lyttelton wrote:

> And how many ways are there still . . . of . . . adulterating what is sold, calling things good which are known to be worthless, even consciously doing work ill, and yet taking the full pay for it.[55]

Adulteration was rife. He referred to the many 'clever contrivances . . . in all professions for "making the ephah small and the shekel great" '[56] – in other words, short measures. Stowell lamented the 'lax and prevalent' practices.[57] Gisborne warned against insider trading and noted that the 'frequency of deceit does not take away the guilt of it'.[58]

The second major concern was the poor treatment of employees. Villiers quoted from John

---

47 Lyttelton, *Sins of Trade and Business*, p. 17.
48 Villiers, 'Gold and Gold-Seekers', p. 148.
49 Boardman, *The Bible in the Counting House*, p. 121.
50 Hugh Stowell, 'The Christian Man in the Business of Life', in *Christianity in the Business of Life: Four Lectures* (London: John F. Shaw, 1858), p. 92.
51 George Fisk, 'The Moral Influence of the Commercial Spirit of the Day', in *Lectures Delivered Before the Young Men's Christian Association, 1847–8* (London: Benjamin Green, 1848), p. 287.
52 Gisborne, *An Enquiry into the Duties of Men*, p. 387.
53 Boardman, *The Bible in the Counting House*, p. v.
54 Stowell, 'The Christian Man in the Business of Life', p. 94.
55 Lyttelton, *Sins of Trade and Business*, p. 12.
56 Lyttelton, *Sins of Trade and Business*, p. 12.
57 Stowell, 'The Christian Man in the Business of Life', p. 95.
58 Gisborne, *An Enquiry into the Duties of Men*, p. 465.

Francis's *Chronicles and Characters of the Stock Exchange* (1849), which said of the financier Nathan Mayer Rothschild that 'Like too many great merchants, whose profits were counted by thousands, he paid his assistants the smallest amount for which he could procure them'.[59] Villiers also linked unfair profits and unfair wages with the truck system – the payment of wages in public houses. This scandalous practice meant that workers gathered in public houses at lunchtimes on payday (often involving behind the scenes arrangements with pub landlords). The pay was delayed until the late afternoon; credit was taken for the drink consumed until the wages were paid and were then required for the discharge of the debt. It was another evangelical, Lord Shaftesbury, who campaigned in Parliament against such practices. Speaking on the Second Reading of the Payment of Wages in Public Houses (Prohibition) Bill in 1883, he said that 'they would find that seven-tenths of the men and every one of the women would cry out in the name of God to give them this legislation'.[60]

The third concern was loss-leading or cross-subsidy. Gisborne gave an example of sugar sold at below its market price so as to gain custom for tea which was sold at a proportionately much greater price. He attacked traders – or 'adventurers', as he put it:

> who endeavour to draw customers to their banking-house, or their shop, by dazzling them with flattering terms and accommodations which are not meant to be continued; or who transact some part of their business, or dispose of some particular article at a losing price, as a lure to the unwary; while they more than repay themselves by unsuspected and exorbitant profits on other branches of their trade.[61]

Gisborne also attacked artificial pricing, customs duty avoidance and the charging of higher prices to the poor – whether by a merchant or a banker.

> If it be wrong in the banker to raise his terms of doing business, or his rate of interest, upon modest or ignorant customers; it is not less wrong in the merchant to extort a higher price than usual from purchasers of a similar description.[62]

A fourth area of evangelical concern was speculation, which Boardman described as 'not commerce, but gambling',[63] characterized by there being no intention to close a deal, simply to trade for the difference. He added that 'a merchant ... is not authorized, in ordinary circumstances, to employ his capital or credit in speculations aside from his proper business'.[64] Stowell counselled against being 'carried away with inordinate love of speculation', and rushing into 'new schemes'.[65]

How did evangelicals respond to these challenges? At the theoretical level the matter was rather complex. Moral discipline was not only seen as essential within market behaviour, but furthermore, as Hilton notes, consequent on the widespread adoption by evangelicals of

---

59 John Francis, *Chronicles and Characters of the Stock-Exchange* (London: Willoughby, 1849), p. 300, quoted in Villiers, 'Gold and Gold-Seekers', p. 150.
60 Earl of Shaftesbury, 'Payment of Wages in Public Houses Prohibition Bill', *Hansard*, House of Lords, 6 March 1883, col. 1571.
61 Gisborne, *An Enquiry into the Duties of Men*, p. 375.
62 Gisborne, *An Enquiry into the Duties of Men*, p. 452.
63 Boardman, *The Bible in the Counting House*, p. 110.
64 Boardman, *The Bible in the Counting House*, p. 103.
65 Stowell, 'The Christian Man in the Business of Life', p. 90.

Malthusian pessimism, 'death was thought to be a lesser calamity than debt'.[66] The market rewarded and the market punished. Evangelical preachers were more practical. The Christian trader was exhorted, first of all, to recognize that his faith and business life could not be separated. J. Baldwin Brown, addressing the Manchester YMCA, urged young men entering business to 'take the whole of your moral nature into it with you'.[67] He was also clear that they must refuse 'from the first to regard business as a thing which must be dealt with on other principles than those which regulate the other departments of your life'.[68] In another lecture in the same series, J. B. Owen made a similar point, 'You cannot be one man in the warehouse and another in the sanctuary';[69] which Stowell spiritualized even further: God 'is not less in the counting-house or the exchange, than He is in the sanctuary'.[70] This unity of body and soul was considerably more prevalent amongst evangelicals than is often credited.

Second, and as a consequence, there were limits to business and trade. Boardman argued that there was 'a line beyond which firms have no moral *right* to extend their business'.[71] Gisborne maintained that some trades were contrary to God's will, most obviously the slave trade:

> The Government which shall allow its subjects to continue the slave trade, now that its nature and effects are thoroughly understood; the merchant who shall fit out the ship; the Captain who shall command it; the manufacturer who shall furnish it with manacles and fetters; will have to answer, each according to the just scale of divine retribution.[72]

Sin, of course, in classic evangelical fashion would lead inevitably to judgment. The unity of body and soul could not be separated from the eschatological calling to account. Gisborne's first general rule, as he called it, was that no-one was authorized to enter into or continue in a business 'which is either in itself unjust and immoral . . . or to impair the happiness of the human race'.[73]

The third response was the need for absolute integrity – as 'patent as the midday sun', according to Baldwin Brown[74] – or as Stowell put it, 'unflinching, unswerving honesty'.[75] Benjamin Gregory in *The Thorough Business Man* (1871), a memoir of the Wesleyan merchant Walter Powell, claimed that Powell 'had not two consciences – a buying conscience, and a selling conscience'.[76] Gisborne noted that in respect of bankers, 'scrupulous integrity and veracity' lay at the heart of their business.[77] Indeed the banker should never 'seek to retain custom at the expense of veracity'.[78]

Fourth, quality alone should sell rather than any duplicitous practices. Powell, according to

---

66 Hilton, *Age of Atonement*, p. 162.
67 Brown, 'The Young Man's Entrance into Life', p. 23.
68 Brown, 'The Young Man's Entrance into Life', p. 21.
69 J. B. Owen, 'Business without Christianity, with some Statistics and Illustrative Incidents', in *Christianity in the Business of Life: Four Lectures* (London: John F. Shaw, 1858), p. 47.
70 Stowell, 'The Christian Man in the Business of Life', p. 72.
71 Boardman, *The Bible in the Counting House*, p. 127.
72 Gisborne, *An Enquiry into the Duties of Men*, p. 369.
73 Gisborne, *An Enquiry into the Duties of Men*, p. 373.
74 Brown, 'The Young Man's Entrance into Life', p. 24.
75 Stowell, 'The Christian Man in the Business of Life', p. 94.
76 Benjamin Gregory, *The Thorough Business Man: Memoirs of Walter Powell* (London: Strahan and Co., 1871), p. 204.
77 Gisborne, *An Enquiry into the Duties of Men*, p. 416.
78 Gisborne, *An Enquiry into the Duties of Men*, p. 439.

Gregory, placed his reliance 'on the superiority of his articles'.[79] Indeed, evangelical resistance to advertising, not least amongst the Quaker businesses, was largely based upon the idea that good quality articles would, in effect, sell themselves.

Fifth, came transparency. Gisborne noted that, not only 'is one of the first duties of an upright trader to keep accurate accounts',[80] but also more broadly:

> To secure himself as far as may be possible both from the risk and from the suspicion of practising duplicity, he will be anxious to lay open, in such a measure as prudence will permit, the principles on which he acts in his profession.[81]

Sinful business behaviour would lead to judgment. Indeed, this was a common theological theme in the evangelical debates around business and commercial practice. The market was a school of discipline with rewards and punishments (wealth on the one hand, bankruptcy on the other), and also a place to grow in faith and be a model to others. J. C. Ryle, reflecting on the failure in 1841 of the family bank in Manchester and Macclesfield, wrote in his autobiography:

> I certainly cannot say I was surprised as much as some, and simply because I was a Christian I had long been vexed with the Sabbath-breaking which took place in connexion with the bank, visits to partners, and consultations about worldly business, and the like, and I had a strong presentiment that such a complete departure from my Grandfather's godly ways, would sooner or later be severely chastised.[82]

The Christian was to be 'the model-man for the conduct of this world's business'.[83] Owen argued that engaging in business without Christianity was greater folly than 'attempting to navigate an unknown sea without chart or compass'.[84] Boardman said that Christianity 'supplies ... one of the best of all schools for the culture of integrity, candour, moderation, decision, generosity'.[85] Indeed, if the market were a school then it should also inculcate a vision and interests beyond 'his own emolument and advantage',[86] and it 'will render him faithful and attentive in the concerns of other men committed to his care, or depending on his conduct'.[87] The banker in particular was exhorted to 'exert himself in doing good by benevolent loans',[88] which would do more good than simple philanthropy. Accepting small deposits was part of this responsibility. The pressure to conform to worldly business methods required 'a rare amount of Christian principle and strength of character to resist'.[89]

The point is that the theological idea of the market as a school of discipleship and discipline formed and shaped the moral character of the merchant which showed itself in honesty and fair dealings, but also in a wider vision of responsibility to society.[90] The quest for integrity in

---

79 Gregory, *The Thorough Business Man*, pp. 204–5.
80 Gisborne, *An Enquiry into the Duties of Men*, p. 395.
81 Gisborne, *An Enquiry into the Duties of Men*, p. 389
82 *Bishop J. C. Ryle's Autobiography: The Early Years*, edited by Andrew Atherstone (Edinburgh: Banner of Truth Trust, 2016), p. 88.
83 Brown, 'The Young Man's Entrance into Life', p. 5.
84 Owen, 'Business without Christianity', p. 33.
85 Boardman, *The Bible in the Counting House*, p. 51.
86 Gisborne, *An Enquiry into the Duties of Men*, p. 373.
87 Gisborne, *An Enquiry into the Duties of Men*, p. 389.
88 Gisborne, *An Enquiry into the Duties of Men*, p. 448.
89 Lyttelton, *Sins of Business and Trade*, p. 18.
90 See further, G. R. Searle, *Morality and the Market in Victorian Britain* (Oxford: Oxford University Press, 1998).

trade would carry a price for the evangelical businessman. He would face scorn and ridicule for standing up for his principles. However, this meant not only the specific practices, but the people, policies and behaviours of those who directed the enterprise. Spencer sums the matter up:

> When not only the trader who adulterates or gives short measures, but also the merchant who overtrades, the bank-director who countenances an exaggerated report, and the railway-director who repudiates his guarantee, come to be regarded as of the same genus as the pickpocket, and are treated with like disdain; then will the morals of trade become what they should be.[91]

Disciplined moral behaviour was not restricted to the narrowly legal. 'My chief design', Gisborne wrote, 'is to put the man of business on guard against being drawn almost imperceptibly into practices' which though not obviously criminal 'yet will be found, on examination, to partake of deceit'.[92] Business may indeed have been ordained by God, evangelicals taught, but its practitioners were not exempted from the judgment of both the invisible hand in the market and, ultimately, the visible hand of judgment.

Capitalism, socialism and philanthropy

To what extent did this evangelical critique of business and wealth find expression in the wider intellectual climate? G. M. Young, in his classic portrait of the Victorian era, asserted that 'the virtues of a Christian after the Evangelical model were easily exchangeable with the virtues of a successful merchant or a rising manufacturer'.[93] The reality was more complex. There were many examples of 'enlightened entrepreneurs', and, as has already been seen, an ideological alliance with the laissez-faire economics of 'political economy'.[94] David Bebbington notes that a 'whole race of successful industrialists, such as the millionaire hosiery manufacturer, Samuel Morley, had been bred in the chapels'.[95] Dominant among these enlightened businesses were the Quakers, many of whom were evangelicals, especially in the banking sector.[96] Nothing is more likely to hone the entrepreneurial spirit than the attempt to extinguish it. Their exclusion from higher education and civic life, led the Quakers to found their own schools and provide business education within their own communities through apprenticeships. Intellectual

---

91 Spencer, *The Morals of Trade*, p. 82.
92 Gisborne, *An Enquiry into the Duties of Men*, p. 383.
93 G. M. Young, *Victorian England: Portrait of an Age* (London: Oxford University Press, 1936), p. 2.
94 A. M. C. Waterman, *Revolution, Economics and Religion: Christian Political Economy, 1798–1833* (Cambridge: Cambridge University Press, 1991); A. M. C. Waterman, 'Theology and the Rise of Political Economy in Britain in the Eighteenth and Nineteenth Centuries', in *The Oxford Handbook of Christianity and Economics*, edited by Paul Oslington (Oxford: Oxford University Press, 2014), pp. 94–112.
95 D. W. Bebbington, *The Nonconformist Conscience: Chapel and Politics, 1870–1914* (London: George Allen and Unwin, 1982), p. 1.
96 Elizabeth Isichei, *Victorian Quakers* (Oxford: Oxford University Press, 1970); T. A. B. Corley, 'How Quakers Coped with Business Success: Quaker Industrialists, 1860–1914', in *Business and Religion in Britain*, edited by David J. Jeremy (Aldershot: Gower, 1988), pp. 164–89; Thomas C. Kennedy, *British Quakerism, 1860–1920: The Transformation of a Religious Community* (Oxford: Oxford University Press, 2001); Mark Freeman, 'Quakers, Business, and Philanthropy', in *The Oxford Handbook of Quaker Studies*, edited by Stephen W. Angell and Pink Dandelion (Oxford: Oxford University Press, 2013), pp. 420–33; Turnbull, *Quaker Capitalism*, pp. 5–10.

expertise was diverted into business.[97] 'Evangelical Quakerism' transformed the 'inner light' into objective standards of moral behaviour, which were reflected in the Quaker 'advices on trade', dealing with debt, accounting, honesty and other business matters. During the period of evangelical ascendancy within the Quaker movement in the mid-nineteenth century, the inner conscience of prudence and honesty was strongly reinforced by the external moral code of Scripture. Nevertheless, in practice, the picture was mixed. Some Quaker merchants provided pension schemes and even profit-sharing, but unions were unwelcome. Hours were long and the Cadburys dismissed young men at the age of twenty-one as they became more expensive, and there is no evidence that Quaker businesses paid above the market rate for their employees.[98] Although the Cadburys took part in the 'model village' experiment, exemplified by Bournville in Birmingham, to the critics this was, at best, paternalism and at worst, social control. Free trade and social conscience often came into conflict. Elizabeth Isichei writes that the 'philanthropic protestations' of the Quakers 'have always seemed to have a hollow ring in the light of their hostility or indifference to Shaftesbury's attempts to limit the working-hours of factory children'.[99]

Although proud of their social conscience, evangelicals generally distanced themselves from both the theoretical and practical claims of socialism, Christian or otherwise. There was a significant gap between the theological and ideological emphases of evangelicals and Christian Socialists, and their respective social action. Evangelical social concern was largely based on the voluntary principle, following Chalmers, whilst allowing for state intervention in the protection of the vulnerable.

Lord Shaftesbury, the doyen of Victorian evangelicalism, once found himself in 1833 sharing a platform with both Robert Owen, one of the founders of trade unionism, and Daniel O'Connell, the Irish radical. It is an illustration of how temporary bedfellows in a common cause did not mean embracing common political or economic principles.[100] Socialism and Chartism were anathema to Shaftesbury, both enemies of the state. In the *Quarterly Review* in 1840, he warned that 'The two great demons in morals and politics, Socialism and Chartism, are stalking through the land'.[101] In this opinion he was not alone. Most of the campaigners against 'child labour' were both evangelicals and Tories for whom any general move in the direction of the acceptance of 'political economy' was constrained by their view of society as organic, based on mutuality and interdependence, sacrifice and duties rather than rights.[102] This led Shaftesbury to argue in Parliament for 'good understanding between the employer and the employed',[103] and indeed:

> for restored affections, for renewed understanding between master and man, for combined and general efforts, for large and mutual concessions of all classes of the wealthy for the benefit of the common welfare, and especially of the labouring people.[104]

---

97 Arthur Raistrick, *Quakers in Science and Industry: Being an Account of the Quaker Contributions to Science and Industry during the 17th and 18th Centuries* (New York: Kelley, 1968), p. 43.
98 Joseph John Gurney, *Hints on the Portable Evidence of Christianity* (London: Arch, 1832); James Walvin, *The Quakers: Money and Morals* (London: John Murray, 1997), Ch. 11.
99 Isichei, *Victorian Quakers*, p. 246.
100 Richard Turnbull, *Shaftesbury: The Great Reformer* (Oxford: Lion Hudson, 2010), p. 83.
101 Lord Ashley, 'Infant Labour?', *Quarterly Review* vol. 67 (December 1840), 180.
102 Peter Dunkley, *The Crisis of the Old Poor Law in England, 1795–1834: An Interpretive Essay* (New York: Garland, 1982), p. 27.
103 Lord Ashley, 'The Ten Hours Factory Bill', *Hansard*, House of Lords, 29 January 1846, col. 392.
104 Lord Ashley, 'Factory Bill', *Hansard*, House of Lords, 10 May 1844, col. 914.

Hence he was as critical of 'class action' by the Chartists as he was of the failure of 'class responsibility' by the aristocracy. Chartism and socialism were symptoms of the perilous conditions of the people who thus, 'suppose that anything must be better than their present condition'.[105] For the socialist, wealth conveyed power which was destructive and had to be restrained; for the evangelical, wealth endowed responsibility and opportunity.

The evangelical understanding of sin was clearly applied to economic and social conditions. Shaftesbury was perhaps the most single-minded social reformer of the nineteenth century and explicitly driven by his evangelical convictions. Oppression of the people, unjust wages, and poor employment conditions, demanded action; it was the failure of those with the responsibility for such action that led to the rise of socialism. So, for example, Shaftesbury described the employment of child sweeps as 'this Satanic system', 'a vile system', and referred to 'the long succession of disgusting and unsurpassed physical and moral cruelties which had been inflicted, and which were still being inflicted, on children of the tenderest years'.[106] Yet, a Tory he remained.

As Bebbington has noted, 'Nonconformists shared the general belief that the remedy for the ills of society lay in sustained voluntary effort', but towards the end of the nineteenth century there was 'a deepened sense of responsibility for the welfare of the people as the circumstances of the poor were increasingly felt to be intolerable'. Hence philanthropy continued, but 'it was no longer thought to be sufficient'.[107] The 'Nonconformist conscience' played an increasingly significant part in politics and economics, contributing to better labour relations, trade unions and the rise of the Independent Labour Party. Dissent was divided, however. Not all business leaders imitated the beneficence of the Congregationalists Titus Salt and William Lever, or the Quakers George Cadbury and Joseph Rowntree. Michael Watts notes several Dissenting employers 'for whom maximising their profits came before the welfare of their workers'. Among the most notorious was the match-making firm Bryant and May, founded by Quaker William Bryant, where harsh working conditions led to a strike in 1888 and the creation of the first British women's trade union.[108]

John Clifford, twice president of the Baptist Union (1888 and 1899), moved from a classic understanding of the priority of the redemption of the individual to, in 1885, describing God as the first socialist and attacking the idea of competition altogether.[109] The publication of *The Bitter Cry of Outcast London: An Inquiry into the Condition of the Abject Poor* (1883) was but one catalyst. In the London dock strike of 1889 another Baptist minister, J. C. Carlile, served on a strike support committee. These individuals, however influential, were a minority and attracted much criticism and little support. In *Social Christianity* (1890), a series of sermons originally preached in London, the Methodist Hugh Price Hughes criticized contemporary Christianity as 'selfishly individualistic'.[110] He added: 'We have constantly acted as if Christianity had nothing to do with business, with pleasure and with politics; as if it were simply a question of private life and prayer meetings'.[111] This was reminiscent of Wilberforce's *Practical View* a hundred years earlier, but Hughes occupied a very different ecclesial, social and, indeed, political position. He recognized the limits of the voluntary principle – the statute book, he said, was 'the national

---

105 Lord Ashley, 'Infant Labour?', 180.
106 Earl of Shaftesbury, 'Chimney Sweeps Bill', *Hansard*, House of Lords, 11 May 1875, cols 443–6.
107 Bebbington, *The Nonconformist Conscience*, pp. 37–8.
108 Michael Watts, *The Dissenters*, vol. 3: *The Crisis and Conscience of Nonconformity* (Oxford: Clarendon Press, 2015), pp. 281–2.
109 Watts, *The Dissenters*, III: 291.
110 Hugh Price Hughes, *Social Christianity* (third edition, London: Hodder and Stoughton, 1890), p. xii.
111 Hughes, *Social Christianity*, p. 21.

conscience'.[112] He lavished praise upon Shaftesbury, who also understood the role of legislation not in place of, but alongside the voluntary principle. So, Hughes wrote: 'An Act of Parliament is not mere tone. It is educational. It teaches the conscience, it strengthens the conscience, and even the most degraded usually realise that what is illegal is wrong'.[113] What then is remarkable is how Shaftesbury and Hughes came to the same conclusion about socialism. Socialism said Hughes was 'illogical and mischievous'.[114] However, he recognized both its appeal and its threat: 'It will be impossible to arrest the Socialistic propaganda unless we infuse into our public life that deep and intense sympathy with the poor'.[115] Clifford, who distanced himself from the Independent Labour Party, wrote to the *Christian Socialist* in June 1891: 'I cannot see my way to the recognition of the public control of Capital'. As Watts comments, 'His enthusiasm for profit-sharing was incompatible with the Socialism which regarded all profit as anathema'.[116]

In a changed context, relationships were becoming institutionalized. Businesses were rapidly expanding with the capital formation enabled by limited liability. The old order was shifting, and evangelicals, so radical and yet so conservative, struggled with these cultural, societal and economic changes as much as everyone else.

Twentieth-century tensions

In the twentieth century, a dichotomy took place. Evangelicals continued to build successful business empires and maintained the classic tradition of philanthropy in support of the voluntary principle. The church was in many ways a 'chaplain to capitalism'.[117] At the same time, some evangelical theologians became more sympathetic towards socialism, although they did not carry the whole of the movement with them. A redistributive tradition arose, driven largely from the margins of evangelicalism.

In North America, evangelical business leaders shaped the direction of the movement. As Eric Baldwin observes, 'access to capital was as crucial for growth for churches as it was for the expansion of the industrial economy in which they were embedded'.[118] Profits from conservative corporations bankrolled conservative preachers in the religious marketplace. An evangelicalism nervous of the 'social gospel' was ripe to be developed into a brand. For example, Henry Parsons Crowell, founder of the Quaker Oats Company, joined the Board of the Moody Bible Institute, Chicago, in late 1901 just as the college struggled for money, identity and purpose following the death of its founder. He quickly took control, recruited new leadership, secured a clear theological branding, and restructured the Institute, paying market level salaries.[119] Crowell also combined forces with the Californian oil executive Lyman Stewart (co-founder of the Bible Institute of Los Angeles) to publish and distribute *The Fundamentals*, using the latest promotional techniques. Business methods were harnessed to secure evangelical orthodoxy. Evangelicals

---

112 Hughes, *Social Christianity*, p. 141.
113 Hughes, *Social Christianity*, p. 140.
114 Hughes, *Social Christianity*, p. 77.
115 Hughes, *Social Christianity*, p. 21.
116 Watts, *The Dissenters*, III: 312.
117 Michael L. Budde and Robert Brimlow, *Christianity Incorporated: How Big Business is Buying the Church* (Eugene, OR: Wipf and Stock, 2007), p. 7.
118 Eric Baldwin, 'Religious Markets, Capital Markets, and Church Finances in Industrializing America', in *Secularization and Religious Innovation in the North Atlantic World*, edited by David Hempton and Hugh McLeod (Oxford: Oxford University Press, 2017), p. 60.
119 Timothy E. W. Gloege, *Guaranteed Pure: The Moody Bible Institute, Business, and the Making of Modern Evangelicalism* (Chapel Hill, NC: University of North Carolina Press, 2015), p. 128.

acted as both consumers and investors, with their success driven by market forces.[120] A similar pattern emerged in Britain, where David Jeremy concluded that 'the impact of business on the churches has on balance been more substantial than the impact of the churches on business'.[121] However, his analysis of business elites found that in 1955 only 40 per cent of the chairmen and managing directors of Britain's largest ninety-six companies had *any* religious connection, limited perhaps to an Anglican funeral. The dominance of the Church of England makes isolating evangelical influence difficult; from a sample of 160 only four were associated with the Methodists, two with the Brethren and one with the Congregationalists.[122] Nevertheless, there were some prominent individuals, such as John Laing (a member of the Brethren) whose family construction company enjoyed phenomenal growth in the mid-twentieth century, enabling him to provide generous financial support to interdenominational evangelical ministry, including Inter-Varsity Fellowship, London Bible College and Billy Graham crusades.[123]

Politically most evangelical business leaders, especially in the United States, leaned to the Right. Surprisingly, however, some evangelical activists by the late twentieth century began to advocate collectivist and socialist economic policies. The 'redistributive tradition' is inextricably linked with the name of R. H. Tawney whose *Religion and the Rise of Capitalism* (1926) – originally a series of lectures in memory of the Christian socialist Henry Scott Holland – criticized the 'naïve and uncritical worship of economic power'.[124] Tawney provided the foreword in 1930 to the first English edition of Max Weber's *Die protestantische Ethik und der Geist des Kapitalismus*, which won a transatlantic readership as *The Protestant Ethic and the Spirit of Capitalism*. The sociological metanarratives of Tawney and Weber were deeply influential but, most remarkably, within a generation they had begun to shape even *evangelical* opinion. In *The Politics of Jesus* (1972), the Mennonite theologian John Howard Yoder stated that 'Jesus is, according to the biblical witness, a model of radical political action'.[125] This took the form of a social ethic, a challenge to the political authorities, and 'the beginning of a new set of social alternatives'.[126] Yoder claimed that Jesus had accepted voluntary poverty for the sake of the kingdom of God and had instructed his disciples to redistribute capital.

These ideas were further popularized among evangelicals by Ronald J. Sider's *Rich Christians in an Age of Hunger* (1977) and by the writings of Jim Wallis, founding editor of *Sojourners* magazine and author of *Agenda for Biblical People* (1976). Sider accepted the Tawney-Weber thesis that the objective of economic affluence had taken centre stage, combined with Yoder's politicization of Jesus, and built an economic and social ethic. He was an early critic of a growth based economy, arguing that the aim was not just a simpler lifestyle but 'to reduce total

---

120 See further, R. Laurence Moore, *Selling God: American Religion in the Marketplace of Culture* (New York: Oxford University Press, 1994); Douglas Carl Abrams, *Selling the Old-Time Religion: American Fundamentalists and Mass Culture, 1920–1940* (Athens, GA: University of Georgia Press, 2001); James Hudnut-Beumler, *In Pursuit of the Almighty's Dollar: A History of Money and American Protestantism* (Chapel Hill, NC: University of North Carolina Press, 2007); *Religion and the Marketplace in the United States*, edited by Jan Stievermann, Philip Goff and Detlef Junker (New York: Oxford University Press, 2015); *The Business Turn in American Religious History*, edited by Amanda Porterfield, Darren E. Grem and John Corrigan (New York: Oxford University Press, 2017).
121 David J. Jeremy, *Capitalists and Christians: Business Leaders and the Churches in Britain, 1900–1960* (Oxford: Clarendon Press, 1990), p. 418.
122 Jeremy, *Capitalists and Christians*, p. 193.
123 F. Roy Coad, *Laing: The Biography of Sir John W. Laing* (London: Hodder and Stoughton, 1979).
124 R. H. Tawney, *Religion and the Rise of Capitalism: A Historical Study* (London: John Murray, 1926), p. 282.
125 J. H. Yoder, *The Politics of Jesus: Vicit Agnus Noster* (Grand Rapids, MI: Eerdmans, 1972), p. 2.
126 Yoder, *The Politics of Jesus*, p. 39.

expenditures ... to the point where you enjoy a standard of living which all persons in the world could share'.[127] Sider's themes in his biblical analysis were liberation and incarnation, the classic emphases of Christian socialism. His prescription included the redistribution of capital, the denunciation of sinful structures on trade, the rejection of consumption, and the hint of a subsistence lifestyle ('living in community'). Sider acknowledged that 'eating less beef or becoming a vegetarian will not necessarily feed one starving child. If millions of Americans and Europeans reduce their beef consumption, but do not act politically to change public policy, the result will not necessarily be less starvation in the Third World'.[128] Therefore the demand must be for socio-political and structural change.[129]

During the widespread recession of the 1970s, among the worst hit communities were Britain's former industrial powerhouses, like the city of Liverpool. The local Anglican bishop, David Sheppard, a prominent evangelical, led calls not only for economic regeneration but for new economic structures. In *Bias to the Poor* (1983), a provocative set of lectures, he attacked the voluntary principle under the guise of social control:

> both charity and paternalism are concepts which are rightly criticised; both offer help, but frequently retain control in the fatherly or charitable hands of someone else, and therefore may then be said to strengthen rather than weaken dependence. That dependence is the enemy of a true sense of responsibility and self worth.[130]

The replacement of the voluntary principle by the state principle (Sheppard did not critique the dangers of dependency on the government) signified a key shift in evangelical approaches to poverty and economics. On both sides of the Atlantic there remained, however, many evangelical advocates of capitalism, albeit a market system built on ethical values – such as the British Conservative politicians Sir Frederick Catherwood, author of *The Christian in Industrial Society* (1964), and Brian Griffiths, author of *Morality and the Market-Place* (1982) and *The Creation of Wealth* (1984). In the United States, *The Poverty of Nations: A Sustainable Solution* (2013) by economist Barry Asmus and theologian Wayne Grudem – a play on Adam Smith's *The Wealth of Nations* – championed the integration of a free market economy with biblical social ethics.

These ideological tensions within evangelicalism were on display during the late twentieth and early twenty-first centuries in the Lausanne Movement. The First International Congress on World Evangelization brought together more than 2,300 evangelical leaders from 150 countries to Lausanne, Switzerland, in 1974. The carefully-crafted Lausanne Covenant affirmed 'that evangelism and socio-political involvement are both part of our Christian duty'.[131] It was a significant moment in the evolution of contemporary evangelical identities, though the covenant was much more muted than some participants desired.[132] The Second Congress, in the Philippines in 1989, was stronger: 'We affirm that the proclamation of God's kingdom of justice and peace demands the denunciation of all injustice and oppression, both personal and structural; we will

---

127 R. J. Sider, *Rich Christians in an Age of Hunger* (London: Hodder and Stoughton, 1977), p. 154.
128 Sider, *Rich Christians in an Age of Hunger*, p. 178.
129 See further, David R. Swartz, *Moral Minority: The Evangelical Left in an Age of Conservatism* (Philadelphia, PA: University of Pennsylvania Press 2012); Brantley W. Gasaway, *Progressive Evangelicals and the Pursuit of Social Justice* (Chapel Hill, NC: University of North Carolina Press, 2014).
130 David Sheppard, *Bias to the Poor* (London: Hodder and Stoughton, 1983), pp. 14–5.
131 Lausanne Covenant (1974), paragraph 5, in *Making Christ Known: Historic Mission Documents from 1974–1989*, edited by John Stott (Carlisle: Paternoster, 1996), p. 24.
132 Brian Stanley, '"Lausanne 1974": The Challenge from the Majority World to Northern-Hemisphere Evangelicalism', *Journal of Ecclesiastical History* vol. 64 (July 2013), 533–51.

not shrink from this prophetic witness'.[133] The Third Congress in South Africa in 2010 explicitly brought environmental concerns to the fore and reaffirmed the general commitment to social action: 'We give ourselves afresh to the promotion of justice, including solidarity and advocacy on behalf of the marginalized and oppressed'.[134] What is remarkable, however, is how little the various Lausanne statements say about the reform of economic systems. This may be the result of the dominant influence (and financial backing) of American advocates of the free market, but it also illustrates the limited impact of more radical evangelical thinkers upon the conservatism and pragmatism of the evangelical movement as a whole. Although some international evangelical relief and development agencies have grown increasingly sophisticated since the 1980s in their methods for combatting global poverty, including attempts to transform economic and political structures, the mainstream movement remains largely individualistic in its outlook.[135] Darren Grem goes further, arguing that the minority status of 'evangelical progressives' in modern America is not merely a result of a failure in persuasion or politics, but of 'money, power, strategy, and appropriation' since big business prefers to back conservative Christianity.[136]

Conclusion

This chapter has examined the trajectory of thought and practice within the evangelical tradition in the understanding of money, wealth and business. The main conclusion is that there was such a trajectory. However, this development was neither uniform nor without ambiguity. The principle of success in business remained throughout; evangelical natural theology and the doctrine of providence guaranteed that. Similarly, the idea of accountability within the market as well as the accountability of the market was a very strong emphasis. Intellectually, evangelicalism associated closely with Adam Smith and political economy but not in an entirely uncritical way. The other classic doctrine of evangelicalism, sin, prevented that and the century of industrialization, the nineteenth century, showed the increasing critique of business practice by evangelical writers whilst not losing sight of the place of business in the eyes of God.

This slightly ambiguous position is well-illustrated by the debates around the introduction of limited liability in 1856, which extended well beyond evangelicalism, but reflected the debate about accountability. Wesley's relatively simplistic critique of wealth and riches remained throughout and indeed gained sophistication. The Quakers illustrate the case in point – their very strong culture and network, together with the interplay of conscience and Scripture, leading to worldly success within a strongly moral framework. The move, in the twentieth century, in a more corporatist direction by at least some evangelical thinkers, has gained some, but only partial traction. It was perhaps that theological commitment to business, formed and shaped by the powerful critique of sin, that uniquely placed the evangelical entrepreneur in a position of both promoting business and doing good in society, not only through philanthropy, but through the application of commercial principles in pursuit of social good. Wealth for the evangelical is always likely to remain ambiguous; but once acquired, through honest means, should be put to good use.

---

133 Manila Manifesto (1989), affirmation 9, in *Making Christ Known*, edited by Stott, p. 231.
134 Cape Town Commitment (2010), paragraph 7c, in John Stott, *Evangelical Truth: A Personal Appeal for Unity, Integrity and Faithfulness* (new edition, Carlisle: Langham Global Library, 2013), p. 128.
135 Amy Reynolds and Stephen Offutt, 'Global Poverty and Evangelical Action', in *The New Evangelical Social Engagement*, edited by Brian Steensland and Philip Goff (New York: Oxford University Press, 2014), pp. 242–61.
136 Darren E. Grem, *The Blessings of Business: How Corporations Shaped Conservative Christianity* (New York: Oxford University Press, 2016), p. 8.

16

EVANGELICALS AND GLOBALIZATION

Philip Jenkins

The most significant theme in the history of Christianity over the past century has been the huge expansion of the faith worldwide, and the decisive shift of its centre of gravity outside Europe.[1] A century ago, Christianity was still clearly a Western religion. Combining Christian numbers in Europe and North America, these continents accounted for 82 per cent of all believers in 1900, and even by 1970, that figure had fallen only to 57 per cent.[2] Since that point however, change has been very marked. Today, Euro-American Christians make up 38 per cent of the worldwide total, and that figure could reach a mere 27 per cent by 2050. Back in 1914, Africa and Asia scarcely featured on the global Christian map. By 2050, though, by far the largest share of the world's Christians will be found in Africa, which should have a billion or more believers. About a third of the world's Christians by that point will be African, and those African Christians will outnumber Europe's by more than two to one. In terms of raw numbers, Latin America and Asia will both be outpacing Europe. By 2050, the nations with the world's largest

---

1 Global Christianity is a flourishing field of writing and research, and one that has only reached full maturity in the present century. See Lamin Sanneh, *Disciples of All Nations: Pillars of World Christianity* (New York: Oxford University Press, 2007); Mark A. Noll, *The New Shape of World Christianity: How American Experience Reflects Global Faith* (Grand Rapids, MI: Baker Academic, 2014); *Global Evangelicalism: Theology, History and Culture in Global Perspective*, edited by Donald M. Lewis and Richard V. Pierard (Downers Grove, IL: InterVarsity Press, 2014); Dana L. Robert, *Christian Mission: How Christianity Became a World Religion* (New York: Wiley-Blackwell, 2009).
2 Throughout this chapter, figures for Christian numbers are drawn from the World Christian Database (hereafter, WCD), produced by the Center for the Study of Global Christianity at Gordon-Conwell Theological Seminary, http://www.worldchristiandatabase.org/wcd/ (accessed 24 February 2018). Although enormously useful, WCD data suffer from two main problems. One difficulty involves traditionally Christian countries that historically supported state churches, where the WCD tends to rely on official church figures for the number of adherents. The notional figures for Britain or Germany, for example, tell us little about actual Christian practice or commitment, or even the number of people who might admit to any kind of Christian identification. Equally problematic are the WCD estimates for countries where Christianity is strictly regulated or regarded with widespread suspicion by government or rival religious communities. Nobody doubts that countries like India and China have sizable Christian populations over and above what is portrayed by the official statistics of those nations, but the size of such shadow populations in these lands is highly debatable. The WCD figures for these countries are substantially larger than many observers would suggest, and almost certainly require adjustment. Given those caveats, though, the WCD data represent by far the best available statistics.

Christian populations will be: the United States, Brazil, Mexico, Nigeria, the Congo, Ethiopia, the Philippines, and China. The Christian world will have turned upside down, and much of that epochal story has taken place just in the past half-century.

This change is enormously significant in its own right, but it is critical for the story of evangelicalism, broadly defined. Although most denominations have gained mightily from global expansion since about 1970, many of the greatest beneficiaries have been evangelical and charismatic groupings. Moreover, older mainline churches that have shared in the general upsurge have often done so by adopting worship styles that would once have seemed decidedly Pentecostal or charismatic.[3]

Christian expansion

Far more than at the height of the missionary expansion of imperial times, the story of evangelicalism has moved decisively to the global stage. Contrary to the expectation of those missionary pioneers, that global transformation was only partially a matter of mass conversions. By far the most important reasons for the change were demographic. According to the World Christian Database, between 1900 and 2010, the number of Christians in Europe grew by 29 per cent, a substantial figure. In Africa, though, the absolute number of recorded believers grew in the same period by an incredible 4,930 per cent, and the comparable growth in Latin America was 877 per cent.[4] Such growth can only be understood in terms of a rapid population increase.

Take for instance the continent of Africa. In 1900, Africa had around 100 million people, or 6 per cent of the global population. In 2005, the number of Africans reached one billion, or 15 per cent of humanity. By 2050, Africa's population will be between two and two and a quarter billion, which will then be about a quarter of the world's people.[5] Those numbers do not count African migrants in Europe and North America. If, therefore, a church was planted in an African nation in 1900, and it merely kept its share of the population, then it would in the subsequent years have grown by over tenfold, a spectacular return on the original investment.

Now set those numbers alongside those for Europe. The 400 million Europeans alive in 1900 would grow to 730 million today, but in relative terms, as a share of global population, Europe was in steep decline. Europeans made up a quarter of humanity in 1900, as against 11 per cent today, and falling to a projected 8 per cent by 2050. In 1900, Europeans outnumbered Africans by four to one. By 2050, Africans should have a three to one advantage over Europeans.

Having said this, conversion is nonetheless a key part of the story. To take the African example again, Christians represented just 10 per cent of the population in 1900, rising to some 46 per cent by the end of the century. In some countries particularly, the Christian share of the population boomed. In the lands that became Nigeria, Christians accounted for 1 per cent of the population in 1900, but 45 per cent by 1970.[6] Taking the continent as a whole, the main

---

3 For the global spread of Pentecostal forms of evangelical religion, see Allan Heaton Anderson, *To the Ends of the Earth: Pentecostalism and the Transformation of World Christianity* (New York: Oxford University Press, 2013); Donald E. Millar and Tetsunao Yamamori, *Global Pentecostalism: The New Face of Christian Social Engagement* (Berkeley, CA: University of California Press, 2007).
4 World Christian Database.
5 Population data are taken from the 'World Population Data Sheet', Population Reference Bureau (2013), at www.prb.org/publications/datasheets/2013/2013-world-population-data-sheet/data-sheet.aspx (accessed 24 February 2018). See also Rakesh Kochhar, '10 Projections for the Global Population in 2050', Pew Research Center (2014) at www.pewresearch.org/fact-tank/2014/02/03/10-projections-for-the-global-population-in-2050/ (accessed 24 February 2018).
6 World Christian Database.

African story of the twentieth century was that about half the population moved from primal, animist religions to one of the great monotheist faiths, and by a four to one margin, they chose Christianity over Islam.

Reasons for such conversions were complex, but much of the story involved rapid and tumultuous social change in the form of mass urbanization and migration, and that is equally true of Asia and Latin America as of Africa. From the 1960s onwards, all these societies were changed radically by the mass migration to cities, and the uprooting of old village communities. The emerging megacities offered little in the way of welfare, education or health, beyond what people could provide themselves, or what they found in religious institutions, whether Christian or Muslim. Those social ministries did much to attract migrants to their faiths. Of their nature, the groups running those outreach efforts tended to be more passionate and even fundamentalist in character, creating an open door for evangelical and charismatic communities. Much of their evangelism is associated with the vast revival meetings and miracle crusades that are a standard fixture of urban life across the Global South.

The nascent churches exercised a special appeal for groups that had been excluded in traditional society, but who could now claim a full share in participation and leadership. In different settings, this usually meant women and ethnic or racial minorities. In the new communities, they gained the power to speak publicly, to find what David Martin famously called 'Tongues of Fire'[7]. Many observers of Latin American religion remark on the great material improvement that evangelical women find in their domestic lives, particularly when their menfolk are induced to give up alcohol and drugs, and acquire habits of thrift. In a fine phrase coined by Elizabeth Brusco, Latin American Pentecostalism is a 'Reformation of Machismo'.[8] At higher social levels, upwardly mobile professional and technically-oriented groups were drawn to churches that interpreted the world in modern and Westernized forms, and this has commonly meant Western-style megachurches.

In speaking generally of 'evangelical and charismatic' churches in this way, questions of theological definition can become confused in the context of Global South Christianity. When seeking a definition of evangelicalism, most scholars turn gratefully to David Bebbington's classic 'quadrilateral', encompassing the four components of activism, biblicism, crucicentrism, and conversionism.[9] Looking at flourishing Global South churches, whether in Brazil, Nigeria or South Korea, it is very easy to find denominations that entirely fit these four defining principles. Unfortunately for purposes of strict accuracy, those same bodies also share many additional characteristics that mark them as charismatic or Pentecostal, above all a belief in continuing spiritual gifts, and often a profound commitment to spiritual warfare.

The confusion is most evident in Latin America where the term 'evangélico' is synonymous with Pentecostal, and attempts to distinguish a separate evangelical identity are met with puzzlement. In Ethiopia, the common word for Protestant is 'Pentay'. Nor are individual denominations any more reliable as a guide. The Indonesian Reformed Evangelical Church is actually Pentecostal, as is the very large Chilean congregation, Jotabeche Methodist Pentecostal Church. With due awareness of the definitional problems, this chapter inevitably transgresses the boundaries commonly erected between evangelicals and charismatics, and also Pentecostals

---

7 David Martin, *Tongues of Fire: The Explosion of Protestantism in Latin America* (London: Wiley-Blackwell, 1993).
8 Elizabeth Brusco, *The Reformation of Machismo: Evangelical Conversion and Gender in Colombia* (Austin, TX: University of Texas Press, 1995).
9 David W. Bebbington, *Evangelicalism in Modern Britain: A History from the 1730s to the 1980s* (London: Unwin Hyman, 1989), Ch. 1.

and neo-Pentecostals. In so much of the Global South, where growth has been so impressive, the labels really have little meaning.

Africa

It was particularly during the First World War that Africa witnessed an upsurge of native churches, usually led by prophetic or messianic figures. These groups became known as African Independent Churches (AICs), although that term has varied in meaning, not least because of its implication that such mainstream denominations as Anglicans or Catholics are somehow not independent. Today, the term is usually understood to represent African-Initiated Churches.

In the past half-century, such movements have attracted a disproportionate share of scholarly attention, with a heavy focus on those that draw on traditional practices. We have valuable accounts of such AICs as South Africa's Shembe movement or its Zion Christian Church, the ZCC.[10] While not diminishing the role of such groups, it would be wildly misleading to suggest that African church life is focused on such groups, with their distinctive practices that outsiders can find odd or troubling. Far more representative of African Christianity are more familiar evangelical or charismatic churches, or indeed mainline denominations that have usually become strongly charismatic in tone.

A typical example of such a thriving and wholly respectable church is ECWA, the Evangelical Church of West Africa, more recently retitled the Evangelical Church Winning All. Although by no means the largest or most significant denomination of its type, it epitomizes many familiar themes. ECWA claims some 5,000 congregations, across Nigeria and neighbouring lands, where it has 3 million active members, with another 3 million regular attenders.[11] Although originally founded by Euro-American missionaries, ECWA has for many years been strictly an African church in its leaders and members, and it bows to no external or colonial authority. It is in fact so entirely African and independent as to raise serious questions about the whole 'AIC' label.

ECWA's story begins in the 1890s with the Soudan Interior Mission, with 'Soudan' referring not to the modern nation but rather to the broad belt stretching across Africa below the Sahara. As the European empires began to break up after the Second World War, SIM began transferring its operation to the new ECWA church, which officially dates from 1954. By 1976, the new entity formally inherited all remaining SIM operations, including its educational, medical and publishing activities, and at that point it began its swift expansion. ECWA soon produced a roster of creative and influential leaders, including influential theologian Byang Kato, who urged the contextualization of the gospel in Africa, but at the same time warned of the syncretistic tendencies he saw among other thinkers of the day. From 1970, the church's Evangelical Missionary Society was headed by Panya Dabo Baba, an early pioneer of mission from Africa to the rest of the world. However familiar we might today find the notion of African missionaries travelling the world, much of the impetus for that South-North mission came from Panya Baba's enterprising vision. ECWA now has some 1,200 missionaries active outside Nigeria, spread across Africa, the Middle East, Europe and the United States.

Apart from any individual, ECWA exercises its influence through its two key Nigerian seminaries. Since 1980, the Jos ECWA Theological Seminary (JETS) has offered theological training

---

10 G. C. Oosthuizen, *The Theology of a South African Messiah* (Leiden: Brill, 1967); Bengt Sundkler, *Zulu Zion and Some Swazi Zionists* (Oxford: Oxford University Press, 1976); *The Story of Isaiah Shembe*, edited by Irving Hexham and G. O. Oosthuizen (Lewiston, NY: Edwin Mellen Press, 1997); Philip Jenkins, 'South African Zionists', *Christian Century* (14 June 2011), 45.

11 Philip Jenkins, 'The African Mainstream', *Christian Century* (31 October 2012), 45.

and higher education not just to its own clergy, but to a wide range of denominations, including Anglicans. It is a key presence in a nation that currently has some 75 million Christians, a number that could increase to 180 million by 2050. ECWA lacks so many of the features that would attract the notice of Western academics. It was not founded by flamboyant messianic prophets, and it has no rituals that bear the traces of shamanic or magical origins. Instead, it is immediately recognizable as a sober evangelical church. Of course, some of its features separate it from Western equivalents, not least in its firm belief in the reality of spiritual healing and exorcism. The church's claimed success in defeating spiritual evil accounts for a major part of its evangelistic success. But this mission always operates within the framework of church order, avoiding anything that might look like Pentecostal excess.[12]

While ECWA grew directly from Western missions, other rising churches were more purely domestic in character. In Ethiopia, for instance, can be seen a story not unlike that of Europe's own Reformation. From the late nineteenth century, individual entrepreneurs translated the Scriptures into native tongues, and new groups emerged outside the dominant Orthodox Church. The real explosion, though, came during the 1970s, when a Communist revolution all but swept away the old religious order. Although Protestants had been a very marginal presence indeed before 1974, today they are 17 million strong, around 18 per cent of the population, and they are multiplying fast.[13]

One successful body is the Ethiopian Evangelical Church Mekane Yesus, EECMY, which is Lutheran – appropriately enough, given the historical parallels to Luther's own day. Originating among foreign missionary bodies, the church achieved its independence in 1969, only a few years before the revolution. Since the 1960s, EECMY has grown from a few thousand baptized members to some 5.5 million. But the Mekane Yesus church is by no means the only force in the Protestant expansion. Even larger is the Kale Heywet ('Word of Life') charismatic church, a thoroughly Bible-centred group with 6.5 million members.[14] Smaller groups include the Meserete Kristos ('Christ is the Foundation'), which is Mennonite. Impossible to count too precisely are the congregations of the thriving but diffuse Mulu Wongel ('Full Gospel') church. Mulu Wongel's main congregation in Addis Ababa is one of Africa's largest megachurches.

In some cases, old AICs became much more obviously evangelical in tone as they made conscious decisions to move towards the Christian mainstream. A century ago, converts in what is now Nigeria developed a passionate spiritual movement committed to immediate spiritual experience, for prophecy, healings and visions. Fervent believers broke away to form societies for prayer and healing, and they attracted the name Aladura, 'Owners of Prayer'. With their strict focus on healing, the believers received an enormous boost during the great epidemics that swept West Africa during and after the First World War.[15]

One heir to that tradition was the Church of the Cherubim and Seraphim, which in turn spawned dozens of breakaways and new plantings. The most significant is the Redeemed Christian Church of God (RCCG), which since the 1970s has come to look ever more Pentecostal in its worship style. The RCCG has also achieved a stunning global reach, with a fiery sense of mission, and it has enjoyed wide success across North America and Europe. The RCCG is in the process of becoming a new global denomination.

12 Jenkins, 'The African Mainstream'.
13 Tibebe Eshete, *The Evangelical Movement in Ethiopia* (Waco, TX: Baylor University Press, 2009).
14 Philip Jenkins, 'Reformation in Ethiopia', *Christian Century* (27 November 2013), 45.
15 Ruth Marshall, *Political Spiritualities: The Pentecostal Revolution in Nigeria* (Chicago, IL: University of Chicago Press, 2009); Paul Gifford, *Ghana's New Christianity: Pentecostalism in a Globalizing African Economy* (Bloomington, IN: Indiana University Press, 2004). For the wider African scene, see Ogbu Kalu, *African Pentecostalism: An Introduction* (New York: Oxford University Press, 2008).

Latin America

In Latin America too, evangelical and charismatic numbers were growing fast, the difference of course being that here, the expansion occurred in lands long since converted to Christianity in its Roman Catholic form. We are not thus comparing like with like, in that this was not Christianization *de novo*.[16] Even so, we see many parallels between the two continents, especially in the forms of faith taken by new believers and their communities. Latin American Pentecostals have much in common with Africa's evangelical churches, and its AICs.

In Africa, many scholars paid insufficient attention to the main thrust of Christian growth because they were paying so much attention to the AICs. In Latin America, meanwhile, much of the Western writing on the religious scene in the 1970s and 1980s focused on liberation theology and the social activist movements within Catholicism, a phenomenon that scholars found ideologically attractive. By the late 1980s, though, liberation movements were stagnant or declining, while Pentecostal and evangélico churches were surging ahead.

By far the most important country in terms of Protestant growth is Brazil. The country's Protestant population has surged from perhaps 1 or 2 per cent in the 1960s to perhaps 20 per cent today, and the boom has no obvious end. Nobody scoffs at claims that Brazil by 2050 might have a Protestant majority, or at boasts of a 'New Reformation'. Protestantism in Brazil is dominated by thriving Pentecostal churches, especially by major denominations like the *Igreja Universal do Reino de Deus* ('Universal Church of the Kingdom of God'), and the *Igreja do Evangelho Quadrangular*, a descendant of the US Four Square Gospel church. One extraordinary success story has been the Assemblies of God, a Pentecostal church founded in the United States in 1914, and which today has some 3 million members in that country. Worldwide, though, it has enjoyed huge success, especially in Brazil. On a typical Sunday, more people attend Assemblies of God churches in the greater São Paulo area than in the whole United States. Those 3 million Assemblies followers in America are overwhelmed by 28 million in Latin America and the Caribbean, and 16 million more in Africa.[17]

In this region above all, can be seen the clear linkage between mushroom urban growth and the rise of popular evangelicalism. All these rising churches are strongly focused on promises of healing, miracles and personal transformation. In sociological terms, evangélicos offer the attractions of a classic sect. They demand high involvement and participation by members, who in return receive significant rewards of emotional satisfaction and intimate fellowship. Believers have joined a tight-knit new family, in which members strive to help each other confront and overcome the pressures of multiple deprivation. Catholics themselves grudgingly admit that Protestant believers are much more active and enthusiastic in their faith than their neighbours, keener about reading the Bible and trying to reshape their lives according to its teachings. The Brazilian Bible Society produces over 4 million Bibles annually, making that country one of the largest producers and consumers of the book worldwide.[18]

---

16 For more on this, see R. Andrew Chesnut, *Born Again in Brazil: Pentecostal Boom and the Pathogens of Poverty* (New Brunswick, NJ: Rutgers University Press, 1997); Daniel Miguez, *To Help You Find God: The Making of a Pentecostal Identity in a Buenos Aires Suburb* (Amsterdam: Free University of Amsterdam, 1997); Virginia Garrard-Burnett, *Protestantism in Guatemala: Living in the New Jerusalem* (Austin, TX: University of Texas Press, 1998); Peter S. Cahn, *All Religions are Good in Tzintzuntzan: Evangelicals in Catholic Mexico* (Austin, TX: University of Texas Press, 2003).
17 Philip Jenkins, 'Astonishing Assemblies', *Christian Century* (14 May 2014), 45.
18 Philip Jenkins, *The New Faces of Christianity: Believing the Bible in the Global South* (New York: Oxford University Press, 2006).

Asia

Asia has only one Christian majority nation, which is the overwhelmingly Catholic Philippines, and in most countries, Christian populations are very small minorities. Even so, the vast numbers in this region mean that those minorities represent quite substantial populations in their own right, and here too, evangelical and charismatic churches have grown dramatically, chiefly from the 1970s. In terms of sheer numbers, the heart of the Asian story is of course China, which now has a Christian population of perhaps 75 million, substantially larger than any European country. Much the largest growth has occurred among unregistered churches beyond the scope of government control, and these are overwhelmingly charismatic or evangelical in nature.[19]

We are on much firmer ground in South Korea, which over the past century has seen its Christian population grow from 1 per cent to around one-third of the whole.[20] Although Catholics and Protestants are both growing, many of the main congregations are evangelical or charismatic in nature. Some of Seoul's spectacular megachurches regularly appear in listings of the world's largest congregations, and they are virtually denominations in their own right. The best known is the Yoido Full Gospel Church, affiliated to the Assemblies of God, and currently claiming 900,000 members, spread among many satellite congregations.[21] The Myung Sung Presbyterian Church is the world's largest congregation in that tradition: Korea has more Presbyterians than the United States itself. After the United States, South Korea is the world's largest supplier of Christian missionaries; all this is happening in a global industrial and financial powerhouse, with huge media assets.

Other centres are less familiar. Although Indonesia is the world's largest Muslim state, it also has perhaps 30 million Christians, with another 8 or 9 million in Vietnam. Malaysia, Singapore and Taiwan all have solid Christian minorities. The nations bordering the South China Sea – China, Vietnam, the Philippines, Indonesia, Malaysia and Taiwan – are home to a combined population of well over 200 million Christians, a number not far short of the United States total. When we read the phrase 'Pacific Rim', we might just as well use the term Christian Arc. And that is all separate from the sizable Christian communities of the Indian subcontinent, at least 40 million strong. Perhaps 300 million Christians now live in Asia, about an eighth of the global total,[22] and most projections see the continent playing a growing role in the churches.

Across this Asian Christian landscape are many charismatic and evangelical churches, usually in the largest cities, and often appealing to upwardly mobile professional groups. The Pentecostal Church of Indonesia has grown from perhaps half a million members in 1980 to 3 or 4 million today. In 2008, the Indonesian Reformed Evangelical Church opened its Messiah Cathedral in Jakarta, a classic megachurch seating 6,000, and a grandiose structure that would not look out of place in Seoul or Singapore. Other megachurches flourish in Jakarta and in Surabaya, the country's second city. Despite the enormous power of Islam in that country, such urban

---

19 Fenggang Yang, *Religion in China: Survival and Revival under Communist Rule* (New York: Oxford University Press, 2011); Nanlai Cao, *Constructing China's Jerusalem: Christians, Power and Place in Contemporary Wenzhou* (Stanford, CA: Stanford University Press, 2010); Lian Xi, *Redeemed by Fire: The Rise of Popular Christianity in Modern China* (New Haven, CT: Yale University Press, 2010).
20 Robert E. Buswell and Timothy Lee, *Christianity in Korea* (Honolulu, HI: University of Hawaii Press, 2007); Timothy S. Lee, *Born Again: Evangelicalism in Korea* (Honolulu, HI: University of Hawaii Press, 2010).
21 Philip Jenkins, *The Next Christendom: The Coming of Global Christianity* (New York: Oxford University Press, 2011).
22 Philip Jenkins, 'Asian Tigers and Megachurches' (2012), www.realclearreligion.org/articles/2012/09/11/asian_tigers_and_megachurches.html (accessed 24 February 2018).

Christians show no concern about hiding their activities out of fear of provoking persecution. We find similar manifestations in India's high tech heartlands. Chennai's New Life Church claims a membership running into the tens of thousands, as do the Full Gospel and Bethel churches in Bangalore.[23]

Popular Christian culture

Throughout the Global South, signs of an evangelical Christian presence abound, and in unsuspected settings. In the streets of a typical black African nation, it is difficult to avoid the pious slogans and declarations of faith that serve as the names of businesses and the mottos painted on buses and taxis. Far from being casual ephemera, such manifestations suggest the omnipresence of faith. That vernacular faith is most evident in the soundscape. As Christian churches grow around the world, then, it is not surprising to find an astonishing efflorescence of hymn composition. We must avoid the loose term 'hymn-writing', as so many of the creators are primarily oral artists, and only gradually do their works find their way into written form. However they are made, though, the sheer abundance and quality of those hymns is overwhelming, whether in Yoruba or Swahili, Tamil or Zulu. Arguably, we live today in the golden age of Christian hymn-making.

In the English-speaking world, successive evangelical revivals left such monuments as 'Amazing Grace' or 'The Old Rugged Cross'. And as in the English-speaking world, hymns do not stand solely on the artistic merits of their words and music. To hear great hymns is to be drawn into a familiar story, which in its way forms part of an epic mythology. The newer Christian world, too, has its legendary hymns, but few as potent as the 'Tukutendereza Yesu', the mighty Luganda song that has since the 1930s become the anthem of evangelical faith across East Africa, especially for the pious *Balokole*, 'the Saved'. The hymn grew out of a revival that emerged in Uganda and Rwanda, and which subsequently transformed churches in Kenya and further afield. Since the 1970s, it has become the standard music heard at the region's frequent revival meetings and crusades, as the words mark the believer's acceptance of Christ. These days, the hymn is a staple of Kenya's booming Christian music industry, and features in up-tempo gospel videos. Across modern East Africa, the 'Tukutendereza' is hard to avoid. Wherever you go, you hear the words of evangelical faith:

Tukutendereza Yesu
Yesu Omwana gw'endiga
Omusaigwo gunaziza
Nkwebaza, Omulokozi

(We praise you Jesus
Jesus Lamb of God
Your blood cleanses me
I praise you, Saviour).[24]

In other ways too, Global South Christians use innovative means to spread the faith. Little known in the West, one of the main expressions of popular evangelical faith in Africa is the

---

23 Philip Jenkins, 'The Clash That Wasn't', *Christian Century* (11 July 2012), 37; Jenkins, 'Astonishing Assemblies'.
24 See Thomas A. Oduro, *Music in the Life of the African Church* (Waco, TX: Baylor University Press, 2008); Philip Jenkins, 'Tukutendereza Yesu', *Christian Century* (25 January 2011), 45.

Nigerian-based video industry. Since the 1990s, popular religious and charismatic videos have appeared in their hundreds, presenting stark calls to spiritual warfare. Such films teach doctrines of deliverance and sanctification while constantly reminding believers of the dangers of occult dabbling. Made largely in a mixture of Yoruba and English, Nigerian Christian videos enjoy a continent-wide distribution through satellite networks and cable channels. These films have spawned imitators in other countries, in Ghana and, now, Kenya, and many have been subtitled for use in French-speaking Africa. So influential have they been that Nigerian Muslims are now producing their own Islamic counterparts in a desperate attempt to catch up.

Coming home

As Christian numbers have swelled in the Global South, so many of those new believers have moved to Europe or North America, bringing their characteristic forms of belief with them. In some cases, such as the RCCG churches, this was a matter of deliberate missionary endeavour. More commonly, families and individuals travelled seeking a better life, and in their new homes they formed churches offering familiar styles of worship and devotion. Whatever the reason, evangelical and charismatic churches of Global South origin are easy to find in any of the Western world's great cosmopolitan cities. In turn, completing the global cycle, those churches reached out to their original homelands.

Although it is an extreme example, we might for instance look at the story of Nigerian Sunday Adelaja, who in 1987 arrived in Minsk, in the former Soviet Union. Within four years, the Soviet Union itself had collapsed, and Adelaja moved to the newly independent nation of Ukraine. In 1994, with a few friends, he formed a Christian mission known as the Word of Faith Bible Church, which ultimately evolved into the Embassy of the Blessed Kingdom of God for All Nations. That circle of friends soon swelled to become one of Europe's most successful evangelical churches, claiming 20,000 members at the main facility in Kiev (Kyiv), and hundreds of daughter and satellite churches around Ukraine.[25] The Embassy also took its 'all nations' title very seriously, with new plants across Western Europe and several of the former Soviet republics. Remarkably too, the membership was overwhelmingly white European in its composition.

Throughout Europe, we find African-derived megachurch pastors, such as Matthew Ashimolowo of London's Kingsway International Christian Centre. This has become a potent transnational ministry headquartered in London, with a strong health and wealth component. Apart from activities in Europe, his church uses television and radio to reach out to Central and Western Africa. In the 1980s, the Congo too became the scene of a charismatic revival that subsequently spilled across Europe. Today, Congolese-founded evangelical and Pentecostal churches abound in Paris, London and Brussels, and these account for some of Europe's largest and most fervent mega-congregations. As older evangelical churches have declined in Europe, they have been powerfully reinforced by these recent arrivals.[26]

---

25 Philip Jenkins, 'Saving the Soviets', *Christian Century* (26 December 2012), 37.
26 The spread of Global South forms of faith to the traditional West has become one of the liveliest themes of research at present. See, for instance, Mark R. Gornik, *Word Made Global: Stories of African Christianity in New York City* (Grand Rapids, MI: Eerdmans, 2011); Jehu Hanciles, *Beyond Christendom: Globalization, African Migration and the Transformation of the West* (New York: Orbis Books, 2008); *Christianity in Africa and the African Diaspora: The Appropriation of a Scattered Heritage*, edited by Afe Adogame, Roswith Gerloff and Klaus Hock (New York: Continuum, 2009); *African Christian Presence in the West: New Immigrant Congregations and Transnational Networks in North America and Europe*, edited by Frieder Ludwig and J. Kwabena Asamoah-Gyadu (Trenton, NJ: Africa World Press, 2011);

Debates and controversies

Globalization has raised many acute questions about the nature of evangelical faith, and especially the proper limits of accommodating to local cultures. This is especially marked in matters of healing, exorcism and spiritual warfare, which are all absolutely central to new Protestant and evangelical churches in the Global South.[27] Significantly, such practices have also been widely adopted by more mainstream congregations, and even Roman Catholics have had to formulate responses to accusations of witchcraft and demonic possession. One visible sign of the new Christianity is the night vigils that are so popular in churches across Africa and Asia, as believers demonstrate their power over the spirits of darkness that once terrorized them. Such very popular services commonly draw attendance in the thousands, sometimes the tens of thousands, who gather for prayer and exorcism. Night vigils flourish among the booming evangelical and Pentecostal churches of South Korea, where hundreds of thousands pass their Friday nights in prayer and praise.

Congregations have few problems finding scriptural justifications for their militant activism in spiritual warfare. The Book of Acts is a fruitful source for such stories and proof texts, as are the words of Jesus himself. Gospel passages like Luke 8 are much valued because the demonic evil there portrayed cannot simply be dismissed as psychosomatic: these are very real devils. The problem of course arises when belief in healing and exorcism meshes so closely with local pagan or pre-Christian practice as to arouse charges of syncretism, a problem that has often arisen in Africa and Asia. In Brazil, the leaders of thriving charismatic churches often have past experience with African-derived pagan healing movements like Umbanda.

Among African churches, witchcraft has been a uniquely sensitive issue. Among pre-Christian primal religions, the detection and destruction of witches was often a vaunted power of charismatic spiritual leaders, and some modern-day Christian pastors seem to have inherited those aspirations. Revival crusades often flaunt a potent anti-witchcraft message, which appeals at least as much in the sprawling cities as it ever did in isolated villages. The most troubling cases of alleged witchcraft involve the supposed misdeeds of children who allegedly carry the curses of witchcraft, and who spread their ills over society. Often, such children are subjected to extreme violence as part of exorcism rituals, while many are altogether expelled from society, to become pariahs. Scandals involving churches obsessed with 'witch-children' have blighted the image of African Christianity in some European countries, particularly Great Britain.

In other ways too, the fervent piety of newer churches lends itself to abuse. Claims of miraculous healings are the standard currency of evangelical revivals, and such stories circulate widely. Some African countries have tried to discourage the media from spreading such stories without clear evidence of their truth, on the principle of enforcing truth in advertising. Ecclesiastical corruption is widespread.

Of more general concern has been the extreme popularity of prosperity theologies. Although the ideas and general style of such churches is chiefly derived from North America, they have become thoroughly at home in Global South communities, where miraculous intervention

---

Afe Adogame, *The African Christian Diaspora: New Currents and Emerging Trends in World Christianity* (New York: Continuum, 2013). For the impact of Global South developments in North America, see Soong-Chan Rah, *The Next Evangelicalism: Releasing the Church from Western Cultural Captivity* (Downers Grove, IL: InterVarsity Press, 2009).

27 There is a fine collection of case studies on the role of healing in global charismatic Christianity in *Global Pentecostal and Charismatic Healing*, edited by Candy Gunther Brown (New York: Oxford University Press, 2011).

often seems like the only plausible way of negotiating the hazards of daily life.[28] In West Africa especially, it is hard to avoid churches with a strong prosperity theme. They find their most ostentatious expression in the wildly successful ministries of preachers like Ghana's Nicholas Duncan-Williams or Nigeria's David Oyedepo. Across Africa, prosperity teachings are central to the ubiquitous culture of revivals and miracle crusades, so much so that they overwhelm more traditional charismatic or Pentecostal doctrines. As distinguished scholars like Paul Gifford, J. Kwabena Asamoah-Gyadu and David Maxwell have shown, the prosperity message has come to dominate the teaching of many new churches, which draw as much on American ideas of Positive Thinking and perky self-help manuals as on any familiar Christian theology.[29]

For all the excesses of some preachers, moreover, most prosperity churches also contribute practically to improving the material lot of their flocks. Their actions belie their simplistic message of 'Just tithe, have faith, and stand back!' Matthew Ashimolowo teaches that poverty and unemployment are manifestations of sin, against which Christians must struggle. In practice, this means that the faithful should relieve other members of the congregation by giving them jobs, while the church sternly teaches habits of thrift and sobriety. Most prosperity churches not only condemn poverty, but also teach invaluable ways of avoiding it, like learning not to fall into debt, and actually saving up in order to buy material goods. Debt is a demon to be defeated. Few communities in the world could fail to benefit from such a lesson, but it is vital for people moving suddenly from a rural setting into an overwhelming African metropolis, with all the consumerist blandishments offered to the poor. In such a setting, being a member of a church offers life-saving access to social networks of mutual aid and support, which teach essential survival skills. Meanwhile, peer pressure helps believers avoid the snares of substance abuse. If the faithful do not actually receive blessings too rich to count, at least their membership of a church vastly enriches their life chances. David Oyedepo has said that the prosperity promise only makes sense in the context of enriching the wider community far beyond the narrow confines of the church.[30]

The wider world

Western churches were slow to come to terms with the rapidly changing realities of the Global South. One pioneering event in the story of globalization was the International Congress on World Evangelization, held at Lausanne in 1974. Despite the enormous significance of this event – and the ambitious character of its public declaration, the Lausanne Covenant – it was initiated by Western churches, with Billy Graham and John Stott in the lead. The call to evangelization still bore memories of the familiar notion that faith came from the Christian world to the outside. Little in the Covenant gave much sense of the radical changes already under way.[31]

In 1989, Manila witnessed a follow-up to Lausanne, but it was the third meeting, in Cape Town in 2010, which really pointed to the massive shift in numbers and influence. Intended to mark the centennial of the famous World Missionary Conference held in Edinburgh in 1910, the Cape Town meeting included a far larger representation of Global South leaders and

28 For the prevalence of American prosperity theology, see Kate Bowler, *Blessed: A History of the American Prosperity Gospel* (New York: Oxford University Press, 2013).
29 See Paul Gifford, *Christianity, Development and Modernity in Africa* (London: Hurst and Co., 2015); J. Kwabena Asamoah-Gyadu, *African Charismatics* (Leiden: Brill, 2005); David Maxwell, 'Delivered from the Spirit of Poverty', *Journal of Religion in Africa* vol. 28 (1998), 350–73.
30 Jenkins, *New Faces of Christianity*, pp. 91–7.
31 *The Lausanne Movement: A Range of Perspectives*, edited by Lars Dahle, Margunn Serigstad Dahle and Knud Jorgensen (Eugene, OR: Wipf and Stock, 2014).

speakers, and a degree of diversity that would have been inconceivable at the first Lausanne event, to say nothing of earlier gatherings. At Edinburgh in 1910, the 1,200 delegates included a thousand from the US and Great Britain combined, besides just four from Asia and none from Africa.[32] At Cape Town, there were 4,000 delegates, including just 530 from the US, Great Britain and Canada combined. African, Asian and Latin American voices predominated. No less strikingly, women made up 35 per cent of delegates.

Limits to growth

So astonishing has been the Christian upsurge over the past generation – specifically in its evangelical-charismatic forms – that we must wonder how long it can be sustained. Theoretically, growth rates like those in Africa cannot continue indefinitely without converting every last person within a generation or two, and that is precisely the future that some have foretold. If things go on as they are, it is said, then Latin America will be Protestant within a generation, and China will convert *en masse* to Christianity. Due caution needs to be used in listening to such projections.

In reality, it is rarely safe to extrapolate trends into the indefinite future: things just do not go on as they are *ad infinitum*. In the case of Christianity, two obvious limits suggest themselves. In Africa especially, expansion over the past century was relatively easy because the target audience for evangelism was chiefly adherents of primal faiths. That market, so to speak, is now largely saturated, and today's Christians confront another fast-growing world religion with enormous popular appeal, namely Islam. For Muslims, apostasy from the faith is an exceedingly serious matter, and evangelistic efforts run the strong risk of inciting mass violence. This does not mean that the age of mass conversions is at an end, but the situation has become much more difficult and, likely, slower. In a country like China too, the government has clearly indicated that it will tolerate Christian expansion only as long as it does not pose a threat to the nation's political order. Christians face severe limits to growth.

Less obvious a challenge, but arguably much more significant in the long run, are demographic factors.[33] I have already shown how demographic changes explain the growth of Global South Christianity, but matters are changing fast, and in much of the world, future trends indicate rising secularization. Several factors shape a country's religious outlook, and prosperity and the reassurance of state welfare provision certainly play a role. A country's fertility rate also tells us much about its attitudes towards religion. When a country develops economically, women are urgently needed to enter the workforce, rather than remain in the home. Meanwhile, shifting religious values place less pressure on women to have large families. In turn, smaller families mean diminished links with religious structures – fewer children to put through religious education or First Communion classes. And couples that have decided to limit families tend to run up against church policies on issues of contraception and abortion. When sexuality is separated from conception and child-rearing, a society becomes more open to non-traditional family structures, including gay unions. Whatever the reason, European experience indicates that countries where the fertility rate falls well below replacement (2.1 children per woman) is facing rapid secularization.

---

32 See Brian Stanley, *The World Missionary Conference: Edinburgh 1910* (Grand Rapids, MI: Eerdmans, 2009).
33 Demographic issues have not received anything like the attention they deserve, but see Eric Kaufmann, *Shall the Religious Inherit the Earth? Demography and Politics in the Twenty-First Century* (London: Profile Books, 2010).

That is the precise situation now facing many countries in Asia and Latin America, and especially the most economically developed. A few decades ago, all had classic Third World population profiles, and very large families. In the 1960s, for instance, Brazil's fertility rate hovered around six children per woman, alarming those who warned of a global population explosion. By 2014, though, Brazil's figure was 1.79, far below replacement. Chile and Uruguay both record similar rates of 1.84. Argentina is still above replacement, but the rate is falling fast. On the Pacific Rim, such nations as South Korea, Singapore and China itself have even lower fertility rates, in fact some of the lowest ever recorded in human history: China stands at 1.55, South Korea at 1.25. Even in the Philippines, the rate since 1960 has fallen from 7.0 to 3.0, still above replacement, but declining rapidly.[34] Worldwide, we are witnessing a social revolution in progress, and a gender revolution.

Arguably, the success of evangelical Christianity itself has contributed to these changes. In the new churches, women acquire greater self-confidence and a new ability to control their lives and personal relationships. They are also encouraged to seek education. Women in the workforce are more likely to define their role differently from their mothers, who had borne very large families. Smaller family size is a gauge of modernization and female empowerment.[35]

But the consequences for institutional religion are damaging. In Latin America especially, we now see signs of secularization that would have been unthinkable not long ago.[36] Nine per cent of Brazilians now say they follow no religion, and the proportion of nones is much higher among the under-20s. As so often, Uruguay emerges as the region's most secular country, with 40 per cent having no religious affiliation.[37] Same sex marriage offers a useful gauge of transformation, particularly as it has been so staunchly opposed by most churches, Catholic and Protestant. Nevertheless, Brazil approved same sex unions in 2004, with gay marriages following subject to some local discretion. Argentina legalized same sex marriage in 2010. Although such countries are a long way from European levels of secularization, the emergence of a triangular political set-up can be foreseen, with evangélicos, Catholics and seculars, and a constantly shifting balance of coalitions and alliances. The one great exception to these demographic patterns is Africa, where classic Global South population profiles show no signs of dramatic change in the near future. As African migrants become ever more numerous in the West, it is likely that their religious ways will also spread, and become more commonplace.

The future church

A variously attributed saying holds that it is very difficult to make predictions, especially about the future. If it is hard to tell where Christians are likely to be found in the greatest numbers, or whether those numbers are growing or shrinking, it is much harder to guess what issues might be agonizing them at any given time. It is wildly unlikely that even the wisest and best informed observer of the evangelical world in 1970, for example, would have predicted the shape of today's Christian world.

---

34 Greg Ip, 'How Demographics Rule the Global Economy', *The Wall Street Journal* (22 November 2015).
35 Women's roles in emerging churches is a thriving research field. From many examples, see Brusco, *The Reformation of Machismo*; Frances S. Adeney, *Christian Women in Indonesia: A Narrative Study of Gender and Religion* (Syracuse, NY: Syracuse University Press, 2003); and Maria Frahm-Arp, *Professional Women in South African Pentecostal Charismatic Churches* (Leiden: Brill, 2010).
36 For themes of secularization, see David Martin, *The Future of Christianity: Reflections on Violence and Democracy, Religion and Secularization* (Farnham: Ashgate, 2010).
37 Philip Jenkins, 'A Secular Latin America?', *Christian Century* (20 March 2013), 45.

Having said that, some writers have dared to make such predictions. In his 2010 book, *The Future Church: How Ten Trends Are Revolutionizing The Catholic Church*, the journalist John L. Allen identified ten megatrends as essential for understanding the coming half-century or so, and to varying degrees, all his comments apply across denominational frontiers, not just to the Roman Catholic church. Specifically, Allen lists his ten trends as follows: a World Church; Evangelical Catholicism; Islam; the New Demography; expanding Lay Roles; the Biotech Revolution; Globalization; Ecology; Multi-polarism and Pentecostalism. Most of these points are self-evident, but some require further elucidation. Under 'Islam', he refers to the threat of violent confrontation and persecution experienced by many Christians in Africa and Asia. At the same time, though, he points to the theological challenges of the encounter with Islam, and the need for Christians to formulate a theology that incorporates that faith into its world-view.[38] It is also striking that so many of his projections involve a reduction of boundaries between Catholics and other Christians, so that Catholics as much as mainline denominations will need to accommodate Pentecostal worship styles, and perhaps attitudes to the workings of the Holy Spirit. His church has always defined itself as One Holy, Catholic and Apostolic. By 2050, he suggests, it will be Global, Uncompromising, Pentecostal and Extroverted. This might be an apt slogan for the evangelical future.

---

38 John L. Allen Jr, *The Future Church: How Ten Trends are Revolutionizing the Catholic Church* (London: Doubleday Religion, 2012).

SELECT BIBLIOGRAPHY AND FURTHER READING

Aalders, Cynthia Y., *To Express the Ineffable: The Hymns and Spirituality of Anne Steele* (Milton Keynes: Paternoster, 2008).
Abraham, William J. and Kirby, James E. (eds), *The Oxford Handbook of Methodist Studies* (Oxford: Oxford University Press, 2009).
Abrams, Douglas Carl, *Selling the Old-Time Religion: American Fundamentalists and Mass Culture, 1920–1940* (Athens, GA: University of Georgia Press, 2001).
Adeney, Frances S., *Christian Women in Indonesia: A Narrative Study of Gender and Religion* (Syracuse, NY: Syracuse University Press, 2003).
Adogame, Afe, *The African Christian Diaspora: New Currents and Emerging Trends in World Christianity* (New York: Continuum, 2013).
Adogame, Afe, Gerloff, Roswith and Hock, Klaus (eds), *Christianity in Africa and the African Diaspora: The Appropriation of a Scattered Heritage* (New York: Continuum, 2009).
Alexander, Estrelda Y., *Black Fire: One Hundred Years of African American Pentecostalism* (Downers Grove, IL: InterVarsity Press, 2011).
Anderson, Allan, *An Introduction to Pentecostalism: Global Charismatic Christianity* (Cambridge: Cambridge University Press, 2014).
Anderson, Allan, *Spreading Fires: The Missionary Nature of Early Pentecostalism* (Maryknoll, NY: Orbis, 2007).
Anderson, Allan, *To the Ends of the Earth: Pentecostalism and the Transformation of World Christianity* (Oxford: Oxford University Press, 2013).
Anderson, Robert Mapes, *Vision of the Disinherited: The Making of American Pentecostalism* (New York: Oxford University Press, 1979).
Atherstone, Andrew and Jones, David Ceri (eds), *Engaging with Martyn Lloyd-Jones: The Life and Legacy of 'the Doctor'* (Nottingham: Apollos, 2011).
Atherstone, Andrew and Maiden, John (eds), *Evangelicalism and the Church of England in the Twentieth Century: Reform, Resistance and Renewal* (Woodbridge: Boydell, 2014).
Atkins, Gareth, Das, Shinjini and Murray, Brian (eds), *Chosen People, Promised Lands: The Bible, Race and Empire in the Long Nineteenth Century* (Cambridge: Cambridge University Press, forthcoming).
Attansai, Katherine and Young, Amos (eds), *Pentecostalism and Prosperity: The Socio-Economics of the Global Charismatic Movement* (New York: Palgrave Macmillan, 2012).
Austin, Alvyn, *China's Millions: The China Inland Mission and Late Qing Society, 1832–1905* (Grand Rapids, MI: Eerdmans, 2007).
Austin, Alvyn and Scott, Jamie S. (eds), *Canadian Missionaries, Indigenous People: Representing Religion at Home and Abroad* (Toronto: University of Toronto Press, 2005).
Balmer, Randall, *Evangelicalism in America* (Waco, TX: Baylor University Press, 2016).
Barclay, Oliver, *Evangelicalism in Britain, 1935–1995: A Personal Sketch* (Leicester: Inter-Varsity Press, 1997).

Select bibliography

Bays, Daniel H. and Wacker, Grant (eds), *The Foreign Missionary Enterprise at Home: Explorations in North American Cultural History* (Tuscaloosa, AL: University of Alabama Press, 2010).

Bebbington, David W., *Evangelicalism in Modern Britain: A History from the 1730s to the 1980s* (London: Unwin Hyman, 1989)

Bebbington, David W., *The Dominance of Evangelicalism: The Age of Spurgeon and Moody* (Leicester: Inter-Varsity Press, 2005).

Bebbington, David W., *Victorian Religious Revivals: Culture and Piety in Local and Global Contexts* (Oxford: Oxford University Press, 2013).

Bebbington, David W. and Jones, David Ceri (eds), *Evangelicalism and Fundamentalism in the United Kingdom during the Twentieth Century* (Oxford: Oxford University Press, 2013).

Bell, Steve and Chapman, Colin (eds), *Between Naivety and Hostility: Uncovering the Best Christian Responses to Islam in Britain* (Milton Keynes: Authentic, 2011).

Bendroth, M. L., *Fundamentalists in the City: Conflict and Division in Boston's Churches, 1885–1950* (New York: Oxford University Press, 2005).

Binfield, Clyde, *George Williams and the Young Men's Christian Association: A Study in Victorian Social Attitudes* (London: William Heinemann, 1973).

Blumhofer, Edith L., *Aimee Semple McPherson: Everybody's Sister* (Grand Rapids, MI: Eerdmans, 1993).

Bowen, Desmond, *The Protestant Crusade in Ireland, 1800–1870: A Study of Protestant-Catholic Relations between the Act of Union and Disestablishment* (Dublin: Gill and Macmillian, 1978).

Bowler, Kate, *Blessed: A History of the American Prosperity Gospel* (New York: Oxford University Press, 2013).

Bradley, Ian, *The Call to Seriousness: The Evangelical Impact of the Victorians* (London: Jonathan Cape, 1976).

Brekus, Catherine A., *Sarah Osborn's World: The Rise of Evangelical Christianity in Early America* (New Haven, CT: Yale University Press, 2013).

Brencher, John, *Martyn Lloyd-Jones (1899–1981) and Twentieth-Century Evangelicalism* (Carlisle: Paternoster, 2002).

Breward, Ian, *A History of the Churches in Australasia* (Oxford: Oxford University Press, 2001).

Brown, Callum G., *The Death of Christian Britain: Understanding Secularisation, 1800–2000* (London: Routledge, 2001).

Brown, Candy Gunther (ed.), *Global Pentecostal and Charismatic Healing* (New York: Oxford University Press, 2011).

Bruns, Roger A., *Preacher: Billy Sunday and Big-Time American Evangelism* (New York: W. W. Norton, 1992).

Brusco, Elizabeth, *The Reformation of Machismo: Evangelical Conversion and Gender in Colombia* (Austin, TX: University of Texas Press, 1995).

Buswell, Robert E. and Lee, Timothy, *Christianity in Korea* (Honolulu, HI: University of Hawaii Press, 2007).

Butler, David, *Methodists and Papists: John Wesley and the Catholic Church in the Eighteenth Century* (London: Darton, Longman and Todd, 1995).

Butler, Jon, *Awash in a Sea of Faith: Christianizing the American People* (Cambridge, MA: Harvard University Press, 1992).

Cahn, Peter S., *All Religions are Good in Tzintzuntzan: Evangelicals in Catholic Mexico* (Austin, TX: University of Texas Press, 2003).

Callahan, Allan Dwight, *The Talking Book: African Americans and the Bible* (New Haven, CT: Yale University Press, 2006).

Campbell, Ted A., *The Religion of the Heart: A Study of European Religious Life in the Seventeenth and Eighteenth Centuries* (Columbia, SC: University of South Carolina Press, 1991).

Carpenter, Joel A., *Revive Us Again: The Reawakening of American Fundamentalism* (New York: Oxford University Press, 1997).

Carpenter, Joel A. and Shenk, W. R. (eds), *Earthen Vessels: American Evangelicals and Foreign Missions, 1880–1980* (Grand Rapids, MI: Eerdmans, 1990).

Carson, Penelope, *The East India Company and Religion, 1698–1858* (Woodbridge: Boydell, 2012).

Carter, Grayson, *Anglican Evangelicals: Protestant Secessions from the Via Media, c.1800–1850* (Oxford: Oxford University Press, 2000).

Case, Jay Riley, *An Unpredictable Gospel: American Evangelicals and World Christianity, 1812–1920* (New York: Oxford University Press, 2012).

Select bibliography

Chandler, Andrew (ed.), *Evangelicalism, Piety and Politics: The Selected Writings of W. R. Ward* (Farnham: Ashgate, 2014).
Chesnut, R. Andrew, *Born Again in Brazil: Pentecostal Boom and the Pathogens of Poverty* (New Brunswick, NJ: Rutgers University Press, 1997).
Coakley, J. F., *The Church of the East and the Church of England: A History of the Archbishop of Canterbury's Assyrian Mission* (Oxford: Oxford University Press, 1992).
Coffey, John, *Exodus and Liberation: Deliverance Politics from John Calvin to Martin Luther King Jr.* (New York: Oxford University Press, 2014).
Coffey, John (ed.), *Heart Religion: Evangelical Piety in England and Ireland, 1690–1850* (Oxford: Oxford University Press, 2016).
Collins, Kenneth J., *The Evangelical Moment: The Promise of an American Religion* (Grand Rapids, MI: Baker, 2005).
Conkin, Paul K., *Cane Ridge: America's Pentecost* (Madison, WI: University of Wisconsin Press, 1990).
Cooper, Kate and Gregory, Jeremy (eds), *Revival and Resurgence in Christian History* (Woodbridge: Boydell, 2008).
Corrigan, John, *Business of the Heart: Religion and Emotion in the Nineteenth Century* (Berkeley, CA: University of California Press, 2002).
Cox, Harvey, *Fire from Heaven: The Rise of Pentecostal Spirituality and the Reshaping of Religion in the Twenty-First Century* (Reading, MA: Addison-Wesley, 1995).
Cox, Jeffrey, *Imperial Fault Lines: Christianity and Colonial Power in India, 1818–1940* (Stanford, CA: Stanford University Press, 2002).
Crawford, Michael J., *Seasons of Grace: Colonial New England's Revival Tradition in its British Context* (New York: Oxford University Press, 1991).
Crisp, Oliver D. and Sweeney, Douglas A. (eds), *After Jonathan Edwards: The Courses of New England Theology* (New York: Oxford University Press, 2012).
Cross, Anthony R., Morden, Peter J. and Randall, Ian M. (eds), *Pathways and Patterns in History: Essays on Baptists, Evangelicals and the Modern World in Honour of David Bebbington* (London: Baptist Historical Society / Spurgeon's College, 2015).
Crouse, Eric Robert, *Revival in the City: The Impact of American Evangelists in Canada, 1884–1914* (Montreal: McGill-Queen's University Press, 2005).
Curtis, Heather D., *Faith in the Great Physician: Suffering and Divine Healing in American Culture, 1860–1900* (Baltimore, MD: Johns Hopkins University Press, 2007).
De Groot, Christiana and Taylor, Marion Ann (eds), *Recovering Nineteenth-Century Women Interpreters of the Bible* (Atlanta, GA: Society of Bible Literature, 2007).
De Jong, J. A., *As the Waters Cover the Sea: Millennial Expectations in the Rise of Anglo-American Missions, 1640–1810* (Kampen: Kok, 1970).
David, Rupert and Rupp, Gordon (eds), *A History of the Methodist Church in Great Britain, volume 1* (London: Epworth Press, 1965).
Dayton, Donald W. and Johnson, Robert K. (eds), *The Variety of American Evangelicalism* (Knoxville, TN: University of Tennessee Press, 1991).
Dochuk, Darren, Kidd, Thomas and Peterson, Kurt (eds), *American Evangelicalism: George Marsden and the State of American Religious History* (Notre Dame, IN: University of Notre Dame Press, 2014).
Eason, Andrew Mark, *Women in God's Army: Gender and Equality in the Early Salvation Army* (Waterloo: Wilfrid Laurier University Press, 2003).
Emerson, Michael and Smith, Christian, *Divided by Faith: Evangelical Religion and the Problem of Race in America* (New York: Oxford University Press, 2001).
Eshete, Tibebe, *The Evangelical Movement in Ethiopia* (Waco, TX: Baylor University Press, 2009).
Espinosa, Gaston, *William J. Seymour and the Origins of Global Pentecostalism: A Biography and Documentary History* (Durham, NC: Duke University Press, 2014).
Etherington, Norman (ed.), *Missions and Empire* (Oxford: Oxford University Press, 2005).
Evans, Christopher H., *The Kingdom is Always but Coming: A Life of Walter Rauschenbusch* (Grand Rapids, MI: Eerdmans, 2004).
Evanson, Bruce J., *God's Man for the Gilded Age: D. L. Moody and the Rise of Modern Mass Evangelism* (Oxford: Oxford University Press, 2003).
Fea, John, *The Bible Cause: A History of the American Bible Society* (New York: Oxford University Press, 2016).

Forbes, Bruce David and Kilde, Jeanne Halgren (eds), *Rapture, Revelation, and the End of Times: Exploring the Left Behind Series* (New York: Palgrave Macmillan, 2004).
Foster, Charles H., *The Rungless Ladder: Harriet Beecher Stowe and New England Puritanism* (Durham, NC: Duke University Press, 1954).
Frahm-Arp, Maria, *Professional Women in South African Pentecostal Charismatic Churches* (Leiden: Brill, 2010).
Frey, Sylvia R. and Wood, Betty, *Come Shouting to Zion: African American Protestantism in the American South and British Caribbean to 1830* (Chapel Hill, NC: University of North Carolina Press, 1998).
Frykenberg, Robert Eric, *Christianity in India: From Beginnings to the Present*, Oxford History of the Christian Church (Oxford: Oxford University Press, 2008).
Frykenberg, Robert Eric (ed.), *Christians and Missionaries in India: Cross-Cultural Communication since 1500* (Grand Rapids, MI: Eerdmans, 2003).
Ganiel, Gladys, *Evangelicalism and Conflict in Northern Ireland* (Basingstoke: Palgrave, 2008).
Garrard-Burnett, Virginia, *Protestantism in Guatemala: Living in the New Jerusalem* (Austin, TX: University of Texas Press, 1998).
Gasaway, Brantley W., *Progressive Evangelicals and the Pursuit of Social Justice* (Chapel Hill, NC: University of North Carolina Press, 2014).
Gauvreau, Michael, *The Evangelical Century: College and Creed in English Canada from the Great Revival to the Great Depression* (Montreal: McGill-Queen's University Press, 1991).
Gauvreau, Michael and Hubert, Hubert (eds), *The Churches and Social Order in Nineteenth- and Twentieth-Century Canada* (Montreal: McGill-Queen's University Press, 2006).
Gibbard, Noel, *The First Forty Years: The History of the Evangelical Movement of Wales, 1948–98* (Bridgend: Bryntirion Press, 2002).
Gifford, Paul, *Christianity, Development and Modernity in Africa* (London: Hurst and Co., 2015).
Gifford, Paul, *Ghana's New Christianity: Pentecostalism in a Globalizing African Economy* (Bloomington, IN: Indiana University Press, 2004).
Gilley, Sheridan and Stanley, Brian (eds), *The Cambridge History of Christianity, vol. 8: World Christianities, c.1815–c.1914* (Cambridge: Cambridge University Press, 2006).
Gloege, Timothy E. W., *Guaranteed Pure: The Moody Bible Institute, Business, and the Making of Modern Evangelicalism* (Chapel Hill, NC: University of North Carolina Press, 2015).
Goodhew, David (ed.), *Church Growth in Britain: 1980 to the Present* (Farnham: Ashgate, 2012).
Goodwin, Daniel C., *Into Deep Waters: Evangelical Spirituality and Maritime Calvinistic Baptist Ministers, 1790–1855* (Montreal: McGill-Queen's University Press, 2010).
Gregory, Jeremy, and McLeod, Hugh (eds), *International Religious Networks* (Woodbridge: Boydell, 2012).
Grem, Darren E., *The Blessings of Business: How Corporations Shaped Conservative Christianity* (New York: Oxford University Press, 2016).
Gribben, Crawford, *Evangelical Millennialism in the Trans-Atlantic World, 1500–2000* (Basingstoke: Palgrave Macmillian, 2011).
Gribben, Crawford and Holmes, Andrew (eds), *Protestant Millennialism, Evangelicalism and Irish Society, 1790–2005* (Basingstoke: Palgrave, 2006).
Gribben, Crawford and Stunt, Timothy (eds), *Prisoners of Hope? Aspects of Evangelical Millennialism in Britain and Ireland, 1800–1880* (Milton Keynes: Paternoster, 2004).
Gribben, Crawford and Sweetnam, Mark (eds), *Left Behind and the Evangelical Imagination* (Sheffield: Sheffield Phoenix, 2011).
Gutjahr, Paul C., *An American Bible: A History of the Good Book in the United States, 1777–1880* (Stanford, CA: Stanford University Press, 1999).
Gutjahr, Paul C., *Charles Hodge: Guardian of American Orthodoxy* (New York: Oxford University Press, 2011).
Hall, Matthew J. and Strachan, Owen (eds), *Essential Evangelicalism: The Enduring Influence of Carl F. H. Henry* (Wheaton, IL: Crossway, 2015).
Hambrick-Stowe, Charles E., *Charles G. Finney and the Spirit of American Evangelicalism* (Grand Rapids, MI: Eerdmans, 1996).
Hammond, Geordan and Jones, David Ceri (eds), *George Whitefield: Life, Context, and Legacy* (Oxford: Oxford University Press, 2016).
Hanciles, Jehu, *Beyond Christendom: Globalization, African Migration and the Transformation of the West* (New York: Orbis Books, 2008).
Hannah, John D., *An Uncommon Union: Dallas Theological Seminary and American Evangelicalism* (Grand Rapids, MI: Zondervan, 2009).

Select bibliography

Harrell Jr., David Edwin, *All Things are Possible: The Healing and Charismatic Revivals in Modern America* (Bloomington, IN: Indiana University Press, 1975).
Harris, Harriet A., *Fundamentalism and Evangelicals* (Oxford: Oxford University Press, 1998).
Hart, D. G., *Deconstructing Evangelicalism: Conservative Protestantism in the Age of Billy Graham* (Grand Rapids, MI: Baker, 2004).
Hartch, Todd, *The Rebirth of Latin American Christianity* (New York: Oxford University Press, 2014).
Harvey, Paul, *Redeeming the South: Religious Cultures and Racial Identities among Southern Baptists, 1865–1925* (Chapel Hill, NC: University of North Carolina Press, 1997).
Hatch, Nathan and Noll, Mark A. (eds), *The Bible in America: Essays in Cultural History* (New York: Oxford University Press, 1982).
Haykin, Michael A. G., *Joy Unspeakable and Full of Glory: The Piety of Samuel and Sarah Pearce* (Kitchener, Ontario: Joshua Press, 2012).
Haykin, Michael A. G. and Stewart, Kenneth J. (eds), *The Emergence of Evangelicalism: Exploring Historical Continuities* (Leicester: Inter-Varsity Press, 2008).
Hays, Christopher M. and Ansberry, Christopher B. (eds), *Evangelical Faith and the Challenge of Historical Criticism* (London: SPCK, 2013).
Heltzel, Peter, *Jesus and Justice: Evangelicals, Race and American Politics* (New Haven, CT: Yale University Press, 2009).
Hempton, David, *Evangelical Disenchantment: Nine Portraits of Faith and Doubt* (New Haven, CT: Yale University Press, 2008).
Hempton, David, *The Church in the Long Eighteenth Century* (London: I. B. Tauris, 2011).
Hempton, David and Hill, Myrtle, *Evangelical Protestantism in Ulster Society, 1740–1890* (London: Routledge, 1992).
Hempton, David, *Methodism and Politics in British Society, 1750–1850* (London: Hutchinson, 1984).
Hempton, David, *The Religion of the People: Methodism and Popular Religion, c.1750–1900* (London: Routledge, 1996).
Heyrman, Christine Leigh, *American Apostles: When Evangelicals Entered the World of Islam* (New York: Hill and Wang, 2015).
Hilton, Boyd, *The Age of Atonement: The Influence of Evangelicalism on Social and Economic Thought, 1785–1865* (Oxford: Clarendon Press, 1986).
Hindmarsh, D. Bruce, *John Newton and the English Evangelical Tradition* (Grand Rapids, MI: Eerdmans, 1996).
Hindmarsh, D. Bruce, *The Evangelical Conversion Narrative: Spiritual Autobiography in Early Modern England* (Oxford: Oxford University Press, 2005).
Holmes, Janice, *Religious Revivals in Britain and Ireland, 1859–1905* (Dublin: Irish Academic Press, 2000).
Holmes, Stephen R., *The Wondrous Cross: Atonement and Penal Substitution in the Bible and History* (Milton Keynes: Paternoster, 2007).
Holtrop, Pieter and McLeod, Hugh (eds), *Missions and Missionaries* (Woodbridge: Boydell and Brewer, 2000).
Hopkins, Mark, *Nonconformity's Romantic Generation: Evangelical and Liberal Theologies in Victorian England* (Milton Keynes: Paternoster, 2004).
Howsam, Leslie, *Cheap Bibles: Nineteenth-Century Publishing and the British and Foreign Bible Society* (Cambridge: Cambridge University Press, 1991).
Hummel, Ruth and Thomas, *Patterns of the Sacred: English Protestant and Russian Orthodox Pilgrims in the Nineteenth Century* (London: Scorpion Cavendish, 1995).
Hutchinson, Mark and Kalu, Ogbu (eds), *A Global Faith: Essays on Evangelicalism and Globalization* (Sydney: Centre for the Study of Australian Christianity, 1998).
Hutchinson, Mark and Wolffe, John, *A Short History of Global Evangelicalism* (New York: Cambridge University Press, 2012).
Irons, Charles, *The Origins of Proslavery Christianity: White and Black Evangelicals in Colonial and Antebellum Virginia* (Chapel Hill, NC: University of North Carolina Press, 2008).
Isichei, Elizabeth, *A History of Christianity in Africa* (Grand Rapids, MI / Lawrenceville, NJ: Eerdmans / Africa World Press, 1995).
Jay, Elizabeth, *The Religion of the Heart: Anglican Evangelicalism and the Nineteenth-Century Novel* (Oxford: Clarendon, 1979).
Jeffrey, David Lyle and Evans, Stephen C. (eds), *The Bible and the University* (Grand Rapids, MI: Zondervan, 2007).

Jeffrey, Kenneth S., *When the Lord Walked the Land: The 1858–62 Revival in the North East of Scotland* (Carlisle: Paternoster, 2002).
Jenkins, Philip, *God's Continent: Christianity, Islam and Europe's Religious Crisis* (New York: Oxford University Press, 2007).
Jenkins, Philip, *The New Faces of Christianity: Believing the Bible in the Global South* (New York: Oxford University Press, 2006).
Jenkins, Philip, *The Next Christendom: The Coming of Global Christianity* (New York: Oxford University Press, 2011).
Jeremy, David J. (ed.), *Business and Religion in Britain* (Aldershot: Gower, 1988).
Jeremy, David J., *Capitalists and Christians: Business Leaders and the Churches in Britain, 1900–1960* (Oxford: Clarendon, 1990).
Jeremy, David J. (ed.), *Religion, Business and Wealth in Modern Britain* (London: Routledge, 1998).
Joiner, Thekla Ellen, *Sin in the City: Chicago and Revivalism, 1880–1920* (Columbia, MO: University of Missouri Press, 2007).
Jones, David Ceri, *'A Glorious Work in the World': Welsh Methodism and the International Evangelical Revival, 1735–1750* (Cardiff: University of Wales Press, 2004).
Kalu, Ogbu (ed.), *African Christianity: An African Story* (Pretoria: University of Pretoria, 2005).
Kalu, Ogbu, *Power, Poverty and Prayer: The Challenges of Poverty and Pluralism in African Christianity, 1960–1996* (Trenton, NJ: Africa World Press, 2006).
Kay, William K., *Apostolic Networks in Britain: New Ways of Being Church* (Milton Keynes: Paternoster, 2007).
Khalaf, Samir, *Protestant Missionaries in the Levant: Ungodly Puritans, 1820–60* (Abingdon: Routledge, 2014).
Kidd, Thomas S., *American Christians and Islam: Evangelical Culture and Muslims from the Colonial Period to the Age of Terrorism* (Princeton, NJ: Princeton University Press, 2009).
Kidd, Thomas S., *George Whitefield: America's Spiritual Founding Father* (New Haven, CT: Yale University Press, 2014).
Kim, Rebecca Y., *The Spirit Moves West: Korean Missionaries in America* (New York: Oxford University Press, 2015).
Kim, Ig-Jin, *History and Theology of Korean Pentecostalism: Sunbogeum (Pure Gospel) Pentecostalism* (Zoetermeer: Boekencentrum, 2003).
Lalleman, Pieter J., Morden, Peter J. and Cross, Anthony R. (eds), *Grounded in Grace: Essays in Honour of Ian M. Randall* (London: Baptist Historical Society / Spurgeon's College, 2013).
Laqueur, Thomas Walter, *Religion and Respectability: Sunday Schools and Working Class Culture, 1780–1850* (New Haven, CT: Yale University Press, 1976).
Larsen, Timothy S., *A People of One Book: The Bible and the Victorians* (New York: Oxford University Press, 2011).
Larsen, Timothy S., *Christabel Pankhurst: Fundamentalism in Coalition* (Woodbridge: Boydell Press, 2002).
Larsen, Timothy S. and Treier, Daniel J. (eds), *The Cambridge Companion to Evangelical Theology* (New York: Cambridge University Press, 2007).
Lee, Timothy S., *Born Again: Evangelicalism in Korea* (Honolulu, HI: University of Hawaii Press, 2010).
Lewis, Donald M. (ed.), *Christianity Reborn: Evangelicalism's Global Expansion in the Twentieth Century* (Grand Rapids, MI: Eerdmans, 2004).
Lewis, Donald M. (ed.), *Dictionary of Evangelical Biography, 1730–1860* (Oxford: Blackwell, 1995).
Lewis, Donald M., *Lighten their Darkness: The Evangelical Mission to Working-Class London, 1828–1860* (Westport, CT: Greenwood Press, 1986).
Lewis, Donald M. and Pierard, Richard V. (eds), *Global Evangelicalism: Theology, History and Culture in Regional Perspective* (Downers Grove, IL: InterVarsity Press, 2014).
Lian, Xi, *Redeemed by Fire: The Rise of Popular Christianity in Modern China* (New Haven, CT: Yale University Press, 2010).
Livingstone, David N., *Dealing with Darwin: Place, Politics, and Rhetoric in Religious Engagements with Evolution* (Baltimore, MD: Johns Hopkins University Press, 2014).
Lloyd, Jennifer, *Women and the Shaping of British Methodism: Persistent Preachers, 1807–1907* (Manchester: Manchester University Press, 2009).
Lotz, David W. (ed.), *Altered Landscapes: Christianity in America, 1935–1985* (Grand Rapids, MI: Eerdmans, 1989).
Lovegrove, Deryck W., *Established Church, Sectarian People: Itinerancy and the Transformation of English Dissent, 1780–1830* (Cambridge: Cambridge University Press, 1988).

Lovelace, Richard F., *Dynamics of Spiritual Life: An Evangelical Theology of Renewal* (Downers Grove, IL: InterVarsity Press, 1989).

Ludwig, Frieder and Asamoah-Gyadu, J. Kwabena (eds), *African Christian Presence in the West: New Immigrant Congregations and Transnational Networks in North America and Europe* (Trenton, NJ: Africa World Press, 2011).

Maddox, Randy, *Responsible Grace: John Wesley's Practical Theology* (Nashville, TN: Kingswood Books, 1994).

Magnum, R. Scott and Sweetnam, Mark S., *The Scofield Bible: Its History and Impact on the Evangelical Church* (Colorado Springs, CO: Paternoster, 2009).

Maiden, John, *National Religion and the Prayer Book Controversy, 1927–28* (Woodbridge: Boydell, 2011).

Mandelbrote, Scott and Ledger-Lomas, Michael (eds), *Dissent and the Bible in Britain, c.1650–1950* (Oxford: Oxford University Press, 2013).

Marsden, George M. (ed.), *Evangelicalism and Modern America* (Grand Rapids, MI: Eerdmans, 1984).

Marsden, George M., *Fundamentalism and American Culture: The Shaping of Twentieth Century Evangelicalism, 1870–1925* (New York: Oxford University Press, 1980).

Marsden, George M., *Understanding Fundamentalism and Evangelicalism* (Grand Rapids, MI: Eerdmans, 1991).

Marshall, Ruth, *Political Spiritualities: The Pentecostal Revolution in Nigeria* (Chicago, IL: University of Chicago Press, 2009).

Martin, David, *The Future of Christianity: Reflections on Violence and Democracy, Religion and Secularization* (Farnham: Ashgate, 2010).

Martin, David, *Tongues of Fire: The Explosion of Protestantism in Latin America* (Oxford: Oxford University Press, 2008).

Mathews, Mary Beth Swetnam, *Doctrine and Race: African American Evangelicals and Fundamentalism between the Wars* (Tuscaloosa, AL: University of Alabama Press, 2017).

McBain, Douglas, *Fire Over the Waters: Renewal Among Baptists and Others from the 1960s to the 1990s* (London: Darton, Longman and Todd, 1997).

McClymond, Michael J., *Embodying the Spirit: New Perspectives on North American Revivalism* (Baltimore, MD: Johns Hopkins University Press, 2004).

McClymond, Michael J. (ed.), *Encyclopedia of Religious Revivals in America* (Westport, CT: Greenwood Press, 2007).

McClymond, Michael J. and McDermott, Gerald, *The Theology of Jonathan Edwards* (New York: Oxford University Press, 2012).

McDannell, Colleen, *Material Christianity: Religion and Popular Culture in America* (New Haven, CT: Yale University Press, 1995).

McDermott, Gerald R. (ed.), *The Oxford Handbook of Evangelical Theology* (New York: Oxford University Press, 2010).

McGrath, Alister E., *Evangelicalism and the Future of Christianity* (London: Hodder and Stoughton, 1994).

McLoughlin, William G., *Modern Revivalism: Charles Grandison Finney to Billy Graham* (New York: Ronald Press, 1959).

McVicar, Michael Joseph, *Christian Reconstruction: R. J. Rushdoony and American Religious Conservatism* (Chapel Hill, NC: University of North Carolina Press, 2015).

Miguez, Daniel, *To Help You Find God: The Making of a Pentecostal Identity in a Buenos Aires Suburb* (Amsterdam: Free University of Amsterdam, 1997).

Miller, Donald and Yamamori, Tetsunao, *Global Pentecostalism: The New Face of Christian Social Engagement* (Berkeley, CA: University of California Press, 2007).

Miller, R. M., Stout, H. S. and Wilson, C. R. (eds), *Religion and the American Civil War* (New York: Oxford University Press, 1998).

Moir, John S. and McIntire, C. T. (ed.), *Canadian Protestant and Catholic Missions, 1820s–1960s* (New York: Peter Lang, 1988).

Moore, R. Laurence, *Selling God: American Religion in the Marketplace of Culture* (New York: Oxford University Press, 1994).

Morden, Peter J., *'Communion with Christ and his People': The Spirituality of C. H. Spurgeon (1834–92)* (Oxford: Regent's Park College, 2010).

Morden, Peter J., *The Life and Thought of Andrew Fuller (1754–1815)* (Milton Keynes: Paternoster, 2015).

Morgan, Sue (ed.), *Women, Religion and Feminism in Britain, 1759–1900* (Basingstoke: Palgrave Macmillan, 2002).

Select bibliography

Murray, Iain H., *Revival and Revivalism: The Making and Marring of American Evangelicalism, 1750–1858* (Edinburgh: Banner of Truth Trust, 1994).

Napper, Joyce, *Christianity in the Middle East* (Larnaca: Middle East Christian Outreach, 1996).

Naselli, Andrew David and Hansen, Collin (eds), *The Spectrum of Evangelicalism* (Grand Rapids, MI: Zondervan, 2011).

Neal, Lynn S., *Romancing God: Evangelical Women and Inspiration Fiction* (Chapel Hill, NC: University of North Carolina Press, 2006).

Newport, Kenneth C. G. and Campbell, Ted A. (eds), *Charles Wesley: Life, Literature and Legacy* (Peterborough: Epworth, 2007).

Newport, Kenneth C. G. and Gribben, Crawford (eds), *Expecting the End: Millennialism in Social and Historical Context* (Waco, TX: Baylor University Press, 2006).

Noll, Mark A., *America's God: From Jonathan Edwards to Abraham Lincoln* (New York: Oxford University Press, 2002).

Noll, Mark A., *Between Faith and Criticism: Evangelicals, Scholarship, and the Bible in America* (second edition, Vancouver: Regent College Publishing, 2004).

Noll, Mark A. (ed.), *God and Mammon: Protestants, Money and the Market, 1790–1860* (New York: Oxford University Press, 2002).

Noll, Mark A., *In the Beginning was the Word: The Bible in American Public Life, 1492–1783* (New York: Oxford University Press, 2015).

Noll, Mark A., *The New Shape of World Christianity: How American Experience Reflects Global Faith* (Downers Grove, IL: InterVarsity Press, 2009).

Noll, Mark A., Bebbington, David W. and Rawlyk, George A. (eds), *Evangelicalism: Comparative Studies of Popular Protestantism in North America, the British Isles, and Beyond, 1700–1990* (New York: Oxford University Press, 1994).

Oak, Sung-Deuk, *The Making of Korean Christianity: Protestant Encounters with Korean Religions, 1876–1915* (Waco, TX: Baylor University Press, 2013).

Offutt, Stephen, *New Centers of Global Evangelicalism in Latin America and Africa* (Cambridge: Cambridge University Press, 2015).

Oxbrow, Mark and Grass, Tim (eds), *The Mission of God: Studies in Orthodox and Evangelical Mission* (Oxford: Regnum, 2015).

Pibworth, Nigel P. (ed.), *The Letters of John Berridge of Everton: A Singular Spirituality* (Kitchiner, Ontario: Joshua Press, 2015).

Piggin, Stuart, *Spirit, Word, and World: Evangelical Christianity in Australia* (Brunswick East, Victoria: Acorn, 2012).

Pope, Robert, *Seeking God's Kingdom: The Nonconformist Social Gospel in Wales, 1906–1939* (Cardiff: University of Wales Press, 1999).

Porter, Andrew, *Religion versus Empire? British Protestant Missionaries and Overseas Expansion, 1700–1914* (Manchester: Manchester University Press, 2004).

Porter, Fran, *Changing Women, Changing Worlds: Evangelical Women in Church, Community and Politics* (Belfast: Blackstaff Press, 2002).

Price, Charles and Randall, Ian M., *Transforming Keswick* (Carlisle: Paternoster, 2000).

Rabotau, Albert J., *Slave Religion: The 'Invisible Institution' in the Antebellum South* (New York: Oxford University Press, 1978).

Rack, Henry D., *Reasonable Enthusiast: John Wesley and the Rise of Methodism* (London: Epworth, 1989).

Rah, Soong-Chan, *The Next Evangelicalism: Releasing the Church from Western Cultural Captivity* (Downers Grove, IL: InterVarsity Press, 2009).

Randall, Ian M., *Communities of Conviction: Baptist Beginnings in Europe* (Schwarzenfeld: Newfeld Verlag, 2009).

Randall, Ian M., *Evangelical Experiences: A Study in the Spirituality of English Evangelicalism, 1918–1939* (Carlisle: Paternoster, 1999).

Randall, Ian M., *Spirituality and Social Change: The Contribution of F. B. Meyer (1847–1929)* (Carlisle: Paternoster, 2003).

Randall, Ian M., *What a Friend We Have in Jesus: The Evangelical Tradition* (London: Darton, Longman and Todd, 2005).

Randall, Ian M. and Hilborn, David, *One Body in Christ: The History and Significance of the Evangelical Alliance* (Carlisle: Paternoster, 2001).

Select bibliography

Rawlyk, G. A. (ed.), *Aspects of Canadian Evangelical Experience* (Toronto: McGill-Queen's University Press, 1997).
Rawlyk, G. A. (ed.), *The Canadian Protestant Experience, 1760 to 1990* (Burlington: Welch, 1990).
Robeck, Cecil and Young, Amos (eds), *The Cambridge Companion to Pentecostalism* (Cambridge: Cambridge University Press, 2014).
Robert, Dana, *Christian Mission: How Christianity Became a World Religion* (Chichester: Wiley-Blackwell, 2009).
Robertson, Darrel M., *The Chicago Revival, 1876: Society and Revivalism in a Nineteenth-Century City* (Metuchen, NJ: Scarecrow Press, 1989).
Robinson, Thomas A. and Ruff, Lanette R., *Out of the Mouths of Babes: Girl Evangelists in the Flapper Era* (New York: Oxford University Press, 2012).
Rosenberg, Carroll Smith, *Religion and the Rise of the American City: The New York City Mission Movement, 1812–1870* (Ithaca, NY: Cornell University Press, 1971).
Rosman, Doreen, *Evangelicals and Culture* (London: Croom Helm, 1984).
Ross, Andrew, *David Livingstone: Mission and Empire* (London: Continuum, 2006).
Ruotsila, Mark, *Fighting Fundamentalism: Carl McIntire and the Politicization of Fundamentalism* (New York: Oxford University Press, 2016).
Sandeen, Ernest, R., *The Roots of Fundamentalism: British and American Millenarianism, 1800–1930* (Chicago, IL: University of Chicago, 1970).
Sanneh, Lamin, *Disciples of all Nations: Pillars of World Christianity* (Oxford: Oxford University Press, 2008).
Sanneh, Lamin, *Whose Religion is Christianity? The Gospel Beyond the West* (Grand Rapids, MI: Eerdmans, 2003).
Sanneh, Lamin and Carpenter, Joel A. (eds), *The Changing Face of Christianity: Africa, the West, and the World* (Oxford: Oxford University Press, 2005).
Sanneh, Lamin and McClymond, Michael J. (eds), *Wiley-Blackwell Companion to World Christianity* (Oxford: Wiley-Blackwell, 2016).
Schwanda, Tom (ed.), *The Emergence of Evangelical Spirituality: The Age of Edwards, Newton, and Whitefield* (New York: Paulist Press, 2015).
Semple, Rhonda Ann, *Missionary Women: Gender, Professionalism and the Victorian Idea of Christian Mission* (Woodbridge: Boydell and Brewer, 2003).
Sensbach, Jon, *Rebecca's Revival: Creating Black Christianity in the Atlantic World* (Cambridge, MA: Harvard University Press, 2005).
Shafer, Axel R. (ed.), *American Evangelicals and the 1960s* (Madison, WI: University of Wisconsin Press, 2013).
Shaw, Mark, *Global Awakening: How Twentieth-Century Revivals Triggered a Christian Revolution* (Downers Grove, IL: InterVarsity Press, 2010).
Shea, William M., *The Lion and the Lamb: Evangelicals and Catholics in America* (New York: Oxford University Press, 2004).
Smith, Christian, *American Evangelicalism: Embattled and Thriving* (Chicago, IL: University of Chicago Press, 1998).
Smith, Mark (ed.), *British Evangelical Identities Past and Present: Aspects of the History and Sociology of Evangelicalism in Britain and Ireland* (Milton Keynes: Paternoster, 2008).
Smith, Mark and Taylor, Stephen (eds), *Evangelicalism in the Church of England, c.1790–c.1900* (Woodbridge: Boydell, 2004).
Smith, Timothy L., *Revivalism and Social Reform: American Protestantism on the Eve of the Civil War* (Baltimore, MD: Johns Hopkins University Press, 1980).
Spence, Martin, *Heaven on Earth: Reimagining Time and Eternity in Nineteenth-Century British Evangelicalism* (Eugene, OR: Wipf and Stock, 2015).
Stackhouse, John G., *Canadian Evangelicalism in the Twentieth Century* (Toronto: University of Toronto Press, 1993).
Stanley, Brian (ed.), *Christian Missions and the Enlightenment* (Grand Rapids, MI: Eerdmans, 2001).
Stanley, Brian (ed.), *Missions, Nationalism and the End of Empire* (Grand Rapids, MI: Eerdmans, 2003).
Stanley, Brian, *The Bible and the Flag: Protestant Missions and British Imperialism in the Nineteenth and Twentieth Centuries* (Leicester: Apollos, 1990).
Stanley, Brian, *The Global Diffusion of Evangelicalism: The Age of Billy Graham and John Stott* (Nottingham: Inter-Varsity Press, 2013).
Stanley, Brian, *The World Missionary Conference, Edinburgh 1910* (Grand Rapids, MI: Eerdmans, 2009).

Steensland, Brian and Goff, Philip (eds), *The New Evangelical Social Engagement* (New York: Oxford University Press, 2014).
Steven, James, *Worship in the Spirit: Charismatic Worship in the Church of England* (Carlisle: Paternoster, 2002).
Stevenson, Peter K., *God in Our Nature: The Incarnational Theology of John McLeod Campbell* (Milton Keynes: Paternoster, 2004).
Stone, Jon R., *On the Boundaries of American Evangelicalism: The Postwar Evangelical Coalition* (Basingstoke: Macmillan, 1997).
Stott, Anne, *Hannah More: The First Victorian* (Oxford: Oxford University Press, 2003).
Stott, Anne, *Wilberforce: Family and Friends* (Oxford: Oxford University Press, 2012).
Stout, Harry S., *The Divine Dramatist: George Whitefield and the Rise of Modern Evangelicalism* (Grand Rapids, MI: Eerdmans, 1991).
Strom, Jonathan, Lehmann, Hartmut and van Horn Melton, James (eds), *Pietism in Germany and North America, 1680–1820* (Farnham: Ashgate, 2009).
Strivens, Robert, *Philip Doddridge and the Shaping of Evangelical Dissent* (Farnham: Ashgate, 2015).
Stunt, Timothy, *From Awakening to Secession: Radical Evangelicals in Switzerland and Britain, 1815–1835* (Edinburgh: T. & T. Clark, 2000).
Sutton, Matthew Avery and Dochuk, Darren (eds), *Faith in the New Millennium: The Future of Religious and American Politics* (New York: Oxford University Press, 2015).
Svelmoe, William, *A New Vision for Missions: William Cameron Townsend, the Wycliffe Bible Translators, and the Culture of Early Evangelical Missions, 1896–1945* (Tuscaloosa, AL: University of Alabama Press, 2008).
Sweeney, Douglas A., *Nathaniel Taylor, New Haven Theology and the Legacy of Jonathan Edwards* (New York: Oxford University Press, 2003).
Sweeney, Douglas A., *The American Evangelical Story* (Grand Rapids, MI: Baker, 2005).
Taves, Ann, *Fits, Trances, and Visions: Experiencing Religion and Explaining Experience from Wesley to James* (Princeton, NJ: Princeton University Press, 1999).
Taylor, W. H., *Antioch and Canterbury: The Syrian Orthodox Church and the Church of England, 1874–1928* (Piscataway, NJ: Gorgias Press, 2005).
Tidball, Derek J., *Who Are the Evangelicals? Tracing the Roots of Today's Movement* (London: Marshall Pickering, 1994).
Thomas, George M., *Revivalism and Cultural Change: Christianity, Nation Building, and the Market in the Nineteenth-Century United States* (Chicago, IL: University of Chicago Press, 1989).
Thorne, Susan, *Congregational Missions and the Making of an Imperial Culture in Nineteenth-Century England* (Stanford, CA: Stanford University Press, 1999).
Tolley, Christopher, *Domestic Biography: The Legacy of Evangelicalism in Four Nineteenth-Century Families* (Oxford: Clarendon, 1997).
Tomlinson, Pete, *The Post-Evangelical* (London: Triangle, 1995).
Turnbull, Richard, *Shaftesbury: The Great Reformer* (Oxford: Lion Hudson, 2010).
Vaudry, Richard W., *Anglicans and the Atlantic World: High Churchmen, Evangelicals and the Quebec Connection* (Montreal: McGill-Queens University Press, 2003).
Wacker, Grant, *America's Pastor: Billy Graham and the Shaping of a Nation* (Cambridge, MS: Belknap Press, 2014).
Wacker, Grant, *Heaven Below: Early Pentecostals and America Culture* (Cambridge, MA: Harvard University Press, 2001).
Walker, Pamela J., *Pulling the Devil's Kingdom Down: The Salvation Army in Victorian Britain* (Berkeley, CA: University of California Press, 2001).
Wallace, W. Jason, *Catholics, Slaveholders and the Dilemma of American Evangelicalism, 1835–1860* (Notre Dame, IN: University of Notre Dame Press, 2010).
Walls, Andrew F., *The Missionary Movement in Christian History: Studies in the Transmission of Faith* (Maryknoll, NY: Orbis, 1996).
Ward, Keith and Wild-Wood, Emma (eds), *The East African Revival: History and Legacies* (Farnham: Ashgate, 2011).
Ward, W. R., *The Protestant Evangelical Awakening* (Cambridge: Cambridge University Press, 1992).
Warner, Rob, *Reinventing English Evangelicalism, 1966–2001: A Theological and Sociological Study* (Milton Keynes: Paternoster, 2007).
Watson, J. R., *The English Hymn: A Critical and Historical Study* (Oxford: Clarendon Press, 1997).

Select bibliography

Watts, Michael R., *The Dissenters: From the Reformation to the French Revolution* (Oxford: Clarendon Press, 1978).
Watts, Michael R., *The Dissenters: The Crisis and Conscience of Nonconformity* (Oxford: Clarendon Press, 2015).
Werner, J. S., *The Primitive Methodist Connexion: Its Background and Early History* (Madison, WI: University of Wisconsin Press, 1984).
Whisenant, James, *A Fragile Unity: Anti-Ritualism and the Division of Anglican Evangelicalism in the Nineteenth Century* (Milton Keynes: Paternoster, 2003).
Wigger, John, *American Saint: Francis Asbury and the Methodists* (New York: Oxford University Press, 2009).
Wilkinson, Paul, *For Zion's Sake: Christian Zionism and the Role of John Nelson Darby* (Eugene, OR: Wipf and Stock, 2008).
Wilson, Linda, *Constrained by Zeal. Female Spirituality amongst Nonconformists, 1825–1875* (Carlisle: Paternoster, 2000).
Winston, Diane H., *Red-Hot and Righteous: The Urban Religion of the Salvation Army* (Cambridge, MA: Harvard University Press, 1999).
Wolffe, John (ed.), *Evangelical Faith and Public Zeal: Evangelicals and Society, 1780–1980* (London: SPCK, 1995).
Wolffe, John, *The Expansion of Evangelicalism: The Age of Wilberforce, More, Chalmers and Finney* (Leicester: Inter-Varsity Press, 2006).
Wolffe, John, *The Protestant Crusade in Great Britain, 1829–1860* (Oxford: Clarendon Press, 1991).
Xi, Lian, *Redeemed by Fire: the Rise of Popular Christianity in Modern China* (New Haven, CT: Yale University Press, 2010).
Yang, Fenggang, *Religion in China: Survival and Revival under Communist Rule* (New York: Oxford University Press, 2011).
Yeager, Jonathan (ed.), *Early Evangelicalism: A Reader* (New York: Oxford University Press, 2013).
Yeager, Jonathan, *Enlightened Evangelicalism: The Life and Thought of John Erskine* (New York: Oxford University Press, 1993).
Ziefle, Joshua, *David du Plessis and the Assemblies of God: The Struggle for the Soul of a Movement* (Leiden: Brill, 2012).

INDEX

Accepting Evangelicals 20
Adams, John Quincy 204
Adelaja, Sunday 275
African Initiated Churches (AICs) 87–8, 167, 270–2
Akenson, Donald Harman 187–8, 197
Akindayomi, Josiah 214
al-Din, Imad 142
al-Kamil, Malik 130
al-Masih, Abd 142
al-Qadir, Abd 137
al-Qaeda 139, 144
Alexander I (tsar) 125
Alexander, Charles 241
Algiers Mission Band 132
Allen, John L. 280
Allen, Richard 28, 202
Alline, Henry 147
Alton, David 107
Ambuofa, Peter 29
American Board of Commissioners for Foreign Missions (ABCFM) 114, 116–7, 119, 121–2, 124, 128, 163, 166
Amirizadeh, Marziyeh 143
Anderson, Allan 224
Anderson, Robert Mapes 78
Anderson, Rufus 121, 166
Annacondia, Carlos 90
Anthony, Susanna 234
Aoko, Gaudencia 86
Arab World Ministries 141
Arabi Pasha 140
Armenian Orthodoxy 116, 118, 125
Arminianism 11, 14, 17, 24, 30, 44–5, 47, 75, 82, 95–6
Arndt, Johann 114
Arthur, William 135, 137

Asamoah-Gyadu, J. Kwabena 277
Asbury, Francis 202, 206
Ashimolowo, Matthew 275, 277
Asmus, Barry 265
Assemblies of God 272–3
atonement 9, 18, 39–56, 64–6
Aulen, Gustav 41, 52
Azariah, V. S. 29

Baba, Panya Dabo 270
Backer, Kristiane 142
Bahnsen, Greg 196
Baker, Heidi 86
Balcombe, Dennis 89
Baldwin, E. F. 139
Baldwin, Eric 263
Baldwin, James 36
Balleine, G. R. 104, 242
Balmer, Randall 4
Bangs, Nathan 153
Baptist Missionary Society 68, 72, 128, 146 7, 163
Barclay, Oliver 4
Barnes, Albert 28
Barrows, Cliff 239
Barth, Karl 52
Bary, Rifqa 143
Bass, Charles 190
Bauder, Kevin 9
Bebbington, David 10–11, 60, 66, 69, 74, 76, 81–2, 90–1, 178, 232, 248, 251, 260, 262, 269
Bediako, Kwame 29
Beech, Carl 228
Beecher, Lyman 99, 102
Beeke, Joel 15
Bell, Rob 5
Bell, Steve 130, 135–7
Bellamy, Joseph 47

Index

Benezet, Anthony 201, 205
Bergler, Thomas 159
Berkouwer, G. C. 104
Berridge, John 46–7
Bible societies 28–9, 31–2, 34, 36, 114–5, 125, 154, 203, 272
Bickersteth, Edward 188
Bickersteth, E. H. 102
Bickersteth, Robert 256
Birks, T. R. 17, 188
Birney, James G. 204, 207
Bivins, Jason C. 194
Blackstone, William 28, 137
Bliss, Philip 31
Boardman, Henry 254, 256–9
Boddy, Alexander 54
Boettner, Loraine 107, 196
Bonnke, Reinhard 29, 54
Booth, Catherine 28, 32–3, 157, 218, 224
Booth, William 28, 157, 218, 224, 239
Boudinot, Elias 28
Bowler, Kate 214
Bradley, Ian 254
Bradley, Mark 141–2
Branham, William 90
Bray, Gerald 9
British Evangelical Council 16
British Syria Mission 130
Broadbent, E. H. 119, 124
Brother Andrew 136, 138–9, 143
Brown, Callum 160
Brown, Christopher Leslie 201
Brown, J. Baldwin 258
Browning, Robert 234
Bruce, F. F. 29, 186
Brusco, Elizabeth 269
Bryant, William 262
Buchanan, Claudius 115
Buchanan, Colin 9, 15–16
Buchman, Frank 243
Bunyan, John 234
Burchell, Thomas 205
Burke, Edmund 164
Burroughs, Eva 224
Burton, John 31
Burwash, Nathanael 28
Buss, Michael 16
Butler, Anthea 199
Butler, Jon 74, 81
Butler, Samuel 247
Buxton, Thomas Fowell 28, 165, 199, 203, 205, 207

Cadbury, George 261–2
Cadman, William 155
Cage, Nicolas 195
Caine, Barbara 151

Calvin, John 23, 41, 237
Calvinism 2, 11, 14, 17, 24, 30, 44–8, 53, 63, 66–7, 70, 75, 95, 103, 122, 128, 153, 164, 196, 202
Cambuslang revival 26, 78
Campbell, Alexander 28
Campbell, John McLeod 48
Campbell, R. J. 50–1
Campolo, Tony 5
Campus Crusade for Christ 34, 118, 124, 190–1
Cane Ridge revival 84–6
Carey, George 13
Carey, William 33, 128, 147, 164–5, 201
Carlile, J. C. 262
Carlson, Carole 191
Carpenter, Joel 159
Carson, D. A. 15, 228
Carter, Kameron 216
Cartwright, Peter 153
Cash, Johnny 193
Cash, June Carter 193
Catherwood, Frederick 265
Catholic Apostolic Church 102
Cecil, Richard 236
Cerullo, Morris 17
Chafer, Lewis Sperry 189–90
Chalke, Steve 17–19, 55
Chalmers, Thomas 151, 251–4, 261
Chaney, Charles 158
Champneys, William Weldon 155
Chapman, Colin 133
Chapman, Jennie 194
Chappell, David 212
Charismatic renewal 4–5, 7, 9, 12, 14, 32, 53–4, 69, 74, 79, 82–3, 85–6, 89–91, 93, 106–8, 113, 125, 132, 160, 162, 170, 215, 226, 236, 239, 268–73, 275–8
Chartism 261–2
Chauncy, Charles 84
Chavasse, Christopher 235
Chavasse, Edith 235
Chavasse, Francis 235, 243
Chavda, Mahesh 90
Cheever, George Barrell 100
Chemin Neuf 93
Chick, Jack 107
Children's Special Service Mission (CSSM) 155
Chilton, David 195
China Inland Mission (CIM) 136, 166, 221
Chiniquy, Charles 105
Cho, Yonggi 89
Choe, Ja-Sil 89
Choquette, Robert 99
Christianity Today 9, 15, 17, 104, 108, 212, 226–7
Christmas, Henry 134
Christophe, Henri 202
Church Association 2, 100–1, 104
Church, Joe 88

Church Missionary Society (CMS) 33, 51, 99,
  114–5, 117, 119–21, 124, 129, 131, 135, 140,
  163, 165–6, 221, 235
Church Pastoral Aid Society (CPAS) 155
Churchill, Seton 129
Churchill, Winston 193
Clapham Sect 100, 165, 218, 220, 234, 240, 254
Clark, Joseph B. 148
Clark, Molliston Madison 206
Clarke, Adam 28
Clarkson, Thomas 199, 202–3, 205
Clements, Roy 19
Clifford, Alan 133
Clifford, John 262–3
Coates, Gerald 236
Cochran, Pamela 225, 228
Coke, Thomas 150, 202
Coker, Daniel 203
Cole, Nathan 27
Colenso, Elizabeth 221
Colenso, William 221
Coleridge, Samuel Taylor 184
Colley, Linda 94
Collins, Kenneth 7
Collinson, Patrick 237
Colson, Charles 107
Comaroff, Jean 171
Comaroff, John 171
Communism 31, 89, 103–4, 108, 110, 113, 120,
  122, 125–6, 137–8, 141, 193, 212, 271
Comstock, Anthony 244
Cone, James 210
Conkin, Paul 86
Cook, James 147, 164
Cooke, Jenny 226
Copeland, Kenneth 89
Copleston, Edward 254
Coppin, Levi 210
Coptic Orthodoxy 119, 121
Corio, Alec 100
Cornish, Samuel 204
Corrigan, John 80, 83
Costas, Orlando 29
Cowper, William 40, 238, 240
Cox, Harvey 79
Cox, Jeffrey 171
Cragg, Kenneth 130, 132
Crawford, Percy 159
Cray, Graham 6
Crisp, Oliver 47
Crosby, Fanny 40, 59
Crossley, Hugh Thomas 156
Crowell, Henry Parson 263
Crowther, Samuel Ajayi 33, 166–7
Cruickshank, George 202
Crusades 130, 136, 138
Cugoano, Ottabah 201

Cumming, John 94
Cunningham, J. W. 135
Cunningham, Richenda 235
Currie, Robert 77

Dabney, Robert 208
Dale, R. W. 2, 49, 53
Darby, John Nelson 28, 184–90, 196–7
Dartmouth, Earl of 201
Darwinism 37–8
Davenport, Frederick 76
Davidoff, Leonore 218, 220
Davie, Donald 237
Davies, Samuel 200
Dawkins, Richard 128
Dawn, Maggi 5
Dayton, Donald 5, 11
Dehqani-Tafti, Hassan 143
DeMar, Gary 195
Denney, James 53
Dewick, E. C. 4
Dickens, Charles 28, 151–2
Dixon, Thomas 211
Dodd, C. H. 53
Doddridge, Philip 42
Doughten, Russell S. 193
Douglas, Mary 86
Douglass, Frederick 204, 216
Douglass, Harlan Paul 158
Doyle, Tom 143–4
Drummond, Henry 2
Dryden, John 234
Duff, Alexander 146, 166
Duncan-Williams, Nicholas 277
Duree, Susannah 46
Durkheim, Émile 80, 83

East African Revival 88, 274
East India Company 33, 128, 163
Eastern Orthodoxy 110–26
Easton, Hosea 204
Edinburgh World Missionary Conference 120, 123,
  168, 277–8
Edwards, Joel 18, 214
Edwards, Jonathan 23–4, 42–3, 47–8, 58–9, 62–3,
  82, 84–5, 127, 144, 183, 202, 205, 216
Edwards, Jonathan Jr 47, 202
Eldredge, John 228
Elias, John 45
Eliot, George 36, 94, 248
Eliot, John 163
Eliot, Philip 102
Elliot, Henry Miers 135
Ellis, Sarah 218
Elmore, Floyd 187
Elrington, Thomas 187
Emerson, Michael 212

Equiano, Olaudah 201, 216
Erskine, John 95, 201
eschatology 28, 97–8, 100–1, 114, 117–8, 154, 164, 166–7, 178–97, 203, 207–8
Esther, Gulshan 143
Ethiopian Evangelical Church Mekane Yesus (EECMY) 271
Evangelical Affirmations 8, 15
Evangelical Alliance (EA) 13, 17–19, 29, 35, 49, 55, 101, 104, 120, 123, 134, 138, 206
Evangelical Church of West Africa (ECWA) 270–1
Evangelical Fellowship for Lesbian and Gay Christians 20
Evangelical Movement of Wales (EMW) 53
Evangelical Orthodox Church 118
Evangelical Theological Society (ETS) 17
Evangelicals and Catholics Together (ECT) 16, 108
Evans, David Morier 255
Ewell, C. Rosalee Velloso 35

Fackre, Gabriel 4
Farningham, Marianne 220–1
Fee, Gordon 228
Fellowship of Evangelical Churchmen (FEC) 15
Fellowship of Independent Evangelical Churches (FIEC) 19
Finke, Roger 78
Finney, Charles 28, 48, 75, 82, 90–1, 102–3, 156, 203, 216
Fischer, Benjamin L. 242
Fisk, George 256
Fletcher, Colin 19
Fletcher, John 97
Fletcher, Mary 97
Flint, Timothy 147
Foote, Julia 32–3
Forbes, Cheryl 226
Foreman, Stephen 144
Forster, Charles 133
Forsyth, P. T. 39, 53
Fosdick, Harry Emerson 3
Foster, Richard 70
Fountain Trust 106
Foxe, John 95, 234
Francis (pope) 93
Francis de Sales 96–7
Francis of Assisi 130
Francis, John 257
Francke, A. H. 111, 113, 163
French, Thomas Valpy 131
Fry, Elizabeth 28
Frykholm, Amy 194
Fuller, Andrew 48, 61–3, 66, 68, 72
Fundamentalism 4–5, 9, 11, 17, 39, 51, 103–4, 112, 127–8, 159, 168–70, 177, 218, 225, 231, 263, 269

Gaebelein, Arno 189
Gairdner, Temple 121, 129–32, 134–5, 139
Gallagher, Sally 228
Garnet, Henry Highland 204
Garnett, Jane 248, 255
Garrison, David 142
Garrison, William Lloyd 199, 207
Gentry, Kenneth 195
George, David 26–7, 202, 216
Gifford, Paul 277
Gilbert, Alan 83
Gill, John 44, 183–4
Gillies, John 75
Gillquist, Peter 118
Gisborne, Thomas 254–60
Gladstone, Jack 203
Gladstone, John 203
Gladstone, W. E. 254
Glock, Charles 78
Glover, T. R. 52
Gobineau, Joseph-Arthur de 167
Goldmann, David 136
Goldsmith, Martin 136, 141
Gorbachev, Mikhail 105
Gordon, Charles 129–30, 220–1
Gordon, Robert 214
Gore, Tipper 245
Gosforth, Jonathan 88
Gough, Hugh 13
Graham, Billy 6, 15, 28, 40, 82, 91, 124, 159–60, 213, 215–6, 239, 264, 277
Grant, George Monro 28
Graves, Richard 187
Gray, James M. 189
Greek Orthodoxy 113, 119
Greenbelt Festival 5
Gregory, Benjamin 258–9
Greig, Pete 91
Grem, Darren 266
Gribben, Crawford 181, 183, 194, 235, 243
Griffiths, Brian 265
Grimke, Francis 210
Grimke, Sarah 36, 207
Grimley, Matthew 246
Gronniosaw, James 201
Groothuis, Rebecca 228
Grotius, Hugo 41, 47
Groves, A. N. 166
Grudem, Wayne 228, 265
Gründer, Horst 173
Guest, Mathew 195
Gumbel, Nicky 14
Gundry, Robert 17
Gushee, David 19
Gutjahr, Paul 36, 102
Gwynne, Llewellyn 129–30, 135

Hackett, Conrad 12
Hagin, Kenneth 89
Haldane, Alexander 9
Haldane, James Alexander 153
Haldane, Robert 153
Halévy, Élie 77, 94
Hall, Catherine 218, 220
Hammon, Briton 201, 216
Hammon, Jupiter 201
Hammond, T. C. 53
Hanegraaff, Hank 77
Hardesty, Nancy 225–6
Harman, Bryant Gray 105
Harper, Michael 69, 113
Harris, Howel 95
Hart, Darryl 8, 14
Hartwell, R. M. 77
Harvey, John 237
Harvey, Paul 212
Haslam, William 57–9, 67
Hatch, Nathan 8
Havergal, Frances Ridley 65, 67, 234–6, 241
Havergal, Maria 235
Havergal, William Henry 236
Haynes, Lemuel 202
Hempton, David 36, 77, 95, 187, 250
Henry, Carl 7–8, 29, 216
Herbert, George 234
Hervey, James 240
Higgins, Michelle 215
Hilborn, David 18
Hill, Christopher 10
Hill, Clifford 134, 138–9
Hill, Grace Livingston 235
Hill, John 2
Hill, Rowland 242
Hillsong 32
Hilton, Boyd 248, 253, 257
Hincks, Edward 187
Hindmarsh, Bruce 45–6
Hinn, Benny 54
Hobsbawn, E. J. 77
Hocking, Joseph 235
Hocking, Silas 235
Hodge, A. A. 50
Hodge, Charles 28, 102
Hogarth, William 95
Hogg, John 140
Holland, Henry Scott 264
Holmes, Janice 156
Holy Trinity Brompton 14, 86, 93, 160
homosexuality 19–20, 176, 226
Hopkins, Samuel 23, 202
Horton, Michael 14
Houston, James 69
Houston, Mary Pritchard 227
Howard, Peter 243

Howsam, Leslie 36
Hughes, Hugh Price 262–3
Hunt, Holman 237
Huntingdon, Countess of 201, 205, 240
Huntingdon, Samuel 176
Huntingdon, William 45
Hussein, Saddam 139
Hybels, Bill 5
hymnody 25–6, 31–2, 40, 55, 59, 64–5, 67, 80, 96,
    111, 157, 181–2, 236–41, 249, 274

Indonesian revival 89–90, 141, 273
Inskip, Thomas 104
Institute for the Study of American Evangelicals 10
International Fellowship of Evangelical Students
    (IFES) 8, 53
International House of Prayer 91–2
Inter-Varsity Fellowship (IVF) 52–3, 169, 236, 264
Iranian Revolution 138, 141
Irish Church Mission 98
Irons, Charles 206, 208
Irving, Edward 2, 186
Isichei, Elizabeth 261
Islam 110, 114–5, 117–8, 121, 125, 127–45, 167,
    176, 183, 193, 196, 269, 273, 275, 278, 280

Jackson, Thomas 238
Jacobs, Harriet 206
James, John Angell 148, 219, 222
James, William 76
Jao, Greg 215
Jay, Elisabeth 241, 246
Jay, William 2, 47
Jeffrey, Kenneth 74–5, 78, 81
Jeffreys, George 54, 158
Jeffreys, Stephen 54
Jenkins, Jerry B. 235
Jenkins, Philip 35, 176
Jennings, Willie 216
Jeremias II (patriarch) 122
Jeremy, David 264
Jessup, Henry 140
Jeyaseelan, Jey 229
Jeyaseelan, Lizy 229
John XXIII (pope) 105
John Paul II (pope) 93
Johnson, Franklin 51
Jones, John Morgan 51
Jowett, John 236, 238, 243
Jowett, William 114, 235
Joynson-Hicks, William 244
Judson, Adoniram 33
Judson, Ann 33
Jung, Carl Gustav 76

Kairanawi, Rahmatullah 131
Kantzer, Kenneth 15

Index

Kaplan, Amy 148, 152
Kato, Byang 270
Keith-Falconer, Ion 129, 135
Keller, Rosemary Skinner 219
Kelly, Thomas 181
Kennedy, John F. 104
Kerr, Cecil 107
Keswick movement 67, 88, 166–8
Khomeini, Ayatollah 141
Kidd, Thomas 127–8
Kidner, Derek 29
Killick, Tim 240
King, Boston 202
King, Coretta Scott 215
King, Martin Luther 198, 208–10, 212–3, 216
Kings, Graham 4
Kisk, Pliny 128
Klemperer, Otto 232
Knibb, William 199, 203, 205
Knox, E. A. 140, 234, 242
Ku Klux Klan 211
Kuhlman, Kathryn 86, 90, 224

Ladd, George 29
Laden, Osama bin 139
LaHaye, Tim 235
Laing, John 264
Lake, Frank 226
Lambert, Bernard 186
Landels, William 219
Landsman, Ned 78
Lang, G. H. 119
Larsen, Timothy 11
Larson, Bob 245
Latourette, Kenneth 171
Lausanne movement 29–30, 35, 112, 118, 120, 123, 160, 169–70, 265–6, 277–8
Lavington, George 95
Lawrence J. B. 149
Lee, Chun Kwan 89
Lee, Jarena 216
Lefroy, George 131
Left Behind series 29, 191, 194–7, 233, 235, 243
Leland, John 206
Leonard, Graham 15
Lever, William 262
Lewis, C. S. 235
Lewis, I. M. 79
Lewis, John 209
Lewis, Sarah 151
Liele, George 27, 201
Lincoln, Abraham 220
Lindsay, Michael 12
Lindsell, Harold 17, 227
Lindsey, Hal 29, 178, 190–6
Lindsey, Jan 191
Ling, Jeff 245

Livingstone, David 38, 165
Lloyd-Jones, Martyn 8–9, 13, 16, 28, 53, 70, 105, 196
Locke, John 95–6
Loescher, Frank S. 211
London City Mission 155
London Itinerant Society 148
London Missionary Society 48, 119, 163, 165, 203
Lord's Army 119, 122
Lovelace, Richard 83
Lowry, Robert 31
Lucaris, Cyril 122
Lull, Ramon 130
Luther, Martin 23, 26, 271
Lyttelton, W. H. 254–6

McAfee, Joseph 148
MacArthur, John 196
Macaulay, Thomas Babington 234
Macaulay, Zachary 202
McAuley, Jerry 156
McBain, Douglas 69
MacBeth, R. G. 150
McCallum, Richard 137
M'Cheyne, Robert Murray 28
McDannell, Colleen 36
Macdonald, Margaret 186
McDowell, Josh 159
Machen, J. Gresham 14, 103
McGrath, Alister 6, 70–1, 235
McIntire, Carl 104
McLaren, Brian 5
McLaurin, C. C. 103
McLeod, Hugh 246
McLoughlin, William 74, 80–3
McNeile, Hugh 100
MacNutt, Francis 90
MacNutt, Judith 90
McPherson, Aimee Semple 28, 82, 86, 158, 224
MacPherson, Dave 186
Maddox, Randy 43
Mallet, Sarah 223
Mallouhi, Christine 130
Malthus, Thomas 252, 254, 258
Mandela, Nelson 214
Margrett, David 202
Marrant, John 201
Marsden, George 6, 10–11
Martin, David 269
Martyn, Henry 128–31, 142
Mascall, Eric 15
Masefield, John 242
Mason, Lowell 31
Mathison, Keith 196
Maxwell, David 277
May, Henry 206
Metzger, Bruce 34

Mill, John Stuart 252
Millar, Sandy 14
millennialism, *see* eschatology
Miller, Donald 89
Milner, Joseph 102
Milton, John 234
Ming-dao, Wang 89
Mohler, Albert 10, 14, 20
Montgomery, Carrie Judd 86
Moody, D. L. 28, 32, 82, 91, 156–7, 166, 211, 216, 239
Moody, Harold 214
Moore, Russell 215
Moral Re-Armament (MRA) 236, 243, 246
Moravians 46, 58, 65, 81, 163, 200
More, Hannah 28, 68, 201, 218, 235–6, 240–1
Morgan, David 237
Morley, Samuel 260
Morris, Leon 53
Morrison, Robert 33
Mote, Edward 31
Mott, John 167
Müller, George 166
Murphy, Cullen 4
Murray, Iain 8, 75, 196
Murrow, David 228
Musk, Bill 133
Muslims, *see* Islam

Naismith, David 155
Nash, E. J. H. 237
National Association of Evangelicals 8, 15, 104, 213
National Evangelical Anglican Congress 55, 106
Nationwide Festival of Light 107, 246
Navigators 124
Nebeker, Gary 187
Neill, Stephen 172
Nestorians 110, 116–7, 120–1, 124
Neve, Arthur 131
Neve, Ernest 131
Newbigin, Lesslie 170
Newman, Francis 36
Newman, John Henry 36, 103, 127–8
Newton, John 45, 60, 205, 216, 238
Noll, Mark 8, 10, 12, 222
Norman, Larry 193
North Africa Mission 140–1
North, Gary 190, 195
Nsibambi, Simeoni 88

Oasis Trust 19
Obama, Barack 216
O'Brien, Brandon 229
Ockenga, Harold 5, 16, 104
O'Connell, Daniel 261
Octavianus, Petrus 29
Oliver, E. H. 150

Oloyede, Jonathan 69
Olson, Roger 6, 11
Oncken, Johann Gerhardt 68
Ondeto, Simeo 86
Orcibal, Jean 96
Orr, J. Edwin 75
Orr-Ewing, Amy 136
Orr-Ewing, Frog 136
Orthodox Presbyterian Church (OPC) 14
Osborn, Sarah 26
Overseas Missionary Fellowship, *see* China Inland Mission
Owen, J. B. 258–9
Owen, Robert 261
Oxford Group Movement, *see* Moral Re-Armament
Oyedepo, David 277

Packer, James I. 7, 15–16, 29, 54–5, 70, 236
Padwick, Constance 129–30, 132–3
Page, Nick 71
Paley, William 254
Palmer, Phoebe 28
Pankhurst, Christabel 225
Parks, Rosa 209
Parshall, Julie 133
Parshall, Phil 133
Parsons, Levi 128
Patmore, Coventry 219–20
Pawson, David 128, 138
Payne, Daniel Alexander 28
Pearce, Samuel 59, 66
Peck, John Mason 154
Pennington, James 204
Pentecost, J. Dwight 189–90
Pentecostalism 4, 11, 18, 20, 28, 32, 50, 54, 68–9, 74–5, 78–9, 82–3, 85–6, 89–92, 105–7, 113, 124–5, 141, 158, 162, 168–9, 175–6, 199, 213, 215, 224, 229, 268–73, 275–7, 280
Perkins, Justin 116
Peterson, Eugene 70
Pierce, Ronald 228
Pfander, Karl Gottlieb 131–2
Pfander Centre for Apologetics 133
Phillips, J. B. 34
Pierson, Arthur T. 189
pietism 4, 26, 33, 111, 113–4, 163, 170, 200, 205
Pietsch, B. M. 37
Pinnock, Clark 17
Piper, John 70, 216, 228
Pius IX (pope) 100
Plessis, David du 69
Plütschau, Heinrich 33
Pobendonostsev, K. P. 119
Pomare II 87
Pope, Alexander 234
Popescu, Teodor 122

Index

Porter, Andrew 172, 254
Powell, Walter 258
Poynter, J. W. 105
Poythress, Vern 196
Prest, Charles 147
Prison Christian Fellowship 107
Promise Keepers 215, 227–8
Prophetic Word Ministries 134
Protestant Association 100, 102
Protten, Christian 200
Protten, Rebecca 216
Public Worship Regulation Act 101
Puritan Studies Conference 16
Pusey, E. B. 127

Quakerism 28, 70, 127, 201–3, 248, 251, 259–63, 266
Quírez, Pedro Arana 29

Raboteau, Albert 84
Rack, Henry 249–50
Ramabai, Mary 33, 86, 224
Rambo, Lewis 76–7
Ramsey, Brooks 212
Ranaghan, Kevin 106
Randall, Ian 67, 70
Ransom, Reverdy 210
Ranyard, Ellen 152
Redeemed Christian Church of God (RCCG) 160–1, 214, 271, 275
Reformation Society 98, 100, 102
Religious Tract Society 154
Renovaré 70–1
revival 1, 11, 25–6, 32, 39–40, 42–4, 50, 57, 73–92, 95, 97–8, 100, 103, 140–2, 144, 152–3, 156–9, 164, 166, 168, 170, 182, 186, 200, 203–4, 209, 221–2, 224, 231, 249, 251, 269, 274–7
Ricardo, David 252
Rice W. A. 135
Richmond, Legh 240–1
Riding Lights Theatre Company 242
Ritschl, Albrecht 49
Robert, Dana 170, 174
Roberts, Evan 50
Roberts, Oral 28, 89–90
Robertson, O. Palmer 196
Rodeheaver, Homer 241
Roman Catholicism 11–12, 16, 22–3, 31, 66, 85–6, 93–111, 114–7, 120, 125, 127, 137, 151, 167–9, 180, 226, 237, 272–3, 276, 280
Romanian Orthodoxy 119, 122
Rookmaaker, H. R. 247
Rosman, Doreen 233–4
Rostampour, Maryam 143
Rothschild, Nathan Mayer 257
Rowland, Daniel 147
Rowntree, Joseph 262

Ruether, Rosemary Radford 219
Runcorn, David 19
Rundle, Robert 99
Rush, Benjamin 201
Rushdoony, Rousas John 195
Russell, Ken 246
Russian Orthodoxy 119–20, 124–5, 137
Ryle, J. C. 2, 49, 61–3, 66–7, 259
Ryrie, Charles 189

Said, Edward 173
St John, Farnham 141
St John, Patricia 141
Salt, Titus 262
Salvation Army 28, 32, 157, 224, 239
Samaritan's Purse 169
Samuel, David 7–8
Sandeen, Ernest 187
Sandifer, David 239
Sankey, Ira D. 239, 241
Sanneh, Lamin 34
Saunders, Prince 203
Saward, Michael 4, 232, 236
Scanzoni, John 226–7
Scanzoni, Letha 225–7
Schaeffer, Edith 226
Schaeffer, Francis 5, 28, 159, 226, 247
Schleiermacher, Friedrich 49
Scofield, C. I. 189–90
Scott, Joan 217
Scott, Thomas 28, 135
Scott, Walter 234
Scripture Union 20
Selby, Hubert 244
Sélen, Mats 101
Semmel, Bernard 83
Seymour, William 68
Shaftesbury, Earl of 9, 257, 261–3
Shah, Hannah 143
Sharp, Granville 205
Sharpe, Sam 203
Shaw, Luci 70
Shaw, Mark 74–5, 81, 92
Shea, Bev 160
Shea, William 109
Shedd, W. A. 122
Sheikh, Bilquis 143
Sheppard, David 107, 245, 265
Shoemaker, Robert 218, 222
Shuck, Glenn 194
Sibthorp, Richard 103
Sider, Ronald J. 264–5
Simeon, Charles 1–2, 65, 236
Simeon Trust 102
Simmons, William 211
Simpson, A. B. 157
Singh, Sundar 29

Index

Sizer, Sandra 80
slavery 25–30, 35, 47, 84, 100–1, 153, 155, 163–5, 173, 198–210, 212, 216, 240, 253, 258
Smail, Tom 69
Smedes, Lewis 8
Smith, Adam 249–53, 255, 265–6
Smith, Christian 108, 212
Smith, Gerrit 207
Smith, Jay 133
Smith, John 203
Smith, Mark 8, 12
Smith, Oswald J. 159
Smith, Reginald Bosworth 134
Smith, Sydney 165
Smith, Timothy 207
Smolinski, Reiner 181
socialism 137, 168, 261–5
Sookhdeo, Patrick 138
Southern Baptist Convention 14, 149, 155, 198, 211, 215
Sovereign Grace Union 16
Spence, Martin 188, 197
Spencer, Herbert 255, 260
Spring Harvest 18
Spurgeon, C. H. 2, 28, 39, 50, 59–60, 62–3, 65–8, 220
Stackhouse, John 11, 15
Stanley, Brian 20–1, 88, 129, 172, 225
Stanton, Elizabeth Cady 36
Stark, Rodney 78–9
Steele, Anne 26, 31, 64, 240
Steinmetz, David 38
Stephen, James 202
Stephen, Jonathan 18–19
Stewart, Lyman 51, 263
Stine, Brad 228
Stone, Barton 85
Stone, Jon 8
Storkey, Elaine 225
Stott, Anne 220
Stott, John 5, 13, 28, 55–6, 105, 128, 169–70, 277
Stout, Harry 83
Stowe, Harriet Beecher 28, 207
Stowell, Hugh 256–8
Strachey, Lytton 130
Stuart, Moses 28
Student Christian Movement (SCM) 52, 123
Student Volunteer Movement (SVM) 167
Stunt, Timothy 186, 197
Sumner, J. B. 254
Sunday, Billy 82, 156
Sung, John 29, 89
Swales, Ann 222–4
Swanepoel, Freek 215
Sweet, Leonard 9
Swift, Wesley 222
Szeryng, Henryk 232

Tadros, Yusef Effendi 131
Talmadge, Herman 212
Tappan, Arthur 155, 203–4, 207
Tappan, Lewis 203–4, 207
Tappan, William 31
Tatford, F. A. 193–4
Taves, Ann 77
Tawney, R. H. 264
Taylor, Dan 44
Taylor, Hudson 166
Taylor, Iain 12
Taylor, Kenneth 34
Tennent, Gilbert 147
Terrett, Sarah 223–4
Terrett, William 223–4
Thomas à Kempis 96
Thomas, George 79
Thompson, E. P. 77–8
Thornton, Douglas 129, 131, 139
Thornton, John 47
Thornton, Henry 201
Tidball, Derek 10, 70–1, 146
Tikhon of Zadonsk 114
Titterton, C. H. 51
Tocqueville, Alexis de 28
Tomlinson, Dave 5–6, 243
Toronto Blessing 77, 85–6
Tosh, John 220
Townend, Stuart 55–6
Townsend, Cameron 34
Trotter, Lilias 132, 135, 139–41, 144
Trotter, Mel 156
Turner, Nat 206
Turner, Victor 86
Turner, William C. 199
Tutu, Desmond 215
Tyndale House 53

Urquhart, Colin 54

Vance, Norman 66
Van Cott, Margaret Newton 222
Vanhoozer, Kevin 12
Vatican Council (second) 105–6, 108
Venn, Henry Jr 102, 166
Venn, Henry Sr 43
Venn, Jane Catherine 234
Vickery, Amanda 218
Victory Churches of India 229–31
Village Itinerancy Society 153
Villiers, Montagu 255–7
Viner, Jacob 253–4
Vineyard movement 32, 91, 132
Vita, Beatriz Kimpa 86

Wacker, Grant 78, 83
Wake, William 111

Walker, David 204
Walker, Samuel 71
Wallace, Anthony 75, 80–1, 92
Wallace, Lew 28
Wallis, Jim 264
Walliss, John 195
Walsh, Walter 98
Walvoord, John F. 190
Walworth, Clarence Augustus 103
Ward, W. R. 10, 25–6, 74, 81
Ward, William 128
Ware, Bruce 17
Warfield, Benjamin 3
Warneck, Gustav 170
Warner, Rob 11, 160
Warner, Susan 36
Warren, Max 170, 172
Warren, Rick 5, 216
Watchman Nee 29, 89
Waterman, Anthony 251, 254
Watson, David 69, 242
Watts, Isaac 25, 31, 43, 64
Watts, Michael 73, 78, 262–3
Watts, Walter 255
Webber, Robert 4
Weber, Max 79–80, 254, 264
Weber, Timothy 4
Weed, John 132
Weed, Ruthie 132
Welby, Justin 13–14, 93
Weld, Theodore Dwight 203, 207
Welles, Orson 191
Wells, David 4, 7, 105
Wells, Ida B. 211
Welsh revival 40, 50, 158
Wenham, John 236
Werner, Julia 77
Wesley, Charles 1, 25, 31, 42, 81, 96–7, 111, 184, 238
Wesley, John 1–2, 11, 23–4, 39, 43–4, 58–9, 62–3, 66, 81, 95–7, 111, 127, 147, 183, 201, 203, 216, 223, 231, 234, 249–51, 255–6, 266
Wesley, Samuel 97
Whately, Richard 254
Wheatley, Phillis, 201–2, 240
Whisenant, Edgar 192
White, Andrew 136
Whitefield, George 1–2, 11, 23–7, 39, 44–6, 60–3, 81, 83, 95–7, 127, 144, 147, 183, 200, 205, 216
Whitehouse, Mary 246
Whitemore, Emma 156

Wilberforce, William 2, 28, 68, 163, 165, 198–9, 201–3, 205, 207, 216, 218, 220, 234, 236, 262
Wiley, H. Orton 29
Willard, Dallas 70
Williams, Edward 48
Williams, Fannie Barrier 210
Williams, Garry 18
Williams, George 156
Williams, Michael 190
Williams, William 33, 42
Wilson, Daniel 115, 137
Wilson, Linda 62
Wilson, Thomas 65
Wimber, John 54, 91, 132
Witherspoon, John 42
Wolffe, John 93, 98, 101
Wong, Wilfred 128
Wood, Arthur 159
Wood, Frederick 159
Wood, Sabria 228
Wood, Wilfred 214
Woodworth-Etter, Maria 86, 90
Worboise, Emma Jane 241
Word Alive 18
World Council of Churches 105, 123, 168
World Vision 124, 169
Worlock, Derek 107
Wright, Nigel 6
Wright, N. T. 9, 125
Wrytzen, Jack 159
Wycliffe Bible Translators 34, 169
Wynkoop, Mildred 29

Xavier, Francis 102
Xiao, Zhao 33

Yoder, John Howard 264
Yoido Full Gospel Church 89, 273
Young, G. M. 260
Young, T. Dinsdale 104
Young Men's Christian Association (YMCA) 156, 166, 255–6, 258
Young Women's Christian Association (YWCA) 166, 241
Yousef, Mosab Hassan 143
Youth for Christ 159
Youth With A Mission (YWAM) 136

Zacharias, Ravi 159
Ziegenbalg, Bartholomäus 33
Zinzendorf, Count von 65, 205
Zwemer, Samuel 129–30, 132, 135, 137, 140
Zwingli, Huldrych 237